570

FF

OF ACPL

P9-DBT-882

1- 4- 54

A GUIDE TO BIRD FINDING

WEST OF THE MISSISSIPPI

A

Guide to

Bird Finding WEST OF THE MISSISSIPPI

By OLIN SEWALL PETTINGILL, JR.

with illustrations by GEORGE MIKSCH SUTTON

New York · OXFORD UNIVERSITY PRESS · 1953

COPYRIGHT 1953 BY OLIN SEWALL PETTINGILL, JR.

LIBRARY OF CONGRESS CATALOGUE CARD NUMBER: 53-9191

PRINTED IN THE UNITED STATES OF AMERICA

825999

FOR MY FATHER AND MOTHER

Preface

This volume is the counterpart of *A Guide to Bird Finding East of the Mississippi* (1951) and is identical with it in organization and style. Much of this text had, in fact, already been prepared when the first volume went to press and remains essentially unchanged except for minor revisions to bring the information up to date.

Like the first volume, this work attempts to cover each state with respect to physiographic regions, natural areas, and the principal ornithological attractions. For the somewhat specialized information I relied heavily on ornithological literature and the generous help of various ornithologists, amateur and professional.

In perusing books, pamphlets, and journals pertaining to plant and animal life of the states west of the Mississippi, I took the liberty of extracting the facts that would prove useful and incorporated many of them in the text. All of the books and pamphlets drawn upon extensively are included in the reference material at the end of this book. Among the journals consulted, the following contained papers of greatest value: *The Auk, The Condor, The Wilson Bulletin, Audubon Field Notes, Audubon Magazine, Journal of Wildlife Management, The American Midland Naturalist, The Murrelet, The Nebraska Bird Review, Iowa Bird Life, The Flicker,* and *South Dakota Bird Notes.*

Without the co-operation of over 300 persons, each one of whom contributed information, the preparation of this guide would have been impossible. When I received information relating to a particular bird-finding area, I wrote it up in my own style, then returned it to the donor for checking. This was a time-consuming procedure and, needless to say, a tax on the generosity of the donor, who had already gone to the trouble of assembling the data. Listed at the end of each chapter are the individuals who helped supply the necessary facts, or who played some other part in the preparation of the chapter. To all of them I am immensely indebted.

Of the many persons who helped with the preparation of the manuscript I wish to single out for my special thanks John W. Aldrich, Roger Tory Peterson, George Miksch Sutton, and Josselyn Van Tyne for their advice, or suggestions, on some of the common names chosen for certain bird species; Harry C. Oberholser not only for carefully going over the manuscript of the Texas chapter, but for giving me his computed total of bird species known to occur in the state; Frederick M. and Marguerite Heydweiller Baumgartner for their critical reading of the Oklahoma chapter and for bringing the lists of species in the chapter's introduction into conformity with the information in their forthcoming *Book of Oklahoma Bird Life;* the following for contributing substantially to the contents of a particular chapter and, later, reading the whole chapter: W. J. Breckenridge, Harvey L. Gunderson, and Dwain W. Warner (Minnesota), Ben B. Coffey, Jr. (Arkansas), Robert B. Lea and George H. Lowery, Jr. (Louisiana), C. J. Henry and Mrs. Robert T. (Ann M.) Gammell (North Dakota), Levi L. Mohler, R. Allyn Moser, and William F. Rapp, Jr. (Nebraska), George G. Williams (Texas), Clifford V. Davis (Montana), Robert J. Niedrach (Colorado), Allan R. Phillips (Arizona), Thomas D. Burleigh (Idaho), Ernest S. Booth and Earl J. Larrison (Washington), and Stanley G. Jewett (Oregon); the following for contributing substantially to three or more area accounts: M. Dale Arvey, L. Irby Davis, W. B. Davis, William R. Eastman, Jr., William H. Elder, Donald S. Farner, Reed W. Fautin, John E. and Margret Galley, Harold C. Hedges, Zell C. Lee, S. Walter Lesher, Karl H. Maslowski, Kenneth D. Morrison, Clifford C. Presnall, Alexander Sprunt, Jr., and John H. Wampole; and Edward F. and Doris Dana and G. Reeves Butchart for their timely assistance with editorial matters and proofreading.

In order to have the accounts of National Wildlife Refuges and National Parks and Monuments correct in all details I made it a custom to send preliminary copies to the Refuge managers and the Park and Monument superintendents or naturalists with the request that they read them for accuracy. I was greatly impressed with their willingness to comply and am deeply grateful to them for their co-operation.

George Miksch Sutton's delightful pen and ink drawings enliven the pages of this volume as they did those of the first and will, I am confident, point up the ornithological attractions of the 22 western states.

Finally, I wish to express my everlasting gratitude to Robert M. Mengel for the fine account of Wyoming's Big Horn Mountains and to the men listed below, who were willing to prepare entire chapters, faithfully following my specifications in regard to organization and style: Gale Monson (Arizona), W. J. Baerg (Arkansas), Charles G. Sibley and Howard L. Cogswell (California), Jean M. Linsdale (Nevada), J. Stokley Ligon (New Mexico), Robert M. Storm (Oregon), William H. Behle (Utah).

The publication of this second volume marks the end of a project that began in 1946. Besides bringing me pleasant acquaintances with ornithologists the country over, the work has served to impress upon me the great diversity of bird-finding opportunities in all of the 48 states. Whereas I once believed that there were only a few states with truly exciting places to find birds, I now know that every state encompasses at least several spots waiting to enrich a bird finder's quest for the interesting and the unusual. All in all, there are enough places in our nation, each peculiarly inviting, to keep the bird finder 'on the go' for a lifetime.

That some parts of this book will be out of date in a relatively short space of time is almost a certainty. The natural processes of plant growth and ecological succession, the commercial and agricultural 'development' of wild areas, the construction of expressways and other new roads—all will create changes and hence make necessary regular revisions or new editions. Users of this volume and its eastern counterpart will be of great service if they will notify me of any changes in environments (including resultant effects on birdlife) and routes that come to their attention.

OLIN SEWALL PETTINGILL, JR.

Carleton College
Northfield, Minnesota
May 1953

Contents

xi

The Plan of This Book

Area Covered. This book covers the 22 states lying wholly, or in part (Minnesota and Louisiana), west of the Mississippi River. In Minnesota and Washington, adjacent Canadian areas are mentioned, and in California one Mexican area. Places for bird finding are chosen with the over-all purpose of showing (1) species of birds; (2) important bird concentrations such as breeding colonies and wintering aggregations; (3) representative types of bird habitats, from ocean beaches and deserts to mountaintops; and (4) the widest possible diversity of birds existing in the vicinity of all the large metropolitan areas and leading vacation centers. Included among the places are the major National Parks and National Wildlife Refuges, a large number of National Monuments, many state and municipal parks and refuges, and numerous private sanctuaries and estates. In addition to bird-finding places, brief mention is made of institutions—museums, colleges, universities, research stations, summer camps, libraries, zoos—that are of ornithological interest in one way or another and state and local ornithological societies.

Birds Covered. Attention is given to all species of birds regularly occurring in the 22 states. Subspecies are ignored for the most part, since they are seldom identifiable in the field.

Terminology. The common or vernacular names of bird species are used. They follow the *Check-List of North American Birds* (fourth edition, 1931, and supplements) of the American Ornithologists' Union, except when the names provided there do not adequately designate species or do not seem appropriate. Listed below are most of the species names used that are at variance with those of the *Check-List*. The technical or scientific names are included in parentheses.

xiii

Arctic Loon (*Gavia arctica*)
Least Grebe (*Colymbus dominicus*)
Leach's Petrel (*Oceanodroma leucorhoa*)
Olivaceous Cormorant (*Phalacrocorax olivaceus*)
Pelagic Cormorant (*Phalacrocorax pelagicus*)
Anhinga (*Anhinga anhinga*)
White-faced Ibis (*Plegadis mexicana*)
Red-shouldered Hawk (*Buteo lineatus*)
Rough-legged Hawk (*Buteo lagopus*)
Ferruginous Hawk (*Buteo regalis*)
Blue Grouse (*Dendragapus obscurus*)
Greater Prairie Chicken (*Tympanuchus cupido*)
Lesser Prairie Chicken (*Tympanuchus pallidicinctus*)
Sage Grouse (*Centrocercus urophasianus*)
California Quail (*Lophortyx californica*)
Mountain Quail (*Oreortyx picta*)
Wild Turkey (*Meleagris gallopavo*)
Rock Sandpiper (*Erolia ptilocnemis*)
Black-legged Kittiwake (*Rissa tridactyla*)
Common Murre (*Uria aalge*)
Flammulated Owl (*Otus flammeolus*)
Whiskered Owl (*Otus trichopsis*)
Great Horned Owl (*Bubo virginianus*)
Common Nighthawk (*Chordeiles minor*)
Lesser Nighthawk (*Chordeiles acutipennis*)
Green Kingfisher (*Chloroceryle americana*)
Yellow-shafted Flicker (*Colaptes auratus*)
Red-shafted Flicker (*Colaptes cafer*)
Acorn Woodpecker (*Melanerpes formicivora*)
Common Sapsucker (*Sphyrapicus varius*)
Hairy Woodpecker (*Dendrocopos villosus*)
Downy Woodpecker (*Dendrocopos pubescens*)
Ladder-backed Woodpecker (*Dendrocopos scalaris*)
Black-backed Woodpecker (*Picoïdes arcticus*)
Three-toed Woodpecker (*Picoïdes tridactylus*)
Rose-throated Becard (*Platypsaris aglaiae*)
Western Kingbird (*Tyrannus verticalis*)
Traill's Flycatcher (*Empidonax traillii*)
Canada Jay (*Perisoreus canadensis*)
Steller's Jay (*Cyanocitta stelleri*)
Scrub Jay (*Aphelocoma coerulescens*)
Arizona Jay (*Aphelocoma ultramarina*)
Common Raven (*Corvus corax*)
Common Crow (*Corvus brachyrhynchos*)
Pinyon Jay (*Gymnorhinus cyanocephalus*)
Black-capped Chickadee (*Parus atricapillus*)

Brown-capped Chickadee (*Parus hudsonicus*)
Black-crested Titmouse (*Parus atricristatus*)
Plain Titmouse (*Parus inornatus*)
Bush-tit (*Psaltriparus minimus*)
White-breasted Nuthatch (*Sitta carolinensis*)
Pygmy Nuthatch (*Sitta pygmaea*)
Brown Creeper (*Certhia familiaris*)
Bewick's Wren (*Thryomanes bewickii*)
Long-billed Marsh Wren (*Telmatodytes palustris*)
Canyon Wren (*Catherpes mexicanus*)
Curve-billed Thrasher (*Toxostoma curvirostre*)
California Thrasher (*Toxostoma redivivum*)
Olive-backed Thrush (*Hylocichla ustulata*)
Veery (*Hylocichla fuscescens*)
Western Bluebird (*Sialia mexicana*)
Blue-gray Gnatcatcher (*Polioptila caerulea*)
Plumbeous Gnatcatcher (*Polioptila melanura*)
Northern Shrike (*Lanius excubitor*)
Loggerhead Shrike (*Lanius ludovicianus*)
Hutton's Vireo (*Vireo huttoni*)
Bell's Vireo (*Vireo bellii*)
Solitary Vireo (*Vireo solitarius*)
Orange-crowned Warbler (*Vermivora celata*)
Nashville Warbler (*Vermivora ruficapilla*)
Audubon's Warbler (*Dendroica auduboni*)
Yellow-throated Warbler (*Dendroica dominica*)
Northern Water-thrush (*Seiurus noveboracensis*)
Yellow-breasted Chat (*Icteria virens*)
Black-capped Warbler (*Wilsonia pusilla*)
Tricolored Blackbird (*Agelaius tricolor*)
Hooded Oriole (*Icterus cucullatus*)
Boat-tailed Grackle (*Cassidix mexicanus*)
Common Grackle (*Quiscalus quiscula*)
Brown-headed Cowbird (*Molothrus ater*)
Summer Tanager (*Piranga rubra*)
Black-headed Grosbeak (*Pheucticus melanocephalus*)
Purple Finch (*Carpodacus purpureus*)
Cassin's Finch (*Carpodacus cassinii*)
Gray-crowned Rosy Finch (*Leucosticte tephrocotis*)
Common Redpoll (*Acanthis flammea*)
Common Goldfinch (*Spinus tristis*)
Lesser Goldfinch (*Spinus psaltria*)
Red Crossbill (*Loxia curvirostra*)
Eastern Towhee (*Pipilo erythrophthalmus*)
Spotted Towhee (*Pipilo maculatus*)
Brown Towhee (*Pipilo fuscus*)

Savannah Sparrow (*Passerculus sandwichensis*)
Sharp-tailed Sparrow (*Ammospiza caudacuta*)
Rufous-crowned Sparrow (*Aimophila ruficeps*)
Pine-woods Sparrow (*Aimophila aestivalis*)
Desert Sparrow (*Amphispiza bilineata*)
Sage Sparrow (*Amphispiza belli*)
Oregon Junco (*Junco oreganus*)
Gray-headed Junco (*Junco caniceps*)
Mexican Junco (*Junco phaeonotus*)
American Tree Sparrow (*Spizella arborea*)
Brewer's Sparrow (*Spizella breweri*)
White-crowned Sparrow (*Zonotrichia leucophrys*)
Lapland Longspur (*Calcarius lapponicus*)

The great majority of common names used are identical with those in Roger Tory Peterson's *A Field Guide to Birds* (1947) and *A Field Guide to Western Birds* (1941). In cases where they are different, cross references are made in the index.

Occasionally it has been worth while to call attention to a subspecies. In such instances, the common name of the subspecies is placed in parentheses before the name of the species: for example, (Red-breasted) Common Sapsucker, (Red-naped) Common Sapsucker.

In a few cases certain species have common names in this volume that are different from those in the first volume. For example, *Vireo solitaria* is called Solitary Vireo here but Blue-headed Vireo in the earlier work. This change has been deemed necessary in view of the fact that common names used in the eastern part of the country are, for one reason or another, unsuitable when applied to the same species in the western part.

Frequently the following terms are used to indicate groups of species:

Waterfowl: swans, geese, ducks
Waterbirds: loons, grebes, albatrosses, shearwaters, fulmars, petrels, pelicans, cormorants, herons, ibises, spoonbills, gallinules, coots, jaegers, gulls, terns, alcids
Shorebirds: oyster-catchers, plovers, surf-birds, sandpipers, avocets, stilts, phalaropes
Alcids: murres, guillemots, murrelets, auklets, puffins
Landbirds: vultures, hawks, eagles, falcons, gallinaceous birds,

doves, parrots, cuckoos, owls, goatsuckers, swifts, humming-
birds, trogons, kingfishers, woodpeckers, passerine birds
Corvids: jays, magpies, ravens, crows, nutcrackers
Parulids: wood warblers
Fringillids: grosbeaks, finches, sparrows, buntings

The technical terms applied by ornithologists to faunal
regions or biological communities are not used, although
the areas are frequently described. Ornithologists consulting this work can, on reading the descriptions, apply the
terms to which they are accustomed.

Names for physiographic features follow in most cases
those used in *Physiography of Eastern United States*
(1938) and *Physiography of Western United States* (1931)
by Nevin M. Fenneman. Names of trees follow quite
closely those in *Knowing Your Trees* (1947) by G. H.
Collingwood and Warren D. Brush.

Organization of the Chapters. Each chapter consists of
an introduction and a series of bird-finding places.

The introduction presents the ornithology of the state,
with particular reference to the physiographic regions and
biological communities, to migration, and to the winter season. The leading paragraph usually points out one or more
matters of outstanding interest pertaining to the state. The
paragraphs that follow take up the regions and communities, describing them briefly and usually mentioning characteristic breeding birds. In the case of the farmlands or
open country (forest edges, brushy lands, pastures, fields,
prairie grasslands, wet meadows, hedgerows, orchards,
dooryards) and the predominant forests, characteristic species are listed, but the lists are by no means complete. In
fact, some species are omitted because they are too commonplace to warrant attention, others because their environmental preferences are too specialized, still others
because their status in the state concerned is questionable.
Listed below are the species left out of such lists in most
of the chapters.

All herons	Prairie Falcon
Red-tailed Hawk	Duck Hawk
Golden Eagle	Sparrow Hawk
Bald Eagle	European or Hungarian
Osprey	Partridge

Ring-necked Pheasant
Woodcock
Wilson's Snipe
Spotted Sandpiper
Great Horned Owl
Long-eared Owl
Common Nighthawk
All swifts
All hummingbirds
Belted Kingfisher
Lewis' Woodpecker
Traill's Flycatcher
Hammond's Flycatcher
Violet-green Swallow
Bank Swallow
Rough-winged Swallow
Cliff Swallow
Common Raven

Common Crow
Dipper
Short-billed Marsh Wren
Canyon Wren
Rock Wren
Robin
Veery
Cedar Waxwing
Starling
Golden-winged Warbler
Blue-winged Warbler
English Sparrow
Yellow-headed Blackbird
Red-wing
Brewer's Blackbird
Brown-headed Cowbird
Lark Sparrow

Following the paragraphs concerned with regions and communities are two or more paragraphs dealing with the peculiarities of migration and winter birdlife. The principal migration routes through the state and their relationships, if any, to the continental flyways are indicated. In most of the chapters an attempt is made to show, by a series of inclusive dates, when one may expect to observe the peak flights of the majority of waterfowl, shorebirds, and landbirds. The dates are not intended to designate when migrations begin and end. Much of the information on winter birdlife is based on recent Christmas bird counts published in *Audubon Field Notes.*

If a state-wide ornithological society exists, the concluding paragraph is usually devoted to it. The official journals mentioned often provided information presented in the chapter.

The accounts of bird-finding places that follow the introduction are presented under the nearest cities or towns that are indexed (with a few exceptions) on the Rand McNally Road Map of the state. Institutions or local ornithological societies are given recognition under the cities or towns where they are located or where their headquarters are based.

Reference Material. At the end of the book are sug-

gested references. Because this work is not a guide to identification of birds or to studies of birds, recommended
guides for these purposes are included. The regional publications are, for the most part, recent ones and are either
still in print or readily available in most ornithological libraries. All will prove useful.

Index. There is one index. Page numbers refer to the
following: (1) Bird-finding places and the states, cities,
and towns under which they have been described. The
bird-finding places are generally those having names
printed in capitals in the text. (2) Species of birds mentioned in connection with the bird-finding places. Species
in the introductions to the chapters are referred to in only
a few instances. (3) Ornithological societies and institutions of ornithological interest.

Hints for the Bird Finder

When Looking for a Particular Kind of Bird. Look up the name of the bird in the index, then consult the pages given. On each page the bird is mentioned in connection with a locality. By reading this information, it is possible to determine how to reach the bird from the city or town under which the locality is listed, what time of year to make the trip, and what to expect by way of terrain, vegetation, and other birds.

When Visiting a State. Consult the chapter on the state, reading first the introduction, which gives the principal features of the state's ornithology. Then read the accounts of bird-finding localities. Reference to a road map and its index will readily locate the cities and towns from which the locality may be reached.

When Visiting a City or Town. Consult the index, where the city or town will appear if it is presented in the book.

When Visiting a National Park. Consult the index to find where the Park is discussed. Route directions to the Park's headquarters from the nearest city or town will be included. Always make a point of going to headquarters and inquiring about the various interpretive services. Find out when the Park naturalist conducts field trips and gives talks on birdlife and other phases of natural history. Ask about the museum, which will provide supplementary information on natural history. Obtain a map of the Park.

When Visiting a National Wildlife Refuge. The National Wildlife Refuges, whose boundaries are marked by the flying-goose signs, are federally owned and are supervised by the Fish and Wildlife Service of the Department of the Interior. Because they contain some of the finest places for birds, many are described in this book. Consult the index. Directions for reaching the headquarters of each Refuge are included with the route directions from the nearest city or town.

Never visit a National Refuge without first going to its headquarters (or writing in advance to the Refuge manager), making known the purposes of the visit and obtaining permission to enter. Permission is usually granted to the bird finder, unless there is a probability that he will disturb endangered species or interrupt special projects. Meals and overnight accommodations are not available at the Refuges. The assistance of the Refuge personnel may be available, if dates of the visit are known several days in advance so that the personnel may make the necessary adjustments in their work schedules.

Although an attempt is made in this book to give pertinent information on the birdlife in the Refuges, the bird finder will do well to supplement it by making inquiries at the headquarters when he obtains permission to enter.

When Visiting State Parks and Refuges. Several of the states (e.g. Iowa and Oklahoma) have refuge and park systems patterned after those of the Federal Government. Both refuges and parks have headquarters. Ordinarily it is necessary to obtain permission before entering refuges. The parks have naturalists available for field trips and lectures (usually in the summer only). Sometimes there are good museums. When certain of these parks and refuges are interesting ornithologically, they are included in this book, together with route directions to their headquarters.

Miscellaneous Precautions. To nearly all bird-finding localities described here route directions are given, making local inquiry unnecessary. Nevertheless, the person using this guide will be wise to check on these directions whenever possible by contacting ornithologists through institutions and local societies, the addresses of which are given in this book.

Before entering any area for birds, the bird finder should always determine the ownership of the property, learn whether or not permission to enter is necessary, and inquire for regulations that must be observed. In so far as possible, this book indicates when areas are restricted in any way.

In most cases in this book, when a wilderness area for

birds is notoriously hazardous, appropriate warnings are given, but the following words of caution are applicable when visiting all such areas: (1) Carry a good map and compass, and consult both before entering. (2) Be informed about the prevalence of venomous snakes and poisonous plants, and be able to recognize them. (3) Wear clothing that will serve as a protection against noxious insects. (4) Observe all camping and fire-building regulations. (5) Carry drinking water in areas where there are extensive deserts.

A well-known habit of certain birds, such as pelicans, cormorants, herons, gulls, and terns, is to gather in colonies or rookeries for breeding purposes. Because these aggregations are always impressive, the locations of a great many are given in this book. The bird finder must bear in mind, however, that a walk into any type of colony can be detrimental to the welfare of the occupants by driving the adults from their nests and bringing severe exposure to the eggs or small young, or by driving older young from their nests and subjecting them to starvation or to attacks by neighboring adults and by predators. Therefore, observe these precautions: *Circle the colony but never go into it.* Do not stay near the colony longer than a few minutes. If the air temperature is decidedly cool, or the sun's rays uncomfortably hot, do not approach the colony at all, but postpone the visit to a time when conditions are more suitable.

How to Help Increase Ornithological Knowledge. In addition to serving as a recreation, bird finding can be a means of increasing ornithological knowledge.

Park superintendents and refuge managers welcome from a bird finder lists of species seen, and accounts of interesting observations made, during his investigation of the areas in their charge. These records are usually filed and later made available, in one form or another, to other bird finders.

Most of the places described in this book warrant further ornithological study. A bird finder visiting them will do ornithology a great service by writing up his observations as papers or general notes and submitting them to ornithological journals, preferably those covering the states or parts of states in which the places are located. The principal journals and the sponsoring organizations to which they may be addressed are mentioned in the pages of this book.

A bird finder can make useful contributions to ornithological information by taking part in the Christmas bird counts, breeding-bird censuses, and migration and winter-bird studies, the results of which are published regularly in *Audubon Field Notes*. Instructions on how to participate may be obtained by writing the National Audubon Society, 1130 Fifth Avenue, New York 28, New York.

Two books—*A Guide to Bird Watching* (1943) by Joseph J. Hickey and *A Laboratory and Field Manual of Ornithology* (1946) by Olin Sewall Pettingill, Jr.—contain helpful suggestions for the bird finder who wants instructions on methods of bird study (e.g. taking censuses) and on how to prepare reports of observations.

A GUIDE TO BIRD FINDING

WEST OF THE MISSISSIPPI

Arizona

BY GALE MONSON

CACTUS WREN

The saguaro cactus is one of the nation's most familiar symbols. To many Americans, it is the mark of the desert. To the people of Arizona, it is the state flower. To the bird finder, it is a famous host to many interesting birds. In its fluted, spiky columns the Gilded Flicker and Gila Woodpecker excavate their nest holes, which are later re-used by nesting Sparrow Hawks, Elf Owls, Screech Owls, Mexican Crested Flycatchers, and Purple Martins; other birds,

3

notably White-winged Doves, find a repast in the bright red fruit that succeeds the crowns of waxy white blossoms. This giant among cacti is found in our country almost exclusively in southern Arizona. It is king among other desert growths, of which the most common are creosote bush, mesquite, paloverde, catclaw, incienso, bur sage, cholla, and prickly pear. These plants, which make up the typical desert floral landscape, are spread over the southern and western parts of Arizona, the portions of the state that are the true desert—home of such birds as the Verdin, Cactus Wren, various species of thrashers, Plumbeous Gnatcatcher, and Desert Sparrow.

Rising above this desert floor in southeastern Arizona are several small but very rugged and wonderfully beautiful mountain chains, among them the Santa Catalinas, the Santa Ritas, the Huachucas (*whah'-choo-kahs*) and the Chiricahuas (*cheery-caw'-wahs*), and the Pinalenos or Grahams. These mountains attain elevations of from 9,000 to more than 10,000 feet above sea level. They are clothed with live oak, manzanita, juniper, and pinyon pine on the lower slopes, and with ponderosa pine, Douglas fir, and other large trees toward the summits. They are as wonderful ornithologically as they are scenically, for here are found such striking birds as the large Blue-throated and Rivoli's Hummingbirds, the Coppery-tailed Trogon, the Rose-throated Becard, the Sulphur-bellied Flycatcher, the Red-faced Warbler, and the Painted Redstart. There are a number of birds in these mountains and adjacent valleys that are found nowhere else in the United States.

Separating the low southern and western parts of Arizona from the higher Colorado Plateau country of the north is the Mogollon Rim (pronounced *moke'-o-yon*)—an irregular, discontinuous escarpment crossing the state in a northwesterly direction. Climbing up its face, the traveler leaves the hot desert and Mexican birdlife and meets a new climate, a new flora, and a new fauna. He is now in a forest of mile upon mile of juniper and pinyon pine; the largest ponderosa pine stand in the world; stretches of dense aspen, Douglas fir, and spruce. Elevations range from about 6,000 feet to well over 11,000 feet on Mt. Baldy in the White Mountains, and to almost 13,000 feet on the San Francisco Peaks. Despite the forest, the country remains true to the desert in that water is scarce: only rarely is there a permanent trout stream; the lakes are few and far apart; canyon floors are usually dry. Many birds typical of the mountainous west make their homes here, including the Red-shafted Flicker, Lewis' and Three-toed Woodpeckers, Canada and Steller's Jays, Robin, Audubon's Warbler, Western Tanager, Black-headed and Evening Grosbeaks, and even Pine Grosbeaks and Green-tailed Towhees. On the lakes are to be found nesting Eared Grebes, ducks, Soras, and Coots, and in some secluded canyons there are breeding American Mergansers, Ospreys, Dippers, and Lazuli Buntings. In the area about Springerville, the bird finder will see among the nesting birds an eastern element, which includes the Catbird, Veery, and Bobolink.

This lofty wooded belt drops on the north to the grand mesas and colored buttes of the Navajo section of the Colorado Plateau. Here are great grassy expanses, pygmy forests of juniper and pinyon, and sagebrush-filled valleys. West of this Navajo land lies the Grand Canyon, cut between the cold Kaibab Forest and the state's loftiest mountains, the San Francisco Peaks, whose highest summit reaches 12,611 feet above sea level. Typical Navajo birds are the Horned Lark, Scrub Jay, and Mountain Bluebird.

Arizona lies almost completely within the drainage basin of the Colorado River. Along it and its chief tributaries within the state—the Gila (*hee'-la*), Salt, Verde, Santa Cruz, San Pedro, and Little Colorado Rivers—lie blocks of irrigated farmlands, luxuriantly green and exceedingly fertile, in sharp contrast with the brown surrounding desert. Cottonwoods and eucalyptus, orange and grapefruit, date palms and pecans, olives and oleanders vie with alfalfa, cotton, melons, lettuce, flax, and small grains. In these low valleys sprawl the largest cities—Phoenix, Tucson, and Yuma. Huge dams have created Roosevelt Lake on the Salt River, San Carlos Lake on the Gila River, and Havasu and Mohave Lakes and Lake Mead on the Colorado.

Such a diversity of topographical features results in so great a variety of vegetation and climate that bird distribution and migrations are complex in the extreme. In ascend-

ing the slopes of any Arizona mountain range, less than a
vertical mile will transport one as far ecologically as would
hundreds of horizontal miles in the central or eastern
states. The low, hot southern desert changes almost imperceptibly from east to west across the state, a rainfall of
about a foot per year at Douglas diminishing to less than
four inches at Yuma. Everywhere in the state there are
small tracts that are 'ecological islands,' differing in major
aspects from the surrounding territory. To illustrate, one
would think of the saguaro and the juniper as occupying
very different natural niches; yet there are 'islands' in
Arizona where they grow side by side. Despite all these
transitions and variations, it is possible to separate the
state into a number of major natural vegetative associations, which largely determine the distribution of the birds
and other animals.

The first of these would be the *southern desert.* The
basic plant is the creosote bush; associated with it in varying degrees of abundance are the saguaro, paloverde, ironwood, catclaw, incienso, bur sage, ocotillo, cholla, and
prickly pear. The creosote-bush association covers most
portions of southern Arizona, excluding the higher mountain ranges, from the San Pedro Valley west to the Colorado River and northwest to the Lake Mead area. There
are also sizable areas of this association in the upper Gila
Valley. Characteristic breeding birds are:

Red-tailed Hawk	Ash-throated Flycatcher
Sparrow Hawk	Common Raven (near moun-
Gambel's Quail	tains)
Road-runner	Verdin
Screech Owl	Cactus Wren
Great Horned Owl	Mockingbird
Elf Owl	Curve-billed Thrasher
Lesser Nighthawk	Crissal Thrasher
Costa's Hummingbird	Plumbeous Gnatcatcher
Gilded Flicker	Phainopepla
Gila Woodpecker	Loggerhead Shrike
Ladder-backed Woodpecker	Brown Towhee
Mexican Crested Flycatcher	Desert Sparrow

Much of the southeastern part of the state is *high grassland,* occupying the territory between the farms and brush-

lands of the valley bottoms, and the bases of the mountain ranges. This association covers the greater part of the Sulphur Springs, upper Gila, upper Santa Cruz, San Pedro, and San Simon Valleys. There are scattered small tracts northwest to beyond Wickenburg, and west to the far side of the Baboquivari Mountains (pronounced *bab'-o-keev'-a-ri*) on the Papago Indian Reservation. Dominant plants are annual and perennial grasses, chiefly grama and tobosa. Years of grazing by cattle and horses have resulted in the replacement of the grasses in many areas by mesquite, yucca, and burroweed. Typical breeding birds are:

Swainson's Hawk	Mockingbird
Scaled Quail	Loggerhead Shrike
Poor-will (rocky sites)	Eastern Meadowlark
Western Kingbird	Scott's Oriole
Say's Phoebe	Grasshopper Sparrow
Horned Lark	Lark Sparrow
White-necked Raven	Botteri's Sparrow

Occurring along the *major watercourses* in southern Arizona are cottonwoods and willows, which grow with high thick brush (mainly mesquite, batamote or seep willow, arrowweed, and tamarisk). In places, mesquite is the principal plant, forming veritable thickets. This association is continually being cleared to make way for irrigated farmland and is usually limited to relatively narrow strips along the streams. It is characterized by the following breeding birds (asterisks denote those not found along the Colorado River):

Green Heron	Mexican Crested Flycatcher
Cooper's Hawk	Black Phoebe
*Mexican Goshawk	Vermilion Flycatcher
*Mexican Black Hawk	*Beardless Flycatcher
Gambel's Quail	Rough-winged Swallow
White-winged Dove	Crissal Thrasher
Ground Dove	Bell's Vireo
Yellow-billed Cuckoo	Lucy's Warbler
Black-chinned Hummingbird	Yellow Warbler
Gila Woodpecker	Yellow-breasted Chat
Ladder-backed Woodpecker	Hooded Oriole (mesquite)
Western Kingbird	Bullock's Oriole
*Cassin's Kingbird	Brown-headed Cowbird

*Red-eyed Cowbird
Summer Tanager
*Cardinal
*Pyrrhuloxia
Blue Grosbeak

Lesser Goldfinch
Abert's Towhee
Song Sparrow (now very
    local except along the
    Colorado)

To the bird finder, perhaps the most interesting plant association is that found on the *lower slopes of the southeastern mountains.* The key plant is the live oak, of which there are a number of species. On the driest slopes is found 'bushy' chaparral, consisting for the most part of manzanita, buckthorn, mountain mahogany, scrub oak, sumac, and cliff rose. In canyon bottoms, usually dry and rocky courses that carry water only during cloudbursts, grow sycamores, ashes, and Arizona walnuts. In such settings are to be found some of the rarest American birds: the Zone-tailed Hawk, the Whiskered Owl, the Rivoli's and Blue-throated Hummingbirds, the Coppery-tailed Trogon, the Rose-throated Becard, and the Sulphur-bellied Flycatcher. Typical breeding species are:

Zone-tailed Hawk
Mearns' Quail
Band-tailed Pigeon
Screech Owl
Whiskered Owl
Elf Owl
Broad-billed Hummingbird
Acorn Woodpecker
Arizona Woodpecker
Olivaceous Flycatcher
Western Wood Pewee
Scrub Jay (chaparral)
Arizona Jay
Bridled Titmouse

Bush-tit
Bewick's Wren
Eastern Bluebird (local)
Blue-gray Gnatcatcher
Hutton's Vireo
Gray Vireo (chaparral)
Black-throated Gray Warbler
Painted Redstart
Hooded Oriole (sycamores)
Scott's Oriole
Spotted Towhee (chaparral)
Rufous-crowned Sparrow
Black-chinned Sparrow (chaparral)

On the higher parts of the southeastern mountains, over great areas of the Mogollon Rim country, along the rims of the Grand Canyon, on the San Francisco Peaks, and atop the great mesas of the Navajo country, there grows a stand of magnificent *ponderosa pine,* with admixtures of Gambel's oak, New Mexican locust, aspen, and big-toothed maple. Breeding birds of this association include the following (those marked with an asterisk are found in the more southern mountains only):

Golden Eagle
Wild Turkey
Band-tailed Pigeon (near oaks or firs)
Flammulated Owl
Pygmy Owl
*Whip-poor-will
White-throated Swift
Broad-tailed Hummingbird
Red-shafted Flicker
Acorn Woodpecker
Hairy Woodpecker
Western Wood Pewee
*Coues' Flycatcher
Violet-green Swallow
Purple Martin
Steller's Jay
*Mexican Chickadee
Mountain Chickadee
White-breasted Nuthatch

Pygmy Nuthatch
House Wren
Robin
Western Bluebird
(Plumbeous) Solitary Vireo
Virginia's Warbler
*Olive Warbler
Audubon's Warbler
Grace's Warbler
*Red-faced Warbler
Brewer's Blackbird
Western Tanager
Hepatic Tanager
Black-headed Grosbeak
Evening Grosbeak
Pine Siskin
Red Crossbill
*Mexican Junco
Chipping Sparrow

On the highest peaks of the state are stands of *alpine forest*—Douglas fir, Engelmann spruce, and aspen, with thickets of willow and alder along streams—that support another association of birds. Here is the ultimate contrast with the low, hot desert; and the birds are as different as those of the Minnesota north woods are from the birds of the Texas plains. The following are characteristic breeders:

Goshawk
Band-tailed Pigeon
Spotted Owl
Saw-whet Owl
Common Sapsucker
Williamson's Sapsucker
Three-toed Woodpecker
Wright's Flycatcher
Western Flycatcher
Olive-sided Flycatcher
Canada Jay (White Mountains)
Red-breasted Nuthatch
Brown Creeper
Hermit Thrush
Mountain Bluebird (openings)

Townsend's Solitaire
Golden-crowned Kinglet
Ruby-crowned Kinglet
Warbling Vireo
Macgillivray's Warbler (mainly White Mountains)
Cassin's Finch
Pine Grosbeak (mainly White Mountains)
Green-tailed Towhee
(Red-backed) Gray-headed Junco
White-crowned Sparrow (White Mountains)
Lincoln's Sparrow (White Mountains)

Above the limits of timber on the San Francisco Peaks and in the White Mountains, American Pipits make their homes and Clark's Nutcrackers are common.

All of the *Navajo country*, except that occupied by the ponderosa-pine and alpine-forest stands, can be divided into areas characterized by three separate types of growth: (1) open, weedy grassland—chiefly grama and galleta grass and snakeweed; (2) sagebrush, greasewood, and saltbush stands; and (3) the pygmy forest of pinyon pine and juniper. In the grassland, the Poor-will, Horned Lark, and Western Meadowlark are virtually the only breeding birds. Birdlife in the greasewood-sagebrush-saltbush type is also scarce; it is typified by such species as the Mourning Dove, Common Nighthawk, Say's Phoebe, Mockingbird, Bendire's Thrasher, Sage Thrasher, Loggerhead Shrike, House Finch, Vesper Sparrow, Desert Sparrow, Sage Sparrow, and Brewer's Sparrow. In the pygmy forest, the following are the typical breeding birds:

Red-tailed Hawk	Plain Titmouse
Sparrow Hawk	Bush-tit
Mourning Dove	Bewick's Wren
Great Horned Owl	Mountain Bluebird
Common Nighthawk	Blue-gray Gnatcatcher
Cassin's Kingbird	(Plumbeous) Solitary Vireo
Ash-throated Flycatcher	Black-throated Gray Warbler
Gray Flycatcher	Spotted Towhee
Scrub Jay	Chipping Sparrow
Pinyon Jay	

In sharp contrast with the rest of the state, there are places along the Colorado River with extensive growths of *cattail and bulrush* that provide a water habitat. Here typical breeding birds are:

Pied-billed Grebe	Ruddy Duck
Double-crested Cormorant	Clapper Rail (local)
Great Blue Heron	Florida Gallinule
American Egret	Coot
Snowy Egret	Long-billed Marsh Wren
Green Heron	Yellow-throat
Black-crowned Night Heron	Yellow-headed Blackbird
Least Bittern	Red-wing
Redhead	Song Sparrow

The bird finder will surely be bewildered by bird migration in Arizona. There are a few well-defined migratory pathways, such as the Colorado River Valley, which are extensively used by waterbirds and landbirds alike. Elsewhere a jumble of mountains, valleys, canyons, mesas, and plains serves to break up migration routes and upset timetables. Some birds migrate only through the mountains; others migrate only through the valleys and plains. Species that migrate through both mountain and valley often do so at different times, and frequently are of different subspecies as well. A few species nest in the lowlands, then migrate to higher elevations for the rest of the summer season; others nest in the highlands, then immediately fly to the lowlands to linger a while before traveling south. Audubon's Warbler is found in the Navajo country only as a transient; in the high mountain country, only as a summer resident; in the lower parts of the state, only as a winter resident. Transient birds often tarry unusually late in Arizona, and the tenderfoot ornithologist is likely to class lingering migrants as summer residents or winter residents. The migrations of some species, such as the Black Phoebe and Phainopepla, are little known. There are some species that occasionally leave their home territory to make unusual flights; among these are the Lewis' Woodpecker, Steller's Jay, and Clark's Nutcracker. These are mountain birds that are seldom seen in the lowlands, even during winter. Some birds are invaders—the Lawrence's Goldfinch from California and the Wood Ibis and Thick-billed Parrot from Mexico. Along the Colorado River, ocean birds from the Gulf of California occasionally put in their appearance.

Arizona's climate being relatively snow-free, many birds come to spend the winters, especially in the warmer parts of the state. Among these are Western Grebes, White Pelicans, and Canada and Snow Geese; a variety of ducks; Marsh and Pigeon Hawks; Sandhill Cranes, Soras, Wilson's Snipe, Spotted and Least Sandpipers, and Greater Yellow-legs; Belted Kingfishers; and Common Sapsuckers. There are also large concentrations of Tree Swallows along the Colorado River; and often great waves of Western and Mountain Bluebirds come to the lowlands, to feed on mistletoe berries and to hawk for insects over the fields. Flocks of American Pipits come to the irrigated fields and pastures, and hordes of Yellow-headed Blackbirds, Red-wings, and Brewer's Blackbirds visit the stockyards and grainfields. There are large gatherings of Lark Buntings from the Great Plains; myriads of Horned Larks and McCown's and Chestnut-collared Longspurs go to the southeastern grasslands. And we must not overlook the cheerful flocks of several species of juncos, and Chipping, Brewer's, and (Gambel's) White-crowned Sparrows that throng the low woodlands and brushlands during the winter months.

AJO (pronounced *ah'-ho*). This copper-mining town in southwestern Arizona is situated on the broad and dusty desert plain. It is the entrance to a fascinating region, the ORGAN PIPE CACTUS NATIONAL MONUMENT (330,690 acres). To reach Monument headquarters, drive 11 miles southeast from Ajo and its suburb, Rowood, on State Route 86; then turn south (right) on the surfaced road that leads through the Monument to Sonoyta, just across the border in old Mexico, and to Rocky Point (Punta Penasco) on the Gulf of California; 21 miles along this International highway is headquarters, on the west side of the road.

The Monument is best known for its array of spectacular cacti, including especially the long-armed organ pipe cactus, so named because of its fancied resemblance to rows of huge organ pipes. The saguaro is abundant, and along the International boundary is found the sinita, or whisker cactus. The cacti provide an interesting and exciting background for the birdlife of the area.

Near headquarters is a large desert wash, lined by mesquite, ironwood, and paloverde. During the delightful winter months, characteristic nesting birds of the southern desert association are found here quite readily, including the Gambel's Quail, Road-runner, Great Horned Owl, Gilded Flicker, Gila Woodpecker, Ladder-backed Woodpecker, Verdin, Cactus Wren, Curve-billed and Crissal Thrashers, Plumbeous Gnatcatcher, Phainopepla, House Finch, and Desert Sparrow; also winter visitants, including the Red-shafted Flicker, Say's Phoebe, Ruby-

crowned Kinglet, Audubon's Warbler, Green-tailed Tow-
hee, Lark Bunting, Brewer's Sparrow, and (Gambel's)
White-crowned Sparrow. In spring and summer, the White-
winged Dove, Elf Owl, Poor-will, Lesser Nighthawk,
Costa's Hummingbird, Mexican Crested and Ash-throated
Flycatchers, Lucy's Warbler, and Hooded and Scott's
Orioles may be added to the list. The rare Harris' Hawk is
also occasionally seen.

BISBEE. In southeastern Arizona, a few miles from the
Mexican border, lies this mining town, ensconced within
the eastern buttresses of the MULE MOUNTAINS.
US Route 80 crosses Bisbee from east to west. On the west-
ern outskirts of town it climbs to a pass in the mountains
and then drops down WEST TOMBSTONE CANYON.
A visit to the upper parts of the Mule Mountains, which
may be reached from the pass, will acquaint the bird finder
with a number of interesting species found in the chaparral
of live oaks, mountain mahogany, manzanita, and agave.
Among them will be the Band-tailed Pigeon, Scrub and
Arizona Jays, Bush-tit, Bewick's Wren, Crissal Thrasher,
Spotted Towhee, and Rufous-crowned and Black-chinned
Sparrows, which are typical breeding birds; other species
will be found during migrations and in winter. A stop anywhere along the lower part of West Tombstone Canyon,
only a few miles below the pass, will reveal birds more
typical of the desert. Among them the bird finder would
see in spring and summer the White-winged Dove, Black-
chinned Hummingbird, Gila and Ladder-backed Woodpeckers, Vermilion Flycatcher, Verdin, Cactus Wren,
Curve-billed Thrasher, Phainopepla, Lucy's Warbler,
Hooded Oriole, Cardinal, Brown Towhee, and Desert
Sparrow. These are species found in the major watercourse
association, with a sprinkling of those from the southern
desert association. The plant assemblage here is quite interesting, consisting of Arizona walnut, small-leafed sumac,
catclaw, mesquite, hackberry, and sycamore. On the water-
shed above Bisbee, near the town, flowers bloom profusely
in the many small canyons in the fall, attracting numerous
migrating hummingbirds, chief among them the Rufous.

CONTINENTAL. This village is on US Route 89, some
27 miles south of Tucson, on the east bank of the Santa
Cruz River. It is almost completely surrounded by wide
irrigated fields with brushy borders, where the bird finder
may see Black Phoebes, Phainopeplas, and Pyrrhuloxias.
During the winter, Audubon's Caracaras have occasionally
been found in the area, as well as great flocks of Lark Buntings in favorable years.

From Continental it is a 12-mile drive southeastward
over a county road up into MADERA CANYON, sometimes called White House Canyon, in the lofty SANTA
RITA MOUNTAINS. The road ends at Roundup Picnic
Grounds, among live oak and juniper. The left-hand foot
trail leads the visitor back and up the northwestern slope
of the Santa Ritas, through mixed oaks and pines, to almost pure pines, where birds typical of this association may
be seen—Zone-tailed Hawks, Band-tailed Pigeons, Broad-
tailed and Rivoli's Hummingbirds, Red-shafted Flickers,
Acorn and Hairy Woodpeckers, Coues' Flycatchers, Violet-
green Swallows, Steller's Jays, Pygmy Nuthatches, Western
Bluebirds, Solitary Vireos, Virginia's Warblers, Olive Warblers, Grace's Warblers, Western and Hepatic Tanagers,
Black-headed Grosbeaks, Red Crossbills, and Mexican
Juncos. Spring and early fall are the best seasons for making such a trip. Of principal interest, however, are the birds
of the sycamores growing in Madera Canyon, for the most
part below the Picnic Grounds. Here, mainly in spring and
summer, a group of species hardly known elsewhere in
the United States may be found—Whiskered Owls, Broad-
billed Hummingbirds, Arizona Woodpeckers, Sulphur-
bellied and Olivaceous Flycatchers, Beardless Flycatchers,
Arizona Jays, Bridled Titmice, Hutton's Vireos, Painted
Redstarts, and Scott's and Hooded Orioles, and, in some
years, even Coppery-tailed Trogons—enough to thrill the
heart of any visiting ornithologist.

FLAGSTAFF. This city's elevation, 6,895 feet above sea
level, places it in the ponderosa pines. Extensive stands of
this fine tree surround the city. Flagstaff is famed for the
variety of its tourist attractions—among them the magnificent San Francisco Peaks towering 6,000 feet above it

to the north, the Walnut Canyon and Wupatki National Monuments (both Pueblo Indian ruins), and Sunset Crater National Monument. The bird finder will have little difficulty in seeing birds typical of the ponderosa-pine forest on spring and summer visits to these places. The loud rattle of the Broad-tailed Hummingbird as it dashes from one flower patch to another soon becomes a familiar sound. Woodpeckers are represented principally by the Red-shafted Flicker and the Hairy Woodpecker. Violet-green Swallows feed above the pine tops. Big Steller's Jays troop through the trees scolding the visitor raucously. A spritely duo of bird species—Mountain Chickadee and Pygmy Nuthatch—seems inseparable from the pine boughs. Robins and Western Bluebirds are at home in this forest. Each patch of low brush has its pair of Virginia's Warblers, with Grace's Warblers above them in the trees. The rich, rolling songs of Western Tanagers and Black-headed Grosbeaks are sometimes, during the quiet summer days, the only bird voices to disturb the silence. During the winter, the landscape is usually snowy, and comparatively few birds are about—mostly woodpeckers, jays, chickadees, nuthatches, and various juncos.

South of Flagstaff, some 20 miles distant, is famous OAK CREEK CANYON. US Route 89A, which threads the Canyon, drops sharply to it from an almost solid stand of ponderosa pine—down into a wooded wonderland of huge alders, willows, ashes, and sycamores. Through the trees rush the waters of rock-bedded Oak Creek; high on either side tower the rocky canyon walls, of marvelous red and yellow hues. Bright butterflies and wildflowers add their colors to the scene. The Canyon is remarkable ecologically, for here the flora and fauna of the ponderosa pine country and the desert regions meet and often intermix. At the north end of the Canyon, at Pine Flat Campground, such birds as the Broad-tailed Hummingbird, Red-shafted Flicker, Hairy Woodpecker, Steller's Jay, Mountain Chickadee, Pygmy Nuthatch, Robin, Virginia's and Grace's Warblers, Painted Redstart, Western Tanager, and Black-headed Grosbeak are common. Only a few miles farther south, at Indian Gardens, are found such desert birds as the Black-chinned Hummingbird, Mexican Crested

Flycatcher, Black Phoebe, (Sonora) Yellow Warbler, (Long-tailed) Yellow-breasted Chat, Bullock's Oriole, (Cooper's) Summer Tanager, Blue Grosbeak, and (Desert) Song Sparrow—together with a goodly representation of many of the birds found at Pine Flat. The number of ecological puzzles in such an area is well-nigh endless. Band-tailed Pigeons are one of the more common birds of the Canyon, as are the White-throated Swifts and Violet-green Swallows that course along its walls. The careful bird finder will find the Red-faced Warbler where there are pines and Douglas firs, and the eastern Indigo Bunting has been known to nest here. In the Canyon two unusual birds to be looked for are the Mexican Black Hawk and Dipper. It would be difficult indeed to imagine any other place in our United States where birds, trees, climate, and geology all so fortunately conspire to form a place of never-ending wonderment to the bird finder. Spring, summer, and fall are the best times to visit it, for then birds are most numerous and active. The winter bird population is relatively small.

Driving 2 miles south of Flagstaff, on US Route 89A, and then 9 miles east, on a paved country route, brings the bird finder to LAKE MARY, set among the pines. Here, during spring, and especially during fall, there are often huge concentrations of Eared Grebes and ducks, including unusual numbers of Lesser Scaup Ducks and Canvas-backs. In late summer and early fall, numerous shorebirds, gulls, and terns are also present. A few miles farther southeast on the same route lies MORMON LAKE, which is larger and has much the same variety of birds. During protracted droughts, however, these lakes dry up completely.

Flagstaff is the home of the MUSEUM OF NORTHERN ARIZONA. To reach it, turn north off US Route 66 in downtown Flagstaff onto Fort Valley Road. Follow the signs for about 3 miles out of town; the Museum is on the left in its natural setting of ponderosa pines. Although its emphasis is on archeology and geology, the Museum has an interesting exhibit of bird specimens arranged according to the life zones on the San Francisco Peaks; and there is a small but choice collection of bird skins numbering about 2,300. There are also about 200 bird skeletons, which, interestingly enough, are used to identify bird bones found in prehistoric Indian ruins.

GRAND CANYON. Arizona's foremost tourist spectacle, GRAND CANYON NATIONAL PARK (645,808 acres), has several kinds of birds commonly associated with it: the White-throated Swifts that dash and skitter along its brink, the Violet-green Swallows that skim heedlessly into the abyss, and the Turkey Vultures and Common Ravens that enjoy gliding on the air currents that rise from the depths. These the visitor will often see with the first glimpse into the mighty chasm.

Grand Canyon Park is so big and varied that it is virtually impossible for the bird finder to see it with any degree of completeness. To visit the SOUTH RIM only, turn off US Route 66, 2 miles east of Williams, onto State Route 64, which after 59 miles ends directly on the South Rim at Grand Canyon Village, the Park headquarters. If the NORTH RIM is the objective, turn south off US Route 89 onto State Route 67 at Jacob Lake, which is 41 miles west of the famous Navajo Bridge, or 31 miles south and east of Fredonia. It is then 44 miles, over the forested Kaibab Plateau, to Bright Angel Point on the North Rim. A trail connects Grand Canyon Village and Bright Angel Point, crossing the Colorado River at the Canyon bottom by means of a suspension bridge at Phantom Ranch. The visitor may hike down this trail to the bottom, or go by mule, in a day's time; and if he desires, he can make an overnight stop at Phantom Ranch.

The North Rim is roughly 1,000 feet higher than the South Rim at Grand Canyon Village, from which it is separated by some 11 miles of space. At this elevation of over 8,000 feet the bird finder is in a forest composed chiefly of spruce, Douglas fir, and aspen, much like what he would encounter far to the north of Arizona. Ponderosa pine is also found, in lower and drier spots. Birds characteristic of the alpine forest association are common: Williamson's Sapsucker, Olive-sided Flycatcher, Clark's Nutcracker, Brown Creeper, Hermit Thrush, Mountain Bluebird, Townsend's Solitaire, Golden-crowned and Ruby-crowned Kinglets, Warbling Vireo, Audubon's Warbler, Western Tanager, Evening Grosbeak, Pine Siskin, and Gray-headed Junco. This is the only place in Arizona where the rare Pileated Woodpecker has ever been found. Great concentrations of Common Ravens and Cassin's Finches may be seen in the open 'parks.' The assiduous bird finder may possibly observe here such Arizona rarities as the Goshawk, Blue Grouse, and Three-toed Woodpecker, and in some years even the Pine Grosbeak.

The lower South Rim is forested by pinyon pine and juniper, with frequent patches of ponderosa pine. Among the common birds are the Broad-tailed Hummingbird, Red-shafted Flicker, Acorn and Hairy Woodpeckers, Western Wood Pewee, Steller's Jay, Mountain Chickadee, White-breasted and Pygmy Nuthatches, Western Bluebird, Black-throated Gray Warbler, Western Tanager, and Chipping Sparrow. Less common, but often seen, are the Sharp-shinned Hawk, Say's Phoebe, Plain Titmouse, Grace's Warbler, Brewer's Blackbird, Black-headed Grosbeak, and Red Crossbill. The bird finder may be thrilled by a glimpse of that seldom-seen bird, the Flammulated Owl. Turkey Vultures, Mourning Doves, White-throated Swifts, Violet-green Swallows, and Common Ravens are usually to be seen. In brushy patches look for Blue-gray Gnatcatchers, Gray Vireos, and Green-tailed Towhees.

A descent into the Canyon from either rim is a marvelous experience for anyone. The bird finder will find it especially so, for he will be able to witness the change in birdlife as he goes from the rim tops to the Canyon bottom, a classical example of zonation. A short distance below either rim, the ponderosa pine gives way to the pygmy forest of the Navajo country—pinyon pines and juniper, together with various other trees and shrubs. Golden Eagles, Poor-wills, Scrub and Pinyon Jays, Bush-tits, House Finches, and Spotted Towhees are to be observed with the first drop in elevation. Pinyon Jays are often abundant. These birds give way, as the bottom is approached, to such species as the Black-chinned Hummingbird, Ash-throated Flycatcher, Say's Phoebe, Canyon and Rock Wrens, Rufous-crowned Sparrow, and Desert Sparrow. In addition, along the River at the bottom, and along the streams that flow into the River, a strange mixture of species is found: Belted Kingfisher, Black Phoebe, Dipper, Lucy's Warbler, (Sonora) Yellow Warbler, Yellow-breasted Chat, Lazuli Bunting, and Song Sparrow. The mesquite and willows at Phantom Ranch are a vivid contrast indeed to the pines of the rims.

During the winters, many of the birds that brighten the higher areas of the Canyon are gone. The hardy woodpeckers, jays, nutcrackers, chickadees, and nuthatches are still present, however, and the bird finder may be fortunate enough to see some of the unusual winter visitors that have been recorded here, such as the Bohemian Waxwing and rosy finches. Townsend's Solitaires and Evening Grosbeaks are common, and Oregon Juncos are abundant. In the Canyon's depths he will also observe that winter changes the birdlife, species that frequent the higher country in summer now being found at lower elevations.

At Park headquarters, a study collection of approximately 500 bird skins and a reference library of about 125 volumes on birds are housed in a building known as the Naturalists Workshop. The skins are of species found in the Canyon area. An exhibit using bird skins as indicators of life zones is located at the Yavapai Observation Station, one mile east of Grand Canyon Village. The bird student should by all means visit the Station.

KINGMAN. In the Hualpai Mountains (pronounced *wall'-pie*), 14 miles south of Kingman by road, is HUALPAI MOUNTAIN PARK, a pine-girt retreat from the surrounding desert. To reach it, turn south off US Route 66, 1.8 miles east of Kingman. The road climbs rapidly southward, from a little more than 3,000 feet above sea level at Kingman to 6,200 feet in the Park. The Park has public campgrounds, as well as rustic cabins, for those wishing to remain overnight or longer.

The Hualpais are high and rugged, with stands of majestic ponderosa pine on the slopes, and some aspen and fir in the deep, cold canyons. They are the only high mountains on the edge of the lower Colorado River Valley. In the Park, which is in the northern and highest portion of the range, the characteristic trees are ponderosa pine and Gambel's oak, with an understory of New Mexican locust, scrub oak, manzanita, and so on. Among the more readily observed birds are the Band-tailed Pigeon, Broad-tailed Hummingbird, Acorn and Hairy Woodpeckers, Western Wood Pewee, Steller's Jay, White-breasted and Pygmy Nuthatches, House and Canyon Wrens, (Plumbeous) Solitary Vireo, Virginia's and Grace's Warblers, Painted Redstart, Hepatic Tanager, and Black-headed Grosbeak. These may be found from May to September. If he is fortunate, the bird finder will see one or two Zone-tailed Hawks— but he must look sharply, for they are easily confused with Turkey Vultures. At night, Flammulated Owls are common, but not easily seen.

During May and in September and late August, small flocks of migrating warblers are common. These include the Orange-crowned, Nashville, Audubon's, Black-throated Gray, Townsend's, Hermit, Macgillivray's, and Black-capped Warblers. Olive-sided and other flycatchers are common then, as are various transient vireos, hummingbirds, and Western Tanagers.

En route to and from the Park, the road passes through several miles of scrub-oak chaparral, the home of such birds as the Scrub Jay, Plain Titmouse, Bush-tit, Bewick's Wren, Blue-gray Gnatcatcher, Gray Vireo, Scott's Oriole, Spotted Towhee, and Black-chinned Sparrow; in October and later, the (Slate-colored) Fox Sparrow is found here.

PARKER. On the Colorado River, some 15 miles above Parker, is PARKER DAM, which has formed beautiful Havasu Lake, part of the HAVASU LAKE NATIONAL WILDLIFE REFUGE. This Refuge is long and narrow, following along the Lake and the Colorado River for a distance of about 50 miles above the Dam, almost to the town of Needles on the California bank. Altogether there are 45,471 acres in Arizona and California. The lower, southern three fifths of the Refuge consists of Havasu Lake proper; the next one fifth is 11 miles of canyon-walled river; and the upper one fifth is swamp and marsh spread over a wide alluvial valley. Refuge headquarters is in Parker.

Havasu Lake proper can be approached by two principal routes. From Parker on State Route 72, the bird finder crosses the Colorado River to the California side, then turns right to follow a surfaced road 16 miles to Parker Dam. Then he drives across the Dam back into Arizona and follows a scenic curving road another mile to the BILL WILLIAMS RECREATIONAL AREA (locally called HAVASU SPRINGS), which consists of a peninsula of some 100 acres. Here it is possible to look for birds from along the bank, or to rent a boat to find birds on the Lake. Another point of entry is from Topock, on US Route 66. To reach the Lake via this route, drive east on US Route 66 for 10 miles, then turn south another 25 miles to the PITTSBURG POINT RECREATIONAL AREA ('Site Six'), which occupies a peninsula almost a mile wide and 2 miles long near the center of the east shore of the Lake. Rental boats are obtainable here, as well as overnight lodgings and meals.

The emphasis, of course, is on waterbirds. Double-crested Cormorants, Great Blue Herons, and American Egrets are found the year round. Large flocks of Eared Grebes frequent the Lake during migration, and numbers of Western and Pied-billed Grebes spend the winters. More than 20 species of ducks have been identified; occasional flocks of all the common American species are to be seen. A flock of more than 1,000 American Mergansers usually winters near Pittsburg Point. During migration, such shorebirds as Long-billed Curlews, Willets, Marbled Godwits, Avocets, Black-necked Stilts, and Northern Phalaropes are frequent. Small numbers of Ring-billed Gulls spend the winter, and in spring large flocks of California Gulls pass through. Graceful-winged Forster's Terns and Black Terns are common migrants. In the scanty vegetation ashore will be found such typical desert birds as Gambel's Quail, Costa's Hummingbird, Ash-throated Flycatcher, Verdin, Plumbeous Gnatcatcher, and Phainopepla.

The river portion of the Refuge is scenically the most spectacular, especially the Devil's Elbow sector. This part can be reached only by boat, best from Topock, where motorboats with or without guides can be rented. The bird finder will be thrilled throughout the year by seeing cormorants, herons, and egrets in this wild setting, and he should be alert for the sight of a Duck Hawk or White-throated Swifts along the canyon walls. If the motor is shut off and the boat allowed to drift quietly with the current, the loud cry of the Canyon Wren may ring out in the impressive silence. In the summer, myriads of Cliff Swallows are at home here, their residence proved in the winter by their mud homes, which still cling under many a projecting cliff.

The swampy portion of the Refuge is crossed at the southern end by US Route 66 at Topock. The swamp is a maze of ponds, channels, and sandbars, with large areas of inundated brush and the most extensive stands of cattails and bulrushes in the state. The swamp is best seen from a boat, which can be rented at one of the concessions near Topock. There are nesting colonies of Double-crested Cormorants, Great Blue Herons, and American and Snowy Egrets. During the winter the swamp is the haunt of large numbers of Canada and Snow Geese, besides ducks of several species, among which the Gadwall, Green-winged Teal, and Buffle-head are the most prominent. Tremendous flocks of White Pelicans pass through in spring and fall. Harris' Hawks are common permanent residents. Coots and Florida Gallinules nest among the cattails. Here, too, are found large flocks of Tree Swallows, which are present from late summer through the winter and into spring. Nesting songbirds include the Long-billed Marsh Wren, (Sonora) Yellow Warbler, Yellow-throat, Yellow-headed Blackbird, and (Desert) Song Sparrow. Along the edges of the swamp, where mesquite, arrowweed, and tamarisk grow thickly, the bird finder from the East and Middle West can soon find several species new to his life list: Gambel's Quail, White-winged Dove (summer only), Roadrunner, Gila and Ladder-backed Woodpeckers, Black Phoebe (except in spring), Vermilion Flycatcher, Verdin, Crissal Thrasher, Plumbeous Gnatcatcher, Phainopepla (except in summer), Lucy's Warbler (spring and summer only), Hooded and Bullock's Orioles (spring and summer only), and Abert's Towhee. Of all localities along Route 66, this swamp is probably the most rewarding to the bird finder.

Let us now leave the Refuge and return to the immediate vicinity of Parker. Parker is near the northern end of the COLORADO RIVER INDIAN RESERVATION, a tract some 35 miles long by 10 to 15 miles wide. This, the home of the Mohave and Chemehuevis tribes, as well as of transplanted Hopis and Navajos, consists for the most part of a wide irrigated valley, with spots of brush and weeds and cottonwood trees that are very attractive to birds. This area is crisscrossed by a good road system. To reach it, simply drive out of Parker to the southwest. During the winter, the bird finder will be struck by the large numbers of Sparrow Hawks, Mourning Doves, Say's Phoebes, Loggerhead Shrikes, House Finches, and (Gambel's) White-crowned Sparrows to be found along the roads. Gambel's Quail, Road-runners, Gila Woodpeckers, Vermilion Flycatchers, Common Ravens, Mockingbirds, Phainopeplas, Western Meadowlarks, Red-wings, Brown-headed Cowbirds, Abert's Towhees, Savannah Sparrows, and Brewer's Sparrows are also common. Along the canals, Great Blue Herons, American Egrets, and Florida Gallinules can be found. Large flocks of Killdeer and American Pipits frequent the moist fields. During the summer months, the Wood Ibis, White-winged Dove, Western Kingbird, Yellow-breasted Chat, Bullock's Oriole, and Blue Grosbeak enliven the scene. Often in the winter, flocks of Robins, Western and Mountain Bluebirds, and Common, Lesser, and Lawrence's Goldfinches are found.

PATAGONIA. This small settlement in southern Arizona lies in the valley of Sonoita Creek, on State Route 82, 20 miles northeast of Nogáles. There are hills covered with live oaks on either side of the valley, with the heights of the Santa Rita Mountains to the west and the lower Patagonia Mountains to the east. By far the most interesting bird country is the Creek bottom, with its small live stream, bordered by large willows, cottonwoods, and ashes, some sycamores, mesquite, and live oaks, and an interesting understory of elderberry, tree tobacco, and the shrubby *Senecio salignus.* The birdlife is an unusual mixture of representatives of the southern major watercourses and the lower southeastern-mountains associations. Gambel's Quail, Ground Doves, Acorn Woodpeckers, Black Phoebes, Bridled Titmice, Verdins, Bewick's Wrens, Cardinals, Pyrrhuloxias, Brown Towhees, and Rufous-crowned Sparrows are among the permanent residents. Zone-tailed

Hawks, Mexican Black Hawks, Mexican Goshawks, Band-tailed Pigeons, Broad-billed Hummingbirds, Olivaceous, Vermilion, and Beardless Flycatchers, Phainopeplas, Lucy's Warblers, Red-eyed Cowbirds, and Summer Tanagers may be seen regularly during the spring and summer. Patagonia is remarkable for the birds that winter there and that are usually found elsewhere in Arizona only during the warmer months, among them *Empidonax* flycatchers and Hepatic Tanagers. Among the rarer American birds that have been seen here are the Violet-crowned Hummingbird and Green Kingfisher.

By going east from Patagonia on the Harshaw road the bird finder may drive about 15 miles into the SAN RAFAEL VALLEY, an interesting grassy expanse where, in summer, (Arizona) Eastern Meadowlarks and Grasshopper Sparrows are found and, during the winter, large flocks of Horned Larks, McCown's and Chestnut-collared Longspurs, and occasionally, the rare Baird's Sparrow.

PHOENIX. This Arizona metropolis, a city of many lawns, shade trees, shrubs, and outlying citrus groves, is set in the heart of the great irrigated Salt River Valley. Frequent bird sights in the city are the Mourning Dove, White-winged Dove, Inca Dove, Black-chinned Hummingbird, Gila Woodpecker, Western Kingbird, Mockingbird, Curve-billed Thrasher, Phainopepla, House Finch, and Abert's Towhee.

Local bird finders have two favorite routes they follow to look for birds. The beginning point of the first is at the origin of North Scottsdale Road east of downtown Phoenix. Going north from Papago Park, this road passes through marginal desert, citrus groves, and irrigated farms to the town of Scottsdale. Common resident birds of this area are Sparrow Hawks, Mourning Doves, Road-runners, Loggerhead Shrikes, and Western Meadowlarks; in summer look for Western Kingbirds and Hooded and Bullock's Orioles; in winter for Lark Buntings and (Gambel's) White-crowned Sparrows. Four and a half miles north of the intersection in downtown Scottsdale of Scottsdale Road and Indian School Road is a small ranch pond, always good for a waterbird record of some kind—perhaps even Canvas-backs or mergansers. Eight miles out, the Air Force's Thunderbird Field No. 2 is on the right; the pavement ends and the 'arboreal desert' begins. With a slightly rising elevation, the terrain becomes rolling, and the road leads through a fine growth of saguaro, ironwood, paloverde, cholla, ocotillo, and a variety of other desert plants. Common resident birds include Red-tailed Hawks, Gambel's Quail, Gila Woodpeckers, Cactus Wrens, Curve-billed Thrashers, and Desert Sparrows. In winter, there are Marsh Hawks, Sage Thrashers, Western and Mountain Bluebirds, and Audubon's Warblers; in summer, White-winged Doves, and Costa's Hummingbirds.

Six and a half miles north of the pavement's end, the road passes beneath the large power transmission line from the Colorado River at Curry's Corner, where the route turns right. Then 1.7 miles through an interesting yucca, catclaw, and ocotillo association lead to a fork in the road. Take the left fork up through the pass between the hills and past the T-Dart Ranch. Pinnacle Peak is on the left —watch for the split in the pinnacle. Two miles from the last fork the route forks again. Take the right one; just around a small, boulder-strewn hill there is a water 'tank,' made by a dam across a ravine. Here may be found desert birds as they come for water. From this point, go right, toward the Verde River; or left, into ranch country (both roads have dead ends, so the return will be over the same route). This trip will acquaint the bird finder with birds of the Phoenix area, especially those of the desert, and is also definitely worth while for desert plants and desert scenery.

A second favorite route of local ornithologists begins at Five Points in downtown Phoenix, leaving therefrom on West Van Buren Street. Beyond the city, the route passes through irrigated farmlands with an abundance of birdlife. The highway shoulders are wide, and stops can be made at almost any spot. Fourteen miles west of Five Points, at a corner of farmland on the right, water drains during much of the year, attracting such birds as ducks, and the Wilson's Snipe, Vermilion Flycatcher, and Bendire's Thrasher.

From here, the route continues west 2.2 miles to the

palm-lined Litchfield Park-Goodyear highway, then turns left (south) one mile to Goodyear, then right (west) one mile to a slight dip in the road which marks a spot where irrigation water collects and often attracts a variety of birds, among them (in winter) American Pipits, Brewer's Blackbirds, and Savannah Sparrows.

West another 4.8 miles, turn left at Perryville; 2.4 miles from Perryville, along the railroad tracks, a weed and brush thicket is worth a stop for Verdins and, in winter, for Lark Buntings, Savannah Sparrows, Brewer's Sparrows, (Gambel's) White-crowned Sparrows, and Song Sparrows.

South 2.7 miles from the railroad tracks, turn right onto US Route 80 toward Liberty. Drive up and down the roads between the fields and along the canals. When the fields are being irrigated or tilled, the bird finder will see flock upon flock of birds—Great Blue Herons, American and Snowy Egrets. Mountain Bluebirds, American Pipits, Audubon's Warblers, Yellow-headed Blackbirds, Red-wings, Brewer's Blackbirds, and Lark Buntings; and, in some winters, Lawrence's Goldfinches. In addition to these, Marsh Hawks and Black Phoebes are common.

This type of country continues westward along US Route 80 as far as Palo Verde, 15 miles west of where the route first touched US Route 80. The bird finder may return to Phoenix from any point along the highway. Back in the city, he will have seen a most interesting portion of the verdant 'Valley of the Sun.'

SAFFORD. Lying in the upper GILA VALLEY in eastern Arizona, Safford is the center of a verdant irrigated district, with the high GRAHAM MOUNTAINS to the south and the lower Gila Mountains to the north. The Valley's many trees—cottonwood, ash, mulberry, umbrella, and others—offer abundant cover to Mourning and White-winged Doves, Inca Doves, Yellow-billed Cuckoos, Gila and Ladder-backed Woodpeckers, Western Kingbirds, Mockingbirds, Phainopeplas, Yellow Warblers, Hooded and Bullock's Orioles, Summer Tanagers, Blue Grosbeaks, House Finches, and Lesser Goldfinches. In the cotton and alfalfa fields, Western Meadowlarks and Red-wings abound. In and along thickets near the Gila River, and in the bordering desert, are Gambel's Quail, Road-runners, Black-chinned Hummingbirds, Vermilion Flycatchers, Verdins, Curve-billed Thrashers, Plumbeous Gnatcatchers, Lucy's Warblers, Cardinals, and Brown Towhees. Limited to the vicinity of the River are Yellow-breasted Chats, Abert's Towhees, and (Desert) Song Sparrows. There are White-necked Ravens about the Valley, and Boat-tailed Grackles are a not uncommon sight near town. These birds are all nesting species, many of them year-round residents. During the winter, large flocks of blackbirds are a feature of the birdlife, as are numerous (Gambel's) White-crowned Sparrows and, occasionally, large numbers of Robins and Western and Mountain Bluebirds.

The Graham (or Pinaleno) Mountains rise rapidly from the Valley floor's 3,000-foot elevation to almost 11,000 feet. Their upper parts are accessible by automobile from Safford. Turn south on US Route 666 in Safford; 11 miles from town, turn right on a road, known as the Swift Trail, that winds up the east face of the Mountains past a summer resort called Pinecrest, or Turkey Flat. The road soon 'tops out' in a saddle and loops on over the mountain top for several miles more. The vistas of the surrounding desert from this road are among the finest in the state. To the bird finder, however, the most interesting aspects are the changes that occur in vegetation and climate, with the corresponding changes in birdlife, from the foot of the Mountains to their summits. Just a few road miles transport one from the hot, cactus-dotted, shrubby desert up through the oak-juniper belt into the tall ponderosa pines, and finally to the cold top elevations where is found one of the most extensive stands of alpine fir and Engelmann spruce in Arizona, with occasional wet grassy patches and aspen glades.

In the desert lowland at the foot of Swift Trail, the bird finder may seek the Gambel's Quail, Ash-throated Flycatcher, Verdin, Cactus Wren, Plumbeous Gnatcatcher, and Desert Sparrow. In the oak-juniper belt (with tall sycamores along the canyons), look for the Zone-tailed Hawk, Arizona Woodpecker, Olivaceous Flycatcher, Arizona and Scrub Jays, Bridled Titmouse, Bewick's Wren, Blue-gray Gnatcatcher, Hutton's Vireo, Black-throated Gray Warbler, Scott's Oriole, and Rufous-crowned Sparrow. Among the pines, watch for the Band-tailed Pigeon, Broad-tailed Hummingbird, Red-shafted Flicker, Hairy Woodpecker, Coues' Flycatcher, Violet-green Swallow, Steller's Jay, Mountain Chickadee, White-breasted and Pygmy Nuthatches, Robin, (Plumbeous) Solitary Vireo, Olive Warbler, Grace's Warbler, Red-faced Warbler, Painted Redstart, Western and Hepatic Tanagers, Black-headed Grosbeak, and Mexican Junco. Where fir and spruce grow as in the Canadian north woods, search for the Western Flycatcher, Red-breasted Nuthatch, Brown Creeper, Hermit Thrush, and Golden-crowned Kinglet. There are few such places in our country where the bird finder can, within a few hours' time—if desired, in little more than one hour's time—see birds of such extremes of environment.

SUPERIOR. Five miles west of this copper-mining town with its big smelter chimney, turn left off US Route 70 to visit the BOYCE THOMPSON SOUTHWESTERN ARBORETUM. This is one of the show places of the Arizona desert, having 1,700 acres of native plants, and 30 acres of irrigated vegetation. Here there are different kinds of plants from many foreign countries, as well as those representing the southwest. Although the Arboretum is dedicated mainly to the propagation of native and exotic desert plants, totaling some 3,000 varieties, it is also a remarkable place to find birds. Its unusual site, at the foot of Picket Post Mountain, plus the experience of wandering among the many showy and interesting growths, make bird finding an extraordinary pleasure. Many dry-land birds, including the Gambel's Quail, White-winged Dove, Black-chinned and Costa's Hummingbirds, Gila and Ladder-backed Woodpeckers, Ash-throated Flycatcher, Plumbeous Gnatcatcher, Black Phoebe, Verdin, Rock Wren, Curve-billed Thrasher, Phainopepla, Hooded and Bullock's Orioles, Cardinal, House Finch, Brown Towhee, and Desert Sparrow, are readily observed. The photographing of birds while they are nesting is forbidden in the Arboretum.

TOMBSTONE. This formerly rip-roaring mining town in southeastern Arizona serves as a starting point for expeditions into some of Arizona's best birdlands. It is set in a *Mortonia* and catclaw desert. A mile and a half northeast of town, on the Gleeson Road, WALNUT GULCH is crossed. Here an interesting aggregation of birds may be found, especially in the spring and summer. The Gulch is a sandy wash, lined by trees and shrubs such as Arizona walnut, desert willow, *Sageretia,* small-leafed sumac, hackberry, and honeysuckle. Vegetatively, it defies classification, but it fits most nearly into the southeastern grassland association. Gambel's Quail, White-winged Doves, Black-chinned Hummingbirds, Ladder-backed Woodpeckers, Western Kingbirds, Ash-throated Flycatchers, Verdins, Cactus Wrens, Mockingbirds, Curve-billed Thrashers, Hooded and Scott's Orioles, and Desert Sparrows are common. The sharp-eyed bird finder will detect such unusual birds as the Lucy's Warbler and Rufous-crowned Sparrow.

Tombstone is a gateway to the HUACHUCA MOUNTAINS (pronounced *whah'-choo-kah*), a bird wonderland if there ever was one. Travel northwest from town 3 miles on US Route 80, then 16 miles west on State Route 82, and turn south for 10 miles on State Route 92 to Fort Huachuca. At this point, in the foothills of the Huachucas, the visitor can go west on the Canelo road. Some of the finest, and most nearly virgin, grassland in the state is found here. The bird finder will delight in looking for the Scaled Quail, Horned Larks, White-necked Ravens, and Botteri's Sparrows. The Huachuca Mountains proper can be penetrated from State Route 92 east and south of Fort Huachuca via a number of canyons—Garden, Huachuca, Miller, Ramsey, Carr, and others. All are famous in Arizona's ornithological history. It is best to make local inquiry concerning routes and accessibility because of changes in ownership and Forest Service regulations. At least one of the canyons should be open to the public, and all are good bird-finding spots, any time of the year. To see the unusual Mexican species, however, it is best to be on hand in late spring and early summer. The dominant vegetation along these canyons is live oak and sycamore, with chaparral of varying composition on the higher parts of the canyon slopes. The list of strange birds to be seen is a long one; included are the Mearns' Quail, Whiskered Owl, (Stephens') Whip-poor-will, Rivoli's and Blue-throated Hummingbirds, Coppery-tailed Trogon, Arizona Woodpecker, Sulphur-bellied Flycatcher, Olivaceous Fly-catcher, Buff-breasted Flycatcher, Arizona Jay, Bridled Titmouse, Hutton's Vireo, and Painted Redstart. The higher portion of the Huachucas, which reaches above 9,000 feet, is accessible by the REEF ROAD, which turns off State Route 92 at an inn about 10 miles south of Fry. A spectacular drive carries one up into the pine belt. Here birds typical of this association may be found, besides such rarities as the Spotted Owl, Coues' Flycatcher, (Vorhies') Brown-throated Wren, Olive Warbler, Grace's Warbler, Red-faced Warbler, and Mexican Junco.

Seventeen miles northwest of Tombstone, near the small farming center of St. David, US Route 80 crosses the SAN PEDRO RIVER. Verdant farms occupy the valley, with fine stands of large cottonwoods and willows and good growths of mesquite in their uncultivated sections. Birds of the major watercourse association are plentiful, especially Gila Woodpeckers, Western Kingbirds, Vermilion Flycatchers, Bewick's Wrens, Mockingbirds, Phaino-peplas, Lucy's and Yellow Warblers, Yellow-breasted Chats, Bullock's Orioles, and Abert's Towhees.

TUCSON. This is a 'birdy' city. Its trees and shrubbery attract many birds in addition to the ubiquitous English Sparrow. Trim little Inca Doves flutter from lawns and alleys up into the oleanders and palms; their *coo-coo* call is one of the most frequently heard bird voices. Black-chinned Hummingbirds may be seen feeding at lantana and jasmine, and their nests are often found in low-hanging branches of olive and paloverde. Gila Woodpeckers are noisy inhabitants of date palms, large cottonwoods, and eucalyptus. Purple Martins, which nest in saguaros outside the city, may often be seen flying over, en route to their roosts. Verdins scold from mesquite and catclaw remnants of the original desert vegetation. Cactus Wrens and loudly calling Curve-billed Thrashers skulk in every tract of thick shrubbery. Phainopeplas are attracted from time to time by pepper trees and other fruit-bearing plants. Hooded Orioles nest in palms and cottonwoods. Cardinals, brighter in Arizona than elsewhere, are often seen almost in mid-city. House Finches bid fair to outnumber English

PHAINOPEPLA

Sparrows; their beautiful song is heard the year round. During the winter, when Hummingbirds, Martins, and Orioles are no longer found, (Gambel's) White-crowned Sparrows populate the hedges and sing their dreamy songs on warm, sunny days.

Tucson is the starting point for a delightful drive into the SANTA CATALINA MOUNTAINS. From the junction of North Stone Avenue and Speedway, a few blocks north of downtown Tucson, drive east 7 miles on Speedway, leaving the city behind. Then turn left, continuing on pavement another 2 miles. A second turn to the left will take one 7 miles to SABINO CANYON on the south side of the Mountains, a popular picnicking spot where sycamores and saguaros grow almost side by side, and unusual birds may be found, including the Broad-billed Hummingbird, Beardless Flycatcher, Red-eyed Cowbird, and, in winter, Black-chinned and Fox Sparrows.

If the side trip to Sabino Canyon is not made, continue on the pavement without turning left. The road crosses mesquite-lined Rillito Creek and bears left toward the Mountains. It is soon apparent that the car is climbing, and suddenly the road is winding sharply upward, along saguaro-studded hillsides. Turkey Vultures float by at this level, and White-throated Swifts may dash alongside. Farther on, after more climbing and winding, the road enters MOLINO BASIN, where there are many evergreen oaks, junipers, and agaves. This is the live-oak belt, the home of Arizona Woodpeckers, Scrub and Arizona Jays, Bridled Titmice and Bush-tits, Bewick's Wrens, Blue-gray Gnatcatchers, Hutton's Vireos, Black-throated Gray Warblers, Scott's Orioles, Spotted Towhees, and Rufous-crowned Sparrows. All of these may be seen any month of the year, excepting the Gnatcatcher, Warbler, and Oriole. Continuing onward and upward, the road enters a ponderosa-pine forest, with its own assemblage of bird kinds. The bird finder will want to look especially for Band-tailed Pigeons, Coues' Flycatchers, Violet-green Swallows, Steller's Jays, Mountain Chickadees, Pygmy Nuthatches, Grace's Warblers, Virginia's Warblers, Olive Warblers, Red-faced Warblers, Painted Redstarts, Western and Hepatic Tanagers, Evening Grosbeaks, Red Crossbills, and Mexican Juncos.

The mountain road eventually reaches its end at cool SUMMERHAVEN, about 50 miles by road, but less than 20 miles as the raven flies, from Tucson, and at an elevation of 8,000 feet above sea level, more than a mile higher than Tucson. The pines almost disappear from north-facing slopes and are replaced by Douglas fir, white fir, and aspen. Here the bird finder can get acquainted with such alpine birds as the Spotted Owl, Red-breasted Nuthatch, Brown Creeper, Golden-crowned Kinglet, Orange-crowned Warbler, and Pine Siskin—certainly not the birds one would expect to find almost within sight of saguaro cactus. On this brief journey, beginning among palms and cacti, Inca Doves and Cactus Wrens, and ending among spruce and fir, nuthatches and kinglets, we have passed through four distinct associations of birdlife. There are few places in the world where such a feat can be accomplished so easily. The road is open all year, and bird finding here is always interesting; the best months, however, are April and May, and August and September.

In the environs of Tucson there are large stretches of the southern-desert association, where most of the birds characteristic of it may be found. It is a rare experience to search for birds among the huge saguaros, which are perhaps at their best in the SAGUARO NATIONAL MONUMENT (63,284 acres). To reach the Monument, travel east from downtown Tucson on Broadway for about 10 miles, then turn left and follow the signs on a zigzag course for approximately 7 miles more to headquarters. A winding road then leads through the remarkable cactus forest.

Through Tucson itself, and to the north and south, winds the SANTA CRUZ RIVER. It is normally a dry riverbed but on occasion becomes a silt-laden torrent. Along it in many places are heavy growths of brush and occasional cottonwoods or willows—often readily accessible to the bird finder—and irrigated farms. Species representative of the major watercourse association may readily be found here; of these, the Ground Dove, White-winged Dove, Vermilion Flycatcher, Lucy's Warbler, Pyrrhuloxia, and Abert's Towhee are of special interest. Such species of casual occurrence as the Black-bellied Tree-duck and West Mexican Kingbird have recently been found breeding here. To the south and east of Tucson, in mesquite-lined, grassy, desert swales, the rare Rufous-winged Sparrow may be observed.

Tucson bird enthusiasts have formed the Tucson Bird Study Club, which meets twice monthly from November to May. Inquiry may be made concerning the Club at the Arizona State Museum, on the UNIVERSITY OF ARIZONA campus in Tucson. In the Museum are 120 mounted birds, including a pair of Quetzals. Also on the campus, in the Department of Zoology in the Chemistry-Physics Building, is a study collection of 3,000 bird skins and 250 sets of eggs, including four skins of the Coppery-tailed Trogon and one of the California Condor. The skins are almost exclusively those of Arizona birds. There is a good collection of bird reference books in the University library, including complete sets of leading American ornithological journals.

WILLCOX. This ranching center lies in the heart of the famous Sulphur Springs Valley. To the south is found mirage-afflicted Willcox Dry Lake (or Playa), which is ordinarily dry but sometimes holds water and is then attractive to waterfowl, shorebirds, and even gulls and terns. Willcox is ringed by mountain ranges—the Winchesters, Dos Cabezas, Dragoons, and Chiricahuas—all of which have spots interesting to the bird finder, but the Chiricahuas, because of their altitude, size, and proximity to the Mexican border, are the most notable. Any of the west-slope canyons, as well as the wild area atop the peaks, will reward the visitor with unusual bird sights. Local inquiry should be made about the accessibility of these places.

At the northern end of the Chiricahua Mountains is the 10,694-acre CHIRICAHUA NATIONAL MONUMENT (known also as the Wonderland of Rocks), where wind and water have carved spectacular rock formations. To reach it, leave Willcox on the well-maintained county road that runs east and south, through the ghost town of Dos Cabezas, about 38 miles to the entrance of the Monument. Headquarters of the Monument is in Bonita Canyon, which is well worth exploring for birds. The road to Massai Point, an observation lookout, climbs the Canyon. Sycamores, Arizona cypresses, and live oaks grace the Canyon bottom; on the north-facing slopes are pines and junipers, on the south-facing slopes, yuccas, century plants, and cacti. In spring and summer, look for such birds as the Band-tailed Pigeon, (Stephens') Whip-poor-will, White-throated Swift, Black-chinned, Broad-tailed, and Broad-billed Hummingbirds, Arizona Woodpecker, Olivaceous and Coues' Flycatchers, Steller's and Arizona Jays, Plain and Bridled Titmice, Canyon and Rock Wrens, Blue-gray Gnatcatcher, Hutton's Vireo, Black-throated Gray and Grace's Warblers, Painted Redstart, Scott's Oriole, Western Tanager, and Rufous-crowned Sparrow.

YUMA. The irrigated fields and orchards about this city in southwestern Arizona attract many birds of special interest to the bird finder. Extensive acreages of grapefruit, oranges, dates, and pecans afford habitat to birds that dwell in trees, while fields of alfalfa, small grains, flax, melons, and carrots attract birds that like open areas. Canals and drainage ditches harbor various waterbirds, including Green Herons, Least Bitterns, and Florida Gallinules. During the winter, hundreds of American Egrets feed in flooded fields, often under large, swirling flocks of Ring-billed Gulls. In the fall, the same fields attract Killdeer, 'peeps,' Dowitchers, Avocets, Black-necked Stilts, and American Pipits, and occasionally flocks of the rare Mountain Plover may be seen. Road-runners and Gambel's Quail are frequent sights along the roads, and large gatherings of Mourning Doves are common the year round. During the late summer, hordes of White-winged Doves descend on the grainfields. Ground Doves are often flushed among the citrus groves. In the town itself, the assiduous bird finder will see Inca Doves. Both of these diminutive doves are permanent residents. Burrowing Owls perched on telephone poles are common sights during the winter. Gila Woodpeckers are everywhere, and brilliant male Vermilion Flycatchers are frequent at all seasons. Yuma is known for its tremendous autumn flocks of Tree, Barn, and Cliff Swallows that flash about over the fields and bead telephone and fence wires by the thousands. The Cactus Wren, strangely enough, has adapted itself to this irrigated country. Mockingbirds nest commonly. Phainopeplas and Loggerhead Shrikes perch on every hand. Wintering flocks of Yellow-headed Blackbirds, Red-wings, and Brewer's Blackbirds consort with feeding cattle. Songs of Western Meadowlarks are fluted from the alfalfa fields every month of the year. (Gambel's) White-crowned Sparrows gather during the fall and winter along the fencerows and hedges.

On the Colorado River north of Yuma is the IMPERIAL NATIONAL WILDLIFE REFUGE. It consists of the backed-up waters of IMPERIAL DAM, and 46,791 acres in Arizona and California. To reach the Dam, which is at the south end of the Refuge, cross the Colorado River at

Yuma into California on US Route 80, drive half a mile west, then turn right and go by oiled road to Bard, thence by gravel road past Laguna Dam to Imperial Dam, a distance of 18 miles from Route 80. Imperial Dam itself is a vantage point from which to observe waterbirds that may be about, especially during September and October. Birds to be seen then include Eared and Western Grebes, White Pelicans, Double-crested Cormorants, Great Blue Herons, American and Snowy Egrets, Black-crowned Night Herons, Canada and White-fronted Geese, several species of ducks, Coots, Ring-billed Gulls, Caspian Terns, Forster's Terns, and Black Terns. On a small pond to the west of the road approaching Imperial Dam the bird finder may be fortunate enough to see Least Grebes, which nest there.

By crossing the River, by means of a bridge below the Dam, back into Arizona and following the canal that feeds from the Dam for a distance of about 2 miles, MITTRY LAKE is reached. This, a seepage backwater area of the Colorado River, about 3 miles long by half a mile wide, is a mecca for waterbirds, particularly during September and October. Pied-billed Grebes dot the water everywhere, Western Grebes dive on being approached, and White Pelicans fish in large flocks. Occasionally a Brown Pelican is seen. Numerous Double-crested Cormorants and white egrets (both species) by the hundreds fly about or stand in the shallows. Wood Ibis and White-faced Ibis seek out the shallow, muddy-bottomed areas, where Roseate Spoonbills have also been seen. Ducks of several species may be observed, including the rare Fulvous Tree-duck, and nesting Redheads. Harris' Hawks rest on the dead bushes. If the shoreline has receded sufficiently to leave the mud exposed, throngs of shorebirds congregate, especially Snowy Plovers, Killdeer, Wilson's Snipe, Least and Western Sandpipers, Dowitchers, Avocets, and Black-necked Stilts. Mittry Lake is also a rendezvous for myriads of swallows; and Long-billed Marsh Wrens, Yellow-throats, and Song Sparrows abound along its margins.

Contributing authorities: H. C. Bryant, Harry L. Crockett, Steve Gallizioli, Fred Gibson, Joe T. Marshall, Jr., Allan R. Phillips, Charles Wallmo.

Arkansas

BY W. J. BAERG

PILEATED WOODPECKER

'Arkansas, although long known as a paradise for sportsmen, has been strangely neglected by ornithologists.' So
wrote Arthur H. Howell in his *Birds of Arkansas,* published
40 years ago, and the statement is still true, even though
there have been significant efforts to make known the birds
of the state. Albert Lano (1860–1928), although totally
blind, was a very active teacher of ornithology in northwest
Arkansas for many years. His ability to identify all local
birds by song or call note, his genuine enthusiasm, and his
unwavering advocacy of bird protection (only the Sharp-
shinned and Cooper's Hawks being excepted) made bird

students of many children who heard him. When some-
one complained of difficulties in recognizing birds by sound,
he would reply: 'That is because your ears are tuned for
but two things, the ring of the dinner bell and the ring of
the silver dollar.'

The state's total area, 52,725 square miles, is divided
about equally into two main regions: the lowlands of the
Coastal Plain and the uplands. Both drain into the Mississippi River, which forms the state's eastern boundary.

The lowlands lie roughly east and south of a line drawn
from Corning in northeastern Arkansas, through Little
Rock, Arkadelphia, and De Queen, to the Oklahoma
boundary. The eastern lowlands constitute the wide flood
plain of the Mississippi (sometimes referred to as the Mississippi Delta), broken by a long series of hills known as
Crowley's Ridge, which vary in width from half a mile to
12 miles and extend about 150 miles from the Missouri line
near Piggott to Helena. According to one theory, the Ridge
represents an uneroded bank between two former channels of the Mississippi River. Much of this flood plain, together with the bottomlands of the big rivers—the St.
Francis, the White, and the Arkansas—which cross it to
join the Mississippi, contains vast swamps supporting fine
stands of bald cypress, tupelo, overcup oak, water locust,
and other trees associated with southern swamps. Some of
the most extensive of these swamps are in the counties adjacent to the Missouri Bootheel in the extreme northeast.
In the bigger swamps, conditions are generally ideal for
the nesting of such birds as the Double-crested Cormorant,
Anhinga, Great Blue Heron, American Egret, Green
Heron, Black-crowned Night Heron, Wood Duck, Black
Vulture, Red-shouldered Hawk, Barred Owl, Pileated
Woodpecker, Prothonotary Warbler, and Parula Warbler.
Moreover, there is always a possibility of finding a pair
or two of Little Blue Herons, Yellow-crowned Night
Herons, Mississippi Kites, Bald Eagles, and Swainson's
Warblers. The rare Bachman's Warbler should always be
looked for in the swamps around the Bootheel wherever
there is a heavy undergrowth of canebrake; in days gone
by, the species was considered relatively common in this
part of the state. The lowlands west of the flood plain are

level to somewhat rolling. The remaining forests are mainly loblolly and short-leaf pines, mixed with hardwoods such as black and post oaks. Wooded swamps similar to, but usually smaller than, those in the flood plain occur along the rivers that traverse the area.

The uplands, occupying the remaining portion of the state northwest of the lowlands, comprise mountainous country cut by the southeastward-flowing Arkansas River into two subregions: the Ozarks on the north and the Ouachita Mountains (pronounced *wash'-i-ta*) on the south. The Ozarks are a continuation of the dissected plateau of the same name in Missouri, and they are similarly picturesque though somewhat higher. Several peaks attain altitudes in excess of 2,000 feet. The Ouachita Mountains are more rugged and have elevations greater than those in the Ozarks. Two peaks, Magazine Mountain and Blue Mountain, reach 2,850 feet, the highest points in the state. Both the Ozarks and Ouachita Mountains are forest-covered. In the Ozarks hardwoods predominate, principally oaks, gums, hickories, maples, and ashes. On the south and west slopes are short-leaf pines, intermingled with the hardwoods or, often, in pure stands. The Ozarks are widely known as 'the land of the white oaks.' In the Ouachita Mountains the situation is reversed, with short-leaf pines predominating and hardwoods intermingled or occurring in pure stands on the better sites. Much of the larger timber has been cut. There is, however, considerable virgin timber in the National Forests, and many second-growth stands over the region are now becoming commercially important. In the forests of both the Ozarks and the Ouachita Mountains birds are relatively scarce in variety of species and numbers of individuals. Ornithologically, however, these highlands are of interest, for they constitute the southernmost limits of the regular breeding range of several northern species, namely, the Black-billed Cuckoo, Whip-poor-will, Blue-winged Warbler, Yellow Warbler, Oven-bird, Scarlet Tanager, and Common Goldfinch.

A few scattered areas of prairie grassland once existed in the state, particularly in the western part, but they have become farmlands, as have many of the forested areas in the lowlands and in the valleys of both the Ozarks and

Ouachita Mountains. The bird finder, when passing through rural districts during the late spring and summer, should watch for species on the eastern or northern limits of their ranges. Among them are the Scissor-tailed Flycatcher (most likely to be noticed on telephone wires in the western half of the state), the Western Meadowlark (in fallow fields or grassy roadsides of extreme western Arkansas), and the Painted Bunting (most likely to be seen in the vicinity of shrubby places near the roads in eastern and southern Arkansas). Today the following birds breed regularly on the farmlands (fallow fields, pastures, meadows, fencerows, brushy areas, woodland borders, orchards, and dooryards) and in the woodlands (including the lowland and upland forests):

FARMLANDS

Bob-white
Killdeer
Mourning Dove
Barn Owl
Red-headed Woodpecker
Eastern Kingbird
Eastern Phoebe (chiefly northern Arkansas)
Purple Martin
Bewick's Wren (northern Arkansas)
Carolina Wren
Mockingbird
Catbird
Brown Thrasher
Eastern Bluebird
Loggerhead Shrike

White-eyed Vireo
Prairie Warbler
Yellow-throat
Yellow-breasted Chat
Eastern Meadowlark
Orchard Oriole
Common Grackle
Cardinal
Blue Grosbeak
Indigo Bunting
Dickcissel
Eastern Towhee
Grasshopper Sparrow
Pine-woods Sparrow
Chipping Sparrow
Field Sparrow

WOODLANDS

Cooper's Hawk
Red-shouldered Hawk
Broad-winged Hawk
Yellow-billed Cuckoo
Screech Owl
Barred Owl
Chuck-will's-widow
Yellow-shafted Flicker
Pileated Woodpecker

Red-bellied Woodpecker
Hairy Woodpecker
Downy Woodpecker
Red-cockaded Woodpecker (pine forests only)
Crested Flycatcher
Acadian Flycatcher
Eastern Wood Pewee
Blue Jay

Carolina Chickadee
Tufted Titmouse
White-breasted Nuthatch
Brown-headed Nuthatch (pine
  forests only)
Wood Thrush
Blue-gray Gnatcatcher
Yellow-throated Vireo
Red-eyed Vireo
Warbling Vireo
Black and White Warbler
Prothonotary Warbler

Worm-eating Warbler (chiefly
  northwestern Arkansas)
Parula Warbler
Cerulean Warbler
Yellow-throated Warbler
Pine Warbler (pine forests
  only)
Louisiana Water-thrush
Kentucky Warbler
Hooded Warbler
American Redstart
Baltimore Oriole
Summer Tanager

The lowlands in eastern Arkansas, like the Yazoo-Mississippi Delta in western Mississippi, lie in the path of the great Mississippi flyway; hence enormous numbers of waterbirds, waterfowl, shorebirds, and landbirds pass through this part of the state twice yearly. Many loiter and feed, meanwhile forming huge concentrations—for example, the masses of geese and ducks in the Big Lake National Wildlife Refuge (see under Blytheville) and the White River National Wildlife Refuge (see under Stuttgart). In most of Arkansas, the main flights may be expected within the following dates: waterfowl, 20 February—1 April, 20 October—15 December; shorebirds, 15 April—20 May, 10 August—15 October; landbirds, 25 March—5 May, 10 September—5 November.

Arkansas has a large wintering population of waterfowl, many Canada Geese, Mallards, Pintails, Lesser Scaup Ducks, and others preferring to remain here rather than to continue south. The state also serves as wintering ground for many passerine birds that breed in the more northern latitudes. These include Brown Creepers, Robins, Hermit Thrushes, Golden-crowned and Ruby-crowned Kinglets, Myrtle Warblers, Harris' Sparrows (western part of the state), White-crowned Sparrows, White-throated Sparrows, Swamp Sparrows, and Song Sparrows.

BLYTHEVILLE. From Blytheville in northeastern Arkansas drive west on State Route 18 to Manila, then east for 2.5 miles on a gravel road, passing an airport, to the BIG LAKE NATIONAL WILDLIFE REFUGE (9,522 acres).

Headquarters is located in the Refuge at the end of the road.

Big Lake was formed by the earthquake disturbances of 1811–12 that likewise caused the creation of Reelfoot Lake in Tennessee. Included in the Refuge area are about 3,000 acres of open water (principally Big Lake and five smaller bodies of water) and 3,000 acres of swampland where cypresses, willows, and buttonbushes are the conspicuous cover. The major ornithological attractions are the waterbirds and waterfowl, best seen from boats, which are always available. It is impossible to reach different parts of the Refuge with a car but various places on Big Lake can be approached on foot by lanes.

The Prothonotary Warbler is an exceedingly common breeding bird, its song being heard seemingly everywhere from mid-April through June. Among other species nesting commonly on the Refuge are the Wood Duck (about 150 pairs), Crested Flycatcher, Wood Thrush, and Red-eyed Vireo. American Egrets, Snowy Egrets, Little Blue Herons, and (occasionally) Wood Ibises appear in the late summer. Double-crested Cormorants are seen, sometimes in large numbers, in the late fall and early winter months. Nearly all of the geese and ducks using the Mississippi flyway may be observed from late fall to spring, though much less commonly in the winter months. The following populations were estimated in the fall of 1949: Mallard, 100,000; Blue-winged Teal, 8,000; Gadwall, 5,000; Blue Goose, 3,000; Pintail, 2,000; Green-winged Teal, 1,500; Black Duck, 1,000; Baldpate, 1,000; other species of waterfowl, 3,900. Because the Refuge is isolated from human habitation, species of hawks and owls are well represented the year round. These include the Cooper's Hawk, Red-tailed Hawk, Red-shouldered Hawk, Great Horned Owl, Barred Owl, and Screech Owl. Also well represented the year round are species of woodpeckers such as the Red-bellied and Pileated. The latter has the local name of 'Good God,' undoubtedly because of the impression that it makes on a person who sees it for the first time.

FAYETTEVILLE. The Fayetteville region in extreme northwestern Arkansas has a wide range of habitats: wooded hills, large cultivated fields, shaded streams, and several lakes. Much of it is covered with timber, exclusively hardwoods. Oaks are dominant; other trees are sweet gum, black gum, sycamore, American elm, hickory, maple, willow, hackberry, black walnut, and black cherry. Various fruit-bearing shrubs are abundant.

The city itself is the seat of the UNIVERSITY OF AR-KANSAS. In its Museum and Entomology Department there are about 600 bird skins, 100 bird mounts, and nearly 2,000 sets of eggs. Library facilities include the standard ornithological books and journals. Courses in ornithology are given upon sufficient demand.

About 15 miles west of Fayetteville on State Route 16 is LAKE WEDINGTON, a 100-acre body of water used for recreational purposes. University ornithologists find it excellent for waterbirds and waterfowl in the fall and winter. Beginning in late August, Blue-winged Teal arrive. These are soon followed by Mallards, Gadwalls, Lesser Scaup Ducks, Redheads, and Coots. The Lesser Scaup Ducks and Coots become the most abundant species. Others more or less common are the Black Duck, Baldpate, Pintail, Green-winged Teal, Canvas-back, American Golden-eye, and Hooded Merganser. The country surrounding the Lake is wooded and hilly, with sufficient elevation to attract such northern or upland species as the Whip-poor-will and Scarlet Tanager, and yet holds a typical association of southern birdlife, including the Chuck-will's-widow and Wood Thrush.

DEVIL'S DEN STATE PARK (4,320 acres), in densely wooded hill country notable for its deep rock fissures, is frequently visited by ornithology classes of the University. This is reached by going south from Fayetteville on US Route 71 for 10 miles, then turning right at West Fork on State Route 170 and proceeding 18 miles to the entrance. Park headquarters is situated on Lee's Creek, reached by a road winding down a steep slope. Here there are cabins and camping facilities. Most any of the foot trails and bridle paths leading off to the wooded sections of the Park will yield a variety of birds, among them the Wood Thrush, Red-eyed Vireo, and Scarlet Tanager.

HOPE. In the southwestern corner of the state, near the Red River, GRASSY LAKE is well worth a visit. Although the Lake is owned by a sportsmen's club, bird finders not only are welcomed but are assisted in getting to spots of interest. To reach the Lake, take US Route 67 southwest from Hope to the town of Fulton, and turn northwest on a gravel road (State Route 32) to the property, which is 6 miles distant.

The Lake, about 7 miles long and 1½ miles wide, was formed by damming a small tributary creek of the Red River. Since the water is nowhere very deep, the Lake contains an abundance of pondweeds, several big patches of waterlilies, and many cypress trees. Very little of the surface is entirely open.

Anhingas are very common throughout the year. In summer they join Great Blue Herons and American Egrets to nest in a few old cypress trees in conditions as crowded as those to be observed in the rookery in the White River National Wildlife Refuge (see under Stuttgart). The Egrets tend to outnumber the Great Blue Herons. A few Black-crowned Night Herons usually join the colony, but their nests are widely scattered. Other birds commonly breeding at Grassy Lake are Wood Ducks (broods are in evidence in the early summer), Pileated Woodpeckers, and Prothonotary Warblers. Well-stocked with fish and producing a rich supply of aquatic plants, the Lake attracts large numbers of ducks, which begin to congregate in October.

HOT SPRINGS. The famous mineral hot springs in the Ouachita Mountains, now embraced by HOT SPRINGS NATIONAL PARK (1,019 acres), have been known to the white man since 1541, when they were reportedly visited by Hernando de Soto. Owing to the fact that the area has been given protection for a long period—it became a Federal Reservation in 1832 and a National Park in 1932—its natural resources, including its birdlife, have prospered by a minimum of interference. Though having no remarkable bird aggregations, it is a moderately good spot for finding birds characteristic of the Arkansas uplands. A recent report from the Park listed 138 species.

In general, the Park comprises rolling to hilly country (maximum elevation, 1,320 feet), about three fourths of which is forested. Nearly 75 per cent of the trees are second-growth loblolly and short-leaf pines growing on the slopes; the remainder, chiefly deciduous trees such as sweet gums, black gums, American elms, persimmons, hawthorns, and various oaks, stand along the streams. Breeding birds considered at least fairly common in the Park include the Turkey Vulture, Yellow-billed Cuckoo, Whip-poor-will, Red-bellied Woodpecker, Red-headed Woodpecker, Crested Flycatcher, Eastern Phoebe, Eastern Wood Pewee, Rough-winged Swallow, Blue Jay, Carolina Chickadee, Tufted Titmouse, White-breasted Nuthatch, Carolina Wren, Mockingbird, Catbird, Wood Thrush, Eastern Bluebird, Blue-gray Gnatcatcher, Loggerhead Shrike, White-eyed Vireo, Black and White Warbler, Pine Warbler, Prairie Warbler, Louisiana Water-thrush, Yellow-breasted Chat, Orchard Oriole, Summer Tanager, Indigo Bunting, and Chipping Sparrow.

Hiking trails, bridle paths, and winding roads lead through the Park and permit access to the best wooded sections.

LITTLE ROCK. This capital city lies on the Arkansas River near the center of the state. The foothills of the Ouachita Mountains rise to the west, and the Arkansas lowlands stretch eastward and southward. US Route 70 between Little Rock and Memphis (Tennessee) crosses the lowlands to the east and passes the following places of ornithological interest.

HILL LAKE, 12 miles from Little Rock, is a meander cutoff of the Arkansas River, which winds along near the highway for several miles. The Lake is partly marsh and partly open water, and much of it is overshadowed by cypresses. A road (unnumbered) crosses the Lake on a fill and proceeds southward to connect with State Route 30. The surrounding country is chiefly cotton land interrupted by farm buildings, hedgerows, and groves of trees. On the Lake, from October to April, one is almost certain to see a few species of ducks, Pied-billed Grebes, and perhaps hundreds of Double-crested Cormorants. On muddy shores, a few shorebirds—Lesser Yellow-legs, Pectoral Sandpipers, and Semipalmated Sandpipers—may be found in April, early May, and September. Prothonotary Warblers are common summer residents where the borders of the Lake are wooded, while Yellow-throated Vireos are equally common summer residents in the rows of pecan trees on each side of the highway.

Lonoke, 23 miles from Little Rock, is surrounded by a rice-growing area with shallow reservoirs and ponds. Local directions can be obtained for reaching some of the larger ponds designed especially to attract waterfowl, which are abundant in fall, spring, and mild winters. These places are not closed to hunting, and thus visits are not generally advisable during the open season. Herons are common in the late summer at the ponds and in the rice fields. One and a half miles before reaching Lonoke on Route 70, a road on the right leads to the STATE FISH HATCHERY. This Hatchery comprises 267 acres and includes 57 rearing ponds. Some of these ponds are usually drained and attract moderate numbers of migrating shorebirds, including the Stilt Sandpiper. In summer, Bell's Vireos have been found in the weeping willows along the ponds. Among other summer residents in the general vicinity are Yellowthroats, Indigo Buntings, and Dickcissels.

Near Hazen, 43 miles from Little Rock, watch the roadside ditches where cattails and waterlilies are rooted in shallow water. Here in summer one should see King Rails and an occasional Purple Gallinule, an uncommon species this far north. In this section of the state, during the winter, long, strung-out flocks of blackbirds may be seen in the late evenings and early mornings, moving to and from their roosts.

PARIS. This coal-mining town in the Ouachita Mountains is on State Route 22 about 40 miles east of Fort Smith, which is on the western boundary of Arkansas. To the southeast looms MT. MAGAZINE, one of the highest peaks in the state, whose summit may be reached by proceeding southward from Paris for approximately 20 miles over the Mount Magazine Road. From the summit the road continues southward to Havana, on State Route 10. A trip over this scenic route to the top of the mountain, with exploratory stops here and there, affords an excellent opportunity to observe the birdlife inhabiting some of the highest country between the Appalachians and the Rockies. Upland birds to be looked for especially are the Black-billed Cuckoo, Black and White Warbler, Oven-bird, and Scarlet Tanager. The Road-runner has been reported by several observers, and appears to be definitely established as a resident.

STUTTGART. Sometimes called the Rice Capital, this town in east-central Arkansas lies on a level plain of nearly impervious clay, which appeared to be useless for farming until rice culture was developed. Not long ago enormous numbers of transient and wintering geese and ducks visited rice fields in the evening and at night to feed on the harvested shocks, but now that rice is harvested by combine and stored in large concrete bins, these 'raids' have decreased greatly. Hordes of Red-wings, accompanied by Common Grackles, Brown-headed Cowbirds, and Starlings, feed on the rice from its 'milk stage' in September until November, when it is removed from the fields. For this damage the birds repay the farmers by again visiting the fields in the late spring to feed on the armyworms that prey upon the newly growing rice crops. In addition to the ever-present blackbirds and Starlings, other birds occur in impressive numbers. In the spring and summer, some of the commonest breeding birds are the Sparrow Hawk, Bob-white, Killdeer, Common Nighthawk, Loggerhead Shrike, Yellow-throat, Eastern Meadowlark, Dickcissel, and Field Sparrow. Innumerable swallows (Tree, Bank, Rough-winged, Barn) congregate on the telephone wires beginning in the late summer; meanwhile, Great Blue Herons, American Egrets, Little Blue Herons, and sometimes Snowy Egrets begin visiting the wet rice fields to feed on minnows, crayfish, and insect larvae. Marsh Hawks are remarkably numerous over the entire rice-growing area in the fall and winter.

Among the best bird-finding areas in Arkansas is the WHITE RIVER NATIONAL WILDLIFE REFUGE east of Stuttgart. Headquarters is on the eastern edge of the village of St. Charles, which is reached from Stuttgart by taking State Route 30 south to DeWitt (24 miles), turning left (east) on State Route 1, and driving 16 miles. The road is paved for the entire distance but is narrow in places.

The Refuge (roughly 2.5 to 6 miles wide and 50 miles long) comprises 116,390 acres lying along the White River. About 90 per cent is timbered with cypresses, gums, sycamores, elms, maples, and other trees characteristic of the dense bottomland forests of the Lower Mississippi. Water areas include, in addition to the main river channel, about 170 lakes and innumerable channels and bayous. The lakes vary in size from a few acres to several hundred; some deep ones are permanent, while others go dry in the summer. All the water areas are subjected to an annual overflow. There are no true marshes, although a few shallow lakes produce marsh-type vegetation. Waterfowl foods have been propagated in certain places where the water level can be controlled.

Waterfowl are the Refuge's greatest attraction and constitute the main reason for its establishment. Their appearance in the fall begins when the Blue-winged Teal arrive in late August. In the following month they come in increasing numbers and are joined during the last days of the month by Canada Geese and Mallards. The Canada Geese rapidly increase until in late November as many as 6,000 may be seen on one lake. Mallards, though no longer in the enormous numbers of former years, steadily increase through the fall to become the dominant waterfowl by December. (As many as 120,000 were observed on 20 December 1949.) Other ducks appearing in considerable numbers are Pintails and Green-winged Teal. Most of the waterfowl remain until February.

Perhaps the Refuge's second greatest attraction is the heron rookery, where several hundred pairs of Great Blue Herons and American Egrets, together with a large number of Anhingas and a few pairs of Black-crowned Night Herons, occupy a group of giant cypresses standing in an area of only a few acres. In each great tree all four species may be observed nesting together. In May, when the nestlings are well grown, the colony is a noisy spectacle: the young clamoring for food, the adults arriving and departing in a deafening volume of loud croaks, squawks, and chucks.

The Wood Duck is a common breeding bird on the

Refuge, and there are a few aeries of the Bald Eagle. Many birds partial to bottomland forests and their brushy margins abound. Breeding species include the Pileated Woodpecker, Red-bellied Woodpecker, Crested Flycatcher, Acadian Flycatcher, Prothonotary Warbler, Parula Warbler, Yellow-throated Warbler, Louisiana Water-thrush, and Summer Tanager; winter residents, the Common Sapsucker, Eastern Phoebe, Golden-crowned and Ruby-crowned Kinglets, Purple Finch, Savannah Sparrow, Slate-colored Junco, and White-throated Sparrow. Snowy Egrets and Little Blue Herons, and sometimes Wood Ibises, are visitants in the late summer.

Very few roads lead to the Refuge; hence it is not readily accessible by car. Bird finders visiting the Refuge should make inquiries at headquarters about the location of the heron rookery and other places for birds, and how they may be reached.

Contributing authorities: Ben B. Coffey, Jr., T. H. Holder, Terrell Marshall, Joe Morton, Peter J. Van Huizen.

California

BY CHARLES G. SIBLEY AND HOWARD L. COGSWELL

CALIFORNIA CONDOR

California has been described in superlatives so often that
there are few who have not heard that it possesses the biggest trees, the highest mountain, and the lowest desert in
the United States, as well as the largest flying bird in the
world—the California Condor. But even for those more interested in variety than in size there is, perhaps, no comparable area in North America. A motorist may observe
shearwaters before breakfast and before sunset see Clark's
Nutcrackers and Cactus Wrens.

The topography of California is so diversified that a brief

description is certain to be inadequate. From Oregon to the Mexican border is a distance of 780 miles; west to east the width varies from 150 to 350 miles. The dominant topographical feature is the great range of the Sierra Nevada in the east, 385 miles long and averaging 80 miles in width. The Sierra rises as it trends southward to culminate in Mt. Whitney (see under Bishop), 14,496 feet above sea level and the highest point in the United States; 40 other peaks in the range exceed 10,000 feet. Mt. Shasta in northern California is 14,161 feet, and Mt. Lassen (see under Redding), the only volcano recently active in the United States, is 10,453 feet. The Coast Ranges, fringing the ocean for 500 miles and averaging 30 miles in width and 3,000 feet in elevation, parallel the Sierra Nevada, with the Great Valley lying between. The Tehachapi Range on the south and the Siskiyou Mountains on the north complete the encirclement of the Valley, which thus forms a vast inland bowl over 400 miles long and averaging 50 miles in width. The southeastern third of the state is occupied by the Mohave and Colorado Deserts, together covering more than 24,000,000 acres. From the summit of Mt. Whitney it is only 60 miles to Death Valley, the lowest spot in the United States. West of the Deserts rise the San Bernardinos, the San Gabriels, and the San Jacintos, with peaks of over 10,000 feet.

The principal drainage system of the state is composed of the Sacramento and San Joaquin Rivers and their tributaries, which carry the runoff from the Sierra Nevada to San Francisco Bay. These rivers and those that drain seaward from the northern Coast Ranges, such as the Klamath, Eel, and Russian Rivers, flow the year round; but numerous small streams in the more arid sections of the state contain water only during the winter and spring.

The climate of California is as diverse as its topography. The lowlands and coastal areas enjoy the mild winters of which Californians are justly proud, but winter in the mountains earned for the Sierra Nevada its Spanish name, which means 'snowy range.' Over most of the state the rains fall between October and April, summer rains being rare. Annual rainfall varies from 80 inches along the northwest coast to less than 5 inches in the deserts. Along the coast summer fogs maintain a cool, moist climate, permitting the growth of the coastal redwood and its associates.

It is apparent that such variations in climate and topography will have proportional effects upon the plants and animals. The bird finder in California thus enjoys a much greater variety of habitats, and consequently of birds, than he will find in an inland area of low relief; 439 species of birds are recorded from the state, and of these, 273 breed there.

The Great Valley of California was originally an area of grassland, with extensive marshes near the rivers. Parts of it were arid and not used for agriculture. Today the entire Valley is used for farming and pasture, its orchards, vineyards, and grainfields being in a large measure dependent on irrigation. Over 14,000,000 acres in the state are under cultivation. In addition to the Sacramento and San Joaquin Valleys, the Santa Clara, Salinas, Napa, and Imperial Valleys are largely devoted to agriculture.

With irrigation and the planting of many types of trees and shrubs, the avian habitats have been both modified and multiplied. Many native, and a few introduced, species of birds are more abundant in the fields and farmyards, along roadsides, and in city parks than in any natural plant association. Birds that occur commonly in man-made habitats are the following:

Sparrow Hawk
California Quail
Ring-necked Pheasant
Killdeer
Mourning Dove
Chinese Spotted Dove (southern California)
Barn Owl
Burrowing Owl
Anna's Hummingbird
Red-shafted Flicker
Western Kingbird
Black Phoebe
Barn Swallow
Cliff Swallow
Scrub Jay
Yellow-billed Magpie
Common Crow

Bush-tit
Mockingbird
Robin
Loggerhead Shrike
Yellow Warbler
Western Meadowlark
Hooded Oriole (southern California)
Bullock's Oriole
Brewer's Blackbird
House Finch
Common Goldfinch
Lesser Goldfinch
Spotted Towhee
Brown Towhee
White-crowned Sparrow
Song Sparrow

Grassland occupies approximately 10 per cent of the area of the state; small patches occur widely in the lowlands, but the most extensive areas are in the southern and western portions of the Great Valley and in a belt around the Valley at the base of the surrounding hills. The grassy areas of the lowlands are green from November through May; those of northern California and the montane meadows of the Sierra Nevada are green throughout the summer. Typical birds of the low altitude grassland include:

Swainson's Hawk
Prairie Falcon
Sparrow Hawk
Killdeer
Mourning Dove
Burrowing Owl
Western Kingbird
Say's Phoebe
Horned Lark

Common Raven
Common Crow
Loggerhead Shrike
Western Meadowlark
Brewer's Blackbird
Brown-headed Cowbird
Grasshopper Sparrow
Lark Sparrow

The foothills encircling the Great Valley support a park-like woodland whose principal components are the Digger pine and the blue oak. The valley oak often occurs on the more level areas. In the northwestern part of the state, areas of oak woodland are usually dominated by the Oregon oak; in the central Coast Ranges and in southern California, by coast live oak. The following species are associated in the breeding season with the oaks or with the intervening open areas (filled by grasses, other herbaceous plants, or low shrubs). Many of the same species are also found in riparian situations:

Cooper's Hawk
Red-tailed Hawk
Golden Eagle
Sparrow Hawk
California Quail
Mourning Dove
Screech Owl
Black-chinned Hummingbird
Anna's Hummingbird
Red-shafted Flicker
Acorn Woodpecker
Nuttall's Woodpecker

Ash-throated Flycatcher
Western Wood Pewee
Violet-green Swallow
Scrub Jay
Plain Titmouse
Bush-tit
White-breasted Nuthatch
House Wren
Western Bluebird
Blue-gray Gnatcatcher
Hutton's Vireo
Black-throated Gray Warbler

Bullock's Oriole   Lesser Goldfinch
Brewer's Blackbird   Brown Towhee
Brown-headed Cowbird   Lark Sparrow
Black-headed Grosbeak   Chipping Sparrow
House Finch

Few species occurring in streamside thickets and trees are restricted to that habitat. Most of them occur also in either the chaparral or the oak-woodland associations. Riparian trees in the arid regions of the state are largely cottonwoods, willows, and sycamores. The humid coastal region and the mountain canyons of southern California are characterized by alders, big-leaf maple, coast live oak, and California-laurel, with a dense ground cover of thimbleberry, wild rose, snowberry, blackberry, coffeeberry, and bracken fern. The following birds breed in riparian situations in the state:

Red-shouldered Hawk   Warbling Vireo
California Quail   Yellow Warbler
Screech Owl   Yellow-throat
Great Horned Owl   Yellow-breasted Chat
Long-eared Owl   Black-capped Warbler
Black-chinned Hummingbird   Bullock's Oriole
  (southern California)   Brown-headed Cowbird
Red-shafted Flicker   Black-headed Grosbeak
Downy Woodpecker   Blue Grosbeak
Black Phoebe   Lazuli Bunting
Traill's Flycatcher   Common Goldfinch
Western Flycatcher   Lesser Goldfinch
Western Wood Pewee   Spotted Towhee
Bush-tit   Brown Towhee
House Wren   Lincoln's Sparrow (moun-
Bewick's Wren   tains)
Olive-backed Thrush   Song Sparrow
Bell's Vireo

Before agricultural development there were extensive marshes in the river bottoms of the Sacramento and San Joaquin Valleys. Today there are only remnants of these. Some marshy areas have been set aside as wildlife refuges for breeding and wintering waterfowl. Small patches of fresh-water marsh association will be found in the shallows of most lakes and ponds and in the sloughs and back-waters of the larger rivers. Cattails, bulrushes, sedges, and willows are the usual dominant emergent plants. Species that breed in fresh-water marshes or along the shores of lakes or streams are the following:

Eared Grebe	Sora
Western Grebe	Florida Gallinule
Pied-billed Grebe	Coot
Double-crested Cormorant	Killdeer
Great Blue Heron	Spotted Sandpiper
American Egret	Avocet
Snowy Egret	Black-necked Stilt
Green Heron	Wilson's Phalarope
Black-crowned Night Heron	Forster's Tern
American Bittern	Caspian Tern
Mallard	Black Tern
Gadwall	Short-eared Owl
Pintail	Belted Kingfisher
Cinnamon Teal	Black Phoebe
Wood Duck	Long-billed Marsh Wren
Redhead	Yellow-throat
Ruddy Duck	Yellow-headed Blackbird
American Merganser	Red-wing
Marsh Hawk	Tricolored Blackbird
Virginia Rail	Song Sparrow

Harlequin Ducks breed on torrential mountain streams in the Sierra Nevada, and the Dipper is found on turbulent permanent streams in the mountains and near the coast.

Coniferous forests cover more than one fifth of the state: most of northern California above the valleys, except for the northeast corner, which is invaded by the Great Basin sagebrush and juniper; the Sierra Nevada south to Kern County; the San Bernardinos, San Jacintos, Lagunas, and other mountains in southern California; the inner Coast Ranges, south to Napa County; and the Santa Cruz and Santa Lucia Mountains, which border the ocean from San Francisco Bay to San Luis Obispo. From Monterey northward, the coastal coniferous forest is dominated by the towering coastal redwood, which with its associates (Douglas fir, madrone, tanbark oak, black oak, golden chinquapin, California-laurel) forms a belt 450 miles long and one to 50 miles wide. Patches of closed-cone pine (Monterey, Bishop, knobcone, Torrey) occur at intervals along the coast.

The montane coniferous forest of the Sierra Nevada may, for ornithological convenience, be roughly divided at the 6,000-foot level. Below this point the dominant trees are the ponderosa pine, sugar pine, incense cedar, Douglas fir, white fir, and black oak. Above 6,000 feet the lodgepole pine, Jeffrey pine, red fir, and western white pine are characteristic, while near timber line whitebark, foxtail, or limber pine and mountain hemlock form an open subalpine forest. In the following list, the symbols H (high, mainly above 6,000 feet), L (low, mainly below 6,000 feet), and C (coastal) indicate the distribution of the more common breeding birds of the coniferous forests. Species occurring in all three divisions are unmarked. Most species occurring in the Sierra Nevada also range into the inner Coast Ranges of northern California, but in the following list these species are not considered 'coastal,' since they do not usually occur in the redwood or coastal pine associations:

Sharp-shinned Hawk (L, C)
Blue Grouse (H, L, north coast)
California Quail (C)
Mountain Quail
Band-tailed Pigeon (L, C)
Screech Owl (L, C)
Great Horned Owl
Pygmy Owl
Common Nighthawk (H, L)
Vaux's Swift (C)
Allen's Hummingbird (C)
Calliope Hummingbird (H, L)
Red-shafted Flicker
Pileated Woodpecker
Acorn Woodpecker (L, C, in oaks)
(Red-breasted) Common Sapsucker (H, L, north coast)
Williamson's Sapsucker (H)
Hairy Woodpecker
White-headed Woodpecker (H, L)
Hammond's Flycatcher (H)
Western Flycatcher (C)

Western Wood Pewee
Olive-sided Flycatcher
Violet-green Swallow
Tree Swallow
Steller's Jay
Clark's Nutcracker (H)
Mountain Chickadee (H, L)
Chestnut-backed Chickadee (C)
White-breasted Nuthatch
Red-breasted Nuthatch (H, local coastally)
Pygmy Nuthatch (pines only)
Brown Creeper
Winter Wren (mainly C, local L)
Robin
Varied Thrush (north coast)
Hermit Thrush
Olive-backed Thrush (L, C)
Western Bluebird (L, C)
Mountain Bluebird (H)
Townsend's Solitaire (H)
Golden-crowned Kinglet
Ruby-crowned Kinglet (H, L)
(Cassin's) Solitary Vireo

Warbling Vireo
(Calaveras) Nashville War-
 bler (L)
Audubon's Warbler
Hermit Warbler (H, L, local
 coastally)
Macgillivray's Warbler
Western Tanager
Black-headed Grosbeak

Evening Grosbeak (H)
Purple Finch (L, C)
Cassin's Finch (H)
Pine Grosbeak (H)
Pine Siskin
Red Crossbill (H, local
 coastally)
Oregon Junco

The dense stands of woody shrubs that occupy large tracts of the arid foothills in the state are composed of plants the early Spanish settlers called 'la chaparra.' The place where they grow, in accordance with Spanish word structure, is therefore 'chaparral.' Chaparral is characteristic of the dry inner Coast Ranges along the west side of the Sacramento and San Joaquin Valleys and reaches its greatest extent in southwestern California. It occupies nearly 10 per cent of the surface of the state, or approximately 10,000,000 acres. The component plants vary greatly but are always stiff, heavily branched, woody perennials. The manzanitas, scrub oak, chamise, mountain lilac or buckthorn (several species), poison oak, baccharis, and certain sages are plants of the arid chaparral. Along the coast and in riparian situations in the Sierra there occurs a moister phase that is often characterized as 'soft chaparral.' The component plants are usually different, but the growth form is similar, and the bird associates are nearly the same. Macgillivray's Warbler breeds in this type, both coastally and in the Sierra. At middle altitudes (4,000 to 8,000 feet) in the Sierra Nevada a chaparral association of mountain mahogany, snowbush, huckleberry oak, and manzanita is found. Wright's Flycatcher, the Green-tailed Towhee, and the Fox Sparrow are the common birds breeding in this montane chaparral, with the Nashville Warbler where scattered trees are admixed. The following species are characteristic of low-altitude chaparral:

Poor-will
Costa's Hummingbird (south-
 ern California)
Ash-throated Flycatcher
Scrub Jay

Bush-tit
Wren-tit
Bewick's Wren
California Thrasher
Blue-gray Gnatcatcher

58 A Guide to Bird Finding

Orange-crowned Warbler
Lazuli Bunting
Lesser Goldfinch
Spotted Towhee
Brown Towhee
Rufous-crowned Sparrow
Sage Sparrow
Black-chinned Sparrow
(Nuttall's) White-crowned
Sparrow (coastal)

Where the Great Basin impinges upon the eastern side of the Sierra Nevada, pinyon pine, juniper, and sagebrush are the dominant plants. This semidesert association is found in the northeastern corner of the state (eastern Modoc and Lassen Counties), in the central-eastern portion (Mono and Inyo Counties), in western Kern County, on the higher ranges in the Mohave Desert, and along the lower slopes of the southern California mountains fronting on the desert. The common birds of this association include:

Swainson's Hawk
Sparrow Hawk
Sage Grouse
Mourning Dove
Poor-will
Ash-throated Flycatcher
Gray Flycatcher
Horned Lark
Scrub Jay
American Magpie
Common Raven
Pinyon Jay
Plain Titmouse
Bush-tit
Sage Thrasher
Blue-gray Gnatcatcher
Loggerhead Shrike
Gray Vireo
Vesper Sparrow
Desert Sparrow
Sage Sparrow
Brewer's Sparrow

The Mohave Desert extends northward to Death Valley and westward to the San Gabriel and Tehachapi Mountains. Its altitude varies from 2,000 to 5,000 feet, with peaks rising to over 7,000 feet in some of the desert ranges. The lower Colorado Desert extends eastward from the Salton Sink to the Colorado River. The motorist crossing these deserts will pass through mile after mile of dull-green creosote bush. In the washes occur mesquite, paloverde, ironwood, and smoke tree; the few permanent streams are bordered with cottonwood and willow. The angular Joshua tree is a prominent feature in the Mohave, while the spiny, red-flowered ocotillo is characteristic of the Colorado Desert. Over 20 species of cacti occur, at least half of which are found in both deserts. The giant saguaro occurs at a few scattered localities near the Colorado River. The commoner breeding birds of both the Mohave and Colorado Deserts are:

Prairie Falcon	Common Raven
Sparrow Hawk	Verdin
Gambel's Quail	Cactus Wren
Mourning Dove	Rock Wren
Road-runner	Mockingbird
Screech Owl	Leconte's Thrasher
Great Horned Owl	Plumbeous Gnatcatcher
Burrowing Owl	Phainopepla
Lesser Nighthawk	Loggerhead Shrike
Poor-will	Scott's Oriole
Costa's Hummingbird	House Finch
Ladder-backed Woodpecker	Desert Sparrow
Say's Phoebe	

The following species are found only in the Colorado Desert:

White-winged Dove	Crissal Thrasher
Gila Woodpecker	Hooded Oriole
Vermilion Flycatcher	Abert's Towhee

California's coastline is approximately 1,200 miles in length, nearly one tenth of the entire coastline of the United States. It is extremely varied, with rocky cliffs and headlands providing shelter for small bays and sandy beaches. The mild climate along the coast permits numerous transient shorebirds and waterfowl to spend the winter. The bays of Humboldt, Tomales, Bolinas, San Francisco, Monterey, Morro, Newport, and San Diego provide shelter from ocean storms. Rocky headlands and offshore islets have nesting sites for Brown Pelicans, Double-crested Cormorants, Brandt's Cormorants, Pelagic Cormorants, Western Gulls, Common Murres, Pigeon Guillemots, and Tufted Puffins. The following lists include residents, transients, and winter visitants. An asterisk indicates that the species nests along the California coast. Species in the first list occur on all types of coast or on coastal waters.

Common Loon	Western Grebe
Arctic Loon	*Brown Pelican
Red-throated Loon	*Double-crested Cormorant
Horned Grebe	White-winged Scoter

Surf Scoter
Red-breasted Merganser
Ruddy Turnstone
Hudsonian Curlew
Willet
Red Phalarope
Northern Phalarope
Glaucous-winged Gull
*Western Gull

Herring Gull
California Gull
Ring-billed Gull
Short-billed Gull
Bonaparte's Gull
Heermann's Gull
*Forster's Tern
Caspian Tern

Rocky shores provide nest sites or forage areas for the following:

*Brandt's Cormorant
*Pelagic Cormorant
*Duck Hawk
*Black Oyster-catcher
 Surf-bird

Black Turnstone
Spotted Sandpiper
Wandering Tattler
*Common Murre
*Pigeon Guillemot

Sandy beaches and adjacent dunes are the favored habitat of the following species:

*Snowy Plover
 Semipalmated Plover
 Black-bellied Plover
 Long-billed Curlew
 Knot
 Baird's Sandpiper
 Least Sandpiper
 Dowitcher
 Western Sandpiper

Marbled Godwit
Sanderling
*Least Tern
Royal Tern
*Horned Lark
American Pipit
*Savannah Sparrow
*(Nuttall's) White-crowned
    Sparrow

On the more sheltered bays and estuaries the bird finder may see the following winter visitants:

Eared Grebe
Pied-billed Grebe
White Pelican
Black Brant
Pintail
Baldpate

Canvas-back
Lesser Scaup Duck
American Golden-eye
Ruddy Duck
Coot
Belted Kingfisher

A group of the most interesting and least-known birds occurs within a few miles of the coast. From the excursion boats to Catalina (see under San Pedro) or from a chartered fishing boat out of Monterey or Newport Beach, it is possible to see Black-footed Albatrosses, often within the range of a few feet. Sooty Shearwaters (occurring literally by the million) are the most abundant offshore species during the summer. They may often be seen from shore. Less common than the Sooty Shearwaters are the Black-vented and Pink-footed Shearwaters. The Black-vented nests on islands offshore from Lower California, while the Pink-footed and Sooty are visitors from the Southern Hemisphere. A frequent winter visitor is the Fulmar, which breeds far to the north.

Four species of petrels breed on offshore islands along the California coast. Of these, the Fork-tailed, Leach's, and Ashy have been recorded offshore the entire length of the state. The Black Petrel has been observed as far north as San Francisco. The Pomarine and Parasitic Jaegers and the Sabine's Gull occur as transients, while the Black-legged Kittiwake is a winter visitor.

Among the alcids, the most abundant is probably the Common Murre, which is a resident. Pigeon Guillemots are likely to be seen at any time of year, but the Rhinoceros Auklet is a winter visitor. The Xantus' Murrelet and the tiny Cassin's Auklet both breed on offshore islands and are winter visitants along the coast.

The only species of North American bird whose nest has not been found by ornithologists is the Marbled Murrelet. This species occurs commonly in winter along the coast of the northern half of the state and in summer has been observed flying inland in Humboldt County on the north coast. Probably ornithologists will eventually find that the Marbled Murrelet nests inland in the dense forests of the northwestern part of the state.

Every tidal mud flat along the coast has its quota of wintering and transient shorebirds, and most species also occur on the mud flats and fresh-water marshes in the interior. The commoner shorebirds found on mud-flat areas are the Semipalmated Plover, Killdeer, Black-bellied Plover, Long-billed and Hudsonian Curlews, Willet, Greater Yellow-legs, Least Sandpiper, Red-backed Sandpiper, Dowitcher, Western Sandpiper, Marbled Godwit, Avocet, and Black-necked Stilt.

The vegetation of the coastal salt marshes of California is dominated by pickleweed, spartina grass, and the com-

posite genus, *Grindelia*. Few bird species are entirely restricted to salt marshes, but many wintering shorebirds retire to rest in the marshes when high tides cover their
feeding areas on the near-by mud flats. Wintering ducks
find refuge on tidal sloughs and ponds; herons and egrets
visit the marshes to feed. Breeding birds include the Marsh
Hawk, Clapper Rail, Short-eared Owl, and Savannah and
Song Sparrows. During the winter these residents are
joined by Virginia Rails, Soras, Long-billed Marsh Wrens,
American Pipits, and Yellow-throats. The rare and elusive
Black Rail is known to breed at Mission Bay (see under
San Diego), and it has been observed in winter at Tomales
Bay and San Francisco Bay. When the highest tides of
the year flood the salt marshes, it is often possible to see
the secretive Rails which at other times remain well hid-
den in the pickleweed tangles.

In most of California there are no sharply distinct migration periods such as eastern observers experience; multitudes of transients pass through the state over such extended seasons that there is never a time of year when
none is on the move. Northward-bound landbird transients
sweep into the state from the southeast, passing across the
deserts and adjacent foothills with little regard for their
normal habitats. One main lane leads up from Imperial
Valley along the Little San Bernardino Mountains (see
under Twentynine Palms) and then splits into two: (1) a
major route following the southern foothills of the San
Bernardino and San Gabriel Mountains to the Tehachapi
Range and the Sierra Nevada or the central valley; (2) a
route along the north bases of the San Bernardinos and the
San Gabriels, thence across the western Mohave Desert
and up the east flank of the Sierra Nevada. Swainson's and
other hawks, Vaux's Swift, hummingbirds, swallows, flycatchers, thrushes, vireos, warblers, orioles, and tanagers
move in waves along both of these routes; and those that
use the second may switch to the first one again at the
Tehachapis. Parallel spring routes in the low mountains of
San Diego and Orange Counties converge with these two
routes above Los Angeles, while many swallows continue
to the northward along the coast or valleys near the coast.
In the San Francisco Bay and central valley regions, how-

ever, there seem to be less spectacular movements, the
birds gradually arriving and departing, with few or no
waves. Only a few species, such as the Vaux's Swift, Rufous
Hummingbird, Townsend's Warbler, and Western Tanager, pass along the north Coast Ranges in numbers. Olive-
backed Thrushes are very widespread as transients and may
be heard overhead at night along any of these routes.

At the beginning of the southward migration, from late
June into September, most small landbirds use the high-
altitude route, the foothills being hot and dry at this season. In July the flower-carpeted meadows of the high
Sierra are in the noisy possession of hordes of Rufous Hummingbirds already southward bound; and by late August
an amazing array of transients and up-mountain, post-
breeding wanderers spreads to and above the timber line.
Participating in this altitudinal movement, an important
aspect of western migration, are flycatchers, most of the
vireos and warblers, Swainson's Hawk, Robin, Hermit
Thrush, Olive-backed Thrush, Western Tanager, Black-
headed Grosbeak, Purple and Cassin's Finches, and even
the familiar Brewer's Blackbird. The southward-bound
transients find spring just past at these altitudes and flowers
and insects plentiful, even though night temperatures may
be near freezing and winter not far off.

Many species that nest in the mountains carry out a
complementary down-mountain migration as the cold
weather sets in, the Mountain Quail making the trip of some
25 to 40 miles down the west slope of the Sierra on foot.
Meanwhile the Blue Grouse moves up into the snow to
feast on fir needles all winter. By October the foothills are
teeming with transients, particularly the later warblers and
numerous fringillids.

Waterfowl and shorebirds in spring use the same
routes along the southern California mountains in passing from the Imperial Valley to the coastal areas, or
into the central valley with its series of marshes. Flocks
of White Pelicans, geese, and gulls are especially frequent high over the mountains, the California and
Ring-billed Gulls following an almost east-west route
from the coast across the central part of the state to
reach breeding grounds in the Great Basin. Similarly,

in the north, the main movement of waterfowl is northeastward from the Sacramento Valley wintering grounds to
the elevated Modoc Plateau and the Great Basin region.
A strictly coastwise route is used by Black Brant, many gulls
and terns, some shorebirds, and by loons and scoters, which
may be counted as they pass headlands. The pelagic birds,
including lines of millions of shearwaters, are usually farther offshore but may be watched from a few favored points
(see under Monterey, San Diego, and Santa Barbara). The
case of the Heermann's Gulls, which are often said to migrate northward from Mexican breeding grounds, is really
one of radial migration after nesting, for they also move
southward to Guatemala. A general timetable of migration periods follows:

Shearwaters .... all year; peaks of Sooty Shearwater,
                        May—June; September
White Pelican .... October—April

Waterfowl and most
  waterbirds .... (August), September—
                        December; February—April
Hawks .... February—early April; September—
                        November
Most shorebirds ...... April—early May; late July—
                        October
Phalaropes, terns ..... May; (July), August—September
Vaux's Swift .... late April—early May; August—
                        September
Hummingbirds .... February—April (May); (June),
                        July—September
Flycatchers .... April—May; July—September
                        (October)
Swallows .... March—April; late August—
                        September
Olive-backed Thrush .. late April—May; late August—
                        September
Vireos and warblers ... April—early May; August—Septem-
                        ber (October)
Orioles, Black-headed
  Grosbeak .... late March—early May;
                        August—early September
Western Tanager ..... late April—May; August—
                        September
Sparrows .... March—April; late September—
                        November

For the bird finder, winter in California holds special attractions. There are as many species of birds to be found at
the lower altitudes from October to April as during the
rest of the year; and many of the species are present in
far greater numbers than are any of the summer birds.

Beginning as early as August with the arrival of flocks
of Pintails, the winter waterfowl population of the Sacramento Valley is estimated at many millions from November
through February. In the moist stubble fields one can then
see, often from a paved road, flocks of several thousand
Canada or White-fronted Geese and scores of thousands
of Mallards, Pintails, Baldpates, and Green-winged Teal.
Snow Geese and Shovelers are also abundant, but they
keep somewhat closer to the ponds and marshes of the
refuges and gun clubs, as do the diving ducks, such as the
Canvas-back, Lesser Scaup Duck, American Golden-eye,
Buffle-head, and Ruddy Duck. Whistling Swans and Sandhill Cranes are common in several places in December and
January. Throughout the state, ducks winter abundantly
on all bodies of water where food and protection are provided; Coots are ubiquitous and are exceedingly abundant
in many places; large numbers of Eared and Western
Grebes frequent the larger lakes; both the American and
the Snowy Egrets winter commonly in central and southern California.

Along the seashore the common winter birds include
three kinds of loons, five grebes, three cormorants, eight
gulls, and a variety of shorebirds and waterfowl, as well as
alcids and other pelagic species that frequent rocky headlands. From Santa Barbara southward, Western Grebes
congregate in flocks of thousands to fish just beyond the
breakers. The larger bays all along the coast support great
rafts of Black Brant and diving ducks. Many thousands of
the smaller shorebirds winter in the San Francisco Bay
region and southward; the larger species are most common along the southern coast, where in a single midwinter
flock there may be hundreds of Willets, Dowitchers, Marbled Godwits, and Avocets and dozens of curlews.

Throughout the state at the lower altitudes, in city and
country, the following winter visitants are normally common from October to March or April in almost any habitat
that provides food and escape cover:

Sharp-shinned Hawk   Audubon's Warbler
Cooper's Hawk   Oregon Junco
Robin   White-crowned Sparrow
Hermit Thrush   Golden-crowned Sparrow
Ruby-crowned Kinglet   Fox Sparrow
Cedar Waxwing

Besides these, several species are common winter visitants to certain habitats or regions: Band-tailed Pigeon, in or near oak woodland; (Red-breasted) Common Sapsucker, in foothill orchards and in pepper and oak trees; Myrtle Warbler, in the northwest coast region and (less commonly) to the south in riparian and near-by habitats; Townsend's Warbler, in live oaks, riparian woodland, or 'redwood border'; Varied Thrush, in the northwest coast region and, erratically throughout the state, in canyon and oak woodland; Lewis' Woodpecker (erratic in occurrence), in oaks; Golden-crowned Kinglet (erratic in occurrence), in conifers and other evergreens.

In the open fields of the valleys, flocks of California and Ring-billed Gulls, with some Herring Gulls, follow the plows; Ferruginous and Rough-legged Hawks join the resident hawk species, the latter chiefly in the north. Many American Pipits, Red-wings, Tricolored Blackbirds, and Savannah Sparrows roam about the grasslands and fields, the Red-wings and Tricolored Blackbirds often in huge massed flocks with which may be associated Brewer's Blackbirds, a few Brown-headed Cowbirds, and (recently) occasional Starlings. Vesper Sparrows are widespread but only locally common. Say's Phoebes and Mountain Bluebirds favor fields with little or no vegetation, and flocks of Mountain Plovers are frequent in similar situations along the west side of the San Joaquin Valley (State Route 33) and in the Imperial Valley. The deserts also receive winter influxes of several species that nest in other habitats to the north—for example, the Bewick's Wren, Sage Thrasher, Blue-gray Gnatcatcher, and the Sage, Chipping, Brewer's, and White-crowned Sparrows. The cold northeastern part of the state receives northern visitors not found in other regions, such as the Gray-crowned and Black Rosy Finches, Common Redpoll, American Tree Sparrow, and Lapland Longspur, but there are fewer resident species there, and the greatest variety of winter birdlife is to be found in the foothills of the Sierra Nevada and the southern Coast Ranges, and along the coast where the temperature is seldom below freezing.

BAKERSFIELD. In the cultivated farmland along US Route 399 west from Greenfield (8 miles south of Bakersfield on US Route 99) may be found all of the breeding-bird species on the farmland-urban and grassland lists, including in winter hundreds of Mountain Bluebirds and sparrows, and hordes of Red-wings and Tricolored Blackbirds. Seventeen miles west of Greenfield the highway crosses the usually dry Kern River and the accompanying water-bearing canal. Just beyond, the Tupman Road leads northward and parallels Buena Vista Slough. At 2.6 miles along this road (near Tupman) a sign marks the entrance to the headquarters of the STATE ELK PRESERVE ZOO-LOGICAL PARK, where most of the remaining elk native to this central valley are maintained. The 1,100-acre Preserve includes cottonwood-willow strips along the Slough and adjacent areas of grassland and saltbush. There are many herons, egrets, occasional Wood Ducks, and (in summer) Lesser Nighthawks, Bell's Vireos, Blue Grosbeaks, and many more common riparian-woodland birds.

Return to Route 399 and turn right to Taft, skirting the Elk Hills through extensive sagebrush areas. A short walk through any of this country offers a chance to see Leconte's Thrashers and Sage Sparrows, both of which nest here, the latter occurring even more commonly in winter flocks. At Taft turn right on State Route 33 and drive north through Blackwells Corners, 42 miles from Taft. Route 33, beyond Blackwells Corners, traverses a wintering ground of the Mountain Plover. From the road literally hundreds of Mountain Plovers may be seen feeding on the most barren flats or in the short grasses bordering the cultivated fields.

The birdlife in the southern Sierra Nevada, easily reached east and south of Bakersfield, is similar to that of the same type of country farther north in the Sierra (for example, in Yosemite National Park; see under Merced). Anywhere in the open foothill grazing country north, east, and south of Bakersfield, however, there is a chance of seeing Cali-

fornia Condors—especially when ground-squirrel poison-
ing is being carried out on a large scale in spring. One of
the favored tours to see spring wildflowers is a drive south
from Bakersfield on Route 99 for about 10 miles, then east
on an unnumbered road over Kern Mesa to Arvin. This
route, due east of Arvin, leads near 6,935-foot BEAR
MOUNTAIN, an outpost of the Tehachapi Range and one
of the roosting sites of non-breeding Condors. Though the
Condors may be feeding at a great distance from the roost,
patient watching of the mountain top and slopes below
it as the morning sun begins to warm them and create good
flying conditions may enable the bird finder to see these
magnificent birds in flight. Condors are also frequently
seen flying over Route 99 in the stretch between Gorman
and Lebec, midway between Bakersfield and Los Angeles.

West of Lebec (41 miles south of Bakersfield on Route
99) rises 8,826-foot MT. PINOS, where most of the
coniferous-forest birds are common. The Blue Grouse and
Ruby-crowned and Golden-crowned Kinglets are found,
chiefly in the firs north of the summit. Clark's Nutcrackers
are especially common along the steep north slopes, the
(Red-breasted) Common Sapsucker, White-headed Woodpecker, and Pygmy Nuthatch in the pines, the Green-tailed
Towhee and Fox Sparrow in the high-altitude buckthorn
thickets. It is possible to see Condors flying overhead anywhere in the region.

Perhaps of even greater interest to many bird finders
will be the sagebrush-filled valleys to the northeast and
south of Mt. Pinos—CUDDY VALLEY and LOCKWOOD
VALLEY, respectively. In the short gray shrubs, which
dominate all but the creek-bed areas of these Valleys, Lark
and Brewer's Sparrows are common summer residents, Sage
Sparrows nest in lesser numbers, and Lawrence's Goldfinches are occasional breeders. In fall and winter flocks
of Pinyon Jays are frequent here, as well as in the surrounding pinyon country.

To reach Mt. Pinos and the Valleys, turn west from Route
99 just south of Lebec and pass through the village of
Frazier Park. The road divides 3.5 miles beyond this, leading to Cuddy Valley (right) and Lockwood Valley (left).
Half a mile along the Lockwood Valley road is Chuchupate

Ranger Station (Los Padres National Forest), where information may be obtained in summer about roads and
trails in the area; 3.5 miles beyond this point, a dirt road
to the right leads 10 miles and 3,600 feet upward in altitude nearly to the summit of Mt. Pinos. It is one-way most
of the distance, the return being by a shorter and steeper
route. A new road up from the head of Cuddy Valley is under construction. National Forest public camps are maintained on the Mountain and near Frazier Park.

BERKELEY. The relatively advanced state of knowledge
about California birds can be directly attributed to the
work and influence of Joseph Grinnell, Director of the
UNIVERSITY OF CALIFORNIA MUSEUM OF VERTE-
BRATE ZOOLOGY from its founding in 1907 until his
death in 1939. Perhaps his greatest contribution was the
development of methods and standards, which were passed
on to his students.

The Museum of Vertebrate Zoology (Room 2593, Life
Sciences Building) has an ornithological collection of approximately 120,000 study skins, 10,000 skeletons, 10,000
sets of eggs, and a library of 500 volumes in addition to a
large collection of scientific reprints. The Biology Library
of the University is housed in the same building and contains all of the important books and journals of ornithology.
No public exhibits are maintained.

The Northern Division of the Cooper Ornithological
Society meets at 8:00 P.M. on the first Thursday of each
month on the University of California campus. Persons interested in birds are cordially invited to attend the meetings. Further information may be obtained from the office
of the Museum of Vertebrate Zoology. *The Condor,* bimonthly publication of the Cooper Ornithological Society,
is edited at the Museum and published in Berkeley.

STRAWBERRY CANYON, on the campus of the University of California and readily accessible by paved road,
provides a wide variety of habitats for the landbirds of the
central Coast Range. From the Stadium the road leads east
up the north side of the Canyon. Keep right when the
road forks at the poultry house. The south side of the
Canyon is thickly wooded with coast live oaks, buckeyes,

California-laurel, madrone, and patches of planted pines, redwoods, and other conifers. Alders, willows, live oaks, laurels, and big-leaf maples occur along the creek. The north side of the Canyon is mostly grassland with patches of chaparral in the ravines. The Botanical Gardens are reached by driving to the end of the paved road. Here among semiformal, varied plantings is an excellent bird-finding area. Birds are plentiful throughout the year, with April and May the favored months.

BERKELEY AQUATIC PARK is reached by driving west on University Avenue to 6th Street. Turn left (south) one block to Addison Street, turn right (west), and drive four blocks to the Park. A paved drive encircles the area. The winter (October to March) concentrations of ducks, gulls, and shorebirds are the primary avian attractions. Avoid Sundays and holidays during good weather.

The foot of University Avenue leads to BERKELEY MUNICIPAL PIER and BERKELEY YACHT HARBOR. Both provide vantage points for observing wintering loons, grebes, ducks, and gulls.

MOUNT DIABLO STATE PARK (1,957 acres) offers optimal conditions for observing birds of the chaparral and blue oak–Digger pine associations. From Berkeley take State Route 24 through the low-level tunnel to Walnut Creek. There are two possible entrances to the Park. (1) Turn left on State Route 21 at its junction with Route 24 in Walnut Creek, drive approximately 4 blocks to the first stop light, turn right, following signs, and continue north-east for 2.2 miles to a right turn marked with a sign showing the way to Mt. Diablo. (2) Turn right on State Route 21 and continue 6.3 miles to Danville, turn left, and follow the signs 3.3 miles to the south entrance of the Park. Both routes lead to the summit (3,849 feet), from which the view on a clear day is remarkable. Look for (Bell's) Sage Sparrows in the chaparral. In the blue oak–Digger pine woodland is an assemblage of bird species markedly different from those of the Berkeley side of the hills. Nuttall's Woodpeckers, Ash-throated Flycatchers, White-breasted Nuthatches, Blue-gray Gnatcatchers, Lark Sparrows, and Chipping Sparrows are sure to be found if a visit is made in April or May.

BISHOP. This bustling supply center for many high-altitude Sierra Nevada resorts, and outfitting center for fishermen, packers, and hikers, is at the northern end of the long trough of OWENS VALLEY, at the point where numerous streams converge to form the Owens River. In the fields and brushlands, from the vicinity of Bishop southward, California Quail, Ring-necked Pheasants, Roadrunners, Burrowing Owls, American Magpies, Common Ravens, Bush-tits, Lesser Goldfinches, and Savannah Sparrows are to be found all year. In summer (Pacific) Common Nighthawks forage daily over the Valley from nesting grounds on higher mountains to the west, and the Lesser Nighthawk is found in limited numbers nesting on the floor of the Valley, this area being one of the few places where both may be seen. The Bell's Vireo, Yellow-breasted Chat, Yellow-headed Blackbird, and Blue Grosbeak nest along the streams or irrigation ditches; many other riparian-woodland species and the Lewis' Woodpecker are found in the cottonwoods lining the Owens River and its tributaries. Winter visitants in the open Valley include the Marsh Hawk, American Pipit, Audubon's Warbler, and the Vesper, Sage, White-crowned, and Lincoln's Sparrows.

From Bishop southward for 119 miles, US Route 6 (uniting with US Route 395) parallels one of the greatest fault scarps in the world, marked by the east face of the Sierra Nevada, which rises abruptly to 10,000 feet above the floor of Owens Valley, affording spectacular scenery all along the way. Side roads lead from the main highway westward up many of the rugged canyons. For the bird finder interested in nesting Pine Grosbeaks, White-crowned Sparrows, and especially in Gray-crowned Rosy Finches, the roads leading to the highest altitudes are the following: (1) from Lone Pine, 59 miles south of Bishop, a road up Lone Pine Canyon ends at Whitney Portal, 8,371 feet, beyond which is a 7-mile trail up MT. WHITNEY to Outpost Camp, at 10,350 feet, where Rosy Finches are occasional, and thence to Consultation Lake, where they are common; (2) from Bigpine, 15 miles south of Bishop, a 12-mile road up Bigpine Creek to beyond Glacier Lodge, below the largest of the Sierran glaciers;

(3) from Bishop, the Bishop Creek Road to SABRINA LAKE, 9,170 feet, and SOUTH LAKE, 9,750 feet—either of which is a several-mile hike away from Rosy Finch breeding areas; (4) from Tom's Place, 25 miles northwest of Bishop on Route 395, the Rock Creek road ends in LITTLE LAKES VALLEY at over 11,000 feet—Rosy Finches should be found close by; (5) from near Casa Diablo Hot Springs, 42 miles northwest of Bishop on Route 395, the Mammoth Lakes road, ending at about 9,000 feet, just short of MAMMOTH PASS, where Rosy Finches occur in summer and just south of which they have nested. All of these high-altitude roads and trails are open, of course, only in summer; they are not 'highways,' and it is usually advisable to check with the Inyo National Forest ranger stations in Bishop, Bigpine, or Lone Pine before attempting them.

On the MONO PLATEAU, north of Bishop, with its sagebrush valleys and scattered pine forests, there are a few places where the Sage Grouse may still be found: (1) the vicinity of Casa Diablo Hot Springs, and (2) Whitmore Hot Springs and Benton Crossing, 1 and 4 miles, respectively, east of Route 395, about 37 miles north of Bishop. Other species of the Great Basin sagebrush habitat are also to be found in this area.

BRAWLEY. IMPERIAL VALLEY is a portion of a roughly triangular trough; the surface of the Salton Sea, which lies in the Valley north of Brawley, is 244 feet below sea level. Irrigated fields have to a great extent supplanted the natural deserts of the Valley floor, and the greatest variety of landbirds is found in the mesquite, catclaw, and paloverde bushes along the New and Alamo Rivers or the many canals, which the roads cross at intervals. Nearly all of the species on the desert list are here, with many of the farmland and grassland birds also common, especially in winter. From late March through April hordes of transient swifts, swallows, vireos, warblers, tanagers, and fringillids sweep up the Valley, almost disregarding their usual habitats; one of the biggest concentrations is the scores of thousands of Tree Swallows that appear about 5 to 9 April.

Birds associated with irrigated fields, such as the White-faced Ibis and the Wood Ibis, waterfowl, the Greater and Lesser Yellow-legs and other shorebirds, Ring-billed Gulls, pipits, and blackbirds, change their feeding grounds as one field or another satisfies their particular requirements; hence the bird finder must drive about in order to find the best locations on any given date. Secondary highways, such as State Route 111 either way from Brawley or the road east and south to Alamorio and Holtville, are better than US Route 99 for this purpose.

At the southern end of Salton Sea is the SALTON SEA NATIONAL WILDLIFE REFUGE (38,887 acres). To reach Refuge headquarters, go northwest on US Route 99 to Vendel's Service Station, 11.6 miles from Brawley, then turn north and drive 4 miles along the dirt road. Much of the upland field and the thousand-acre marshy portion of the Refuge can be reached by patrol roads from headquarters. From November through January there are hundreds of thousands of ducks of a dozen species (especially Pintails, Baldpates, and Green-winged Teal), thousands of Snow Geese, hundreds of Canada and White-fronted Geese, numbers of White-faced Ibises, Long-billed and Hudsonian Curlews, Dowitchers, and smaller shorebirds. Yellow-headed Blackbirds and Red-wings abound, with the greatest concentrations in March and April. White-faced Ibises, American and Snowy Egrets, Dowitchers, Black-necked Stilts, and Ring-billed Gulls are also particularly abundant transients. Outstanding nesting species are the White Pelican, Fulvous Tree-duck, Clapper Rail, Florida Gallinule, Black-necked Stilt, Gull-billed Tern, and Caspian Tern. The height of the nesting period for the Pelican and Terns is May and early June, about a month later for the others. Wood Ibises are common post-breeding visitors throughout the Valley from mid-July until about 1 October, during which time the temperature in the sun is likely to deter all but the most ardent bird finders. It is, however, frequently comfortable early and late in the day.

The California State Division of Fish and Game maintains the IMPERIAL WATERFOWL REFUGE and public shooting grounds, at several places in the Valley, with present headquarters reached by going north on State Route

111 from Brawley to 3.6 miles north of Calipatria; thence
west on K lateral road (easily identified by the high water
tank at Estelle, one mile east of the highway) across the
Alamo River (3.5 miles); and then right on the first road.
Much of the land included in this area is open field, flooded
in the fall to accommodate large numbers of ducks and
some geese. The old headquarters area along the Alamo
River on State Route 111, 7.5 miles north of Brawley, includes extensive cattail and bulrush marshes where rails,
gallinules, and Yellow-headed Blackbirds are common;
willow thickets in which the very pale (Desert) Song Sparrow may be found at any time of the year (together with
other subspecies during the winter); and cottonwood trees
which harbor a few Ground Doves, and Gila and Ladder-
backed Woodpeckers. The Vermilion Flycatcher and typical desert birds are to be found in the dry shrubland bordering the marsh. Burrowing Owls have nested for years
under the dirt entrance road, which leads east from the
highway just north of the river crossing.

For a close view of the SALTON SEA, a visit to Mullet
Island is recommended; from December to February one
may see Mountain Plovers, Sage Thrashers, Mountain Bluebirds, or a flock of Sandhill Cranes (Lesser Sandhills, as a
rule) in the alfalfa fields passed en route. The Cranes
usually fly back at dusk to roost on the shore west of Mullet Island. In fall and winter, Snowy Plovers, Marbled
Godwits, Avocets, and other shorebirds frequent the shores
of the shallow bays on either side of the Island; the sea itself may be dotted for miles with Eared and Western
Grebes and various waterfowl. Wintering Savannah Sparrows along the shore include some of the large-billed forms
from Baja California. Privately-owned Mullet Island is
really a low rocky hill on the shore of the Sea north of the
mouth of the Alamo River. It is past the unique 'mud pots,'
at the end of a 5.5-mile dirt road extending westward from
State Route 111, 17 miles north of Brawley. Cabins have
been for rent here at times, and camping is permitted for a
fee.

DEATH VALLEY JUNCTION. Included within the
boundaries of DEATH VALLEY NATIONAL MONU-

MENT are 2,891 square miles of superlative, eroded desert scenery, in the 165-mile-long Valley and precipitous bordering mountains. Of the total area, 550 square miles are below sea level, reaching at Bad Water the lowest point in North America (−279.6 feet). Telescope Peak, 15 miles away in the Panamint Mountains, attains an elevation of 11,045 feet. Today the motorist may drive at any time of year over paved roads through passes that were frequently unattained goals to the wagon trains a century ago. Monument headquarters is 35 miles north of Death Valley Junction on State Route 190. There are several entrances to the Monument. Within and near the Monument, accommodations for visitors range from large inns and hotels to trailer parks and public campgrounds. The Monument naturalist will direct visitors to the areas of greatest interest to them.

On areas below sea level, mostly covered with salt deposits and sand dunes, few birds are to be found (e.g. the Turkey Vulture, Common Raven, Say's Phoebe); but along the streambeds entering the Valley are growths of mesquite and arrowweed that harbor nesting Gambel's Quail, Costa's Hummingbirds, Verdins, Lesser Goldfinches, and many others. In and near the several permanent watering places around the edges of the Valley and on the floor, many transients congregate, especially in April and October: the Great Blue Heron, American and Snowy Egrets, American Bittern, most of the dabbling ducks, Cooper's Hawk, Coot, Mourning Dove, Rough-winged Swallow (which nests locally), American Pipit, Audubon's Warbler, Yellow-headed Blackbird, and the Savannah, Vesper, and Chipping Sparrows. Species breeding in the vicinity of the larger springs include the Yellow Warbler, Yellow-breasted Chat, Red-wing, Bullock's Oriole, Brown-headed Cowbird, and House Finch. The area around Furnace Creek Ranch (on Route 190 south of headquarters) is ideal for seeing most of these birds, and the marshy-bordered spring at Eagle Borax Works (on a side road south of headquarters and west of Route 190) is a good second. In December and January, Canada Geese may be found here, and Wood Ducks are frequent visitors, especially in the fall. Common wintering landbirds, some of which stay into April, include the American Magpie, Sage Thrasher, Blue-gray

Gnatcatcher, and the Sage, Brewer's, and Song Sparrows.

The height of the nesting season is mid-April, when the shrub-dotted slopes at medium altitudes in the Monument have nesting Road-runners, Burrowing Owls, Leconte's Thrashers, and Desert Sparrows. The Prairie Falcon, Great Horned Owl, White-throated Swift, Ash-throated Fly-catcher, and Rock Wren nest where cliffs or rock-jumbles provide suitable crevices; and the Canyon Wren is found in the deeper canyons. Although the lowermost steep slopes of the mountains around the Valley are practically devoid of vegetation, there is an extensive pinyon pine–juniper woodland belt at higher altitudes, and small areas of bristle-cone pine and limber pine near the highest peaks. Birds typical of the pinyon pine–juniper woodland may be seen along the Mahogany Flat Road, which runs eastward from a point on the Jayhawker Trail, 4 miles within the western Monument boundary. (The Jayhawker Trail is a recently paved road from Trona, California, through Emigrant Canyon to a junction with State Route 190 in the Monu-ment.) From the end of the Mahogany Flat Road, a 7-mile trail leads to Telescope Peak, passing through pines on the way. The Clark's Nutcracker, Mountain Chickadee, White-breasted Nuthatch, Mountain Bluebird, Oregon Junco, and even the Evening Grosbeak, Red Crossbill, and, occa-sionally, other montane species are to be found here. Spec-tacular views of Death Valley, 2 miles below, are also to be enjoyed on this climb.

EL MONTE. Most of the natural river-bottom vegetation and associated abundant birdlife along valley streams near Los Angeles has been cleared away for 'development' pur-poses; but at and near the National Audubon Society's SAN GABRIEL RIVER WILDLIFE SANCTUARY are several areas of black cottonwood, willow, alder, and syca-more, with tangles of wild grape, blackberry, straggly gooseberry, and creek dogwood, which total about 100 acres. The Sanctuary headquarters, at 664 N. Durfee Ave-nue, El Monte, is about 3 miles (along Durfee) south from Valley Boulevard in El Monte. Trails into the woodland and riverbed areas begin here, and the visiting bird finder will be welcomed. The stated purposes of the Sanctuary include the preservation and protection of the river bottomland, with its wildlife, and nature and conservation education—for which latter program a small nature museum and library are maintained at headquarters. Information about local Audubon Societies and other bird clubs in southern California can be obtained by writing the director of the Sanctuary at the address given above. A regularly scheduled field trip within the Sanctuary starts from headquarters at 9:00 A.M. on the second Sunday of each month.

The valleys of the San Gabriel River and the paralleling Rio Hondo converge between two ranges of low grassy hills, just below the Sanctuary, to a 2-mile gap (Whittier Narrows), which forces up subsurface water for streams that flow the year round. This factor is responsible for the dense undergrowth and several wooded swamps in the Sanctuary area, as well as for the fertility of the surrounding farmland. Birds are plentiful at any time of year; all of the valley species on the riparian-woodland list and most of those of the urban-farmland and grassland lists are regular breeders. In the fall and winter the wild grapes and berries provide food for Mockingbirds, Robins, Hermit Thrushes, Cedar Waxwings, and hosts of fringillids. Long-billed Marsh Wrens and Lincoln's Sparrows are common in the wet weedy areas along the riverbed in winter. White-throated Swifts are mid-day aerial visitors through late December and January. Orange-crowned Warblers, Myrtle Warblers, Townsend's Warblers, and Black-capped Warblers winter in small numbers along with the abundant Audubon's Warbler. A few Cassin's Kingbirds and Phainopeplas also winter frequently.

The Cardinal, introduced from the east before 1923, is now a common resident in the woodland areas. (Red-bellied) Red-shouldered Hawks are still fairly common residents and White-tailed Kites are of intermittent occurrence, sometimes nesting. A regular but rare visitor in February and March is the Gray Flycatcher.

Winter visitants and transients associated with the stream or adjacent small ponds in the valley include the Great Blue Heron, American and Snowy Egrets, American Bittern (all these stay through the summer in small numbers), the Pied-billed Grebe, a few of the dabbling ducks, Ruddy

Duck, American Merganser, Virginia Rail, Sora, Florida
Gallinule (which has nested here), Coot, Wilson's Snipe,
Spotted Sandpiper, Solitary Sandpiper (rare, in mid-April),
Greater Yellow-legs, Least and Western Sandpipers, and
Belted Kingfisher. The Osprey is an occasional spring
transient, and the Duck Hawk and Pigeon Hawk are frequent in winter. When the dam across Whittier Narrows
below the Sanctuary is completed, more water will be
present in the Sanctuary and should encourage the presence
of greater numbers of waterbirds, waterfowl, and shorebirds.

Spring migration at the Sanctuary extends from February
(Turkey Vulture, Allen's Hummingbird, and Tree Swallow) through April (Vaux's Swift and most passerine
birds) into May (Purple Martin and Western Tanager).
Nesting activity, beginning with Bush-tits in February,
reaches a peak in May, when nearly all species have eggs
or young, and drops off gradually through June and July
with second broods. Besides the more common riparian-
woodland species, the following nest in or near the Sanctuary: Green Heron, American Bittern, Yellow-billed Cuckoo
(rare), Cassin's Kingbird, Traill's Flycatcher, Tree Swallow, Olive-backed Thrush, Yellow-breasted Chat, Blue
Grosbeak, Lawrence's Goldfinch, and Grasshopper Sparrow.

EUREKA. A visit to the Humboldt Bay region of the
northern coast is worth while at any season of the year. For
waterbirds and shorebirds the winter months (October to
March) will be the most productive. US Route 101 (both
north and south of Eureka) passes close to the east side of
Humboldt Bay, and from it many favorable spots may be
seen. EUREKA SLOUGH is crossed by a concrete bridge
at the northern city limits. Park on the shoulder of the road,
and search the adjacent waters and mud flats for waterbirds and shorebirds. Between Eureka and Arcata, a distance of 8 miles, the highway parallels the Northwest
Pacific Railroad, both running along the top of a levee between the Bay and reclaimed pastureland. Birds of the
fields and grasslands will be seen on the east side of the

road, and birds of the mud flats and tidal sloughs on the west.

At Arcata a paved road turns west from Route 101, 9 miles to Samoa, traversing slough-cut pastureland, for approximately 6 miles, to MAD RIVER SLOUGH. Waterbirds and waterfowl will be found on the Slough; just south of the bridge is a large mud flat where shorebirds occur in abundance, including large flocks of Marbled Godwits in migration. From Mad River Slough to Samoa the road winds amid sand dunes covered with beach pine and huckleberry. Wintering Myrtle and Audubon's Warblers occur in this habitat. From Samoa continue south. The dunes flatten out and are covered with yellow lupine, which blooms in April. In winter, Fox and Song Sparrows are common. Stop at any convenient place along this stretch and walk to the ocean beach. Wintering species include shorebirds of the sandy beach, such as Sanderlings; Baird's Sandpipers are not uncommon.

The road leads south from Samoa for approximately 6 miles to the NORTH JETTY, where a parking area is available. Look for cormorants—Double-crested, Brandt's, and Pelagic—and other waterbirds including Common Murres in the wave-swept channel. Out on the rocks of the Jetty look for Surf-birds, Wandering Tattlers, and Black Turnstones. It was on this Jetty that the California records for the Rock Sandpiper were obtained. On the dry sand at the base of the Jetty one may find Knots and Ruddy Turnstones.

FRESNO. The bird finder visiting the SAN JOAQUIN VALLEY in central California in summer will do well to seek higher and cooler elevations if he expects much variety, but when snows in the Sierra Nevada force the birds to warmer lowlands a visit to ROEDING PARK (157 acres) will be worth while. Over 60 wintering species have been recorded in this Park, on US Route 99 at the north edge of the city.

For waterbirds, bird enthusiasts of the Fresno region visit Mendota, 35 miles west of Fresno on State Route 180. Near the town of Whites Bridge, wintering Sandhill Cranes and Whistling Swans may be seen. In the spring Black

Terns nest in the rice fields along the road just east of Mendota.

Yellow-billed Cuckoos and Blue Grosbeaks are special attractions to the bird finder in the San Joaquin Valley. Both these and other riparian species will be found in April and May in the willows, cottonwoods, and sycamores along the San Joaquin River, approximately 11 miles north-west of Fresno on US Route 99.

SEQUOIA and KINGS CANYON NATIONAL PARKS (386,560 and 454,600 acres) provide access to the west-ern flank of the Sierra Nevada. Only a small portion of these areas may be reached by car, but the 'back country' is accessible to the hiker. The entrances to both Parks may be reached from Fresno by driving east on State Route 180. The headquarters for both Sequoia and Kings Can-yon is at Ash Mountain in Sequoia. Maps and detailed in-formation regarding trails are available at the entrances and headquarters.

During the summer, nature hikes are led by ranger naturalists and illustrated campfire talks are given on the natural history of the Parks. There is a museum at Giant Forest in Sequoia. Camping facilities are provided at many places. Lodging and meals are available at Giant Forest and General Grant Grove in Sequoia, and at Cedar Grove in Kings Canyon.

At comparable altitudes the birdlife is similar to that of Yosemite National Park (see under Merced). The Blue Grouse, Mountain Quail, White-throated Swift, Black Swift, Calliope Hummingbird, Pileated Woodpecker, Dip-per, Canyon and Rock Wrens, Black-throated Gray War-bler, Western Tanager, and Fox Sparrow are among the more interesting summer-resident species at lower eleva-tions. Birds of the high country are the same as those of Yosemite.

LOS ANGELES. (Near-by areas only; outlying ones dis-cussed under Pasadena, Santa Monica, El Monte, and San Pedro. See also under Newport Beach, Santa Ana, San Bernardino, Bakersfield, and Santa Barbara for areas within a one-day auto trip from Los Angeles.) For the visitor to Los

Angeles whose bird finding may be limited to the downtown area, a few city parks are worth a visit.

In MacARTHUR PARK are small twin lakes, which
teem with waterfowl and gulls from October through
March. Most of the gulls come to the Park daily from
roosting areas somewhere on or near the coast. California
and Ring-billed Gulls are the common species, with
Glaucous-winged, Herring, and Heermann's Gulls in small
numbers. The wintering population of Lesser Scaup Ducks
is about 200; only the Coots are more plentiful. Joining
these in the eager fight for kernels of grain that visitors
toss from shore are lesser numbers of Gadwalls, Baldpates,
Pintails, Shovelers, Redheads, Ring-necked Ducks, and
Canvas-backs. Ruddy Ducks are common, too, but they,
with the Eared and Pied-billed Grebes and Double-crested
Cormorants, stay farther from shore. Other species of
ducks and waterbirds occasionally drop in and rarities
show up with astonishing frequency. The landbirds found
in MacArthur and other city parks include the Chinese
Spotted Dove, Ringed Turtle Dove, Anna's Hummingbird,
Black Phoebe, Mockingbird, Hooded Oriole (after late
March), Brewer's Blackbird, House Finch, Brown Towhee,
and Song Sparrow. To reach the Park from downtown,
drive or take a bus 1.5 miles westward on Wilshire Boulevard (between 6th and 7th, west of Grand Avenue) to
Alvarado Street, beyond which the Park lies on either side
of the Boulevard.

ECHO PARK (31 acres) is similar to MacArthur Park,
but occasionally it has some additional species (egrets,
mergansers, Forster's Terns). To reach it, go west on Temple Street to Glendale Boulevard (1.5 miles from Civic
Center) and then north to the Park, which is on the right.

Three miles south of the downtown area along Figueroa
Street (US Route 6) is Exposition Park, in the northwest
corner of which is the LOS ANGELES COUNTY MU-
SEUM OF HISTORY, SCIENCE, AND ART. The bird
hall of the Museum displays most of the species found in
southern California—about 500 mounted specimens arranged by habitats—and there are excellent habitat groups
of large mammals, both American and African. The most

unusual attraction is the hall with skeletons and recon-
structed models of the mammals and birds that lived in the
Los Angeles area in late Pleistocene time, all from the
wealth of material excavated from the La Brea tar pits. Included are the saber-toothed tigers, giant ground sloths,
mammoths and mastodons, and many birds no longer in
existence, such as the asphalt stork, pygmy goose, several
huge vultures, a caracara, and a turkey. Mounted skeletons
of 14 Pleistocene birds are on display. The tar pits themselves have been set aside as a city park (Allen Hancock
Park), which is on Wilshire Boulevard, 3.25 miles from
downtown. The ornithological study collections of the Museum include about 24,000 skins, 18,000 skeletons, and
great numbers of bones from the La Brea deposits. Curators
can provide helpful information for visiting bird finders.

Adjoining Exposition Park on the north is the campus of
the UNIVERSITY OF SOUTHERN CALIFORNIA. The
University offers ornithology and natural-history courses
in the spring and/or summer. Its collection of over 1,200
study skins of birds belonging to the Allen Hancock Foundation pertains chiefly to the islands and adjacent mainland
of the eastern tropical Pacific. The Cooper Ornithological
Society, Southern Division, meets at 8:00 P.M. on the fourth
Tuesday of each month in the Architects Building on the
U.S.C. campus.

The UNIVERSITY OF CALIFORNIA AT LOS ANGE-
LES, at 405 Hilgard Avenue, is 12 miles from downtown
via Wilshire and Westwood Boulevards. Courses in ornithology and vertebrate natural history, as well as opportunities for ornithological research, are offered here. The large
campus is a good bird-finding area; over 100 species of birds
characteristic of oak and riparian woodland, chaparral, and
open field have been recorded in this place. The University
now has the Donald R. Dickey Research Collection, temporarily housed at 2205 West Adams Boulevard. The Collection includes approximately 36,000 study skins and 2,000
skeletons of birds, as well as a large associated library.

The best park from the bird finder's standpoint is GRIF-
FITH PARK (3,761 acres), by far the largest in Los Angeles, including over 5 square miles of chaparral-covered
mountain slopes and live oak–sycamore woodland, as well

as small willow riparian areas and a large golf course and other lawn areas. The east and north parts of the Park are reached from downtown via Glendale Boulevard past Echo Park to Riverside Drive, thence left to the entrance, just past Los Feliz Boulevard, a total distance of 5.5 miles. A left turn on Los Feliz Boulevard leads to the Western and Vermont Avenue entrances in the southwest part of the Park. In the latter is the planetarium, to the east of which, in Vermont Canyon, is a tiny 'bird sanctuary' where California Quail and other woodland-border species are found. The adjacent chaparral slopes are good for Fox Sparrows in winter. Above the planetarium, winding roads give access to the slopes of 1,652-foot Mt. Hollywood and join other roads from the north end of the Park. Municipal bus lines lead into or near the Park from several directions; and numerous trails enable those with a hiking urge to stretch their legs.

The greatest variety of habitats is found near the zoo on the northeast side of the Park. Here are great live oaks and sycamores with resident Anna's Hummingbirds, Acorn, Downy, and Nuttall's Woodpeckers, Scrub Jays, Plain Titmice, Bush-tits, Hutton's Vireos, and Purple Finches. Common as summer residents in the canyon above the zoo are: Black-chinned Hummingbird, Western Flycatcher, Western Wood Pewee, House Wren, Orange-crowned Warbler, and Black-headed Grosbeak. The Poor-will, Costa's Hummingbird, and Phainopepla are found on the chaparral slope to the north. At any time of year, but particularly in winter, a flock of White-throated Swifts may be seen flying about Bee Rock, which juts from the mountainside high above the zoo. In winter, visitants to the lawn areas include Lark and Chipping Sparrows, and (Red-breasted) Common Sapsuckers are to be seen regularly in the pepper trees lining some of the roads and paths. Nearly all of the species of oak-woodland and chaparral lists are to be found somewhere in the Park. Common spring transients include: flocks of Turkey Vultures and Swainson's Hawks, Allen's and Rufous Hummingbirds, all of the swallows, many vireos and warblers (with peak in late April), especially the Black-throated Gray, Townsend's, Hermit, and Macgillivray's, as well as the Olive-backed Thrush and Western Tanager, which remain common into May. Particularly good spots during the migration are Mineral Wells Picnic Grounds and vicinity (north of the golf course) and the area on the south side of the Park from the Western Avenue entrance to the section near the planetarium.

The zoo itself is free and is open from 8:00 A.M. to 4:30 P.M. daily; it has a collection of nearly 400 live birds, including about 50 American species, especially herons, spoonbills, waterfowl, hawks, doves, owls, and corvids.

LOS BANOS. Winter-visiting bird finders in central California should not fail to go to the LOS BANOS WATERFOWL REFUGE. This 3,000-acre state-operated Refuge, including natural and artificial ponds and some farmland, is approximately 4 miles northeast of Los Banos. Drive east on State Route 152 and turn left just before crossing the railroad tracks at the edge of town. (This road is just west of Canal Farm Inn.) Drive north 3 miles to Henry Miller Avenue, turn right (east), and continue for half a mile to the Refuge headquarters. The best time to visit the area is from October to February. Peak concentrations of birds appear during the waterfowl hunting season. Some of the more spectacular species present in winter are Whistling Swans, Canada Geese, White-fronted Geese, Snow Geese, and Sandhill Cranes. All species of ducks that winter in fresh-water areas in California will be found here, and wintering shorebirds are abundant. Although numbers of species and individuals are smaller in the breeding season, the bird finder will see Black-necked Stilts, Avocets, Forster's and Black Terns, and if very fortunate, he may find Fulvous Tree-ducks and White-faced Ibises.

MERCED. Less than 70 miles east from Merced on State Route 140, within the boundaries of YOSEMITE NATIONAL PARK (760,951 acres), the ornithologist will find all of the avian associations of the Sierra Nevada. The floor of Yosemite Valley, at an elevation of 4,000 feet, will offer riparian species along the Merced River; birds of the montane-coniferous forest and deciduous woodland occur in the wooded portions of the Valley. From the Valley the bird finder may hike or drive into the 'high country,' where species characteristic of the high-altitude montane forests will be encountered.

A museum with excellent bird exhibits is located at Park headquarters, Government Center. Persons interested in any phase of natural history should first visit the museum, where information about the naturalist program of guided trips and illustrated talks, literature, and maps are available.

On the Valley floor in summer every camper's table is a feeding station for Steller's Jays, Robins, Western Tanagers, Black-headed Grosbeaks, and Oregon Juncos. White-throated Swifts and Violet-green Swallows are usually in sight overhead. Occasionally Golden Eagles and Black Swifts will be seen. Six species of woodpeckers may be found in the Valley. Look for the Pileated Woodpecker in large dead pines above Mirror Lake, and for Red-shafted Flickers, Acorn Woodpeckers, Hairy Woodpeckers, Downy Woodpeckers, and White-headed Woodpeckers in the oaks, cottonwoods, and old apple orchards.

Dippers are common in the summer along all the streams below 8,000 feet. Spotted Sandpipers, Western Flycatchers, Yellow Warblers, and Song Sparrows are streamside birds. Olive-backed Thrushes and Macgillivray's Warblers will be found near Happy Isles, while (Calaveras) Nashville Warblers will reward a search of the talus slopes along the south side of the Valley.

Other Valley species are the Band-tailed Pigeon, Great Horned Owl, Pygmy Owl, Saw-whet Owl, Western Wood Pewee, Red-breasted Nuthatch, Brown Creeper, Canyon Wren, (Cassin's) Solitary and Warbling Vireos, Brewer's Blackbird, and Chipping Sparrow. Hermit Thrushes may be found along Tenaya Creek above Mirror Lake.

Above the Valley floor at Glacier Point the Blue Grouse come near the hotel porch for crumbs, and Fox Sparrows nest in the chaparral behind the hotel. Watch for the Townsend's Solitaire nests (marked by a trailing 'apron' of pine needles) in the cut banks of the highway from Chinquapin to Glacier Point.

In Tuolumne Meadows there are Clark's Nutcrackers, Mountain Bluebirds (nesting in dead lodgepole pines), Pine Grosbeaks, Red Crossbills, and White-crowned and Lincoln's Sparrows (nesting in shrubs along streams).

From Tioga Pass, on the eastern border, at 9,941 feet, it is a short hike to Saddlebag Lakes on the north or to Dana Glacier on the south. This is Gray-crowned Rosy Finch country. Look for these birds at the base of rocky cliffs or foraging on the snow and ice. It is also sometimes possible to see Golden Eagles, Williamson's Sapsuckers, and Rock Wrens.

MONTEREY. The MONTEREY PENINSULA offers great diversity for bird finders: rocky shores, sandy beaches, bay and ocean, pine and oak woods. The more determined will not be satisfied until they have taken a trip offshore to see the pelagic species. Boats may be chartered at the Municipal Pier in Monterey. This is an expensive venture and usually necessitates considerable planning and the organization of a group to share the expense. The bird finder will be repaid for his trouble by being able to see the Black-footed Albatross and shearwaters of several species in any season, and Sabine's Gulls and possibly petrels in the spring and fall. In the winter months a number of alcids, including Common Murres, Cassin's Auklets, and Rhinoceros Auklets will be seen without fail. If the boat is chartered and no experienced local observer is present, have the skipper head west from Point Pinos for 5 or 6 miles in order to find the maximum concentration of pelagic birds. Take along a supply of 'chum' (sardines, suet, stale bread, or anything edible), in order to attract the birds to the boat. To insure complete comfort, get a supply of anti-seasick drug, dramamine. It can be obtained only by prescription, but it works.

The Pacific Grove Museum (Central and Forest Avenues in Pacific Grove, 3 miles northwest of Monterey) contains displays of mounted birds, most of which are excellently done and well labeled. A list of the birds of the Monterey Peninsula may be obtained here.

Follow the signs from Pacific Grove to the north entrance to Seventeen Mile Drive (admission 50 cents per car). The Drive passes through extensive groves of Monterey pine and along several miles of rocky shoreline. Stop at Bird Rock (watch for sign) to observe the breeding colony of Brandt's Cormorants. From Cypress Point watch for the passing lines of Sooty Shearwaters in summer or for migrating loons in spring and fall. From the Carmel gate of Seventeen Mile Drive continue south along the Carmel waterfront to the mouth of the Carmel River. The exposed flats at the River mouth are favored by shorebirds (July to August, especially). Look carefully for the rare but regular Baird's Sandpiper. In the winter this area is favorable for waterfowl.

POINT LOBOS RESERVE STATE PARK (admission 25 cents per car) is 7 miles south of Monterey on State Route 1. This 336-acre preserve is the site of a natural grove of Monterey cypress and large tracts of Monterey pine. Ask for a map at the gate and drive to the end of the road near the south boundary. A trail leads to a point from which Bird Island may be seen. This is the northernmost breeding place of the Brown Pelican on the Pacific coast. Brandt's Cormorants nest on the flat surfaces of Bird Island, Pelagic Cormorants on the ledges of the cliffs. Western Gulls also nest here. On near-by rocky shores look for Black Oyster-catchers (resident), Black Turnstones (winter), and Wandering Tattlers (spring and fall). Pigeon Guillemots breed on rocky islets and cliffs at several places on Point Lobos.

In the stands of Monterey pines the bird finder should listen for the calls of the Pygmy Owl and Pygmy Nuthatch and watch for the Steller's Jay, Chestnut-backed Chickadee, Brown Creeper, and Oregon Junco. A pair of White-tailed Kites is often seen in Carmelo Meadow north of the warden's cottage.

From Point Lobos south to PFEIFFER BIG SUR STATE PARK (707 acres) on State Route 1 is 24 miles. The highway follows the coastline, often high above the waves on rocky cliffs. There are several points of interest en route. Stop at Hurricane Point, 1.2 miles south of Bixby Creek (look for the sign) and 13.5 miles south of the Point Lobos entrance. From Hurricane Point look down at the large rock offshore, where there is a colony of several hundred Common Murres during the breeding season.

One of the rarest of North American mammals, the sea otter, may be seen in the kelp beds along this stretch of coast. Places where the animals are often seen include the area just south of Mal Paso Creek, 2.7 miles south of Point Lobos; kelp beds offshore opposite the intersection of the Palo Colorado Road, 9.3 miles south of Point Lobos; and at Hurricane Point, between the mainland and the Murre colony rock. It is not a simple matter to distinguish the animals at a distance, and a telescope is a great advantage.

Pfeiffer Big Sur State Park contains stands of the coast redwood with its usual associates. Watch for Dippers along the Big Sur River. Among the more interesting species breeding within the Park are the Winter Wren, Audubon's Warbler, and Western Tanager. Steller's Jays will come to a picnic table and will often approach to within a few inches of a person's hand—if the hand is offering food. Camping and picnicking facilities are excellent. Numerous trails will permit the ornithologist to gain access to a variety of habitats including riparian, oak woodland, and chaparral.

On Route 1, 17 miles north of Monterey, is the town of Moss Landing, at the mouth of ELKHORN SLOUGH. To the bird finder this area is attractive for its ponds, salt marshes, tidal mud flats, and sandy beaches. In the spring and fall, transient shorebirds are the main attraction; during the summer the breeding Snowy Plovers, Avocets, Black-necked Stilts, and Forster's and Least Terns will repay a visit. The wintering waterbirds and ducks complete the year-round picture.

A concrete bridge crosses Elkhorn Slough just north of Moss Landing. Stop on the road shoulder and look for shorebirds if the tide is low, or for loons, grebes, and ducks if the mud flats are covered by water. Continue north approximately 0.5 mile and turn left on an oiled road leading over a causeway across the lagoon. Stop on the causeway and search the tidal areas north and south of the road. Continue on to the end of the road at the mouth of Elkhorn Slough. Park and walk up the beach. In the summer, the sandy beach above the level of the tide is the breeding site of Snowy Plovers and Least Terns.

The Monterey Peninsula Audubon Society publishes *The Sanderling* (mimeographed; monthly) and meets on the third Friday evening of each month at the Sunset School in Carmel. The organization may be contacted through the headquarters office in Point Lobos Reserve State Park.

MORRO BAY. The only tidal estuary of any size between San Francisco and Santa Barbara is triangular Morro Bay. Most of its northeast shore and adjacent marshy areas, as well as the long sand-dune peninsula opposite it, are included in MORRO BAY STATE PARK (about 1,600 acres). This is reached by driving south from State Route 1 in the business district of Morro Bay. There are camping and picnic areas and boats for rent near the Park headquarters, a mile south of town. The mile-wide salicornia marsh has several winding tidal channels along which large numbers of herons and egrets, waterfowl, and shorebirds congregate during most of the year. Long-billed Curlews are here by the hundreds in August and September, and scores of Great Blue Herons stand in the marsh in December. The open flats of the Bay beyond hold thousands of probing shorebirds at low tide, and the sandier areas have Baird's Sandpipers (late July to September), Knots (fall), and all the western plovers. Hundreds of Black Brant feed in the Bay in winter but retire across the sand dunes to the open ocean when disturbed. Loons, grebes, pelicans, cormorants, diving ducks, and all of the gulls that occur on the coast are to be found in the Bay in winter, especially in the U-shaped harbor and channel portion west of town.

MORRO ROCK, a tall dome-shaped island just offshore from the mouth of the Bay, has recently been connected with the mainland and one can walk out to it and to the breakwater beyond it (when the waves are not too high). Opportunity is thus provided for seeing Surf-birds, turnstones, and other shorebirds of the rocky-coast habitat. Brown Pelicans, all three species of cormorants, and various gulls roost on the rock. All the western species of terns are to be expected in and about the mouth of the Bay during migration.

NEWPORT BEACH. The coast and adjacent low hills, fields, and marshes of which this beach city is the center have many excellent bird-finding spots within easy range of the Los Angeles metropolitan area.

Extending 3 miles inland from the yacht harbor and fishing center of Newport Bay, UPPER BAY still has large salt-marsh and mud-flat areas, dominated by hosts of fiddler crabs, herons, and shorebirds. The road parallels the east shore of the Bay, leaving US Route 101A at a point almost opposite the road marked 'Balboa Island'; the Island is in the lower or outer bay in the opposite direction. In Costa Mesa (just northeast of Newport Beach on State Route 55) 17th, 19th, and 22nd Streets lead to the top of the bluffs overlooking the west side of Upper Bay.

All of the shorebirds of the mud-flat list, as well as the rarer transients such as Knots, and Pectoral and Baird's Sandpipers, are found on the tide flats or sand bars in the Bay. Snowy Plovers and Least Terns, to a great extent driven from their ancestral nesting haunts on the beaches by the summer crowds of people, now nest in limited numbers on the alkaline flats and artificial sand islands around such estuaries as Upper Bay. There is some evidence that Avocets, Black-necked Stilts, and Caspian Terns have nested here also; and a visitor who walks out on a dyke crossing the middle of the Upper Bay is guaranteed a noisy reception from them during June and July. Clapper Rails nest commonly in the marsh, and Black Rails have been seen here. Most of the dabbling ducks, Lesser Scaup Ducks, Ruddy Ducks, and some Buffle-heads are regular wintering waterfowl, and White Pelicans are sometimes present in winter, contrasting in plumage and habits with the resident Brown Pelicans. The upper part of the Bay is dyked off into salt ponds that attract large numbers of phalaropes in migration, the Northern Phalarope predominating over the Wilson's Phalarope, and the Red Phalarope occurring but rarely.

As to landbirds, the tree tobacco and spring flowers along the bluff east of Upper Bay are gathering points for hummingbirds. Blue Grosbeaks nest here in May and June; Cactus Wrens sing regularly and add to their nests in the prickly-pear clumps all during the fall. Common Ravens have nested on the vertical cliffs, and the farmland above them is superb country for Horned Larks, various wintering sparrows, Marsh Hawks and other wintering hawks, including, on occasion, both Rough-legged and Ferruginous. White-tailed Kites are found in the moister swales —for instance, at the head and on the west side of the Bay.

The harbor of Newport Beach is also one of the best

places from which to charter a boat for an offshore trip to observe pelagic birds. Inquiry among the many boat operators docking in the fish cannery area opposite 28th to 31st Streets will usually enable the bird finder to make the necessary arrangements.

Along the coast highway (US Route 101A) northwest of Newport Beach are several spots always alive with birds. The best one is on BOLSA LAGOON (property of the Bolsa Chica Gun Club) beyond the oil-well area north of Huntington Beach, where great numbers of waterfowl are found in winter (on non-hunting days). With good binoculars the Lagoon, on the right of the highway, can be scanned from the car. As Sunset Beach is neared, there are mud flats in the Lagoon that hold thousands of shorebirds at ebb tide. Burrowing Owls are resident across the Lagoon on the slight knoll that may be traversed on Los Patos Avenue from the south end of Sunset Beach. In the flat land beyond, there are many smaller gun clubs whose ponds hold a great many waterfowl, easily seen from the roads when hunting is not going on. White-faced Ibises are regular here in migration, occasional in winter.

Drive south on US Route 101A to US Route 101, turn left and drive 3 miles to SAN JUAN CAPISTRANO MISSION, with its nationally famous Cliff Swallows. Experienced bird finders will not, of course, expect the Swallows to conform as faithfully in arrival and departure dates (19 March, 23 October) as the legend would have them, and they must not be disappointed if White-throated Swifts are the only prominent aerial foragers here on the appointed days.

OAKLAND. LAKE MERRITT is world famous as a refuge for wintering waterfowl. Although located in the heart of the city, this 155-acre salt-water Lake is visited annually by thousands of ducks and waterbirds. A feeding and banding station is on the northeast arm of the Lake at the intersection of Bellevue Avenue and Perkins Street. During the winter the ducks are fed daily at 3:30 P.M.

The largest concentration of birds at Lake Merritt will be found between November and April, when the Eared Grebe, Western Grebe, Pied-billed Grebe, Double-crested

Cormorant, American and Snowy Egrets, Mallard, Pintail, Baldpate, Canvas-back, Lesser Scaup Duck, American Golden-eye, Ruddy Duck, Coot, several species of gulls, and Forster's Terns are among the commoner species. A number of geese have been pinioned and have become very tame. A small amount of food will bring dozens of wild ducks to a person's feet. Photographic opportunities are excellent.

Favorable areas for landbirds are numerous in the vicinity of Oakland. One of the best is SEQUOIA PARK (entrance on Joaquin Miller Road). The fine stands of second-growth coast redwood are native, but the Monterey pines and cypresses in the 182-acre Park have been planted. Among the breeding birds to be expected are the Hairy Woodpecker, Olive-sided Flycatcher, Steller's Jay, Chestnut-backed Chickadee, Red-breasted Nuthatch, Brown Creeper, Wren-tit, and Oregon Junco. Although decidedly uncommon, the Saw-whet Owl, Hermit Thrush, and Audubon's Warbler have been found breeding in or adjacent to the Park.

BAY FARM ISLAND is a mecca for shorebird enthusiasts from late July until May. Migration periods in spring and fall produce the greatest numbers, mid-April, when the northbound transients are in nuptial plumage, being especially rewarding. Wintering flocks are present from November to March. The best time for a visit is the first hour after high tide. Tide tables may be obtained at sporting-goods stores and Shell service stations.

To reach Bay Farm Island, take High Street west to San Jose Avenue, turn left and proceed two blocks to Peach Street, turn right and continue on across the bridge to the Bay Farm Island side. If the tide is low, the mud flats adjacent to the bridge will be exposed. Knots are often seen here in the spring. From this point there are several possible routes. (1) Turn left on Doolittle Drive and continue along the Municipal Golf Course. Watch the mud flats and open water of San Leandro Bay on the left for shorebirds and waterbirds. (This area is being rapidly modified by filling and dredging, so that what is good mud flat this year may be a rock wall next.) Turn around at Oakland Airport and return to the bridge. (2) Drive straight ahead from the bridge on Maitland Drive. On the right is a levee which obstructs the view. Stop any place along this stretch and get out to inspect the tidal flats on the other side of the levee. (This area is also slated for filling and modification.) Continue along Maitland Drive to Island Road; turn right and drive to the end of the road. Walk to the bay shore, and then turn right and walk along the shore. Mud and sand flats extend on both sides of the levee, which circles back to the bridge. (3) Return to Maitland Drive and turn right. Continue to the end of Maitland Drive, park, and inspect the bay shore and mud flats.

Among the more abundant birds to be expected in suitable habitats on Bay Farm Island are the Eared Grebe, Western Grebe, American Egret, several species of dabbling and diving ducks, the Clapper Rail, Killdeer, Black-bellied Plover, Hudsonian Curlew, Willet, Least Sandpiper, Red-backed Sandpiper, Dowitcher, Western Sandpiper, Marbled Godwit, Sanderling, Avocet, several species of gulls, Forster's Tern, Caspian Tern, Short-eared Owl, and American Pipit.

The OAKLAND PUBLIC MUSEUM, 1426 Oak Street, maintains a collection of mounted birds. The Museum is open from 10:00 A.M. to 5:00 P.M. on weekdays, 1:00 to 5:00 P.M. on Sundays and holidays.

OCEANSIDE. Just south of this coastal city is the MAXTON BROWN SANCTUARY, consisting of Buena Vista Lagoon, which is crossed by US Route 101 just back from the ocean beach. Roads circle the 1.5-mile-long portion of the Lagoon and the bordering fresh-water marsh, which is inland from the highway. Great concentrations of ducks, a few White-fronted and Snow Geese, numbers of White Pelicans, and upward of 10,000 Avocets gather here in the fall and winter. It is the one place on the coast where Wood Ibises occur regularly from about 1 June to mid-September, although flocks may also be seen at times around the lagoons in the mouths of other valleys of San Diego County. Birds nesting commonly at the Maxton Brown Sanctuary include the Pied-billed Grebe, Cinnamon Teal, Ruddy Duck, Virginia Rail, Sora, Florida Gallinule, and others of

the fresh-water marsh and lake list. The ocean beach itself along Oceanside and south to Carlsbad is sandy, with
the appropriate birds to be found in season. Terns—
Forster's, Common, Least, Royal, Caspian, Black, and occasionally Elegant—occur in September. The mouth of the
San Luis Rey River, which Route 101 crosses by a high
bridge at the north end of Oceanside, is also a good area
for waterfowl, shorebirds, and some riparian-woodland
species.

From Second Street in downtown Oceanside a road
leads inland along the SAN LUIS REY VALLEY, where
White-tailed Kites are common the year round, and where
most of the open farmland and grassland birds are also
to be found. The road to the San Luis Rey Valley joins
US Route 395, along which, between Bonsall and Escon-
dido, there are foothill areas of woodland and chaparral.
From either of these towns well-marked roads lead to
PALOMAR MOUNTAIN, atop which the world's largest
telescope is located. The winding road up the Mountain
passes through black oak, Coulter pine, and big-cone spruce
forests similar to those of Cuyamaca Rancho State Park
(see under San Diego), and there is more of the same in
Palomar Mountain State Park on a side road to the north.
The peak, however, is covered with a dense oak and mixed
chaparral in which California Thrashers and Black-chinned
Sparrows nest.

PALM SPRINGS. At the head of the date-garden areas
of COACHELLA VALLEY and close to the steep desert
face of MT. SAN JACINTO, this resort town is convenient
for winter and spring bird finding. The same desert areas
may be reached from Indio, below sea level near the center of the Valley, which slopes on into the Salton Sea to
the south (see under Brawley).

There are birds to be found in so many places on the
desert, here and there by roadsides, that it is difficult to
direct bird finders to given spots. Spring tourists will
usually want to drive many of the roads out from both
towns to see the splendid and colorful wildflowers that
follow a winter in which any significant rains fall, and in
so doing they may find most of the desert birds. In the

creosote bush–cactus–burroweed association, which covers most of the gentle upland slopes, the breeding birds are similar to those found near Twentynine Palms and in Death Valley. The low, sparse shrubland on the more alkaline plains attracts wintering Say's Phoebes, Mountain Blue-birds, and Brewer's Sparrows. But it is in the mesquite, cat-claw, paloverde, and smoke trees of the low, sandy washes that one commonly finds, in any season, the Verdin, Crissal Thrasher, Plumbeous Gnatcatcher, and Abert's Towhee. There are such areas along State Route 111 near Cathedral City south of Palm Springs; on State Route 195, 2 miles west of Mecca (south of Palm Springs on Route 111), and along US Route 99, 6 miles west of Mecca.

The same association, often in close proximity to wil-lows and sycamores, occurs in the canyons at the base of Mt. San Jacinto—for example, in Chino Canyon (reached by a 2-mile road leading west from Route 111 at 1.5 miles north of Palm Springs), and in Tahquitz, Andreas, and Palm Canyons (reached by well-marked roads leading west from Route 111 south of Palm Springs). The native fan palms of Palm Canyon, set amid gigantic boulders, are a great scenic attraction; and the bird finder will readily locate the Ladder-backed Woodpecker, Canyon and Rock Wrens, and (in winter) several of the riparian-woodland species, as well as the Poor-will, Townsend's Solitaire, and others.

Summer residents arriving in the Coachella Valley as early as February include the Costa's Hummingbird, which does not usually get to the Pacific slope until late March or April. The Phainopepla also nests in February and March near Palm Springs, long before the species arrives on the Pacific slope. The height of the general nesting season, however, is in April. The northwesternmost known nesting ground of the Vermilion Flycatcher is on an irrigated ranch one mile south of Mecca on Lincoln Street.

To get to the higher altitudes, with a grand view of the whole Coachella Valley and the Salton Sea trough and of the desert ranges eastward, a drive up the Palms to Pines Highway (State Route 74) is recommended. This road leaves Route 111, 12.9 miles southeast of Palm Springs, and climbs along a broad alluvial fan where typical desert plants and birds are found. It then leads up the mountain by the switchbacks of Seven Level Hill, where ocotillo and agave blooms add to the colorful scene in spring. Chuckwalla lizards and Rock Wrens live in the crevices of the rocky prominences here, and Prairie Falcons nest near by. Higher up, the Highway passes through a belt of pinyon pines and junipers, where most of the birds typical of the more extensive areas of this habitat are found, although several do not occur this far south. Beyond Pinyon Flat, which is 15 miles from Route 111, the Highway soon reaches the Jeffrey pines of Hemet Valley, leaving the desert behind. Although Hemet Valley and the reservoir in it are 2,300 feet lower in elevation, they offer bird-finding opportunities somewhat comparable with those of Bear Valley in the San Bernardinos (see under San Bernardino).

Thirty-five miles from Route 111 a 4.5-mile side road leads north to Idyllwild, at 5,300 feet, the headquarters of MOUNT SAN JACINTO STATE PARK (12,708 acres). There are public campgrounds amid pines and cedars at headquarters, and the trail to the 17 square miles of primitive high country starts from the end of Fern Valley Road in Idyllwild. The birdlife of this region is quite similar to that of the San Bernardinos; and the views from the summit of 10,805-foot San Jacinto are unsurpassed.

PASADENA. (A detailed map of Los Angeles and adjacent cities will be most helpful in this area.) Traversing the western part of Pasadena, from the base of the San Gabriel Mountains southward into Los Angeles, is the ARROYO SECO, a broad gully between the old alluvial fan, on which most of the city is built, and the San Rafael Hills to the west. In the southwest part of the city a 1.25-mile stretch of the Arroyo is in more or less natural condition and is traversable on bridle- and footpaths from several directions. A good mid-point of entry is from Arroyo Boulevard just south of La Loma Road, 1.5 miles from downtown Pasadena; drive south on Fair Oaks Avenue, right (west) on West California Street to its end, then left one block on Arroyo Boulevard. There are huge sycamores and oaks and a strip of alders and willows along the stream, with soft-leaved shrubs, blackberry, and ivy on the Arroyo banks south of La Loma Road, while to the north the floor of the Arroyo has a more scattered dry shrubland, with oaks or chaparral on the banks.

Throughout the year Band-tailed Pigeons gather in the treetops, in some winters in flocks of considerable size; they nest scatteringly in the near-by live oaks. Other breeding birds include the Purple Finch, Common Goldfinch, and most of the species of oak-woodland and chaparral lists. Common as summer residents (March or April through August) are the Black-chinned Hummingbird, Western Flycatcher, Western Wood Pewee, House Wren, Bullock's Oriole, and others of the riparian-woodland list. White-throated Swifts congregate about the Colorado Street Bridge to the north of this area, especially in spring; migrating swallows are numerous in March and April, vireos, warblers, and Black-headed Grosbeaks in late April, and *Empidonax* flycatchers, Olive-sided Flycatchers, and Western Tanagers through May.

State Route 118, 5 miles northwest from Fair Oaks Avenue and Colorado Street in Pasadena, crosses Devil's Gate Dam, on the west side of which is OAK GROVE PARK. The entrance is the first road to the right after crossing the Dam and near-by bridge; for nearly a mile to the northward the live oaks are more or less solid, broken only here and there by bits of chaparral on steep banks or by grassy and boulder-strewn areas on the lower flats. These mixed habitats attract most of the birds on the chaparral list as well as those of the oak woodland. Common winter visitants include the White-breasted Nuthatch, Western Bluebird, Orange-crowned Warbler, Townsend's Warbler, Lark Sparrow, Oregon Junco, and Chipping, White-crowned, Golden-crowned, and Fox Sparrows. Phainopeplas nest here in June. In the spring the live oaks here or anywhere along the base of the San Gabriel Mountains are hosts to most of the transient perching birds, the greatest numbers appearing during spells of intermittent showery weather in late April or early May.

About 16 miles northwest of Pasadena on State Route 118, 2 miles beyond Sunland, the route crosses TUJUNGA WASH, where tall yuccas bloom in profusion in late spring, and cactus and spinescent bushes create a desert-

like aspect. In the Wash east of the highway, the diligent
bird finder may locate some of the few Cactus and Rock
Wrens or Sage Sparrows that are resident here. Other recommended areas in this vicinity are the HANSEN FLOOD
CONTROL RESERVOIR, to the left of the highway, 4
miles beyond Sunland (for waterfowl in winter and Golden
Eagles upon occasion), and LOPEZ CANYON, reached
by a road leaving the highway on the right, 4.8 miles from
Sunland. At first this road leads through large fields devoted
to raising flowers and flower seeds, which attract huge
flocks of goldfinches—Common, Lesser, and Lawrence's
—in autumn, with sometimes a few Pine Siskins; and beyond, in the Canyon, there are oak-woodland and chaparral areas.

The higher SAN GABRIEL MOUNTAINS are easily
reached from Pasadena via the Angeles Crest Highway
(State Route 2), which leads north from Route 118 in
La Cañada. The Highway climbs above Arroyo Seco Canyon to an elevation of 4,666 feet at Red Box Gap, 13.6 miles
from Route 118. From here one may take a road right,
which leads to Mt. Wilson with its observatory and views
of the city below, or continue on Route 2 higher into the
San Gabriel Mountains to the pine forests of Charlton
Flats (8 miles), Chilao (11 miles), and Buckhorn Flat (20
miles)—the last at an elevation of 6,300 feet. Birds to be
found here are much the same as those of the San Bernardino Mountains (see under San Bernardino), except
for the species associated with mountain meadows and
lakes, which are absent here. Eventually the Crest Highway will be continued near the crests of some of southern
California's most scenic mountains all the way to Big Pines.

For a sample of a relatively unspoiled wooded canyon
with a fine mountain stream, visit SANTA ANITA CAN-
YON in the San Gabriel Mountains. Drive east from
Pasadena on US Route 66 to Arcadia, then north on Santa
Anita Avenue, from the north end of which a paved road
leads 3.5 miles up the mountainside and ends at Chantry
Flat amid golden oaks and big-cone spruces. One of the
few stands of madrone (here merely tall shrubs) in southern California is found on the slope above Chantry. In the
oaks and spruces and in the near-by tall chaparral areas,

many spring transients characteristic of the foothill areas are found; as nesters there are such species as the Olive-sided Flycatcher, Violet-green Swallow, Steller's Jay, Solitary Vireo, Orange-crowned and Black-throated Gray Warblers, Purple Finch, and Oregon Junco. From the end of the road, a three-quarter-mile, well-traveled trail leads to the bottom of the Canyon and stream. Here the Western Flycatcher, Western Wood Pewee, Dipper, House Wren, Canyon Wren, Warbling Vireo, Yellow Warbler, and Black-headed Grosbeak are among the more common breeding birds. In winter and early spring both the Canyon and the Flat frequently receive influxes of down-mountain transients such as the Mountain Chickadee, Brown Creeper, Townsend's Solitaire, and Pine Siskin.

The LOS ANGELES STATE AND COUNTY ARBO-RETUM, in the western part of Arcadia, is reached by taking Route 66 east from Pasadena about 5 miles to Old Ranch Road and turning right. (The turn is opposite the old Santa Anita railroad station and is marked by signs on Route 66.) The Arboretum is a place of varied habitats and abundant birdlife. There is a small pond and marshy border, a bit of riparian woodland with dogwood and grape thickets, Engelmann and coast live-oak woodland, tall eucalyptus and other planted trees, and near-by open fields. The common birds are most of those on the urban, riparian, and oak-woodland lists. A few (Red-bellied) Red-shouldered Hawks have persisted. Owls roost in the palm trees, and Hooded Orioles nest in the palms in May. Band-tailed Pigeons, (Red-breasted) Common Sapsuckers, Orange-crowned and Townsend's Warblers, and Chipping and Lincoln's Sparrows are among the regular winter visitors. Lewis' Woodpeckers occur regularly some winters; Steller's Jays and Mountain Chickadees are also often present from August to February as a result of post-breeding dispersal.

REDDING. LASSEN VOLCANIC NATIONAL PARK, 52 miles east of Redding on State Route 44, was established to preserve the spectacular volcanic area surrounding Mt. Lassen. Within the 161 square miles of the Park are numerous volcanic cones, hot springs, lava flows, and other evidences of vulcanism. Mt. Lassen was the scene of the most recent volcanic activity in the United States. It was in violent eruption in 1914 and 1915 and did not become quiescent until 1921.

State Route 44 joins State Route 89 in the northwest corner and together they become the Lassen Peak Loop, a 30-mile highway that winds and twists through the Park to its southwest corner. There are excellent camping facilities throughout the Park. Accommodations and meals are available from May to October at Manzanita Lake, Park headquarters. The Loomis Memorial Museum at Manzanita Lake contains natural-history exhibits; Park naturalists are on duty here during the summer season.

Birds of the montane coniferous forest, including the Pileated and White-headed Woodpeckers, Steller's Jay, Clark's Nutcracker, Red-breasted Nuthatch, Dipper, Townsend's Solitaire, Audubon's Warbler, Cassin's Finch, Red Crossbill, Green-tailed Towhee, and Fox Sparrow, will be found in the Park.

SACRAMENTO. WASHINGTON LAKE attracts wintering waterfowl and shorebirds and is the breeding site of waterbirds of the fresh-water-marsh habitat. From Sacramento drive west on US Route 40 approximately 4 miles to the beginning of the Yolo Causeway. Just as the highway rises to go over the Causeway a dirt road leads to the left and winds along the south shore of Washington Lake for nearly 3 miles. The Lake is a large, open body of water with irregular bulrush-bordered shores.

Nesting White-tailed Kites and (Red-bellied) Red-shouldered Hawks will be found in April and May along the Garden Highway (State Route 16) northwest of Sacramento. The Highway runs along the top of the levee bordering the west bank of the SACRAMENTO RIVER. Stop frequently and inspect the willows, cottonwoods, and valley oaks along the River. In the fall and winter the open farmland to the west of the Highway is a resting and feeding area for White-fronted and Snow Geese.

In order to be certain of seeing Black-chinned Hummingbirds and Blue Grosbeaks in central California, the bird finder should seek the type of riparian association found at Bridge House, 23 miles southeast of Sacramento on State Route 16. In the spring these and other species, such as the Nuttall's and Lewis' Woodpeckers, Western Kingbird, Ash-throated Flycatcher, and (Long-tailed) Yellow-breasted Chat (in abundance), will be found along the gravelly, winding CONSUMNES RIVER. A few Wood Ducks nest in the area. Park near the bridge and walk along the old road, which leads along the west side of the River.

SAN BERNARDINO. From this inland valley city, State Route 18 leads up and over the SAN BERNARDINO MOUNTAINS to the north and out onto the MOHAVE DESERT beyond. The San Bernardinos, although steep and rugged for the most part, are unique among the southern California ranges in having an extensive area of gentle topography at a fairly high altitude, with several large mountain lakes and adjoining meadows. Birdlife is consequently present in much greater variety.

From downtown San Bernardino drive 5 miles north on Sierra Way to where State Route 18 begins a 10-mile climb through the chaparral belt and across the heads of several small wooded canyons. Stops for chaparral birds are easily made at the several large parking places along the highway; Costa's Hummingbirds (summer) and Rufous-crowned Sparrows are common in the sage-covered foothills. From April to July Black-chinned Sparrows may be heard singing from the end of the switchback, 2.5 miles above the upper end of the Waterman Canyon Road.

For the next 30 miles Route 18 is known as the Rim of the World Drive, since it skirts for several miles the upper edge of the steep chaparral slopes from which there are excellent views of much of the valley and the distant San Jacinto and Santa Ana Mountains. Soon, however, Route 18 enters a forest—ponderosa pine, incense cedar, and black oak—through which several roads (including State Route 2) lead to LAKE ARROWHEAD (elevation 5,106 feet), 2 miles to the north. Many coniferous-forest birds are common here; but the forest comes right down to the shore of the Lake and there are fewer waterfowl and shorebirds than at 7-mile-long BIG BEAR LAKE (6,750 feet) in Bear Valley, 21 miles farther along the Rim of the World Drive.

At Big Bear Lake the road divides: one branch goes south of the Lake through the village of Big Bear Lake; one branch goes north of the Lake through Fawnskin. These branches are joined by crossroads at and west of Big Bear City. Thus it is possible to encircle the Lake in a car. On the south shore the best bird finding is from or near two roads that lead out onto points in the Lake, the first a mile west of the town of Big Bear Lake, the second a mile east. Also the area east of town from Eagle Point to the east end of the Lake is good. On the north shore the best area for waterfowl is Grout Bay at Fawnskin.

When the water level of Big Bear Lake is normal, the concentrations of Coots in the fall and winter are among the largest known at any single location, estimates of up to 200,000 having been made for the whole Lake. Transient shorebirds include the Wilson's Snipe, Willet, Greater and Lesser Yellow-legs, Least Sandpiper, Dowitcher, Western Sandpiper, Avocet, Black-necked Stilt, and Wilson's and Northern Phalaropes. Ring-billed Gulls are commonest through the winter, with California Gulls, Herring Gulls, and Bonaparte's Gulls occurring chiefly as transients, as well as Forster's Terns, Caspian Terns, and Black Terns. Late April to May and September to October are the best times for all these birds; but thousands of ducks are at their peak in November. Canvas-backs and the hundreds of wintering American Mergansers arrive later and are most numerous in midwinter. Bald Eagles winter regularly, and Ospreys are transients. In late May and June many Pied-billed Grebes, Coots, and a few waterfowl nest in the weedy area at the east end of the Lake, Cinnamon Teal being the most common duck, with fewer Mallards, Pintails, Redheads, and Ruddy Ducks. Killdeer, Spotted Sandpipers, and Horned Larks nest along the open-pastured shore in May.

The meadows back from the Lake (e.g. near the mouth of Rathbone Creek east of Eagle Point or in the center of the Valley east of the Lake) are foraging areas for Ferruginous Hawks (winter), Sparrow Hawks, Western Kingbirds (summer), Say's Phoebes, Western and Mountain Bluebirds, Western Meadowlarks, and Savannah Sparrows. Violet-green and Cliff Swallows also forage over the meadows, the Cliff Swallows regularly placing their mud nests on the tall boles of ponderosa pines along the south side of the Valley.

The pine forests that surround both Arrowhead or Big Bear Lakes have most of the breeding birds characteristic of coniferous forests of the Sierra Nevada, although several species are found only at the higher altitudes south of Big Bear: for example, the Williamson's Sapsucker, Clark's Nutcracker, Red-breasted Nuthatch, Townsend's Solitaire, Ruby-crowned Kinglet, Cassin's Finch, and Red Crossbill.

BALDWIN LAKE, in the east end of Bear Valley, 2 miles beyond Big Bear Lake, is without an outlet and is intermittently dry for periods of years. When it holds water, however, its waterfowl population is greater than that on Big Bear, with a large Eared Grebe nesting colony, a small one of Yellow-headed Blackbirds, and possibly nesting Wilson's Phalaropes. The dry flats south of the Lake and the moister meadows up the slope from them are two of the best places to find Pinyon Jays the year round. From State Route 18, north of the Lake, a dirt road leads around the east side, passing through a broad slope of Great Basin sagebrush in which Green-tailed Towhees and Brewer's Sparrows nest in May and June.

Beyond Baldwin Lake, Route 18 drops sharply down to the Mohave Desert, with particularly good bird-finding spots at the foot of each of the three steep grades. On the first 'flat,' a side road marked 'Rose Mine' leads to the right through an island of Joshua trees and shrubs amid pinyons, oaks, and junipers. Here the high-desert birds and some of the oak-woodland birds are found; and in the sparse vegetation of the low ridge to the north of the flat a few Gray Vireos summer regularly. Complete desert conditions are encountered below the next grades, with birdlife comparable to that of the creosote-bush and Joshua-tree areas described under Twentynine Palms and Palm Springs.

On the edge of San Bernardino between South E Street and Colton Avenue, south of the National Orange Show, about 250 acres of valley riparian woodland are included in the WARM CREEK WILDLIFE REFUGE, where

birds typical of that habitat and also those species associated with permanent valley streams (see under El Monte)
can be found. Information for reaching the Refuge and
permission to enter it, as well as a means of contacting the
San Bernardino Audubon Society officials who have charge
of the area, can be obtained by telephoning San Bernardino
82-3240.

SAN DIEGO. BALBOA PARK contains 1,400 acres of
wooded canyons, brushy borders, and eucalyptus groves in
which the common breeding birds of the urban list as well
as many winter visitants may be found. The SAN DIEGO
ZOO (also called the ZOOLOGICAL GARDENS) and
the NATURAL HISTORY MUSEUM are close together
east of Park Boulevard, which extends north through the
Park from downtown. The Zoo, open to visitors daily for a
small admission fee, is noted for its successful outdoor
maintenance of large mammals and its huge, tree-enclosing
cages for flying birds. Over 1,000 caged or tame birds are
on display, including many tropical and Pacific island forms
rarely seen in captivity, and about 50 species of North
American birds. Wild birds are also encouraged in the Zoo
grounds; several hundred ducks come and go daily during
the winter, and Black-crowned Night Herons roost and
nest in the tall trees over the animal pits. The Natural History Museum, a separate institution operated by the San
Diego Society of Natural History, has extensive mounted
displays of native birds and a scientific study collection of
over 31,000 bird skins and 500 egg sets, mainly from the
southwestern United States and Baja California. The Society conducts field trips to local points for various kinds
of nature study, about which information may be obtained
at the Museum, as well as helpful suggestions on bird-
finding areas in the San Diego region.

In the northeast corner of the city is SAN DIEGO
STATE COLLEGE, which offers an ornithology course in
the spring semester with field trips in the region. To reach it,
go out US Route 80 to a point, 8 miles from downtown,
where a sign marks the turn (left) to the campus, which is
on the brink of ALVARADO CANYON. In the Canyon
there are willow thickets and sycamores, scattered wood-

land, and sagebrush areas. Many species on the chaparral and riparian-woodland lists nest here, and the April migration brings warblers, among them the Black-throated Gray, Townsend's, and Black-capped, and a host of other birds.

CUYAMACA RANCHO STATE PARK includes about 30 square miles of black oak–Coulter pine forest, live-oak woodland, and chaparral. Headquarters are 47 miles from San Diego in Green Valley. Drive east on Route 80, then north on State Route 79 for 6.5 miles. Cuyamaca Peak on the west side of the Park reaches 6,515 feet in altitude and has a ponderosa-pine forest on the higher slopes. Several of the coniferous-forest birds (White-headed Woodpecker, Mountain Chickadee, Pygmy Nuthatch) reach the southern limit of their distribution in the state here or at Laguna Mountain to the southeast. Lower elevations in the Park have the birds typical of the oak-woodland and chaparral habitats; many waterfowl, Avocets, Black-necked Stilts, and phalaropes may be found on Cuyamaca Reservoir (east of Route 79 in the north end of the Park) when the water level is low. Several camping and picnic areas are near State Route 79 in the Park and dirt roads and trails lead to various points at the higher altitudes. From Julian, 10 miles farther north, the Colorado Desert and Salton Sea (see under Brawley and Palm Springs) are quickly reached via State Route 78.

At MISSION BAY, between Ocean Beach and Pacific Beach of northwest San Diego, one or two Louisiana Herons winter regularly, as well as numbers of Black Brant, Baldpates, Buffle-heads, and other waterfowl. There are salt marshes, in which Black Rails have been found nesting, and mud flats, with all of their transient and wintering birds, on the south and north shores of the Bay, east of a causeway that crosses its middle part. To reach this go north on US Route 101 past the Marine Base to Barnett Street, then turn left and soon right on Midway Drive, which crosses the causeway.

From Ocean Beach, just southwest of Mission Bay, the Sunset Cliffs Road leads along the top of a bluff overlooking sandy and rocky beaches where birds of both these habitats can be found. Migrating Black-vented and Sooty Shearwaters are often seen here close to shore.

At LA JOLLA, 7 miles north of Ocean Beach along Mission and La Jolla Boulevards, there are wave-worn caves in the sea cliff just below the center of town. A nesting colony of Brandt's Cormorants is situated here, and Surf-birds, Wandering Tattlers, and others of the rocky-shore list forage at tide level in the proper season.

Across the harbor portion of SAN DIEGO BAY opposite the city is Coronado (reached by ferry from the southern end of Pacific Highway in San Diego), where boats may be rented for cruising on the Bay. Large concentrations of Black Brant and diving ducks congregate in the long south half of the Bay in winter, and terns are common transients. Least Terns nest abundantly south of Coronado on the sands of the narrow isthmus between the Bay and ocean that is traversed by State Route 75. Royal and Elegant Terns occur in flocks during the post-breeding dispersal period.

From the harbor of San Diego Bay it is possible, upon advance arrangements with Custom Offices and charter-boat companies, to go to the northernmost of Mexico's LOS CORONADOS ISLANDS, 8 miles offshore just below the border, where there are breeding colonies of the Black Petrel, Brown Pelican, Xantus' Murrelet, Cassin's Auklet, Western Gull, and other waterbirds.

SAN FRANCISCO. The visitor to GOLDEN GATE PARK will see little evidence to indicate that the entire area now covered by woods, lawns, flower beds, and lakes has been developed from barren sand dunes within the past 80 years. The long narrow Park covers 1,013 acres between Stanyan Street and the ocean. The North American Hall of the CALIFORNIA ACADEMY OF SCIENCES (open 10:00 A.M.–5:00 P.M. daily, no charge) contains excellent habitat groups of the birds and mammals of California. The research collection of the Academy contains over 63,000 bird skins and its library has more than 2,600 volumes pertaining to ornithology. Simson African Hall and the Steinhart Aquarium are immediately adjacent to the North American Hall.

Stow Lake is the largest of the artificial lakes in Golden Gate Park and will attract the bird finder interested in waterfowl. Wintering ducks may be approached and photographed at close range. The Mallard, Baldpate, Pintail, Shoveler, Redhead, Ring-necked Duck, Canvas-back, and Ruddy Duck are among the species to be expected.

To the epicure, the world-famous CLIFF HOUSE, on the Great Highway, is known for its cuisine, but the ornithologists of central California have long used its observation deck as a convenient vantage point from which to see transient Surf-birds and Black Turnstones. March and April, and from August to October, are the favorite periods, although both species have been seen in nearly every month of the year. Search the rocks directly below the Cliff House. In April and August look for migrating Wandering Tattlers on the same rocks. In late summer huge numbers of shearwaters, mostly Sooty Shearwaters, are frequently seen offshore. Sea lions, Brown Pelicans, (Farallon) Double-crested Cormorants, and Brandt's Cormorants share the Seal Rocks offshore from the Cliff House.

The SAN FRANCISCO ZOOLOGICAL GARDENS (known locally as FLEISHHACKER ZOO) are at the intersection of Sloat Boulevard (State Route 5) and the Great Highway. The avian attractions of the Zoo include over 800 birds, 200 of which are North American species. A large aquatic aviary contains a number of waterfowl, and pinioned cranes of several kinds may be seen in the open paddocks. Penguins and flamingos are among the exotic attractions. As usual, a large percentage of the caged birds are parrots and macaws.

LAKE MERCED is a short distance south of Fleishhacker Zoo and may be reached by driving south on the Skyline Boulevard and turning left on Lake Merced Boulevard. Formerly, Laguna de la Merced was a single body of water that was connected with the ocean in winter. Today the Lake is divided into two parts, both permanently cut off from the sea. Certain salt-water invertebrates, however, still inhabit its now fresh waters. From late autumn to early spring large numbers of Eared Grebes, Western Grebes, and Pied-billed Grebes may be seen here, as well as numerous wintering ducks and gulls. One of the best points for observation is the parking area along the Boulevard at the southeastern end of the southernmost lake.

At any season one may see Soras and Florida Gallinules close to the cattails and rushes bordering the shore. This same habitat is the home of Long-billed Marsh Wrens and Yellow-throats during the summer.

The bird finder who wishes to observe nesting seabirds in central California will find them at POINT REYES, approximately 50 miles by road north of San Francisco. Take US Route 101 across the Golden Gate Bridge to State Route 1 and turn left. Stop at STINSON BEACH, where the road passes along the shore of Bolinas Bay, and look for waterbirds and shorebirds. (Red-bellied) Red-shouldered Hawks are often seen along this stretch. Continue on through Olema and, just before reaching the hamlet of Point Reyes Station, take the left turn toward Inverness. Follow the road around the west side of Tomales Bay to Inverness. Stop wherever there is a turnout and look for waterbirds on Tomales Bay. Black Brant winter, often in large numbers. Many other species of waterfowl will be seen in the winter. A stop in the Bishop pines, approximately 2 miles beyond Inverness, may be rewarded by the sight and sound of Pygmy Nuthatches. Continue on to the lighthouse area at Point Reyes, where a public parking place is designated. Walk down the steps toward the lighthouse as far as the Coast Guard caretaker will allow visitors to go, and search the rocks and water below for Brandt's and Pelagic Cormorants, Common Murres, Pigeon Guillemots, and Tufted Puffins. Keep an eye and ear open for Duck Hawks, Common Ravens, and Rock Wrens, which frequent the rocky point. If the caretaker will permit a descent along the trail on the west side of the Point, it is possible to reach a spot directly above the Murre colony. The courtship display of the Brandt's Cormorants is worth the entire trip. The nesting season is from May to July, but a visit at any time of year is rewarding.

Of the more extensive areas of coastal redwood forest the nearest to San Francisco is MUIR WOODS NATIONAL MONUMENT (504 acres). This trip may be combined with a visit to Point Reyes. Take US Route 101 to Manzanita and turn left on Route 1 for 2.5 miles to the right turn marked with a sign showing the direction to the Monument. The variety of birdlife is not great, but certain species will be found here that are rare outside the red-woods. Spotted Owls are resident but only the extremely fortunate bird finder will see or hear one. Look for Steller's Jays, Chestnut-backed Chickadees, Brown Creepers, an occasional Dipper along the creek, and breeding Winter Wrens and Hermit Thrushes. Pygmy Owls are present and may be found in the daytime.

The mouth of Tomales Bay is reached from DILLONS BEACH, which, from mid-October through March, is a vantage point for the observation of wintering loons (3 species), grebes, ducks, and shorebirds. April is a good time to observe the shorebird migration. Across the mouth of the Bay, on the rocky shores of Tomales Point, Harlequin Ducks spend the winter. Black Brant and other waterfowl winter in the Bay. To reach Dillons Beach, continue north on Route 1 to the village of Tomales. A left turn, indicated by a sign, leads to the Dillons Beach resort area (4 miles), where the car must be left. (There is a charge for parking.) Walk south along the Beach to the mouth of the Bay.

SAN JOSE. ALUM ROCK PARK (629 acres), 7 miles east of San Jose, is a deeply cut, wooded canyon in the hills that bound the east side of the Santa Clara Valley. From downtown San Jose, drive east on Santa Clara Street, which becomes Alum Rock Road at the city limits. The road is well marked with signs. There are picnic tables, fireplaces, and many trails in the area. Along permanent Penitencia Creek the canyon bottom is heavily wooded with coast live oak, buckeye, willow, sycamore, white alder, and big-leaf maple. The north walls of the east-west canyon are clothed with patches of chaparral, grass, and Digger-pine and blue-oak woodland. Rufous-crowned Sparrows are common in the blue-gray patches of sagebrush. From the chaparral the songs of the Wren-tit and California Thrasher are heard, and Golden Eagles are often seen soaring overhead. Dippers have nested for several years along the Creek, and the tumbling song of the Canyon Wren is to be heard in the breeding season. White-throated Swifts have been known to nest in the rocky cliffs of the canyon walls. Although a visit at any time of year is rewarding, the best months are April, May, and June. Bird finders will prefer to avoid Sundays and holidays, when the Park is crowded.

At the southern tip of San Francisco Bay is the village of ALVISO, departure point for bird finders intent upon locating marshbirds and shorebirds in this area. From San Jose, drive north on First Street, which becomes the Alviso–San Jose Road at the city limits.

The Southern Pacific Railroad has conveniently provided dry-shod access to the marshland. Park as close as possible to the tracks on the north side of town and walk out on the railroad fill, which leads for 3 miles across sloughs and marshes. There is ample room to get off the tracks when a train passes. Birds of the salt marshes and mud flats will be found. Try to arrive as the tide is beginning to ebb. It is of special interest to observe birds during the extremely high tides of the year. A tide of more than 6.6 feet (Golden Gate level) will force the marsh dwellers out from cover and will often afford unusually favorable opportunities for observation of Clapper Rails and Short-eared Owls. There is always a chance of seeing the elusive Black Rail during such tides, and in the winter both Virginia Rails and Soras are often present.

Los Esteros Road (State Street) leaves Alviso to the northeast and runs along the margin of the marsh. Stop at the first sharp bend (about 0.6 mile from Alviso); if the tide is out, there will be exposed mud flats and marshland to the north of the Road. The Road continues for 1.5 miles through marshland to Zanker Road. Visits at any season will yield results, with the best shorebird concentrations occurring in August, September, April, and May.

MT. HAMILTON is the site of the Lick Observatory of the University of California. The 18 miles of twisting paved road to the summit (4,209 feet altitude) pass through Digger-pine and blue-oak woodland. April and May are the months recommended for a visit. Follow directions for Alum Rock Park but take the right turn (watch for the sign) approximately 5 miles east of San Jose. On a clear day the view alone is well worth the trip.

SAN JOSE STATE COLLEGE, 4th and San Fernando Streets, has a teaching collection of approximately 1,000 bird skins and a library of over 100 volumes pertaining to ornithology. A course in ornithology is given in the spring quarter. The Santa Clara Valley Audubon Society meets at the College on alternate months. For information, call at Room 100, Science Building.

SAN PEDRO (south of Los Angeles). CABRILLO BEACH (reached by going south on Pacific Avenue to 36th Street, then turning left), at the foot of a 2-mile long breakwater protecting outer Los Angeles Harbor, is a conveniently reached spot for the study of the common wintering loons, grebes, cormorants, diving ducks, shore-birds, and gulls. There is a rocky shore within walking distance outside the breakwater, and Fulmars, small alcids, and other pelagic birds are sometimes seen from the break-water itself. The city of Los Angeles operates a MARINE MUSEUM in one end of the pavilion building just south of the base of the breakwater. Mounted specimens of most of the seashore and pelagic birds, as well as of a great many of the fish, mollusks, and other animals found in the near-by ocean, are on display.

The high rocky cliff at Point Fermin, a few blocks west and south of Cabrillo Beach, allows no entry to the shore-line below, but west from Point Fermin, Paseo del Mar and Palos Verdes Drive, which it joins, follow the coastline in a scenic drive around the hills overlooking the ocean. There are a number of good stopping points. One and three quarters miles west of Point Fermin Park there is a steep road going down from Paseo del Mar to WHITE'S POINT. This is one of the few spots around the Palos Verdes Hills, which lie between San Pedro and Redondo Beach, where one can easily get down to the habitat of transient and wintering Surf-birds and Wandering Tattlers; but the hu-man visitors on weekends keep many of the birds away. Other points to reach the rocky shoreline are at PORTU-GUESE BEND, 3 miles west of White's Point, and at BLUFF COVE in Palos Verdes Estates on the west side of the hills. The latter is reached by a trail down from Paseo del Mar, 3½ blocks west of the Palos Verdes School; Tat-tlers are common in May and in August, and near by there are roosts of Brandt's Cormorants and White-throated

Swifts. This drive also offers opportunities for seeing most of the open-field birds and, in shrubby areas facing the ocean, nesting (Dusky) Orange-crowned Warblers.

SANTA CATALINA ISLAND, 20 miles offshore from San Pedro, is the only one of the 'channel islands' of southern California to which regular passenger boat service is maintained. The fishing and resort town of Avalon near the southeast end of the Island is the terminus of the Catalina Steamship Line, which leaves the foot of Avalon Boulevard in Wilmington (just north of San Pedro) once each weekday and twice (or more) daily on weekends. Tickets may be obtained at the pier or at the offices of the Pacific Electric Railway in Los Angeles or suburban cities.

From the steamer, Sooty Shearwaters may be seen almost any time of year, and Fulmars and alcids or other pelagic birds in winter or during migration. From Avalon, excursion boats are operated to the 'Seal Rocks' at the southeast end of the Island, on which Brandt's and Pelagic Cormorants are common and near which Bald Eagles nest in February and March. At certain times, runs are also made all the way around the 21-mile-long Island, and glass-bottomed boats operate in Avalon Bay over beautiful submarine gardens. Transportation overland on the rugged Island is difficult, and permission must be secured from the Island Company to leave the Avalon area. Within it, however, there are many birds, including the resident subspecies of the Allen's Hummingbird, Horned Lark, Bewick's Wren, Loggerhead Shrike, House Finch, and Spotted Towhee. Other species occurring regularly are the Western Flycatcher, Barn Swallow, Common Raven, Bush-tit, Rock Wren, Mockingbird, Lesser and Lawrence's Goldfinches, Chipping Sparrow, and (in winter) Audubon's Warbler, White-crowned Sparrow, Golden-crowned Sparrow, and Fox Sparrow. The breeding (Dusky) Orange-crowned Warbler usually emigrates to the mainland for the winter.

A mile from Avalon is the famous BIRD PARK (admission free), which has about 3,000 live birds of 450 species on display in a 20-acre outdoor zoo. Nearly all the birds are exotic species, from all regions of the world.

SANTA ANA. In the Santa Ana Mountains southeast of Los Angeles is one of the most unusual bird sanctuaries in the country—the DOROTHY MAY TUCKER SANCTUARY. Here hummingbirds of six species are attracted to a battery of feeders along a shelf just outside the screen of a 24-foot porch on which one may sit and watch at the range of 2 or 3 feet. The Sanctuary, which grew from a modest test-tube feeder in 1926 to feeding places for nearly 200 birds, was presented to the California Audubon Society in 1941 by Mr. B. F. Tucker in memory of his wife, for whom it is named.

The Anna's Hummingbird is a resident, and the Black-chinned and Costa's arrive for the summer in late March or early April, while the Rufous, Allen's, and Calliope are transients, chiefly in early April, February and March, and late April, respectively. In the fall migration, large numbers stay into October in this favorable spot, long after the main migration at higher altitudes. Many feeding trays and nest boxes, as well as a small stream under large live oaks, cottonwoods, and sycamores and the adjacent sage- and chaparral-covered slopes, bring many birds of these habitats to the 9 acres of the Tucker Sanctuary. In April, when the greatest variety of hummers is present, SANTIAGO CANYON (popularly called Modjeska) below the Sanctuary is likely to contain almost any of the landbirds that migrate through southern California.

From Santa Ana drive north on Main Street to Chapman Avenue, turn right and follow this street through the town of Orange toward Irvine Park. Five and a half miles from Orange there is an intersection. The main road continues one mile to Irvine Park. Turn right and continue on this road past the upper end of Irvine Lake (Santiago Reservoir), 13 miles from Santa Ana. Two miles past the Lake there is a fork in the road. The left branch leads up Silverado Canyon (also a good bird-finding area). Take the right branch up Santiago Canyon and past the Modjeska Home. At a point 3.6 miles from the Silverado fork, the main road turns to climb over the ridge to the right of the Canyon. Just before this turn, take a road up the main Canyon for about a mile to the Sanctuary, which is marked by a sign.

SANTA BARBARA. Situated picturesquely on a 3-mile-wide gentle slope between steep mountains and the sea, Santa Barbara has long been an ornithological center. It was home to Ralph Hoffman and W. Leon Dawson, authors of two of the most-used books on California birds. The SANTA BARBARA MUSEUM OF NATURAL HISTORY, 2559 Puesta del Sol Road, has excellent exhibits of California birds, mammals, reptiles, and other animals and of the geology and climates of the region. There are about 500 mounted birds, some in habitat groups, others in systematic arrangement. The scientific collections, representing the whole Pacific Coast, include over 3,200 bird skins and 4,500 sets of eggs.

MISSION CANYON, between the Museum and the Santa Barbara Mission, is alive with birds all year. A mixture of native live-oak and sycamore woodlands, with shrub and tree plantings around near-by residences and in Rocky Nook Park just above the Museum, brings in all of the widespread wintering species. Varied Thrushes and Townsend's Warblers are present some years. The Allen's Hummingbird and Hutton's Vireo nest here in March or before, but the height of the nesting season is in April and early May, when the Cooper's and (Red-bellied) Red-shouldered Hawks, Band-tailed Pigeon, Hairy Woodpecker, Canyon Wren, Olive-backed Thrush, Yellow-breasted Chat, Purple Finch, and Oregon Junco have eggs or young. At the same time many transient warblers are passing through, and a late flight of Bullock's Orioles comes in early May, apparently birds that breed far to the north.

The BOTANIC GARDENS, a mile farther up the Canyon along Mission Canyon Road, are below open sagebrush and chaparral slopes; Phainopeplas are common here in the summer.

Drive north from the Museum on Mission Canyon Road for 3 blocks, then left on Laurel Canyon Road, and north on the San Marcos Pass Road (State Route 150), which passes through chaparral and live-oak woodland and crosses the crest of the Santa Ynez Mountains only 13.5 miles from downtown Santa Barbara. Many soaring hawks can be seen and there is a splendid view out over the city and offshore islands. Where Route 150 reaches the bottom of the grade north of the Pass, a side road leads eastward (right) up the Santa Ynez Valley. At PARADISE CAMP COUNTY PARK, 2.5 miles up this road, there are large cottonwoods, willows, and sycamores along the stream, and coast live oaks and deciduous valley oaks on the flats. The summer birdlife here is a combination of all of the oak-woodland and most of the riparian species; and the canyon above the Park offers opportunities for exploring the rugged back country, which is mostly chaparral-covered. California Condors still range here, but they are more likely to be seen from vantage points around their nesting area itself (now wisely closed to the public), such as from Pine Mountain Summit (5,300 feet), which is reached by driving east from Santa Barbara on Route 150 to Ojai, then north for 34 miles on US Route 399, or from Mt. Pinos (see under Bakersfield). In the more open, drier part of the Santa Ynez Valley to the west, Yellow-billed Magpies reach the southern limit of their breeding range and may be seen from Route 150 at various places along the Valley, which Route 150 follows west to a point near the coast, beyond Lompoc.

At the southeast entrance to Santa Barbara, between Route 101 and Cabrillo Boulevard, is ANDRE CLARK BIRD REFUGE—a park lake to which Eared and Western Grebes, many cormorants, hundreds of waterfowl, and hordes of Coots and gulls come in winter. A little separate pond on the opposite side of US Route 101 is frequented by Ring-necked and other ducks.

The harbor area along West Cabrillo Boulevard is good for general and sandy-seacoast birds. HENDRY'S BEACH, about a mile west of the lighthouse, is better in that it has a good sandy beach and there is less chance of being disturbed by crowds. Besides the usual coastwise species, Sooty Shearwaters and some Pink-footed and Black-vented Shearwaters that occur with them are frequently seen migrating or rafting on the ocean close to shore.

The new campus of SANTA BARBARA COLLEGE of the University of California is west of the city on the heights of Goleta Point, in the seaward face of which Bank Swallows have nested some years. The present campus is in the city on Alameda Street near the Museum. A vertebrate-natural-history course (including birds) is taught here in the spring, and a Nature Study and Conservation In-

stitute is held each August in co-operation with the Museum
and Botanic Gardens.

SANTA MONICA. On the west side of the Los Angeles
metropolitan area are excellent beach and foothill bird-
finding areas, the SANTA MONICA MUNICIPAL PIER
and YACHT HARBOR at the end of Colorado Avenue
being one. From the Pier in winter, Eared Grebes and
Western Grebes and occasionally Red-throated or other
loons may be watched as they dive for fish. Brown Pelicans,
Double-crested Cormorants, and all of the gulls gather in
large numbers on the breakwater or, if undisturbed, on
the beach. Brandt's and Pelagic Cormorants occur regularly in small numbers. Heermann's Gulls are abundant
from July to February; and most of the terns, including occasional Elegant Terns, are present in September.

Drive southward on US Route 101A (Lincoln Boulevard,
between 7th and 9th Streets) for 3.2 miles to Washington
Street, thence right for 1.75 miles to Speedway and left for
1.75 miles to the mouth of BALLONA CREEK in Playa del
Rey. Snowy Plovers and other species of the sandy-shore
list are found on the wide beach to the north and south of
two jetties, which attract rocky-shore species as well. Many
loons, grebes, and scoters forage in the near-by ocean in winter. Surf-birds and Black Turnstones have been seen here
every month of the year. Continuing inland along the Creek
are long, rock levees, the south one overlooking remnant
salt-marsh areas and alkali flats in which Least Terns nest.
A few Clapper Rails and Short-eared Owls are still found
beyond the oil wells north of the levees.

Almost any of the canyons in the Santa Monica Mountains north of the city provide the opportunity to see oak-
woodland and chaparral birds; but TAPIA PARK, farther
west in the heart of the Santa Monica Mountains, has, as
well as these habitats, tall cottonwoods and willows along
the stream. Hence, breeding birds of the riparian woodland
are also to be found here. Band-tailed Pigeons, (Red-
breasted) Common Sapsuckers, and all of the widespread
species (see under winter birdlife in the introduction) are
common in winter. To reach the Park, drive west from
Santa Monica on US Route 101A for 9 miles, turn right,

and follow a winding road (over a mountain and into a canyon) for 10.5 miles.

Coastal points along Malibu Road (Route 101A), west of Santa Monica, which are frequently worth while are: DUME POINT, reached by a side road leaving the highway at the top of the hill in 'Malibu Riviera,' 19 miles from Santa Monica, for birds of the open-field and rocky-shore habitats; and, just west of Dume Point, ZUMA BEACH COUNTY PARK, where there is a fine sandy beach and willow thicket and sycamore woodland just inland from it, with a consequent variety of landbirds. Rock Wrens live on the sea cliffs at Dume, all three species of cormorants roost here, and there may be large numbers of loons, Western Grebes, scoters, and gulls on the ocean below in winter.

SCOTIA. The famous Redwood Highway (US Route 101) south from Scotia passes through many fine stands of the coast redwood. Although each of the many groves and state parks is worthy of exploration by the bird finder, only one will be mentioned here.

Drive south from Scotia on Route 101 for 16 miles to Dyerville, where the DYERVILLE FLATS grove contains the tallest known redwood, the Founders' Tree, which is 364 feet in height. For the bird finder, there are two special times of the year. During the last part of April or the first half of May, nesting Varied Thrushes will be heard and possibly seen near the Flat Iron Tree. Turn west from Dyerville on an improved road to the Flat Iron Tree, park, and listen for the moaning, whistled notes of this bird, whose calls carry a considerable distance. Chestnut-backed Chickadees, Winter Wrens, and Black-capped Warblers are other breeding species. Look for Dippers along the creeks and for American Mergansers and Ospreys along the Eel River (adjacent to Route 101 at Dyerville). In mid-June the principal avian attraction is the Vaux's Swift. It is not necessary to leave Route 101 to see this western counterpart of the Chimney Swift hawking overhead. Tree Swallows are also abundant. In willow thickets along streams will be found Yellow Warblers, Yellow-breasted Chats, and Song Sparrows.

STOCKTON. In the Sierran foothills, 30 miles northeast of Stockton, is CALAVERAS RESERVOIR. Take State Route 8 east and, approximately one mile before reaching Valley Springs, turn right on a gravel road with a sign indicating the way to Calaveras Dam. The Dam is 3 miles from the turnoff. A parking space is provided. The rolling country is wooded with Digger pines and blue oaks interspersed with chaparral areas of chamise, manzanita, and buckthorn. The avian associates of these vegetational types will be found. The Reservoir is the winter refuge of Canada Geese and other waterfowl. Bald Eagles are occasionally seen here, and Golden Eagles are not uncommon. October to April is the favored season for a visit.

The delta of the great Sacramento–San Joaquin drainage system is the winter home of many transient waterfowl. The marshes have been dyked and drained but the birds continue to make use of cornfields and pastures that were once marshland. Numerous sloughs and canals provide the necessary habitat for marshbirds. From Stockton drive west for approximately 13 miles on State Route 4 (Borden Highway) to VICTORIA ISLAND. Flocks of White-fronted and Snow Geese will usually be found between November and March. Whistling Swans are not uncommon. Look for White-tailed Kites either hovering over open fields or perched in dead or leafless trees. Most of the species of fresh-water ducks that winter in California will be found on the sloughs and ponds. Numerous side roads are available for exploration but be cautious about dirt roads in wet weather.

TRUCKEE. Since 1948 the National Audubon Society has operated the AUDUBON CAMP OF CALIFORNIA in the upper coniferous-forest belt just west of the Sierran crest and not far northwest of Lake Tahoe on the California-Nevada line. The Camp occupies Sugar Bowl (Ski) Lodge at the head of SUMMIT VALLEY (altitude nearly 7,000 feet). To reach the Lodge from Truckee, drive 12.3 miles west on US Route 40 across Donner Pass (elevation 7,135 feet) to Soda Springs; turn left (south) here, cross the railroad tracks, and then turn left again, following the dirt road past the north shore of Lake Van Norden to the Lodge at the end of the road (3.5 miles from Soda Springs). Watch for Mountain Bluebirds in the vicinity of the stables and the meadow near the Lake.

The Audubon Camp usually has five two-week sessions running consecutively from mid-June to late August. Teachers, youth leaders, and other persons (all must be 18 years of age or older), regardless of professional background or recreational interest, may attend. The Camp's principal purpose is to teach conservation by developing an appreciation of the out-of-doors and demonstrating the interrelationship between animals, plants, soils, and water. Through daily guided field trips, persons enrolled for any one of the sessions become acquainted with a variety of habitats, both terrestial and aquatic, and their animal occupants. Further information about the Camp, including the cost of enrollment, may be obtained by writing the National Audubon Society, Room 201, 693 Sutter Street, San Francisco 2, California, or (in summer) the Director, Audubon Camp of California, Norden, California.

The forest of red fir, lodgepole pine, and western white pine near Sugar Bowl Lodge has such regularly nesting birds as the (Red-breasted) Common Sapsucker, Williamson's Sapsucker, Hammond's Flycatcher, Hermit Thrush, Townsend's Solitaire, Golden-crowned and Ruby-crowned Kinglets, Audubon's Warbler, Western Tanager, Evening Grosbeak, Cassin's Finch, Pine Grosbeak, and Pine Siskin, as well as other species on the coniferous-forest list. In the small meadow with willow and mountain-alder thickets, or on the borders of the cleared ski slopes, are found the summer-resident Calliope Hummingbird, Traill's Flycatcher, Black-capped Warbler, White-crowned and Lincoln's Sparrows, and (in July and August) hordes of transient Rufous Hummingbirds. Goshawks, Blue Grouse, Mountain Quail, and Red Crossbills occur frequently in the summer; Black-backed Woodpeckers, rarely. Clark's Nutcrackers are sometimes observed near the Lodge but are more readily found on MT. LINCOLN (8,383 feet), which forms one wall of the spectacular 'Sugar Bowl,' where snows drift to a depth of 50 to 60 feet in winter. Bird finders wishing to undertake the 2-mile climb up the mountain, especially in the early summer before the snows have gone, should inquire at the Lodge for the best route.

In DONNER PASS, north of the highway summit (US Route 40), is a sparse growth of pines and junipers interspersed with low montane chaparral in which breeding Green-tailed Towhees are common, and with extensive rocky areas where Common Nighthawks and Rock Wrens nest. Just north of Route 40 at a point half a mile west of the Pass, Wright's and Olive-sided Flycatchers and Nashville, Macgillivray's, and Black-capped Warblers may be heard on a slope that supports about 7 acres of soft chaparral, admixed with young pines and firs. A half-mile walk up a logging road, starting just west of the ski lift of the Donner Ski Ranch, will enable one to find these and other nesting birds.

There is a very different bird-finding area in the MARTIS VALLEY, reached from Truckee by a road going south from Route 40 east of the Southern Pacific Railroad Station. After crossing the railroad tracks and the Truckee River, the road continues for 5 miles to the open sagebrush flats of the Valley, where Horned Larks, Sage Thrashers, Green-tailed Towhees, and Vesper and Brewer's Sparrows nest, and where Swainson's Hawks forage.

The Dipper is frequent along the TRUCKEE RIVER— one pair has been found nesting each year in a section close to US Route 40, 5 to 6 miles east of Truckee, beyond the Agricultural Inspection Station.

Bird finding comparable to that of the middle altitudes in Yosemite National Park (see under Merced) and magnificent scenery may be enjoyed during a 73-mile tour around LAKE TAHOE, reached by driving 15 miles (1.2 miles west, then south) from Truckee on State Route 89. The Lake itself, because of its great depth, attracts few waterbirds; but at the south end lies a large marsh, the western part of which is accessible to bird finders willing to wade from the U.S. Forest Service campground (east of Camp Richardson on Route 89, 41 miles from Truckee). Birds nesting in the marsh include the Eared Grebe, American Bittern, Canada Goose, Mallard, Cinnamon Teal, Forster's and Black Terns, Wilson's Phalarope, Long-billed

Marsh Wren, Yellow-headed Blackbird, and Red-wing. (For other birds that may be found in the vicinity of Lake Tahoe, see under Reno in the Nevada chapter.)

TULELAKE (on the north-central border of California). The vegetation of northeastern California is mostly sage-brush and juniper, but more ducks and geese nest in this section than in any other part of the state. Three NATIONAL WILDLIFE REFUGES—TULE LAKE, LOWER KLAMATH, and CLEAR LAKE—are near the Oregon line. All three Refuges are administered from the Tule Lake Refuge.

Tule Lake Refuge has an area of 37,337 acres, of which 13,000 acres are water; 30 nesting islands have been provided for pelicans, cormorants, geese, ducks, and gulls. Nesting waterfowl include the Canada Goose, Mallard, Gadwall, Pintail, Cinnamon Teal, Redhead, and Ruddy Duck. During migration the great flights of waterfowl include species that nest in the Arctic and spend the winter in the valley marshes of California. The largest concentrations occur in September and October, when, in addition to the breeding species, the ornithologist will see Whistling Swans, White-fronted and Snow Geese, Green-winged Teal, Shovelers, Ring-necked Ducks, Canvas-backs, American Golden-eyes, and Buffle-heads. Ducks and geese are by no means the only avian attractions. Other nesting species dependent upon water include Western and Eared Grebes, White Pelicans, (Farallon) Double-crested Cormorants, Great Blue Herons, Green Herons, Black-crowned Night Herons, American and Snowy Egrets, White-faced Ibises, Willets, Avocets, Black-necked Stilts, California Gulls, Forster's Terns, Caspian Terns, and Black Terns. On the adjacent, dry, sage-covered plains are found the birds of the Great Basin, including the Sage Grouse, Sage Thrasher, Lark Sparrow, and Brewer's Sparrow.

Lower Klamath and Clear Lake Refuges (21,460 and 34,616 acres) have many similar aspects but each presents something of peculiar interest. More than 200 species have been recorded for all the Refuge areas.

The bird finder is advised to obtain information on places of greatest interest at the time of his visit. This he may do by calling at the Refuge Office in Tulelake on week-days or at headquarters on weekends or holidays.

To reach Tule Lake headquarters, take the East-West Road at the south end of Tulelake and drive 5 miles west to Hill Road. Turn left (south) and proceed 0.5 mile to headquarters on the right side of the road.

Lower Klamath headquarters may be reached by driving 3 miles north from Tulelake on State Route 139, turning left on the State Line Highway, and continuing for 9.5 miles.

Clear Lake headquarters is reached by driving south from Tulelake on Route 139 for 18 miles and turning left at the railroad overpass on the Forest Service road to Doublehead Mountain. The Refuge is 9 miles from this turnoff.

TWENTYNINE PALMS. (Reached from Palm Springs by driving north on State Route 111 to US 99, turning right for 4 miles, and then left on the road to Morongo.) Twenty-nine Palms is a resort town on the southern Mohave Desert and the headquarters of the JOSHUA TREE NATIONAL MONUMENT (575,934 acres). There are many dirt roads in the Monument, and most maps show only a few of them, so that it is advisable for the bird finder to visit head-quarters before entering the area.

Spring is by far the best time to visit the desert foothills and mountains of the Monument, for if there have been any significant rains during the winter, the ground between the scattered shrubs becomes a many-hued carpet of blos-soming annuals. The grotesque arms of the Joshua trees are capped with mammoth columns of creamy white flowers in late March and April. Besides the unending variety of desert scenery provided by woodlands of Joshua tree and of pinyon pine and desert juniper, there are several oases where willows and cottonwoods and available water attract birds from a considerable surrounding area. There are also several active gold mines and many imposing rock outcrops, from one of which (Keys View), at an elevation of 5,000 feet, there is a magnificent view of the low-lying Colorado Desert.

At Twentynine Palms, Phainopeplas nest in March when

most of the winter visitants are still on hand; other species
of the desert list nest chiefly in April and early May. Most
of the springs within the Monument area are near the
boundary between the pinyon-juniper woodland of the
higher slopes and the creosote-bush and cactus desert of
the lower altitudes, with the Joshua trees overlapping
both habitats. Good bird-finding areas south and west from
Twentynine Palms are Quail Springs, Barker Dam, Pinyon
Wells, and Lost Horse Valley (en route to Keys View).
The Gambel's Quail, Ladder-backed Woodpecker, Costa's
Hummingbird (summer resident), Cactus Wren, Rock
Wren, Scott's Oriole (summer resident), and Desert Sparrow are all easily found about these springs. Mountain
Quail are sometimes found in the same areas with the Gam-
bel's Quail, although the two tend to nest at different al-
titudes. Gray Vireos are local summer residents in the
low, sparse shrubs on the not too rocky slopes. Golden
Eagles and Prairie Falcons are present throughout the year.
Pinyon Jays nest at the higher altitudes but may be found
almost anywhere in the Monument at other times.

Common winter species include those widespread over
the state and, in addition, the Anna's Hummingbird, Canyon Wren, Western Bluebird, Mountain Bluebird, Townsend's Solitaire, Chipping Sparrow, and Brewer's Sparrow.
In April and October many warblers pass through and may
be seen both around the springs and flitting from bush to
bush across the desert. The Black-throated Gray is especially common, but the Orange-crowned, Macgillivray's,
and Black-capped, as well as the Yellow-throat, also occur.
Other transients are the House Wren, Hermit and Olive-
backed Thrushes, Lawrence's Goldfinch, Green-tailed
Towhee, and the swallows, especially the Violet-green.

Near the southern border of the Monument is Cottonwood Spring, reached by a 41-mile dirt road from Twentynine Palms through the Pinto Basin or by a 5.6-mile road
extending northward from US Route 60 at a point 25.5
miles east of Indio. At the Spring there is a small grove of
cottonwood trees and a few palms about a pool with willows and bulrushes—and it is on the main line of migration, which follows along the Little San Bernardino Mountains and into coastal southern California to the west.

WILLOWS. Bird finders motoring through the Sacramento Valley on US Route 99W will hardly need to leave the highway to visit SACRAMENTO NATIONAL WILDLIFE REFUGE, 7 miles south of Willows. The Refuge headquarters is a quarter mile east of the highway. The turn-off is marked and the steel tower is a good landmark. Approximately half of the 10,776 acres are marshy, with numerous ponds that are accessible by car. The Refuge is best visited in the fall and winter, when the transient and wintering waterfowl are in greatest numbers. From 15 August to 15 January the ducks are present, with Pintails, Mallards, and Baldpates in order of greatest numbers. The other fresh-water ducks will also be found. There are geese in great numbers in December and January, with the Snow Goose most abundant. Canada, White-fronted, and Ross' Geese are winter visitors. Nesting birds are few but include American and Snowy Egrets, Mallards, Green-winged and Cinnamon Teal, and Killdeer.

Contributing authorities: Elmer C. Aldrich, John R. Arnold, John E. Chattin, J. H. Comby, Paul Covel, Mrs. C. H. Daugherty, John Davis, Keith L. Dixon, Vernon Ekedahl, C. Bert Harwell, Albert C. Hawbecker, Donald V. Hemphill, Verna Johnston, L. Floyd Keller, Mrs. Junea W. Kelly, Carl B. Koford, Arnold Lane, H. Elliott McClure, Alden H. Miller, Edward J. O'Neill, Robert T. Orr, Frank A. Pitelka, Bruce F. Provin, W. Dan Quattlebaum, Egmont Z. Rett, Howard J. Sargeant, Milton L. Seibert, George L. Sherman, Arnold Small, Mrs. Marguerite Angelo Smelser, Miss Emily Smith, Emerson A. Stoner, Robert W. Storer, Mrs. O. M. Stultz, Robert R.Talmadge, Mrs. Josephine Vaughn, Laidlaw O. Williams.

Colorado

WHITE-TAILED PTARMIGAN

In Colorado 1,500 peaks attain 10,000 or more feet of elevation; 300 exceed 13,000 feet; and 52 rise above 14,000 feet.
Between the lowest point (3,350 feet), near the Kansas line,
and the highest point (14,431 feet), on the summit of Mt.
Elbert, there is an altitudinal range of nearly 2 miles; moreover, Colorado as a whole has a mean altitude of 6,800
feet—higher than that of any other state. Quite naturally
visitors in Colorado become elevation conscious, and this
is especially true of those in search of birds, for finding
different species is as much a matter of changing from one
altitude to another as of covering miles of territory.

Not all of Colorado is mountainous; the towering mountains lie only across the central part of the state, from the northern to the southern boundary, and in the southwest. East of the mountains are extensive plains, and west of them is a high plateau. From east to west, the plains, the mountains, and the plateau constitute three major natural regions, each occupying roughly a third of the state.

The eastern plains, a segment of the Great Plains, are a vast expanse of prairie extending for some 200 miles in a gradual upward slope from the eastern boundary to about 5,500 feet at the base of the mountain foothills. The sole natural interruptions of an otherwise slightly undulating terrain are occasional sandhills and mesas and the shallow river valleys, notably those of the Platte and Arkansas Rivers and their tributaries, which drain most of the area. Short grasses—chiefly grama and buffalo—yuccas, and cacti are the prominent native vegetation, except for scrub oaks on the sandhills, stretches of sagebrush, and (along streams or in moist draws) small stands of trees—cottonwoods, box-elders, and willows, together with clumps of wild plum, wolfberry, chokecherry, and other shrubs. Though relatively dry, the plains are used for farming and cattle raising; hence their monotony is relieved in part by cultivated fields, by lines of fences, by widely scattered farm buildings, ranch houses, and small communities, most of which are sheltered by tree plantations. Birdlife is characteristically western, yet a few species of eastern affinities (e.g. the Eastern Phoebe, Blue Jay, Eastern Bluebird, and American Redstart) occur in the river valleys. Throughout the plains the species listed below breed regularly in most wooded tracts (tree plantations and deciduous growth along streams), or in open country (prairie grasslands, sagelands, fallow fields, wet lowlands, brushy places, woodland edges, and dooryards). Certain of these species (marked with an asterisk) also breed in suitable places in the valleys, foothills, and (sometimes) higher slopes of the adjoining mountains.

WOODED TRACTS

*Sharp-shinned Hawk
*Cooper's Hawk
 Yellow-billed Cuckoo

Screech Owl
Barn Owl
Red-shafted Flicker

*Hairy Woodpecker
*Downy Woodpecker
Blue Jay
*Black-capped Chickadee
*White-breasted Nuthatch

*Red-eyed Vireo
*Warbling Vireo
American Redstart
Bullock's Oriole
*Black-headed Grosbeak

OPEN COUNTRY

Turkey Vulture
Swainson's Hawk
Ferruginous Hawk
Marsh Hawk
Greater Prairie Chicken
Lesser Prairie Chicken
(mainly southeastern
Colorado)
Mountain Plover
Killdeer
Mourning Dove
Road-runner (mainly south-
ern Colorado)
Burrowing Owl
Red-headed Woodpecker
Eastern Kingbird
Western Kingbird
Say's Phoebe
*Horned Lark
Barn Swallow
*American Magpie
White-necked Raven
*House Wren
Bewick's Wren (mesa
country)
Mockingbird
Catbird
Brown Thrasher
*Mountain Bluebird

Loggerhead Shrike
Bell's Vireo
Yellow-throat
Yellow-breasted Chat
Western Meadowlark
Common Grackle
Blue Grosbeak
Lazuli Bunting
Dickcissel
Common Goldfinch
Lesser Goldfinch (mainly
southern Colorado)
Spotted Towhee
Lark Bunting
*Savannah Sparrow
Grasshopper Sparrow
*Vesper Sparrow
Cassin's Sparrow (mainly
southeastern Colorado)
*Chipping Sparrow
Clay-colored Sparrow
Brewer's Sparrow
*Song Sparrow
McCown's Longspur (north-
eastern Colorado only)
Chestnut-collared Longspur
(northeastern Colorado
only)

The mountains are part of the Rocky Mountain system or 'Rockies,' which form, in the United States, a barrier between the Great Plains on the east and the several plateaus on the west. In Colorado they are high, massive granite uplifts grouped into ranges; all trend north and south and are bordered by sedimentary foothills. The east-ernmost of the major ranges are the Front Range (north) and the Sangre de Cristo Range (south), while those of greatest height and grandeur to the west are the Park Range (north), the Sawatch and Elk Ranges (central), and the San Juan Mountains (south). Winding from Wyoming to New Mexico across the Colorado Rockies, dividing them into eastern and western slopes, is the Continental Divide. This follows the crest of the Park Range, swings eastward and proceeds southward along the Front Range, and then meanders southwestward along the Sawatch Range and through the San Juan Mountains.

Behind the eastern ranges is a chain of four wide and elevated valleys locally referred to as 'parks.' From the Wyoming line south these are the North, Middle, and South Parks (all west of the Front Range) and the San Luis Valley (west of the Sangre de Cristo Range). Originally grasslands, they are now for the most part cut up into farms and ranches. No bird species are peculiar to the parks but such species as the Western Meadowlark, Vesper Sparrow, and Savannah Sparrow are common as in other agricultural areas of the state. In the San Luis Valley (see under Saguache) are numerous marshy lakes and ponds that attract a surprising variety of nesting waterbirds, ducks, and marshbirds.

Like all high mountains, the Rockies in Colorado show from base to summit a vertical succession, or belts, of plant associations. The elevations at which these occur depend on such factors as latitude, exposure, soil, and moisture, while their width depends on the steepness of the slope. East of the Continental Divide the slopes have, in general, an abrupt incline, and therefore their plant associations are narrow and well-defined.

The lower foothills at the edge of the plains, with a surface characteristically rough and dissected, support a scrub, or 'pygmy,' forest consisting of juniper, pinyon pine, and scrub oak, as well as mountain mahogany and other shrubs. Low ridges and rims of canyons that are sometimes quite far from the main ranges have the same growth. In this type of environment, which is invariably warm and dry, the Poor-will, Scrub Jay, Pinyon Jay, Blue-gray Gnatcatcher, and, particularly in the scrub oaks, the Virginia's Warbler, Green-tailed Towhee, and Spotted Towhee are regular breeding residents. Above the pygmy forest, on the more uniform surface of the higher foothills, is an open forest of ponderosa pine, lodgepole pine, and Douglas fir —the preferred nesting habitat of the Band-tailed Pigeon, Williamson's Sapsucker, Pygmy Nuthatch, Western Bluebird, Solitary Vireo, and Western Tanager.

Along the watercourses, where cottonwoods, aspens, willows, chokecherries, alders, wild raspberries, snowberries, wild roses, and other deciduous trees and shrubs thrive, the Broad-tailed Hummingbird, Warbling Vireo, Yellow Warbler, Oven-bird, and other species found also in the wooded stream bottoms on the plains are common summer residents. Elevations reached by the pygmy forest and by the ponderosa-pine and Douglas-fir association differ over the state. In northern Colorado, the pygmy forest extends, on the average, up to 6,000 feet. The pine-fir association attains 7,800 feet, beginning at 6,000 except on the Front Range, where it begins at the plains, since there is no pygmy forest. In southern Colorado, the pygmy forest extends up to 7,000 feet, and, on southern slopes that are excessively hot and dry, much higher; thus the pine-fir and the higher associations begin at correspondingly greater altitudes.

Above the forests of the foothills is a heavy mountain forest at elevations averaging from 7,800 to 10,200 feet in northern Colorado and from 8,500 to 10,800 feet in the south. At lower levels the tree growth is a mixture of lodgepole pine and quaking aspen, with the addition of white fir in southern Colorado. Blue spruce, alder, and willow commonly fringe the bogs and cool streams. At the higher levels the timber is an almost pure stand of Engelmann spruce, except on cooler slopes, in shaded ravines, and near bogs and streams, where it is intermixed with alpine fir. Breeding more frequently in this forest than elsewhere in the mountains are the Goshawk, Blue Grouse, Pygmy Owl, Hammond's Flycatcher, Wright's Flycatcher, Olive-sided Flycatcher, Canada Jay, Red-breasted Nuthatch, Brown Creeper, Hermit Thrush, Olive-backed Thrush, Townsend's Solitaire, Golden-crowned and Ruby-crowned Kinglets, Black-capped Warbler, Cassin's Finch, Red Crossbill, and (in willow thickets) Lincoln's Sparrow.

Between the mountain forest and the timber line, reached in northern Colorado at an average elevation of 11,200 feet and in southern Colorado at 11,800 feet, is the subalpine forest, in which spruce and fir are stunted and, on the front ranges and others, gradually replaced by limber pine, alpine fir, and bristlecone pine, the characteristic trees of the timber line. Above timber line are alpine meadows, where mats of grasses and perennial flowering plants are interspersed with thickets of low-growing willows. Loose boulders, cliffs, and talus slopes, cold streams and lakes derived from melting snow, and, even in midsummer, low temperatures and winds of high velocity characterize this bleak region. In the subalpine forest few bird species are represented that cannot also be found in the mountain forest below. From mountain forest to timber line, changes in birdlife involve mostly a steady reduction in numbers of individuals. At the timber line, however, where widely spaced dwarf conifers meet alpine willows, Pine Grosbeaks and White-crowned Sparrows nest commonly. Above timber line, the Horned Lark is often observed as a summer resident of the larger meadows, and the Common Raven is occasionally seen patrolling a precipice where it probably nests, but the three breeding species of regular occurrence are the White-tailed Ptarmigan, the American Pipit, and the Brown-capped Rosy Finch.

A number of species nest widely over the forested slopes of the Colorado Rockies, their habitat preferences being less restricted than those already mentioned. Among those that nest here regularly are the following:

Three-toed Woodpecker (more common on higher forested slopes)	Clark's Nutcracker Mountain Chickadee Audubon's Warbler
Violet-green Swallow Tree Swallow	Macgillivray's Warbler (deciduous thickets)
Steller's Jay (most common on lower forested slopes)	Pine Siskin Gray-headed Junco

Other species in the Rockies are confined during the breeding season to the following situations: Prairie Falcon, to cliffs in the foothills; White-throated Swift, to cliffs at all elevations save those above timber line; Lewis' Woodpecker, to open areas near forests in the foothills; (Red-

naped) Common Sapsucker, to aspens at all elevations;
Traill's Flycatcher, to shrubs on stream borders at lower
elevations; Western Flycatcher, to well-shaded spots near
streams or buildings below 9,000 feet; Western Wood
Pewee, to forests containing either ponderosa pine or aspen;
Dipper, to fast-flowing mountain streams; Canyon Wren,
to cliffs below 9,000 feet; Rock Wren, to rough, rocky
slopes at all elevations; House Finch, to the vicinity of human habitations, both in the foothills and on the adjoining
edge of the plains.

West of the Continental Divide, the mountain slopes
are comparatively gradual, with the result that the plant
associations not only occupy belts of considerable width but
tend to overlap extensively; nevertheless the sequence
and elevations of the plant associations are essentially the
same as on the eastern slopes.

Most of the high plateau west of the mountains in
Colorado is part of the Colorado Plateau, the greater part
of which lies in eastern Utah, northern Arizona, and northwestern New Mexico. Lofty ridges and occasional broad
mesas between deep meandering canyons and valleys, each
with similar tributaries, characterize the terrain. Quite appropriately, the section of the Colorado Plateau lying in
Colorado and eastern Utah is referred to as the canyon
lands. The floors of the canyons and valleys (elevations
4,500 to 6,000 feet) are typically arid or desert-like; year-
round streams are few, and the vegetation consists to a
large extent of sagebrush and cacti. An exception may be
found in the large river valleys (e.g. the Colorado River
Valley) where the floors are several miles wide and have
moist flood plains with soils suitable for farming. On the
canyon and valley slopes, from 6,000 to 8,500 feet, grows
a pygmy forest of pinyon pine and juniper, together with
antelope brush, serviceberry, mountain mahogany, and
other shrubs. Where slopes extend from 8,500 to 10,500
feet, as on the big mesas (e.g. Grand Mesa, described in
this chapter under Grand Junction), there is a succession
of foothills and mountain forests with associated birdlife
comparable to that of the Rockies to the east. In the extreme north, the high plateau of western Colorado is part
of the Wyoming Basin—an area of sagebrush plains (ele-

vation 6,000 feet) flanked by rough country in which the
principal plant cover is a sparse growth of junipers. Trees
and shrubs such as cottonwood, willow, and buffaloberry
are confined to the banks of streams.

On the high plateau of western Colorado, the following
species are among those considered characteristic of the
sagebrush country (the sagebrush-studded floors of canyons and valleys and the sagebrush plains) and of the
pygmy forests on canyon and valley slopes:

SAGEBRUSH COUNTRY

Sage Grouse (not common)   Western Meadowlark
Scaled Quail (southern   Vesper Sparrow
   plateau)   Lark Sparrow
Burrowing Owl   Desert Sparrow
Horned Lark   Sage Sparrow
Sage Thrasher   Chipping Sparrow
Loggerhead Shrike   Brewer's Sparrow

PYGMY FOREST

Poor-will   Blue-gray Gnatcatcher
Gray Flycatcher   Gray Vireo
Scrub Jay   Black-throated Gray Warbler
Pinyon Jay   Spotted Towhee
Plain Titmouse   Brown Towhee (southern
Bush-tit   plateau)
Bewick's Wren

The streams, small lakes, and reservoirs on both sides of
the mountains and in the mountain parks attract modest
numbers of transient waterbirds, waterfowl, and shorebirds
during the spring and fall; at the same time, the mountain
valleys that trend north and south are paths for many transient landbirds. Periods during which peak flights may be
expected are as follows: waterfowl, 1 March—10 April,
15 October—10 December; shorebirds, 25 April—25 May,
5 August—10 October; landbirds, 10 April—10 May, 5
September—1 November.

There is no place in Colorado where one may expect to
observe tremendous aggregations or waves of migrating
birds, but the mountains nevertheless provide a fertile field
for the study of vertical migration. This is especially true
on the front ranges, where different altitudinal environ-

ments are readily accessible by highways (see under Loveland, Denver, and Boulder, for example). Certain species, such as the Brown-capped Rosy Finch, move down the mountains in the fall. In the spring a reverse movement occurs. Migrations from one level to another are said to take place with the same regularity, and to be initiated by the same factors, as horizontal migrations from one latitude to another.

In the late summer and early fall, Marsh Hawks, Prairie Falcons, Sparrow Hawks, Mourning Doves, Eastern Kingbirds, Pinyon Jays, Western Meadowlarks, and other species that breed in the open country, foothills, or mountain parks occur frequently at high altitudes, even on alpine meadows. This phenomenon is explained by some authorities as being the result of an up-mountain wandering prior to a down-mountain return and subsequent southward migration. A few authorities advance the explanation that it represents a lingering during an early, though normal, north-to-south migration via high elevations. Before either explanation can be accepted, further investigation is necessary.

Winter birdlife in the valleys and foothills of the Rockies contains an interesting mixture of species from the north and northwest, species that breed during the summer on the adjacent high slopes, and species resident in the immediate vicinity. Christmas bird counts made near Fort Collins, Greeley, Boulder, Denver, and Colorado Springs —cities in close proximity to the front ranges—usually comprise between 40 and 50 species, and occasionally more. Rarely do the totals fail to include huge numbers of Red-wings, several species of juncos (e.g. the White-winged, Slate-colored, Oregon, Gray-headed), Lewis' Woodpeckers, Townsend's Solitaires, and American Tree Sparrows. Other species quite commonly represented include the Cassin's Finch, Evening Grosbeak, and White-crowned Sparrow. If lakes and reservoirs have been visited during the counts, the Mallard, Pintail, and Green-winged Teal will be among the waterfowl recorded.

BOULDER. This city in the eastern foothills of the Rockies is the site of the UNIVERSITY OF COLORADO, which offers elementary and advanced courses in ornithology. The University of Colorado Museum, on the campus on the southern edge of Boulder, has a collection of ornithological materials that includes 2,515 skins, 387 mounts, and 1,575 egg sets. The greater part of the collection was made in Colorado, but there is a fair representation of skins from Central America and northern South America.

The birdlife of the Front Range immediately west of Boulder illustrates particularly well the altitudinal changes in species from foothill canyons and forests to timber line and alpine meadows. To see this altitudinal succession to advantage, a pleasant trip may be made (preferably in July) from Boulder, at an elevation of 5,530 feet, to the cool alpine meadows of MT. AUDUBON, whose summit reaches 13,223 feet. This involves a climb of approximately 35 miles by car plus a little over 2 miles on foot. An indication of the birds that may be expected in the early summer is given in the paragraphs below.

Drive west from Boulder to Nederland on State Route 119, which at once enters BOULDER CANYON. Its stream, Boulder Creek, is lined near the mouth with cottonwoods, willows, and various shrubs that provide habitats for such birds as Macgillivray's Warblers, Black-headed Grosbeaks, Lazuli Buntings, and Spotted Towhees. On the south-facing slopes of the Canyon are scattered stands of ponderosa pine, while on the north-facing slopes are close stands of small Douglas fir. At a point 9 miles up the Canyon, park the car and take a foot trail on the right to Boulder Falls, 75 yards distant, for a likely glimpse of Dippers, which may be feeding young in a near-by nest. At this same spot, look for Steller's Jays.

At Nederland, 18 miles west of Boulder and just beyond the large Barker Reservoir, turn north on State Route 160 to Ward, 12 miles north. Here, at an altitude of 8,000 to 9,000 feet, the highway passes through a forest of lodgepole pine and aspen. Birds to be expected along the way include the Olive-sided Flycatcher, Violet-green Swallow, Steller's Jay, Mountain Bluebird, Cassin's Finch, Pine Siskin, Green-tailed Towhee, and, possibly, the Band-tailed Pigeon and Red Crossbill.

At Ward take a rough road to the left (marked by a sign

'Brainard Lake') and proceed about 3 miles to RED ROCK LAKE (elevation 10,100 feet), a small shallow body of glacial water partly bordered by shrubs. Walking around the Lake, one may chance to see or hear a number of species, among them the Spotted Sandpiper, Canada Jay, Clark's Nutcracker, Mountain Chickadee, Ruby-crowned Kinglet, Audubon's Warbler, Black-capped Warbler, Pine Grosbeak, Gray-headed Junco, White-crowned Sparrow, and Lincoln's Sparrow.

At Brainard Lake (elevation 10,300 feet), 2 miles from Red Rock Lake, take the Buchanan Pass Trail up Mt. Audubon, reaching the timber line east of the peak, about 2 miles' walking distance from the Lake. The climb, which goes as high as 1,000 feet above Brainard Lake, requires about two hours; it is rigorous and should not be attempted unless one is in good physical condition. Possibly a Blue Grouse may be seen from the Trail; some of the other species seen will be identical with those at Red Rock Lake. At the rocky area of the timber line, begin looking for White-tailed Ptarmigan. Protectively colored, they are difficult to find; but, if discovered, they may be approached closely before they become unduly alarmed. For other birds of the alpine region, follow the rock cairns (the Trail itself becomes less evident above the timber line) for another half mile above and west of the big permanent snowbank on the east side of the mountain. American Pipits are numerous in the alpine meadows in the vicinity of the snowbank and may be observed giving their aerial displays of sound and wing action. A few Horned Larks may also occur here. In addition to seeing the White-tailed Ptarmigan and American Pipits, perhaps the greatest reward for the climb is the opportunity to watch Brown-capped Rosy Finches, sometimes as many as 200 at a time, searching on the snowbank for insects that have been blown onto its surface and been immobilized there by the cold temperature.

COLORADO SPRINGS. Just northwest of this plains city (elevation 5,900 feet), lying in central Colorado almost in the shadow of Pikes Peak, is a point of great scenic interest—THE GARDEN OF THE GODS. To reach it, drive west from the business district on Colorado Avenue (US Route 24) and turn right on Ridge Road, which leads to the entrance. In this city park, great masses of red rock, some curiously ridged and pinnacled, loom above an area that is partly grassland and partly covered by thickets of scrub oaks and stands of pinyon pine and juniper. Among the birds nesting in the park, the most conspicuous are the White-throated Swift, Violet-green Swallow, and Cliff Swallow, all of which occupy the precipices of the higher rock formations.

Of considerable ecological interest in central Colorado is the BLACK FOREST (elevation 7,000–7,500 feet), a rolling area of 150,000 acres, timbered with a nearly pure stand of ponderosa pine and situated between the Great Plains and the slopes of the Rockies. Only along the creeks is the coniferous growth interrupted—by willows and aspens, associated with adjoining patches of alder, chokecherry, mountain mahogany, wild rose, and other shrubby growth. Typical, uncleared sections of the Forest may be reached from Colorado Springs by driving north for 18 miles on US Route 87, then turning right on State Route 50 and proceeding for about 6 miles. Some of the species breeding regularly in the pine and creek environments are the Mourning Dove, Broad-tailed Hummingbird, Hairy Woodpecker, Western Wood Pewee, Black-capped Chickadee, White-breasted Nuthatch, Pygmy Nuthatch, House Wren, Western Bluebird, Solitary Vireo, Warbling Vireo, Yellow Warbler, Audubon's Warbler, Pine Siskin, Lesser Goldfinch, Green-tailed Towhee, and Gray-headed Junco.

CORTEZ. In extreme southwestern Colorado, 51,333 acres of the canyon lands comprise MESA VERDE NATIONAL PARK, established in 1906 by the Federal government for the purpose of conserving and protecting the remains of prehistoric Indian villages, scores of which are on mesa tops and in canyon caves. Their remarkable state of preservation and romantic settings, coupled with their archeological importance, are sufficient to excite the interest of the most apathetic visitors. In fact, the ancient ruins are so much the focal point of interest to visitors that the Park's fauna and flora are usually overlooked. While understandable, this is unfortunate, for the Park has a biota that may be considered typical of the high, semi-arid country of the southwestern United States. Plants and animals are sharply restricted in variety and numbers. For the bird finder it is fascinating to observe the kinds of birds that tolerate the rather severe conditions of this environment.

Geologically, the area embraced by the Park consists of one tableland or plateau—Mesa Verde—with a general elevation of 8,000 feet. On the north it has a 2,000-foot escarpment facing out over a rather dry plateau and, beyond that, the broad Montezuma Valley; on the south it is skirted by the canyon of the Mancos River, or Mancos Canyon, which has a depth of nearly 2,000 feet. Except for the north rim and its escarpment, the Mesa is strangely cut by many deep, steep-walled, ramifying canyons, all trending southward and converging on Mancos. On a topographic map this complex canyon system resembles the branching of a dense shrub, with Mancos Canyon as the main stem and the Mesa's canyons the branches emerging from one side. A relatively thick growth of pinyon pine and juniper occurs on the uncut surfaces of the southern half of the Mesa; a cover of scrub-oak thickets, interspersed with open areas in which grasses, sagebrush, and rabbitbrush are common, is distributed along the north rim. In certain spots, such as the heads of canyons, there are small stands of Douglas fir and ponderosa pine, while in the pinyon-pine and juniper forest and on the upper canyon walls are shrubs such as the mountain mahogany and serviceberry.

The Park entrance, or checking station, is on US Route 160 about midway between Cortez and Mancos. Useful maps and a schedule of guided trips to the ruins may be secured here. From the entrance it is 20 miles to headquarters, which is in the Park on the west rim of Spruce Tree Canyon; here there are various facilities including a store, post office, campgrounds, meal services, and overnight accommodations, and, in addition, an archeological museum. Spruce Tree Lodge, operated by the Mesa Verde Company, offers quarters ranging from tents to de luxe cabins. Rates and reservations may be obtained by writing the Company, whose address is Mesa Verde National Park, Colorado. Meal services and accommodations are available

only during the Park season, which extends from 15 May
to 15 October.

One of the best places for birds on Mesa Verde is on the
north rim, which the entrance road soon follows after ascending the north escarpment at its eastern end. From here,
while taking in, on the right, the magnificent view of
Montezuma Valley and, on the left, the sweeping panorama
of the Mesa's canyon-gashed surface sloping downward
from the road, the bird finder may well see a few Turkey
Vultures, White-throated Swifts, and Common Ravens, and
perhaps one or two Red-tailed Hawks and Golden Eagles.
It is also possible to hear Canyon Wrens singing below the
rim. A side road to the right, 10 miles from the entrance,
leads to Park Point (8,572 feet altitude), the highest elevation in the Park. Not far west of this side road, the entrance
road passes three canyon heads on the left and then bears
south to headquarters, passing additional canyon heads on
the way. In the vicinity of headquarters, as well as on the
north rim and in some of the canyon heads passed by the
entrance road, there are habitats suitable for the following
birds, which breed here regularly: Blue Grouse, Mourning
Dove, Poor-will, Common Nighthawk, Broad-tailed Hum-
ingbird, Lewis' Woodpecker, Say's Phoebe, Violet-green
Swallow, Steller's Jay, Scrub Jay, American Magpie, Pinyon Jay, Plain Titmouse, Bush-tit, Bewick's Wren, Mountain Bluebird, Blue-gray Gnatcatcher, Virginia's Warbler,
Black-throated Gray Warbler, Western Tanager, and
Brown Towhee.

DEL NORTE. An enjoyable trip for both birds and scenery
in southwest-central Colorado is up the RIO GRANDE
VALLEY from Del Norte, following the river through
Creede almost to the headwaters near the Continental Divide in the San Juan Mountains.

From Del Norte (elevation 7,778 feet) drive west on
US Route 160 to State Route 149, one mile west of South
Fork (elevation 8,250 feet). Between these points the road
traverses grassy flats dotted with sagebrush, while along
the Rio Grande are willows and cottonwoods. From South
Fork, take State Route 149, which climbs through a cut
between hills covered with ponderosa pine, pinyon pine,

and juniper to Masonic Park, 4 miles distant; farther on, 13 miles from South Fork, Route 149 winds through Wagon Wheel Gap, a narrow chasm with highly colored cliffs interrupted at intervals by small wooded parks. From Wagon Wheel Gap to 20 miles beyond Creede (elevation 8,854 feet) the Route traverses a broad upland with grassy prairies and meadows, marshes, and ponds. Eventually, the road ascends to Spring Creek Pass (elevation 10,901 feet) on the Continental Divide, 44 miles from Creede.

Most of the landbird species to be observed in the Valley also occur at similar elevations in the Gothic area (see under Gunnison), but the Valley has, because of the numerous marshy areas, such additional breeding birds as the Pied-billed Grebe, Snowy Egret, Gadwall, Green-winged Teal, Cinnamon Teal, Shoveler, Ring-necked Duck, Lesser Scaup Duck, Ruddy Duck, Coot, Long-billed Marsh Wren, Yellow-headed Blackbird, and Brewer's Blackbird.

At Creede, arrangements may be made for a side trip to WHEELER NATIONAL MONUMENT (300 acres),* at an elevation of over 11,000 feet near the crest of the La Garita Mountains, an eastward extension, or high divide, of the San Juan Mountains between the Rio Grande and the Saguache River. The trail leaves the north edge of town and winds around Mammoth Mountain toward the Monument, a distance of 8 miles. (The Monument may also be reached from Wagon Wheel Gap, first by 3 miles of automobile road through private lands and then by 6 miles of foot trail up Fellows Creek.)

Wheeler Monument embraces bizarre formations—pinnacles and abrupt chasms—resulting from volcanic activity and erosive forces. All are in sharp contrast to the surrounding country, which is richly forested with conifers, Engelmann spruce for the most part. Owing to the Monument's isolation, few bird finders have, apparently, visited the area. Such birds as the Canada Jay, Clark's Nutcracker, Brown Creeper, Hermit Thrush, Ruby-crowned Kinglet, Audubon's Warbler, Pine Grosbeak, and Pine Siskin undoubtedly breed in the forests, but whether any species use the for-

---

* In 1950 Wheeler National Monument, a property of the National Park Service, was transferred to the U.S. Forest Service. It is now part of Rio Grande National Forest.

140   *A Guide to Bird Finding*

mations for nesting or other purposes is yet to be determined.

Guides, saddle and pack horses, and camping supplies are available at Creede. To allow ample time for bird finding, a two-day trip is recommended, with an overnight stay at the Monument.

DENVER. On mile-high plains, with short-grass prairie on the east and the foothills and Front Range of the Rockies on the west, Denver has in its vicinity numerous prairie lakes and several 'Mountain Parks' where birds occur in great enough variety to delight any bird finder. The Mountain Parks are recreational areas owned and maintained by the city and are reached by highways leading south and west from downtown thoroughfares. All have such facilities as shelters, tables, outdoor fireplaces, and water supplies.

Of the many trips for birds to be taken in the Denver area, the one that terminates with a drive to the summit of MT. EVANS (elevation 14,259 feet) over the highest automobile road in the United States is the most exciting, particularly for those unfamiliar with the birdlife of the high country west of the Great Plains. Directions for this trip, including side trips to three of the Mountain Parks, follow.

Drive west from Denver on US Route 40; 10 miles from the city limits, turn left onto State Route 93 and drive to RED ROCKS PARK (639 acres). Here ponderosa pines and junipers stand in striking contrast to the brilliant hues of oddly upturned and eroded rock strata; among the breeding birds to be expected are the Prairie Falcon, White-throated Swift, Violet-green Swallow, Cliff Swallow, Scrub Jay, Canyon Wren, Rock Wren, Lazuli Bunting, Green-tailed Towhee, Spotted Towhee, and, interestingly, the domesticated Rock Dove, which here has reverted to its natural cliff-dwelling habits. In winter, Gray-crowned, Black, and Brown-capped Rosy Finches and four species of juncos may be found in the Park area.

Return to Route 40 and continue 5 miles to the GENESEE MOUNTAIN PARK GAME RESERVE (2,403 acres), the largest of the Denver Mountain Parks, situated higher in the foothills. On the left is a gravel road that leads into the area. Much of the Park is forested. Open stands of ponderosa pine and Douglas fir comprise the principal growth, but here and there are aspen groves and, in the ravines, a variety of deciduous trees. It is an excellent spot for such woodland nesting birds as the Pygmy Owl, Saw-whet Owl, Broad-tailed Hummingbird, (Red-naped) Common Sapsucker, Williamson's Sapsucker, Western Wood Pewee, Steller's Jay, Black-capped Chickadee, Mountain Chickadee, Pygmy Nuthatch, Red-breasted Nuthatch, White-breasted Nuthatch, Western Bluebird, Mountain Bluebird, Townsend's Solitaire, Solitary Vireo, Warbling Vireo, Western Tanager, and Gray-headed Junco.

Again continue on Route 40 to Idaho Springs and turn left onto State Route 103, which ascends gradually to Echo Lake at an elevation of 10,605 feet in ECHO LAKE PARK (about 50 acres). In the boggy habitat around the Lake, there is little difficulty in finding, during the height of the singing period in June, Black-capped Warblers, White-crowned Sparrows, and Lincoln's Sparrows. Behind the Lake, on the slopes that are densely wooded with Engelmann spruce and alpine fir, more arduous searching will uncover some of the high-mountain birds, including the Three-toed Woodpecker, Clark's Nutcracker, Canada Jay, Ruby-crowned Kinglet, Audubon's Warbler, Hermit Thrush, and the shy but colorful Pine Grosbeak.

Beyond Echo Lake the road winds upward toward the summit of Mt. Evans. At the timber line (11,500 feet), where stunted and twisted trees meet rock slides and alpine meadows, are the breeding habitats of Rock Wrens, Cassin's Finches, and White-crowned Sparrows. Along the road from the timber line to the summit (the last few yards must be covered on foot) are alpine meadows, with dense clusters of wildflowers in June and early July. Here the birds most likely to be seen are White-tailed Ptarmigan and American Pipits, but other birds should be looked for: Horned Larks nesting on the wider alpine meadows; one or more Common Ravens flying about near precipitous cliffs; and Brown-capped Rosy Finches searching for insects and seeds, frequently in the vicinity of snow patches.

In the early fall the meadows just above the timber line are likely places for seeing Blue Grouse, which wander up to them.

On the return trip to Denver, it may be desirable to turn right at Echo Lake on State Route 68 and proceed until the road joins Route 40 at Bergen Park (26 acres). Though this Park is small, its forest growth and birdlife compare favorably with those of Genesee Park.

For an entirely different bird-finding trip in the Denver area, drive northeast from the city on US Route 6 to BARR LAKE DRAINAGE AREA, 12 miles from the city limits. This is characterized by many prairie lakes and drainage pools, shallow and often bordered by marshes or muddy flats. Many birds breed in the Area, and the following can usually be observed with fair regularity: Eared Grebe, Pied-billed Grebe, Double-crested Cormorant, Snowy Egret, Black-crowned Night Heron, American Bittern, Mallard, Pintail, Blue-winged Teal, Cinnamon Teal, Shoveler, Redhead, Ruddy Duck, Virginia Rail, Sora, Coot, Wilson's Snipe, Willet, Avocet, Wilson's Phalarope, Forster's Tern, Black Tern, Yellow-throat, Red-wing, Savannah Sparrow, and Song Sparrow. A small rookery of Double-crested Cormorants and Black-crowned Night Herons is situated in dead trees at the south end of Barr Lake, a reservoir in the Area east of Route 6. Gulls, waterfowl, and many kinds of shorebirds are abundant in the Area during migrations; Canada Geese, Mallards, a few Pintails, American Golden-eyes, and American Mergansers winter regularly.

In Denver, the DENVER MUSEUM OF NATURAL HISTORY, in City Park on the west side of Colorado Boulevard between East 17th and East 26th Avenues, has an ornithological collection consisting of 25,000 skins (representing mainly the Rocky Mountain region), 5,000 egg sets, and 1,000 mounts. The mounts, mostly from Colorado, are instructively grouped according to altitudinal associations. An impressive feature of the public exhibits is a superlative series of habitat groups depicting western bird and mammal life of various environments from plains to high country. Also in City Park, between York Street and Colorado Boulevard and East 17th and East 26th Avenues, are the DENVER ZOOLOGICAL GARDENS, with over 1,500 birds on display. Especially outstanding is the collection of waterfowl, many of which are wing-free and commonly fly over the duck lake and its island.

DURANGO. This shipping center for a rich farming section in southwestern Colorado is a good starting point for a profitable bird-finding jaunt in the ANIMAS RIVER VALLEY. Drive north from Durango on US Route 550, a paved road, which passes up the Valley on the west side. About 14 miles from Durango, turn right on a gravel road (no route number) and proceed to Baker Bridge, the site of a former settlement on the east bank of the Animas River. Elevations of the Valley floor range from about 6,500 feet at Durango to 7,000 feet at Baker Bridge. Ponds, a few marshy areas, and grassy meadows, with cottonwoods and willow clumps along the River, characterize the uncultivated parts of the Valley floor, while on the near-by hillsides are extensive pygmy forests of scrub oak and pinyon pine and also forests of ponderosa pine and Douglas fir. Some of the common breeding birds to be expected in suitable habitats are the Sparrow Hawk, Band-tailed Pigeon, Broad-tailed Hummingbird, Lewis' Woodpecker, Cassin's Kingbird, Western Wood Pewee, Steller's Jay, Scrub Jay, Pinyon Jay, Black-capped Chickadee, Bush-tit, White-breasted Nuthatch, Mountain Bluebird, Loggerhead Shrike, Virginia's Warbler, House Finch, Lesser Goldfinch, and Lark Sparrow.

From the turnoff to Baker Bridge, Route 550 continues northward to Montrose, providing a scenic drive through the high, rugged San Juan Mountains, where the Animas River rises. Hundreds of peaks, some of them greatly sharpened by glacial erosion, exceed 13,000 feet and a few reach above 14,000 feet. The area has been little explored ornithologically.

FORT COLLINS. In the Agricultural Building on the south side of the campus of COLORADO AGRICULTURAL AND MECHANICAL COLLEGE at Howes Street is an ornithological collection consisting of 1,400 skins and 635 mounts. Eighty-six of the mounts are in habitat displays. A course in ornithology is offered during the spring quarter and summer session; graduate work leading to a master's degree in ornithology is available.

Two and a half miles north of Fort Collins on the west side of US Route 87 is TERRY LAKE, a reservoir, near the northern shore of which lies an island where Great Blue Herons, Black-crowned Night Herons, Double-crested Cormorants, and (sometimes) Snowy Egrets nest. To reach this colony, continue north on Route 87 for 2 miles; turn left on the first county road beyond the Lake; drive west half a mile and park by a marsh just north of the island; then walk south along the marsh through a cotton-wood grove to the point of a peninsula opposite the island. Here one may easily observe the nests 100 yards away. Early in the season, from mid-March to mid-May, watch for Eared Grebes, Western Grebes, Pied-billed Grebes, and numerous ducks on the Lake; later in the season watch for one or two Snowy Egrets.

An excellent place near by for observing transient water-fowl in the spring is a small pond just north of Terry Lake. To reach it, return toward Route 87 for a quarter of a mile, then walk north through a pasture. Mallards, Gad-walls, Baldpates, Pintails, Green-winged Teal, Blue-winged Teal, Cinnamon Teal (occasionally), Shovelers, Redheads, and Ruddy Ducks may be seen and, in addition, grebes and Coots. Transient shorebirds (e.g. Lesser Yellow-legs) often stop to feed here, while Avocets nest regularly on the shores.

FORT MORGAN. Since the surrounding country here in northeastern Colorado is mainly farmland or dry, barren plains, birdlife is concentrated along the South Platte River, particularly around a series of spring-fed ponds, known as the MUIR SPRINGS, extending for 2 miles along the River northwest of town. From US Route 6 in Fort Morgan, drive north on West Street for 0.5 mile, west for 0.5 mile, then northwest and north for 1.2 miles to a point where the ponds first come into view. Park the car and follow the paths on the many dykes that rim the ponds. In the cattails and quillreeds bordering the ponds such birds as the American Bittern, Cinnamon Teal, Marsh Hawk,

Virginia Rail, Sora, Wilson's Snipe, Yellow-headed Black-bird, and Red-wing may be found nesting. Some of the birds that may also be found nesting in the adjacent cot-tonwoods, willows, and shrubs are the Sparrow Hawk, Screech Owl, Red-shafted Flicker, American Magpie, Black-capped Chickadee, Yellow Warbler, Yellow-throat, Yellow-breasted Chat, Bullock's Oriole, Black-headed Grosbeak, Lazuli Bunting, and Song Sparrow.

GRAND JUNCTION. In west-central Colorado, where an angle is formed by the confluence of the Colorado and Gunnison Rivers, rises 'the grandfather of all mesas,' GRAND MESA. Actually a fragment of a great lava cap, it is sometimes referred to as the largest flat-topped moun-tain in the United States. A drive over the level top of this great plateau at an elevation of 10,500 feet from the start-ing point at Grand Junction at 4,583 feet cannot fail to impress even the most sophisticated traveler. Besides un-rivaled scenery, the trip has, for the bird finder, abundant rewards.

Early summer is the time for observing the greatest variety of birds. Of the several routes over the Grand Mesa, the following is suggested because the road conditions are the best. Other routes, however, will do just as well for bird finding since the birdlife is much the same along all of them.

From Grand Junction, drive southeast on US Route 50. At Whitewater, turn left (east) on an unnumbered road which joins Lands End Road, loops up to the rim of the Mesa, and then crosses the Mesa to join State Route 65. Turn right onto Route 65 and proceed to State Route 92; turn right onto Route 92 and again right, onto Route 50 at Delta, to return to Grand Junction. The entire trip, about 130 miles, can be made in a day. Should one wish to make a more leisurely trip, taking two days, there are over-night accommodations at Skyway, which may be reached from Lands End Road by turning left onto Route 65.

Sharply contrasting environments are passed through in the journey to the top of the Mesa. First is the valley floor of the Gunnison River, where desert-like wastes alternate with irrigated and highly cultivated farmlands and ranches.

Next is the steep slope of the Mesa with its pygmy forest of scrub oak, pinyon pine, and juniper. Finally, on top of the Mesa, are meadows bright with wildflowers, small blue lakes, and extensive stands of Engelmann spruce and other conifers. (Grand Mesa does not rise above the timber line and thus has no true alpine meadows.) Almost anywhere along the way one is likely to see a Sparrow Hawk, Violet-green Swallow, or Mountain Bluebird—species the bird finder will recognize as old friends if he has been in Colorado very long; but most of the different kinds of birds dwell in particular places and hence must be searched for with their habitat preferences in mind.

Where Lands End Road leaves Route 50 in the Gunnison Valley, Ring-necked Pheasants and Gambel's Quail may be observed, especially in the early morning and late afternoon, on the farmlands and brushy deserts. Horned Larks are common and other birds that occur regularly include Red-tailed Hawks, Swainson's Hawks, Mourning Doves, Western Kingbirds, Say's Phoebes, Sage Thrashers, Loggerhead Shrikes, Western Meadowlarks, and Brewer's Sparrows. Barn and Cliff Swallows frequently fly low over the cultivated fields to catch insects. As the road climbs to meet the main slope of the Mesa and farms become smaller and fewer, one should begin looking for Common Ravens. The oak thickets along Kannah Creek, about 10 miles from Whitewater, have many nesting American Magpies and are worth investigating for Western Tanagers. Above the Creek, in growths of aspen, scrub oak, pinyon pine, and juniper, are Ash-throated Flycatchers, Scrub Jays, Pinyon Jays, Plain Titmice, Bush-tits, and Spotted Towhees.

At the rim of the Mesa, not far from the road, is a rugged promontory known as Lands End; on it is a glass-walled shelter house. Overlooking a tremendous stretch of western Colorado, Lands End makes a fine vantage point from which to watch the soaring of Turkey Vultures and Golden Eagles and the circling-sailing-flickering flights of White-throated Swifts. Back from the edge of the dropoff are spruces, whose seed-bearing cones often attract Clark's Nutcrackers. From Lands End across the top of the Mesa meadows alternate with spruce groves whose edges should,

upon inspection, reveal Red-shafted Flickers, Williamson's
Sapsuckers, Three-toed Woodpeckers, Steller's Jays, Mountain Chickadees, Pygmy Nuthatches, Ruby-crowned Kinglets, Cassin's Finches, Pine Grosbeaks, Pine Siskins, White-
crowned Sparrows, and other birds liking the coniferous
forests of Colorado's high country.

WHITE-THROATED SWIFTS

While in Grand Junction no visitor will want to miss
COLORADO NATIONAL MONUMENT (18,311 acres),
which embraces a section of the great escarpment on the
south side of the Colorado River Valley. Here, produced by
the prolonged effects of erosion, are immense canyons with
precipitous walls of red sandstone, gigantic, curiously
carved monoliths towering as high as 500 feet, and other
formations of herculean proportions.

The Monument is reached from Grand Junction by
driving southwest on the Monument highway across the
Colorado River to the eastern boundary, about 5 miles distant. Once in the Monument, the visitor should proceed to
Cold Shivers Point and take the famous Rimrock Drive,
the construction of which was a remarkable engineering
feat—the road was laid along meandering edges of great

chasms. The road passes Monument headquarters, where there is a public picnic area and campground, and eventually reaches the northern boundary. From here one may return to Grand Junction by taking a Monument road across the Colorado River to Fruita, on US Route 50, and there turning right.

The woody vegetation of Colorado Monument is sparse, consisting principally of scattered pinyon pine, juniper, and low shrubs. Breeding birdlife is thinly diffused. Turkey Vultures, Red-tailed Hawks, Sparrow Hawks, Mourning Doves, Say's Phoebes, Horned Larks, and Loggerhead Shrikes are likely to be seen from the Rimrock Road. Others to be observed by listening or searching with field glasses from the many overlooks along the way are Scrub Jays, Pinyon Jays, Plain Titmice, Bewick's Wrens, Canyon Wrens, Rock Wrens, Sage Thrashers, Spotted Towhees, Lark Sparrows, and Brewer's Sparrows. Bird finding is more productive in the late spring and late summer, when birdlife is considerably augmented by rosy finches, juncos, and other fringillids. Where the roads cross the Colorado River there are usually ducks, such as Mallards and Baldpates and, in the late summer, Great Blue Herons, Snowy Egrets, Black-crowned Night Herons, and White-faced Ibises.

GREELEY. Though the plains in eastern Colorado seem dull when compared with the mountainous terrain in the rest of the state, no bird enthusiast will find them so in the spring and early summer (April through June), when they come to life with the songs and nesting activities of countless birds. One place in northeastern Colorado, if visited in the spring according to the following directions, will show the birdlife of the plains at its best.

Drive north from Greeley on US Route 85 to a point 7 miles north of Nunn where a roadside sign indicates the CENTRAL PLAINS EXPERIMENTAL RANGE. This is the southwest corner of an area containing 21 sections in which grazing is scientifically controlled by the federal government for experimental purposes. Here can be found most types of habitat existing in this part of the country and the birds characteristic of them.

At the sign, turn east off the highway and drive slowly,

watching for such conspicuous birds as Swainson's Hawks, Golden Eagles, Horned Larks, and Western Meadowlarks. At least one or two pronghorn antelopes should be seen. A Burrowing Owl on the banks beside the road is always a possibility.

One and a half miles east of the highway, a fencerow begins on the north side of the road and marks the start of good territory for Sparrow Hawks, Common Nighthawks, Mourning Doves, Western Kingbirds, and especially Lark Buntings. One and a half miles east of the point where the fencerow begins, a double fencerow goes north. Pass through the gates here into the range to the northwest, in which grow short grasses and cacti. Follow a dimly outlined trail across it. McCown's Longspurs, as well as Horned Larks, should flush up ahead of the car. With time and careful searching on this range one may be able to turn up a pair of Mountain Plovers and, with luck, a pair of Long-billed Curlews. Proceed to the northwest corner of this section. To the north are a small grove of cottonwoods and an old stone building. Go through the gate, and drive north as far as possible, then walk the rest of the way to the building. Once at the building, turn east to a water hole. Eastern Kingbirds, American Magpies, and occasionally a pair of Swainson's Hawks nest in the cottonwood grove; Blue-winged Teal, Red-wings, and sometimes Killdeer and Avocets nest in the vicinity of the water hole.

Return to the road via the double fencerow; continue east for one mile, and then turn left. Two miles north are the headquarters buildings, under the eaves of which Cliff Swallows nest. A mile farther north, turn right through a gate and follow the fence to a windmill. Park here and walk north through a section of range grown to short grasses and saltbush. There is very little grazing here, and it is good habitat for Lark Buntings and Brewer's Sparrows, Horned Larks and Western Meadowlarks. It is also rattlesnake country.

The COLORADO STATE COLLEGE OF EDUCATION, at 16th Street between 8th and 10th Avenues, offers a course in bird study. The Museum of Natural History in Crawford Hall has the following ornithological collection, mostly from Colorado: 1,200 skins, 475 mounts, and 230 egg sets. A noteworthy feature is an extensive collection of hummingbird skins.

GUNNISON. The Gothic area in west-central Colorado, west of the Continental Divide, is situated in the Elk Range, which, though small in extent, is deemed one of the most commanding in the Rocky Mountain system. Here are wide valleys, steep slopes, and lofty, isolated peaks with elevations ranging from 8,900 to 14,259 feet (Castle Peak). Lakes, rivers, marshes, valley meadows, mountain forests, alpine meadows, and regions of perpetual snow are some of the habitats represented within the area. Such is the setting of the ROCKY MOUNTAIN BIOLOGICAL LABORATORY.

The Laboratory, owned and administered by an independent corporation comprised of scientists from colleges and universities in different parts of the country, offers summer courses in biology to both graduate and undergraduate students and provides opportunities for research. Course work, of six-weeks' duration, extends from the first of July to mid-August. The mailing address is Crested Butte, Colorado. To reach the Laboratory by car, drive north from Gunnison for 29 miles on State Route 135 to Crested Butte, then right on State Route 327 for 9 miles to Gothic, once a prosperous gold and silver mining town but now completely taken over by the Laboratory.

Gothic (or the Laboratory) lies at the northern end of a long meadowy valley (elevation 8,900–9,500 feet) encircled by seven peaks, which reach heights varying from 12,000 to 13,500 feet. Through the valley, which is park-like in appearance, meanders the East River, bordered in places by willow thickets and aspen groves. The forest growth on the adjacent mountains from valley floor to timber line at 11,500 feet consists principally of Engelmann spruce mixed with Douglas fir and aspen.

Not far from the Laboratory is the GOTHIC NATURAL AREA (905 acres), which has been permanently set aside by the U.S. Forest Service for research purposes. About 500 acres of the Area is a virgin-spruce and fir forest; the rest of the tract consists of alpine meadows, marshes, and grassy parks. Both the Laboratory and the Natural Area are within the boundaries of Gunnison National Forest.

' One Laboratory investigator, who is familiar with birds of the forests and open country in north-central United States and had not previously looked for birds in the Rocky Mountains, considered the birds in the Gothic area 'difficult to dig out.' This is because he had to cover a considerable amount of territory in order to find both variety of species and large numbers of individuals. Any bird finder accustomed to dense populations will have the same experience in the Rocky Mountains.

Among the birds that are common in the valley areas —willow thickets, aspen groves, grasslands, and so on— and are therefore often seen near the Laboratory during the summer are the following: Swainson's Hawk, Sparrow Hawk, Mourning Dove, Broad-tailed Hummingbird, Red-shafted Flicker, (Red-naped) Common Sapsucker, Western Flycatcher, Violet-green Swallow, Cliff Swallow, House Wren, Warbling Vireo, Western Meadowlark, Brewer's Blackbird, Vesper Sparrow, and Lincoln's Sparrow. Dippers nest along the East River and its tributaries; Red-tailed Hawks and Golden Eagles sometimes soar over the valley. Other species that range more widely, from valley to timber line, include the Blue Grouse, Mountain Chickadee, Hermit Thrush, Mountain Bluebird, Ruby-crowned Kinglet, Audubon's Warbler, Pine Siskin, and White-crowned Sparrow. Canada Jays, Clark's Nutcrackers, Pine Grosbeaks, and Gray-headed Juncos, although sometimes present in the valley during the summer, are more common in the spruce-fir forests on the higher slopes. Spotted Sandpipers may be seen at Emerald Lake, at an altitude of 10,-000 feet, about 5 miles northwest of the Laboratory, while in the meadows along the East River, between the Laboratory and Emerald Lake, Red-wings nest in considerable numbers.

LOVELAND. In the Front Range of the Rockies in north-central Colorado, there is hardly an easier or more exciting way of seeing birds than to drive from Loveland to the village of Estes Park, thence across ROCKY MOUNTAIN NATIONAL PARK to its western entrance at Grand Lake

Village, a distance of 82 miles. By making stops at different elevations and vegetational associations, it is possible to identify an astonishing variety of birds. Although the Park is open the entire year, its main highway, the Trail Ridge Road, is closed (above 10,000 feet) from October or November to the first of June because of snow. Bird finding is profitable any time but best in mid-June, when most species are in full song.

Rocky Mountain Park embraces 405 square miles of mountain terrain, which has no elevation lower than 7,800 feet; 65 peaks exceed 10,000 feet; the highest, Longs Peak, reaches 14,255 feet and is a perennial favorite among mountain climbers the world over. The Continental Divide runs southward across the Park from the northwest corner, separating the area almost centrally into eastern and western portions. Forests are extensive and are characterized at lower elevations by open stands of ponderosa pine, with blue spruce in the sheltered gorges on the eastern side of the Park and willow and aspen along the streams; at elevations of 8,000 to 9,500 feet, by dense stands of lodgepole pine and aspen; and at elevations above 9,500 feet, by Engelmann spruce and alpine fir joined toward the timber line (11,000 feet) by limber pine, which becomes stunted and twisted and with the dwarfed spruce and fir forms the so-called 'wind timber.' While the splendid forests are distinctive features, the Park's great charm may be attributed less to them than to a great variety of scenic attractions—the spectacular peaks and the wide intervening valleys, the gulches and gorges flanked by precipitous cliffs and talus slopes, the alpine meadows carpeted with a profusion of wildflowers, the small glaciers wedged in the heads of gorges, the mirrored pools and lakes, and the cascading streams—and the abundance of wildlife, which includes, in addition to birds, the American elk, mule deer, bighorn sheep, beaver, and many smaller mammals.

Park headquarters is in the village of Estes Park, 4 miles east of the Park, where there are hotel and cabin accommodations. Other hotel and cabin accommodations are available in the Park, as well as in Grand Lake Village just west of the Park. Naturalist services include guided field trips and illustrated talks during the summer season (15

June—1 September). The Moraine Park Museum, inside the National Park near the Thompson River entrance, has numerous natural-history exhibits including habitat displays of mountain birds and mammals. The Fall River Pass Museum, in the northern part of the National Park, features animal and plant life characteristic of the high country.

Directions for a June trip from Loveland (elevation 4,983 feet) to the highest point (12,183 feet) on the Trail Ridge Road in Rocky Mountain National Park are given below. Stops for bird finding are selected for the chief purposes of showing variety of species and vertical succession.

Drive west from Loveland on US Route 34 to ESTES PARK (elevation about 7,500 feet). The last couple of miles before reaching Estes Park will be through a typical mid-mountain park of open grassy meadows with scattered stands of ponderosa pine. An occasional Vesper Sparrow may be found in the meadows, and Mountain Bluebirds are frequent near the pines. Many more breeding birds—e.g. the Broad-tailed Hummingbird, Violet-green Swallow, Tree Swallow, House Wren, Yellow Warbler, House Finch, Pine Siskin, and Chipping Sparrow—may be found in the village.

From the main street in Estes Park, turn right and drive west 5 miles to the Fall River entrance to Rocky Mountain National Park. Obtain here detailed maps of the Park, together with a schedule of naturalist services.

One mile from the entrance is Horseshoe Park, a large grassy meadow with several ponds at the western end. In their vicinity, at an elevation of 8,000 feet, a few Mallards and Red-wings often nest.

A little farther on, at a sign designating Fall River Lodge, turn right and drive past this establishment to Roaring River. The aspen growth south of the road is worth investigating for Downy Woodpeckers, (Red-naped) Common Sapsuckers, Western Wood Pewees, House Wrens, Warbling Vireos, Audubon's Warblers, Macgillivray's Warblers, and, perhaps, a Blue Grouse, Black-headed Grosbeak, or Evening Grosbeak. In the large aspens near the River, look for holes in which Violet-green Swallows nest. South of the aspens, along Fall River, is an area of shrubby willows where *Empidonax* flycatchers, Yellow Warblers, Black-capped Warblers, and Lincoln's Sparrows occur.

Return to the highway, turn right to Deer Ridge Chalet, then right again on the Trail Ridge Road. After passing through Hidden Valley, in which there is a series of beaver dams, the highway swings sharply to the left and begins a steep grade. About a mile farther on, it switches back to the right. Before taking this turn—called Many Parks Curve—stop the car in the parking place and look for birds in the adjacent tree growth, which consists mainly of lodgepole pine mixed with Engelmann spruce. Canada Jays, Clark's Nutcrackers, and Mountain Chickadees, as well as Steller's Jays and Gray-headed Juncos, are some of the birds that may be expected here. From Many Parks Curve the highway continues to climb. After a mile or two it passes through a virgin forest of towering spruces and firs. In this tree association, the bird population is not high, but if the area is worked intensively, preferably above the road, it should yield Canada Jays, Mountain Chickadees, Hermit Thrushes, Pine Grosbeaks, Ruby-crowned Kinglets, Gray-headed Juncos, and, with luck, a Three-toed Woodpecker. Then stop at Rainbow Curve, the next big parking space. Here least chipmunks and Say's ground squirrels are tame and easily fed, and it is possible to see a pika or two. The parking space is a good point from which to hear the songs of the Townsend's Solitaire and to see Common Ravens in flight.

Not far above Rainbow Curve the highway climbs through the timber line (11,500 feet elevation) with its stunted limber pine or wind timber. This is the favorite habitat of White-crowned Sparrows. Just above the timber line, park opposite the stone cabins, under the eaves of which Mountain Bluebirds sometimes nest. Among the rocks along the ridge to the south, Rock Wrens are summer residents. Above the alpine meadows on the other side of this ridge, Horned Larks and American Pipits are likely to be giving their flight songs. The same meadows may have White-tailed Ptarmigan but these are hard to find. If they are not here, try some of the other alpine meadows and rock piles near the highway as it continues its ascent from the stone cabins.

Next, stop at Iceberg Lake, which is above 12,000 feet; walk to the edge of the cirque on the left and peer over its edge to view the steep walls; Brown-capped Rosy Finches are likely to be perched on the ledge shelves or moving to and from their nests in various crevices. A few rods up, above Iceberg Lake, the Trail Ridge Road reaches its highest point (12,183 feet) and then descends to the Fall River Pass Museum at 11,797 feet. The meadows in the vicinity of the Museum are a fine place for White-tailed Ptarmigan, as well as for Horned Larks and American Pipits.

From the Fall River Pass Museum, the bird finder may return to Loveland or continue across the Continental Divide to the western entrance of the Park at Grand Lake.

MONTROSE. The weirdly spectacular Black Canyon of the Gunnison River in western Colorado is famous for its 50 miles of sheer walls consisting of schists, predominately bluish-black, with white, gray, pink, and red granitic intrusions. The BLACK CANYON OF THE GUNNISON NATIONAL MONUMENT embraces 14,464 acres, including the most formidable 10-mile section of the Canyon. In places here the rims of the chasm are as close as 1,300 feet, yet the depth ranges from 1,730 to 2,425 feet.

Because the Canyon itself is so exceedingly rugged, it supports little vegetation; nevertheless, there are draws along the rims containing a dense growth of pinyon pines, junipers, and scrub oaks. Obviously, these forested draws are the best spots for birds. During the summer, some of the species to be observed regularly either in the draws or from vantage points along the rims are the Red-tailed Hawk, Sparrow Hawk, Golden Eagle, Blue Grouse, White-throated Swift, Broad-tailed Hummingbird, Violet-green Swallow, Steller's Jay, Scrub Jay, American Magpie, Mountain Chickadee, Mountain Bluebird, and Virginia's Warbler.

Both the north and south rims of the Canyon are accessible by car during the late spring and summer. To reach the south rim, drive 8 miles east on US Route 50, then 9 miles northward over State Route 347, a graded road. To reach the north rim, it is necessary to drive 22 miles northwest

on Route 50 to Delta, then east and south for 39 miles on
State Route 92 to a point south of Crawford, where a
marked, graded road, on the right, leads to the rim, 14 miles
distant.

SAGUACHE. In the San Luis Valley, 9 miles south of
Saguache (pronounced *sah'-watch*) along US Route 285
(east side), are the RUSSELL LAKES, shallow bodies of
water fringed by marshes in which bulrushes are the predominant growth. Here, in a mountain park at an elevation of 7,580 feet, may be found nesting, beginning in May,
a remarkable variety of waterbirds, ducks, marshbirds, and
shorebirds, including the Eared, Western, and Pied-billed
Grebes, Snowy Egret, Black-crowned Night Heron, American Bittern, White-faced Ibis, Mallard, Gadwall, Pintail,
Blue-winged and Cinnamon Teal, Redhead, Ruddy Duck,
Virginia Rail, Sora, Coot, Avocet, Wilson's Phalarope,
Long-billed Marsh Wren, Yellow-throat, Yellow-headed
Blackbird, and Red-wing.

WALSENBURG. From this city (elevation 6,200 feet)
among the foothills in southeast-central Colorado, the road
to Cucharas Pass (elevation 9,994 feet) in the Sangre de
Cristo Range follows the CUCHARAS RIVER VALLEY.
In the late spring and summer, bird finding is very good in
many spots near the highway.

From Walsenburg, take US Route 160 southwest for 10
miles, then turn left on State Route 111 and proceed to La
Veta. Between Walsenburg and La Veta the Valley is broad
and has fertile soils used extensively for crop production.
Peaks of the Sangre de Cristo Range rise in the west, but
the eye-catching scenic features are the massive twin mountains, East Spanish Peak (12,683 feet) and West Spanish
Peak (13,623 feet), which stand apart from the Range on
the south. Red-shafted Flickers, Western Kingbirds, American Magpies, Mountain Bluebirds, Western Meadowlarks,
Bullock's Orioles, and House Finches are common in this
part of the Valley, as are Lewis' Woodpeckers, which should
be watched for on telephone poles.

From La Veta, continue on Route 111, which soon ascends through the gradually narrowing Cucharas River

Valley to Cucharas Pass. Here the Valley floor has meadow-land dotted with ponds and with marshes fringed by cat-tails and willow clumps, while the slopes of the Valley have pinyon pine and scrub oak giving way at higher elevations to pine, fir, and aspen. Among the birds to be expected, if stops are made during the climb through the Valley, are Band-tailed Pigeons, Violet-green Swallows, Steller's Jays, Common Ravens, Macgillivray's Warblers, Western Tana-gers, and Green-tailed Towhees.

Contributing authorities: Gordon Alexander, Alfred M. Bailey, Paul H. Baldwin, J. Frank Cassel, Mrs. Carl N. (Allegra E.) Collister, Edward F. Dana, Mrs. Virginia S. Eifert, William Fer-guson, John E. Galley, Mrs. John E. (Margret) Galley, Harry W. Hann, Mrs. John N. Hough, Clyde P. Matteson, Robert J. Niedrach, Fred Mallery Packard, Ronald A. Ryder, James M. Stauffer, Harvey E. Stork, Don Watson.

Idaho

CLARK'S NUTCRACKER

In no other state is the birdlife so little known as in Idaho. Fewer than a dozen papers listing the kinds of birds in specific localities are available, and the first check-list of Idaho birds, admittedly of a preliminary nature, has only recently been published. There still exist today, in the very heart of the state, over a million acres of ruggedly beautiful, mountainous country—appropriately designated a Primitive Area—where the presence of certain bird species can only be assumed. Idaho is still an ornithological frontier.

Idahoans will be the first to admit that their state lacks geographical unity. No great mountain chain, valley, or arid plain belongs exclusively to Idaho; those that occur here are shared with one or more of the six bordering states. The same may be said of Idaho's biota. Despite this peculiarity, 'the parts of other states' that comprise Idaho have some of the choicest scenery and, for the visiting bird finder, some of the most attractive settings for birds that he will come upon anywhere in the United States.

In southern Idaho, the widest part of the state, the principal physiographic feature is the Snake River Plain, which extends about 375 miles in length, from the eastern to the western boundary, looping southward during its course, and averaging between 75 and 100 miles in breadth. Mountain ranges clearly mark most of the Plain's boundaries. Some form abrupt rims; others encroach upon the Plain in parallel formation, leaving long peninsulas of the Plain between them. The Snake River, as it cuts through the Plain from Wyoming to the Oregon line, drops from 6,000 to 3,000 feet; on the north and south the Plain itself rises gradually from the River, like the sides of a shallow trough, to altitudes approaching 6,000 or 7,000 feet at the base of the mountain ranges.

The Snake River Plain was once desert-like, its rolling surface covered with sagebrush, greasewood, and clumps of grasses, in some places as far as the eye could see. The only major interruptions were localities—for example, the Craters of the Moon National Monument (see under Arco) —where lava beds, lava flows, and other rock features of volcanic origin discouraged vegetation, and along watercourses and in coulees where there were trees (cottonwoods, aspens, willows) and various shrubs. Today much of the Plain that is without rock has become a productive agricultural area. Under extensive irrigation, the lands adjacent to the Snake River yield Idaho's famous potatoes, as well as sugar beets, peas, alfalfa, and fruits. Upon the higher lands near the mountains, away from the River and beyond reach of irrigation, acres upon acres of wheat come from soils that were once thought useless for cultivation.

In southwestern Idaho, southwest of the Snake River Plain, is the Owyhee country (pronounced *oh-wy'-he*), a vast highland roughly embraced by Owyhee County. Arid and bleak in aspect, broken by canyons and ridges, and by occasional mountain ranges with peaks rising to 7,000 feet, it is an inhospitable land that has only sparse human population and few roads. Sagebrush and associated plants find sufficient soil in scattered spots; alder, cottonwood, aspen, wild currant, and wild rose grow along the small number of watercourses; and meadows and marshes exist in the few watered valley bottoms. Elsewhere the country is desert. In southeastern Idaho—the rest of the state south of the Snake River Plain—the country is decidedly different. Here are many small mountain ranges, all running north and south, with peaks in some cases attaining heights of 10,000 feet. Their slopes frequently have stands of pinyon pine, juniper, and mountain mahogany. (For an indication of some of the birds that may be expected in these mountain areas, see under Burley.)

Alternating with the mountain ranges are valleys of varying width which have elevations between 4,000 and 5,000 feet. In nearly all of the valleys there are streams with borders of deciduous trees and shrubs and broad stretches of sageland. Several have fine lakes and marshes. Through irrigation, many of the sagelands have been converted into areas for crop production.

Throughout the Snake River Plain and the mountain valleys to the south, the following breeding birds may be expected in the open country (sagelands, agricultural lands, wet meadows, brushy places, and the vicinity of dwellings) and in the wooded stream bottoms. Species marked with an asterisk also breed in the mountains elsewhere in the state.

OPEN COUNTRY

Turkey Vulture
Swainson's Hawk
Marsh Hawk
Sage Grouse
Killdeer
*Mourning Dove
Burrowing Owl
Short-eared Owl
Eastern Kingbird
Western Kingbird
Say's Phoebe
Horned Lark
Barn Swallow

*American Magpie
Bush-tit
*House Wren
Sage Thrasher
Loggerhead Shrike
Yellow Warbler
Yellow-throat
Yellow-breasted Chat
Western Meadowlark
Lazuli Bunting
House Finch
Vesper Sparrow
Sage Sparrow

Chipping Sparrow
Brewer's Sparrow

Song Sparrow

WOODED STREAM BOTTOMS

Screech Owl
Red-shafted Flicker
°Hairy Woodpecker
Downy Woodpecker
Wright's Flycatcher

Western Wood Pewee
Black-capped Chickadee
Warbling Vireo
Bullock's Oriole
Black-headed Grosbeak

The development of agriculture in southern Idaho has had profound effects on birdlife. In the reclamation of the sagelands, the numbers of Sage Grouse, Sage Thrashers, and other birds preferring that type of environment have been markedly reduced; conversely, birds such as Robins, Yellow Warblers, Bullock's Orioles, and Black-headed Grosbeaks have undoubtedly increased because of the growth of orchards and of tree and shrub plantations about homes. The creation of irrigation reservoirs and canals in this region of few natural lakes and marshes has greatly extended drinking and resting places for waterbirds, waterfowl, and shorebirds; where water levels have been sufficiently stabilized to permit the growth of aquatic plants, feeding and breeding grounds for such birds have also been augmented. As a result of these artificial basins and watercourses, water-loving birds have shown a notable increase in southern Idaho. There is no better evidence of this fact than in the Minidoka National Wildlife Refuge (see under Rupert) and in the Deer Flat National Wildlife Refuge (see under Nampa), where storage reservoirs with controlled water supply attract impressive congregations of grebes, cormorants, herons, geese, ducks, shorebirds, gulls, and terns for loitering, feeding, and nesting purposes.

Central Idaho, that part of the state lying between the Snake River Plain and the Panhandle (here defined as the remainder of the state north of Lewiston and Idaho County), embraces a vast section of the northern Rocky Mountains. A great many peaks exceed 10,000 feet; Mt. Borah, 12,655 feet, is the highest point in the state. The general topography, some of the roughest in the United States, is a veritable maze of mountain ranges and intermittent valleys, with a remarkable assortment of deep sun-less canyons, steep bare ridges, and jagged peaks—all so commonplace in this area that only the most formidable have names. Dense forests blanket the wider valleys and sometimes extend high up the adjacent slopes. Almost entirely coniferous, save for scattered aspen groves, the forests consist principally of Douglas fir, grand fir, and western red cedar, and occasionally of ponderosa pine, at elevations below 5,000 feet; Engelmann spruce, alpine fir, and lodgepole pine between, roughly, 5,000 and 7,000 feet; and whitebark pine from 7,000 feet to the timber line at about 7,500 feet. There are a few somewhat level surfaces above the timber line that are typical alpine meadows. Hidden away in nearly all parts of this great wilderness are lovely lakes, frequently forest-bordered, and, like many of the other physiographic features here, often nameless.

Contributing in no small measure to the grandeur of central Idaho is the Salmon River, which gouges a deep path through seemingly impervious terrain from its source in the Sawtooth Mountains near Galena Peak. For 100 miles it takes a northeastward course, gathering volume from its tributaries and passing through Cronks Canyon (the Royal Gorge of Idaho) and the Miniature Grand Canyon. Near the Montana line the River, already a turbulent stream, bends abruptly westward and enters the forbidding, 200-mile-long canyon bearing its name. By the time the Salmon River has descended 2,000 feet, receiving additional tributaries on the way, and emerged from its high-walled chasm at Riggins near the Oregon line, it is a roaring torrent. On seeing its final miles through the Canyon, one readily understands how it earns another name, 'The River of No Return.' To navigate upstream through the Salmon River Canyon is unthinkable; but to come downstream is possible (see under Hailey) provided the person making the expedition loves adventure and is willing to equip himself with the proper craft and obtain the assistance of an experienced guide.

US Route 93 goes through part of central Idaho on the east, and US Route 95 traverses the western portion. Only along these highways is the country settled and agriculturally productive. The rest of central Idaho is comparatively undisturbed. Roads, in most cases secondary or un-improved, connect a few areas; towns, resorts, mines, and ranches are small in number and far between. Midway between Routes 93 and 95, and bounded on the north by part of the Salmon River Canyon, are 1,087,744 acres, designated as a Primitive Area, in which construction of roads, trails, and other improvements is not allowed; in addition, there are many thousands of outlying acres which, though not set aside, still exist in their natural state and will doubtless remain so for many years to come.

While the mountain fastnesses of central Idaho are ac-cessible only to hardy bird finders willing to organize pack trips by trail, or even by unmarked route, some of the most delightful and scenic spots are accessible by car and are not too far from quite satisfactory accommodations (see under Boise, Hailey, and Riggins). Since information is limited, it is impossible to tell just which coniferous for-ests, canyons, rocky slopes, or mountain meadows close to the road will, upon exploration, yield the longest list of birds, but the species listed below should be expected to breed regularly in this area.

Goshawk	Hermit Thrush
Sharp-shinned Hawk	Olive-backed Thrush
Blue Grouse	Mountain Bluebird
Franklin's Grouse	Townsend's Solitaire
Ruffed Grouse	Ruby-crowned Kinglet
Pygmy Owl	Solitary Vireo
Pileated Woodpecker	Red-eyed Vireo
Common Sapsucker	Orange-crowned Warbler
Williamson's Sapsucker	Nashville Warbler
Black-backed Woodpecker	Audubon's Warbler
Three-toed Woodpecker	Western Tanager
Olive-sided Flycatcher	Evening Grosbeak
Tree Swallow	Cassin's Finch
Canada Jay	Pine Grosbeak
Steller's Jay	Black Rosy Finch
Clark's Nutcracker	Pine Siskin
Mountain Chickadee	Red Crossbill
White-breasted Nuthatch	Oregon Junco
Red-breasted Nuthatch	White-crowned Sparrow
Pygmy Nuthatch	Fox Sparrow
Brown Creeper	Lincoln's Sparrow

The many precipitous slopes and deep canyons that characterize so much of the rough country in both central and southern Idaho are often favorite breeding localities of such bird species as the following:

Turkey Vulture	Violet-green Swallow
Golden Eagle	Cliff Swallow
Prairie Falcon	Common Raven
Mountain Quail	Canyon Wren
White-throated Swift	Rock Wren

The Idaho Panhandle is a mixture of lesser mountain ranges, beautiful lakes, and coniferous forests. Resorts, farmlands, many towns, and one large city (Coeur d'Alene) interrupt the natural landscape, which enjoys a fairly heavy rainfall and is thus more verdant than southern Idaho. Bird-finding possibilities in the Panhandle are undoubtedly rich. (For an area with various, and representative, bird habitats, see under St. Maries.) Among the peculiarities of the birdlife are the Western Bluebird and several species of eastern affinities (e.g. Catbird, Cedar Waxwing, Northern Water-thrush, American Redstart, Bobolink), which are not found regularly in the breeding season elsewhere in the state.

Observations on bird migration in Idaho have been made principally in southern Idaho, on several of the reservoirs (see under Idaho Falls, Nampa, and Rupert). Here large numbers of transient waterfowl and small numbers of shorebirds, gulls, and terns gather. Remarkably few small-landbird species—the Northern Shrike, Common Redpoll, Slate-colored Junco, and American Tree Sparrow among them—appear regularly in the state, and then only as transients or winter residents. Most of the species listed for Idaho nest at least somewhere in the state. Throughout southern Idaho the main migratory flights take place within the following dates: waterfowl, 10 March—20 April, 10 October—25 November; shorebirds, 1 May—1 June, 1 August—1 October; landbirds 15 April—20 May, 25 August—20 October.

Owing to Idaho's generally high elevation, winters are cold and not very productive ornithologically. Open water in southern Idaho sometimes holds large wintering populations of waterfowl, for example in the Deer Flat National Wildlife Refuge (see under Nampa). Northwest-central Idaho and the Panhandle, where the elevations are the lowest in the state, have the mildest winter conditions. In the vicinity of Lewiston may be found what is probably the greatest variety of landbirds, including the Mourning Dove, Cedar Waxwing, Golden-crowned Kinglet, Audubon's Warbler, Western Meadowlark, Red-wing, Brewer's Blackbird, Evening Grosbeak, Common Goldfinch, Savannah Sparrow, Oregon Junco, and White-crowned Sparrow.

ARCO. For weird, unworldly landscape, CRATERS OF THE MOON NATIONAL MONUMENT is almost unrivaled. Here have been set aside 48,183 acres of cinder cones, craters, fissure eruptions, lava flows, caves, and tunnels—some of the most striking of the volcanic phenomena that prevail over wide areas of the Snake River Plain. On first seeing this vast panorama of black and gray desolation, the bird finder will conclude that it is devoid of birds except for Poor-wills, Horned Larks, Violet-green Swallows, Common Ravens, and Rock Wrens, but on closer inspection he will discover patches of juniper, limber pine, aspen, and various shrubs that hold small numbers of such birds as the Traill's Flycatcher, Loggerhead Shrike, Robin, Yellow Warbler, Yellow-throat, and Fox Sparrow.

Craters Monument is traversed by State Route 22 and US Route 20 between Arco and Carey. Headquarters, at Arco, is 20.5 miles from the north (Arco) entrance. At the west (Carey) entrance there are overnight accommodations.

BOISE. Idaho's capital and largest city, Boise (pronounced *boy'-see*), lies on the Boise River in the Upper Boise Valley of the Snake River Plain. At an elevation of only 2,741 feet and sheltered on the north by the Boise Range, it is favored by mild winters.

For a profitable summer bird-finding trip, drive southeastward and then northward from Boise on State Route 21 to Idaho City (almost a ghost town) in the Boise Basin, a distance of about 45 miles. The last 25 miles of the trip is through BOISE NATIONAL FOREST, notable for its

fine stands of pine and spruce. As the road approaches
Idaho City it passes numerous ponds, created by placer-
mining operations and now choked to some extent with
vegetation. Nearly all of these water areas attract a few
nesting waterbirds, ducks, and shorebirds. Blue Grouse,
Ruffed Grouse, California Quail (recently introduced), and
many other birds should be found in their vicinity.

If the bird finder has time and camping equipment, he
may wish to continue on State Route 21 past Lowman (82
miles from Boise) to Stanley (127 miles from Boise) on
State Route 93. (For an account of the bird-finding possibilities on State Route 93, see under Hailey.) Before making the trip, the bird finder should inquire at Idaho City
about the condition of the road, which has been under construction a long time. Like the trip on State Route 93, this
is through wild, rough country that has been little explored
ornithologically.

BURLEY. Two good spots for bird finding, off the beaten
path, are GOOSE CREEK and the CITY OF ROCKS.
The best time for observing breeding birds is in May and
June. To reach Goose Creek, drive south from Burley on
State Route 27 for 22 miles, to Oakley; then take a good
gravel road (unnumbered) south to a point within 2 miles
of the Idaho-Utah line. Here, in the vicinity of Goose Creek,
are low ridges, covered with pinyon pine, juniper, and
mountain mahogany, where such birds as the Ash-throated
Flycatcher, Gray Flycatcher, Scrub Jay, Pinyon Jay, Plain
Titmouse, Blue-gray Gnatcatcher, and Black-throated Gray
Warbler may be found nesting.

To reach the City of Rocks, drive south from Burley on
State Route 27 for 22 miles, to Oakley, then southeast on
an unpaved road (unnumbered) for 14 miles. This is an
arid, 25-square-mile area marked by sheer cliffs and by
curious pinnacles of rock towering hundreds of feet above
the floor of a valley. Pinyon pine, juniper, and mountain
mahogany, though sparse, are the predominating vegetation; aspen and whitebark pine also occur. Some of the
breeding birds that may be expected here are the following: Turkey Vulture, Golden Eagle, Prairie Falcon, Burrowing Owl, Poor-will, White-throated Swift, Black-

chinned Hummingbird, (Red-naped) Common Sapsucker, Say's Phoebe, House Wren, Rock Wren, Hermit Thrush, Mountain Bluebird, Virginia's Warbler (apparently found nowhere else in the state), Audubon's Warbler, Green-tailed Towhee, Lark Sparrow, Gray-headed Junco, Brewer's Sparrow, and Fox Sparrow.

GOLDEN EAGLE

Another good spot off the beaten path is MT. HARRISON, reached from Burley as follows: Drive east on US Route 30S to Declo (9 miles), turn south on an unnumbered road to Albion (9 miles), and then continue south a short distance over a road that ascends Mt. Harrison via Howells Canyon. The road goes almost to the top. Near the top, in a lovely setting at the head of Howells Canyon and accessible by an easy trail from the road, is Lake Cleveland. The mountain slopes (elevations 4,500–8,000 feet) differ in their vegetation accordng to exposure, those on the north being covered with pine and fir and those on the south with sagebrush. During a trip up Mt. Harrison in June, some of the nesting birds to be expected are the Blue Grouse, Clark's Nutcracker, Dipper, Hermit

Thrush, Townsend's Solitaire, Ruby-crowned Kinglet, Audubon's Warbler, Macgillivray's Warbler, Cassin's Finch, Pine Siskin, Green-tailed Towhee, and Oregon Junco.

HAILEY. Undoubtedly Idaho's longest and most magnificent scenic highway is US Route 93 between Hailey, in the southern foothills of the Sawtooth Range, and Salmon City, in the Upper Salmon River Valley. For 192 miles the road traverses a wilderness of lofty peaks, awesome canyons, mountain-walled lakes, and great coniferous forests; by countless switchbacks, it climbs to heights of breathtaking grandeur and descends into deep valleys. Features that stand out in the memory of anyone who takes this route are the ascent of Galena Summit (elevation 8,752 feet), the highest point in Idaho accessible by car; the lovely drive through Challis National Forest with its fine stands of ponderosa pine, lodgepole pine, Douglas fir, and Engelmann spruce; and the trips through Cronks Canyon (the Royal Gorge of Idaho), the Miniature Grand Canyon, and the Upper Salmon River Canyon. Side trips to Sun Valley, the setting of the much-publicized luxury resort (reached from Ketchum), and to idyllic Stanley Lake (reached from Stanley), flanked by tall conifers and reflecting several immense peaks of the Sawtooth Range, provide other memorable features. (One desiring real adventure may arrange at Salmon City for a boat trip down the Salmon River Canyon.) Since stretches of the highway are in poor condition, anyone making the trip should first make local inquiry at either Hailey or Salmon City. Good campsites and limited overnight accommodations are available at several points along the way.

Despite the fact that this vast area has been penetrated by highway for a number of years and has become notable for its superlative scenery, its birdlife is still unknown. That its heights attract eagles, that its forests hold grouse, owls, flycatchers, jays, and fringillids, and that its canyons provide nesting sites for falcons, swifts, swallows, and wrens are almost certainties; but which species they are and in what abundance they occur remain to be learned. This is virgin territory for the bird finder desiring to make discoveries.

IDAHO FALLS. The bird finder interested in waterfowl will enjoy visiting the CAMAS NATIONAL WILDLIFE REFUGE (10,535 acres), 38 miles north of Idaho Falls on the Snake River Plain. To reach it, drive north from Idaho Falls on US Route 91. At a point 3 miles north of the Union Pacific Depot in the little town of Hamer, turn off the highway onto a road going west. This leads to headquarters, 2 miles distant, and is the only entrance to the Refuge. Various parts of the preserve may be reached by car.

The Refuge consists roughly of 6,000 acres of low, sandy knolls and 4,000 acres of flat, marshy areas with numerous small ponds, all of which may be flooded. Camas Creek flows for 8 miles through the Refuge from the northeast to the southwest corner, while in the southeastern and southern part of the Refuge are two permanent bodies of water, Sandhole Lake (90 acres) and Rays Lake (200 acres). The predominant vegetation on the Refuge is sagebrush, with interspersed native grasses on the uplands and cattails and bulrushes in the marshes.

By the first of June the nesting of the following waterfowl is well under way: Canada Goose, Mallard, Gadwall, Pintail, Green-winged Teal, Blue-winged Teal, Cinnamon Teal, Shoveler, Redhead, Canvas-back, Lesser Scaup Duck, and Ruddy Duck. Other breeding birds to be found at the same time are Willets and Avocets on the periphery of wet places, and Sage Grouse and Long-billed Curlews on the knolls. In the fall, from mid-October to the first of December, huge numbers of transient Canada Geese and ducks greatly increase the waterfowl population, providing an impressive spectacle.

LEWISTON. Situated in extreme northwest-central Idaho at the confluence of the Clearwater and Snake Rivers and at an altitude of 720 feet—the lowest point in the state— this city is picturesquely hemmed in by mountains and steep, bare ridges devoid of trees and shrubs. Sheer cliffs and rocky slopes are characteristic features of the landscape. It was on the present site of Lewiston that Lewis and Clark stopped for several days during their arduous journey to the Pacific Coast.

The Clearwater and Snake Rivers bound the city on the

north and west, while extending southward from the outskirts is rolling country with cherry orchards, grainfields,
and homes. Owing to Lewiston's low elevation, the protection afforded by the adjacent ridges and mountains, and
the proximity of agricultural lands, birdlife is varied and
abundant. Some of the common breeding birds in the immediate vicinity of Lewiston are the Mourning Dove,
Rufous Hummingbird, Lewis' Woodpecker, Western Kingbird, Say's Phoebe, Western Wood Pewee, Horned Lark,
Violet-green Swallow, Black-capped Chickadee, Cedar
Waxwing, Warbling Vireo, Western Meadowlark, Bullock's
Oriole, Brewer's Blackbird, House Finch, Common Goldfinch, and Lazuli Bunting. A surprising number of species
pass the winter in the area. Christmas bird counts yield, for
example, usually between 25 and 35 species, and include
the Mourning Dove, Golden-crowned Kinglet, Audubon's
Warbler, Western Meadowlark, and White-crowned Sparrow, which are rarely found commonly elsewhere in the
state during the winter months.

MONTPELIER. This city (elevation 5,941 feet) in the
southeastern corner of Idaho lies toward the northern end
of high, lovely Bear Lake Valley, which is closely flanked by
mountains. Although some of the land in the lower part of
the Valley is under cultivation and the upper areas are
given over to farming and grazing, it is an exceptionally fine
place for the study of waterfowl; large numbers of ducks
and geese may be found nesting.

The largest body of water in the Valley is BEAR LAKE
(30 miles long and about 7 miles wide), which straddles
the Idaho-Utah line. An important summer resort, this Lake
is principally a resting area for ducks and geese during
migration. When there is sufficient water, a few ducks
sometimes nest around its marshy borders.

North of Bear Lake lies small, shallow MUD LAKE,
which merges northward into DINGLE SWAMP. The vegetation bordering Mud Lake and standing in the wettest
part of the Swamp consists principally of cattails and bulrushes. On slightly higher ground there is an abundance
of grasses, sedges, and rushes, most of which is harvested as

wild hay. On still higher ground, where the soil is not too alkaline, grain is raised; elsewhere there is a wild growth of greasewood and other salt-tolerant plants. A large canal, the Bear Outlet Canal, designed to carry water pumped from Bear Lake into Bear River, cuts northward across Dingle Swamp. Several streams, chiefly from the Bear River Range on the west of the Valley, also drain into the bottom-lands.

Large colonies of Snowy Egrets and Black-crowned Night Herons occupy Dingle Swamp, and a colony of Double-crested Cormorants has taken over one island in Mud Lake. Other breeding birds in this area include the Western Grebe, Pied-billed Grebe, American Bittern, Canada Goose, several kinds of ducks, Forster's Tern, and Black Tern. Also nesting in the vicinity are the following shore-birds: the Killdeer, Wilson's Snipe, Long-billed Curlew, Spotted Sandpiper, Willet, Avocet, and Wilson's Phalarope.

To reach Bear Lake, Mud Lake, and Dingle Swamp, drive south from Montpelier on US Route 30N. Just beyond Wardboro, when Route 30N turns east, continue south on a country road to the very small town of Dingle. From Dingle, go south about 9 miles (Dingle Swamp is on the right) and turn right on the road to St. Charles, which passes between Mud Lake and Bear Lake; bird finding should be very productive here between May and July. For an alternate route from Dingle, follow a dirt road directly west to Paris (where it intersects US Route 89). This road crosses Dingle Swamp and is thus a fine vantage point for observing nesting birds. In order to see the nesting colonies of Egrets and Night Herons, travel west from Dingle on the dirt road to the large Bear Lake Outlet Canal; turn south onto a rather poor road and follow along the east bank of the Canal for about a mile. The colonies, which can be reached only by wading, will be discovered in the Swamp to the eastward by watching the movements of the birds through field glasses.

MOSCOW. The 600-acre campus of the UNIVERSITY OF IDAHO is centered on a hill on the southeastern edge of this Panhandle city. In the Science Hall is a collection of about 2,000 bird skins representing 270 species, mostly from the northwestern states. A course in ornithology, offered in the second semester, meets in this building.

Moscow is surrounded by rolling farmlands, actually a continuation eastward of the Palouse Country of eastern Washington. Mountains and heavily forested areas are not far distant. Common breeding birds beyond the city's outskirts—in the deciduous woods, pastures, fields, and shrubby places—include the Marsh Hawk, Long-eared Owl, Calliope Hummingbird, Red-shafted Flicker, Traill's Flycatcher, Wright's Flycatcher, Western Wood Pewee, Violet-green Swallow, Rough-winged Swallow, Black-capped Chickadee, House Wren, Catbird, Veery, Mountain Bluebird, Warbling Vireo, Macgillivray's Warbler, Yellow-breasted Chat, American Redstart, Bullock's Oriole, Black-headed Grosbeak, Lazuli Bunting, House Finch, Common Goldfinch, Savannah Sparrow, Grasshopper Sparrow, Fox Sparrow, and Song Sparrow.

An interesting spot for birds is MOSCOW MOUNTAIN (elevation 4,200 feet), which may be reached by driving east 2 miles on State Route 8, turning north and then proceeding 8 miles; or by driving north 5 miles on US Route 95 and then taking the first turn east at the foot of the Viola grade. On the Mountain's slopes, which are covered for the most part with western red cedar, ponderosa pine, Douglas fir, white fir, lodgepole pine, white pine, and aspen, may be found a rich variety of nesting birds such as the Sharp-shinned Hawk, Ruffed Grouse, Pygmy Owl, Vaux's Swift, Rufous Hummingbird, Pileated Woodpecker, Olive-sided Flycatcher, Steller's Jay, Mountain Chickadee, Chestnut-backed Chickadee, Red-breasted Nuthatch, Pygmy Nuthatch, Brown Creeper, Winter Wren, Varied Thrush, Olive-backed Thrush, Western Bluebird, Solitary Vireo, Orange-crowned Warbler, Townsend's Warbler, Western Tanager, Evening Grosbeak, Cassin's Finch, Pine Siskin, Spotted Towhee, and Oregon Junco.

NAMPA. Just south of this city, which lies in the highly developed agricultural area at the extreme west end of the Snake River Plain, is the DEER FLAT NATIONAL WILDLIFE REFUGE (10,267 acres), an important nest-

ing ground and stopping point during migration for great
numbers of waterbirds and waterfowl. Headquarters may
be reached from Nampa by taking US Route 30 south for
7 blocks, turning west on Lone Star Road (oil-surfaced)
for 3.5 miles, and turning south for 1.5 miles and west a
quarter of a mile on a gravel road. Nearly all parts of
the Refuge are easily accessible by roads.

The Refuge consists primarily of Lake Lowell (Deer
Flat Reservoir), an artificial body of water 9 miles long
and 2.5 miles wide, with a surface, when filled, of some
9,800 acres. The Lake has considerable shallow water, with
bulrushes and other emergent plants. Just below the upper
dam, which is west of headquarters, is a marsh of 20 acres,
with cattails the predominating vegetation. Cottonwoods,
black locusts, willows, and various shrubs stand along the
shore of the Lake and the several radiating canals; sagebrush and native grasses constitute the principal cover on
the adjacent higher ground. On a small island at the east
end of Lake Lowell is a colony of several thousand pairs of
California Gulls. Other birds that may be found nesting
in suitable situations in the Refuge are the Eared Grebe,
Western Grebe, Double-crested Cormorant, Great Blue
Heron, Black-crowned Night Heron, Coot, Canada Goose,
Mallard, Green-winged Teal, Cinnamon Teal, Avocet, and
Black-necked Stilt. White Pelicans and White-faced Ibises
are frequent visitants but apparently do not nest. Some of
the species that breed regularly in the general vicinity of
the Refuge are the following: Bob-white, Ring-necked
Pheasant, Killdeer, Mourning Dove, Common Nighthawk,
Say's Phoebe, Horned Lark, Bullock's Oriole, Brewer's
Blackbird, and House Finch. The nesting of most species
is under way by the first week of May.

From the third week of February to the end of April
transient waterfowl are present, but the populations are
greatest in mid-March. Fall migration is first evident in
the second week of August, when the shorebirds—Greater
and Lesser Yellow-legs, Dowitchers, Western Sandpipers,
and others—begin appearing in large numbers. During
the second and third weeks of November waterfowl concentrations reach their peak. At this time the most common
species are, in order of abundance, the Mallard, Baldpate,

Green-winged Teal, Pintail, Shoveler, Canada Goose, White-fronted Goose, Snow Goose, Lesser Scaup Duck, Redhead, Canvas-back, American Golden-eye, and Ruddy Duck. Tens of thousands of Mallards and smaller numbers of other waterfowl stay on the Refuge throughout the winter, depending on the weather conditions. Most waterfowl are gone from 20 December to 31 January.

The SNAKE RIVER NATIONAL WILDLIFE REFUGE (355 acres), administered by the Deer Flats Refuge, comprises 69 islands in the Snake River. Forty of them, each with less than an acre of surface, are low-lying and covered with a dense growth of willows; the others, larger and higher, have willows on their borders, but their interiors support a desert type of vegetation. Used by Canada Geese and large numbers of Mallards as nesting grounds, the islands are also occupied by Mourning Doves, American Magpies, Brewer's Blackbirds, and many other landbirds. Since the Refuge is maintained for nesting waterfowl, it is closed to the public from 1 February to 31 August. The islands, however, may be viewed at any time by driving south from Nampa on 12th Avenue (State Route 45), then taking a road to the right just before crossing the Snake River. This road proceeds downstream along the River's edge, from which the islands may be easily seen.

POCATELLO. The second largest city in the state and one of the principal railroad centers west of the Mississippi, Pocatello in southeastern Idaho is also the seat of IDAHO STATE COLLEGE. This institution, on the east side of the city, offers a second-semester course in ornithology. Classes meet in the new Liberal Arts Building, where there is a collection of about 500 bird skins and other ornithological materials.

US Route 30N going north and west from Pocatello reaches the Snake River at American Falls, 25 miles away. At a point about 10 miles northeast of American Falls, the highway begins passing fairly close to the AMERICAN FALLS RESERVOIR, a huge body of water 26 miles long and 12 miles wide, formed by the damming of the Snake River for irrigation purposes. It may be profitable to stop occasionally and scan the Reservoir for waterbirds and waterfowl.

US Route 30N goes southwest from American Falls, roughly paralleling the Snake River for about 24 miles. The drive is picturesque, with fine views of the Snake River Valley and its irrigated plains and, in the distance to the north and south, of numerous mountain ranges. Birds one is likely to see along the River in the summer months are White Pelicans, Double-crested Cormorants, and California Gulls. These birds and others—for example, various ducks, Forster's Terns, Caspian Terns, and Black Terns—are common here in the spring and fall. American Golden-eyes and American Mergansers frequent certain parts of the River in the winter.

RIGGINS. This tiny town (elevation 1,800 feet) is in a deep chasm and is near the point where the Salmon River, on emerging from the Salmon River Canyon, is joined by the Little Salmon River and makes a sharp bend north. Overnight accommodations are available. Situated almost midway between the Panhandle and southern Idaho in highly scenic country, Riggins makes an excellent base for interesting ornithological explorations. Rugged mountain slopes, sheer cliffs, coniferous forests, rushing streams, and sequestered lakes lie in all directions. Thus there are different habitats for a great variety of birds, including both Blue and Ruffed Grouse, Mountain Quail, Violet-green Swallows, Steller's Jays, Dippers, and Canyon Wrens.

From Riggins it is possible to drive east for a short distance up the SALMON RIVER CANYON. Vegetation is sparse, except for brush along the water's edge, and birdlife is necessarily limited. The more spectacular part of the Canyon, many miles farther up the Salmon River, is not accessible by car.

South from Riggins, US Route 95 follows the Little Salmon River up LITTLE SALMON RIVER CANYON through wonderfully mountainous country. Now and then the highway passes near the base of forested slopes or traverses a meadow where the bottom of the Canyon widens. These spots should yield a fascinating array of birds.

RUPERT. The Snake River Plain, in the vicinity of Rupert in south-central Idaho, was once entirely desert-like except for scattered wet-weather marshes and the willow-bordered banks of the Snake River and its tributaries. But around the first of the century the Minidoka Dam was built across the Snake River northeast of Rupert, forming Lake Walcott, a huge reservoir for irrigation. This body of water soon provided food and cover for many waterfowl, and in 1909 it was established by President Theodore Roosevelt as part of the Minidoka Reservation for the protection of native birds. The name was later changed to MINIDOKA NATIONAL WILDLIFE REFUGE. Recently, some of the shallow bays were cut off by dykes in order to assure a more stabilized water supply for aquatic plants when the level of the reservoir drops. Such units have served to attract still more waterfowl.

Lake Walcott is generally deep, with abrupt shorelines, but there are places near the shore, in the dammed-off upper reaches of the bays, and around low islands where the water is shallow enough for cattails, bulrushes, and other marsh vegetation. The variety and numbers of birds that now breed regularly in this artificial environment are truly astounding. These include not only many pairs of Canada Geese, Mallards, Gadwalls, Pintails, Redheads, Lesser Scaup Ducks, Ruddy Ducks, and other waterfowl, but the following, which occupy particularly some of the islands (e.g. Bird and Tule Islands) or their marshy borders: Horned Grebes, Western Grebes (uncommon), Double-crested Cormorants, Great Blue Herons, Snowy Egrets, Black-crowned Night Herons, American Bitterns, Coots, Yellow-headed Blackbirds, and Red-wings. The nesting season for all of these birds extends from April through June. Important as the area has become for nesting birds, it is even more important for migrating waterfowl. At times in the fall, geese and ducks number as many as 100,000 individuals.

Lake Walcott and the Snake River make up only 10,000 of the 22,123 acres embraced by the Refuge. The rest of the area has a sandy surface partly covered by sagebrush and clumps of native grasses. Such birds as the Sage Grouse, Sage Thrasher, Lark Sparrow, Sage Sparrow, and Brewer's

Sparrow presumably still breed here regularly, as they did on much of the Snake River Plain before irrigation.

Headquarters of the Minidoka Refuge, at Minidoka Dam 10 miles northeast of Rupert, may be reached by driving north from Rupert on an unnumbered country road to one mile past Acequia, then turning right (east) at the Minidoka Dam sign. Headquarters is in a lava-rock building on the point north of the Dam.

Normally, the south side of the Refuge, which is accessible by car, is the most advantageous for bird observations. At Walcott Park, a public recreation area in the immediate vicinity of headquarters, boats may be hired for visiting Bird and Tule Islands. Permission to land on the Islands during the nesting season must be obtained at headquarters.

ST. MARIES. The town of St. Maries (elevation 2,145 feet), southeast of Coeur d'Alene Lake in the Panhandle, lies on low hills; but in its immediate vicinity, where the St. Maries River merges with the St. Joe River, there are wide bottomlands, the rich soils of which are used for growing fruits and crops. Some of the bird species regularly occurring as summer residents in the fields, wet meadows, pastures, orchards, and shrubby places, in the remaining deciduous woods along the two watercourses, and about the farm buildings are the following: Sparrow Hawk, Killdeer, Mourning Dove, Common Nighthawk, Black-chinned Hummingbird, Rufous Hummingbird, Calliope Hummingbird, Red-shafted Flicker, Downy Woodpecker, Eastern Kingbird, Western Wood Pewee, Violetgreen Swallow, Tree Swallow, Rough-winged Swallow, Barn Swallow, Cliff Swallow, American Magpie (permanent resident), Black-capped Chickadee, House Wren, Catbird, Mountain Bluebird, Cedar Waxwing, Red-eyed Vireo, Warbling Vireo, Yellow Warbler, American Redstart, Bobolink, Western Meadowlark, Bullock's Oriole, Brewer's Blackbird, Black-headed Grosbeak, Lazuli Bunting, Common Goldfinch, Spotted Towhee, Savannah Sparrow, Chipping Sparrow, and Song Sparrow.

West of St. Maries the St. Joe River continues on its course to enter Coeur d'Alene Lake and is flanked much of its way by COEUR D'ALENE SLOUGH—a wet lowland consisting of a few stretches of open water, cattail marshes, cottonwood and willow swamps, and mud flats. State Route 5, west from St. Maries, follows the Slough for about 5 miles, making this interesting area readily accessible by car. Included among the nesting birds that should be looked for here in late May, June, and early July are the Pied-billed Grebe, American Bittern, Mallard, Cinnamon Teal, Wood Duck, Virginia Rail, Sora, Coot, Wilson's Snipe, Black Tern, Veery, Northern Water-thrush, Yellow-throat, Yellow-headed Blackbird, and Red-wing. When this low-land is flooded in the spring (late March and April), it is attractive to numerous waterfowl, particularly the Whis-tling Swan (usually in flocks of from 15 to 75 individuals), Canada Goose, Baldpate, Pintail, Green-winged Teal, Blue-winged Teal, Shoveler, Redhead, Ring-necked Duck, Canvas-back, Lesser Scaup Duck, and Hooded Merganser. Also attracted in the spring (and during the winter, as long as there is open water) are American Golden-eyes and American Mergansers. Ducks occur commonly on the Slough in the fall (October and November), but the Slough is open to hunting, which makes observations un-satisfactory. Shorebirds, such as the Solitary Sandpiper, Pectoral Sandpiper, Baird's Sandpiper, Dowitcher, West-ern Sandpiper, and Northern Phalarope, frequent the mud flats in late August and September, more rarely in May.

Farther west on State Route 5, 12 miles from St. Maries, is HEYBURN STATE PARK, a recreational and camping area, the northern part of which touches on Coeur d'Alene Lake. Of the Park's 7,838 acres, about 2,300 go to make up four charming lakes: Chatcolet, Hidden, Round, and Benewah; the rest is covered by timber, mostly coniferous except along the watercourses. Among the birds that should be found in the Park are the Ruffed Grouse, Spotted Sand-piper, Great Horned Owl, Pygmy Owl, Belted Kingfisher, Pileated Woodpecker, Lewis' Woodpecker (in open tim-ber), Hairy Woodpecker, Wright's Flycatcher, Steller's Jay, Chestnut-backed Chickadee, Pygmy Nuthatch, Olive-backed Thrush, Ruby-crowned Kinglet, Solitary Vireo, Red-eyed Vireo, Audubon's Warbler, Macgillivray's Warbler, American Redstart, Western Tanager, Evening Grosbeak,

Pine Siskin, Red Crossbill, Oregon Junco, and Fox Sparrow.

Far to the east of St. Maries lies the 'main division' of ST. JOE NATIONAL FOREST, embracing rough, mountainous terrain with altitudes ranging from 2,400 feet on the St. Joe River, which cuts through the division from the east, to 7,000 feet on the higher peaks. Most of the area, except ridge tops, burned-over spots, and the few alpine meadows, is forested with western red cedar, western white pine, and ponderosa pine at lower elevations, western white pine, Douglas fir, and western larch at intermediate elevations, and Engelmann spruce, lodgepole pine, alpine fir, and whitebark pine at higher elevations to timber line. From St. Maries, an unnumbered road, in fairly good condition but suitable only for summer travel, reaches Avery in the main division via St. Joe City and Calder. To reach this road, drive north from St. Maries on US Route 95A; just outside of town, cross the St. Joe River and turn east. At Avery, 50 miles from St. Maries, various Forest Service roads lead off into the Bitterroot and St. Joe Mountains. There are few, if any, overnight accommodations east of St. Maries, so if one is planning to stay any length of time, he should take camping equipment. Before making the trip, the bird finder will be wise to inquire at the National Forest headquarters in St. Maries for information about the most interesting places for birds and their accessibility by road or trail.

On the whole, the bird species in the main division of St. Joe National Forest are those that occur also in Heyburn State Park and near-by areas of low elevation, but the forests at high altitudes in the division have attracted additional species. Careful searching during June or early July in timbered places above 4,000 feet should yield the following breeding species, considered to be of regular occurrence: Goshawk, Sharp-shinned Hawk, Red-tailed Hawk, Blue Grouse, Franklin's Grouse, Vaux's Swift, (Red-naped) Common Sapsucker (usually in aspen tracts), Black-backed Woodpecker, Three-toed Woodpecker, Olive-sided Flycatcher, Canada Jay, Common Raven, Clark's Nutcracker, Mountain Chickadee, Red-breasted Nuthatch,

Brown Creeper, Winter Wren, Varied Thrush, Hermit
Thrush, Townsend's Solitaire, Golden-crowned Kinglet,
Nashville Warbler, Townsend's Warbler, Cassin's Finch,
and Pine Grosbeak. In brushy places bordering lakes and
streams above 4,000 feet, one should find the Black-capped
Warbler and Lincoln's Sparrow. Other species that may
be seen are the Dipper along fast-flowing streams, the Rock
Wren on rocky slopes near ridge tops, and the White-
crowned Sparrow at the timber line.

SODA SPRINGS. This southeastern Idaho town, rich in
early history and the site of many cold mineral springs, is
also the take-off point for GRAYS LAKE, which, in the
opinion of one Idaho ornithologist, is 'possibly the outstanding area in the state for abundance and variety of birdlife.' June is the best time for bird finding.

From Soda Springs, take State Route 34 north. This
goes to the southwest side of the Lake, a distance of 30
miles. Here a road turns off left and goes north along the
west side. Route 34 swings eastward for 5 miles around
the south end of the Lake to a junction with a road on
the left that proceeds first northward on the east side, then
around the north end of the Lake, eventually meeting the
west-side road. Grays Lake is thus encircled by roads. In
their vicinity are many attractive campsites.

Grays Lake occupies a high plateau (elevation 6,400
feet), flanked on the east and north by the Caribou Mountains, with peaks rising as high as 10,000 feet, and on the
west by the lower Little Valley Hills. Though a large body
of water with a 41-mile shoreline, Grays Lake is nevertheless very shallow and to a large extent choked with bulrushes and other emergent plants. Numerous channels
meander through the vegetation, and in spots there are
open stretches of water. Among the birds that are attracted
to this great marshy area for nesting purposes are the
Sandhill Crane (about 150 pairs), 13 kinds of ducks, including the Gadwall, Green-winged Teal, Blue-winged
Teal, Cinnamon Teal, Shoveler, and Ruddy Duck, and the
following: Eared Grebe, Canada Goose, Wilson's Snipe,
Long-billed Curlew, Willet, Avocet, Wilson's Phalarope,
Franklin's Gull, Forster's Tern, Black Tern, Long-billed

Marsh Wren, and Yellow-headed Blackbird. Adjacent to the Lake the Bobolink nests in meadowlands, and the Lincoln's Sparrow in wet, brushy places.

The mountain ridges bordering Grays Lake have a cover of lodgepole pine, limber pine, Douglas fir, and aspen, with intermittent patches of serviceberry, chokecherry, snowberry, wild rose, and other shrubby growth. Birds breeding on the lower elevations are such species as the Broadtailed Hummingbird, Calliope Hummingbird, Catbird, Orange-crowned Warbler, Macgillivray's Warbler, Western Tanager, Black-headed Grosbeak, Lazuli Bunting, and Fox Sparrow. At higher elevations nest the Blue Grouse, (Red-naped) Common Sapsucker, Hammond's Flycatcher, Steller's Jay, Townsend's Solitaire, Cassin's Finch, Pine Grosbeak, Green-tailed Towhee, Oregon Junco, and White-crowned Sparrow.

Contributing authorities: M. Dale Arvey, Thomas D. Burleigh, F. Sheldon Dart, W. B. Davis, Edson Fichter, Ralph L. Hand, C. Lynn Hayward, Frank B. Jacox, Victor E. Jones, Wallace M. Leonard, William H. Marshall, Wilbert A. Rodgers, Henry J. Rust.

Iowa

UPLAND PLOVER

Early March along the Missouri River in western Iowa marks the arrival of Snow and Blue Geese from their winter's stay in Louisiana. Snow still remains in patches on the bluffs, and ice has not yet disappeared from the streams and ponds when the first flocks appear high overhead, pursuing an ancestral course that leads steadily northward —from the Missouri River at Sioux City to the Big Sioux River and thence, by way of the Red River of the North, into Canada. By mid-March, the 'waveys' are moving by the hundreds of thousands, their V-formations making zigzag patterns across the sky. Over certain areas, as if by prearrangement, they break ranks and descend rapidly on set wings, each bird wheeling dizzily, sometimes tumbling headlong or slipping sidewise, and finally alighting close to others to feed and loiter. Such is the case at the Forney Lake State Refuge (see under Sidney), where, every spring, Snow and Blue Geese gather in such great numbers that they cover acres of ground. There are few spectacles like it in the United States.

From the Mississippi River on the east to the Missouri and Big Sioux Rivers on the west, Iowa is topographically much the same—a level to slightly rolling plain with only subtle differences here and there. Elevations vary from 477 feet at Keokuk in the southernmost point of the state to 1,675 feet near Sibley in the northwestern corner. With a soil rich and arable, the Iowa scene is one of cornfields and other cultivated tracts, square or oblong with straight roads and highways running along section lines. Spaced almost evenly are sets of tree-sequestered farm buildings—each comprising a white house, red barn, and tall silo close to a pasture where dairy herds graze. Also spaced evenly, though farther apart, are the towns, each with its church spire and grain elevator. This monotony, albeit one of un- qualified prosperity, is relieved only at intervals by the wooded bluffs and river valleys. Some of the bluffs, such as those along the Mississippi in the northeast, are as high as 400 feet and are separated by richly forested ravines.

The greater part of Iowa was once prairie grassland, a vast biotic community which has all but disappeared. Near Cherokee, a small section of original prairie has remained untouched through the years as a private preserve, while in the vicinity of the Iowa Lakeside Laboratory at West Okoboji Lake (see under Spirit Lake), there is a bit of prairie that has been partly restored. Woodlands, made up chiefly of oak, hickory, maple, elm, green ash, basswood, and cottonwood, were confined to areas along rivers and streams, to the borders of lakes and sloughs, and (particu- larly in the eastern part of the state) to the plain—as prairie groves. Where the grassland and woodlands came together, there were usually rank weeds, shrubby thickets, and low trees. Few, if any, of the original woodlands still stand. Like the prairie, the majority have been destroyed to make way for farming; others have long since been replaced by second- and third-growth timber. Although birdlife has been considerably altered by these changes, the number of species still occurring in Iowa is impressive. Over 135 are known to breed, at least 25 are regular winter visitants, and 148 are spring and fall transients. Prairie species may be found in such places as fallow fields and grassy pastures. Forest and forest-edge birds are abundant in the larger timbered tracts, most of which are situated in the big river valleys. Today, throughout Iowa, the following species may be found breeding regularly in the farmlands (fallow fields, pastures, wet meadows, shrubby areas, and dooryards) and woodlands (including remains of prairie groves).

FARMLANDS

Marsh Hawk
Bob-white
Killdeer
Upland Plover
Mourning Dove
Barn Owl
Red-headed Woodpecker
Eastern Kingbird
Eastern Phoebe
Horned Lark
Tree Swallow
Barn Swallow
Purple Martin
House Wren
Catbird
Brown Thrasher
Eastern Bluebird

Loggerhead Shrike
Yellow Warbler
Yellow-throat
Bobolink
Eastern Meadowlark
Western Meadowlark
Common Grackle
Cardinal
Indigo Bunting
Dickcissel
Common Goldfinch
Eastern Towhee
Grasshopper Sparrow
Vesper Sparrow
Chipping Sparrow
Field Sparrow
Song Sparrow

WOODLANDS

Cooper's Hawk
Red-shouldered Hawk
Broad-winged Hawk
Yellow-billed Cuckoo
Black-billed Cuckoo
Screech Owl
Barred Owl
Whip-poor-will
Yellow-shafted Flicker
Red-bellied Woodpecker

Hairy Woodpecker
Downy Woodpecker
Crested Flycatcher
Eastern Wood Pewee
Blue Jay
Black-capped Chickadee
Tufted Titmouse
White-breasted Nuthatch
Wood Thrush
Blue-gray Gnatcatcher

Red-eyed Vireo	Baltimore Oriole
Warbling Vireo	Scarlet Tanager
Oven-bird	Rose-breasted Grosbeak
American Redstart	

There are differences in breeding birdlife from border to border in Iowa but these are relatively slight, a situation to be expected in an area whose physiographic features show remarkable uniformity. The Blue-winged Warbler breeds regularly only in eastern Iowa and the Prothonotary Warbler, Cerulean Warbler, Louisiana Water-thrush, and Kentucky Warbler occur primarily as summer residents in eastern and southern Iowa; the Western Kingbird, Brewer's Blackbird, and Lark Sparrow nest mostly from the central part of the state westward; the Bell's Vireo breeds from border to border but is considered fairly common only in the western and southern sections; the Least Flycatcher and Savannah Sparrow may be found regularly in the summer in the extreme north, and the Turkey Vulture and Acadian Flycatcher in the southern half of the state; the Yellow-breasted Chat is fairly common as a nesting bird in southern Iowa and northward in the valleys of the Mississippi and Missouri.

Marshes with cattails, bulrushes, sedges, and other aquatic plants are found for the most part in the lake region of the northwestern part of the state and on the bottoms of the Mississippi and Missouri. Many of the marshes in the lake region hold small breeding populations of Black Terns, Yellow-headed Blackbirds, and Swamp Sparrows. In nearly all the large marshes of Iowa the following birds breed regularly:

Pied-billed Grebe	Sora
American Bittern	Florida Gallinule
Least Bittern	Coot
King Rail	Long-billed Marsh Wren
Virginia Rail	Red-wing

An estimated 50,000 ducks, chiefly the Blue-winged Teal, which is the most common, and the Mallard and Ruddy Duck, are reared in and around the marshes of northwestern Iowa. The Wood Duck breeds along the Mississippi in notable numbers and, less abundantly, around streams and ponds to the west.

The Mississippi and Missouri Valleys on the state's eastern and western boundaries, respectively, are the chief migration routes for birds breeding in north-central North America; hence Iowa is a very good spot for observing many transient waterfowl, waterbirds, shorebirds, and landbirds. Of equal importance as far as heaviness of traffic is concerned, the two routes nevertheless differ from each other with respect to the species using them. Such northern passerine birds as the Yellow-bellied Flycatcher, Winter Wren, Hermit Thrush, Veery, and various warblers—the Golden-winged, Parula, Magnolia, Black-throated Green, Blackburnian, Chestnut-sided, and Canada—are much more abundant in the Mississippi Valley. The Connecticut Warbler follows this route—rarely, if ever, the Missouri route. Whistling Swans are more often seen along the Mississippi, but most other waterfowl appear more commonly along the Missouri. This is true not only of the Blue and Snow Geese, whose spring movements provide the state's outstanding ornithological feature, but also of Gadwalls, Redheads, and others. In addition to waterfowl, birds to be found more frequently in the Missouri Valley than in the Mississippi are the Eared Grebe, White Pelican, Northern Phalarope, Franklin's Gull, and Harris' Sparrow. In Iowa, the main migratory flights in the spring and fall may be expected within the following dates: waterfowl, 10 March—20 April, 10 October—25 November; shorebirds, 1 May—1 June, 1 August—1 October; landbirds, 15 April—20 May, 25 August—20 October.

Horned Larks, Brown Creepers, Cedar Waxwings, Purple Finches, Pine Siskins, Common Goldfinches, Slate-colored Juncos, American Tree Sparrows, and Lapland Longspurs are common during Iowa winters, but the state is too far south to be within the regular winter range of several species of northern fringillids. Thus Common Redpolls, Red Crossbills, and Snow Buntings appear only occasionally, while Evening and Pine Grosbeaks are rare visitors. Few ducks pass the winter in Iowa, because most of the waterways freeze over; yet wherever water containing a sufficient food supply remains open, one may be almost certain to find ducks, particularly American Goldeneyes and American Mergansers. Christmas bird counts made at Des Moines average between 40 and 50 kinds of birds, at Davenport and Sioux City between 25 and 35. The Des Moines count is consistently higher, owing partly to the presence of 5 to 10 species of ducks on the Impounding Reservoir.

The Iowa Ornithologists' Union, with nearly 400 members, publishes a quarterly journal called *Iowa Bird Life* and meets every May and September, at various places in the state. One may contact this organization through the Department of Wildlife Management of Iowa State College at Ames or the State Conservation Commission in Des Moines.

ALGONA. An excellent place for waterbirds, waterfowl, and open-country birds is the UNION SLOUGH NATIONAL WILDLIFE REFUGE (2,075 acres), reached from Algona by going north on US Route 169 through the town of Burt. Two miles north of Burt on the same highway, turn east and drive for 4 miles on an improved gravel road to the Refuge. Headquarters is in Burt. The Refuge consists of a large natural marsh with open water (formerly drained for agricultural purposes but now restored by the construction of four dykes) and about 600 acres of land used for crops and grazing. In the marsh, bulrushes, sedges, pondweeds and other aquatic plants, both emergent and submersed, grow in rich profusion, thus providing ample nesting cover for such birds as Pied-billed Grebes, Least Bitterns, Virginia Rails, Long-billed Marsh Wrens, and Yellow-headed Blackbirds. Waterfowl breeding in the marsh, or in suitable localities elsewhere on the Refuge, are the following (listed in the order of decreasing abundance): Mallard, Pintail, Blue-winged Teal, Baldpate, Wood Duck, Lesser Scaup Duck, Ruddy Duck, and Hooded Merganser. The Refuge provides a haven for waterfowl in the spring and fall, the peaks of abundance being reached in April and October. In addition to many Ring-necked Pheasants, some of the open-country birds nesting on the Refuge are the Upland Plover, Horned Lark, Bobolink, and Western Meadowlark.

AMES. IOWA STATE COLLEGE has a small ornithological collection consisting of 1,285 skins (in the Science

Building) and 500 mounts (in the Museum Annex), representing chiefly Mississippi Valley species. There are over 1,200 books and bound volumes of periodicals on birds in the central College Library. Courses offered include Bird Study (of raptorial and song birds) and Game Birds, as well as Techniques in Wildlife Management, Wildlife Administration, and Wildlife Conservation, which are concerned in part with birds.

The central part of the 2,000-acre campus is attractively landscaped with a broad sweep of lawn and well-grouped trees and shrubs. Of special interest to ornithological students is PAMMEL WOODS, a preserve of 30 acres at the northwest corner. This tract, lying along Clear Creek, is well forested with oak and hickory on higher ground, maple and basswood on the lower. Thickets of sumac, hazelnut, and elderberry occur in the more open areas. Some of the species of birds found nesting here at one time or another are the Cooper's Hawk, Mourning Dove, Barred Owl, Ruby-throated Hummingbird, Yellow-shafted Flicker, Red-bellied Woodpecker, Red-headed Woodpecker, Crested Flycatcher, Blue Jay, Black-capped Chickadee, White-breasted Nuthatch, House Wren, Catbird, Brown Thrasher, Wood Thrush, Red-eyed Vireo, Cardinal, Rose-breasted Grosbeak, Common Goldfinch, and Eastern Towhee.

BOONE. LEDGES STATE PARK in central Iowa, 6 miles south of Boone via State Route 164, is in pleasing contrast to the monotony of the surrounding farmland. Here the visitor drops down into a scenic valley, walled by huge sandstone ledges, to find trees, shrubs, and wildflowers growing in rich profusion. Pease Creek descends rapidly through the valley to join the Des Moines River within the Park's boundaries. All parts of the Park, comprising 698 acres, are easily accessible by good foot trails, automobile roads, and rustic bridges.

Bird finding is at its best here in the late spring and summer. A few predators, such as the Cooper's, Red-tailed, and Red-shouldered Hawks, nest regularly. The chants of Whip-poor-wills can be heard during the evening. Eastern Phoebes find suitable nesting sites under bridges and overhanging ledges, Rough-winged Swallows in the tile drains emerging from bridge abutments. Along the tree-shaded edges of the Des Moines River, Wood Duck broods, Green Herons, and Black-crowned Night Herons are commonly observed. Among the other birds known to occur during the nesting season are the Wood Thrush, Blue-gray Gnat-catcher, Bell's Vireo, Cerulean Warbler, Scarlet Tanager, Rose-breasted Grosbeak, and Indigo Bunting. Further information on the birdlife in the Park may be obtained at the Trading Post in the lower picnic area or at the custodian's residence near by.

CEDAR FALLS. During the 26 years that the Iowa Ornithologists' Union has been taking a Sunday-morning field trip at its annual May convention (in 15 localities well scattered over the state), the largest combined total number of species (150) was counted on 8 May 1937, at Cedar Falls in the east-central part of the state. Most of the region is intensely cultivated with wooded sections limited to the borders of rivers, creeks, and sloughs where the trees consist of oak, hickory, sugar maple, and basswood on the uplands, ash and silver maple in the lowlands.

With the exception of GOOSE LAKE, no single area is particularly impressive for bird finding. Goose Lake, 7 miles northwest of Cedar Falls, is only a small pond (36 acres) in a sandy prairie. It seems to owe its interesting bird population to the fact that it is relatively undisturbed; since it is in a treeless basin, its approaches are visible in all directions from the pond itself. There are a dozen smaller ponds scattered in an area stretching half a mile west and south and a mile east, with bulrush marshes and sandy prairie interspersed. Goose Lake may dry up completely during a summer with low rainfall. Nesting birds in this area include the Pied-billed Grebe, American Bittern, Least Bittern, Blue-winged Teal, Marsh Hawk, Sora, Coot, Black Tern, Long-billed Marsh Wren, Bobolink, and several sparrows—Grasshopper, Vesper, Clay-colored, and Swamp. From 15 March to 15 April about 200 ducks can usually be found in the vicinity, with 10 species present on almost any early April day. In order of abundance these are: Blue-winged Teal, Lesser Scaup Duck, Mallard, Ring-necked Duck,

Shoveler, Pintail, Baldpate, Green-winged Teal, Redhead, Canvas-back, Gadwall, Ruddy Duck, Wood Duck, Buffle-head, American Golden-eye, Hooded Merganser, and Red-breasted Merganser. Geese, in spite of the name of the Lake, occur only rarely. Other regular spring transients include the Horned Grebe, Eared Grebe, Black-crowned Night Heron, Osprey, Pigeon Hawk, King Rail, Virginia Rail, Yellow Rail, Florida Gallinule (sometimes nests), Semipalmated Plover, Wilson's Phalarope, Ring-billed Gull, Franklin's Gull (fall), Bonaparte's Gull, Forster's Tern, Tree Swallow, Cliff Swallow, Short-billed Marsh Wren, Palm Warbler, Yellow-headed Blackbird, Savannah Sparrow, Sharp-tailed Sparrow, and Lincoln's Sparrow. Seen less regularly are the Whistling Swan, Black-bellied Plover, Willet, Dowitcher, Knot, Hudsonian Godwit, American Pipit, Leconte's Sparrow, Henslow's Sparrow, and Baird's Sparrow.

To reach Goose Lake, drive 2.4 miles west on US Route 20 from the junction with US Route 218 in Cedar Falls; north on County Route K for 2.7 miles; west on County Route Z (unmarked and sometimes impassable in spring floods) for 1.3 miles; and finally half a mile north on a lane to the west side of a farmyard, at the end of the road, where locked gates prevent further driving. Goose Lake, half a mile to the northeast, is owned by Waterloo sportsmen, who use it for fall shooting, but bird finders are welcome except during the hunting season. The best procedure is to walk around the lakeshore and then visit the ponds to the east.

CEDAR RAPIDS. There are a number of opportunities for bird finding at Cedar Rapids, an industrial city in the rolling farmland of east-central Iowa.

Within the city limits is CEDAR LAKE, covering about 100 acres, where numerous migrating waterfowl congregate. Owing to the fact that its waters are constantly used for industrial purposes, it fails to freeze over in the winter. Hence such ducks as the American Golden-eye and Hooded Merganser frequently remain through the winter months, even when temperatures dip below zero. Cedar Lake can be approached from the center of the city by turning north on Twelfth Street from First Avenue East.

South of the city, a marshy, 40-acre slough called SWAN LAKE attracts not only transient waterfowl but also shore-birds and marshbirds. Among the species to be observed are the Virginia Rail, Greater and Lesser Yellow-legs, Red-backed Sandpiper, Dowitcher, and Wilson's Phalarope. Snow and Blue Geese and the Sharp-tailed Sparrow may sometimes be seen in the fall. In June and early July the Least Bittern is known to nest regularly and broods of Wood Ducks frequently make an appearance. Swan Lake is reached from Cedar Rapids by going 11.8 miles south from the city limits on US Route 218, then west 1 mile, south 1 mile, and finally west again for another mile.

LAKE MACBRIDE STATE PARK (784 acres) is reached by going farther south on Route 218 to North Liberty (18 miles from Cedar Rapids), then turning north-east on State Route 382 for 5 miles. In the Park is Lake Macbride, a 246-acre body of water formed by a dam just below the confluence of two small creeks. In the spring and fall, transient Green-winged Teal are exceptionally abun-dant here, though they are exceeded in number by tran-sient Mallards, Blue-winged Teal, Pintails, and Lesser Scaup Ducks. In the timbered country that surrounds the Lake, landbird finding is often rewarding.

COE COLLEGE, on First Avenue between Twelfth and Thirteenth Streets in Cedar Rapids, has in its museum, on the top floor of Science Hall, a series of bird mounts and a few skins representing Iowa species. The Cedar Rapids Bird Club meets regularly at Coe College on the first Mon-day evening of each month during the academic year. Field trips and public lectures are among the Club's activities. The organization may be contacted through the Division of Biological Sciences at Science Hall.

CHEROKEE. A small but nonetheless authentic piece of virgin prairie is the AURELIA FARM MEADOW (20 acres), owned by Nestor L. Stiles of this city. Never having been plowed or grazed, the vegetation exists today in prac-tically the same condition as it once did over much of the state. The area is well worth a visit in the spring, when the prairie flowers are in bloom. Some of the birds nesting on the tract are the Bobolink, Western Meadowlark, Grass-hopper Sparrow, and Savannah Sparrow. The Meadow, southwest of Aurelia Cemetery and 1.5 miles from the center of town, is closed to the public and may not be entered without the guidance of the owner. Bird finders are welcome if they will first make an appointment with Mr. Stiles, who may be reached at the Cherokee State Bank.

COUNCIL BLUFFS. Lake Manawa in LAKE MANAWA STATE PRESERVE (1,045 acres) is a meander cutoff of the Missouri River and lies on flat, alluvial bottomland. The north side is developed with cottages and recreational facilities, but southward between the Lake and the Missouri the land is forested, principally with cottonwood, boxelder, and willow. Here in late May, June, and early July, Crested Flycatchers and Tree Swallows occupy abandoned woodpecker holes in willow stubs, and Bell's Vireos breed commonly in marginal thickets. On the sandy southern shore of the Lake, and on a long sand spit extending in an easterly direction from the south shore, Piping Plovers and Least Terns find suitable nesting habitat.

Lake Manawa is just south of Council Bluffs and may be reached by going south on State Route 192 (South Seventh Street), which leads to the Park and to a road encircling the Lake. The woods, sandy shore, and sand spit on the south side are only a short walk from the road.

DAVENPORT. In this urban area, which consists of Davenport on the Iowa side of the Mississippi, and Rock Island and Moline on the Illinois side, the best spot for bird finding is CREDIT ISLAND PARK (about 2.5 miles in length and half a mile in width), belonging to the city of Davenport. Much of the Island has been developed for recreational purposes, with golf courses, picnic grounds, and an artificial lagoon, but the remainder has a bottomland forest of silver maple, American elm, hackberry, swamp white oak, basswood, cottonwood, and willow. Breeding birds of the forest include the Wood Duck, Red-shouldered Hawk, Barred Owl, Red-bellied Woodpecker, Crested Flycatcher, Tufted Titmouse, White-breasted Nuthatch, Warbling Vireo, Prothonotary Warbler, American Redstart, and (in open areas) the Bewick's Wren. In May and September as many as 23 species of transient warblers may be found in the forest and in the wooded parts of recreational areas. In late March and April and late October and November, the shallow harbor on the north side of the Island attracts many ducks, including the Black Duck, Ring-necked Duck, Lesser Scaup Duck, American Golden-eye, Buffle-head, Hooded Merganser, American Merganser, and Red-breasted Merganser. Great Blue Herons, American Egrets, and Black-crowned Night Herons are fairly common near the shore in late summer. If, during May, August, and early September, the water in the harbor recedes to expose mud flats, the Black-bellied Plover, Red-backed Sandpiper, Dowitcher, and other shorebirds—altogether 14 species—sometimes make an appearance. From the Island's south side, which faces the Mississippi channel, huge numbers of Herring and Ring-billed Gulls, and smaller numbers of Caspian Terns and Black Terns may be seen in the spring and fall. The outstanding attraction in the winter is the Bald Eagle, which occurs in large numbers (sometimes as many as 40) along the River from the time the surface freezes (usually mid-December) until the break-up (toward the end of February). To reach the Park, drive west from Davenport on US Route 61 to Schmidt Road, turn left, and follow a well-marked road.

The DAVENPORT PUBLIC MUSEUM, 704 Brady Street, has a small collection of skins of North American birds and over 500 bird mounts, representing many North American and some South American and Asiatic species.

DES MOINES. Iowa's capital city lies in the central part of the state, where the gently rolling agricultural land is broken up by the Des Moines River and its tributary, the Raccoon River. Near the city are two areas that are of interest to bird finders.

The new DES MOINES WATERWORKS IMPOUNDING RESERVOIR (200 acres), 12 miles southwest of the business district, is excellent for transient waterbirds and waterfowl. This is reached by driving west on Grand Avenue (State Route 90), then turning south on State Route 123 to the airport. From the airport turn west on

State Route 28. The first road to the right beyond the curve leads to the Reservoir, around which there is an 8-mile drive. There are two gates to the drive, both of which close at sundown. From mid-October to early December, and from mid-March through April, large flocks of the more common ducks can be seen on the Reservoir, and there is a possibility of observing such irregular or uncommon visitants as the Horned and Eared Grebes, White Pelican, Blue Goose (especially in the fall), American Golden-eye, Buffle-head, and Ruddy Duck. In the open areas adjacent to the Reservoir the Eastern and Western Meadowlarks and the Dickcissel are common in late spring and summer. At this same time of year, look for the Bell's Vireo, which is known to nest near the Reservoir in places where there are shrubby thickets.

Approximately 6 miles north of the intersection of Grand and Second Avenues, State Route 60 passes through MARGO FRANKEL WOODS (about 113 acres). During late April and May, transient landbirds pass through this hardwoods area in great numbers. At the height of migration, which occurs in the first half of May, it is possible to list 85 species. Among birds known to breed here are the Cooper's Hawk, Great Horned Owl, and Whip-poor-will. A spring-fed stream on the west side of the highway is attractive to the Spotted Sandpiper and Louisiana Waterthrush.

Most of the bird finders residing in this city belong to the Des Moines Audubon Society, which may be contacted through the Public Library on First Street between Walnut and Locust Streets. Activities of the organization consist of publishing *The Warbler* (bimonthly), sponsoring public lectures, conducting monthly field trips, and operating a small sanctuary at 853 Twenty-eighth Street.

DUBUQUE. In the environs of this city, whose business district lies close to the Mississippi River, at the foot of high bluffs, are several places for bird finding recommended by the Dubuque Audubon Club.

EAGLE POINT PARK (133 acres), at the termination of Shiras Avenue in the northeast corner of Dubuque, is a wooded area on the bluffs overlooking the Mississippi.

Included in its wide variety of breeding birds are the Pileated and Red-bellied Woodpeckers, Wood Thrush, Blue-gray Gnatcatcher, and Scarlet Tanager.

Below the GOVERNMENT LOCKS and DAM NUMBER 11 on the Mississippi, transient waterbirds and ducks gather in considerable numbers. American Egrets appear in the late summer; Lesser Scaup Ducks in the spring and fall; American Golden-eyes, American Mergansers, and Red-breasted Mergansers in the winter. A few Bald Eagles are not infrequently seen in the winter. The Dam may be reached by turning east onto Lincoln Avenue at the end of Rhomberg Avenue, or by proceeding across High Bridge.

Immediately north of the city limits, US Route 52 passes a stretch of marshes where Virginia Rails, Soras, Long-billed Marsh Wrens, and many other marsh-inhabiting species may be found nesting in late May and June.

The Dubuque Audubon Club meets every month of the year, except during the summer, in the Biology Room of the Senior High School. Field Trips are taken regularly. Contact the organization through the High School.

IOWA CITY. The largest ornithological collection in Iowa is maintained by the Museum of Natural History, on the third floor of Macbride Hall, Jefferson Street at Capitol Street, on the east-side campus of the UNIVERSITY OF IOWA. Ornithological research materials consist of 20,000 skins and 8,000 egg sets, mostly of North American species. Bird Hall, separated from Mammal Hall by the balcony of the auditorium, has a fine exhibit of 1,276 bird mounts, but its outstanding feature is the Laysan Island Cyclorama, a remarkably detailed and realistic representation of the famous Pacific island bird refuge. The Museum is a department in the University's School of Fine Arts and has the distinction of being one of the few institutions, if not the only institution, in the United States to offer instruction in the scientific and artistic technique of museum curatorship and exhibition.

LANSING. The bottoms of the Mississippi from Lansing north to the Minnesota line are included in the great UPPER MISSISSIPPI RIVER WILDLIFE AND FISH

REFUGE (headquarters address: Box 269, Winona, Minnesota). The Refuge consists of a maze of channels, small green islands, ponds, shady sloughs, marshes, and wooded swamps. In any season of the year, except in the winter, bird finding is invariably rewarding. In the spring and fall, Canada Geese and several species of ducks (e.g. Mallard, Baldpate, Lesser Scaup Duck) are abundant, and Common Loons and Double-crested Cormorants appear in considerable numbers. Small flocks of Whistling Swans occasionally linger on isolated stretches of water for a few days in early spring. In late summer and early fall, American Egrets can be found along sloughs and ponds. Migrating Bald Eagles and Ospreys are not unusual. Breeding birds include the following: in marshes, the Mallard, Blue-winged Teal, Marsh Hawk, King Rail (not common), Virginia Rail, Sora, Long-billed Marsh Wren, and Yellow-throat; in the bottomland woods and wooded swamps, the Great Blue Heron, Black-crowned Night Heron, Wood Duck (quite common), Cooper's Hawk, Red-shouldered Hawk, Barred Owl, Prothonotary Warbler, Louisiana Water-thrush, and American Redstart.

State Route 182 going north from Lansing to New Albion, a distance of 12 miles, skirts the Mississippi bottoms —the Refuge is on one side and the high rocky bluffs on the other. Yellow-breasted Chats breed in fair numbers in thickets adjacent to the highway and may sometimes be seen on telephone wires. During migration in May, Connecticut Warblers may be found on the wooded banks of the Upper Iowa River where Route 182 crosses this River just south of New Albion. The only satisfactory way to explore the Refuge for birds is by boat. At New Albion arrangements may be made with a commercial fisherman for a powerboat trip. If possible, secure the fisherman's services as a guide, thus avoiding the possibility of getting lost in the network of channels.

MT. VERNON. This is the home of CORNELL COLLEGE, which offers a summer-school course in ornithology and has one of Iowa's best ornithological libraries, the core of which was the personal collection of the late T. C. Stephens.

OTTUMWA. A meat-packing city of some 33,000 people, Ottumwa lies on the Des Moines River in southeastern Iowa, about 75 miles from the Mississippi and 35 miles from the Missouri line. In the city itself there are two particularly good places for bird finding. One, commonly known as COMMUNITY GARDENS, is on a large island in the Des Moines River, practically in the center of the city. To reach it, drive west along Main Street to Wapello Street, then to the left across railroad tracks and a channel of the River. Continue straight ahead for a mile to the gate; park the car here and proceed on foot over any one of several roads that lead past willow-bordered ponds and through areas forested with maple, cottonwood, basswood, boxelder, elm, and their thick undergrowth. From mid-July to the first of October, American Egrets and other herons are usually quite common in the ponds; from mid-April to late May, transient warblers and other small landbirds pass through the woods, sometimes in impressive numbers. One local ornithologist has, in recent years, observed a total of 149 species in Community Gardens.

A second place for bird finding, HAMILTON PARK, is in the northern part of the city. The Park is reached by driving north on Court Street to Woodland Avenue, then right (east) on Woodland Avenue for two blocks to the end of the street. Leave the car here and walk downhill into an area on the left where a great variety of trees such as elms, catalpas, maples, oaks, locusts, mulberries, hickories, and wild cherries form a heavy forest cover. Like Community Gardens, Hamilton Park is attractive to transient landbirds. During the noon hour on 14 May 1945, 21 species of warblers were recorded by a local ornithologist in an area less than a quarter of a city block in size. Bird species breeding regularly in Hamilton Park include the Red-tailed Hawk, Barred Owl, Red-bellied Woodpecker, Crested Flycatcher, Eastern Wood Pewee, Wood Thrush, Yellow-throated Vireo, Yellow Warbler, Yellow-throat, and Eastern Towhee.

LAKE WAPELLO STATE PARK (1,131 acres), southwest of Ottumwa, is a wooded area in which is located Lake Wapello, an artificial body of water covering 287 acres. Canada Geese, Snow Geese, Blue Geese, and many

ducks visit the Lake in early spring and in the fall. Small
flocks of White Pelicans appear on occasion, usually in
early May. Among the landbirds known to nest in the Park
are the Mockingbird, Orchard Oriole, and Scarlet Tanager.
One end of the Lake is quite marshy and consequently attractive to bitterns, rails, and other marshbirds. To reach
the Park from Ottumwa, go south for 14 miles on US Route
63, then turn right on State Route 273 to Lake Wapello,
a distance of about 13 miles.

SIDNEY. In extreme southwestern Iowa, about midway between Sidney and Hamburg on US Route 275, take State
Route 2 west for 2 miles. At the top of a bluff, turn onto a
short, dead-end road (State Route 239) leading to the
custodian's residence in WAUBONSIE STATE PARK
(620 acres). Near by is the Overlook, where one may obtain
a remarkable view—of Nebraska, across the Missouri River,
9 miles to the west; of Missouri, 4 miles to the south; and,
if one has good eyesight (or imagination), of Kansas, 40
miles southwest.

The Overlook is on a high loess bluff. From it, footpaths
lead over the crests of neighboring bluffs, mostly grass-
covered, and down through wooded ravines to a valley floor
about 300 feet below. Various shrubs, such as dogwood,
coralberry, and wild plum, grow commonly on the slopes of
the bluffs, while redbuds and papaws are abundant in the
ravines—conspicuously so in May, when they come into
bloom. Birds of special interest to be found in various parts
of the Park from the middle of May through July are both
the Scarlet and Summer Tanagers, as well as the Wood
Thrush, Blue-gray Gnatcatcher, Bell's Vireo, Kentucky
Warbler, Yellow-breasted Chat, Orchard Oriole, Indigo
Bunting, Lark Sparrow, and Field Sparrow. The Tanagers
and Kentucky Warbler can be heard along the trails that
lead from the Overlook through the wooded ravines to the
east, north, and west of the custodian's residence. To find
the Chat, take the trail south from the Overlook past the
shelter, then to the top of the ridge along the service road
for half a mile. The birds prefer the plum thickets that
thrive along the fence of this ridge. The Bell's Vireo often
occurs here, too. Another place to find the Bell's Vireo is in

a brushy area just outside the entrance gate. The Lark Sparrow and Field Sparrow have their territories on the prairie ridges west of the Overlook, reached by following the ridge road south for a quarter of a mile and then west.

One of the best places in western Iowa for seeing the remarkable spring concentrations of Snow Geese and Blue Geese is FORNEY LAKE STATE REFUGE (856 acres), which may be reached from Sidney as follows: proceed north on US Route 275 to its intersection with State Route 145, then turn west on State Route 145 to Thurman, and continue west on County Route D to McPaul; then turn north on County Route G, which soon passes the west side of the Lake. The Geese appear in the Forney Lake area in early March, when winter has begun to retreat. Sometimes late winter storms force them southward for short periods. The concentrations usually reach a peak, often as great as half a million or more, between 10 and 20 March. With binoculars or a telescope, one may obtain excellent views of the birds as they loiter about the Lake. Since they are characteristically restless and noisy, the slightest disturbance, such as a passing airplane, causes the entire multitude to take off in a swirling mass of white and gray forms and a deafening clamor of voices. Early in the morning, large numbers fly off to feed on waste grain in near-by cornfields, while in the late afternoon, especially at sunset, there is another heavy movement as the birds return for the night. Throughout the day small groups return and depart—the shuttling back and forth between feeding and loitering grounds is almost constant. The immense numbers of Snow and Blue Geese, the latter outnumbering the former about 20 to 1, practically eclipse the other waterfowl: small flocks of Canada Geese, scattered numbers of White-fronted Geese, and small flocks of ducks, including Mallards, Baldpates, Pintails, Redheads, and American Mergansers.

SIOUX CITY. This, the second largest city in the state, covers over 45 square miles of bottomlands and bluffs along the western boundary, where the Big Sioux and Floyd Rivers meet the Missouri and where, across the Iowa boundary, South Dakota meets Nebraska. Outside the city

200 A Guide to Bird Finding

limits are timbered areas, oxbow lakes (meander cutoffs), marshy sloughs, and great stretches of farmlands that were once marshlands and prairie. Because these physiographic features are attractive to a wide variety of birds, opportunities for bird finding are seemingly limitless—a situation fully enjoyed by the Sioux City Bird Club.

The MISSOURI RIVER BOTTOMS southeast of the city comprise vast grainfields, together with a few marshy places, patches of willows and shrubs, and groves of cottonwoods, elms, hackberries, boxelders, maples, basswoods, and ashes. Here and there huge ditches and dykes have been constructed to control the water level. Between 19 and 28 March, or earlier if the season is earlier, the Bottoms between Luton and Hornick are the locale of Sioux City's topnotch ornithological attraction—the enormous goose and duck concentrations. One of the best spots for witnessing the spectacle may be reached as follows: Drive southward from the city on State Route 141, pass the Old Hanson Trading Post 8 miles from the city limits, and turn right at an unpaved crossroad 2 miles farther on. Follow the road for half a mile to the Williams Farm; continue on this road for another half a mile to a small wooden bridge over a ditch. Cross the ditch and bear left on a road paralleling it. (The road has a gravel surface as far as the Williams Farm, but thereafter it is gumbo and unsuitable for travel in wet weather.) Soon after passing the Williams Farm, one will begin to see hundreds, and frequently thousands, of geese (Snow and Blue Geese, smaller numbers of Canada Geese, and a few White-fronted Geese) and ducks (Mallards, Gadwalls, Baldpates, Green-winged and Blue-winged Teal, Redheads, Ring-necked Ducks, Canvas-backs, and Lesser Scaup Ducks), feeding or resting on the partially flooded fields. Excellent views may be obtained from the road and near-by dyke beyond the wooden bridge. At the time of the waterfowl concentrations, other birds that may be observed in suitable habitats include Pied-billed Grebes, Coots, Short-eared Owls, Red-bellied Woodpeckers, Red-breasted Nuthatches, Winter Wrens, Eastern Bluebirds, Golden-crowned and Ruby-crowned Kinglets, Yellow-headed Blackbirds, and American Tree Sparrows.

In the wide valley of the Missouri directly south of Sioux

City are several areas, especially BROWERS LAKE, BROWNS LAKE WOODS, and BROWNS LAKE, that are excellent for a rich variety of birds. To reach these spots, proceed south on US Route 75 through Sergeant Bluff to the road to the airport on the right (State Route 378). Follow the airport road for about 10 rods, then turn left on Inside Road, which immediately passes southward. Browers Lake is about 2 miles from the last turn and is worthy of field work any spring, early summer, or fall day. Numerous transient species stop here. Eastern Bluebirds, Black-capped Chickadees, and several species of woodpeckers nest in dead trees that stand at the northern end of the Lake. Many Red-wings and a few Long-billed Marsh Wrens also find suitable nesting sites.

Continue southward on Inside Road. Browns Lake Woods (40 acres) is on the left about 2 miles from Browers Lake. The terrain here is quite low and often partly flooded in early spring. In some places there are fine stands of bottomland timber; in other places there are thickets of gooseberry, dogwood, and prickly ash, and patches of bluegrass. In late April and early May, Harris' Sparrows are often very common. After mid-May, summer-resident Orchard Orioles and Indigo Buntings and a pair or two of Blue Grosbeaks may be expected. From about 10 to 15 May one can count on seeing enormous waves of warblers, frequently as many as a dozen species.

Again continue on Inside Road, this time to a point 7 miles from Route 75, and watch for a sign on the left indicating the road to BIGELOW STATE PARK (40 acres). Turn left, then left again at the Park entrance not far beyond. Browns Lake, an oxbow, is in the Park. A few ducks always appear on this body of water in the spring, but in late April or early May it is more attractive to White Pelicans (over 800 have been counted at one time), Herring Gulls, Ring-billed Gulls, and Franklin's Gulls. Only a short walking distance from the shore of the Lake are timbered spots where Red-tailed Hawks, Great Horned Owls, Barred Owls, and Red-bellied Woodpeckers are known to breed. From 4,000 to 6,000 Mallards usually winter on Browns Lake.

LOGAN PARK CEMETERY and STONE STATE

PARK, both on the northwestern outskirts of Sioux City, are convenient for good bird finding the year round. Logan Park Cemetery occupies 100 acres of rolling country that was once virgin prairie. From its entrance, on the west side of Stone Park Boulevard (State Route 12), winding drives lead to all parts. Although the area is extensively landscaped, the introduction of many trees and shrubs, native as well as exotic, has provided the Cemetery with splendid cover and food for woodland and forest-edge birds. The presence of pines, cedars, spruces, and other conifers has encouraged the Pine Siskin to become a permanent resident and the Red Crossbill a frequent winter visitant. Great numbers of passerine species, including the Olive-backed and Gray-cheeked Thrushes and the Lincoln's and Harris' Sparrows, pass through in migration (late April and early May, September and early October). Stone State Park (912 acres) is comprised of loess bluffs and wooded valleys along the east bank of the Big Sioux River. Its entrance on the west side may be reached by driving west from Sioux City on US Route 77 (Gordon Drive) to the junction with Military Road, then turning right and following directional signs to the Park, about 2 miles distant. Unlike Logan Park Cemetery, much of this area exists in its natural wild beauty. The valleys are heavily wooded with ash, hawthorn, elm, basswood, boxelder, cottonwood, and several species of oaks and are carpeted with wildflowers in the spring; on the more exposed slopes wild plum, sumac, and other shrubs grow in dense thickets. All parts of the Park are readily accessible by well-marked trails and bridle paths. Members of the Sioux City Bird Club consider Stone Park as good for transient birds as Logan Park Cemetery and better for breeding birds. From the last week of May some of the species that may be found nesting in Stone Park are the Cooper's Hawk, Red-tailed Hawk, Yellow-billed Cuckoo, Red-bellied Woodpecker, Crested Flycatcher, Wood Thrush, Bell's Vireo, Scarlet Tanager, Indigo Bunting, Eastern Towhee, and Lark Sparrow.

The Sioux City Bird Club may be contacted through the Chamber of Commerce, 1210 Badgerow Building. This organization of 600 members publishes *The Dickcissel* (quarterly), holds regular meetings every third Tuesday of the month in the Art Center (613½ Pierce Street) at 7:30 P.M., and sponsors such activities as field trips and public lectures.

SPIRIT LAKE. Dickinson County, bordering the Minnesota line in northwestern Iowa, embraces the state's principal lake region. The county seat, Spirit Lake, is named for the largest lake in the group (also the largest natural lake in the state), which lies directly north.

Because of the varied bird habitats afforded by the lakes themselves and their immediate surroundings, the lake region is decidedly productive ornithologically. It is estimated that no less than 90 bird species breed in the region, while regular transient and wintering species easily double that number. WEST OKOBOJI LAKE, southwest of the town of Spirit Lake, occupies the center of this region and possesses a combination of habitats that makes for good bird finding. About 5.5 miles long by 2.5 miles wide at one point, it has many small bays and peninsulas, making it exceptionally picturesque. Willows, cottonwoods, boxelders, green ashes, wild plums, clumps of buckbrush, and (on higher ground) bur oaks border much of the Lake, usually in a narrow fringe, but in several localities to a depth of a mile. Among the woodland and forest-edge birds known to breed here are the Yellow-billed and Black-billed Cuckoos, Hairy and Downy Woodpeckers, Western Kingbird, Blue Jay, Black-capped Chickadee, White-breasted Nuthatch, House Wren, Catbird, Brown Thrasher, Yellow-throated Vireo, Red-eyed Vireo, Warbling Vireo, Yellow Warbler (very common), Baltimore Oriole, Rose-breasted Grosbeak, and Indigo Bunting. The Cooper's Hawk, Crested Flycatcher, and Wood Thrush nest in the deeper woods. Grassy meadows and marshes with rushes, sedges, and cattails also border the Lake in a few places, creating nesting situations for such species as the Pied-billed Grebe, Least Bittern, King Rail, Virginia Rail, Coot, Forster's Tern, Black Tern, Long-billed Marsh Wren, Short-billed Marsh Wren, Yellow-throat, Yellow-headed Blackbird, and Swamp Sparrow. Where there are drier meadows, the Upland Plover may be found nesting.

West Okoboji and the other larger lakes of the region

attract fair numbers of transient geese and ducks during the last of March and early April. A few Common Loons and Double-crested Cormorants always show up at the same time. From mid-April through the first week of May, White Pelicans are in evidence, sometimes in flocks of 200 or 300 individuals. In August, a few American Egrets appear and in early September immense numbers of Franklin's Gulls gather on the water and feed in the surrounding farmland.

Bird finders coming to West Okoboji in the summer are welcome to visit the IOWA LAKESIDE LABORATORY (open from early June through August), on the west shore of the Lake, overlooking Miller's Bay, to obtain information on the exact locations of the best bird habitats. The Laboratory may be reached by driving west from Spirit Lake on State Route 9 for 4 miles, then turning left on State Route 32 and proceeding 3.5 miles to the entrance road. First opened in 1909, the Laboratory is operated by three state colleges as a summer station for undergraduate and graduate work in field biology. Part of the Laboratory grounds is a restored prairie of over 50 acres where one may find nesting Bobolinks, Western Meadowlarks, and Grasshopper Sparrows.

Contributing authorities: Charles C. Ayres, Jr., Albert C. Berkowitz, Homer R. Dill, J. Harold Ennis, Martin L. Grant, Fred T. Hall, George O. Hendrickson, Henry Herrmann, James Hodges, Myrle L. Jones, Mrs. Myrle L. Jones, Miss Zell C. Lee, Thomas Morrissey, R. Allyn Moser, Mrs. Harold R. (Helen) Peasley, Fred J. Pierce, F. L. R. Roberts, Mary Price Roberts, Milfred J. Smith, Charles A. Stewart, Bruce F. Stiles, Nestor L. Stiles, Robert F. Vane, Mrs. Robert F. (Jean Witmer) Vane, William Youngworth.

Kansas

AMERICAN MAGPIE

Rectangular Kansas, in the geographical center of the United States, has no mountains or extensive forests, no natural lakes or navigable rivers. Kansas is grassland—or, in the words of a famous native Kansan, William Allen White, a 'slanting slab of prairie sod.'

The 410-mile stretch of Kansas terrain between Missouri and Colorado rises steadily at an average of 8 feet per mile, or 3,401 feet altogether. The surface is alternately flat or rolling, and occasionally interrupted by low hills and ravines. The lowest point (743 feet elevation) lies in the southeastern corner of the state; the highest (4,135 feet) lies on the western boundary.

Most of eastern and central Kansas, roughly two thirds of the state, was originally open, tall-grass prairie. Trees were restricted to particular areas. For example, silver maples, elms, boxelders, sycamores, green ashes, cottonwoods, and willows bordered rivers and streams; oaks and hickories stood on the uplands in the extreme eastern part of the state. Today, the rich soils of eastern and central Kansas have become valuable agricultural and grazing lands. Small 'general' farms of two or three hundred acres, with pastures for dairy herds and fields for hay and diversified crops, are prevalent in eastern Kansas; in central Kansas, on the other hand, the farms commonly exceed 300 acres and are specialized either for growing wheat or for raising cattle. In general, the country is less open than it was, for, as a result of extensive tree planting, there are now many groves, shelterbelts, and orchards. In contrast to most areas, settlement here has brought about an increase, rather than a decrease, in tree growth.

Western Kansas, the remaining third of the state, lies on the Great Plains, an area of greater dryness. Winds here seem never to stop: western Kansas has the reputation of being one of the windiest localities in the interior of the United States. Great sections of the terrain are as flat as a land surface can possibly be. The predominant natural cover of short grasses, chiefly buffalo and grama, is used in places for grazing, but a great proportion has been plowed under for the cultivation of wheat and sorghum. Some parts of western Kansas have a desert-like aspect characterized by an abundance of sagebrush, cacti, and yuccas; others have eroded gullies and river valleys where cottonwoods, willows, and various shrubs occur. But all in all, the landscape is one of sameness—grainfields and cattle ranges spreading to the level of the horizon, relieved only by a set or two of farm buildings or a small town.

Like other states lying entirely on the interior plains, Kansas is a meeting point of eastern and western avifaunas. Birdlife in eastern Kansas is principally eastern in composition. Central Kansas shows the loss of a few eastern species and the addition of a few western, but in total number of species regularly represented, it is predominantly eastern. Western Kansas has a birdlife that is more characteristically western, though a surprising number of eastern species occasionally appear. Below are listed bird species breeding more or less regularly in eastern or western Kansas, and rarely in both places:

EASTERN KANSAS

Red-shouldered Hawk
Broad-winged Hawk
Barred Owl
Chuck-will's-widow (mainly southeast)
Whip-poor-will
Yellow-shafted Flicker
Red-bellied Woodpecker
Crested Flycatcher
Eastern Wood Pewee
Tufted Titmouse
Carolina Wren
Wood Thrush
White-eyed Vireo
Yellow-throated Vireo
Kentucky Warbler
Orchard Oriole
Scarlet Tanager (mainly northeast)
Summer Tanager
Cardinal
Rose-breasted Grosbeak
Indigo Bunting
Eastern Towhee

WESTERN KANSAS

Ferruginous Hawk
Scaled Quail (southwest only)
Mountain Plover
Burrowing Owl
Red-shafted Flicker
Say's Phoebe
American Magpie
White-necked Raven
Rock Wren
Mountain Bluebird
Bullock's Oriole
Black-headed Grosbeak
Cassin's Sparrow (southwest only)

Over the state from border to border, the following species are known to breed regularly in open country (prairie grassland, pastures, fallow fields, meadow-like lowlands, brushy places, and dooryards) or in large wooded tracts:

OPEN AREAS

Turkey Vulture
Swainson's Hawk (common westward)
Marsh Hawk
Bob-white
Killdeer
Upland Plover
Mourning Dove
Road-runner (southern Kansas)
Barn Owl
Red-headed Woodpecker

OPEN AREAS (*Cont.*)

Eastern Kingbird
Western Kingbird (common westward)
Scissor-tailed Flycatcher (southern Kansas)
Eastern Phoebe (rare westward)
Horned Lark
Barn Swallow
Purple Martin (mainly eastern Kansas)
House Wren
Bewick's Wren (southern Kansas)
Mockingbird
Catbird
Brown Thrasher
Eastern Bluebird
Loggerhead Shrike

Bell's Vireo (mainly eastern Kansas)
Yellow Warbler
Yellow-throat
Yellow-breasted Chat
Eastern Meadowlark (eastern Kansas)
Western Meadowlark (common westward)
Common Grackle
Blue Grosbeak
Painted Bunting (southern Kansas)
Dickcissel
Common Goldfinch
Lark Bunting (common westward)
Grasshopper Sparrow
Chipping Sparrow
Field Sparrow

WOODED TRACTS

Cooper's Hawk
Yellow-billed Cuckoo
Screech Owl
Hairy Woodpecker
Downy Woodpecker
Blue Jay
Black-capped Chickadee
Carolina Chickadee (southern Kansas)

White-breasted Nuthatch
Blue-gray Gnatcatcher (eastern Kansas)
Red-eyed Vireo
Warbling Vireo
American Redstart
Baltimore Oriole

Though lying in the path of the central flyway, which bears a heavy traffic of waterbirds, waterfowl, and shorebirds, Kansas has relatively few places where these birds may stop to feed and loiter. Cheyenne Bottoms (reached from Great Bend) is undoubtedly the most prominent because of the extent of its water area; some of the others are Lake McKinney (reached from Lakin), Lake Shawnee (reached from Topeka), Wyandotte Lake (reached from Kansas City), and the larger rivers that flow eastward across the state. Small landbirds whose habitats are woods and thickets are similarly limited in stopping places; hence they gather in enormous numbers in the groves or tracts of trees and shrubs on river bottoms. Bird finding in these isolated spots, which literally swarm with birds at the height of migration, is an exciting experience for the person accustomed to forested sections of the country where birds are more scattered during their seasonal movements. In Kansas, the main migration flights may be expected within the following dates: for waterfowl, 1 March—10 April, 15 October—10 December; shorebirds, 25 April—25 May, 5 August—10 October; landbirds, 10 April—10 May, 5 September—1 November.

Eastern Kansas lies well within the regular winter range of the Harris' Sparrow and numerous other passerine species, including the Brown Creeper, Golden-crowned Kinglet, Slate-colored Junco, American Tree Sparrow, White-crowned Sparrow, Song Sparrow, and Lapland Longspur. Christmas bird counts made in the vicinity of the larger cities in eastern Kansas record between 40 and 50 species, occasionally more. Not infrequently a few western species, such as the Red-shafted Flicker, Spotted Towhee, and Oregon Junco, are noted.

The Kansas Ornithological Society meets annually at a different place in the state during the third or fourth week of April, usually on a weekend. The *Kansas Ornithological Society Bulletin* is published quarterly. The organization may be contacted through either the Museum of Natural History at the University of Kansas in Lawrence or the Department of Zoology at Kansas State College in Manhattan.

ATCHISON. Bird finders in Atchison invariably go to JACKSON PARK (200 acres) in early May for the warbler migration. Situated on a bluff high above the Missouri River, this public area has undisturbed woods and thickets which attract such transient warblers as the Black and White, Tennessee, Orange-crowned, Myrtle, and Blackpoll. Birds to be found here in the summer months include the Tufted Titmouse, Catbird, Brown Thrasher, Wood Thrush, White-eyed Vireo, Bell's Vireo, Red-eyed Vireo, Warbling Vireo, Yellow Warbler, Kentucky Warbler, and Cardinal.

To reach the Park, drive south on Sixth Street (US Route 73) to the city limits and turn left to the entrance. In the Park, automobile roads wind along the edges of steep bluffs where there are turnouts for views of the Missouri Valley. Some of the best places for birds lie close to the road.

For excellent bird-finding areas (especially for waterfowl and waterbirds) across the Missouri River from Atchison, see under Kansas City and St. Joseph in the Missouri chapter.

BALDWIN CITY. This city in extreme east-central Kansas is the home of BAKER UNIVERSITY, where there is a small museum with 375 mounted birds—largely of local species—on the second floor of Parmenter Commons. The Baldwin Bird Club welcomes visitors to its meetings, which are held on the third Wednesday evening of each month, from September through May, in Mulvane Hall on the University campus. Field trips, though not regularly scheduled, are an integral part of the Club's program. A course in ornithology, with emphasis on field identifica- tion, is given during the second session of the summer school.

One of the productive spots for winter birds and spring transients is a region southwest of town called the SAND- PITS, reached by driving south on Sixth Street to Orange Street, then right on Orange Street for half a mile to a creek. Leave the car and walk south along the creek for half a mile, through an undisturbed stand of deciduous trees (chiefly oak, elm, hickory, and walnut) with fre- quent exposed ledges on the west side of the creek. In winter it is possible, during a trip on foot, to observe 25 to 30 species, among them the Screech Owl, Great Horned Owl, Barred Owl, Red-shafted Flicker, Common Sapsucker, White-breasted Nuthatch, Winter and Carolina Wrens, Golden-crowned Kinglet, Purple Finch, Spotted Towhee, and American Tree, Harris', White-crowned, and Song Sparrows. In the spring, between mid-April and mid-May, an abundance of transients may be found.

BIG HILL, the best place for nesting birds, is 3 miles north from the center of town on an all-weather road (no route number) to Vinland. The Hill has the largest undisturbed woods in the vicinity. Watch the roadside shrubbery for Bewick's Wrens, Bell's Vireos, Blue Grosbeaks, and Painted Buntings. Whip-poor-wills, Chuck-will's-widows, Acadian Flycatchers, Yellow-throated Vireos, Red-eyed Vireos, Parula Warblers, and Kentucky Warblers occupy the woods at the foot of the Hill. Drive along the base of the Hill, which extends north about a mile, to the railroad crossing. Park the car and walk half a mile or so west along the tracks, which follow a steeply banked creek, to a secluded place called the Cliffs, a part of the Big Hill area. Here, in a narrow valley, the Wood Thrush, White-eyed Vireo, Louisiana Water-thrush, and Scarlet and Summer Tanagers are usually summer residents.

GREAT BEND. From this grain and oil center, whose name derives from its location on a wide curve of the Arkansas River in central Kansas, drive north on US Route 281 to Hoisington, turn right (east) at Hoisington on State Route 4, go 1.6 miles beyond the tiny town of Redwing, turn right, and then drive as far as the road goes. This leads to a typical section of an enormous marsh, the CHEYENNE BOTTOMS, 8 miles long and about 3 or 4 miles wide, and covering roughly 18,000 acres. The best times to visit this area are the spring and fall—especially the fall, during October and November, when it attracts one of the greatest concentrations of waterfowl on the central flyway. During wet springs and falls most of the area is under water; nevertheless the water is not deep, and one may wade through cattails and reeds over the entire marsh. Some of the summer-resident species are the Marsh Hawk, King Rail, Coot, Long-billed Marsh Wren, Yellow-headed Blackbird, and Red-wing. Canada Geese, Snow Geese, and Blue Geese, several species of ducks, Sandhill Cranes, Franklin's Gulls, Least Terns, and Black Terns are among the common transients.

The Cheyenne Bottoms have recently been acquired by the Kansas Fish and Game Commission for the purpose of creating a permanent lake by means of a series of dams. When this project has been completed, habitat conditions for both breeding and transient waterbirds and waterfowl will be greatly improved.

The ROBL BIRD-BANDING STATION, a private refuge (160 acres) owned by Mr. Frank W. Robl and open to bird finders, is reached by going east from Great Bend on US Route 50N to Ellinwood, then straight north of town for about 2½ miles. The property comprises level terrain, much of which is used for producing winter wheat. A fenced 16-acre area has a small pond of less than 2 acres, which is fed by a windmill. This small body of water is indeed a place for bird finders desiring close views of waterfowl by the hundreds, sometimes (particularly in the fall) by the thousands.

The most abundant geese are the Canada and White-fronted; the most abundant ducks, the Mallard, Gadwall, Baldpate, Pintail, Green-winged Teal, Blue-winged Teal, and Shoveler. Appearing in small numbers are the Redhead, Ring-necked Duck, Canvas-back, and Lesser Scaup Duck; occasionally a Black Duck or a Wood Duck is seen. The maximum numbers are present in October, November, and December, but impressive numbers occur in March and early April. Both geese and ducks arrive at daylight within the fenced area, where food is provided, and spend the day, then leave at nightfall. Many of the Canada Geese and Mallards stay in the vicinity all winter, while a few pairs of Canada Geese also stay all summer, nesting near the pond or by a small creek not far away.

Another ornithological feature of the refuge is the presence of Sandhill Cranes, which stop regularly in October and March.

Since 1924 Mr. Robl has banded nearly 20,000 ducks and has obtained more than 2,000 returns, some from such distant points as Alaska, Central America, Cuba, Trinidad, and Jamaica.

HAYS. In the west-central part of the state the FORT HAYS KANSAS STATE COLLEGE has a collection of 600 bird mounts representing species of this locality. The collection is in the College Library Building on the campus, at the west end of 6th Street. The College offers a course in ornithology.

This 80-acre campus, bordered on two sides by Big Creek and well-planted with deciduous and coniferous trees and shrubs, is the best area in the vicinity for small landbirds. Some of the breeding species are the Mourning Dove, Yellow-shafted Flicker, Eastern Kingbird, Western King-bird, Blue Jay, Mockingbird, Catbird, Brown Thrasher, Warbling Vireo, Yellow Warbler, Orchard Oriole, Baltimore Oriole, and Black-headed Grosbeak. Southeast of the campus on the 3,600-acre tract of the FORT HAYS AGRI-CULTURAL EXPERIMENT STATION are pastures where one may find such birds as the Bob-white, Killdeer, Upland Plover, Horned Lark, Western Meadowlark, Lark Bunting, Grasshopper Sparrow, and Field Sparrow.

One of the notable eagle roosts in western Kansas is in the CEDAR BLUFFS AREA on the Saline River north of town. To reach this area, which is good for other birds of prey as well, drive north from Hays on US Route 183 for about 15 miles. After crossing the Saline River, take the first dirt road to the left (about a quarter of a mile beyond the River). Follow this road 4 or 5 miles until it turns south and recrosses the River. Just after this crossing of the River, at the point where the main road again turns right, turn left and zigzag for a mile or so eastward toward the Cedar Bluffs. Then park the car, and take a path (somewhat indistinct) to the foot of the cedar-covered Bluffs. The eagles, both Golden and Bald, arrive about the first of November and remain until mid-March. They roost at night in the large elms and cottonwoods at the foot of the Bluffs, and frequently loiter in the vicinity during the day.

HUGOTON. In extreme southwestern Kansas the Cimarron River has cut deeply through the dry, undulating sage-brush country, producing cliffs and terraces along a looping course. Numerous tributaries also cut deeply, forming steep-sided coulees, called the CIMARRON RIVER CANYONS. Both the stream and its tributaries are dry most of the year, but the Canyons hold sufficient moisture to support cottonwoods, willows, and shrubby thickets.

The Canyons are fascinating spots for the bird finder. Oasis-like, they contain the only tree growth in an area of many square miles and thus hold remarkable concentrations of woodland and brush-loving birds. And there is al-

ways an element of the unexpected, for the Canyons are
situated about midway between eastern and western
avifaunas, and they attract species from both. Some of the
breeding birds known to occur are Swainson's Hawk, Great
Horned Owl, Poor-will, Red-shafted Flicker, Ladder-
backed Woodpecker, Eastern Kingbird, Western Kingbird,
Crested Flycatcher, Say's Phoebe, Eastern Wood Pewee,
Blue Jay, American Magpie, Black-capped Chickadee,
Bewick's Wren, Rock Wren (where the sides of the
Canyons are steep), Mockingbird, Brown Thrasher, Red-
eyed Vireo, Yellow Warbler, Orchard Oriole, Baltimore
Oriole, Bullock's Oriole, Summer Tanager, and Cardinal.

The Cimarron River may be reached from Hugoton by
going north on US Route 270 for about 15 miles, or by
going west on State Route 45 and north on State Route
51. The Canyons, of which there are many, may be reached
by walking from either highway along the riverbed. April
through June is the best time of year for visiting the Canyons.

On the drive to the Cimarron River from Hugoton across
the sagebrush country the following birds are likely to be
observed during the spring and summer: Lesser Prairie
Chicken, Bob-white, Scaled Quail (near abandoned farm
buildings), Mourning Dove, Burrowing Owl (in prairie-
dog towns), Horned Lark, White-necked Raven, Eastern
Bluebird, Western Meadowlark, Lark Bunting, Lark Sparrow, and Cassin's Sparrow. If the trip is made in winter,
Mountain Bluebirds will be seen.

KANSAS CITY. WYANDOTTE COUNTY PARK (1,500
acres), embracing Wyandotte Lake (330 acres), is a fine
recreational area northwest of this city in the hills at the
edge of the Missouri River Valley. Take State Route 5
from the city to the southern entrance, 9.5 miles distant.
The Park is open the year round, and bird finding is good
at any time.

Much of the area is woodland, with 27 kinds of trees,
including hackberry, basswood, willow, sycamore, and oak.
A drive around Wyandotte Lake gives ready access to the
best parts of the woodland as well as to brushy edges, open
grassy spaces, and the Lake itself. Wood Thrushes, Ken-

tucky Warblers, Orchard Orioles, Baltimore Orioles, and Indigo Buntings are common breeding birds, while Spotted Towhees and Harris' Sparrows occur regularly in the spring and fall. The Lake attracts as many as 15 species of transient waterfowl in March, early April, October, November, and December. Gulls (the Herring, Ring-billed, and Franklin's) and terns (the Forster's, Common, Least, Caspian, and Black) appear frequently in April, early May, September, and October. Bonaparte's Gulls are sometimes present during October and November.

For a somewhat specialized bird-finding area, drive southwest from Kansas City on State Route 32 to Bonner Springs. At Bonner Springs turn left on State Route 7, cross the Kansas River, and drive south from the bridge for about half a mile. The bird finder will then be in an area of grain and alfalfa fields that extend approximately a mile east and a mile southwest. During late July and August, flocks of Buff-breasted Sandpipers—sometimes as many as 50 in a flock—stop here; quite often a flock also contains Killdeer and Upland Plovers. The fields most likely to attract the birds are those in which the alfalfa has been cut over and raked. In these same fields, transient Bobolinks stop briefly in May and Dickcissels spend the summer. When crossing the Kansas River in the late spring and summer, look over the adjacent riverbanks for Bank Swallow colonies, some of which contain 500 or more breeding pairs.

For additional bird-finding areas that are easily reached from this city, see under Kansas City in the Missouri chapter.

LAKIN. Unlike most prairie towns in southwestern Kansas, Lakin, on US Route 50, has a reservoir in its vicinity —long, narrow LAKE McKINNEY. To reach it, drive east from town on Route 50 for one mile. The Lake stretches northeast for about 7 miles. Much of the Lake is bordered by cattails and other aquatic vegetation, with wheat fields extending beyond in all directions, but at the southern end of the Lake there are broad mud flats and a few cottonwoods and willows standing between them and the highway.

Lake McKinney is worth a passing inspection at any time of the year, but it is particularly good for bird finding in April and early May, when the mud flats are visited by a heavy transient shorebird population that includes such species as the Snowy Plover, Willet, Baird's Sandpiper, Dowitcher, Stilt Sandpiper, Avocet, and Black-necked Stilt. Earlier, in March, a few transient Snow and Blue Geese sometimes loiter on the mud flats along the shore. White Pelicans, Double-crested Cormorants, and Black-crowned Night Herons are of frequent occurrence in the late spring and summer. If the bird finder is lucky, he may see transient Sandhill Cranes and Long-billed Curlews feeding in the neighboring wheat fields, the former in March, the latter in April and early May.

LAWRENCE. The campus of the UNIVERSITY OF KANSAS is attractively situated on Mount Oread, or 'the Hill,' overlooking the Kansas (Kaw) River Valley on the north and on the Wakarusa River Valley on the south. In the Museum of Natural History at the northwest corner of 14th Street and Oread Avenue is housed an excellent ornithological collection containing about 20,000 skins (representing mainly Kansas and certain parts of Mexico) and 10,000 skeletons. The skeleton collection is outstanding, containing an unusually good series of species not well represented in the collections of other institutions. The public exhibits include habitat groups, and noteworthy among these are four that show Missouri Valley birdlife in the four seasons, and one depicting typical plants and animals of a pioneer homestead on the Great Plains of western Kansas. On the main floor is a 550-foot panorama of North American animal life from the Arctic to the Mexican tropics. In the building a second-semester course in elementary ornithology and a summer course in natural history, with emphasis on birds, are given.

About 5 miles northwest of Lawrence lies an oxbow lake of the Kansas River called LAKEVIEW, which is reached by driving north on US Route 59, then west on US Route 40 to the Country Club, turning right, and proceeding north for 2 miles, west for 1.5 miles, and then north again for 1.5 miles. Nearly a mile long and from 150 to 200 yards wide, Lakeview is superb in the spring (usually the second and third weeks of March) for migrating geese. As many as 30,000 Canada, White-fronted, Snow, and Blue Geese (the last two predominating) have been estimated at one time.

The UNIVERSITY OF KANSAS NATURAL HISTORY RESERVATION, with undisturbed woodlands and shrubby places, has an excellent variety of breeding birds, including the following: Yellow-billed Cuckoo, Crested Flycatcher, Eastern Wood Pewee, Black-capped Chickadee, Tufted Titmouse, Catbird, Brown Thrasher, Blue-gray Gnatcatcher, White-eyed Vireo, Bell's Vireo, Warbling Vireo, Scarlet Tanager, Cardinal, and Indigo Bunting. Immediately outside of the Reservation are grasslands and intermittent hedgerows that support such birds as the Upland Plover, Eastern and Western Kingbirds, Eastern Meadowlark, Dickcissel, Grasshopper Sparrow, and Field Sparrow. The Reservation may be reached by going east 1.5 miles from the intersection of US Routes 24 and 40 (2 miles north of Lawrence), then north 3 miles on a gravel road to a sign that indicates the area. Permission to look for birds should be obtained from the resident naturalist, whose home and adjacent laboratory are on the Reservation within view of the road.

MANHATTAN. This city, with its abundance of shade trees and other greenery, lies just west of the confluence of the Kansas (Kaw) and Big Blue Rivers. Northwest of the city on a low hill is the pleasingly landscaped campus of KANSAS STATE COLLEGE. The Museum of Natural History in Fairchild Hall contains a synoptic collection of 325 mounted birds and, in addition, 550 bird skins, mostly from Kansas. Second-semester and summer courses in ornithology, given by the Department of Zoology, make good use of this material.

Parts of the city and the College campus are very favorable for many of the smaller landbirds. In one dooryard on the west side of Manhattan a total of 86 species have been observed over a period of 25 years. Outside of the city are numerous prairies, many of which are pastured, and wooded areas on the flood plains bordering the Kansas and Big Blue Rivers. Probably the spot most frequently visited

by bird students at the College is the MARLATT ME-
MORIAL PARK (160 acres), a recreational area northwest
of the city. Principally prairie land, it is nevertheless partly
wooded with both native and introduced trees and shrubs.
The Bob-white, Upland Plover, Yellow-billed Cuckoo,
Horned Lark, Mockingbird, Blue-gray Gnatcatcher, Bell's
Vireo, Orchard Oriole, Dickcissel, Eastern Towhee, Grasshopper Sparrow, and Field Sparrow are a few of the
species that may be found breeding. Transients in the
spring and fall include the Black and White Warbler, Tennessee Warbler, Myrtle Warbler, Black-poll Warbler,
White-crowned Sparrow, Fox Sparrow, and Lincoln's Sparrow. Such birds as the Slate-colored Junco, American Tree
Sparrow, Harris' Sparrow, and White-throated Sparrow are
usually quite common in the winter. Marlatt Park may be
reached from Manhattan by turning north one block west
of the traffic light at Anderson and 17th Streets and following the only well-defined road northwest for 4.4 miles.

MEDICINE LODGE. Between 10 May and 10 September, one is almost certain to see a few Mississippi Kites
along the first 10 to 15 miles of US Route 160 east or west

MISSISSIPPI KITES

of this town. Nests of the birds may be readily found by searching in some of the adjacent groves.

STOCKTON. One of the most accessible eagle roosts in western Kansas is just 6 miles southwest of Stockton on the Solomon River. From 1 November to 15 March, both Golden and Bald Eagles, together with Red-tailed Hawks and other large birds of prey, are frequently observed here. A recent winter census revealed the presence of 90 birds of prey, including 60 eagles, of which 40 were Bald Eagles in fully adult ('white-headed') plumage. To reach the roost go south from Stockton on US Route 183. Just after crossing the bridge over the Solomon River turn right on a dirt road and proceed westward for 5 or 6 miles. The roost is in a quarter-mile section of cottonwood trees along the River.

TOPEKA. According to the Topeka Audubon Society, this capital city's best year-round bird-finding area, one that will produce the greatest variety of birds, from Common Loons to Song Sparrows, is the 606-acre woodland park that includes LAKE SHAWNEE, a 411-acre reservoir. The park is southeast of the city and may be reached by driving south on Kansas Avenue and turning left on 29th Street, which leads to the park entrance. A drive encircles the Lake. There are picnic grounds—some on good vantage points—but no camping is permitted.

Lake Shawnee is bordered by a few patches of cattails and, on higher ground, by fields, groves of oaks and evergreens, and brushy thickets. Across the dam northeast of the Lake are a number of fish-breeding ponds choked with cattails. Bird finding is especially productive from the first of September to the last of November, when migration is in full swing. At such time a list of birds observed on the Lake and in its immediate surroundings will quite likely include the Common Loon, Pied-billed Grebe, Eared Grebe, White Pelican, Double-crested Cormorant, Mallard, Pintail, Blue-winged Teal, Shoveler, Redhead, Canvas-back, Lesser Scaup Duck, American Merganser, Killdeer, Lesser Yellow-legs, Least Sandpiper, Ring-billed Gull, Franklin's Gull, Rough-winged Swallow, Barn Swallow, Cliff Swallow,

Brewer's Blackbird, Red-wing, American Tree Sparrow (not in September), Field Sparrow, and Harris' Sparrow. White-fronted, Snow, and Blue Geese are of frequent occurrence in mid-March and mid-October.

Mallards usually remain all winter and are sometimes joined by American Mergansers and Coots. American Tree Sparrows are winter residents. Great Blue Herons, American Egrets, Green Herons, and Little Blue Herons are possibilities in late summer and early fall.

GAGE PARK (146 acres), west of the city on 10th Avenue, is a recreational area with open, grassy spots, many oak trees, and clusters of shrubs. Landbird finding is rewarding here when warblers and other small passerines are migrating in early May. This is also a convenient place in the winter for finding flickers (sometimes both the Red-shafted and Yellow-shafted), Red-bellied Woodpeckers, Black-capped Chickadees, Tufted Titmice, Red-breasted Nuthatches, Golden-crowned Kinglets, Cedar Waxwings, Cardinals, Purple Finches, and Pine Siskins.

SILVER LAKE, 12 miles west of the city on US Route 24, is an old meander cutoff of the Kansas River that covers 180 acres. Shallow and marked with many dead willow stumps, it contains cattails and other emergent aquatic plants which attract a heavy breeding population of Red-wings. Prothonotary Warblers find suitable nesting sites in the large willows, cottonwoods, and elms that stand on the shore. From late April through May, and from late July through September, Silver Lake is one of the most productive spots in the Topeka area for shorebirds, provided the water level is sufficiently low to expose mud flats.

The STATE MUSEUM on the fourth floor of the Memorial Building at the corner of 10th and Jackson Streets contains the N. S. Goss collection of mounted birds representing 756 species. The specimens are in glass cases, where they are arranged according to family groups.

The Topeka Audubon Society, which may be contacted through either the Central Bank and Trust Company (701 Kansas Avenue) or the Topeka Public Library (8th and Jackson Streets), has 200 members, who sponsor a series of public lectures and enjoy taking numerous field trips.

The Society's official publication, *Topeka Audubon News,* appears quarterly.

WICHITA. The lush vegetation of Wichita's city parks, standing out in contrast to the monotonous wheatlands that stretch away from the city for many miles in all directions, is a mecca for brush and woodland birds. Two rivers, the Arkansas and the Little Arkansas, which join within the city limits, and several near-by bodies of water attract many waterbirds and waterfowl. The bird finding is remarkably good for a municipality as highly industrialized as Wichita.

OAK PARK (about 40 acres) occupies a point of land formed by a bend in the Little Arkansas River and may be reached by going north on Broadway and turning left on 11th Street, which traverses the area. The eastern half of the Park has a rather dense woods of oak, walnut, and cottonwood, with brushy edges, while the western half is quite open and has two small ponds. An exciting time for bird finding here comes in April and early May, when such species as the following are passing through: Least Flycatcher, Olive-backed Thrush, Gray-cheeked Thrush, Ruby-crowned Kinglet, Cedar Waxwing, Black-poll Warbler, Myrtle Warbler, White-crowned Sparrow, and White-throated Sparrow. Birds to be seen in the summer include the Mourning Dove, Yellow-billed Cuckoo, Common Nighthawk, Red-headed Woodpecker, Eastern Kingbird, Crested Flycatcher, House Wren, Catbird, Brown Thrasher, Red-eyed Vireo, Warbling Vireo, Orchard Oriole, Baltimore Oriole, and Rose-breasted Grosbeak. Winter bird finding is good in the Park, for the year-round populations of Belted Kingfishers, Yellow-shafted Flickers, Red-bellied Woodpeckers, Hairy Woodpeckers, Black-capped Chickadees, Tufted Titmice, Robins, Cardinals, and Common Goldfinches are augmented by the arrival of Red-shafted Flickers, Brown Creepers, Golden-crowned Kinglets, Slate-colored Juncos, and Harris' Sparrows.

SIMS MEMORIAL PARK (183 acres), on the east bank of the Arkansas River, reached by continuing on 11th Street for one mile west of Oak Park, is largely open prairie, with some thickets on the sand dunes by the River. Several birds are found here that do not occur in Oak Park: throughout the year, the Bob-white and Eastern and Western Meadowlarks; in spring, fall, and occasionally in winter, the Eastern Bluebird; in summer, the Scissor-tailed Flycatcher, Mockingbird, Bell's Vireo, and Field Sparrow.

For migrating waterbirds and waterfowl, drive west from Broadway in Wichita on 13th Street (becomes Stanley Drive, then Parker Avenue) for 3 miles to BIG SLOUGH, a stream that parallels the Arkansas River for many miles, and flows through poorly drained marshland. More of this same type of habitat may be reached by continuing west from Big Slough for 2.3 miles, then north 2 miles on a section-line road. Here there is a shallow lake which sometimes covers the road. The surrounding territory is largely grassy plain. Lists of birds made in March, early April, October, and November usually contain the Pied-billed Grebe, Great Blue Heron, American Bittern, Canada, Snow, and Blue Geese (mainly in March), Mallard, Gadwall, Baldpate, Pintail, Blue-winged Teal, Shoveler, Redhead, Canvas-back, Lesser Scaup Duck, Ruddy Duck, Marsh Hawk, Coot, Lesser Yellow-legs, Yellow-headed Blackbird, and, occasionally, the Sandhill Crane.

Contributing authorities: Donald J. Ameel, Ivan L. Boyd, L. B. Carson, John C. Dean, Eugene W. Dehner, William R. Eastman, Jr., John E. Galley, Mrs. John E. (Margret) Galley, Frank C. Gates, Richard R. Graber, Mrs. Richard R. (Jean) Graber, Harold C. Hedges, Frank W. Robl, Harrison B. Tordoff.

Louisiana

BROWN PELICANS

The great bird artist, John James Audubon, once declared Louisiana his 'favorite portion of the Union.' In its vast coastal marshes and deep woods, he found a richness of birdlife that inspired him to draw birds in greater number and excellence. Today when the bird finder explores the coastal marshes, places that ornithologists recognize as having some of the largest bird populations in the United States, and works along the forest byways of West Feliciana Parish, he will fully understand why Louisiana meant so much to Audubon.

Louisiana lies entirely on the Coastal Plain. Lower

Louisiana is a strip of lush coastal marshes, 10 to 40 miles wide, lying along the Gulf of Mexico. Upper Louisiana, the remainder of the state, is an upland area of low rolling hills and bottomlands. The maximum elevation, 535 feet, is near Liberty Hill in northwestern Louisiana. Bordering the Mississippi River, which cuts through the state, is a broad bottomland, averaging 50 miles in width, which roughly divides the upland area into the Uplands of the Florida Parishes, north of Lake Pontchartrain and east of the Mississippi, and the West Louisiana Uplands, west of the Mississippi and north of the coastal marshes. Apart from the Mississippi, the most important watercourses are the Red River, flowing into the Mississippi from the northwest, and the Sabine River, forming much of the western boundary and emptying into the Gulf.

Both the Uplands of the Florida Parishes and the West Louisiana Uplands have, along their southern extremities, extensive flats forested with long-leaf and slash pines, often mixed with stands of hardwoods, principally black and post oaks, and mockernut hickory. Characteristic nesting birds are Red-cockaded Woodpeckers, Brown-headed Nuthatches, Pine Warblers, Prairie Warblers, and Pine-woods Sparrows.

The moist alluvial bottomlands of the Mississippi and of the other large rivers have dense forests. In lower or backwater areas where the soil is poorly drained, overcup oak, water locust, cypress, and tupelo grow commonly, but on higher, well-drained areas the common trees are sweet gum, green ash, swamp red oak, willow oak, water oak, elm, and pecan. Some of the birds breeding regularly in the bottomland forests are listed below (species marked with an asterisk may also occur regularly on the pine-oak uplands).

Red-shouldered Hawk
Broad-winged Hawk
Yellow-billed Cuckoo
Screech Owl
Barred Owl
Chuck-will's-widow
*Yellow-shafted Flicker
Pileated Woodpecker
Red-bellied Woodpecker
Hairy Woodpecker

Downy Woodpecker
Crested Flycatcher
Acadian Flycatcher
Eastern Wood Pewee
*Blue Jay
Carolina Chickadee
Tufted Titmouse
White-breasted Nuthatch
    (northern Louisiana)
Wood Thrush

*Blue-gray Gnatcatcher
Yellow-throated Vireo
Red-eyed Vireo
Warbling Vireo
Prothonotary Warbler
Swainson's Warbler
Parula Warbler

Yellow-throated Warbler
Louisiana Water-thrush
Kentucky Warbler
Hooded Warbler
*Baltimore Oriole
Summer Tanager

Upper Louisiana was originally forested in its entirety (except near the western boundary, where the surface supported prairie vegetation), but today about half of upper Louisiana is occupied by settlements and farmlands (fields, brushy lands, thickets, and dooryards), where the following birds may be found nesting:

Bob-white
Killdeer
Mourning Dove
Barn Owl
Red-headed Woodpecker
Eastern Kingbird
Purple Martin
Carolina Wren
Mockingbird
Catbird (mainly northern
  Louisiana)
Brown Thrasher
Eastern Bluebird
Loggerhead Shrike
White-eyed Vireo

Yellow-throat
Yellow-breasted Chat
Eastern Meadowlark
Orchard Oriole
Common Grackle
Cardinal
Blue Grosbeak (mainly north-
  ern Louisiana)
Indigo Bunting
Painted Bunting
Dickcissel
Eastern Towhee
Chipping Sparrow
Field Sparrow

For the bird finder the outstanding attractions of upper Louisiana are the beautiful Feliciana Parishes north of Baton Rouge. A typical spot, once a favorite of Audubon, is St. Francisville, on the Mississippi. In this quiet community there are unfrequented roads, small fields, and thicketed ravines, together with several ante-bellum plantations noted for their deep woods and dignified houses shaded by moss-hung trees and surrounded by lawns with flowering shrubbery and lovely gardens. In such a setting, where habitats are many and varied, birdlife is unusually rich.

The coastal marshes of lower Louisiana are a flat plain of rushes, cord grasses, bulrushes, and quillreeds interrupted by a maze of shallow lakes, bayous, bays, and man-made canals. Scrubby trees, such as willows and hackberries, find foothold only where there are small ridges of sand and shells. Near the coast the water is generally salt or brackish; farther inland it gradually becomes fresh. Except where the Mississippi Delta spreads out into the Gulf, the seaward side of the marshes is protected by a barrier of sand beaches that rise to crests called cheniers (locally pronounced *shin-years*), so named because they support groves of live oaks. A few 'land islands' a mile or more in diameter rise out of the marshes between the cheniers and the interior uplands. These are usually bordered by cypress and tupelo, while a variety of dry-land hardwoods grows in their interiors. Nesting birds of the coastal marshes, including the tree-covered ridges, cheniers, and land islands, are the following:

Olivaceous Cormorant	Fulvous Tree-duck (a few)
Anhinga	Mottled Duck
Great Blue Heron	King Rail
American Egret	Clapper Rail
Snowy Egret	Purple Gallinule
Louisiana Heron	Florida Gallinule
Little Blue Heron	Willet
Green Heron	Black-necked Stilt
Black-crowned Night Heron	Forster's Tern
Yellow-crowned Night Heron	Long-billed Marsh Wren
American Bittern	Yellow-throat
Least Bittern	Red-wing
White-faced Ibis	Orchard Oriole
White Ibis	Boat-tailed Grackle
Roseate Spoonbill (a few)	Seaside Sparrow

The coastal marshes undoubtedly constitute Louisiana's major ornithological attraction. This the bird finder will believe once he visits the 25,000 inhabitants of 'Bird City' on Avery Island (see under New Iberia), cruises along canals of remote and unspoiled Rainey Wildlife Sanctuary (see under Abbeville), and tours the miles of marshes and cheniers in Cameron Parish (see under Sulphur).

Offshore in the Gulf are sand and shell islands, covered with grasses and fringed with mangrove thickets. Notable among them are the large islands of the Timbalier group westward from the Delta and of the Chandeleur group

northeastward. Birds known to breed regularly on these islands (and occasionally on inaccessible beaches of the
mainland) are the following:

Brown Pelican	Least Tern
American Oyster-catcher	Royal Tern
(relatively rare)	Cabot's Tern
Wilson's Plover	Caspian Tern
Willet	Black Skimmer
Laughing Gull	Common Nighthawk
Forster's Tern	Seaside Sparrow

Unfortunately for the bird finder, the islands are not
readily accessible. Although East Timbalier Island has fine
colonies of Brown Pelicans and terns, its great distance
from ports, coupled with the scarcity of craft for hire at
reasonable prices, makes it impossible to reach by ordinary means. The islands of the Chandeleur group are more
accessible—if the bird finder does not object to the great
expense of chartering a powerboat at Gulfport, Mississippi,
the nearest port. Many birds nest on these islands, which
include North Island (chiefly Brown Pelicans) and Isle au
Pitre (American Oyster-catchers, Royal Terns, Cabot's
Terns, Caspian Terns).

The bottomlands of the Mississippi comprise Louisiana's
chief migratory route for waterbirds, waterfowl, shorebirds,
and landbirds in their journeys to and from northern latitudes. In the fall it becomes a veritable bottleneck, where
birds from both northeastern and north-central North
America converge in their southward flight. During these
journeys, impressive numbers of grebes, cormorants, herons,
ducks, gulls, and terns loiter on bayous and meander cutoffs, while tremendous waves of small landbirds move
through the hardwoods.

By far the most interesting aspect of migration in Louisiana is the spring return of landbirds across the Gulf. If at
the time of migration the weather in lower Louisiana is
warm, or mild, the birds with northern destinations proceed inland some distance before coming to land, or else
settle down in the deeply wooded bottomlands in such a
widely dispersed fashion that they are not easily detected.
The coastal area thus appears to be an ornithological

'hiatus.' But if, as a result of inclement weather, a cold front or 'norther' sets in, the birds are forced to accept the first land reached, which is usually the islands and cheniers. The coastal area is then flooded with birds. As soon as the weather clears or mild temperatures occur, the birds disappear. This remarkable phenomenon has been frequently observed at various localities, notably at Grand Isle (see under Thibodaux). Should the bird finder be present there in the spring (1 April to 10 May) at the time of a norther, he will count more birds in an hour or two than he can record in a decade of faithful searching during fair weather.

The following migration timetable applies chiefly to birds passing through Louisiana: for shorebirds, 15 March—15 May, 15 August—20 October; for landbirds, 15 March—5 May, 15 September—10 November.

During the winter, the coastal marshes of lower Louisiana teem with waterfowl. West of the Delta may be seen thousands upon thousands of Blue Geese, probably the bulk of the entire Blue Goose population. Mixed with them are great numbers of Snow Geese, and smaller numbers of Canada and White-fronted Geese. Grebes, cormorants, herons, ducks, gulls, and terns abound along the entire coast. The wintering populations of shorebirds are always impressive, but the species present are subject to great variation, making it impossible to say with certainty which species will be found. Upper Louisiana is the wintering ground of many passerine birds, including Hermit Thrush, Golden-crowned and Ruby-crowned Kinglets, Solitary Vireo, several warblers, and numerous fringillids. Where there are small lakes, reservoirs, bayous, and meander cutoffs, waterbirds and ducks frequently stay from fall to spring.

The Louisiana Ornithological Society comprises a group of amateur and professional ornithologists who conduct census trips and hold meetings throughout the year. The organization may be contacted through the Museum of Zoology, Louisiana State University, Baton Rouge.

ABBEVILLE. About 26,000 acres of coastal marshes, cut by lakes, canals, and bayous, make up the PAUL J. RAINEY WILDLIFE SANCTUARY, owned by the National Audubon Society. Seven miles of beach form its southern boundary on the Gulf of Mexico; Vermilion Bay marks its northern boundary. In the center of the Sanctuary, on a man-made island, are the wardens' residence, the boathouse, other maintenance buildings, and a small guest house. From November to March, the Sanctuary is ideal for witnessing one of Louisiana's ornithological marvels— the huge assemblage of wintering Blue Geese. There are few spectacles anywhere in North America as impressive as these noisy birds, rising, huge flock after huge flock, from feeding grounds in the marshes, cruising overhead in V-shaped formation, and swirling down to rest on bays and lagoons. In the Sanctuary and its immediate vicinity the goose population frequently approximates 50,000, an estimate that is considered conservative.

Visit the Sanctuary and accompany the wardens on a powerboat trip through the canals. An authorization, obtainable from the National Audubon Society, 1130 Fifth Avenue, New York City 28, is required. If the trip is made in winter, quite naturally it will be highlighted by enormous concentrations of Blue Geese, but it will be further enriched by many Snow Geese and ducks, as well as grebes, herons, gulls, and terns. Species that will be seen frequently from the boat are White Pelicans, Brown Pelicans, Great Blue Herons, American Egrets, Snowy Egrets, Louisiana Herons, Little Blue Herons, Green Herons, White-faced Ibises, Mottled Ducks (the only waterfowl nesting in the Sanctuary), Marsh Hawks, Sparrow Hawks, Laughing Gulls, Gull-billed Terns, Forster's Terns, Royal Terns, Black Skimmers, Long-billed Marsh Wrens, Loggerhead Shrikes, Yellow-throats, Red-wings, Boat-tailed Grackles, and occasionally a Vermilion Flycatcher. Even if the trip is made in the spring after the geese are gone, it will not be devoid of enjoyment. In the summertime, the abundant birds include Least Bitterns, Eastern Kingbirds, Orchard Orioles, and occasionally Purple Gallinules. An inspection of the beach will soon reveal Wilson's Plovers and Common Nighthawks nesting on the gravelly, shell-covered parts above reach of the tides and Willets higher up on the beach among the grasses. A wading jaunt through the marshes will undoubtedly turn up King Rails and Seaside Sparrows.

BATON ROUGE. On the campus of LOUISIANA STATE UNIVERSITY, 3 miles south of this capital city, is the Museum of Zoology, which houses an excellent collection of 19,000 bird skins representing principally southeastern United States and Mexico. The University offers both elementary and advanced courses in ornithology, provides graduate training leading to an advanced degree, and sponsors important expeditions to Mexico.

Students of ornithology at the University consider two near-by areas particularly good for bird finding: NEW UNIVERSITY and CITY PARK LAKES, on the east side of the campus; CONRAD POINT, on the Mississippi River 5 miles south of the University.

New University and City Park Lakes, close together, have 8 miles of shoreline and may be reached by proceeding east on Dalrymple Drive. Throughout the winter months one may see many Pied-billed Grebes, Double-crested Cormorants, Coots, and ducks, including Gadwalls, Pintails, Blue-winged Teal, Ring-necked Ducks, and Lesser Scaup Ducks. Many kinds of herons frequent the Lakes in the summer.

To reach Conrad Point, drive west to the east levee of the Mississippi and proceed southward, on a gravel road that parallels the levee, to the Point, where the River bends eastward. On the River side of the levee, the batture (elevated riverbed) is covered with willows and cottonwoods; the borrow pit (ditch along levee) on the other side often contains water. On the batture, many transient landbirds gather during migration, March to May, and August to November. The peaks of warbler migrations occur in the last two weeks of April and the last two weeks of September. In the late spring and summer, Swallow-tailed Kites may be observed occasionally. University students have found Conrad Point and its vicinity a gold mine for unusual birds such as the Wilson's Phalarope, Flammulated Owl, Ash-throated Flycatcher, and Black-throated Blue Warbler.

BURAS. The Mississippi River Delta, reaching out into the Gulf of Mexico, is virtually a cluster of islands separated by the river outlets or passes. The sides of the islands bordering the passes are a few feet above the high-tide mark and are the locations of a few settlements, but elsewhere the islands are so low as to form salt marshes and mud flats of great extent. Offshore from the Delta are the Mud Lumps—masses of clay and silt, each one a few feet above the high-tide mark and averaging an acre of surface. Such is the Delta country, long known to ornithologists for its variety and abundance of waterbirds and waterfowl.

The DELTA NATIONAL WILDLIFE REFUGE comprises 48,789 acres of marshland on several islands of the Delta's east side. The nearest point to the Refuge that can be reached by car is Venice, a village of trappers, fishermen, and citrus growers, 15 miles south of Buras on State Route 31. Persons visiting the Refuge are usually picked up at the Engineer's Dock in Venice. If a bird finder wishes to tour the Refuge, he must communicate with the Refuge manager (address: Pilottown) well in advance of the trip so that a boat can be sent to meet him. Since a full day is necessary for a worth-while tour, he should bring a picnic lunch and arrange to be picked up at 8:00 A.M. and returned in the late afternoon. Food supplies and overnight accommodations are not available at the Refuge but can be obtained at Buras.

A trip to the Refuge is rewarding in any season because one may always see—flying over the outlets and marshes or perching on the mud flats, jetties, and pilings—such a wide variety of birds as White Pelicans, American Egrets, White-faced Ibises, Laughing Gulls, Royal Terns, and Black Skimmers. Ducks and geese are everywhere abundant from October to March; Man-o'-war-birds from March to November; shorebirds from February to June and from August to November. Brown Pelicans nest in great numbers on the Mud Lumps from February to July.

An exciting and profitable way to see the Delta country is by powerboat from Empire. No guide is necessary but it is essential to have a Coastal Survey Map of the Empire area, which may be obtained in the map store at 142 Chartres Street, New Orleans. In Empire, which is 7 miles north of Buras on State Route 31, turn west off the highway just south of the metal drawbridge, stop at the small boat docks, and rent a speed hull from one of the fishermen. By making local inquiry and using the map, the bird finder can easily navigate through the bayous to the Gulf Coast and explore the mud flats of Adams and Bastian Bays. In the fall, winter, and spring, the thrills of bird finding are many because waterbirds, waterfowl, and shorebirds abound.

JENNINGS. For observing large concentrations of wintering waterfowl and methods of waterfowl management, visit the LACASSINE NATIONAL WILDLIFE REFUGE, 21 miles southwest of Jennings. To reach the Refuge, take State Route 25 south from Jennings to Lake Arthur, then State Route 98 west from Lake Arthur. Just outside of town, follow the sign that points the way to the Refuge over an improved gravel road turning south. One may reach the Refuge headquarters by car, but the Refuge itself can be explored by powerboat only.

The Refuge consists of 31,125 acres of salt and brackish marsh with a maze of bayous and man-made canals. Twig rushes, cut grasses, and bulrushes constitute the predominating vegetation. The only trees on the area are three live oaks near the headquarters.

Waterfowl particularly abundant in the winter are Canada Geese, Mallards, Black Ducks, Pintails, Green-winged and Blue-winged Teal, and Ring-necked Ducks, but many other species occur in smaller numbers.

The nearest point where good meals and lodging can be obtained is Lake Charles, west of Jennings on US Route 90.

NEW IBERIA. From New Iberia on US Route 90, drive southwest on State Route 25 for 2.3 miles, then turn south on State Route 445 and travel a distance of 6 miles to a toll gate marking the entrance to privately owned AVERY ISLAND. A road toll is charged. Circular in shape, with a diameter approximating 3 miles, Avery Island is surrounded by coastal marshes and cypress swamps. On the Island are several woodland areas and a development comprising homes, schools, shops, hothouses, a factory, a salt mine, and an oil field. Of special interest to the bird finder are Jungle Gardens and Bird City. An entrance fee is charged.

Jungle Gardens consist of more than 200 acres surrounding the home of the late Edward Avery McIlhenny. In addition to native flora, it contains an extraordinary array of exotic plants, ranging from immense palms and giant bamboos to huge beds of camellias, azaleas, irises, and chrysanthemums. Special landscaping has produced sunken gardens and mirrored pools at numerous points. Birds such as Tufted Titmice, Carolina Wrens, Mockingbirds, Yellow-breasted Chats, Orchard Orioles, Boat-tailed Grackles, and Cardinals are common everywhere, as the bird finder will soon discover when he walks along the footpaths winding through the area.

Bird City, in the southern section of the Jungle Gardens, is a 35-acre pond bordered by buttonwood trees and willows, where 30,000 or more Snowy Egrets and Louisiana Herons nest from late March to July. Other residents of Bird City, though they occur in smaller numbers and are somewhat overshadowed, are Anhingas, Little Blue Herons, Green Herons, and Purple Gallinules.

Both the pond and its heron colony were developed by E. A. McIlhenny, neither having existed prior to 1893. As the colony increased in size, the pond was enlarged. When, in recent years, the breeding population became so enormous as to cause a shortage of nesting sites and nesting materials, elevated platforms of bamboo were placed in the pond as supports for nests, and carloads of twigs were gathered at distant points and heaped on specially constructed benches, from which they could be gathered by the birds at will. The colony soon doubled in size. For the bird finder a watchtower has been erected in the pond and connected to the shore by a footbridge. From the top of the tower he may view the entire colony: birds nesting in the bordering shrubs, the Snowy Egrets standing out as conspicuously as patches of snow; birds nesting on the platforms, a setting so unnatural as to seem ludicrous; birds resting; birds fishing in the shallows; birds skirmishing; birds displaying; birds incessantly arriving and departing. Such is Bird City!

NEW ORLEANS. Hemmed in by marshland, New Orleans lies between the south shore of shallow Lake Pontchartrain and the Mississippi River. South and west of the city the chain of coastal refuges (see under Abbeville, Buras, Jennings, Sulphur, Thibodaux) extends across the state. Adjacent to New Orleans are numerous bayous and lakes where waterbirds are abundant and waterfowl and shorebirds are commonly found in the fall, winter, and spring. An excellent way to see birds in this area is to drive to one of the small fishing villages on the lakes and bayous, rent a 'pirogue,' and paddle out into the marshes (an important Louisiana rule: be fully protected against mosquitoes in any season).

In New Orleans, CITY PARK, extending between City Park Avenue and Robert E. Lee Boulevard, is a large recreational area with splendid groves of live oaks, exotic trees, ornamental shrubs, formal gardens, and lagoons. The breeding population of birds is small, but transient kinglets, vireos, warblers, and fringillids abound in April, early May, September, and early October.

In the Presbytère, on the southwest corner of Chartres and St. Ann Streets, is the Natural History Division of the LOUISIANA STATE MUSEUM (open daily except Mondays), where there are various habitat groups and synoptic collections of Louisiana fauna, including birds.

Directly across St. Charles Avenue from Tulane University is AUDUBON PARK, which has on exhibit over 400 captive birds, about one fourth of which are American. The Park owns one of the rare Whooping Cranes, which may be seen, with the permission of the Director, when it is not on public exhibition. In the Park is a bronze statue of John James Audubon, unveiled on 26 November 1910.

About 21 miles east of the city, US Route 90 crosses Chef Menteur Pass, a tideway connecting Lakes Pontchartrain and Borgne. The bird finder may drive off the highway to the right just before crossing the Long-Simpson Bridge. Here on the edge of the Pass is FORT MACOMB, the ruins of a century-old fortification, which harbors a small population of landbirds. Of chief interest in this area are the swamps and mud flats. These may been seen to advantage from the Louisiana and Nashville Railroad tracks. On foot, skirt the old fortification to the right and walk a quarter of a mile to the railroad tracks, which run as an earthen rampart through the marshland. One mile down the tracks away from the Pass the swamps give way to mud flats, which may be surveyed easily from the tracks. The best point for observation is near a railroad-signal post. Numerous transient birds are conspicuous on this marsh, including the Great Blue Heron, Louisiana Heron, Little Blue Heron, American Egret, Snowy Egret, White-faced Ibis (uncommon), various ducks, Black-necked Stilt, Willet, Greater and Lesser Yellow-legs, Dowitcher, and Pectoral Sandpiper. Occasionally in August and September Wilson's Phalaropes may be seen here.

Beyond Chef Menteur Pass US Route 90 goes northeast for 9 miles on St. Catherines Island. To the right is Lake Catherine, opening into Lake Borgne; to the left is Lake Pontchartrain. Adjacent to the highway embankment are marshes where, from May through July, Clapper Rails, Long-billed Marsh Wrens, and other marshbirds nest. At one point near the south side of the road there is a sandy area where a large nesting colony of Least Terns becomes established in late May. Bald Eagles may occasionally be viewed from the highway in the late winter, spring, and summer. Their aeries will be noted in tall trees not far away. In many spots close to the highway, grebes, cormorants, a few geese, and ducks may be readily observed from October to April; shorebirds from August to June; herons, gulls, and terns at all times of the year.

ST. FRANCISVILLE. It was here in West Feliciana Parish on the banks of the Mississippi that John James Audubon found his 'happy land.' For five months, beginning on 18 June 1821, he lived at Oakley, the James Pirrie plantation, and studied birds near by in 'the most beautiful of all Louisiana's beautiful woods.' Birdlife was rich in variety and abundance, inspiring him to produce some of his finest paintings, including those of the male Wild Turkey, the Mockingbirds defending their young from rattlesnakes, the Baltimore Orioles at the nest, the assemblage of Carolina Paroquets, and the Ivory-billed Woodpeckers. Although the Carolina Paroquets and Ivory-billed Woodpeckers have since vanished, and the populations of many other species that were his subjects have been reduced, St. Francisville is still one of the best spots in Louisiana to find birds, both transient and breeding. Each year at Christmastime orni-

thologists at Louisiana State University make a census of
the St. Francisville area, invariably finding more than 100
species.

The Oakley plantation house, three-storied and with
quaint shuttered porches, still stands today, surrounded by
moss-hung live oaks, yellow poplars, and magnolias. Remote and secluded, it is an enchanting place, approached
only by one roadway through a deep woods. Recently the
plantation—the house and a hundred encompassing acres
—was purchased by the state and restored to resemble as
far as possible the Oakley that Audubon saw when he arrived in 1821. It is now called AUDUBON MEMORIAL
STATE PARK.

Oakley can be reached from St. Francisville by driving
east on US Route 65 for 2.2 miles, then turning left on
State Route 323 and proceeding 3.1 miles to the entrance,
which is on the right. Breeding birds of the plantation
include the Red-bellied Woodpecker, Acadian Flycatcher,
Eastern Wood Pewee, Carolina Chickadee, Tufted Titmouse, Carolina Wren, Wood Thrush, Blue-gray Gnatcatcher, Parula Warbler, Yellow-throated Warbler, Kentucky Warbler, Hooded Warbler, Summer Tanager, and
Cardinal.

In the center of St. Francisville, enclosed in an elaborate
cast-iron fence, are Grace Church and an adjoining cemetery shaded by a grove of magnificent live oaks. On the
western side of the fence is a deep ravine with a dense
growth of shrubs and small trees. From December to
March this spot is a delight to any bird finder who desires to obtain a long list of wintering landbirds. A few
of the birds he will be likely to record are Eastern Phoebes,
Catbirds, Bewick's Wrens, Hermit Thrushes, Solitary
Vireos, Orange-crowned Warblers, Myrtle Warblers, Rose-
breasted Grosbeaks, Eastern Towhees, and White-throated
Sparrows.

East of the center of St. Francisville, reached by taking
roads leading from town, are fine stands of pine where,
in May and June, one may find breeding the Red-cockaded
Woodpecker, Brown-headed Nuthatch, Pine Warbler,
Prairie Warbler, and Pine-woods Sparrow.

For wintering waterbirds and waterfowl in the St. Francisville area, cross the Mississippi on the St. Francisville Ferry and proceed to FALSE RIVER, a narrow lake formed when a meander of the Mississippi was cut off. On reaching the north end of the lake 7 miles from the Ferry, follow a road around the east side of the lake, a distance of about 7 miles. Among the birds that may be viewed from October to March are Horned Grebes, Pied-billed Grebes, Double-crested Cormorants, Ring-necked Ducks, Canvas-backs, Lesser Scaup Ducks, Buffle-heads, Ruddy Ducks, Coots (abundant), Ring-billed Gulls, and Bonaparte's Gulls.

SHREVEPORT. Northwest of the city limits, in agricultural country, is CROSS LAKE, a large water impoundment about 10 miles in length, with an irregular shoreline. The northern side of the Lake is very productive ornithologically. Here, bordering the Lake at different locations, are cypresses, willows, mud flats, grassy marshes, and wooded swamps. Back from the Lake, on higher ground, are abandoned fields, open shrubby areas with thick tangles, and woods composed of oaks and pines (loblolly and short-leaf). The entire area is readily accessible: leave Shreveport on Milam Street (which becomes Blanchard Road outside the city) and drive to North Shore Drive; turn left (west) on North Shore Drive and continue west along the Lake. When North Shore Drive (paved) turns north, continue west on West Shore Drive (dirt surface) to a dead end on the west side of the Lake, 12 miles from the city limits.

From the list of birds known to occur in the late spring and summer, the following are selected to show the bird-finding opportunities: Turkey Vulture, Black Vulture, Wood Duck, Red-shouldered Hawk, Bob-white, Purple Gallinule, Barred Owl, Chuck-will's-widow, Pileated Woodpecker, Red-bellied Woodpecker, Acadian Flycatcher, Brown-headed Nuthatch, Carolina Wren, Mockingbird, Wood Thrush, Loggerhead Shrike, White-eyed Vireo, Prothonotary Warbler, Yellow-throated Warbler, Pine Warbler, Kentucky Warbler, Yellow-breasted Chat, Orchard Oriole, Summer Tanager, Cardinal, Blue Grosbeak, Indigo Bunting, Painted Bunting, Dickcissel, Pine-woods Sparrow.

Among the winter birds are many White-throated Sparrows and great hordes of Red-wings, Rusty Blackbirds, Common Grackles, and Brown-headed Cowbirds. Other winter species to be found regularly are Winter Wrens, Bewick's Wrens, Hermit Thrushes, Orange-crowned Warblers, Myrtle Warblers, Eastern Towhees, Vesper Sparrows, and Field Sparrows. Horned Grebes, Double-crested Cormorants, and Coots pass the winter on the Lake.

Immediately south of Shreveport, State Route 20 passes through open agricultural country where on telephone wires and fences one may regularly see such nesting birds as Scissor-tailed Flycatchers, Loggerhead Shrikes, Eastern Meadowlarks, Indigo Buntings, and Dickcissels.

In the LOUISIANA STATE EXHIBIT MUSEUM, on the Fairgrounds at the end of Edgar Street, are several excellent exhibits of modern design depicting Louisiana's natural resources, including wildlife. The Museum is open on weekdays from 10:00 A.M. to 6:00 P.M., on Sundays from 1:00 to 6:00 P.M.

SULPHUR. In extreme southwestern Louisiana, 142,717 acres of coastal marshland comprise the SABINE NATIONAL WILDLIFE REFUGE. Much of this area is cut up by bayous, man-made canals, alligator ponds, and potholes. Calcasieu Lake (pronounced *kal'-ka-shoe*), 14 by 18 miles in greatest diameter, bisects the eastern section of the Refuge, and Sabine Lake, 7 by 14 miles, forms the western boundary. Both Lakes are brackish and are surrounded by great stretches of three-square bulrushes and cord grasses. In the interior of the Refuge, away from the brackish water of the Lakes, is marsh containing mostly fresh water, with vegetation such as twig rushes, freshwater bulrushes, and quillreeds. Here and there are a few 'islands' covered with scrub willows, chinaberries, and hackberries.

Hordes of birds winter on the Refuge, from 15 October through 15 March, reaching peaks of greatest abundance in December and January. The goose population alone is estimated to be 60,000 Snow and Blue Geese, 5,500 Canada Geese, and 250 White-fronted Geese. Other species represented in impressive numbers are ducks (e.g. Mallards, Gadwalls, and Pintails) and shorebirds (e.g. Wilson's Snipe, Greater and Lesser Yellow-legs, and Black-necked Stilts). In April, May, and September thousands of transient shorebirds gather on the mud flats in Calcasieu and Sabine Lakes. In June, large colonies of Great Blue Herons, American Egrets, and Louisiana Herons become established on several of the islands and in some instances are joined by a few pairs of Olivaceous Cormorants, Anhingas, and Roseate Spoonbills. Other nesting birds regularly found are Green Herons, Least Bitterns, Mottled Ducks, Clapper Rails, Purple Gallinules, and Black-necked Stilts.

To reach the Refuge, drive south from Sulphur on State Route 104 (an improved shell road) which passes the Refuge headquarters, 27 miles from Sulphur, and crosses the east end of the Refuge. Satisfactory meals and lodging may be obtained at Hackberry, 18 miles from Sulphur on the same route.

Route 104 passes close to Calcasieu Lake, where thousands of geese can be seen either loitering on the water or grazing in the adjoining marsh. Shorebirds may also be watched to advantage. The bird finder may walk along the shore of the Lake, since the shoreline is high enough to offer firm footing, but, in general, the Refuge is so vast and the footing so insecure that the bird finder cannot investigate it by himself. Furthermore, the insects are sometimes extremely abundant, making a lengthy journey inadvisable. It is possible, however, to take a boat trip through the Refuge with Refuge personnel while they perform their routine duties. Arrangements must be made before arrival by writing the Refuge Manager, Sabine National Wildlife Refuge, Sulphur. No more than three or four persons can be taken at one time.

Along the coast of the Gulf of Mexico, south and southeast of the Sabine Refuge, are the CAMERON PARISH CHENIERS, narrow, oak-covered ridges slightly above the level of the marshland on the north and the Gulf on the south. They have small settlements and well-drained ground on which fine cotton is grown. In their vicinity is some of the best bird-finding country in Louisiana.

From the Sabine Refuge, continue south on State Route 104 to the coast, 38 miles from Sulphur. Turn right (west) at Holly Beach on State Route 292, and proceed on the Cheniers for 14 miles to Johnsons Bayou. During this trip along the coast the bird finder will get excellent views of such birds as Brown Pelicans, Laughing Gulls, Royal Terns, and Black Skimmers. Return to Route 104 (Holly Beach) from Johnsons Bayou and continue straight east, crossing Calcasieu Pass on the state-operated ferry to Cameron.

FULVOUS TREE-DUCKS

In Cameron, lodging and food may be obtained at the Cameron Hotel, an old establishment often patronized by bird finders. The village of Cameron, with its small plain homes shaded by oaks, is surrounded by a vast expanse of marshland teeming with wildlife. It is so intimately associated with the marsh that marsh mammals and birds in the neighborhood fearlessly accept it as part of their environment. Muskrats run up and down the streets, and Snowy Egrets look for food in the roadside ditches.

At Cameron, State Route 104 becomes State Route 42. At Creole, east of Cameron on State Route 42, the bird finder may take two different trips: (1) Turn right (south) and take State Route 292 eastward, crossing the Mermentau River at Grand Chenier and following the Cheniers eastward to the end of the road. (2) Continue straight ahead (east) for about 15 miles to Little Chenier at the end of the road. Both trips will lead through areas rich in birdlife.

In the marsh north of Little Chenier there is a place locally called 'the Burn,' where about a thousand White-faced Ibises have established a colony. Since the intervening marsh cannot be easily crossed on foot, it is necessary to hire one of the local Cajuns to provide transportation in a 'mud boat'—a motor craft especially designed for traveling through marshes. During the trip, the bird finder is almost certain to see Fulvous Tree-ducks, as well as enormous numbers of egrets and herons.

TALLULAH. In the Mississippi bottomlands of northeastern Louisiana there existed until recently 82,500 acres of forest, over four fifths of which was virgin timber. Sweet gum, swamp red oak, green ash, pecan, persimmon, and magnolia grew to massive size on the higher ground; huge cypresses fringed the sluggish streams and bayous. Known as the SINGER PRESERVE, the forest became famous as one of the last known refuges of the Ivory-billed Woodpecker. In spite of the fact that the Singer Preserve was set aside as a state wildlife sanctuary, lumber companies have secured logging rights to the entire area. Although some parts of the Preserve are still untouched, notably parts on the eastern side, total destruction is only a matter of time. Even now it is doubtful whether the handsome Ivory-bill still exists.

The eastern side of the Singer Preserve may be explored in part by driving 10 miles south from Tallulah on US Route 65 and turning west at Alligator Bayou onto a dirt road that leads into the forest as far as the Tensas River, about 6 miles distant. Pairs of Ivory-billed Woodpeckers have been known to nest over 40 feet up in some of the giant trees that are on high ground on either side of the road, halfway to the River.

THIBODAUX. GRAND ISLE, a narrow strip of land 7 miles long, is one of the few islands on the Gulf Coast accessible by car and is perhaps the best place to witness, after a spring norther, the remarkable concentrations of migrating small landbirds. Thousands of flycatchers, vireos, and warblers gather in the live oaks and oleanders covering the island and swarm around the many dwellings, even entering through open windows. One has to see the sight to appreciate it fully.

Grand Isle is 40 miles west of the Mississippi Delta and can be approached by car from Thibodaux: Go southeastward on State Route 29 for 15 miles to Raceland, then southward on State Route 78, paralleling the west bank of Bayou Lafourche, to Golden Meadow, where Route 78 becomes State Route 622. Proceed on Route 622, crossing Bayou Lafourche and passing through Leeville, where Route 622 becomes State Route 620, and over a vast stretch of marshland (excellent for waterbirds and waterfowl) to the bridge to Grand Isle.

Contributing authorities: John H. Baker, James Brown, Fred R. Cagle, Vandiver L. Childs, Robert B. Lea, George H. Lowery, Jr., Kent E. Meyers, Charles M. Parker, Edward M. Simmons, George G. Williams.

Minnesota

COMMON LOON

In 1867, Thomas Sadler Roberts, a youth of nine years, moved to Minnesota. As chance would have it, he possessed a smoldering interest in birds which in time flared into an intensive ornithological undertaking—a statewide study of Minnesota's birds. Through his life to his death in 1946, he labored with boundless energy and produced in his later years *The Birds of Minnesota*, one of the greatest works in the annals of American ornithology. The bird finder who will roam within Minnesota's borders today should first peruse this masterpiece, for there is a wealth of information to be used and enthusiasm to be shared. This accomplished, he can appreciate and more fully enjoy the April multitudes of geese at Mud Lake and Lake Traverse (see under

Wheaton), the May throngs of shorebirds and warblers near Frontenac, the rich variety of marsh-dwelling birds, including Franklin's Gulls, in the Mud Lake National Wildlife Refuge (see under Thief River Falls), the nesting flycatchers, thrushes, warblers, and fringillids in Itasca State Park (see under Park Rapids), and the many other avian rewards awaiting him.

In general, Minnesota has a gently rolling surface with an average elevation above sea level of only 1,200 feet, but its four corners show considerable variation: in the northeast, rugged hills that are almost mountains; in the northwest, flat, monotonous prairie; in the southeast, high hills and deeply cut ravines; in the southwest, an undulating, sometimes flat surface, interrupted by a ridge called the Coteau des Prairies. The highest elevation in the state, 2,230 feet, is reached in the Misquah Hills of the extreme northeastern part, while the lowest elevation, 602 feet, is the 200-mile strip of land bordering Lake Superior.

Despite the fact that the elevation of the state is relatively low, it possesses the headwaters of three of the great drainage systems of North America. In Itasca Park, the Mississippi begins its southward course, soon joined by the Minnesota River from the west and the St. Croix from the north; in the northeast, the St. Louis River and numerous streams cascade eastward into Lake Superior of the St. Lawrence River system; along the western boundary, the Red River of the North rises to flow northward into the Hudson Bay outlet.

Scattered over the state, though concentrated more heavily in the northern part, are some 10,000 lakes, which, together with the rivers, streams, and their permanent expansions, provide the state with a water surface approximating 5,637 square miles—more fresh-water area than any other state possesses. This fact accounts in no small measure for Minnesota's outstanding ornithological attractions. Red Lake (Minnesota's largest), Mille Lacs, Lake of the Woods, Rainy Lake, Mud Lake, Lake Traverse, and Swan Lake are the abodes of thousands of transient waterfowl. The picturesque rocky islands in Mille Lacs, Lake of the Woods, and Rainy Lake often have colonies of Double-crested Cormorants, Herring Gulls, and Common Terns.

Spirit and Hennepin Islands in Mille Lacs, each less than an acre in extent, with boulders heaped high above the water, have not only colonies of Common Terns but also Purple Martins, which nest under the boulders.

Throughout Minnesota, except in the southeastern section, are large marshes with aquatic plants (i.e. emergent bulrushes, cattails, quillreeds, and sedges; submersed pondweeds, bladderworts, and duckweeds), which provide ideal conditions for breeding waterfowl and for many varieties of marsh-loving birds. King Rails and Florida Gallinules nest commonly in large marshes in the southern part of the state. In wet grassy lowlands near the marshes and lakes of southern and western Minnesota, a few nesting Wilson's Phalaropes may be found. Birds to be looked for in the larger marshes of western Minnesota are the Holboell's Grebe (mainly northwestern and west-central part), the Horned Grebe (mainly northwestern part), the Eared Grebe, the Franklin's Gull, and the Forster's Tern. The following birds breed regularly in nearly all large marshes throughout the state:

Pied-billed Grebe	Coot
American Bittern	Black Tern
Least Bittern (except northern Minnesota)	Long-billed Marsh Wren
	Yellow-headed Blackbird
Virginia Rail	Red-wing
Sora	Swamp Sparrow

In Minnesota's most scenic country—the Lake Superior shore (commonly called the North Shore), the gorge of the St. Croix River, and the bluffs overlooking the Mississippi south of Red Wing—are bold escarpments that are still sites of Duck Hawk aeries. Perhaps the most picturesque site of all is Gwinn's Bluff, which towers 550 feet above the Mississippi, a short distance southeast of Winona.

Minnesota has parts of three great biological realms: the northern coniferous forest in the northeast and north-central sections of the state; the open prairie along the western boundary and the southwestern section; the deciduous forest, a belt interposed between the coniferous forest and the prairie grassland, extending diagonally from the southeastern corner of the state to the northern boundary. Transi-

tion areas where these realms come together provide some
of the finest places for bird finding.

The coniferous forest has fared better in Minnesota than
in states farther east. Since much of the land on which it
exists is unsuited for agriculture, only fires and lumbering
have brought devastation, and this has been offset by extensive reforestation and the early reclaiming of lands by
government agencies. Even today there are virgin stands of
pine. The principal trees of the upland coniferous forests
are white pine, red pine, jack pine, white spruce, and
balsam fir; of the lowlands and bogs, black spruce, tamarack, and white cedar. Where cutting or fires have occurred, birches, aspens, red maples, and other deciduous
trees are temporarily dominant. Breeding birds characteristic of the coniferous forest are the following:

Spruce Grouse	Parula Warbler
Common Sapsucker	Magnolia Warbler
Black-backed Woodpecker	Black-throated Blue Warbler
Olive-sided Flycatcher	Myrtle Warbler
Canada Jay	Black-throated Green Warbler
Brown-capped Chickadee	Blackburnian Warbler
Red-breasted Nuthatch	Northern Water-thrush
Brown Creeper	Mourning Warbler
Winter Wren	Canada Warbler
Hermit Thrush	Purple Finch
Olive-backed Thrush	Pine Siskin
Golden-crowned Kinglet	Red Crossbill
Solitary Vireo	White-winged Crossbill
Black and White Warbler	Slate-colored Junco
Nashville Warbler	White-throated Sparrow

The deciduous forest is continuous from the southeastern corner of the state to the northern boundary, except
where it is divided by an irregular peninsula of prairie extending from the southern boundary near Albert Lea and
Austin north to the Mississippi Valley between Red Wing
and St. Paul. Expectedly, the deciduous belt shows changes
in composition along its 400-mile course. In the southeastern corner, river birch, swamp white oak, white oak, black
sugar maple, and Kentucky coffeetree grow on the Mississippi Valley bottomland, while black oak, honey locust,
shellbark hickory, and black walnut predominate on the

adjacent bluffs and uplands. Birds that regularly nest here, though not much farther north in the state, are the following:

Red-shouldered Hawk	Blue-winged Warbler
Red-bellied Woodpecker	Cerulean Warbler
Tufted Titmouse	Louisiana Water-thrush
Blue-gray Gnatcatcher	

Farther north, across the prairie peninsula, from the vicinity of Faribault north to the vicinity of St. Cloud, is the 'Big Woods' section of the deciduous belt, once a dense forest of hardwoods—sugar maple, basswood, red oak, and American and slippery elms—but now reduced to patches here and there. From St. Cloud north to the boundary, the deciduous belt is less imposing, with elm, boxelder, bur oak, aspen, and black cherry prominent in upland areas that have not been cleared for farming, and willow and cottonwood in the lowland areas, such as bottomlands along streams. On the prairie side of the deciduous belt are prairie groves (islands of deciduous trees separated from the main belt by prairie) and bottomland forests (peninsulas of deciduous trees extending into the prairie along rivers and streams). In general, the tree composition of these groves and forests is similar to that of adjacent parts of the deciduous belt.

The original prairie region of Minnesota was open grassland with only scattered shrubs, but nearly all of it has been turned into farmland and is no longer recognizable. A few Swainson's Hawks and Burrowing Owls may occasionally be found in the extreme western part of the state. In the northwestern part, in the Red River Valley, there are suitable, undisturbed areas where the Sprague's Pipit, Baird's Sparrow, Leconte's Sparrow, Sharp-tailed Sparrow, and Chestnut-collared Longspur may be found, though not so abundantly as farther west in North Dakota.

Among the birds that nest regularly in the deciduous forest from boundary to boundary (including prairie groves and bottomland woods) and on Minnesota farmlands (fields, pastures, wet meadows, brushy lands, and dooryards) are the following:

248   *A Guide to Bird Finding*

DECIDUOUS FOREST

Broad-winged Hawk
Ruffed Grouse
Yellow-billed Cuckoo
Black-billed Cuckoo
Screech Owl
Barred Owl
Whip-poor-will
Yellow-shafted Flicker
Hairy Woodpecker
Downy Woodpecker
Crested Flycatcher
Least Flycatcher
Eastern Wood Pewee

Blue Jay
Black-capped Chickadee
White-breasted Nuthatch
Wood Thrush (southern half
  only)
Yellow-throated Vireo
Red-eyed Vireo
Warbling Vireo
Oven-bird
American Redstart
Baltimore Oriole
Scarlet Tanager
Rose-breasted Grosbeak

FARMLANDS

Marsh Hawk
Greater Prairie Chicken (al-
  most extirpated)
Killdeer
Upland Plover
Mourning Dove
Red-headed Woodpecker
Eastern Kingbird
Eastern Phoebe
Horned Lark
Tree Swallow
Barn Swallow
Purple Martin
House Wren
Catbird
Brown Thrasher
Eastern Bluebird
Loggerhead Shrike
Yellow Warbler

Yellow-throat
Bobolink
Eastern Meadowlark
Western Meadowlark
Common Grackle
Indigo Bunting
Dickcissel (southern Minne-
  sota)
Eastern Towhee
Savannah Sparrow
Grasshopper Sparrow
Henslow's Sparrow (southern
  Minnesota)
Vesper Sparrow
Chipping Sparrow
Clay-colored Sparrow
Field Sparrow (southern
  Minnesota)
Song Sparrow

Minnesota has two heavily used migration routes: the Mississippi Valley and the Red River Valley. In the spring, waterbirds, waterfowl, shorebirds, and passerine birds move up the Mississippi to the vicinity of Minneapolis and St. Paul, where the traffic divides, one part of it going north along the St. Croix River Valley and thence to the vicinity of Duluth and along the North Shore of Lake Superior, the other part continuing to follow the Mississippi but eventually veering off westward. With the exception of Whistling Swans, most waterfowl use the Red River route more commonly than the Mississippi route. This is particularly true of geese. White Pelicans usually follow the Red River route, rarely the Mississippi route. In their northward flight, the majority of birds taking the Red River route first fly up the Missouri River Valley and the Big Sioux River Valley, then to the Red River and directly northward. Apparently fall migration occurs along the same routes. A Minnesota migration timetable follows. *Northern Minnesota* (northernmost third of the state): for waterfowl, 1 April—5 May, 15 September—1 November; for shorebirds, 1 May—1 June, 1 August—15 September; for landbirds, 25 April—1 June, 15 August—1 October. *Southern Minnesota* (southernmost third of the state, including Minneapolis and St. Paul): for waterfowl, 25 March—20 April, 5 October—15 November; for shorebirds, 1 May—1 June, 1 August—25 September; for landbirds, 20 April—25 May, 20 August—10 October.

Minnesota winters are generally severe, with several periods of sub-zero temperatures, but they do not have the extreme cold and dryness of the western plains states at the same latitude. In southern Minnesota, winter residents include the Horned Lark (northern races), Northern Shrike, Purple Finch, Common Redpoll, Lapland Longspur, and Snow Bunting. Winter visitants of irregular occurrence are the Bohemian Waxwing, Evening Grosbeak, Pine Grosbeak, and Red and White-winged Crossbills. The Red-breasted Nuthatch, Brown Creeper, Pine Siskin, Slate-colored Junco, and American Tree Sparrow are found, sometimes commonly, in sheltered areas, but the majority of individuals leave the state. Winter visitors to the woods, bogs, or open country in the extreme northern part of the state are the Snowy Owl, Hawk Owl, Great Gray Owl, and Common Raven.

The Minnesota Ornithologists' Union publishes a quarterly, *The Flicker*, and meets annually on a Saturday in mid-May in a different part of the state. The organization may be contacted through the Minnesota Museum of Natural History, University of Minnesota, Minneapolis 14.

BAUDETTE. About 365 miles north of Minneapolis and St. Paul, between Baudette on the Canadian border and the Red Lakes to the south, is the 'Big Bog Country,' a level wilderness of seemingly limitless proportions. Part of it is now the RED LAKE GAME REFUGE of about 300 square miles. If the bird finder wishes to find northern-forest species in undisturbed surroundings, here is the place.

From Baudette, drive west on State Route 11 to Roosevelt, a distance of 20 miles. At Roosevelt, turn south on County Route S, and continue for about 15 miles to Norris Camp in the Refuge. This is an information center, office of the supervisor, and main entrance to the 225 miles of service roads passing through the Refuge. Although permission to enter the Refuge and use the roads is not required, it is advisable for the bird finder to notify the supervisor of his intentions and to find out which roads are the most interesting ornithologically. There are no public accommodations, but camping is permitted at Norris Camp and other specified places. The bird finder should not venture from the roads unless he is equipped with a reliable compass.

Much of the Refuge is typical northern 'quaking' bog with sphagnum mat on which black spruces, tamaracks, and white cedars grow thickly in some places, sedges and deciduous shrubs in others. Here and there are islands, sometimes of aspen, sometimes of red pine and jack pine. Among the birds to be found on a trip through the Refuge in the late spring and early summer are Canada Jays, near the frequently used campsites; Red and White-winged Crossbills in the red pines and other conifers; Spruce Grouse, Brown-capped Chickadees, and Golden-crowned Kinglets in the spruce bogs; Black-backed Woodpeckers on the edge of spruce bogs and in areas where there are dead trees and stumps. Of the daytime predators, the Red-tailed and Broad-winged Hawks are the most common, the Goshawk, Marsh Hawk, and Sparrow Hawk less common but often seen; of the nocturnal predators, only the Great Horned Owl is common enough to be mentioned. A few Pigeon Hawks have been found nesting in the Refuge.

In the winter the Refuge is occasionally visited by the

Hawk Owl, Great Gray Owl, Richardson's Owl, and Common Raven.

DETROIT LAKES. From this community in west-central Minnesota, travel 9 miles northeast on State Route 34 to an intersecting county road; turn left and drive north for another 9 miles to the headquarters of the TAMARAC NATIONAL WILDLIFE REFUGE. Obtain permission here to pass over roads leading to parts of the Refuge where there are good opportunities for finding birds.

This preserve of 29,108 acres has vast, level uplands, 16 large lakes, 13 smaller lakes, many marshes, and wet lowlands. It is of special interest to the bird finder in that it is in the region of transition between the western prairies, the northeastern coniferous woods, and the southern hardwoods, thereby attracting birds characteristic of all three natural realms. A thorough survey of the birds inhabiting the Refuge should yield a list of great length and interest.

On trips along Refuge roads in June and July, one can be almost certain of seeing Holboell's Grebes, Bald Eagles, and broods of such species as the Wood Duck, American Golden-eye, and Ruddy Duck. The Pileated Woodpecker is known to nest in the Refuge and can be found by careful search.

DULUTH. A group of experienced bird finders residing in this port city have found MINNESOTA POINT a gold mine for many kinds of birds, though it is only a short distance from Superior Avenue in the business district. Minnesota Point is a 7-mile strip of land extending into Lake Superior and separating it from Superior Bay. Formerly connected with the mainland, it is now severed by the Duluth Shipping Canal, over which passes the famous Aerial Bridge. Although the Point is built up with homes and stores for about half its length, there are excellent places for birds at the 200-acre recreation ground landscaped with pine, spruce, and many shrubs, and on the broad, sandy beaches and open water of both the Lake and Bay sides.

To reach these places from the city, turn off Superior

Avenue on Lake Avenue and proceed toward the Aerial Bridge, following Lake Avenue. After crossing the Bridge, take Minnesota Avenue, which passes down the Point as far as 43rd Street, where the recreation ground begins. From 43rd Street one may take Bayside Boulevard to Sky Harbor.

Although the beaches and outlying waters are good for bird observations all along the way, those beyond Sky Harbor are especially productive. Through May, and from early September to early October, one can see not only the expected varieties of shorebirds (Semipalmated Plovers, Ruddy Turnstones, Greater and Lesser Yellow-legs, Pectoral Sandpipers, Least Sandpipers, Red-backed Sandpipers, Semipalmated Sandpipers, Sanderlings) but also Golden and Black-bellied Plovers, Hudsonian Curlews, Knots, White-rumped Sandpipers, Baird's Sandpipers, Dowitchers, Stilt Sandpipers, and an occasional Buff-breasted Sandpiper. Offshore birdlife warrants attention. From November to the first of April a few Glaucous Gulls are almost invariably seen with the Herring Gulls; in April, late October, and November the Old-squaw and many other ducks make their appearance; in late April, May, and October, Bonaparte's Gulls show up in considerable numbers; in June, oddly enough, a few Red-throated Loons are sometimes seen. Over many parts of the Point, in April, May, September, and October, there are frequent flights of such hawks as the Sharp-shinned and Cooper's. The recreation ground almost always attracts interesting migrating and wintering birds. The trees and shrubs bring great numbers of small (migrating) landbirds. (One day in mid-May, 17 species of warblers were noted.) In winter, chances are good for seeing Evening Grosbeaks, Pine Grosbeaks, Common Redpolls, Pine Siskins, and both Red and White-winged Crossbills. The open, treeless stretches sometimes invite American Pipits in the early spring and late fall, Horned Larks and Lapland Longspurs in the late fall and winter (mid-November to April).

SANDBAR ISLAND, in Superior Bay about 100 feet offshore from Minnesota Point, between 19th and 24th Streets, has a small colony of Common Terns and at least one pair of nesting Piping Plovers, beginning in late May.

For a small fee, boys living on Minnesota Point across from the Island can probably be prevailed upon to provide transportation by rowboat.

From the last of August to mid-November many hawks, eagles, and falcons may be seen in southward migration from the 1,100-foot bluffs that overlook Duluth. The predators tend to fly low—sometimes they can be looked down upon from the tops of the bluffs—and not infrequently they pass so close to an observer that he can identify them without the aid of field glasses. The more common species may be seen at the following times: Duck Hawk, Pigeon Hawk, and Sparrow Hawk, last week of August and first half of September; Goshawk (in immature plumage), Sharp-shinned Hawk, and Cooper's Hawk, first three weeks of September; Marsh Hawk and Osprey, second and third weeks of September; Broad-winged Hawk (the species occurring in the most spectacular numbers), third week of September; Goshawk (in adult plumage), Red-tailed Hawk, and Rough-legged Hawk, October and the first half of November, but most common during the first half of October. Golden and Bald Eagles show up at various times throughout the migration period. For the widest variety of predators in greatest numbers, the time to visit the bluffs is any day during the third week of September, preferably between 9:00 A.M. and 2:00 P.M. To reach what is considered, in the opinion of Duluth Bird Club members, the best vantage point for viewing the migration, drive north on 45th Avenue East from Superior Avenue; proceed to the end of 45th Avenue, turn left on Summit Avenue, and go to Skyline Drive, which is the first road on the right; follow Skyline Drive to the first lookout, a drive-off for cars and the spot for observations.

A course in ornithology is given each year in the Science Building of the UNIVERSITY OF MINNESOTA, DULUTH BRANCH. Bird finders wishing to get in touch with members of the Duluth Bird Club, a very active organization, may do so by making inquiries at the Science Building.

ELY. In the northeastern corner of Minnesota, called the Arrowhead Country because of its shape, are 3,728,932

acres comprising SUPERIOR NATIONAL FOREST, the
largest National Forest in the United States. Within its
boundaries are more than 5,000 lakes, ranging in size from
a few acres to 70 square miles, and tremendous stretches
of beautiful forests. For 108 miles along its northern border, which is also the International border, over a million
acres are reserved as three separate roadless areas, while
across the border Canada has set aside a great roadless
area named Quetico Provincial Park. By International
agreement, travel by canoe is the only approved method
of transportation, and the area is thus kept in a primitive
condition. This International, roadless territory is familiarly
referred to as the Quetico-Superior Canoe Country.

Much of the terrain of the Superior National Forest is
rugged, and in some places so hilly as to be semi-
mountainous. The lakes, crystal clear and cool, have shorelines varying from ledges and loose rock to sandy beaches,
and are linked by rivers and streams that greatly facilitate
travel by canoe. The forests are primarily of white pine, red
pine, jack pine, white spruce, white cedar, and tamarack,
sometimes mixed with stands of white birch, yellow birch,
aspen, ash, and sugar maple. Where there is muskeg country—and there is a considerable amount of it—deciduous
shrubs, such as Labrador tea and leather-leaf, grow abundantly. The birdlife in Superior National Forest has not
been intensively investigated, but, judging by the forests,
it is safe to say not only that the birdlife is strongly typical
of northern coniferous forests, but also that certain species
have higher populations here than in any other wilderness
of the United States. At any rate, let the bird finder come
and see for himself.

A choice of every conceivable type of travel awaits the
bird finder. He may go on foot, by car, by canoe, or by airplane, depending on his inclinations, financial resources,
physical stamina, and available time. Ely, an iron-mining
and summer-resort town 120 miles northeast of Duluth, is
the most practicable place from which to begin ornithological explorations. From here, three routes by car are recommended, and no one is to be preferred to the others, since
all pass through equally attractive country. Along each
road are free picnic areas and campgrounds. (1) State

Route 1, going east to the North Shore Drive along Lake
Superior. This traverses 60 miles of varied, wild country.
The birds along side roads leading to lookout towers, logging operations, lakes, and rivers warrant investigation. (2)
The Fernberg Road (State Route 221), leaving Ely through
Winton and extending for 20 miles east and north into
lake country. Side roads branch off to resorts on such lakes
as Snowbank and Moose. The Fernberg Road terminates
in a fork, the right one going to Fernberg Lookout Tower,
where there is an excellent coniferous forest. (3) Echo
Trail, sometimes called the Ely-Buyck Road, passing nearly
50 miles northwest from Ely through majestic stands of
virgin white, red, and jack pines. Probably no forest in
Minnesota is more picturesque. Eventually it leads to the
famous LaCroix region, noted for its lakes with steep rocky
shores and the deep forests that hide them. The bird
finder can imagine the opportunities in store. If a canoe trip
is preferred, the services of several outfitters and guides
may be obtained through the Minnesota Arrowhead Association in Duluth, or the Ely Commercial Club in Ely.
A trip by air may be arranged through the same agencies.
Arrangements for a trip must be made in advance, for the
air services are in great demand.

Before taking trips into Superior National Forest, it is
most advisable to call at the headquarters of the U.S. Forest Service in Ely to obtain maps of the area and information relative to route conditions. Canoe trips are possible
from 10 May, at which time the lakes are ice-free, to 15
October, when the freeze-up begins. Travel over the dirt
and gravel roads is not recommended until after 1 June,
when they become fairly dry. Useful to anyone planning
an extended trip into the Forest is *Memoranda for Canoe
Country* (1953) by Calvin Rutstrum. Available through
the Burgess Publishing Company, 426 South Sixth Street,
Minneapolis 15, Minnesota, this little booklet contains pertinent information about the problems of canoeing and
camping in this wilderness country.

FARIBAULT. A fine remnant of the Big Woods and at
the same time an excellent spot for woodland birds is
NERSTRAND WOODS STATE PARK, about 14 miles

east of Faribault. This forest of approximately 1,400 acres, 270 of which are state-owned, is entirely deciduous, the predominant tree species being sugar maple, basswood, American and slippery elms, and red oak. Much of it is still in a virgin condition, although on several privately owned tracts there has been considerable cutting. The scenic attractions of the Park, in addition to its majestic stands of timber, are a rolling terrain and Prairie Creek with its two waterfalls. Fortunately, Nerstrand Woods have not been 'developed,' even though they are a state park; hence their natural beauty remains undisturbed. The only indications of state ownership are metal signs marked 'State Game Refuge.' Several roads, not suitable for automobiles but ideal for bird finding, lead to all important areas. Birds can be seen in greatest number from the second week of May, when the warbler migration is at its height, to the middle of July. In mid-May it is not unusual to record 75 species, including the Red-tailed Hawk, Broad-winged Hawk, Pileated Woodpecker, Red-bellied Woodpecker, Blue-gray Gnatcatcher, Cerulean Warbler, and Scarlet Tanager.

Nerstrand Woods can be reached from Faribault by taking State Route 60 going east. After driving 8.8 miles, turn north on a gravel road. (A small schoolhouse is located at this turn, on the left.) Continue north 2.2 miles to a church, then right one mile, then north again for 2 miles to a crossroad, which leads (one mile on the right) to the village of Nerstrand and (one mile on the left) to the Nerstrand Woods; both village and forest can be seen from this point. Turn left and drive to the Woods. Within the Woods, a wood road, not made for automobiles, soon begins on the right. Park the car here and walk along the wood road, which eventually dips down toward Prairie Creek, the best place for birds.

A rather large heron rookery is located on an island in SHIELDS LAKE about 10 miles west of Faribault. To reach it from this city, turn off US Route 65 on State Route 21 and continue on the highway through Shieldsville. Shields Lake will be seen on the left just beyond the town. The rookery is on the only island, which is about one mile from the highway side of the Lake. After the fishing season opens in May, boats are available at one or more of the docks near the highway. The island's several acres of surface are covered entirely by trees, mostly elm, maple, and boxelder. The rookery occupies the tops of the tallest trees on the eastern end of the island, which rises rather abruptly to some 35 feet. The adult population consists of about 250 pairs of Great Blue Herons, 25 pairs of Black-crowned Night Herons, and (recently) a few pairs of American Egrets. Any time from the middle of May to the middle of July is best for visiting the colony, because during this period there are young in the nests. The bird finder will be much impressed by what he sees: the island's park-like appearance, owing to the clearing away of underbrush by the cattle that wade across the channel from the pasture on the west shore; the enormous trees with dozens of nests in their loftiest branches; the hubbub among awkward young and stately adults that begins as soon as the bird finder arrives and continues until he leaves.

FRONTENAC. Near this village, which is about 60 miles southeast of St. Paul, is a well-known shorebird rendezvous called SAND POINT, a wave-built sand and gravel spit reaching into Lake Pepin (pronounced *pep'-in*). Any day in May when the water level is such that the Point is not submerged, there is not only ample opportunity to see the usual varieties, from Semipalmated Plovers to Sanderlings, but a better than fifty-fifty chance of viewing such rarities (in eastern Minnesota and the interior of eastern United States) as the Willet, Knot, White-rumped Sandpiper, and Buff-breasted Sandpiper—all of which have been seen here from time to time. A trip in mid-May need not be entirely for shorebirds, because the warbler migration may be observed in the woods bordering the Lake, in the shade trees and shrubs along the old cemetery and streets of the village, and in the swamp near the Methodist Camp. Among the oaks, elms, cottonwoods, willows, and fruit trees, it is possible to identify at least 20 species when a good wave is passing. The Prothonotary and Cerulean Warblers, which do not range much farther north, are particularly interesting parulids to be observed.

To reach Sand Point and vicinity, proceed south, through

the village of Frontenac, on US Route 61 for about one mile, cross Wells Creek, and turn left toward Lake Pepin, leaving Route 61. After the road again crosses Wells Creek, Villa Maria (a girls' school, whose gray-shingled building with red spire is a conspicuous landmark) will be seen on the left, and Sand Point will be seen on the right, extending into the Lake. From here a very poor road leads to the Point; it is often not passable by car. The Methodist Camp, on a small point of the lakeshore, is directly ahead on the road, about one mile past Villa Maria.

McGREGOR. In east-central Minnesota, the RICE LAKE NATIONAL WILDLIFE REFUGE is an inviting wilderness area of 15,240 acres, 4,000 of which are water surface. Surrounding Rice Lake are extensive wet lowlands with islands of tamarack, while in the Lake itself are large beds of wild rice and luxuriant growths of aquatic plants, including bulrushes, cattails, and various pondweeds. A 3-acre island in Rice Lake has a colony of about 15 pairs of Double-crested Cormorants and a Great Blue Heron rookery of approximately 30 pairs. All nests are in aspen and basswood. The upland portions of the Refuge support stands of mixed hardwoods, such as maple, ash, and elm, and some stands of fir and spruce. Woodcock nest in a few localities. In the vicinity of the headquarters and on several trails leading away there are excellent opportunities to watch the warbler migration in May. A few Mallards, Black Ducks, Blue-winged Teal, Wood Ducks, Baldpates, and Hooded Mergansers breed on the Refuge, but the waterfowl are in much greater abundance during migration, particularly in October.

To reach the Refuge, drive south from McGregor on State Route 65 to the very small town of East Lake (5 miles); then turn right (west) onto an unnumbered dirt road, which leads directly to headquarters on the north side of the road overlooking the east end of Rice Lake.

MINNEAPOLIS. Few cities in the United States are more active ornithologically than Minnesota's largest. Three separate organizations, the Minneapolis Audubon Society, the Minneapolis Bird Club, and the Minnesota Bird Club, unite a host of amateur ornithologists who hold regular meetings and study birds with a fervor that would startle the dyed-in-the-wool professional. If there is an underlying cause—and there is—it is the impetus that the late Dr. Thomas Sadler Roberts provided. The majority of the present members were among his students, friends, and admirers.

Dr. Roberts was for many years Professor of Ornithology at the UNIVERSITY OF MINNESOTA, where he gave a stimulating course in ornithology and wrote his monumental two-volume work, *The Birds of Minnesota*. He was also director of the MINNESOTA MUSEUM OF NATURAL HISTORY, an adjunct of the University, on the campus at the intersection of University and 17th Avenues. This handsome modern building, the most up to date among museums of its kind, was the result of his initiative and planning. No bird finder should miss visiting its thrilling interior—the foyer, the 150 well-designed teaching exhibits, and particularly the habitat groups, which, by means of their faithfulness to detail, realistic mounts and backgrounds, and expert lighting, convey the observer to the environments they represent. The Swallow-tailed Kite and the Sandhill Crane groups are truly gems. The Museum's ornithological collection includes over 10,000 bird skins, well representing not only Minnesota, but also other parts of North America and the Philippines; in addition there are 600 bird mounts and 1,700 egg sets. The Museum Library contains 1,000 bound volumes. A course in ornithology, offered by the University's Department of Zoology in the second and third quarters of the academic year, is conducted in this building. The Museum is open from 9:00 A.M. to 5:00 P.M. on weekdays (including Saturdays) throughout the academic year, and from 2:00 to 5:00 P.M. on Sundays and holidays. Summer hours are from 9:00 A.M. to 4:30 P.M. on weekdays, and from 2:00 to 5:00 P.M. on Saturdays, Sundays, and holidays.

Minneapolis has so many beautiful parks, lakes, and tree-shaded byways suitable for good bird finding that it is not possible to say which is better than the others. Resident bird finders seem to agree, however, that THEODORE WIRTH PARK, a 681-acre tract, half a mile wide and extending for $2\frac{1}{3}$ miles along the western border of the city, ranks close to the top for the greatest number and variety of landbirds. It is also fairly good for other birds. One particularly energetic bird finder has positively identified 215 species here over a period of 16 years. The Park's diversity of birdlife is accounted for in a large measure by its varied habitats. The terrain, which is rolling, includes open spaces, glens, springs, three lakes (Theodore Wirth Lake, Birch Pond, and Brownie Lake), rivulets, and a meandering stream. Oaks, birches, elms, willows, boxelders, and numerous conifers, together with many deciduous shrubs, cover much of the area. In winter, the Park is decidedly attractive to birds, owing to the presence of certain springs that remain open in sub-zero temperatures, shrubs and evergreens, which hold their fruit and seeds in cold weather, and feeding stations that supplement the natural food supply.

The Park is 3 miles west from downtown Minneapolis and can be reached in 10 minutes by five thoroughfares, namely, 19th Avenue North, Plymouth Avenue, Olson Memorial Highway, Glenwood Avenue, and Wayzata Boulevard (US Route 12). While almost any section of the Park will be productive, a recommended starting point is where Glenwood Avenue crosses the Park near Theodore Wirth Lake. Footpaths lead from here to all the worth-while areas. On a bird walk through the Park in mid-May, it is possible to find 100 species. Some of the birds to be looked for are the Winter Wren, Black-throated Blue Warbler, Connecticut Warbler (late May), Harris' Sparrow, and White-crowned Sparrow. Summer-resident birds invariably include the Green Heron, Crested Flycatcher, Eastern Bluebird, the Yellow-throated, Red-eyed, and Warbling Vireos, Rose-breasted Grosbeak, and Field Sparrow. Cardinals occur the year round. Through the winter, species to be seen, some more regularly than others, are the Pileated Woodpecker, Red-breasted Nuthatch, Brown Creeper, Golden-crowned Kinglet, Bohemian Waxwing, Evening Grosbeak, Pine Grosbeak, Common Redpoll, Pine Siskin, and American Tree Sparrow.

The THOMAS SADLER ROBERTS BIRD SANCTUARY, about 5 miles from downtown Minneapolis, is also a good spot for birds. This is a part of Lyndale Park, north of Lake Harriet, in the southwestern residential district. The entrance is across Lake Harriet Boulevard from the bandstand. The Sanctuary, which comprises a fenced area of 31 acres, is long and narrow, with a tree- and shrub-bordered path and a marsh through which a stream passes. In spite of the relatively small size of the Sanctuary, nearly two thirds of the species on the Minnesota list have been seen here over the years.

Another pleasant place to find birds in any season is the vicinity of the IZAAK WALTON BASS PONDS, about 12 miles south from downtown Minneapolis in the bottomland of the Minnesota River. The Bass Ponds are three artificial bodies of water, surrounded by willows and low shrubs and filled by a spring-fed stream that arrives through a near-by glen. Adjacent to the Ponds are miles of marshy bottomland with shrubs, scattered trees, sedges, grasses, mud flats, and some open water. From October to April, flocks of American Pipits are frequently noticed on the frozen mud flats, while single Northern Shrikes are sometimes seen, posed conspicuously on a lone tree or shrub. Although the Ponds are well worth looking over for waterbirds and waterfowl, the marshy bottomland is better. Regularly occurring, eye-catching birds, with the approximate time they are usually found, are as follows: Horned Grebes (last half of April); American Egrets (August and September); Whistling Swans (last week of March to the middle of April); Snow and Blue Geese (November and April); the majority of ducks (first of October through November, last week of March to middle of April); Forster's and Common Terns (last week of April to middle of May); Caspian Terns (middle of May to June). On the low bluffs above the bottomland and in the glen near the Ponds is an excellent deciduous woods providing habitats for many nesting birds, including the Pileated and Red-bellied Woodpeckers.

The Ponds and vicinity may be reached by taking Cedar Avenue (State Route 36) south to County Route 1 and turning left. After 0.8 mile, a narrow gravel road (marked) turns off to the east for the Ponds. The property belongs to the Izaak Walton League, but bird finders are welcome.

When the waterbird and waterfowl migrations are at

their height, satisfactory views, particularly with a spotting scope, can be obtained from the CEDAR AVENUE BRIDGE, which crosses a section of the bottomland marshes described above. When coming from Minneapolis, continue south on Cedar Avenue instead of turning left on County Route 1. The Bridge is a short distance beyond. (Cars may not be parked on the Bridge.)

Common Loons and Red-breasted Mergansers are found on LAKE NOKOMIS in April soon after the ice breaks up and in November until the coming of ice drives them away. The birds are easily seen from Cedar Avenue, which passes over the west end of the Lake about 6 miles from downtown Minneapolis.

The Minneapolis Audubon Society sponsors public lectures, conducts field trips in March, April, and May in the Roberts Sanctuary and other spots, and meets the first Friday of each month (except the summer months) at 2:00 P.M. in the Walker Branch Library, 2901 Hennepin Avenue. The Society may be contacted through the Library. The Minneapolis Bird Club, an organization of about 400 children and their parents, publishes *The Kingfisher* (monthly), takes field trips by chartered bus, operates an exhibition booth at the annual State Fair, and gives a bird-identification course each year. The Club may be contacted through the Public Library Museum (1001 Hennepin Avenue), where it meets at 8:00 P.M. on the first and third Tuesdays of every month. The Minnesota Bird Club is made up of nearly a hundred University of Minnesota students and local people with an interest in bird study beyond that of most amateurs. The Club's program consists of a meeting, beginning at 8:00 P.M., on the first Wednesday of each month, October through June, in the Minnesota Museum of Natural History. All three of these Minneapolis organizations welcome visitors.

NORTHFIELD. The CARLETON COLLEGE ARBORETUM, an area of 360 acres, extends from the campus proper northward along the Cannon River. Here are alluvial flood plains of varying width along the River, bluffs cut by ravines, and upland woods and prairie. About half of the area is wooded. Red maple, boxelder, willow, ash, and cottonwood grow commonly in the lowland; red oak predominates on the bluffs; and black walnut and various small trees and shrubs (e.g. wild crabapple, hawthorn, and hazel) occur in certain parts of the uplands. Introduced trees and shrubs have been planted in sections of the Arboretum near the campus. Perhaps the most picturesque parts of the Arboretum are Carleton Creek, which meanders along the edge of the Arboretum from the north part of the campus to the Cannon River, and the George Huntington Lyman Memorial Lakes, which have been formed by impounding the waters of Carleton Creek. Over 150 species of birds may be found during the year, the results largely of two factors: the diversity of environments and the assortment of feeding stations, nesting boxes, and other devices for attracting birds. Six miles of foot trails and seven miles of bridle trails are maintained, making all parts of the Arboretum readily accessible. The best area for bird finding is along the Nature Trail, which begins on the edge of the campus near the mouth of Carleton Creek and threads its way northward for three miles near the Cannon River. The Trail first passes through mature lowland woods, especially good for warblers during the spring and fall migrations. Farther along it emerges on a hazel prairie, then closely parallels the River where small trees and shrubs form dense cover.

The entrance to the Nature Trail is through a rustic gate beside a parking lot and can be reached from US Route 65 by turning north in Northfield Square on State Route 19 and driving for about half a mile. Carleton College will be passed on the right. On approaching the bridge over Carleton Creek, the gate and parking lot will be noticed on the left, the Lyman Memorial Lakes on the right. If the bird finder wishes to look further for birds after following the Nature Trail, he can take the trail skirting the north shore of the Lakes. To get to this trail, simply step out on Route 19 from the parking lot, cross the bridge, and proceed along the shore, where the trail will soon be picked up.

The Arboretum and the north shore of the Lyman Lakes are at their ornithological best in the first, second, and third weeks of May when the migration of small landbirds is under way. Some of the transient species that may be expected at this time are the Yellow-bellied Flycatcher, Hermit Thrush, Olive-backed Thrush, Gray-cheeked Thrush, Veery, Solitary Vireo, Philadelphia Vireo, Black and White Warbler, Tennessee Warbler, Nashville Warbler, Parula Warbler, Magnolia Warbler, Black-throated Green Warbler, Blackburnian Warbler, Chestnut-sided Warbler, Black-poll Warbler, Northern Water-thrush, Connecticut Warbler, Mourning Warbler, Black-capped Warbler, and Canada Warbler. Among the birds that may be found nesting after the middle of May are the following: Red-headed Woodpecker, Crested Flycatcher, Traill's Flycatcher, Eastern Wood Pewee, Rough-winged Swallow, White-breasted Nuthatch, House Wren, Catbird, Brown Thrasher, Wood Thrush, Cedar Waxwing, Red-eyed Vireo, Warbling Vireo, Oven-bird, American Redstart, Baltimore Oriole, Scarlet Tanager, Cardinal, Rose-breasted Grosbeak, and Indigo Bunting.

ST. OLAF COLLEGE, on a hill overlooking Northfield from the west, offers a second-semester course in ornithology, which is centered in Holland Hall. The College may be reached by taking US Route 65 northwest from Northfield Square for one quarter of a mile, then turning left on St. Olaf Avenue.

PARK RAPIDS. ITASCA STATE PARK, midway between Park Rapids and Bemidji on US Route 71 and 225 miles northwest of Minneapolis and St. Paul, enfolds 31,976 acres of natural beauty and charm. Within its boundaries are 300 clear lakes, magnificent virgin stands of red and white pines, and great stretches of young forests. It goes without saying that there are birds to be found, many of them.

Lake Itasca, the largest of the lakes and the source of the Mississippi River, has much to offer. Ospreys and Common Loons fish in its waters; a pair of Bald Eagles rear their young in a nest near its western arm across from Chambers Creek; ducks, including many Wood Ducks, frequent Floating Bog Bay and the entire western shore; Turkey Vultures occasionally loiter in the vicinity.

The woods of Itasca Park are predominantly northern coniferous. In addition to the primeval portions, there are extensive stands of jack pine, balsam fir, white cedar, tamarack, black spruce, and white spruce mixed with scattered stands of white birch, aspen, and sugar maple. Birds of particular interest are the following: Whip-poor-wills (in the woods near Squaw Lake); Pileated Woodpeckers (Bear Point, northwest of Lake Itasca; also the northeast corner of the Park); Black-backed Woodpeckers (in the woods southwest of Lake Itasca); Olive-sided Flycatchers, Red-breasted Nuthatches, Brown Creepers, and Winter Wrens (in the tamarack and black spruce bog near Nicollet Cabin); Brown-capped Chickadees (at Garrison Point, near the southwest extremity of Lake Itasca; also at Iron Springs, one mile north of the Park); Hermit Thrushes (in several places, including the edges of Floating Bog Bay and near the road to LaSalle Springs); Golden-crowned Kinglets (in the tamarack and black spruce bog along LaSalle Creek near the northern boundary); Solitary Vireos (near openings in coniferous woods and bogs); Eastern Towhees (along the road to Squaw Lake); Slate-colored Juncos and White-throated Sparrows (along the Bohall Trail and along Nicollet Creek). Roads and well-marked footpaths pass near all the places where these birds may be seen. The warbler migration begins during the middle of August, at which time it is possible to find over 20 species, both summer residents and transients.

The Park has campgrounds, picnic areas, and tourist accommodations. Douglas Lodge, on Lake Itasca about half a mile from the Route 71 entrance, is an exceptionally fine hotel and cabin development. Less expensive cabin developments are immediately adjacent to the north boundary of the Park.

The UNIVERSITY OF MINNESOTA FORESTRY AND BIOLOGICAL STATION, on the east shore of Lake Itasca, offers graduate and undergraduate work in several branches of field biology. Members of the Station have recorded over 150 species of birds, but no more than 125 are usually recorded in any one summer.

A map of the Park, distributed free of charge by the Divi-

sion of State Parks, State Office Building, St. Paul 1, will
enable the bird finder to locate all places desired. Copies
can usually be obtained at Douglas Lodge.

PRESTON. One of the most charming parts of southern
Minnesota, off the beaten path, are the CARIMONA and
FORESTVILLE WOODS, over 2,000 acres of little-
disturbed hardwoods—walnut, butternut, maple, elm, and
oak—with some white pine. These fine forests occupy the
valley walls (some are quite steep cliffs) of the south
branch of the Root River and the adjacent uplands. The
birdlife is especially interesting because of its southern
affinities, e.g. permanent-resident Red-bellied Woodpeckers and Tufted Titmice, summer-resident Turkey Vultures,
Blue-gray Gnatcatchers, and Blue-winged and Cerulean
Warblers. Nests of the Vultures are to be looked for on
the cliffs; those of the Blue-winged Warblers on the
ground in grassy or shrubby clearings.

At the southwest edge of Preston, 35 miles south of
Rochester, turn west from US Route 52 on County Route
D to Carimona. At the west edge of Carimona, near the
remains of a large brick building, turn north (right) with
County Route D and continue for about a mile to a fork
in the road. The road bearing right (north) is County Route
10, which goes through Carimona Woods, about three
quarters of a mile beyond this fork; the road bearing left
(west) is the continuation of County Route D. To reach
Forestville Woods, continue again on County Route D for
about 5 miles to a brick-fronted building, all that is left
of the village of Forestville. The Forestville Woods surround it.

ROCHESTER. Bird finders are welcome to visit MAYO-
WOOD, the country estate of the late Dr. C. H. Mayo, now
owned by Dr. C. W. Mayo. It contains beautiful, 50-acre
Mayowood Pond, created by damming the south fork of
the Zumbro River. Adjacent to the pond are hills covered
by 1,500 acres of mixed hardwoods, mostly second growth,
but including some magnificent virgin stands. The area is
not entirely wooded, however; there are several marshes
close by and numerous pastures, brushy hillsides, and

plowed fields. Mayowood is an exceptionally fine place for a variety of birds, perhaps the best in southeastern Minnesota. Canada Geese, Blue-winged Teal, and Wood Ducks nest here. Not infrequently Canada Geese and Mallards remain through the winter, sometimes by the thousand. Red-shouldered Hawks, Ruffed Grouse, Pileated Woodpeckers, and Blue-winged Warblers are some of the landbirds known to breed in Mayowood; Tufted Titmice and Carolina Wrens are sometimes seen and may breed. Both the Eastern and Western Meadowlarks occur as summer-resident birds, providing an exceptional opportunity to compare the vastly different songs of the two species.

To reach Mayowood, drive south from Rochester on US Route 63 for about one mile. Just past the Fair Grounds take the first turn to the right. This road leads to Mayowood Pond, a distance of 3 miles. There are paths on both sides of the Pond that lead away from it for distances of several miles. Mayowood is best in early May, when the bird population is swelled by waves of small transient birds, particularly warblers.

ST. CHARLES. Typical of the upper Mississippi River bottomland country is WHITEWATER STATE PARK, midway between Winona and Rochester. At St. Charles on US Route 14, take State Route 74 north to the Park, 6 miles distant. The Park's 688 acres include a deep, broad valley (through which Route 74 descends) with precipitous limestone walls ascending in a spectacular manner from 300 to 400 feet above the valley floor. Whitewater River and several converging creeks pass through the valley. Although the surrounding territory is undulating farmland, the Park is densely forested with mature, mixed hardwoods and some white pine and red cedar. Certain parts of the Park have been developed for recreational purposes —golfing, picnicking, camping, and swimming—but this does not interfere with good bird finding. From glades near the camping area, Woodcock take off for their crepuscular flights; Duck Hawks patrol the cliffs near the golf course; Whip-poor-wills repeat their night-time calls from the woods bordering the River; Turkey Vultures loiter on warm air currents rising from the valley; Louisiana Water-thrushes sneak along the edges of secluded streams; Cliff Swallows set up their colonies under a highway bridge and on some of the perpendicular valley walls; Blue-winged Warblers are at home in the thick shrubs and secondary growth near the picnic area. There are wilder places in the Park, disturbed only by footpaths, where one may see an occasional Pileated Woodpecker and Ruffed Grouse. A bird-finding trip to Whitewater State Park between April and mid-July is almost certain to be rewarding. Overnight cabins are available in the Park.

ST. PAUL. About 8 miles from the business center of this capital city is the LAKE VADNAIS MUNICIPAL FOREST which members of the St. Paul Audubon Society consider one of their best areas for birds in any season. Here are two lakes, a woods, bog, and near-by fields—a distinctly varied country that has yielded in five years' time a list of 171 species. Lake Vadnais and Sucker Lake, parts of the St. Paul municipal water system, have a total surface of about 250 acres. In the migration season waterbirds and waterfowl can often be seen here, but not in great numbers. Perhaps the Wood Duck, which likes the tree-fringed edges of both Lakes from spring to fall, is the most distinguished occupant. The woods, comprising 235 acres, are mainly of coniferous trees (red pine, white pine, white spruce) mixed with a few stands of ash, oak, and aspen. Several Great Horned and Barred Owls seem to make it their home the year round. The woods are especially notable for attracting warblers and other birds that are characteristic of coniferous forests in the northern part of the state. Golden-crowned Kinglets have been found breeding here, establishing the southernmost breeding record for the state. During the winter, Brown-capped Chickadees, Brown Creepers, Bohemian Waxwings, Evening Grosbeaks, Pine Grosbeaks, Common Redpolls, Slate-colored Juncos, and American Tree Sparrows are often reported. In the fall and winter, Goshawks and Rough-legged Hawks make a regular appearance. The bog (Savage Lake), which covers about 100 acres, is surrounded by deciduous woods.

To reach the Lakes and Forest described above, leave

St. Paul on Rice Street (State Route 49), drive north to
County Route F, and turn east (right) on F. This passes
between the Lakes (Sucker is on the north), where the
best part of the Forest is situated. Park the car here, and
take footpaths to the Lakes through the Forest. The bog
is about 1.5 miles from Lake Vadnais. It may be reached
in several ways, one of which is to turn east off State Route
49 onto State Route 36. Drive to McMenemy Street and
turn north. The bog is a short distance beyond, on the left.
The Lake Vadnais Forest is a restricted area, but bird finders are welcome. However, if any part of the Forest is to be
penetrated, permission should be obtained from the keeper,
who lives on the 'between the lakes' road.

In the Administration Building of the UNIVERSITY OF
MINNESOTA FARM CAMPUS, on Cleveland Avenue
north of Como Avenue, work in wildlife management is
regularly given. A small collection of bird skins, mostly of
waterfowl and game birds, is available for study purposes.

COMO PARK ZOO in Como Park, between Lexington
and Hamline Avenues, has a small collection of exotic
waterfowl and other birds. During the winter most of them
are kept in a new limestone building of modern design.

The St. Paul Audubon Society, which may be contacted through the St. Paul Public Library, 90 West 4th
Street, publishes *The Cardinal* (monthly except June, July,
and August), sponsors a series of public lectures, and
manages a 10-acre bird sanctuary in Como Park.

THIEF RIVER FALLS. A must on the itinerary of any
bird finder visiting northwestern Minnesota is MUD LAKE
NATIONAL WILDLIFE REFUGE. Here are 60,744
acres of uplands, marsh, and open water that are teeming
with wildlife. During the season of 1948, the estimated
total of waterfowl that used the marsh was 77,000, and the
estimated production of young was 27,000. Not only are
there heavy populations of birds, but also many mammals,
namely, 1,600 deer; 30 to 40 moose; great numbers of
muskrats, minks, and beavers; a few skunks, weasels, rac-
coons, and bobcats; an occasional black bear and timber
wolf.

The upland terrain of the Refuge is very flat, with varied

wildlife habitats. These include many abandoned farmlands that are reverting to tree growth; scattered groves of
aspen, ash, and elm, with shrub undergrowth; large areas
of willows; and several spruce-tamarack bogs. Ruffed and
Sharp-tailed Grouse are well represented, the latter frequenting the Refuge boundaries near farmlands during
their 'dancing' season in April and during the summer.
Small colonies of Cliff Swallows are established under
bridges and eaves of buildings, while many Tree, Bank,
and Barn Swallows have found acceptable nesting sites. The
Short-eared Owl is seen regularly and probably breeds. A
list of landbirds breeding on the Refuge and passing
through it in migration would no doubt be most impressive.

The entire marsh of more than 20,000 acres is exceedingly rich in aquatic plants: large contiguous areas of cattails, quillreeds, and bulrushes; a good variety of submerged aquatics, such as pondweeds, bladderworts, and
waterweeds. With such a quantity of vegetation suitable for
cover and food, it is quite natural that the marsh attracts
an abundance of waterfowl. Mallards, Gadwalls, Baldpates,
Pintails, Blue-winged Teal, and Shovelers nest commonly;
Wood Ducks, Redheads, Ring-necked Ducks, Lesser Scaup
Ducks, and Ruddy Ducks nest less commonly, but nevertheless in fair numbers. Nesting waterbirds of special interest
are Holboell's Grebes, Horned Grebes (a few), Double-
crested Cormorants, Great Blue Herons, Black-crowned
Night Herons, Franklin's Gulls, and Black Terns. A colony
of 500 pairs of Great Blue Herons is located in an adjacent
spruce-tamarack bog. The Black-crowned Night Herons
and Cormorants nest on islands in the marsh and on the
banks of drainage ditches. Hundreds of Yellow-headed
Blackbirds nest in the quillreeds.

Mud Lake Refuge is 24 miles northeast of Thief River
Falls and can be reached from State Route 32 by turning
east on a gravel road (County Route E) half a mile north
of the village of Holt; 11 miles along this Route, the Refuge
headquarters will be seen adjacent to the highway. Parts
of the Refuge can be reached by car, provided permission
is first obtained at headquarters.

TWO HARBORS. Perhaps the best spot for diversity of birdlife on Minnesota's scenic North Shore Drive (US Route 61) is GOOSEBERRY FALLS STATE PARK (637 acres), 15 miles northeast of Two Harbors. Except for camping and picnicking grounds, and footpaths, it is relatively undisturbed. The Gooseberry River, a turbulent stream with two picturesque waterfalls about 30 feet in height, rushes through the Park into Lake Superior. The bold rocky shore and riverbed are devoid of vegetation, but elsewhere there are mixed woods containing birch, aspen, fir, and spruce, with many shrubs such as alder and dogwood. Paths running beside the River from the lakeshore to the second (upper) falls are the best vantage points for seeing the greatest number of birds. Some of the nesting birds that are observed here in June and July are the Red-breasted Nuthatch, Olive-backed Thrush and Veery, seven warblers (Black and White, Parula, Magnolia, Black-throated Green, Blackburnian, Chestnut-sided, Mourning), the Pine Siskin, and the White-throated Sparrow. Duck Hawks, whose aeries are on the near-by shoreline escarpments, are sometimes observed. Transient shorebirds are often numerous on the shore, close to the mouth of the River, between 1 August and 25 September.

Each year, BEAVER ISLAND has a small colony (about 150 pairs) of Herring Gulls and several nesting Red-breasted Mergansers. This 4-acre island, covered in part by stands of dwarf conifers, is a quarter of a mile offshore from White Rock Resort. To reach it, continue northeast on US Route 61 from Two Harbors and Gooseberry Falls State Park to East Beaver Bay, then turn right and proceed one mile. Arrange with one of the local fishermen for a boat to the Island.

WHEATON. One of Minnesota's greatest ornithological spectacles is the goose migration in spring at MUD LAKE and LAKE TRAVERSE, long narrow bodies of water forming part of the state's western boundary. On a day in the first week of April it is not unusual to see many thousands of geese—mostly Snow and Blue Geese, with small groups of Canada Geese and scattered numbers of White-fronted Geese. Several hundred White Pelicans and Whistling Swans, in addition to thousands of ducks, invariably swell the throng. The best place to begin watching the geese is in the vicinity of the interstate bridge where the two Lakes adjoin.

The bridge is reached from Wheaton by taking State Route 27 southwest for 5 miles, then State Route 117 for the final mile. It will be observed from the bridge that the Lakes have marshy shores rising to cultivated territory on the Minnesota side, and high, grassy bluffs on the South Dakota side. In order to get a true impression of the number of geese, one should explore these shores. From the bridge, then, drive along roads paralleling the Lakes on either side, north to White Rock and south to Browns Valley. At points where the roads come close to the Lakes, hike down to the shores. On one's approach, sometimes wave upon wave of honking birds will take to the air ahead. If possible, plan the trip to Mud Lake and Lake Traverse so as to be present near evening, when flocks of geese start coming in from the grainfields, where they have been feeding during the day, to settle on the water for protection at night. Since most of the territory surrounding the Lakes is privately owned, permission is necessary before crossing overland from road to shore. In early April the paralleling roads may sometimes be so muddy as to be impassable by car, and the winds that frequently sweep in from the prairie may be sharp and penetrating, making warm clothing desirable. Good food and lodging can be obtained at the Palmer House in Wheaton.

Contributing authorities: Walter J. Breckenridge, Harvey L. Gunderson, Mrs. Josephine Daneman Herz, Pershing B. Hofslund, Robley W. Hunt, F. Raymond Keating, Jr., Olga Lakela, Frank R. Martin, Kenneth D. Morrison, Harvey E. Stork, Gustav A. Swanson, Milton D. Thompson, Dwain W. Warner.

Missouri

GREATER PRAIRIE CHICKEN

In spring days long ago, the Missouri prairie resounded at sun-up to the low, vibrant 'booms' of the Greater Prairie Chicken. The setting for these sounds was a grassy knoll, ridge, or meadow. Here were the assembled males, each vigorously maintaining his territory by a succession of strange antics: quick flights by each bird straight upward, followed, after a drop to the ground, by cackles and baleful squawks; charges, as one bird rushed after another; direct encounters, as two birds attacked each other by slapping their wings, or by striking with their bills and feet. The principal feature, however, was the booming display, which was climaxed by rapidly stamping the feet, bringing the pinnated neck feathers to a forward position, inflating the bright orange air sacs, and rendering the three-syllabled doleful sound, *old-mul-doon.* Today the booming of this fine bird may still be heard in Missouri, but in a few areas only. Both species and habitat have been greatly depleted by man.

The prairie is one of the three distinctive physiographic regions in Missouri, occupying most of the state north of the Missouri River and a part southwest of it—roughly a section west of a line drawn from Boonville on the Missouri southward through Versailles, Clinton, Appleton City, El Dorado Springs, Greenfield, and Joplin to the western boundary. Throughout, the Missouri prairie is level to rolling country, dissected by numerous rivers and their tributaries. Originally grassland, with deciduous trees along the watercourses, or in isolated groves, it is now the principal farming district. The remaining population of Greater Prairie Chickens, recently estimated at 13,000 individuals, may be found where large acreages of grassland are now permanent pasture or hayland. Other birds commonly sharing this environment with the Prairie Chickens are the Upland Plover, Horned Lark, Western Meadowlark, and Grasshopper Sparrow.

The Ozarks, the second region, occupy the rest of the state south of the prairie except the southeastern lowlands, which is the third region, extending as far north as Cape Girardeau on the Mississippi and west to points near Poplar Bluff and Naylor. In general, the Ozarks are a broad upland, or plateau, interrupted by innumerable wide valleys, though in several places there are many knobs and peaks with intervening sharp, deep valleys. Few localities have elevations exceeding 1,400 feet. The St. Francis Mountains, in the eastern Ozarks, have a landscape that is rugged, even mountainous. Here Taum Sauk Mountain reaches 1,772 feet, the highest point in the state. Another scenic locality, made famous through the novel, *The Shepherd of the Hills,* by Harold Bell Wright, is west and north of Lake Taneycomo in the southwestern Ozarks (see under Branson). The Ozarks are for the most part tree-clad, though summits of certain knobs and ridges are naturally treeless, or 'bald,' while other areas have been cleared for settlement and agricultural pursuits. The forests vary in character. Those on most slopes are quite open; the timber, predominantly post oak, blackjack oak, and hickory, is medium-sized at lower elevations, but becomes stunted as higher elevations are approached. Birdlife is usually disappointing both in variety of species and in numbers of individuals. In some parts of the Ozarks, on the lower slopes and valley floors, there once stood forests of short-leaf pine and red cedar mixed with bur oak, black oak, walnut, sycamore, black gum, hackberry, boxelder, black cherry, and other deciduous trees. In the remnants of these forests— for example, the tract south of Round Spring State Park (see under Salem)—bird finding is decidedly rewarding, for here dwell an interesting combination of southern, pine-loving birds—the Red-cockaded Woodpecker, Brown-headed Nuthatch, Pine Warbler, and Pine-woods Sparrow —and birds preferring the dense hardwoods.

The southeastern lowland, which includes the Peninsula or Bootheel that projects into Arkansas, represents a widening of the Mississippi flood plain south of Cape Girardeau. With an elevation less than 400 feet above sea level and only 10 to 20 feet above the Mississippi, its numerous shallow ponds, meander cutoffs, and bayous increase many times their size by flooding early in the year, yet are almost dry in the late summer. Dense bottomland forests and swamps containing trees of immense size once stood here, and still do in certain places, such as in Big Oak Tree State Park (see under Charleston). Sycamore, cottonwood, bald cypress, tupelo, sweet gum, magnolia, tulip tree, pecan, persimmon, catalpa, sassafras, various oaks, and other trees characteristic of southern lowlands are common. Expectedly this region attracts bird species not found regularly elsewhere in the state. The Double-crested Cormorant, Anhinga, Little Blue Heron, Yellow-crowned Night Heron, Black Vulture, and Swainson's Warbler are among the species known to breed here. Such rarities as the Swallow-tailed and Mississippi Kites and the Bachman's Warbler will probably be discovered by intensive searching. It is surprising—and certainly regrettable—that so fascinating a region has been neglected ornithologically. Bird finders who have visited it are few indeed.

Although not a physiographic region as such, the forested bottomlands and bluffs along the Mississippi north of Cape Girardeau, the Missouri, and the other big rivers in the state serve greatly to enrich Missouri birdlife. Though mostly second-growth, the cottonwoods, sycamores, sugar maples, boxelders, elms, and willows that stand on the bottomlands, and the oaks, hickories, and walnuts on the bluffs provide habitats for birds, some of which would not otherwise occur in the state to any marked extent.

Throughout Missouri, the following birds breed regularly in the forests (including bottomland woods, the Ozark forests, and remnants of prairie groves) and farmlands (fallow fields, pastures, wet meadows, fencerows, brushy draws, woodland borders, orchards, and dooryards):

FORESTS

Cooper's Hawk
Red-shouldered Hawk
Broad-winged Hawk
Yellow-billed Cuckoo
Screech Owl
Barred Owl
Chuck-will's-widow (chiefly southern Missouri)
Whip-poor-will
Yellow-shafted Flicker
Pileated Woodpecker (chiefly southeastern Missouri)
Red-bellied Woodpecker
Hairy Woodpecker
Downy Woodpecker
Crested Flycatcher
Acadian Flycatcher
Eastern Wood Pewee
Blue Jay
Black-capped Chickadee (chiefly northern and central Missouri)
Carolina Chickadee (chiefly southern Missouri)
Tufted Titmouse
White-breasted Nuthatch

Wood Thrush
Blue-gray Gnatcatcher
Yellow-throated Vireo
Red-eyed Vireo
Warbling Vireo
Prothonotary Warbler
Worm-eating Warbler (chiefly Ozarks)
Parula Warbler
Cerulean Warbler
Yellow-throated Warbler (chiefly southern Missouri)
Oven-bird
Louisiana Water-thrush
Kentucky Warbler
Hooded Warbler (chiefly southern Missouri)
American Redstart
Baltimore Oriole
Scarlet Tanager (chiefly northern Missouri)
Summer Tanager
Rose-breasted Grosbeak (except extreme southern Missouri)

FARMLANDS

Marsh Hawk
Greater Prairie Chicken (locally in prairie region)
Bob-white
Killdeer
Upland Plover (chiefly northern prairie region)
Mourning Dove
Barn Owl
Red-headed Woodpecker
Eastern Kingbird
Eastern Phoebe
Horned Lark
Barn Swallow
Purple Martin
House Wren (except southern Missouri)
Bewick's Wren (except northern Missouri)
Carolina Wren
Mockingbird
Catbird
Brown Thrasher
Eastern Bluebird
Loggerhead Shrike
White-eyed Vireo
Bell's Vireo
Yellow Warbler
Prairie Warbler (chiefly southern Missouri)
Yellow-throat
Yellow-breasted Chat
Eastern Meadowlark
Western Meadowlark
Orchard Oriole
Common Grackle
Cardinal
Blue Grosbeak (chiefly western and southern Missouri)
Indigo Bunting
Dickcissel
Common Goldfinch
Eastern Towhee
Grasshopper Sparrow
Henslow's Sparrow (chiefly northern Missouri)
Vesper Sparrow (chiefly northern Missouri)
Chipping Sparrow
Field Sparrow
Song Sparrow (northern Missouri only)

The Mississippi River on the eastern boundary and the Missouri River, which sweeps across the state from the western boundary, bring through Missouri the birds that habitually follow these great river valleys during migration. On their bottomlands and on adjacent areas enormous numbers of birds may be found: waterbirds, waterfowl, and shorebirds on the countless sand or mud bars, lakes, ponds, sloughs, meander cutoffs, and marshes; landbirds in the weed patches, brushy thickets, and woods. White Pelicans, Double-crested Cormorants, Bald Eagles, and various geese, ducks, gulls, and terns are the most conspicuous transients, but careful inspection of the thickets and woods is almost certain to reveal in the proper season impressive waves of small landbirds. The bottomlands of the Missouri north of Kansas City and of the Mississippi in the vicinity of St. Louis are, in the spring and fall, among the best

places for bird finding in the state. As in Iowa, a number of
northern species of passerine birds—for example, the
Yellow-bellied Flycatcher, Winter Wren, Gray-cheeked
Thrush, Philadelphia Vireo, Bay-breasted Warbler, and
Canada Warbler—move more commonly along the Mississippi in eastern Missouri than they do farther west. Conversely, a few species such as the Orange-crowned Warbler
and Harris' Sparrow are more commonly seen in migration
in the western part of the state. The following timetable
indicates when one may expect the main spring and fall
migratory flights through Missouri: waterfowl, 1 March—
10 April, 15 October—10 December; shorebirds, 25 April
—25 May, 5 August—10 October; landbirds, 10 April—
10 May, 5 September—1 November.

Though too far south to be within the regular winter
range of such northern fringillids as crossbills and redpolls,
Missouri is nevertheless a common wintering ground for
Slate-colored Juncos, American Tree Sparrows, and others.
In southern Missouri, especially in the southeastern lowland, the following birds winter commonly: Red-breasted
Nuthatch, Brown Creeper, Hermit Thrush, Golden-
crowned and Ruby-crowned Kinglets, Myrtle Warbler,
White-crowned Sparrow, White-throated Sparrow, Fox
Sparrow. The Woodcock is said to winter here in fair numbers, but confirmation is lacking. Large aggregations of
waterfowl, mainly Mallards and Pintails, with fewer numbers of other species, pass the winter in southern Missouri
on ponds and other bodies of water where the food supply
is sufficient. One such place is the Basin in the Mingo National Wildlife Refuge, reached from Poplar Bluff. Christmas bird counts made in the state are highest in the St.
Louis and Kansas City areas, where totals often range between 50 and 65 species.

The Audubon Society of Missouri, with a membership of
about 600, publishes a monthly bulletin, *The Bluebird,* and
owns and operates the Springdale Bird Sanctuary (see under Cape Girardeau). It meets in the fall at various places
throughout the state. The organization may be contacted
through the Missouri Conservation Commission, Jefferson
City.

BRANSON. In the Ozarks of southwestern Missouri, Forsyth Dam impounds the waters of the White River to form LAKE TANEYCOMO, a narrow, S-shaped body of water about 15 miles in greatest length. The near-by bluffs and ravines have a rather open woods, the principal growth on the slopes being oak and hickory with scattered stands of short-leaf pine, red cedar, walnut, and other trees. Stretches of shrubby growth appear commonly. Directly to the north and west of Lake Taneycomo is a typical section of *The Shepherd of the Hills* country. Among the birds breeding regularly in the woods and shrubby areas around Lake Taneycomo are the Yellow-billed Cuckoo, Acadian Flycatcher, Carolina Chickadee, Tufted Titmouse, Carolina Wren, Mockingbird, Wood Thrush, White-eyed Vireo, Yellow-breasted Chat, Orchard Oriole, Summer Tanager, Blue Grosbeak, and Indigo Bunting. In the lowland woods along watercourses are such summer residents as the Parula Warbler, Cerulean Warbler, Louisiana Water-thrush, Kentucky Warbler, and American Redstart. The Lake itself is considered noteworthy as a resting place for waterfowl during migration. Branson, a resort town on Lake Taneycomo, is a good spot from which to begin bird finding, since various roads lead from there to different places along the Lake and into the rugged hill country to the north (via US Route 65) and west (via State Route 80). One should not miss obtaining the fine view of the Ozarks from Dewey Bald (7 miles west of Branson on Route 80), a 1,341-foot hill.

BROOKFIELD. The SWAN LAKE NATIONAL WILDLIFE REFUGE in north-central Missouri embraces altogether 10,675 acres lying on the bottomlands of the Grand River. Two artificial pools, Swan and Silver Lakes, occupy 1,100 and 3,050 acres respectively, while the rest of the area consists of 2,500 acres of heavy timber (principally oak, hickory, pecan, walnut, maple, elm, and sycamore), 2,500 acres of agricultural lands, and 1,827 acres of bluegrass meadow. The maximum waterfowl concentrations on the two pools occur in March and November. At such times, as many as 125,000 ducks have been estimated, the species being mainly the Mallard and Pintail with fewer numbers of Black Ducks, Gadwalls, Baldpates, Green-winged and Blue-winged Teal, Shovelers, Redheads, Ring-necked Ducks, Canvas-backs, Lesser Scaup Ducks, and Ruddy Ducks. About 25,000 Snow and Blue Geese have also been estimated in the spring, and smaller numbers, usually about 10,000, in the fall. Spring and fall populations of Canada Geese each average about 30,000 individuals. Coots occur in equally impressive numbers. Although a few Wood Ducks find suitable localities for nesting, the Refuge is not considered a breeding area for waterfowl. Nevertheless it is not without an excellent variety of other breeding birds. Of special interest are the Greater Prairie Chickens, whose booming activities begin in February and last until June, with peak performances in April. To reach the Refuge from Brookfield, proceed west on US Route 36 for 5 miles and turn left to Sumner, taking first County Route N south and then County Route E west for a distance of 12 miles. At Sumner, go south 3 miles on an unimproved road to headquarters, on the west side of the Refuge. Roads through the Refuge are not open to the public, but bird finders may make arrangements for a guided tour by writing in advance to the Refuge manager (address: Sumner).

CAMDENTON. When the Ozarks are in their autumn splendor, bird finding around the LAKE OF THE OZARKS is at its best, for at that time of year one may see an interesting combination of resident and transient species. A favorite spot of Missouri Audubon Society members is the area on the Hahatonka Arm of the Lake, reached as follows: From Camdenton, drive west about 2 miles on US Route 54 to a bridge over the Lake. Instead of crossing the bridge, turn left and proceed 3 miles to the Hahatonka Cabin Camp; enter, and park the car. (Although this property is open to bird finders, it is advisable to ask permission before entering.) Walk up the tree-covered shore one mile to the big spring, or hire a boat at the dock to search for birds along the shore. The wooded hillside that rises back of the Camp is excellent territory for small landbirds. Members of the Missouri Audubon Society, meeting here regularly in mid-October, have listed as many as 74 species in one trip. Some of the species they always expect to find are the Pied-billed Grebe, Double-crested Cormorant, Green-winged Teal, Cooper's Hawk, Ring-billed Gull, Pileated and Red-bellied Woodpeckers, Bewick's and Carolina Wrens, Wood Thrush, Eastern Bluebird, Cedar Waxwing, Solitary Vireo, Orange-crowned Warbler, Myrtle Warbler, Black-capped Warbler, Purple Finch, Harris' Sparrow, and White-crowned Sparrow. Lake of the Ozarks, 129 miles long, with a shoreline of more than 1,300 miles, was formed by Bagnell Dam across the Osage River near US Route 54 north of Camdenton. Winding roads lead to nearly all parts of this octopus-shaped body of water, thus making easily accessible many of the coves and wooded slopes where bird finding can be productive.

CAPE GIRARDEAU. Two miles north of this city, which overlooks the Mississippi at a point 150 miles downstream from St. Louis, is the SPRINGDALE BIRD SANCTUARY (25 acres), owned and operated by the Audubon Society of Missouri. Its northern boundary is scenic Cape Rock Drive, from which it may be reached. Running through the Sanctuary is Cape Creek, bordered by patches of weeds and briars, willow thickets, and stands of cottonwood and sycamore. From this stream a wooded slope rises to a high ridge on which are open fields, an old orchard, and a dense woods. For one wishing to find some of the more common birds characteristic of the Missouri countryside, the Sanctuary is considered excellent. Some of the birds definitely known to breed in the area are the Eastern Phoebe, Acadian Flycatcher, Purple Martin, Blue Jay, Carolina Chickadee, Tufted Titmouse, Carolina Wren, Eastern Bluebird, Blue-gray Gnatcatcher, Prothonotary Warbler, and Field Sparrow. Visitors are welcome to use the trails, which lead to the most interesting parts of the Sanctuary.

CHARLESTON. An excellent example of flood-plain forest in the bottomlands of the Mississippi in southeastern Missouri just northeast of the Bootheel is embraced by BIG OAK TREE STATE PARK (1,007 acres). Much of the forest contains virgin timber, the rest well-developed second growth. Some of the commonest trees are oak, cottonwood,

282   *A Guide to Bird Finding*

cypress, sweet gum, tupelo, and persimmon. Many attain giant size—for example, the famous 'Hunter's Oak' that is 128 feet in height and has a circumference of 23 feet 5 inches. The epiphytic fern, *Polypodium,* grows on the trunks and branches of some of the larger trees. Grassy Lake, a small body of water, usually dries up by late summer. As many as 65 species have been observed here during the breeding season, including the Little Blue Heron, Yellow-crowned Night Heron, Black Vulture, and Swainson's Warbler, as well as the following: American Egret, Wood Duck, Red-shouldered Hawk, Yellow-billed Cuckoo, Pileated Woodpecker, Red-bellied Woodpecker, Red-headed Woodpecker, Crested Flycatcher, Acadian Flycatcher, Carolina Chickadee, White-breasted Nuthatch, Carolina Wren, Wood Thrush, Blue-gray Gnatcatcher, Red-eyed Vireo, Prothonotary Warbler, Parula Warbler, Cerulean Warbler, Yellow-throated Warbler, Kentucky Warbler, Hooded Warbler, and Summer Tanager. The passage of passerine birds through the area during migration in April, early May, and September is heavy—which is to be expected in view of the Park's location with respect to the Mississippi flyway. The abundance of Northern Water-thrushes, for example, is frequently impressive. Common among the wintering species are the Brown Creeper, Hermit Thrush, Golden-crowned and Ruby-crowned Kinglets, Myrtle Warbler, and the White-crowned and White-throated Sparrows. The Park, about 24 miles south of Charleston, can be reached by driving south from Charleston on State Route 55 for 6 miles, then taking State Route 105 for 4 miles to East Prairie. At East Prairie, drive east on County Route V and south on County Route A for the remaining 14 miles.

COLUMBIA. The UNIVERSITY OF MISSOURI, extending across the south side of this city, has long been one of the centers of wildlife research in the United States. An undergraduate course in ornithology is offered by the Zoology Department in Lefevre Hall. Material emphasized includes the structure, identification, habits, and economic importance of Missouri birds. Other studies related to ornithology are offered in the following courses: Principles of Wildlife Conservation, Animal Ecology, and Wildlife Management.

The EAST ASHLAND CONSERVATION AREA is a favorite locale with Columbia bird observers. This is a 2,250-acre tract of wild land which the University of Missouri administers as an experimental wildlife area. Cover types include grassland, woodland edge, oak-hickory woods, and a pine plantation. A virgin stand of sugar maples occurs along Brushy Creek at the south end of the Area. This variety of habitat attracts a great variety of transient and breeding passerine birds. In April and September, Leconte's Sparrows are abundant in the many abandoned fields grown to broom sedge. Some of the birds to be found breeding in the Area, beginning in May, are the Worm-eating Warbler, Prairie Warbler (in the pine plantation), Kentucky Warbler, Summer Tanager, Blue Grosbeak, and Lark Sparrow. The Area may be reached by driving 16 miles south from Columbia on US Route 63 to the town of Ashland, thence on a gravel road 2¼ miles east and half a mile south to the northwest boundary of the Area.

During the past decade, technical personnel of the Missouri Conservation Commission have been making studies of the Greater Prairie Chickens that occupy small areas east of Columbia. The birds gather on their booming grounds in January and reach peak activity in the first two weeks of April; by the end of June, they cease to appear. One of the booming grounds may be reached by driving east from Columbia on US Route 40. On coming to a point 2¾ miles west of Kingdom City, a stretch of native prairie grass will be seen on the right (south) side of the highway. This is the location of the booming ground; others are situated within 2½ miles north and west of this point. The best dates for observation are between the second week of March and the third week of April, when booming usually occurs regularly each day: from half an hour before sunrise until two or three hours later, and from an hour before sundown until dusk. If observations are to be made within 100 yards of the booming ground, it is necessary for the observer to conceal himself, in either a car or a blind, before the arrival of the birds.

KANSAS CITY. Just within the southeastern limits of Kansas City lies SWOPE PARK (1,346 acres), a recreational center possessing exceptional natural beauty. Rocky hills drop steeply into deep ravines and the valley of the Blue River; oaks and hickories cover the slopes, while stately elms and sycamores are abundant in the lowland areas. Landscaped gardens, two golf courses, and two lakes—the Lagoon for bathing and boating and the Lake of the Woods for fishing—add variety to the scene. Bird finding is good in any season. Turkey Vultures nest among remote lime-stone outcroppings, White-eyed and Bell's Vireos in hedge-rows and shrubby edges of woods, Acadian Flycatchers, Yellow-throated Vireos, and Scarlet and Summer Tana-gers on forested hillsides. Barred Owls and Whip-poor-wills can be heard in the evenings during the early summer. Waves of landbirds pass through the Park in the spring and fall, those in April and October containing many Harris' Sparrows, those in early May and September num-erous warblers, such as the Tennessee, Orange-crowned, Myrtle, and Black-poll. The Park is situated southeast from the corner of Swope Parkway and 63rd Street and may be reached from the heart of the city by going south on US Route 71 (the Paseo) and then east (left) on Meyer Boulevard. Winding drives lead to all parts of the Park. Within the Park, near the entrance from Meyer Boulevard, are the SWOPE PARK ZOOLOGICAL GARDENS with a collection of birds, mostly native and exotic waterfowl, on a small lake.

Because Kansas City is in the Missouri Valley—on the Missouri River where it turns eastward from the state's western boundary—hosts of waterbirds, waterfowl, and shorebirds pass through the vicinity during the spring and fall. Excellent vantage points for observation are north of the city, and may be conveniently reached by leaving the city on US Route 71 and then turning left on State Route 45. This highway follows the Missouri River northward over flat marshy bottomlands intersected by streams, back-waters, meander cutoffs, lakes, and lagoons, whose water levels fluctuate seasonally, being especially high in March and April. The following five spots, passed by Route 45, are highly recommended for bird finding:

1. HORSESHOE LAKE, near Farley about 20 miles north of Kansas City, is a meander cutoff where ducks and

shorebirds gather in notable numbers, the former in March, October, and November, the latter in late April, May, late August, and September. Among the shorebirds it is sometimes possible to identify a few of the more unusual species, for example, the Golden Plover, Baird's Sandpiper, Redbacked Sandpiper, Stilt Sandpiper, and Hudsonian Godwit.

2. BEVERLY LAKE, about 5 miles farther north between East Leavenworth and Beverly Station, is similarly attractive to ducks and shorebirds. Having marshy borders with a rich growth of emergent aquatic plants, it provides nesting cover for such birds as American Bitterns, Least Bitterns, King Rails, Virginia Rails, Soras, Florida Gallinules, Long-billed Marsh Wrens, and Yellow-headed Blackbirds.

3. IATAN MARSHES, west and southwest of Iatan about 12 miles north of Beverly Station, is equally fine for nesting marshbirds and, in the late summer, for visiting herons: Great Blue Herons, American Egrets, Blackcrowned Night Herons, and occasionally a few Snowy Egrets, immature Little Blue Herons, and Yellow-crowned Night Herons.

4. BEAN LAKE, west of the village of Bean Lake and about 2 miles north of Iatan, attracts not only ducks, but also flocks of White Pelicans (usually in April, September, and October) and Snow and Blue Geese (in March).

5. SUGAR LAKE, southwest of the junction of Route 45 with US Route 59 and about 5 miles north of Bean Lake, is an irregularly shaped, shallow body of water connected to the Missouri River at its westernmost end. Marshy borders are conspicuous here and there. From late February to early April, and again in late October and November, the 400-acre surface of Sugar Lake is alive with ducks: Mallards, Gadwalls, Baldpates, Pintails, Green-winged and Blue-winged Teal, Shovelers, Redheads, Ring-necked Ducks, Canvas-backs, Lesser Scaup Ducks, American Golden-eyes, Buffle-heads, Ruddy Ducks, Hooded Mergansers, American Mergansers, and Red-breasted Mergansers. In March enormous numbers of Canada, Snow, and Blue Geese, and fewer numbers of White-fronted Geese, may be seen loitering along the shores, or flying to and from their feeding grounds in near-by fields. For shorebirds,

marshbirds, and herons, Sugar Lake is as good as the four spots previously mentioned. Just south of the junction with Route 59, Route 45 passes the easternmost arm of Sugar Lake and the entrance road to LEWIS AND CLARK STATE PARK (on the left), which occupies 60 acres of the Lake's shore. Both this arm and the Park are good places from which to make observations. Other places may be found on the northern shore, parts of which are near the left side of Route 59 going westward from its junction with Route 45. Across the Missouri River from Kansas City are two worth-while bird-finding areas. (For information, see under Kansas City, Kansas.)

Most of the persons residing in Kansas City and vicinity who are interested in birds belong to the Burroughs Nature Club, which may be contacted through the Kansas City Museum at 3218 Gladstone Boulevard. This organization publishes the *Burroughs Club Bulletin* (bimonthly), conducts spring and fall field trips, and sponsors a series of public lectures.

ST. JOSEPH. In this northwestern Missouri city, which overlooks the Missouri River from bluffs on its eastern side, members of the St. Joseph Audubon Society generally search for landbirds by going east on Mitchell Avenue Road. This highway passes through open farming country, then comes to an end, 5 miles from the business district, at a small stream known as HUNDRED AND TWO RIVER. Here there are brushy thickets and deciduous woods where migrating warblers, fringillids, and other passerine birds throng during late April, early May, and September. The height of the spring warbler migration comes during the first week of May. For waterbirds, waterfowl, and shorebirds, Audubon Society members visit either Sugar Lake (for information, see under Kansas City), southwest of St. Joseph on US Route 59, or the SQUAW CREEK NATIONAL WILDLIFE REFUGE (6,809 acres), northwest of the city.

Except for a small area on hilly bluffs, most of the Squaw Creek Refuge is on the flat bottomlands of the Missouri River. About one half is open water; the remainder consists of marshes, several hundred acres of farmland, and a few small wooded sections. The spectacular ornithological attractions are the tens of thousands of Snow and Blue Geese that stop off on their way north in mid-March, the many hundreds of White Pelicans that appear in September and October, and the huge aggregations of ducks that collect on the pools from October to January. Migrating shorebirds are numerous in late April and May. Although the Refuge is not a breeding area for ducks, the marshes with their rich growth of cattails, bulrushes, and other aquatic plants bring in the summer an association of breeding birds that includes Least Bitterns, King Rails, Florida Gallinules, Long-billed Marsh Wrens, and Yellow-headed Blackbirds. Herons of many kinds show up in the late summer. Among the birds to be expected in the winter are Rough-legged Hawks, Bald Eagles, Marsh Hawks, Red-bellied Woodpeckers, Horned Larks, Slate-colored Juncos, American Tree Sparrows, and White-throated Sparrows. Recently, during the last week of December, Canada Geese estimated at 30,000 and Mallards estimated at 60,000 were present on the pools. To reach the Refuge from St. Joseph, drive north on US Route 59 to Mound City, a distance of 46 miles, then turn directly south on Bluff Road (a county highway), which leads to the Refuge headquarters.

The ST. JOSEPH MUSEUM at 11th and Charles Streets is a Gothic-style sandstone structure containing a natural-history collection of 4,000 items. The bird collection comprises about 500 mounts and 1,700 eggs from all over the world. Persons desiring information on where to find birds in the St. Joseph region may contact, through the Museum, members of the St. Joseph Audubon Society.

ST. LOUIS. From the Mississippi just south of the points where the Illinois River enters from the east and the Missouri River from the west, this enormous city and its numerous suburbs spread out westward over many miles of flat to gently undulating terrain. Despite the dense settlement and the vigorous industrial activities, there exists in this region, even within the limits of the city itself, a surprising array of good bird-finding areas—lakes, ponds, lagoons, and marshes for migrating waterbirds, waterfowl, and shorebirds; forested tracts for many different kinds of landbirds.

The best year-round area in the city itself is FOREST
PARK (1,380 acres), one of the largest natural parks in
any United States city. About two miles west of downtown
St. Louis, it extends from Lindell Boulevard on the north
to Oakland Avenue on the south, from Kingshighway
Boulevard on the east to Skinker Boulevard on the west. A
group of small lakes and connecting waterways, open fields,
and hilly woodland offer a variety of habitats. The spot of
special interest is an undisturbed, unlandscaped tract of
hardwood forest back of the Art Museum, almost in the
center of the Park's western half. On four Sunday mornings
in April and May, the St. Louis Audubon Society conducts
the Forest Park Bird Walks. In a single morning, with expert leaders, it is possible to record as many as 75 species,
including the Pied-billed Grebe, Black-crowned Night
Heron, Blue-winged Teal, Wood Duck, Coot, Solitary Sandpiper, Lesser Yellow-legs, Red-bellied Woodpecker, Common Sapsucker, Crested Flycatcher, Rough-winged Swallow, Carolina Chickadee, Tufted Titmouse, Brown
Creeper, Mockingbird, Wood Thrush, Olive-backed
Thrush, Blue-gray Gnatcatcher, Philadelphia Vireo, Worm-
eating Warbler, Magnolia Warbler, Louisiana Water-
thrush, Baltimore Oriole, Eastern Towhee, White-crowned
Sparrow, and Lincoln's Sparrow. The Bird Walks, open
to the public, start at 7:30 A.M. from the Jefferson Memorial
(facing DeBaliviere Avenue on Lindell Boulevard), reached
by Lindell bus or Forest Park streetcar.

Occupying 83 acres in the southwestern part of Forest
Park is the ST. LOUIS ZOOLOGICAL Park (open daily
from 8:00 A.M. to 6:00 P.M.), famous the world over for
the excellence and variety of its exhibits. The birds, of which
there are about 1,000 specimens, representing 450 species
(the majority foreign), are exhibited in three divisions: the
Tropical Bird House and Wing, the huge Outdoor Bird
Cage, and the Waterfowl Lakes. In the Tropical Bird
House there are many rare exhibits, but the striking feature
is the natural beauty of several of the settings used to display specimens. Here are birds amid tropical and semitropical vegetation that grows directly from the soil. Five
large exhibits are behind glass, while a sixth, the largest, is
a swamp exhibit without glass or any covering. Visitors

entering the building come face to face with this immense scene of 15 or more species of birds feeding in the water, wading through a dense tangle of aquatic plants, or flying about in trees that tower overhead. The Primate, Anthropoid, and Reptile Houses contain exhibits as striking as those in the Tropical Bird House. The Zoological Park may be reached by taking the Forest Park streetcar, or by driving over US Route 40 (City Route 50—the Express Highway through Forest Park) and turning north at Hampton Avenue.

Perhaps the best year-round area for bird finding outside of the city is CREVE COEUR LAKE. This is reached by taking US Route 40A (St. Charles Rock Road) west from the city; about 10 miles from the city limits, turn left on Creve Coeur Mill Road for about 4 miles, then left on Marine Avenue, which soon passes the Lake on the northeast side. Situated in the bottoms of the Missouri River, this shallow body of water has muddy shores bordered by willow thickets, shrubs, and tall rushes, while a bluff rising from the eastern shore is well covered by woods. March, October, and November are the best months for finding many kinds of ducks; April, May, August, and September for herons, gulls, terns, and warblers. Some of the species recorded from time to time are the Common Loon, Yellow-crowned Night Heron, Red-breasted Merganser, Broad-winged Hawk, Ruddy Turnstone, Willet, and Avocet. The willow thickets here and in other places along the Missouri are used as roosts by innumerable Red-wings and Common Grackles, together with lesser numbers of Rusty Blackbirds and Brown-headed Cowbirds, during late February, March, October, and early November, and sometimes during the coldest months. In the early evening the gathering of these hordes among the willows is an impressive sight.

From Route 40A, 1.5 miles west of Creve Coeur Mill Road, turn right on Taussig Road. For two miles this road passes through the TAUSSIG ROAD AREA (so designated by the St. Louis Audubon Society), an extension of mud flats on the bottomlands of the Missouri. Here thousands of shorebirds (e.g. Semipalmated Plovers, Wilson's Snipe, Greater and Lesser Yellow-legs, Pectoral Sandpipers, Dowitchers) feed and loiter in late April, early May,

290 A Guide to Bird Finding

late August, and September. Many kinds of herons, such as American Egrets and Great Blue Herons, appear in the late summer and early fall; American Pipits are fairly common visitants in April and October.

The narrow strip of land between the Mississippi and Missouri Rivers at their confluence just north of the city is flat and marshy, with cultivated fields, grassy meadows, and shallow lakes. The extent to which it is covered by water depends on the rainfall. This entire area, known to bird finders as the St. Charles Marshes, is excellent for a multitude of waterbirds and waterfowl. Although much of the land is privately owned, a great many birds can be seen from the main highway (State Route 94), which goes from St. Charles to Alton, Illinois, traversing the entire area. Three specific places in the St. Charles Marshes are outstanding for birds.

1. DARDENNE MARSHES (covering about 3 square miles), privately owned and fenced. Permission to enter the property, except during the hunting season, may be arranged through the St. Louis office of the National Audubon Society, 1207 North Seventh Street, St. Louis 6. The Marshes may be reached by taking US Route 40A west from St. Louis to St. Charles, then right on Route 94 for 3 miles to County Route B (just beyond Boschertown), left on Route B to County Route C, right on County Route C to the first gate on the left, which marks the entrance to the property. From the gate, the road connects with many unimproved roads (passable only in dry weather) running through the Marshes, crossing small streams, and passing muskrat ponds, partly submerged woodlands, and open grassland. The diversity of habitats brings a great number of birds during the spring and fall migrations, and in the winter. Some of the species that have been listed in the late fall and winter are the White Pelican, Mallard (very abundant), Black Duck, Pintail, Ring-necked Duck, Canvasback, Lesser Scaup Duck, American Golden-eye, Ruddy Duck, Red-tailed Hawk, Red-shouldered Hawk, Rough-legged Hawk, Bald Eagle, Marsh Hawk, Sparrow Hawk, Short-eared Owl, Red-bellied Woodpecker, Red-headed Woodpecker, Horned Lark, Carolina Chickadee, Black-capped Chickadee, Carolina Wren, Mockingbird, Logger-

head Shrike, European Tree Sparrow, Rusty Blackbird, Eastern Towhee, American Tree Sparrow, White-crowned Sparrow, White-throated Sparrow, Fox Sparrow, and Swamp Sparrow.

2. MARAIS TEMPS CLAIR is a marsh-bordered lake, reached by proceeding as outlined above to St. Charles, then right on Route 94 through Boschertown and Orchard Farm for 11 miles. The lake appears on the right of the highway. The marshes around the lake are privately owned, but they may be entered, except during the hunting season, after first obtaining permission through the St. Louis office of the National Audubon Society. Bird finding is worth while along the highway itself, since it passes close to the lake. Marais Temps Clair is particularly good for transient waterbirds and shorebirds, and for transient and wintering waterfowl. On several occasions as many as 23 species of ducks have been observed. Short-eared Owls are frequently seen on the surrounding marshes between October and April.

3. WEBER LAKE, actually an arm of the Mississippi, may be reached from Route 94 by turning north on a road that leaves Route 94 opposite Marais Temps Clair. (The direction of Weber Lake is indicated by a sign.) Once on this road, take the first right turn and drive to the end. This small body of water and the willow-lined shore are an excellent area for finding birds in the winter, as well as in the spring and fall. Old-squaws are occasionally seen on the Lake between November and April.

Twenty-five miles west of the city the Missouri Conservation Commission maintains the ROCKWOODS RESERVATION (3,000 acres), a section of very rough country with steep hills and narrow valleys, for the most part forested with oak and hickory. An excellent spot for finding warblers during the height of their migration in the first week of May, it is equally good for diurnal birds of prey: nesting Turkey Vultures, Cooper's Hawks, Red-shouldered Hawks, Broad-winged Hawks, and Sparrow Hawks; migrating Sharp-shinned Hawks and others; wintering hawks, including such rarities as the Goshawk. A natural-history museum adds interest to the Reservation, while well-marked nature trails make readily accessible some of the best vantage points for bird finding. To reach the Reservation, proceed west on US Route 50; at Glencoe Road, turn left and drive one mile to the museum. A resident state naturalist, who has his headquarters in the museum, will provide the bird finder with directions to the best vantage points.

For small landbirds the year round, one of the outstanding places in the St. Louis region is the MISSOURI BOTANICAL SOCIETY ARBORETUM (1,600 acres) at Gray Summit, 30 miles west of the city. Take US Route 66 west to the junction with US Route 50 at the village of Gray Summit. Soon after this junction (Route 66 is joined with Route 50 for 6½ miles), Route 66 passes the Arboretum on the left. Several hundred acres of the tract, lying along the Meramec River bottomland, comprise fields and woodland, where wildflowers, trees, and shrubs from other sections of the state have been introduced. Among the interesting birds that can be found breeding are the Woodcock, Prairie Warbler, Blue Grosbeak, and Lark Sparrow.

Across the Mississippi in Illinois are several places that are popular among the St. Louis bird students. These are Grand Marais State Park; the Mississippi Bottomlands, along the east side of the Mississippi; Horseshoe Lake; Pere Marquette State Park; and Swan Lake, in the Upper Mississippi Wildlife and Fish Refuge. (For information, see under East St. Louis and Grafton in the Illinois chapter of *A Guide to Bird Finding East of the Mississippi,* the eastern counterpart of this volume.)

No account of bird-finding opportunities in the St. Louis region would be complete without calling special attention to the European Tree Sparrow mentioned in a foregoing paragraph. This species, a resident in the British Isles, Europe, and northern Siberia, was introduced in the St. Louis region in 1870. At that time about 20 individuals were released in a residential section on the south side of the city. By 1877, a small colony had become permanently established in the same neighborhood. Despite the subsequent intrusion of the English Sparrow and its tendency to bully its Old World colleague, the Tree Sparrow prospered and soon appeared in other spots around the city, including East St. Louis, across the Mississippi. Today the species may be found in many places within a radius of 50 miles from the city limits, chiefly in the suburban districts and rural communities about homes and farms. Though non-migratory, individuals frequently gather in large flocks during the fall and winter, sometimes joining flocks of English Sparrows. Before looking for the bird, the bird finder should familiarize himself with the field marks used to distinguish it from the English Sparrow, which it closely resembles.

The St. Louis Audubon Society, in addition to conducting the Forest Park Bird Walks, publishes the *Bulletin* (quarterly), sponsors an annual series of public lectures, and undertakes several outings and field trips during the year. The organization, which is a branch of the National Audubon Society, may be contacted through the St. Louis office of the National Audubon Society (see above) or the Chamber of Commerce.

SALEM. In south-central Missouri on State Route 19, between Salem and Eminence, is the so-called PINEWOODS, a privately owned tract of 10,800 acres through which flows the clear, spring-fed Current River. The topography is quite rugged, owing to outcroppings of sandstone and limestone. Until 1947 the tract contained the last extensive stand of virgin short-leaf pines in Missouri, but that year the pines were cut, except for a strip preserved as a roadside park on each side of the highway for about a mile. Most of the oaks, hickories, and other trees remained untouched. Because of the different habitats—especially the remaining strip of pines, the hardwoods with their heavy undergrowth, and the open brushy areas resulting from lumbering operations—at least 67 species of birds have been observed here in June during the breeding season. Closely associated with the pines are the Red-cockaded Woodpecker, Brown-headed Nuthatch (one nesting record), Pine Warbler, and Pine-woods Sparrow. Other birds include the Sharp-shinned Hawk, Red-tailed Hawk, Barred Owl, Chuck-will's-widow, Whip-poor-will, Pileated Woodpecker, Eastern Wood Pewee, Carolina Chickadee, Bewick's Wren, Carolina Wren, Blue-gray Gnatcatcher, White-eyed Vireo, Black and White Warbler, Worm-eating Warbler, Blue-winged Warbler, Cerulean Warbler, Yellow-throated Warbler, Prairie Warbler, Oven-bird, Kentucky Warbler,

Scarlet Tanager, Indigo Bunting, and Eastern Towhee. The Osprey appears regularly along the Current River during the late spring and summer, and probably nests in the vicinity.

SULLIVAN. A fine spot in which to find small landbirds in east-central Missouri is MERAMEC STATE PARK (7,153 acres), one of the major recreational areas in the state, located just east of the town of Sullivan, on State Route 114. A public playground, as well as a forest preserve and game refuge, it consists of an unbroken tract of rolling woodland with modern cabins and dining lodge (open from Memorial Day to Labor Day), camping facilities, and miles of nature trails. Among the natural features are many springs, more than 20 caves (including Fisher's Cave, which is open to the public during the summer months), and the clear waters of the Meramec River, which tumbles swiftly through a narrow valley.

Both the Chuck-will's-widow and Whip-poor-will and both the Parula and Cerulean Warblers nest in the Park during the summer, while earlier in the year, about the first week of May, many other warblers (e.g. the Tennessee, Nashville, Myrtle, Black-throated Green, Black-poll, and Canada) pass through in migration. In the winter, the brushy bottomlands near the entrance to Fisher's Cave are attractive to great numbers of fringillids, such as Slate-colored Juncos, American Tree Sparrows, White-throated Sparrows, Fox Sparrows, Swamp Sparrows, and Song Sparrows. Specific information on the birdlife of the area may be obtained from the naturalist, who has his headquarters in a nature museum near the dining lodge.

Contributing authorities: Rudolf Bennitt, Homer R. Bolen, William J. Bremser, Jr., Miss Tommy Brown, James Earl Comfort, Mrs. William G. (Hattie Ettinger) Conway, Roy E. Coy, Lee R. Crail, James Cunningham, Jr., Eugene W. Dehner, Herbert H. Dill, William H. Elder, Lloyd F. Gunther, Harold C. Hedges, William A. Jenner, William N. Kelley, J. Marshall Magner, Mrs. J. Marshall (Ernestine) Magner, G. E. Moore, Esther L. O'Connor, Clair T. Rollings, Simon Rositzky, Paul Q. Tulenko, G. E. Wood.

Montana

WESTERN GREBES

In May the Western Grebes return to their favorite marshes in the prairie lakes of Montana and at once begin their courtship displays. From then until July they perform, usually in twos, their varied and fantastic antics—'water skimming,' 'weed tricks,' 'head-waggling bouts,' 'penguin struts,' 'ghost dives,' 'swan gliding,' and 'habit preening.' A description would require paragraphs, at best inadequate. To be fully appreciated, these antics must be seen—and they may be readily observed by any bird finder who will take the time and make the effort to visit such a spot as Lake Bowdoin in the Bowdoin National Wildlife Refuge (see under Malta) in late May or June, select a vantage point overlooking the marsh, and simply watch.

Montana, the third largest state, has two major natural divisions: the Prairie Region, roughly the eastern two thirds of the state, and the Mountain Region, the remaining western third. The meeting of the two divisions is along a line running diagonally across the state in a northwest-southeast direction.

The Prairie Region lies on the Missouri Plateau, a part of the Great Plains, with elevations ranging from 1,900 feet in the northeast to 4,500 feet at the edge of the Mountain Region. Eastward across the Prairie Region flow Montana's principal eastern rivers, the Missouri and the Yellowstone, to their confluence just across the North Dakota line. The valleys of these great waterways and their main tributaries are deep and broadly terraced, in places severely dissected by erosion, forming typical badlands, or flanked by high ridges, sometimes showing bold cliffs and striking formations such as pinnacles and 'tables.' Where the terrain has a rough character of this sort, birds such as Say's Phoebes, Bank and Cliff Swallows, Rock Wrens, and perhaps a Prairie Falcon or Golden Eagle may be expected. Beyond the valleys are the smooth rolling plains that dominate the topography of the Prairie Region; yet the plains do not extend for many miles without being interrupted by flat-topped buttes and gravelly mesas of varying heights. In the west, interruptions are even more pronounced, for here small, isolated mountain groups—for example, the Little Rocky, Big Snowy, Bearpaw, Highwood, and Crazy Mountains—rise 3,000 to 4,000 feet above the plains in widely separated localities.

The plains of the Prairie Region, though modified in varying degrees by cultivation or grazing, are mainly grassland, but the grass associations differ according to conditions of soil and moisture. The higher plains, including most hills and mesas, are relatively dry and thus support a short-grass association. Since they are generally unsuited to crop production, they are used to a great extent for grazing cattle and show little change. Favorite habitats for both Horned Larks and McCown's Longspurs, the higher plains are also, if not too greatly disturbed, the most attractive areas in the state for breeding Long-billed Curlews. The lower plains, having greater moisture, were originally long-grass prairie, but are now largely agricultural in character. Nevertheless there are meadows, pastures, and haylands that have grasses, either native or introduced, which provide cover for species of birds—the Bobolink, Savannah Sparrow, Chestnut-collared Longspur, and others—that may have typified the birdlife of the long-grass prairie over the state. In scattered localities are stretches of sagebrush where Sage Grouse, Clay-colored Sparrows, and Brewer's Sparrows regularly reside. Groves of cottonwood, aspen, boxelder, and other deciduous trees together with thickets of willow and various shrubs (e.g. silverberry, buffaloberry, snowberry, wild rose) grow along the watercourses and in sheltered coulees (trench-like ravines); shrubby thickets also grow in draws (shallow ravines) and occasionally spread out to some extent on the adjacent prairie. These wooded environments, especially when isolated by broad expanses of prairie, often contain surprisingly large numbers of birds and varieties of species. Some of the higher hills, mesas, buttes, and ridges have a cover of juniper which, in the southern part of the Prairie Region, holds small nesting populations of Pinyon Jays. On the prairie-surrounded mountains in the western Prairie Region, the vegetation and associated birds are identical with those of the Mountain Region.

No discussion of the Prairie Region and its birds would be adequate without mentioning the thousands of small reservoirs or 'farm ponds' in the unglaciated, southern half of the Prairie Region and their attractiveness to nesting ducks. Each of these ponds (about one to every 3.8 miles) is estimated to yield every year one to two broods of ducks. The species represented are the following, listed in order of decreasing abundance: Mallard, Pintail, Blue-winged Teal, Green-winged Teal, Baldpate, Gadwall, and Shoveler.

Because of the great variation in the physiography of the Prairie Region, there is no species of bird that can be said to occur everywhere; yet a great number of species range widely. Listed below are the species that breed more or less regularly throughout the Prairie Region in timbered areas, along watercourses, and in coulees, or in the open country (prairie grasslands, haylands, pastures, fallow fields, meadow-like lowlands, brushy places, and dooryards).

These same species, unless otherwise indicated, breed in similar situations in the prairie-like valleys of the Mountain Region. Species marked with an asterisk breed also at high altitudes in both the Prairie and Mountain Regions.

OPEN COUNTRY

Swainson's Hawk
Ferruginous Hawk
Marsh Hawk
Sharp-tailed Grouse
Sage Grouse
Killdeer
Long-billed Curlew
Upland Plover (Prairie Region)
Mourning Dove
Burrowing Owl
Short-eared Owl
Red-headed Woodpecker
Eastern Kingbird
Western Kingbird
Say's Phoebe
Horned Lark
*Tree Swallow
Barn Swallow
American Magpie
House Wren
Catbird
Brown Thrasher (Prairie Region)
*Mountain Bluebird
Sprague's Pipit (Prairie Region)
Loggerhead Shrike

Yellow Warbler
Yellow-throat
Yellow-breasted Chat
Bobolink
Western Meadowlark
Common Grackle (Prairie Region)
Lazuli Bunting
Common Goldfinch
Spotted Towhee
Lark Bunting
Savannah Sparrow
Grasshopper Sparrow
Baird's Sparrow (eastern Prairie Region)
Vesper Sparrow
Sage Sparrow (southern Prairie Region)
*Chipping Sparrow
Clay-colored Sparrow (Prairie Region)
Brewer's Sparrow (Prairie Region)
Song Sparrow
McCown's Longspur (Prairie Region)
Chestnut-collared Longspur (Prairie Region)

WOODED TRACTS

*Cooper's Hawk
Black-billed Cuckoo (Prairie Region)
Screech Owl
*Red-shafted Flicker
*Hairy Woodpecker
*Downy Woodpecker
*Wright's Flycatcher

*Western Wood Pewee
*Black-capped Chickadee
*White-breasted Nuthatch
Red-eyed Vireo
Warbling Vireo
American Redstart
Bullock's Oriole
Black-headed Grosbeak

The Mountain Region embraces various ranges in the Rocky Mountains, nearly all of which trend in a north-south direction. The Prairie Region meets the easternmost ranges —the Lewis, Big Belt, Bridger, Absaroka, Beartooth, and the northern tip of the Big Horn—along their eastern foothills. A few of the ranges in the Mountain Region are separated by broad valleys, but most of them are close together, separated (sometimes indistinctly) only by narrow valleys, or even by canyons. The broad valleys are generally flat to rolling, and are typically treeless except near streams. It is thus not surprising to find here many species of birds characteristic of the Prairie Region (see preceding paragraphs). Elevations in the Mountain Region begin at 1,800 feet in the Kootenai River Valley (the lowest point in the state), in the extreme northwest, and reach 12,850 feet on the summit of Granite Peak (the highest point) near Yellowstone National Park in the southeast. The elevations of the valley floors usually range between 3,000 and 5,000 feet. Only a few mountains exceed 10,000 feet, but there are dozens that reach about 9,000. The Continental Divide zigzags northward over several of the ranges, passing west of many of the highest peaks, including Granite Peak.

The higher ranges in the Mountain Region are notably rugged, with craggy ridges and peaks; those in Glacier National Park (see under Glacier Park) are the most extreme in this respect and thus the most scenic. Coniferous trees characterize the forests, although cottonwoods, aspens, alders, willows, and other deciduous growth occur in the lower valleys and ravines, usually near streams, or, in the case of aspens, in groves on the lower slopes. In the foothills and mountains up to about 6,000 feet in the south and 5,000 feet in the north are forests of ponderosa pine and Douglas fir and (not infrequently) belts of juniper. Between 6,000 and 8,500 feet in the south and between 5,000 and 7,500 feet in the north, lodgepole pine becomes the predominant forest growth, but there are also stands of Douglas fir, Engelmann spruce, and limber pine. As the elevation increases, alpine fir appears. West of the Continental Divide, where there is greater humidity, the forests show a different character, especially in the northwest.

Here western white pine, western larch, western red cedar, western hemlock, and grand fir are common, sometimes at elevations much lower than 5,000 feet. Above 8,500 feet in the southern Mountain Region and above 7,500 feet in the northern, begins the stunted or subalpine forest consisting mainly of alpine fir and limber pine with some whitebark pine. This continues to the timber line at 9,000 feet in the south and 8,000 feet in the north. Where the mountains reach far above the timber line an alpine region exists. In parts of Glacier National Park the various forest belts described above are, as a rule, correspondingly lower, with the result that the alpine region sometimes begins at 6,500 feet.

Since most of the main mountain ranges in both the Mountain and Prairie Regions are so close together as to be practically continuous, the species of birds inhabiting them are much the same throughout; but there are nonetheless a few differences between the ranges owing to latitude, elevation, humidity, vegetation, and other factors. For example, the Varied Thrush is evidently found only in the northern mountains west of the Divide, the Black Rosy Finch and Green-tailed Towhee in the southern mountains, and the Pinyon Jay in the juniper belt east of the Divide. Listed below are birds that breed regularly (unless otherwise indicated) in the forests of all the major mountain ranges.

Goshawk
Sharp-shinned Hawk
Blue Grouse
Franklin's Grouse
Ruffed Grouse
White-tailed Ptarmigan
(above timber line in northern mountains)
Pygmy Owl
Pileated Woodpecker (northern mountains)
Common Sapsucker (generally below 7,500 feet)
Williamson's Sapsucker
Black-backed Woodpecker

Three-toed Woodpecker
(southern mountains)
Olive-sided Flycatcher
Violet-green Swallow
Canada Jay
Steller's Jay
Common Raven
Clark's Nutcracker
Mountain Chickadee
Red-breasted Nuthatch
Brown Creeper
Winter Wren (northwestern mountains)
Hermit Thrush
Olive-backed Thrush

Townsend's Solitaire
Golden-crowned Kinglet
Ruby-crowned Kinglet
American Pipit (above timber line)
Solitary Vireo
Orange-crowned Warbler (in deciduous thickets)
Audubon's Warbler
Townsend's Warbler (northwestern mountains)
Northern Water-thrush
Macgillivray's Warbler (in deciduous thickets below 7,500 feet)
Black-capped Warbler (in deciduous thickets above 7,500 feet)
Western Tanager
Cassin's Finch
Pine Grosbeak (subalpine forest)
Pine Siskin
Red Crossbill
Oregon Junco
White-crowned Sparrow
Fox Sparrow (western mountains)
Lincoln's Sparrow (in deciduous thickets of western mountains)

Contributing immeasurably to Montana's attractiveness as a place for bird finding are the prairie lakes, the majority of which are in the northern Prairie Region. Usually shallow and quite marshy, with an abundance of cattails and quillreeds, they frequently hold an impressive breeding population of waterbirds, waterfowl, Yellow-headed Blackbirds, and Red-wings. In their immediate vicinities, Willets, Avocets, and Wilson's Phalaropes frequently nest. The larger the lakes, the more open water they have and the more likely they are to be used as breeding grounds by Western Grebes, Canada Geese, Ring-billed Gulls, Common Terns, and, sometimes, White Pelicans and Double-crested Cormorants. Outstanding among the larger prairie lakes for variety of birds are Medicine Lake and Lake Bowdoin (see under Culbertson and Malta, respectively).

In the Mountain Region lie a number of bodies of water that hold a good array of birds, though they do not have the immense populations of the prairie lakes. The beautiful Red Rock Lakes in the extreme southwest (see under Monida) have nesting Trumpeter Swans, and the reservoir in the Nine-pipe National Wildlife Refuge (see under Ronan) has nesting Western Grebes, both Horned and Eared Grebes, and numerous ducks. In the northwest there are glacial lakes of varying size; most are very deep and bordered by willow thickets and coniferous forests. Flathead Lake (see under Polson) is the largest, but not so interesting ornithologically as the smaller, more remote lakes farther north. Several in Glacier National Park, away from disturbances by man, offer the best chances for seeing broods of American and Barrow's Golden-eyes, Harlequin Ducks, and American Mergansers. A pair or two of Common Loons often occupy the same lakes.

In the spring and fall, great numbers of transient Canada Geese, ducks, and shorebirds pass through the Prairie Region, stopping on the larger lakes for feeding and loitering. Medicine Lake and Lake Bowdoin, once famous hunting grounds but now Federal preserves, are two of the best places for seeing large aggregations. Fairly impressive numbers of waterfowl and shorebirds also visit suitable bodies of water (e.g. the reservoirs in Nine-pipe and Pablo National Wildlife Refuges) of the Mountain Region. The timbered tracts in all of the river valleys throughout the state show evidence of the spring and fall movements of small landbirds, though nowhere is the number of birds particularly great. Some of the species to be expected in the valleys of the eastern Prairie Region are the Tennessee Warbler, Orange-crowned Warbler, Myrtle Warbler, Blackpoll Warbler, Slate-colored Junco, American Tree Sparrow, Harris' Sparrow, and White-throated Sparrow. In the Mountain Region, most of the landbirds moving through in migration are northern representatives of the same species that breed in the Region itself; hence there are few different species to be observed during the spring and fall. The main migration flights in Montana take place within the following dates: waterfowl, 20 March—25 April, 15 September—15 November; shorebirds, 1 May—1 June, 1 August—15 September; landbirds, 15 April—1 June, 15 August—1 October.

As in North Dakota, the Prairie Region of Montana offers generally unproductive bird finding in the winter. The low temperatures, the persistent snow, and the lashing of bitter winds make conditions unfavorable for all but the hardiest of bird species—and the hardiest of bird finders. For a day's search over a wide stretch of plains and in a well-wooded river valley or coulee, several Rough-legged Hawks, a few flocks of Common Redpolls, Lapland Long-

spurs, and Snow Buntings, perhaps a small flock of American Tree Sparrows, one or two Northern Shrikes, and a half-
dozen or so permanent-resident species are considered good
results. The Mountain Region, particularly that part west
of the Continental Divide, which enjoys the milder climate
of the Pacific slope, has additional birds in winter. These
include Mallards, Pintails, American Golden-eyes, and a
few other ducks on spring-fed bodies of water, Dippers near
the shallow rapids of open streams, Townsend's Solitaires,
Pine Grosbeaks, Evening Grosbeaks, and, occasionally,
Bohemian Waxwings in forested valleys. Christmas bird
counts taken at such points as Kalispell in the northwest
and Bozeman in the southwest usually yield between 20 and
25 species.

BIGTIMBER. From this cattle-ranching center in south-
central Montana, State Route 19 goes north through Harlowton and Judith Gap to Moore over the grass-covered
foothills of the Crazy, Little Belt, and Big Snowy Mountains; now and then it crosses a brush- and willow-bordered
stream. Along this 85-mile stretch of oiled road one is likely
to encounter rather unusual concentrations of breeding
birds.

Within easy view from the highway are several spots
where Sharp-tailed Grouse perform early-morning courtship 'dances' with surprising indifference to human observers. The spots are easily found, as they are between
12 and 20 miles north of Bigtimber and within a few feet
of the highway. Though peak activity is usually reached
during the last week of April and the first week of May, the
birds may nevertheless be seen on their dancing grounds
from the time the snow disappears until well into June. The
performances begin half an hour before sunup and continue
for two or three hours.

Long-billed Curlews may be seen or heard almost any
place beginning about 25 miles south of Harlowton. They
arrive in April, nest in late May and June, and often congregate in flocks of two to three hundred before leaving in
early September. Wherever they nest, they are invariably
vociferous when disturbed. If the bird finder as much as
walks over the general nesting area, the birds fly toward

him, then circle and alight on a near-by knoll, meanwhile pouring out an endless series of shrill whistles and angry rattles.

The smaller prairie birds may be seen by the thousands in the spring and early summer, particularly between Harlowton and Judith Gap. Horned Larks, Lark Buntings, Mc-Cown's Longspurs, and Chestnut-collared Longspurs fly up from the roadsides ahead of the car. Between Judith Gap and Moore, where the highway traverses wheat country, diurnal predators appear in wider variety than in most other parts of the state. Such species as the Red-tailed Hawk, Swainson's Hawk, Ferruginous Hawk, Golden Eagle, Marsh Hawk, Prairie Falcon, and Sparrow Hawk are to be expected. American Magpies are unusually common and their nests may be easily found in the willows along the streams. Say's Phoebes and Mountain Bluebirds are frequent around buildings; the former are also frequent near bridges, as are Barn and Cliff Swallows. Spotted Sandpipers and Wilson's Phalaropes may usually be observed around the borders of the numerous farm ponds, which are also nesting habitats for a few ducks and, occasionally, a pair of Pied-billed or Eared Grebes. Savannah and Vesper Sparrows are not uncommon in grassy areas adjoining the ponds. Where the highway crosses brush-bordered streams, Common Goldfinches, Spotted Towhees, and Yellow-throats are in evidence.

BOZEMAN. MONTANA STATE COLLEGE, conspicuous on a hill in the southwest corner of town, offers a summer course in ornithology. Interested visitors are always welcome on the class field trips. In the Museum of Vertebrate Zoology on the top floor of Lewis Hall are approximately 1,000 study skins of Montana birds as well as several ornithological exhibits. The Museum is open to visitors between 8:00 A.M. and 5:00 P.M. every day except Saturday afternoons, Sundays, and holidays. Check-lists of Montana birds are available for the asking.

There are probably few places in Montana holding as wide a variety of landbirds in so small an area as the vicinity of the Federal Fish Hatchery, 5 miles northeast of Bozeman on the Bridger Canyon Road. Its richness of birdlife is not surprising when one takes into consideration the varied environment. Here, meeting the rich farmlands of the Gallatin Valley, are mountain forests of spruce, fir, and pine, ravines choked with tangles of wild rose, snowberry, and dogwood, and a swift stream that is bordered by chokecherry, serviceberry, willow, and hawthorn and overhung by towering cliffs of rock. An early morning trip to this spot in May, June, or July should yield 50 or more bird species.

The Hatchery is easy for newcomers to find because of its proximity to Montana State College's giant block-letter 'M,' a conspicuous landmark on a slope visible from the city. To reach the area, turn north from US Route 10 on Rouse Street (becomes Bridger Canyon Road) and drive north and then east for 5 miles to a sign marking the Federal Fish Hatchery. Drive through the Hatchery grounds and out the stone exit gate, then turn left, continue about a hundred yards, and park the car. Examine the telephone wires overhead for an occasional Calliope Hummingbird. Beyond, to the left, is Bridger Creek, flanked by trees and brush where such breeding birds may be found as the Hammond's Flycatcher, Western Wood Pewee, Black-capped Chickadee, Veery, Warbling Vireo, Audubon's Warbler, Macgillivray's Warbler, American Redstart, Black-headed Grosbeak, and Pine Siskin. To the right, rising abruptly from the road, is a knoll covered with conifers on the north and west sides and grasses on its south and east sides. By taking the two-hour walk around it, one should be able to observe a large number of birds, including the Violet-green Swallow, Steller's Jay, Clark's Nutcracker, Olive-backed Thrush, Mountain Bluebird, Townsend's Solitaire, Ruby-crowned Kinglet, Lazuli Bunting, Evening Grosbeak, Cassin's Finch, both the Green-tailed and Spotted Towhees, White-crowned Sparrow, and other nesting species. Just over the saddle on the east side of the knoll, the Ruffed Grouse often drums and the Golden Eagle sometimes soars overhead. The Spotted Sandpiper and Dipper are likely to be seen by the stream to the north of the knoll, and the Western Tanager in the near-by conifers. The jutting face of the rock to the north of the knoll is occupied by Cliff Swallows and, occasionally, Violet-green and Rough-winged Swallows.

CULBERTSON. In the northeastern corner of Montana, the MEDICINE LAKE NATIONAL WILDLIFE REFUGE is a fine area for finding waterbirds, waterfowl, and birds frequenting the upland prairie. Medicine Lake and six man-made bodies of water comprise about 12,300 of the Refuge's 31,457 acres; marshy areas producing cattails, sedges, and bulrushes, about 18,500 acres; wild grasslands and cultivated lands, about 600 acres.

Breeding birds associated with the water areas of the Refuge include island colonies of White Pelicans, Double-crested Cormorants, Great Blue Herons, California Gulls, Ring-billed Gulls, and Common Terns, together with Canada Geese, a large variety of ducks, and the following: Horned Grebes, Eared Grebes, Western Grebes, Black-crowned Night Herons, American Bitterns, Willets, Avocets, Forster's Terns, and Black Terns. Among the birds to be found nesting in the grasslands are Sharp-tailed Grouse, Bobolinks, and Baird's Sparrows. For most all species, nesting is under way by the first week of June. Large aggregations of transient waterfowl may be observed on Medicine Lake and the other bodies of water of the Refuge during late March, April, late September, and October.

The Medicine Lake Refuge is crossed by State Route 16 at a point 16 miles north of Culbertson on US Route 2. Headquarters lies 2.5 miles east of Route 16, from which it may easily be seen. Most parts of the Refuge may be reached by car.

FORT PECK. Established in 1936, the FORT PECK GAME RANGE of some 950,000 acres extends from the town of Fort Peck in northeastern Montana up the Missouri River for about 150 miles. About one fourth of the Range is occupied by the Fort Peck Reservoir, formed by 4-mile-long Fort Peck Dam across the Missouri River at Fort Peck. Owing to the marked fluctuation in the Reservoir's water level from season to season, natural plant growth is impeded, and hence this great body of water attracts few birds. The remainder of the Range comprises rolling prairie sparsely covered with grasses and sagebrush and interrupted in many places by coulees. Sage Grouse, Horned

Larks, Rock Wrens, Lark Buntings, Lark Sparrows, Brewer's Sparrows, McCown's Longspurs, and Chestnut-collared Longspurs are some of the more common avian inhabitants.

Directly below Fort Peck Dam, seepage gives rise to Duck Creek, which empties almost immediately into the slow, meandering Missouri. White Pelicans, Double-crested Cormorants, and a few breeding ducks are present here in the spring and summer; in winter there are hordes of ducks. During one winter season recently over 3,000 ducks were banded, and of these about 800 were caught during the first two hours of trapping operations.

Beyond the point where Duck Creek empties into the Missouri, a mile or so below the Dam, are cottonwoods and brushy thickets that hold a wide variety of summer-resident passerine birds. To reach this productive spot, drive eastward from Fort Peck and across the top of the Dam; near the east side, between the group of control shafts and the large spillway, turn left on a road that goes down along the east and then south bank of the Missouri and ends. Duck Creek is passed along the way. At the end of the road are the cottonwoods and thickets in which may be found such birds as Western Wood Pewees, Catbirds, Brown Thrashers, Yellow Warblers, American Redstarts, Bullock's Orioles, and Spotted Towhees.

GLACIER PARK. The 1,583 square miles of GLACIER NATIONAL PARK in northwestern Montana have some of the most exceptional scenery in the Rocky Mountains. Here, through the prolonged effects of glaciation, are immense peaks with steeply cut walls, lofty cirques holding the remnants of great glaciers, broad U-shaped valleys separated by high, sharp-edged ridges, and 200 or more picturesque, blue-green lakes, some in deeply-carved basins and others held by morainic dams. Many streams, arising partly from melting glaciers and snowfields, speed down to the valleys, frequently plunging during their course in foaming cascades.

The mountains in Glacier Park form together a double line, running in a northwest-southeast direction for 45 miles. The easternmost line—a segment of the Lewis Range

—fronts on the Great Plains, while the westernmost—the Livingstone Range—slopes down to the Flathead Valley. Southward over the mountains meanders the Continental Divide, thus making a natural separation of the Park into two sides. Elevations in the Park range from 10,448 feet at the summit of Mt. Cleveland, the highest point, down to 4,483 feet at St. Mary Lake on the east side and 3,154 feet at Lake McDonald on the west side.

Coniferous trees characterize the forests. Those on the east side are mainly lodgepole pine and Douglas fir, giving way higher up to Engelmann spruce, alpine fir, and white-bark pine, while those on the west side, where there is greater moisture, are predominantly western white pine, western hemlock, western larch, grand fir, and ponderosa pine. Only in a few places are there deciduous trees—for example, near lakes and streams are cottonwood and willow thickets and on some of the slopes of the east side are groves of aspen. Because of the generally high terrain, all forests are restricted to the lower valleys and slopes. Much of the Park, including the higher valleys, is therefore above timber line and is alpine in character. Where there is soil, mosses and hardy wildflowers grow in profusion. In early July, following the slow retreat of the last snowbanks, wildflowers are at their best, the blooms of the bear grass, shooting star, glacier lily, larkspur, gentian, carpet pink, Indian paintbrush, and others giving lavish color to benches, gentle slopes, and valley meadows.

Complementing the aforementioned attractions are the mammals. So much of the Park is open country that a visitor cannot be within its boundaries very long before viewing some of the bigger species: mountain goats and bighorn sheep moving sure-footedly along the ledges of cliffs at dizzy heights; moose feeding in boggy creek bottoms; mule and white-tailed deer grazing in the forest openings; and perhaps a coyote skulking over a meadow, or a black bear patroling a stream. The smaller mammals are remarkably numerous, particularly the marmots and pikas on the high talus slopes and the squirrels and chipmunks at the timber line and below. Always a special delight to the visitor are the handsome golden-mantled squirrels, many of which are very tame and confidently solicit food.

Amid the superlative scenery, the richness of flora, and the abundance of mammals, birdlife seems to be eclipsed. The truth is that, owing to the high elevation coupled with the wide extent of treeless terrain, birds are limited in numbers and variety. A few species such as Golden Eagles, Ospreys, Rufous Hummingbirds, Violet-green Swallows, Clark's Nutcrackers, and Mountain Bluebirds range widely and a few others such as American Pipits, Macgillivray's Warblers, and Western Tanagers confine themselves to specific habitats, but in no case is any species especially abundant. Moreover, no bird family is represented by any notable number of species save the grouse family, an exception that provides an outstanding ornithological feature. In all, there are five species: the Sharp-tailed Grouse in the low, burned-over areas and the Ruffed Grouse in the aspen groves on the east side; the Franklin's Grouse in the pine-fir forests on the west side; the Blue Grouse in all coniferous forests from about 5,000 feet elevation to the timber line; and the White-tailed Ptarmigan above the timber line.

The bird finder must be reminded that Glacier Park, unlike most other large National Parks, has limited access to cars. It is crossed by only one road, the spectacular Going-to-the-Sun Highway, from the St. Mary entrance on the east side across the Continental Divide to the West Glacier entrance on the west, a distance of 50 miles. There are two other roads, both on the east side, entering separately and running short distances to Many Glacier and Two Medicine, respectively. Glacier Park is primarily a 'trail park,' most of its primeval wilderness being accessible only by trails. For the visitor who prefers traveling on foot or riding horseback, there are over 1,000 miles of trails into the 'back country.'

Embracing as it does so much high country, the Park has a relatively brief season each year (15 June to 15 September), at which time its concessions (e.g. hotels and cabins) are open. For several weeks before and after the regular season, there are accommodations on privately owned land in the Park and outside. Ranger naturalists, stationed at Lake McDonald, Avalanche Creek Campground, Logan Pass, Going-to-the-Sun Point, Many Glacier, and Two Medicine, are available for interpreting the Park's

natural-history features. Guided nature walks, illustrated
lectures, and campfire talks are other services rendered by
these men. Ranger-naturalist program schedules may be
obtained at the checking station at any one of the entrances
to the Park.

Despite the general scarcity of birds in Glacier Park,
there are localities where the bird finder can achieve results
as worth while as those in any other northern Rocky Mountain area. Some of the most promising spots, with directions
for reaching them, are indicated in the following paragraphs. The birds mentioned are those that may be found in
early July.

From the town of Glacier Park, just east of the southeast-
ernmost extremity of the Park itself, drive northward on US
Route 89 (Blackfeet Highway), passing the turnoffs to the
Two Medicine and St. Mary entrances, and continue to the
town of Babb, a distance of 38 miles. Leave the numbered
highway here and proceed 8.5 miles west, on the Park
road, to the Many Glacier entrance. Obtain a detailed map
of the Park at the checking station and continue 4 miles
to Many Glacier, where there is a fine hotel on Swiftcurrent Lake (elevation 4,861 feet). Cabins and campgrounds
are in the general area.

Many Glacier is considered one of the best places for
birds in the Park. Its small aspens and alpine firs—new
growth following a fire in 1936—are attractive to such birds
as Canada Jays, Oregon Juncos, and Chipping Sparrows.
Well worth following is a trail going west from the hotel
along the shore of Swiftcurrent Lake, across Swiftcurrent
Creek, and then south and around the shore of Lake Josephine. Summer-resident Spotted Sandpipers should be observed frequently and, in late summer, there is always a
possibility of seeing one or more broods of Harlequin Ducks
on the Lakes. Both bodies of water have bordering willow
thickets frequented by Macgillivray's Warblers and White-
crowned Sparrows. Near the eastern shores there are also
a few patches of thick conifers where Blue Grouse and
Varied Thrushes may be found. From the southern end of
Lake Josephine a trail leads up to Grinnell Lake (about
3 miles distant) and Grinnell Glacier (6 miles distant), over

which Golden Eagles often soar. For scenery alone, a trip over this trail will prove to be rewarding.

Having explored the Many Glacier area, return to the Blackfeet Highway outside of the Park and go south 6 miles to the St. Mary entrance, then begin a trip westward across the Park on the Going-to-the-Sun Highway.

The Highway west from the St. Mary entrance soon passes close to the north shore of St. Mary Lake, where American Golden-eyes, Barrow's Golden-eyes, American Mergansers, Ospreys, Ring-billed Gulls, and, occasionally, California Gulls may be seen from the car. In the vicinity of Rising Sun (cabins and campgrounds), midway along the Lake, one may expect to find in suitable situations the following summer-resident birds: Sparrow Hawk, Common Nighthawk, Wright's Flycatcher, Tree Swallow, Cliff Swallow, Dipper, Robin, Veery, Macgillivray's Warbler, Western Tanager, Pine Siskin, Oregon Junco, and Chipping Sparrow.

At Logan Pass (elevation 6,664 feet), 18 miles from the St. Mary entrance, the Highway crosses the Continental Divide. Except for the presence of a few stunted conifers, the environment at this point is typically alpine, with terraced benches carpeted with a luxuriant growth of wildflowers. Special birds to be looked for are the White-tailed Ptarmigan, American Pipit, Gray-crowned Rosy Finch, and White-crowned Sparrow. Failing to observe one or more of these species here, the bird finder may try his luck along Hidden Lake Trail. This leads south from the Pass across similar environment. After 2 miles, however, it goes through a small pass and comes to the edge of a cliff overlooking Hidden Lake, 500 feet below. If the bird finder listens carefully, he may hear the songs of Hermit Thrushes rising from among the alpine firs in the vicinity of the Lake.

For a wide variety of birds, the bird finder, having explored Logan Pass, should take the 3½-mile trail to Avalanche Lake. This begins at the Avalanche Creek Campground on the left side of the Going-to-the-Sun Highway, 15½ miles west of Logan Pass, and passes gradually up through a magnificent stand of western red cedar and western hemlock mixed with some lodgepole pine, Douglas fir,

and Engelmann spruce. There is probably no better place
in Glacier Park for Franklin's Grouse than this particular
forest. Seldom is the trail very far from a deep, cool gorge
through which Avalanche Creek rushes noisily. That Dippers may be found here is practically a certainty. Avalanche
Lake, a small body of water of milky color, is bordered by

FRANKLIN'S GROUSE

a dense growth of deciduous shrubs and, farther back, by
mixed conifers and deciduous trees. A high cirque with
cascades spilling over its face looms in the distance. On several occasions Black Swifts have been seen foraging for
insect food in the air above Avalanche Lake. Included
among the species that one may observe in a trip through
the forest to Avalanche Lake and in the vicinity of the
Lake are the following: Common Nighthawk, Rufous Hummingbird, Common Sapsucker, Black-backed Woodpecker,
Wright's Flycatcher, Olive-sided Flycatcher, Violet-green
Swallow, Canada Jay, Steller's Jay, Common Raven, Black-
capped Chickadee, Varied Thrush, Hermit Thrush, Olive-
backed Thrush, Ruby-crowned Kinglet, Red-eyed Vireo,
Warbling Vireo, Townsend's Warbler, Northern Water-

thrush, Macgillivray's Warbler, Yellow-throat, Western Tanager, Cassin's Finch, Pine Siskin, Oregon Junco, Chipping Sparrow, and Fox Sparrow.

About 15 miles beyond Avalanche Lake Campground, the Going-to-the-Sun Highway parallels for about 10 miles the east shore of Lake McDonald, the Park's largest lake. Mallards, American Golden-eyes, Barrow's Golden-eyes, and American Mergansers are the principal summer-resident waterfowl to be seen on the surface. Ring-billed Gulls are common, and occasionally a Bald Eagle makes an appearance. Three miles from the south end of Lake McDonald the Highway reaches the West Glacier entrance at the west boundary of the Park.

HELENA. This capital city (elevation 4,124 feet), built around famous Last Chance Gulch of the Gold Rush days, is well up in the foothills of Mt. Helena. To the northeast, broad Prickly Pear Valley (Helena Valley) descends gradually to the Missouri River some 10 miles away; beyond the Missouri rise the Big Belt Mountains. Several lakes lie along the Missouri, within 25 miles of the city. About 15 miles west of Helena looms the Continental Divide.

Of special interest because of its nesting Canada Geese, as well as its many ducks, is LAKE HELENA, formed by the backing up of the Missouri into the mouth of Prickly Pear Creek. Approximately 3 miles long and 1.5 miles wide, this body of water is very shallow and produces an abundance of cattails and bulrushes. Although the Geese may be seen or heard from almost any spot along the shore, their preferred breeding habitat is in the southern half of the area. It is possible to reach the north margin of Lake Helena by driving north 8 miles on US Route 91, then east 4 miles and south half a mile on well-traveled roads.

US Route 10N over McDONALD PASS (elevation 6,323 feet) on the Continental Divide leads up through a fine coniferous-forest belt to conditions typically subalpine. From parking places along this scenic drive one may walk into adjacent stands of lodgepole pine, Engelmann spruce, and Douglas fir and look for such birds as Franklin's Grouse, Black-backed Woodpeckers, Three-toed Woodpeckers, Canada Jays, Mountain Chickadees, Red-breasted Nuthatches, Brown Creepers, Audubon's Warblers, Black-capped Warblers, and Cassin's Finches. Near the Pass, Clark's Nutcrackers, Oregon Juncos, and, occasionally, Pine Grosbeaks may be observed.

Near the State Capitol Building is a historical museum containing many mounts of native birds and mammals. The museum is open from 8:00 A.M. to 6:00 P.M. during the week and until noon on Saturdays.

MALTA. Lake Bowdoin, a typical prairie lake, has long been an important breeding area for Canada Geese and ducks. Since it is now part of the 15,437-acre BOWDOIN NATIONAL WILDLIFE REFUGE, its continuing importance seems assured. No bird finder passing through northeast-central Montana in June or July should miss visiting the area, for its remarkable variety and large numbers of breeding birds are probably unrivaled elsewhere in the state.

Fed by surface drainage, Lake Bowdoin has strongly alkaline water, the level of which, until recently stabilized by damming, was subject to marked seasonal fluctuations. At present, open water and marsh regularly cover 4,300 acres. Since the water averages between 4 and 5 feet in depth and most of the shore rises abruptly, there is little marsh vegetation; but in the two arms of the Lake—the southeastern and southwestern—the water is sufficiently shallow and the incline of the shore is gradual enough to afford an extensive growth of bulrushes, cattails, and sedges. In the central part of the Lake are several small islands, the largest (Woody Island) having a surface of about 5 acres. Though bordered by a few marshy patches, their interiors are generally barren save for scattered clumps of shrubs (e.g. greasewood) and grasses.

Regular avian inhabitants of Lake Bowdoin marshes (either in the two arms or in other places) include the Eared Grebe, Western Grebe, Canada Goose, Sora, Coot, Black Tern, Yellow-throat, Red-wing, Yellow-headed Blackbird, and the following ducks: Mallard, Gadwall, Baldpate, Pintail, Blue-winged Teal, Shoveler, Redhead, Canvasback, Lesser Scaup Duck, and Ruddy Duck. Canada Geese, Killdeer, Spotted Sandpipers, Willets, Avocets, Wilson's Phalaropes, and Savannah Sparrows nest along the shore of the mainland and on the islands in suitable situations.

Contributing in large measure to Lake Bowdoin's ornithological distinction are the colonies of White Pelicans, Double-crested Cormorants, Great Blue Herons, Herring Gulls, California Gulls, Ring-billed Gulls, and Common Terns that settle each year on the islands, chiefly on Woody and Pelican Islands. The number of breeding pairs in each colony varies greatly from year to year. The White Pelican and Ring-billed Gull colonies are usually large, sometimes having as many as 2,000 and 5,000 pairs, respectively; the colonies of the other species are small—fewer than 200 pairs each. Unless the season is late, the hatching period in all the colonies begins during the first week of June and is over by the last week.

The prairies in the vicinity of Lake Bowdoin attract a few nesting Sharp-tailed Grouse, Long-billed Curlews, and Marbled Godwits, together with great numbers of Horned Larks, Western Meadowlarks, Lark Buntings, and Chestnut-collared Longspurs. Both Bank and Rough-winged Swallows nest locally near the Lake. Other birds to be seen, most frequently near buildings, include Say's Phoebes, Barn Swallows, and Mountain Bluebirds.

Headquarters of the Bowdoin Refuge, situated on the southwestern arm of the Lake, may be reached from Malta by driving 7 miles east on US Route 2, then turning right on the entrance road. The buildings come into view from the highway before turning off. Most parts of the Refuge are accessible by car except during wet weather, when the roads become too muddy for travel. Visits to the islands must not be undertaken without first obtaining permission from the Refuge manager. Generally, visits to the islands are discouraged, since they disturb the nesting birds, but the bird finder may accompany the Refuge personnel on their routine trips, provided he makes arrangements with the manager by correspondence well in advance of the time the trip is to be made.

MILES CITY. US Routes 10, 12, and 212 will bring the bird finder to Miles City, in the heart of the 'boots and saddle' country of eastern Montana. Rolling grasslands and sagebrush flats, buttes, canyons, and coulees, river bottoms, willow thickets, and occasional sloughs characterize the vicinity.

Route 212, passing southeast from the east edge of town, follows the Tongue River and Pumpkin Creek over terrain featured by red buttes and canyons. For the first 15 miles out of town, the country traversed is particularly good for Burrowing Owls, Horned Larks, Sage Thrashers, Lark Buntings, and Lark Sparrows. Pinyon Jays may be expected on the juniper-clad ridges to the east of the highway and Prairie Falcons are likely to be seen in flight almost anywhere.

Fort Keogh, southwest of and adjacent to Miles City, is an old military post used by troops in the days when the Indians were being subjugated. In the vicinity is the MILES CITY FEDERAL FISH HATCHERY, which is well worth a visit for waterbirds, waterfowl, and shorebirds. Take US Route 10 west and south from Miles City; about 2 miles out of town, turn right (the Fort buildings are in view from the highway) and continue for 1.5 miles north and west along the only road to the Hatchery. Leave the car here and proceed on foot between large rearing ponds to grassy sloughs and meadows, where there will be a variety of such birds as grebes, ducks, American Bitterns, Soras, Coots, Wilson's Snipe, and Yellow-headed Blackbirds. About a mile farther west are the sand and gravel bars of the Yellowstone River, which, during May and August, attract numerous transient shorebirds, including Solitary Sandpipers, Greater and Lesser Yellow-legs, Pectoral Sandpipers, Baird's Sandpipers, and Northern Phalaropes. The cottonwood groves and brushy thickets that flank the River are likely spots for Mourning Doves, Red-headed Woodpeckers, Western Wood Pewees, Black-capped Chickadees, Mountain Bluebirds, Warbling Vireos, Yellow Warblers, Yellow-breasted Chats, and Lazuli Buntings.

MISSOULA. Owing partly to its relatively low altitude (3,223 feet) and partly to its location on the Pacific slope of the Continental Divide, this city (often called 'The Garden City' because of its shaded avenues, attractive homes, spacious lawns, and colorful flower beds) enjoys early springs, late falls, and mild winters. Thus there are birds to be found here that are rare in most other parts of the state.

MONTANA STATE UNIVERSITY at the east end of University Avenue has an ornithological collection representing western Montana. Housed in the Biological Museum on the second floor of the Natural Science Building, the material comprises about 1,000 study skins, 150 mounts, and a few egg sets.

The best spots for birds near Missoula is PATTEE CAN-YON south of the city. Two or three morning hours of searching here in April, May, or June should turn up a number of interesting bird species. The following 12-mile drive will take the bird finder to Pattee Canyon by one route and back by another.

In Missoula's business district, turn south from US Route 10 onto Higgins Avenue. After crossing the Clark Fork of the Columbia River and reaching the outskirts of the city, take the Pattee Canyon Road, which is a continuation of Higgins Avenue. Crossing a short stretch of uncultivated grazing land and skirting Mt. Sentinel (which bears on its north slope the University's big letter 'M'), this road leads to the mouth of the Canyon. Once in the mouth of the Canyon, where there are deciduous trees and thick clumps of shrubs, search for such birds as Lewis' Woodpeckers, Varied Thrushes, Veeries, Macgillivray's Warblers, and Bullock's Orioles. Then continue up the Canyon. Above the public campground and picnic area, where Steller's Jays are to be expected, Pattee Canyon Road winds through coniferous woods to the saddle, in the vicinity of which are many high-country birds, including Clark's Nutcrackers, Winter Wrens, Evening Grosbeaks, Pine Siskins, and Oregon Juncos. Calliope Hummingbirds are not uncommon here; a Ruffed Grouse may sometimes be heard drumming; with luck, a Pygmy Owl may be discovered among the lower branches of evergreens. On the other side of the saddle, the Road drops down into the narrow valley of Hellgate River and turns west a short distance south of Milltown. Here Bonner Dam forms a small reservoir that is often attractive to a few ducks and waterbirds. Below the Dam, the Pattee Canyon Road soon reaches US Route 10, on which the bird finder may return to Missoula.

MONIDA. Situated in the east end of the isolated, 6,600-foot high Centennial Valley, the RED ROCK LAKES MIGRATORY WATERFOWL REFUGE (40,008 acres) is one of the most scenic of the many preserves managed by the U.S. Fish and Wildlife Service. It lies under the crest of the Continental Divide, to the south and east, and near the terminations of the Snowcrest and Gravelly Ranges, to the north and west.

The Refuge proper is composed primarily of natural lakes and marshes bordered by upland meadows in a flat terrain, while on hills within the southern boundaries are coniferous forests. The main bodies of water include Upper Red Rock Lake (3,000 acres), Lower Red Rock Lake (2,000 acres), and Swan Lake (1,000 acres). All are fringed by extensive marshes in which sedges are the predominant emergent plants.

The principal ornithological attraction of the Refuge is its Trumpeter Swans. As many as 20 pairs nest, their eggs hatching between 10 and 25 June. Unfortunately these splendid birds are not readily visible, for they frequent the more remote marsh areas; nevertheless, by climbing one of the several knolls overlooking the Lakes, the bird finder may usually observe them quite well with a pair of field glasses, or (better) a telescope. Usually the birds are at least 1.5 miles away, but on rare occasions they may be seen much closer. In order that they will be undisturbed while nesting or rearing their young, visitors unescorted by Refuge personnel are not permitted to enter the marshes from May to September.

Besides the Swans, birds that may be seen on the Refuge in June and July are White Pelicans, Sage Grouse, Sandhill Cranes, Long-billed Curlews, Willets, and many species of ducks. All except the Pelicans nest on the Refuge. In the fall, beginning in September and continuing until the freeze-up, there are moderately large aggregations of waterfowl, including Whistling Swans, which appear in greatest numbers after 15 October.

Refuge headquarters, at Lakeview on the south side of the Refuge, may be reached in a car by leaving US Route 91 at Monida and continuing east through the Centennial Valley for 25 miles. It may also be reached by leaving US Route 191 at Henrys Lake (10 miles west of West Yellowstone, Montana) and proceeding for 28 miles through Red Rock Pass into the east end of the Valley. After leaving either highway the road is generally unimproved and sometimes impassable with an ordinary car, particularly before the first of July and after the middle of September. Inquiry about road conditions should, therefore, be made at Monida, or Henrys Lake (Staley's Spring Lodge). Accommodations may be obtained locally (reservations only from June through August) at the 7L Ranch, about 3 miles west of the Refuge boundary, or at Selby's Elk Lake Resort, a small fishing lodge, with cabins, about a mile from the northeast boundary. A small but pleasant overnight camping area is provided by the Refuge on the shore of Upper Red Rock Lake. For the bird finder willing to rough it, this is an ideal setting during July and August when the weather is mild. Warm clothes are essential, because frosts occur even in midsummer.

POLSON. At Yellow Bay on the east shore of Flathead Lake (elevation 3,000 feet) is the MONTANA STATE UNIVERSITY BIOLOGICAL STATION, reached from Polson by driving east and north for 17 miles on State Route 35. A unit of the University's summer session, the Station is in operation from mid-June to mid-August. Visitors are welcome.

The Station grounds proper comprise 70 acres, forested principally with ponderosa pine, Douglas fir, grand fir, and western larch. Deciduous shrubs and a few cherry orchards are to be found where the timber has been removed. Directly east of the Station are the Mission and Swan Ranges, which rise to altitudes of about 10,300 feet. Some of the breeding birds of regular occurrence in the vicinity of the Station are the following: Cooper's Hawk, Osprey, Ruffed Grouse, Spotted Sandpiper, Pygmy Owl, Pileated Woodpecker, Common Sapsucker, Black-backed Woodpecker, Wright's Flycatcher, Steller's Jay, Common Raven, Mountain Chickadee, Red-breasted Nuthatch, Winter Wren, Varied Thrush, Olive-backed Thrush, Ruby-crowned Kinglet, Solitary Vireo, Audubon's Warbler, Townsend's Warbler, Macgillivray's Warbler, American Redstart, Western Tanager, Black-headed Grosbeak, Evening Grosbeak, Lazuli Bunting, Pine Siskin, Common Goldfinch, Red Crossbill, and Oregon Junco.

Within a two-hour drive from the Station are a variety of avian habitats, ranging from marshes in Nine-Pipe and Pablo National Wildlife Refuges (see under Ronan) to alpine regions in Glacier National Park (see under Glacier Park). Students taking the course in ornithology go on field trips to these places and thus have ample opportunity during the summer to see many kinds of birds.

RONAN. Just north of the National Bison Range in the Flatland Valley lies the NINE-PIPE NATIONAL WILD-LIFE REFUGE (2,021 acres) on gently rolling terrain at about 3,000 feet elevation. About 60 per cent of the area is an irrigation reservoir surrounded by cattails and, on higher ground, by native grasses. Many potholes with marshy vegetation are in the vicinity of the Refuge. North of the Nine-Pipe Refuge is the PABLO NATIONAL WILDLIFE REFUGE (2,868 acres), on terrain of similar type and elevation and containing a reservoir of like size. The vegetation bordering the water comprises not only cattails and grasses but also willows. These two preserves are the most important of the smaller refuges in the state because of the rich variety and relatively large numbers of waterfowl and waterbirds that use the protected areas as breeding grounds in May, June, and July. Here nest a few Canada Geese and the following ducks: Mallard, Gadwall, Baldpate, Pintail, Green-winged Teal, Blue-winged Teal, Cinnamon Teal, Shoveler, Redhead, Canvas-back, Lesser Scaup Duck, and Ruddy Duck. Other breeding birds include the Horned Grebe, Western Grebe, Coot, Black Tern, Yellow-headed Blackbird, and Brewer's Blackbird.

The Nine-Pipe Refuge may be reached from Ronan by driving 5 miles south on US Route 93, then turning right (west) on the Charlo Road and proceeding for 2 miles. To reach the Pablo Refuge from Ronan, drive north for 6 miles on Route 93 and then turn left (west) on a secondary road and proceed for half a mile. All parts of the Refuges are accessible by car, since roads go around both of them.

SIDNEY. A good spot to find breeding ducks in typical prairie surroundings is FOX LAKE, half an hour's drive from Sidney, a trading center near the North Dakota line. About a mile south of Sidney on State Route 14, turn west onto an all-weather county road and continue straight west about 26 miles, passing through the town of Lambert. Fox Lake, a widening of Fox Creek, will appear on the left side of the road just west of the town.

Approximately 1.5 miles long and a quarter of a mile wide, Fox Lake is shallow—not more than 3 feet deep anywhere—and in the summer is a green stretch of waving bulrushes, with cattails in abundance along its treeless margin. Mallards, Gadwalls, Baldpates, Pintails, Green-winged and Blue-winged Teal, and Shovelers are the ducks most likely to be expected in considerable numbers. Rails, blackbirds, and other marsh-loving birds are numerous. In suitable upland situations to the north and south of Fox Creek, where the prairie is rolling, may be found such birds as Burrowing Owls, Horned Larks, Sprague's Pipits, Baird's Sparrows, Clay-colored Sparrows, Brewer's Sparrows, Mc-Cown's Longspurs, and Chestnut-collared Longspurs.

WHITEHALL. In the Tobacco Root Range in southwestern Montana, about halfway between Bozeman and Butte, lies LEWIS AND CLARK CAVERN STATE PARK (2,770 acres), containing one of the biggest limestone caves in the United States. The Park may be reached from US Route 10S by turning north onto an all-weather entrance road, 13.5 miles east of Whitehall, or 5 miles west of the junction of Route 10S with State Route 1.

In this picturesque area are opportunities for both sight seeing and bird finding. Persons wishing to visit Lewis and Clark Cavern (locally called the Morrison Cave) should continue on the entrance road for 4 miles to the parking area near the Cavern entrance at the base of a high cliff. Guides are available here to take visitors through the Cavern from 7:00 A.M. to 9:00 P.M. every day through the summer months. Bird finders should stop on the entrance road half-way between the highway and the Cavern entrance at a spot marked 'Picnic Area and Camp Ground' (elevation about 4,500 feet). This gives access to several interesting bird habitats: to the south, the Jefferson River with adjacent slopes sparsely covered with cactus, yucca, mountain juniper, and sagebrush; to the west, deeply eroded gulllies and rocky outcrops; within a stone's throw to the north, a spruce-fir forest at the mouth of a small canyon that winds invitingly back into the limestone hills of the Tobacco Root Range. During May, June, and July, an exploration of these places should yield a great many species, including the following: Turkey Vulture, Goshawk, Ferruginous Hawk, Golden Eagle, Long-billed Curlew, Rufous Hummingbird, Calliope Hummingbird, Say's Phoebe, Western Wood Pewee, Violet-green Swallow, Canada Jay, Steller's Jay, Common Raven, Pinyon Jay, Clark's Nutcracker, Rock Wren, Sage Thrasher, Mountain Bluebird, Townsend's Solitaire, Ruby-crowned Kinglet, Lazuli Bunting, Cassin's Finch, Pine Siskin, Green-tailed Towhee, Spotted Towhee, Oregon Junco, and White-crowned Sparrow.

WHITE SULPHUR SPRINGS. Probably few Sage Grouse habitats in the West have remained so little changed by man as the thousands of acres of sagebrush flats that reach up and down the SMITH RIVER VALLEY. At an altitude of about 5,200 feet and hemmed in on both sides by mountain ranges, this long, level area along US Route 89 between Livingston and Great Falls is particularly suited to Sage Grouse, despite its extensive use as a cattle range. Although the birds may be found in many places in the Valley, the flats lying adjacent to the highway, 2 to 10 miles south of White Sulphur Springs, hold an unusually heavy concentration. Here in the fall, winter, and spring, in the early morning and toward dusk, it is not uncommon to see hundreds of these large birds moving slowly through the sagebrush or squatting in the open beside the road. And here during the spring, from melting of the snow until early June, it is possible to see their courtship performances. Display activities are best observed in the half-hour periods before and after sunrise. The breeding grounds of the Sharp-tailed Grouse are farther south along this same highway, extending for about 10 miles southward from Ringling. Their activities may be observed at the same season of the year and same time of day as those of the Sage Grouse.

Contributing authorities: Elmo G. Adams, Winston E. Banko, M. E. Beatty, Miss Grace E. Blanchard, Gene H. Crawford, Clifford V. Davis, Donald S. Farner, Karl H. Maslowski, L. R. Newaldt, George A. Petrides, Clifford C. Presnall, John E. Schwartz, Leon C. Snyder, Philip L. Wright.

Nebraska

BURROWING OWLS

Spring in the Platte River Valley means to bird finders one of the country's greatest ornithological shows—an enormous gathering of Sandhill Cranes. At no other point in their long migration through the interior of the continent do these spectacular birds stop in such numbers over such an extended period of time; and at no other point can they be more conveniently watched. Thousands upon thousands roost at night on the sand bars of the broad, shallow Platte River and feed during the day on the level agricultural lands near by (see under Kearney). If disturbed during their daytime foraging, they frequently circle skyward, soaring on set wings like Turkey Vultures, and sometimes almost disappear from view. Occasionally small flocks boldly appear near farmyards, where their lanky forms and long, jerky strides are in comical contrast to the squat shapes and brisk steps of domestic fowl.

In addition to Sandhill Cranes, hordes of other birds visit the state each year, thronging the waterways and crowding the wooded areas. So very exciting is migration in Nebraska that ornithologists here actually give more attention to dates of occurrence and abundance of migrating birds than to nesting records and population densities of the species breeding in the state. As a consequence, published information on the status of breeding birds in Nebraska is relatively meager. This is unfortunate, for the state, extending from the forested bottomlands of the Missouri River to the western plains, is an area where, interestingly, the breeding ranges of many eastern and western species meet and frequently overlap.

Nebraska is a roughly rectangular part of the interior plains, sloping gradually upward from an elevation of 825 feet in the Missouri Valley to 5,300 feet in the Wildcat Hills near the Wyoming line. The North Platte River, entering from Wyoming, joins the South Platte River from Colorado to become the Platte River, which loops southward across the state to enter the Missouri just south of Omaha. Various other rivers, such as the Niobrara, Elkhorn, Loup, and Blue, drain from west to east, eventually joining either the Platte or the Missouri.

Eastern Nebraska (approximately the eastern third of the state from the Missouri River westward for 125 miles) comprises bottomlands and bluffs along the Missouri and low, rolling hills to the west. On the bottomlands, besides cultivated areas, are cottonwood stands, willow thickets, and here and there small, water-filled meander cutoffs and marshes. The neighboring bluffs and their intervening hollows support woodlands, usually open and sometimes extensive, in which shagbark hickory, bur oak, red oak, elm, walnut, green ash, and basswood are among the principal trees. Bordering the woods are low thickets of wild plum, chokecherry, and sumac. West of the bluffs are rolling hills and wide valleys through which streams wend their way in broad, sand-bedded channels. This undulating country was formerly tall-grass prairie, treeless except for cotton-woods, willows, boxelders, silver maples, sycamores, and other deciduous growth lining the watercourses and reaching back into sheltered draws; but it has since been converted into agricultural lands and the once limited tree growth has been augmented by orchards, groves, and other plantations. Birdlife of eastern Nebraska is eastern in its composition, containing a number of species at the western limits of their ranges. Listed below are birds that breed more or less regularly in eastern Nebraska and, in some cases (marked by asterisk), nest in restricted areas farther west.

Red-shouldered Hawk
Broad-winged Hawk
Barred Owl
Whip-poor-will
*Yellow-shafted Flicker
Red-bellied Woodpecker
Crested Flycatcher
*Eastern Phoebe
Least Flycatcher (northeast only)
Eastern Wood Pewee
Tufted Titmouse
*Wood Thrush
Blue-gray Gnatcatcher
White-eyed Vireo (southeast only)

*Bell's Vireo
Yellow-throated Vireo
Louisiana Water-thrush (southeast only)
Kentucky Warbler (southeast only)
*Orchard Oriole
Scarlet Tanager
Summer Tanager (southeast only)
*Cardinal
*Rose-breasted Grosbeak
*Indigo Bunting
*Eastern Towhee

Central and western Nebraska, the remaining two thirds of the state, lies on the Great Plains. Generally higher, more arid, and more sharply dissected than the rolling hills of eastern Nebraska with which they merge imperceptibly, the Great Plains also show considerable variation with respect to physiography. Two regions, in fact, are so distinctive as to require separate description.

North of the Platte and North Platte Rivers is a 24,000-square-mile region of the Great Plains known as the Sandhills. Bounded roughly on the north by the Niobrara River and stretching westward from eastern Nebraska to within 50 miles of the Wyoming line, the Sandhills are countless numbers of dunes 200 or more feet in height with inclines varying from gradual to steep. For the most part they are fixed by a sod of tall and short grasses and a sprinkling of cacti and conspicuous yuccas; thus they are used extensively as grazing lands for cattle. But in places overgrazing and wind action have broken the sod; the wind has then blown out the sand, leaving depressions called blowouts. The sand from these blowouts has drifted over wide areas. Between some of the hills are pockets containing small trees (e.g. hackberries) and shrubby thickets; between others are broad meadows in which rushes and sedges thrive. Here and there, usually between the hills, are groups of ranch buildings around which a few trees have been planted. Scattered throughout the Sandhills are numerous lakes with the majority clustered in the north-central and western sections. Relatively shallow, frequently supporting cattails, bulrushes, and other marsh vegetation, and occasionally bordered by willows and shrubs, these bodies of water are extremely important ornithologically, for they attract a wide variety of breeding and transient waterbirds, waterfowl, and shorebirds. The bird finder interested in exploring the Sandhills should take State Route 2 (Potash Highway) between Grand Island and Alliance; this runs through the heart of the region. If he wishes to investigate certain of the more productive lakes and at the same time see typical sections of the Sandhills, he should take one or more of the trips described in this chapter under Ogallala, Oshkosh, and Valentine.

In the extreme northwest corner of Nebraska the Great Plains drop down to the Missouri Plateau (a northern, topographically different section of the Great Plains) in a north-facing escarpment, the Pine Ridge, which is cut by canyons and eroded near the base to form a strip of badlands. Entering Nebraska from the Wyoming line some 15 miles south of South Dakota, the Pine Ridge curves southward through points south of Crawford and Chadron, then swings northeastward to enter South Dakota near White Clay. South of Crawford and Chadron, it rises almost 1,000 feet in height and has generally sharp slopes that include vertical walls; to the west and east it gradually becomes lower and less abrupt. Over the Pine Ridge, except on the steepest slopes, are stands of ponderosa pine, and near the rim is a sparse growth of juniper. In the deeper canyons are cottonwood, aspen, boxelder, and other deciduous trees, together with various shrubs such as chokecherry, skunk-brush, and buckbrush. This rough country and its fairly extensive coniferous cover brings into the state many birds of western affinities. Thus bird finding here (see under Chadron) will yield results not to be matched anywhere else in the state.

The rest of Nebraska's Great Plains—those north of the Niobrara River, west of the Sandhills, and south of the Platte and North Platte Rivers—consist of slightly uneven tablelands and valley lowlands. On higher ground, wheat, corn, and other grains are cultivated, unless conditions are too arid, in which case the natural cover of short grasses (chiefly grama and buffalo) is retained and used for graz-ing. Crops such as sugar beets, potatoes, and alfalfa are produced in the valleys, particularly where irrigation has been undertaken. Westward the terrain is increasingly broken by ridges, buttes, and canyons. The Wildcat Hills in extreme western Nebraska (see under Scottsbluff) typify these rougher areas. Throughout the Great Plains, deciduous trees and shrubs grow mainly in valleys, shel-tered draws, and canyons, and to some extent about farm-yards, ranch houses, and settlements; in the western part, ponderosa pine and juniper are scattered over the slopes of ridges, buttes, and canyons.

On the Great Plains of Nebraska, including the Sandhills and Pine Ridge, the species listed below breed regularly. Rarely, if at all, do they nest in eastern Nebraska. Species marked with an asterisk occur mainly in the extreme west-ern part of the state.

Swainson's Hawk
Ferruginous Hawk
Greater Prairie Chicken
  (mainly in the Sandhills)
Sharp-tailed Grouse (mainly
  northern part)
*Mountain Plover
Long-billed Curlew (mainly
  in the Sandhills)
Burrowing Owl

*Poor-will
Red-shafted Flicker
Say's Phoebe (uncommon
  eastward)
*Western Wood Pewee
*Violet-green Swallow
American Magpie
*Pinyon Jay
*Rock Wren
Mountain Bluebird

*Solitary Vireo
*Audubon's Warbler
Bullock's Oriole
*Western Tanager
Black-headed Grosbeak

Lazuli Bunting
*Spotted Towhee
Lark Bunting
*White-winged Junco
*Brewer's Sparrow

Throughout Nebraska the following species of birds breed more or less regularly in wooded tracts, or in open country (natural grasslands, agricultural lands, meadow-like lowlands, brushy places, and dooryards):

WOODED TRACTS

Cooper's Hawk
Yellow-billed Cuckoo
Black-billed Cuckoo
Screech Owl
Hairy Woodpecker
Downy Woodpecker
Blue Jay
Black-capped Chickadee

White-breasted Nuthatch
Red-eyed Vireo
Warbling Vireo
Oven-bird (less common west-
  ward)
American Redstart
Baltimore Oriole

OPEN COUNTRY

Marsh Hawk
Bob-white
Killdeer
Upland Plover
Mourning Dove
Barn Owl
Red-headed Woodpecker
Eastern Kingbird
Western Kingbird
Horned Lark
Barn Swallow
Purple Martin (mainly eastern
  Nebraska)
House Wren
Mockingbird (mainly southern
  Nebraska)
Catbird
Brown Thrasher
Eastern Bluebird

Loggerhead Shrike
Yellow Warbler
Yellow-throat
Yellow-breasted Chat
Bobolink
Eastern Meadowlark (mainly
  eastern Nebraska)
Western Meadowlark (com-
  mon westward)
Common Grackle
Blue Grosbeak
Dickcissel
Common Goldfinch
Grasshopper Sparrow
Vesper Sparrow
Chipping Sparrow
Field Sparrow
Chestnut-collared Longspur
  (mainly northern Nebraska)

Spring arrives in this prairie state with a burst. Rivers rise, flooding the bottomlands; temporary ponds and streams appear seemingly everywhere. Waterbirds, geese, and ducks come as soon as the ice goes out, and shorebirds show up later to take full advantage of muddy places left by the receding waters. Flycatchers, kinglets, vireos, and warblers gather in the wooded borders of streams, lakes, and sloughs, or in canyons and city parks. Since these environments are often widely separated by vast stretches of open country, especially in the western part of the state, the birds tend to 'bunch up,' frequently in impressive numbers. Fall comes to Nebraska in a more leisurely manner, and the bird migration is seldom so spectacular, most species passing through the state in a more dispersed and less hurried fashion. The principal migration flights in Nebraska may be experienced within the following dates: waterfowl, 10 March—20 April, 10 October—25 November; shorebirds, 1 May—1 June, 1 August—1 October; landbirds, 15 April—20 May, 25 August—20 October.

In winter, wherever there is open water on the larger rivers and lakes, the bird finder may expect a few ducks (including the American Merganser) and an occasional Herring Gull. Among the more common winter residents in southeastern Nebraska is the Harris' Sparrow. In the central and eastern part of the state there is always a possibility of finding a Red-shafted Flicker, Pinyon Jay, Townsend's Solitaire, White-winged Junco, or Oregon Junco— western species that sometimes move eastward in the winter. As a rule, winter bird finding is more productive in eastern Nebraska near the Missouri River than farther west. For example, Christmas bird counts in the vicinity of Omaha usually total about 30 species; at Chadron, in the northwestern corner, about 18.

The Nebraska Ornithologists' Union holds an annual meeting in May in a different city of the state, conducts field trips during the spring and fall migration seasons, and publishes a quarterly, *The Nebraska Bird Review*. The organization may be contacted through the Nebraska State Museum, Morrill Hall, University of Nebraska, Lincoln.

CHADRON. The bird finder approaching northwestern Nebraska from the east on heavily traveled US Route 20 will notice that the undulating grasslands become increasingly interrupted by buttes, rough gullies, and steep-walled canyons, and that ponderosa pine begins to dot various slopes, especially those on the Pine Ridge to the south. Arriving in the northwest corner, which is much like Wyoming to the west and South Dakota to the north, he is likely to hear his first Poor-will and catch his first glimpses of the Violet-green Swallow, Pinyon Jay, and other western species; at the same time, he may see the last of such eastern species as the Orchard Oriole, Indigo Bunting, and Eastern Towhee. If the bird finder is interested in investigating the mixture of eastern and western birds of Nebraska's northwest corner, Chadron (elevation 3,371 feet) makes a worth-while stopping point.

CHADRON STATE PARK (800 acres) lies 9 miles south of Chadron on Route 19. Almost in the center of the long, narrow Pine Ridge, the Park embraces rough country with a conglomeration of buttes, canyons, and bluffs. Ponderosa pine grows in the higher areas. Along Chadron Creek, which traverses the east side of the Park, and around two small ponds are deciduous trees—cottonwoods, elms, ashes, boxelders, and willows—and low shrubs. Birds that are known to nest in the Park include the Red-tailed Hawk, Prairie Falcon, Poor-will, Red-headed Woodpecker, Downy Woodpecker, Say's Phoebe, Violet-green Swallow, House Wren, Brown Thrasher, Mountain Bluebird, Red-eyed Vireo, Oven-bird, Black-headed Grosbeak, and Lark Sparrow. Other birds that are present in the summer and probably nest are the White-breasted Nuthatch, Audubon's Warbler, American Redstart, and Western Tanager.

Chadron Park is open from 1 June to 1 September, during which time there are housekeeping cabins, camping facilities, horses, and boats available. An auto road winds through the Park from the highway, and several trails lead through canyons and up to the highest bluffs.

HALSEY. A unique project, the creating of a forest, has been under way since 1902 in the NEBRASKA NATIONAL FOREST, BESSEY DIVISION (90,000 acres), which lies 3 miles west of Halsey in central Nebraska. The country here was typical grass-covered, sandhill terrain, devoid of trees and shrubs except in pockets between the hills and on the borders of the Loup and Dismal Rivers and other streams. Planting of trees in this region was started with jack pine and ponderosa pine. Since 1902 the original trees have matured, additional plantings of many varieties of both deciduous and coniferous trees have been made, and a nursery has been established. The forested area, now 30,000 acres, is reached from Halsey on a well-marked gravel road.

While for miles over the treeless countryside that surrounds the Forest the Greater Prairie Chicken, Sharptailed Grouse, Upland Plover, Burrowing Owl, Horned Lark, Western Meadowlark, Grasshopper Sparrow, and Lark Sparrow are among the regular breeding birds, the Forest has brought in great numbers of woodland and forest-edge species—some haunt the river valleys in the east and others are commonly found in the wooded canyons in the west.

Birds that occur in summer either along the rivers or in the forested areas include the Great Blue Heron, Sparrow Hawk, Great Horned Owl, Yellow-shafted Flicker, Redshafted Flicker, Blue Jay, Black-capped Chickadee, House Wren, Catbird, Brown Thrasher, Wood Thrush, Eastern Bluebird, Loggerhead Shrike, Bell's Vireo, Black and White Warbler, Yellow-breasted Chat, American Redstart, Orchard Oriole, Baltimore Oriole, Scarlet Tanager, Cardinal, Black-headed Grosbeak, Blue Grosbeak, Eastern Towhee, and Spotted Towhee. In the winter the Rough-legged Hawk, Pine Grosbeak, Pine Siskin, White-winged Junco, Slate-colored Junco, Oregon Junco, and American Tree Sparrow are to be found.

HASTINGS. The HASTINGS MUSEUM, known also as the House of Yesterday, has 3,500 bird mounts and approximately 400 bird skins, all of North American species. Among several excellent habitat groups is a particularly impressive one of Whooping Cranes. Most of the ornithological collection represents the life work of the late A. M. Brooking. The Museum stands at 14th Street and Burlington Avenue.

HASTINGS COLLEGE, between 7th and 9th Streets at Turner Avenue, offers a course in ornithology each spring.

Northwest of the College, on Eastside Boulevard between 9th and 12th Streets, is HEARTWELL PARK (25 acres), an inviting area consisting of a small artificial pond in a ravine shaded by cottonwoods, willows, and elms. From the last week of April to the middle of May, hosts of transient warblers may be found here and, in addition, Black-crowned Night Herons, Evening Grosbeaks, Lazuli Buntings, and many sparrows.

On the outskirts of Hastings are numerous small lagoons, which vary in water level from year to year, depending on the rainfall. STROMER LAGOON, which usually retains considerable water, offers the best possibilities for seeing waterbirds, waterfowl, and shorebirds in April and early May. White Pelicans, American Egrets, and Avocets are among the transients that may be expected. To reach Stromer Lagoon, drive east from Hastings on US Route 6 to 'Show-Boat' Corner, then turn south and drive 4 miles. The Lagoon will appear on the left side of the road.

The CRYSTAL LAKE RECREATION AREA (63 acres), embracing small Crystal Lake and an adjoining woods along the Little Blue River, is good for bird finding the year round. Three grosbeaks—the Rose-breasted, Black-headed, and Blue—breed here. Red-bellied Woodpeckers are permanent residents. The Area may be reached by driving south from Hastings on US Route 281 to Ayr, then north one mile on State Route 113.

The Brooking Bird Club, which may be contacted through the Hastings Museum, holds regular monthly meetings and many field trips.

KEARNEY. From 15 March to 15 April Sandhill Cranes may be observed almost anywhere along the Platte and North Platte Rivers from Grand Island to the Wyoming border, but the heaviest concentrations apparently occur in the PLATTE RIVER VALLEY between the small towns of Odessa and Elm Creek. The birds, usually in big flocks, should be looked for in the previous year's cornfields, in alfalfa fields, around haystacks, and on pasture lands. A particularly good place is a recently plowed field. Now and then the bird finder may catch sight of a few individuals performing their peculiarly stiff-legged, bounding

dances and, if he is unusually lucky, he may see one of the
few remaining Whooping Cranes (see under Port Lavaca
in the Texas chapter), which are known to linger in the
Platte River Valley during their journey north to Canada.

The best way to find flocks of Sandhill Cranes is to drive
west from Kearney on US Route 30, which parallels the
Platte River on the north and goes through Odessa and
Elm Creek. West of Odessa, start searching from dirt roads
between the highway and the River. Some of these byways
run north and south; others run east and west connecting
them. All pass farmlands that are likely places for Cranes.
(For a part of the North Platte River Valley where Sandhill Cranes may be searched for in a like manner, see under
North Platte.)

LINCOLN. Because of the overlap of ranges of eastern
and western species in the vicinity of this capital city and
the proximity of the migration paths of many shorebirds
and waterfowl, Lincoln bird finders have been able to record about 240 species of resident and transient birds in
recent years.

About 110 species have been seen at various times of
year in ANTELOPE PARK, which extends in a northwesterly and southeasterly direction from its main entrance at
27th (State Route 2) and C Streets. The Park comprises
177 acres bordering Antelope Creek and includes many
varied habitats. Antelope Creek is paralleled roughly by a
road from the main entrance. The banks of the Creek from
A Street northwest to 27th and D Streets are among the
best spots in Lincoln for observing vireos, warblers, and
other transient landbirds (late April and May), since the
habitat varies from deciduous shrubs, aspens, and pines to
a stand of large, old elms at the northwest corner. The
area along the Creek, just east of the pavilion and pine
grove, is particularly favored by sparrows. Although most
of the species commonly seen in Antelope Park are eastern, one should always be on the watch for western transients such as the Red-shafted Flicker, Lazuli Bunting, and
Oregon Junco. Species to be seen through the winter include the Red-breasted Nuthatch, Golden-crowned Kinglet,
Cedar Waxwing, Pine Siskin, and Red Crossbill.

The LINCOLN ZOO, just northeast of the main entrance to Antelope Park, contains a small collection of birds. Many are exotic, but an effort is made to keep a representative selection of North American birds.

Another of the city parks, PIONEERS PARK, has been found to be a good all-year bird-finding area. About 130 species have been found here in recent years. Comprising 600 acres of widely varied terrain, Pioneers Park is southwest of the city; it may be reached by driving west from US Route 77 on South Street, turning left on Park Boulevard (the Gooch Mills is a good landmark for this poorly marked turn), and following the paved road, first southwest, then west on Van Dorn Street across Salt Creek and past the State Hospital turnoff. The Park is 2.5 miles beyond the Gooch Mills; past the State Hospital the route is plainly marked (for about one mile) by a continuous stand of conifers lining the left-hand side of the road. The outstanding botanical feature of the Park is the large number of pine and other coniferous trees that have been planted by the city. Deciduous shrubs grow abundantly in several places. In the winter months the Pinewood Bowl (within the loop of paved road that passes around the Park), a large stand of pines and a few other trees surrounding an open-air theater, is a choice site for finding Long-eared Owls (about 15 usually winter), White-breasted Nuthatches, Red-breasted Nuthatches, Red Crossbills (flocks of 150 or more have been seen), and occasionally a Townsend's Solitaire. The area near the playground is good for observing vireos, warblers, orioles, and sparrows in spring, and for woodpeckers, Brown Creepers, and Golden-crowned Kinglets in the winter. A gravel road leading to pens housing deer, antelope, and bison passes the golf course, where in the late afternoon Short-eared Owls may be seen hunting or sitting on the fence posts. The road also passes several small ponds near which Green Herons nest and where other waterbirds gather during migration.

One of the most productive areas near Lincoln is along the gravel road that is an extension of North 27th Street beyond its intersection with US Route 6. The road is flanked on both sides by a number of small ponds, lakes, and mud flats, the most interesting of which are to be found 2.7,

3.2, 4.4, and 4.8 miles north of Route 6. Of the 140 species of birds that are listed as occurring along this road, the majority are waterbirds, waterfowl, and shorebirds. Canada Geese, White-fronted Geese, Snow Geese, and Blue Geese are common in March. Among the ducks are Mallards, Gadwalls, Baldpates, Pintails, Green-winged Teal, Blue-winged Teal, Shovelers, Redheads, Ring-necked Ducks, Canvas-backs, Lesser Scaup Ducks, Buffle-heads, and Ruddy Ducks. Occasionally a Cinnamon Teal, Wood Duck, or American Merganser may be seen. The shorebirds usually spotted by local bird finders in May, August, and September include the Semipalmated Plover, Golden Plover, Black-bellied Plover, Ruddy Turnstone, Wilson's Snipe, Solitary Sandpiper, Willet, Greater Yellow-legs, Lesser Yellow-legs, Pectoral Sandpiper, Least Sandpiper, Red-backed Sandpiper, Dowitcher, Stilt Sandpiper, Semipalmated Sandpiper, Buff-breasted Sandpiper (fall only), Marbled Godwit, Hudsonian Godwit, Sanderling (usually in the fall), Avocet, and Wilson's Phalarope. Some of the summer-resident landbirds to be found along the roadside or bordering the ponds are the Eastern and Western Meadowlarks, Yellow-headed Blackbird, Blue Grosbeak, Savannah Sparrow, and Henslow's Sparrow. Leconte's Sparrows and Harris' Sparrows are common transients in the spring and fall; and Lapland Longspurs are often very numerous in the winter.

CAPITAL BEACH AMUSEMENT PARK, west of Lincoln, is reached by taking Route 6 west to Burlington Avenue, then turning north 2 blocks. This recreational center on the shore of Salt Lake, the largest body of water in the vicinity of Lincoln, is usually as good for waterbirds, waterfowl, and shorebirds as the North 27th Street area mentioned above. The Park is closed to the public during the waterfowl-hunting season.

The Nebraska State Museum, in Morrill Hall (14th and U Streets) on the campus of the UNIVERSITY OF NEBRASKA, has about 3,500 bird skins and a large number of mounted birds on exhibition. The Museum is open weekdays and Sunday afternoons. A course in ornithology is offered each spring semester by the Department of Zoology.

Most of Lincoln's active amateur and professional ornithologists belong to the Audubon Naturalists' Club, which meets on the third Tuesday of each month at 7:30 P.M. in the auditorium of the Nebraska State Museum. Visitors are welcome. Field trips are conducted throughout the year. The organization may be contacted through the Museum.

NORTH PLATTE. This city, inside the angle formed by the confluence of the North and South Platte Rivers, has in its vicinity some of the state's most productive areas for bird finding in the spring. From early March to the last of May the Rivers and their tributary streams, the valley lowlands and adjacent sandhills, and the many small ponds and wet meadows attract hordes of migrating waterbirds, waterfowl, shorebirds, and landbirds. Wooded tracts, limited for the most part to the borders of watercourses, are oases for masses of tree-loving birds.

One of the best places for flocks of Sandhill Cranes is the NORTH PLATTE RIVER VALLEY between North Platte and Hershey. This may be traversed by driving west from North Platte on US Route 30 for about 3 miles; at the cement-block filling station turn north on a gravel road and drive about 1.5 miles, then turn west on a road that eventually meets another road going south to Hershey on Route 30. The Cranes will be found, from mid-March to mid-April, on the near-by farmlands in situations similar to those in the Platte River Valley (see under Kearney).

The following loop trip (about 15 miles) will lead to some of the richest spots for spring bird finding. Take US Route 83 north from North Platte for about 2 miles to a small bridge over WHITEHORSE CREEK. On both sides of the road, just beyond Whitehorse Creek, are wet meadows where waterfowl and shorebirds gather, especially Shovelers and Greater Yellow-legs. Western Meadowlarks and Red-wings are common on the fence posts and telephone wires. Continue north over the hill, take a left fork, and, about 5 miles from town, stop to view a variety of ducks and a few shorebirds on a small farm pond on the left of the road. One mile beyond, Whitehorse Creek widens into Whitehorse Marsh, where there are Long-billed Curlews and often Great Blue Herons. Another mile be-

yond, ask permission to look for birds from a small dam that
forms JACKSON LAKE, a farm pond on the right of the
road. From this dam one may see ducks on the pond, and,
in the near-by marsh and vicinity, Long-billed Marsh
Wrens, Yellow-throats, Yellow-headed Blackbirds, Savannah Sparrows, Lincoln's Sparrows, and Swamp Sparrows.

Drive north half a mile to where the road turns west.
Park the car and walk a short distance north past a little
cemetery. On the right is a 3-acre woodlot, mostly boxelders, where Great Horned Owls, Yellow-shafted Flickers,
Red-headed Woodpeckers, Hairy Woodpeckers, Downy
Woodpeckers, Black-capped Chickadees, Eastern Bluebirds, and Mountain Bluebirds occur. On the west is a
prairie-dog town with a few Burrowing Owls. In the vicinity
are several small booming grounds of Greater Prairie
Chickens.

The bird finder may return to North Platte by driving
back to a point just beyond Whitehorse Marsh, going
straight south, and then working east and south to Route
83 past numerous farm ponds, marshy places, and wet
meadows.

Another area north of North Platte may be reached by
driving north on Route 83 for 3 miles, turning right on
State Route 92, then left on State Route 92A and right on
State Route 40 to the small town of Stapleton. While crossing this rolling, treeless sandhill country in the spring and
summer, the bird finder should watch for Burrowing Owls
in the prairie-dog towns, and for Marsh Hawks, Horned
Larks, American Magpies, Loggerhead Shrikes, Western
Meadowlarks, Lark Buntings, Vesper Sparrows, Lark Sparrows, and Chestnut-collared Longspurs. Three miles before
reaching Stapleton the road passes along the east side of
AMBLER LAKE (100 acres), which is mainly a large
marsh containing cattails, sedges, bulrushes, and is fringed
by willows and cottonwoods. This body of water, in addition to attracting migrating waterfowl and shorebirds, holds
a population of nesting birds that includes Pied-billed
Grebes, Mallards, Blue-winged Teal, Coots, Long-billed
Marsh Wrens, Yellow-headed Blackbirds, and Red-wings.

Three miles south of town on Route 83 is the NORTH
PLATTE EXPERIMENTAL STATION, where there are

enough deciduous trees and shrubs for Swainson's Hawks, woodpeckers, American Magpies, White-breasted and Red-breasted Nuthatches, Catbirds, Brown Thrashers, Cardinals, and Pine Siskins. Personnel at the Station will give the bird finder directions and permission to inspect the area.

Half a mile east of the Experimental Station on Route 83 is the NORTH PLATTE FISH HATCHERY, where 60 ponds attract hundreds of ducks and shorebirds in both spring and fall.

The best year-round, but the least accessible, bird-finding spot near North Platte is on the south side of the NORTH PLATTE DIVERSION DAM on the Platte River. To reach the southern end of the Dam, continue straight east from the Fish Hatchery for 5 miles (leaving Route 83 when it turns south), bear north at a schoolhouse, continue about one mile, and, after crossing a small wooden bridge over an irrigation ditch, park the car near a small house to the right of the ditch; then walk north a short distance to the Dam. In early June Cliff Swallows nest by the hundreds under the Dam walk. Below the Dam, migrating shorebirds gather on the rocks and exposed sand flats. Above the Dam is a group of dead cottonwood trees—reached by crossing the Dam walk and a stretch of gravel—in which Double-crested Cormorants, Great Blue Herons, and Black-crowned Night Herons nest. Ducks of many kinds, White Pelicans, Herring Gulls, and Ring-billed Gulls frequent this section of the River, while the neighboring woods and thickets are nesting habitats for Brown Thrashers, Bell's Vireos, Red-eyed Vireos, Warbling Vireos, and Common Goldfinches.

LAKE MALONEY (1,650 acres of water surface), one of a chain of artificial lakes about 6 miles south of the city, is reached by going south on Route 83 to the Experimental Station, turning west for one mile, then following a well-traveled road south, west, and south again. Every spring White Pelicans, Double-crested Cormorants, and many herons appear here. When the water is low, the exposed mud flats teem with transient shorebirds, including Lesser Yellow-legs, Pectoral Sandpipers, Baird's Sandpipers, Least Sandpipers, Dowitchers, Semipalmated Sandpipers, and Marbled Godwits.

OGALLALA. The largest reservoir in Nebraska, LAKE McCONAUGHTY (35,200 acres), formed by the Kingsley Dam across the North Platte River, is 6 miles north of Ogallala in an open, rolling area of corn and wheat fields and range lands. In the immediate surroundings of the Reservoir the vegetation consists mostly of grasses and forbs, with occasional cottonwoods and willows. At the western end, in the tops of partly submerged cottonwoods, nest thousands of Double-crested Cormorants. Below the Kingsley Dam is a cattail marsh and a small lake, LAKE OGALLALA, with marshy edges and a border of willows, false indigos, and a few cottonwoods. South of both bodies of water are a number of 'breaks' or canyons in which there is a rich growth of juniper, chokecherry, buckbrush, and wild rose. North of the Lakes the land gradually rises to the sandhill country.

Although the peak periods for birds, in terms of numbers of species and individuals, are during migration from March through May and from August to the last of October, this is wonderful country for bird finding any time of the year. Since there are a number of country roads around the Lakes which, because of the open setting, are easy to find, the bird finder may have a very successful day by just following one small road after another. A trip that touches only the high spots is outlined below.

Drive north from Ogallala on State Route 61 to the Kingsley Dam, an excellent vantage point for observing transient Horned Grebes, Eared Grebes, Western Grebes, Pied-billed Grebes, White Pelicans, Canada and Snow Geese, and ducks—Mallards, Gadwalls, Baldpates, Pintails, Green-winged Teal, Blue-winged Teal, Shovelers, Redheads, Ring-necked Ducks, Canvas-backs, Lesser Scaup Ducks. Below the overhanging concrete spillway of the Dam many thousands of Cliff Swallows begin nesting in June.

At the north end of the Dam, turn right onto State Route 49, which passes Lake Ogallala and the cattail marsh. Here nesting birds include American Bitterns, Long-billed Marsh Wrens, and Red-wings. A small, marshy island in Lake Ogallala supports a colony of Black-crowned Night Herons. On Lake Ogallala in winter, especially if Lake Mc-

Conaughty freezes over, may be found thousands of ducks
—Mallards, American Golden-eyes, and American Mergansers predominating. The breaks south of Lakes Ogallala
and McConaughty give shelter in winter to numerous
Rough-legged Hawks, Bald Eagles, Robins, Common Goldfinches, Pine Siskins, and American Tree Sparrows. In
spring the canyons are alive with migrating sparrows, together with Sparrow Hawks, Yellow Warblers, Myrtle
Warblers, Audubon's Warblers, and Yellow-throats. Nesting birds include the Golden Eagle, Prairie Falcon, Say's
Phoebe, Bank Swallow, Cliff Swallow, American Magpie,
Blue Grosbeak, and probably the Lazuli Bunting.

Return to Route 61 and drive north through a typical
stretch of the Nebraska Sandhills. During wet years there
are many temporary ponds along this highway which attract transient geese, ducks, and shorebirds for resting and
feeding purposes. In the early morning during April and
May the courtship activities of Greater Prairie Chickens
may be observed. One of their booming grounds is on the
right of Route 61 about a mile north of the Dam, and the
several others in the vicinity may be located by following
some of the rather dim trails leading in either direction from
the highway. Beginning in late May, nesting Long-billed
Curlews and a few Avocets should be looked for around
the ponds. Other breeding shorebirds to be expected are
the Killdeer, Wilson's Snipe, Willet, and Wilson's Phalarope. Summer-resident landbirds to be observed commonly
along the highway are the Eastern and Western Kingbirds,
Western Meadowlark, Brewer's Blackbird, Dickcissel, Lark
Bunting (one of the most common birds), Grasshopper
Sparrow, and Vesper Sparrow.

After inspecting this sample of sandhill country, return
on Route 61, and, just before crossing the railroad tracks
on the north side of the Dam, turn right on a dirt road
(leading to Lewellen) which parallels the tracks and the
northern shore of Lake McConaughty. Small roads and
trails lead south from this road to points on the Lake that
are good for observing transient waterbirds and waterfowl.
A few of the thousands of nesting Double-crested Cormorants can be seen from the shore of the Lake just west of the

Otter Creek Recreation Grounds. Other birds to be watched for are White Pelicans (sometimes in flocks of 150 birds or more), Great Blue Herons, and American Egrets.

Along the North Platte River between the west end of the Lake and Lewellen are numerous places where Sandhill Cranes—sometimes as many as 10,000—stop off in the spring and fall. They are best seen from late March to early May and in September and October, either loitering on the sand bars in the River or feeding in the adjoining corn and wheat fields.

At Lewellen turn left, cross the River, and return to Ogallala on US Route 26, or, after crossing the River, take the first left turn and follow the River back to the west end of the Lake opposite the Cormorant colonies. From here proceed along the shore until the road turns right and returns to Route 26 through EAGLES CANYON, a spot attractive to many birds, including a nesting pair of Prairie Falcons, and to mule deer.

OMAHA. The one outstanding spot for birds in the vicinity of Nebraska's biggest city is the FONTENELLE FOREST RESERVE AREA (2,500 acres) along the Missouri River about 2 miles south of the city limits. The Area has two natural divisions, an eastern and a western; railroad tracks run north and south through the Area, roughly following the line between the divisions. The eastern division comprises the Missouri River bottomlands, which support a growth of willows and cottonwoods interrupted by several small farms and marshes. The western division is characterized by steep bluffs and hollows with a cover of virgin timber (oak, hickory, walnut, basswood, elm, ash, and other deciduous species), the largest stand within the state of Nebraska. To reach Fontenelle Forest from downtown Omaha, drive south from Dodge Street (US Route 30) on 13th Street (US Route 75) until (at the city limits) it is crossed by Bellevue Boulevard, which is paved with red brick. Turn left here and follow the Boulevard for about a mile to a sign on the left marking the Fontenelle Forest entrance, then go up the entrance driveway and park the car near the caretaker's house. Maps of trails and other points of interest may be obtained from the caretaker.

Within the Reserve Area is a rich variety of woodland
and forest-edge birds, including the following breeding
species: Red-tailed Hawk, Red-shouldered Hawk, Broad-
winged Hawk, Yellow-billed Cuckoo, Great Horned Owl,
Barred Owl, Whip-poor-will, Ruby-throated Hummingbird,
Red-bellied Woodpecker, Crested Flycatcher, Acadian Flycatcher, Eastern Wood Pewee, Blue Jay, Tufted Titmouse,
White-breasted Nuthatch, Wood Thrush, Blue-gray Gnatcatcher, White-eyed Vireo, Bell's Vireo, Yellow-throated
Vireo, Warbling Vireo, Black and White Warbler, Oven-
bird, Louisiana Water-thrush, Kentucky Warbler, American
Redstart, Baltimore Oriole, Scarlet Tanager, Rose-breasted
Grosbeak, Indigo Bunting, Common Goldfinch, and Eastern
Towhee. The nesting season is usually well under way by
the latter half of May. Transient species that may be ex-
pected during the peaks of migration from mid-April to
mid-May and from mid-September to mid-October are the
Olive-backed Thrush, Gray-cheeked Thrush, Ruby-crowned
Kinglet, Golden-crowned Kinglet, Solitary Vireo, Myrtle
Warbler, Harris' Sparrow, White-throated Sparrow, Fox
Sparrow, and Song Sparrow. In winter Slate-colored Juncos
and American Tree Sparrows may be found.

(For an interesting bird-finding area in Iowa across the
Missouri River from Omaha, see under Council Bluffs in
the Iowa chapter.)

OSHKOSH. Looking north from this town on the North
Platte River in west-central Nebraska, the bird finder will
see the beginning of the rolling, treeless Sandhills, in which
lies the CRESCENT LAKE NATIONAL WILDLIFE REF-
UGE (46,540 acres). To reach the Refuge, drive north
from Oshkosh for 28 miles on State Route 27, which bisects
the Refuge and passes headquarters on Gimlet Lake near
the northern boundary. Since only 8 miles of Route 27 is
state-maintained and the remainder is sandhill trail, the bird
finder should check road conditions before leaving Oshkosh.
Sandhill trails are best during the spring and fall, for in
summer the sand becomes loose and dry, making travel difficult.

Though there are some blowouts and drifting sand, the
hills are in the main excellent range country, covered with

bunch grasses and occasional yuccas. Scattered between the hills are many lakes and numerous potholes with growths of bulrushes and cattails (mostly along the northwest shores); all these water areas are surrounded by meadows. Several of the named lakes, including Crescent (the largest, with 1,000 acres of surface), Island, Gimlet, and Goose, are passed by Route 27. The only conspicuous tree growth on the Refuge is a grove of willows near headquarters.

Both the Greater Prairie Chicken and the Sharp-tailed Grouse are present on the Refuge. Beginning in early June, Avocets and Long-billed Curlews may be found nesting. Other birds known to breed regularly in the Refuge include the Eared Grebe, Western Grebe, Black-crowned Night Heron, Least Bittern, Mallard, Gadwall, Pintail, Blue-winged Teal, Shoveler, Redhead, Ruddy Duck, Coot, Upland Plover, Wilson's Phalarope, Forster's Tern, Black Tern, Burrowing Owl, Long-billed Marsh Wren, Yellow-throat, Yellow-headed Blackbird, Red-wing, Dickcissel, Lark Bunting, and Lark Sparrow. The grove of willows attracts a few pairs of Mourning Doves, Eastern Kingbirds, Western Kingbirds, Warbling Vireos, and Common Goldfinches.

Large numbers of transient ducks, as well as White Pelicans, Snow Geese, and Sandhill Cranes, gather on the Refuge in March, early April, late September, October, and early November. Canada Geese are plentiful in late October and November.

SCOTTSBLUFF. A few pairs of House Finches are year-round residents in this city. State Route 29 south from Scottsbluff in western Nebraska crosses the NORTH PLATTE RIVER to the agricultural center of Gering. The bridge over the River is a good vantage point from which to watch Mallards in winter and great numbers of transient ducks during late March, April, October, and November.

The bird finder who happens to be in Scottsbluff in the summer should drive 7 miles south of Gering on Route 29 to the Wildcat Hills, a narrow strip of broken Great Plains extending eastward from the Wyoming border. Here are many steep-sided buttes and hills, together with canyons and tributary ravines. Although the vegetation is relatively sparse owing to the general dryness of the region, there is sufficient moisture in the canyons to support ponderosa pine, with a sprinkling of juniper, and clumps of skunkbrush, coralberry, and mountain mahogany.

The WILDCAT HILLS BIG GAME REFUGE (entrance on the right of Route 29, 9 miles south of Gering) embraces 852 acres of this region. Although the greater part of the Refuge is fenced to retain bison and is closed to the public, 123 acres is maintained as a recreation ground, with camping and picnic areas. By means of the trails that wind through the recreation area the bird finder may explore canyons or climb to high lookouts. The lack of permanent streams and lakes limits the birdlife to some extent, but a list of the species breeding regularly includes the Mountain Plover, Poor-will, Lewis' Woodpecker, Say's Phoebe, American Magpie, Pinyon Jay, Rock Wren, Mockingbird, Mountain Bluebird, Bullock's Oriole, and Western Tanager.

VALENTINE. South of this ranch town in the north-central part of the state, amid low, treeless hills, lies a group of some 30 named lakes that are the largest of all the lakes in the Sandhills. A number are embraced by the VALENTINE NATIONAL WILDLIFE REFUGE (70,401 acres). Although most of these bodies of water (characteristically long and narrow) are without outlets except at high water, only two or three are strongly alkaline. Nearly all are permanent, unless the seasons are very dry, and support bulrushes, cattails, and other marsh vegetation. Meadowlands, with various rushes and sedges, surround the lakes and merge with the drier, grass-covered uplands.

So far as breeding birds are concerned, this group of lakes, within and outside of the Refuge, is the most important in the Sandhills, for most species of waterbirds, waterfowl, and shorebirds are more abundant here than elsewhere in the region. Breeding species include the Eared Grebe, Pied-billed Grebe, Mallard, Gadwall, Baldpate, Pintail, Green-winged Teal, Blue-winged Teal, Shoveler, Redhead, Canvas-back, Lesser Scaup Duck, Ruddy Duck, Coot, Killdeer, Long-billed Curlew, Upland Plover, Wilson's Phalarope, Forster's Tern, and Black Tern. There are several small colonies of Black-crowned Night Herons. Here and there among the Sandhills are places where the courtship performances of the Sharp-tailed Grouse and the Greater Prairie Chicken may be observed in late March, April, and early May. During the fall migration extremely heavy concentrations of waterfowl and waterbirds occur in this area, attaining a maximum density during late September and October.

To reach the Valentine Refuge, drive south from Valentine for 16 miles on US Route 83, then turn right onto State Route 67, an oiled road, and drive 14 miles. Route 67 passes within sight of headquarters on Hackberry Lake (350 acres). It is possible to drive to the most interesting parts of the Refuge except in winter and early spring. Some of the lakes are open to fishing at certain seasons; others are closed at all times. No camping or open fires are permitted within the Refuge boundaries.

Five and a half miles east of Valentine on State Route 7 is the headquarters of the FORT NIOBRARA NATIONAL WILDLIFE REFUGE (19,122 acres), an area given over principally to the preservation of vanishing species of big game—buffalo, elk, and Texas longhorn cattle. A visit is best made between June and September, when most of the Refuge is accessible by car. While viewing the big game, the bird finder may observe Upland Plovers, which nest regularly, and may perhaps see a few permanent-resident Greater Prairie Chickens and Sharp-tailed Grouse.

Contributing authorities: Joseph T. Armstrong, Jr., Henry E. Baumgarten, Loron C. Bunney, A. D. Campbell, John D. Connors, Miss Doris Gates, William E. Green, Mrs. A. H. Jones, Mrs. John (Willeta) Lueshen, Levi L. Mohler, R. Allyn Moser, Lloyd Ramelli, William F. Rapp, Jr., Carl E. Smith, John H. Wampole, George L. Wiseman.

Nevada

BY JEAN M. LINSDALE

SAGE THRASHER

Opportunities for ornithological discoveries in Nevada are abundant for the person who is willing to leave the highways and railways. Ordinarily, a traveler across Nevada assumes that the desert he sees from the automobile or train covers the state, and that no birds live in the region. Even naturalists sometimes conclude that the state is characterized by absence of animal life, especially birds. In fact, Nevada is one of the last large areas within the United States whose avifauna is little known, for, until recently, scarcely anyone who observed birds in serious fashion had lived here for any length of time. Considering the size of the area, the avian population is composed of few species (310 full species plus 86 additional races) but this circumstance makes for exceptional interest when the birds are studied in detail. The wide dispersal of individuals of most of the species makes it impossible to predict with assurance where in the state any kind of bird will occur, and the same uncertainty applies to the seasonal status of each kind.

Nevada ranks sixth among the states in size. Of its seventy million acres barely four million are in farms and fewer than five hundred thousand are under irrigation. The area considered forest is approximately five million acres, but not much of this is completely covered with timber, and elsewhere trees are sparse.

The plateau of the Great Basin, on which most of Nevada lies, has an altitude between 5,000 and 6,000 feet in the east, from less than 4,000 to 5,000 feet in the west, and between 2,000 and 3,000 feet in the south. The topography is diverse and rugged, with deserts, narrow valleys, and many mountain ranges, from 50 to 100 miles long, running from north to south. On the western border, the slopes rise rapidly to the eastern crests of the Sierra Nevada. At the southern tip, the Colorado River leaves the boundary at below 500 feet altitude.

The only large valley running east and west in the state is the Humboldt River Valley. North of this the mountainous area, which constitutes the divide between the Humboldt and the branches of the Snake River, is broken by many low passes. Nearly all of the rivers in the state empty into lakes without outlets or lose their water by absorption and evaporation as they spread out over the floors of the valleys. Many of the valleys are closed drainage systems, with no stream channels, and are so enclosed by mountains that they would hold large lakes before overflowing. The playas in the valleys characteristically hold water in years of extra rain or snow.

The most striking climatic characteristics of Nevada are its bright sunshine, low annual rainfall in the valleys and deserts, heavy snowfall in the higher mountains, dryness and purity of air, and exceptionally great diurnal ranges in temperature. Reno, at 4,500 feet, has a temperature near the average for the state, with an annual mean of 50 degrees. Highest temperature recorded in the northern section is 112 degrees at Carlin; lowest, −50 degrees at San Jacinto; highest in the southern section, 120 degrees at Logandale; lowest, −21 degrees at Oasis Ranch. Winter temperatures go below zero everywhere except in the extreme south. Average annual precipitation for Nevada is about 9 inches (4.87—15.87 inches). The number of days per year with 0.01 inch or more of precipitation varies from 14 at Clay City, southern Nye County, to 67 at Tahoe. The whole area is within the rain shadow cast by the high Sierra Nevada on the western border, but this influence becomes less pronounced toward the east. In an average year there are 193 clear days, 87 partly cloudy days, and 85 cloudy days.

A high proportion of the birds of Nevada are migratory, obviously on account of the severity of the winter climate. Although about 40 per cent of the species in the state are year-round residents, the figure is usually much smaller when any restricted district on the plateau is considered. Most of the birds recorded in the mountain regions are summer residents. Many species do not leave the region, but move to milder parts of it to escape storms.

A traveler across the middle of Nevada goes over or around more than 20 separate mountain ranges. These mountains provide islands of habitat on a desert plateau, each with its own set of environmental conditions. Among the high peaks are several that dominate their respective ranges: Mt. Rose, 8,933 feet, north of Lake Tahoe in the Carson Range (see under Reno), the only mountain in its vicinity that extends above timber line; Mt. Grant, 11,303 feet, in the Walker River Mountains west of the southern end of Walker Lake; Boundary Peak, 13,145 feet, the highest point in Nevada, on the western boundary at the north end of the White Mountains; Arc Dome, 11,775 feet, the highest of several high peaks in the Toiyabe Mountains (see under Austin) in the center of the state; Wheeler Peak, 13,058 feet, the highest point in the Snake Mountains (see under Ely), just inside the eastern border; Charleston Peak, 11,910 feet, in the Charleston Mountains (see under

Las Vegas), the southernmost of the high mountain peaks, which greatly contrasts with the surrounding desert.

In the higher parts of the mountains, except in the south, there are prominent stands of aspen, and extending still higher are limber pine and Engelmann spruce. Other conifers in the mountains are in scattered small stands that harbor some birds, but the kinds of trees usually do not have a marked effect on the ranges of the birds across the state. Toward the west the association of birds in the forests is almost like the one present across the line in California. Toward the eastern border the conifers are somewhat isolated from the ones in the mountains in Utah, but the birds are much alike on the two sides of the border.

The following arboreal birds are associated with the pines or other coniferous trees on the higher mountains:

Goshawk	Pygmy Nuthatch
Blue Grouse	Brown Creeper
Common Sapsucker	Robin
Williamson's Sapsucker	Mountain Bluebird
White-headed Woodpecker	Townsend's Solitaire
Black-backed Woodpecker	Golden-crowned Kinglet
Three-toed Woodpecker	Ruby-crowned Kinglet
Olive-sided Flycatcher	Solitary Vireo
Steller's Jay	Audubon's Warbler
Clark's Nutcracker	Evening Grosbeak
Mountain Chickadee	Cassin's Finch
White-breasted Nuthatch	Pine Siskin
Red-breasted Nuthatch	Oregon Junco

Meadows in the mountains usually are small and far apart. When they are flooded in the spring and early summer, the abundant moisture, vegetation, and insect food make them concentration points for many kinds of birds. Among the nesting birds are the Broad-tailed Hummingbird, Calliope Hummingbird, Black-capped Warbler, White-crowned Sparrow, Fox Sparrow, and Lincoln's Sparrow.

In the coarse soils of the foothills of the many mountain ranges, junipers and pinyon pines occur in open park-like woodlands. Some characteristic nesting birds are the Pinyon Jay, Plain Titmouse, Bush-tit, Blue-gray Gnatcatcher, Gray Vireo, Virginia's Warbler, and Black-throated Gray

Warbler. These birds are not all limited to this type of vegetation, and some stands of pinyon-juniper, especially in the
southern part of the state, harbor many additional kinds
of birds.

Cliffs and rock slopes are abundant in every section of
Nevada, occurring in a wide range of temperature and
moisture conditions. Among the birds that nest in these
sites are the Osprey, Red-tailed Hawk, Golden Eagle,
Prairie Falcon, Duck Hawk, Sparrow Hawk, White-
throated Swift, Say's Phoebe, Western Flycatcher, Violet-
green Swallow, Cliff Swallow, Canyon Wren, Rock Wren,
and House Finch. In vertical sand banks the Bank and
Rough-winged Swallows and the Belted Kingfisher dig
nesting tunnels.

Nearly all the northern valleys and the desert plateau
area, where the climate has been designated as cold steppe,
originally had a sparse cover of sagebrush with a rich
stand of palatable perennial grasses and weeds. Now the
sagebrush has increased in density, and other plants have
almost completely disappeared—about 70 per cent of the
forage value having been lost. This type of vegetation extends across the north end of the state with broad tongues
along the west border and into the eastern half of the area.
Examples of the type are to be seen close to the towns of
Elko, Reno, Carson City, and Minden (near Carson City).

Birds generally present over the high desert areas include
the following species:

Turkey Vulture	Loggerhead Shrike
Sage Grouse	Brewer's Blackbird
Mourning Dove	Brown-headed Cowbird
Poor-will	Lark Sparrow
Western Kingbird	Desert Sparrow
Horned Lark	Sage Sparrow
Common Raven	Brewer's Sparrow
Sage Thrasher	

In the arid valleys and over extensive areas of alkali
flats, on the cold desert between the southern creosote-
bush desert and the northern sagebrush desert, the prominent shrubs are shadscale and greasewood. Similar altitudinal arrangement of these three zones occurs on the
southern mountains. Within the shadscale area, the shrubs

usually cover less than one tenth of the ground of the stand, the barren ground being covered with small rocks. This is where Horned Larks find huge expanses of habitat suited to their needs. An example of this type of vegetation and the birds associated with it can be seen in the vicinity of Fallon.

The extreme conditions in the southern part of the state resemble those of the California small-leaf-shrub desert. Creosote bush, saltbush, and burroweed are common plants over great areas, with deciduous shrubs, yuccas (including some stands of the Joshua tree), and cacti scattered throughout and with short-lived annuals abundant in the spring months. This type of vegetation extends northward in Nevada to approximately the 37th parallel (Alamo on the east and just south of Tonopah on the west). Characteristic nesting birds are the Gambel's Quail, Road-runner, Poor-will, Lesser Nighthawk, Horned Lark, Loggerhead Shrike, and Desert Sparrow.

In Nevada, the most arid state, the lakes, marshes, rivers, and meadows are naturally important for bird finding. The large deep lakes without islands are generally little inhabited, but they deserve to be visited in any search for birds. Some of the lakes invite special interest because they are remnants of much larger bodies of water that were present in earlier stages in the history of the land. Important lakes are Pyramid, Tahoe, and Washoe Lakes (see under Reno), Carson Lake (see under Fallon), Walker Lake, and Ruby Lake (see under Elko). The man-made Lahontan Reservoir and Lake Mead (see under Boulder City) have already modified the avifauna in their regions.

The non-passerine aquatic birds that nest in Nevada include the 40 species here listed:

Eared Grebe	Black-crowned Night Heron
Western Grebe	American Bittern
Pied-billed Grebe	Least Bittern
White Pelican	White-faced Ibis
Double-crested Cormorant	Canada Goose
Great Blue Heron	Mallard
American Egret	Gadwall
Snowy Egret	Pintail
Green Heron	Green-winged Teal

Blue-winged Teal
Cinnamon Teal
Baldpate
Shoveler
Redhead
Ruddy Duck
American Merganser
Marsh Hawk
Sandhill Crane
Virginia Rail
Sora

Coot
Killdeer
Wilson's Snipe
Long-billed Curlew
Spotted Sandpiper
Avocet
Black-necked Stilt
Wilson's Phalarope
California Gull
Caspian Tern
Black Tern

In the valleys of the northeastern part of the state there are many wet hay meadows and pastures. Birds that nest in these grassy areas and marshlands include the Sandhill Crane, Wilson's Snipe, Long-billed Curlew, Wilson's Phalarope, Long-billed Marsh Wren, Bobolink, Western Meadowlark, Yellow-headed Blackbird, Red-wing, Savannah Sparrow, and Grasshopper Sparrow.

The Truckee, Walker, and Carson Rivers are all mountain streams flowing eastward from the Sierra Nevada. When the snow melts in spring and early summer, these streams run full. The Humboldt (see under Elko) and the Colorado Rivers (see under Boulder City) drain the north and south parts of the area. All these streams attract some birds.

The rivers generally are lined with deciduous cottonwoods or willows and with other trees and bushes that accompany the farming of adjacent land. Among the birds that live in the vegetation here are the following:

Mourning Dove
Yellow-billed Cuckoo
Long-eared Owl
Hairy Woodpecker
Downy Woodpecker
Western Kingbird
Traill's Flycatcher
American Magpie

House Wren
Warbling Vireo
Yellow Warbler
Macgillivray's Warbler
Bullock's Oriole
Lazuli Bunting
Common Goldfinch
Song Sparrow

Not many observations have been made on migration of birds across Nevada. The information available indicates that the main concentrations are along the western border, at the east base of the Sierra Nevada, and extend southward across southern California. Another line of travel parallels the eastern border of the state. Many birds, especially waterfowl, migrate in an east-west direction across the northern part of the state. Some of these enter California in the fall at its northeast corner, and others reach that state at about the latitude of San Francisco Bay. Time of migration is determined partly by the conditions at the points of arrival in the state and along the route across it. The weather and moisture conditions act to shorten or prolong the stay of transient birds and modify their local movements.

In addition to the resident species hardy enough to remain through the winter there are some birds that come in the winter from the north or east. Most of these are not abundant, but it is desirable to keep a watch for them. Among these winter visitants are rosy finches and the following:

Rough-legged Hawk
Ferruginous Hawk
Pigeon Hawk
Mountain Plover
Snowy Owl
Short-eared Owl
American Pipit
Bohemian Waxwing
Cedar Waxwing
Northern Shrike

Common Redpoll
Red Crossbill
Lark Bunting
American Tree Sparrow
Harris' Sparrow
Golden-crowned Sparrow
White-throated Sparrow
Swamp Sparrow
Lapland Longspur

Nevada now has an adequate system of surfaced roads that reach to many places where birds may be seen in abundance, and travel to these places by automobile can generally be made with safety and comfort. In the more remote sections, there is still a certain amount of hazard in traveling into unfamiliar ranges or deserts, and access to some sites may even require a few hours of road building; but with suitable preparation, journeys into these sections may be both safe and highly profitable. Every bird-finding expedition into Nevada should carry an ample supply of food, water, and warm clothing.

AUSTIN. The town site, at 6,594 feet, is in a steep canyon on the west side of the TOIYABE MOUNTAINS, close to the center of the state. This was the base of many of the mining camps in central and eastern Nevada, and the canyon walls are marked with abandoned prospect holes. The population is now reduced to a little more than 500 inhabitants.

In the Toiyabes are numerous small streams that start at high seeps or springs and rush down steep slopes. Some of them disappear among the rocks after running a short distance, others extend as far as the base of the Mountains but rarely farther. Along the lower courses of the streams and on the mountain meadows are willows; inside narrow canyons, dense stands of birches; on flats along the upper streams and on steep moist slopes, aspens; on dry slopes, sagebrush and other shrubs among thin stands of pinyon pine and mountain mahogany.

From Austin many bird-finding localities are accessible —along streams that come down from the Toiyabes and in the valleys on either side of the range. Drive east from Austin on US Route 50 for 11 miles, then turn right on State Route 8A to the GREAT SMOKY VALLEY on the east side of the Toiyabes. Worth-while side trips can be made by turning west off Route 8A near Millett on marked roads up BIRCH CREEK and KINGSTON CREEK CANYONS to campsites from which trails lead into the higher mountains. A large rock outcrop on Birch Creek Meadows attracts many birds, which nest in its crevices. South of Millett, well-marked trails beginning at the mouths of South Twin and North Twin Rivers go to the highest peaks in the Toiyabes. Arc Dome reaches 11,775 feet altitude, and the trip to it passes through a wide variety of conditions and a correspondingly varied association of birds.

Large numbers of migrating birds are present in May and September in Great Smoky Valley. The best time to find the nesting species active is in June, although many of the birds have eggs in May. Favorable localities to see these nesting birds are the vicinity of Millett (on the western side of the alkali flats) and 5 miles south of Millett. The wet meadows, abundant springs, the willows and marsh plants, the heavy thickets of buffaloberry, and the desert plants bordering the alkali flats insure profitable bird finding. Birds present here in the nesting season include the following: Pintail, Cinnamon Teal, Turkey Vulture, Swainson's Hawk, Marsh Hawk, Killdeer, Wilson's Snipe, Western Kingbird, Say's Phoebe, Horned Lark, American Magpie, Common Crow, Long-billed Marsh Wren, Mockingbird, Sage Thrasher, Loggerhead Shrike, Yellow Warbler, Yellow-throat, Yellow-breasted Chat, Western Meadowlark, Yellow-headed Blackbird, Red-wing, Bullock's Oriole, Brewer's Blackbird, Brown-headed Cowbird, Savannah Sparrow, Sage Sparrow, Brewer's Sparrow, and Song Sparrow.

Along the eastern slope of the Toiyabes, in the canyons, in the meadows at middle altitudes, and on the drier wooded or brush-covered slopes another combination of species is present, as follows: Sharp-shinned Hawk, Cooper's Hawk, Red-tailed Hawk, Prairie Falcon, Blue Grouse, Sage Grouse, Poor-will, White-throated Swift, Broad-tailed Hummingbird, Hairy Woodpecker, Wright's Flycatcher, Western Flycatcher, Violet-green Swallow, Cliff Swallow, Scrub Jay, Pinyon Jay, Clark's Nutcracker, Mountain Chickadee, Bush-tit, White-breasted Nuthatch, Dipper, House Wren, Canyon Wren, Rock Wren, Robin, Hermit Thrush, Olive-backed Thrush, Mountain Bluebird, Warbling Vireo, Virginia's Warbler, Audubon's Warbler, Black-throated Gray Warbler, Macgillivray's Warbler, Lazuli Bunting, Cassin's Finch, House Finch, Green-tailed Towhee, Spotted Towhee, Vesper Sparrow, Gray-headed Junco, Chipping Sparrow, Brewer's Sparrow, Fox Sparrow, and Song Sparrow.

BOULDER CITY. Once the construction headquarters for Hoover Dam, Boulder City in southeastern Nevada is now administrative headquarters of the National Park Service, which has charge of the LAKE MEAD NATIONAL RECREATIONAL AREA (689,827 acres in Nevada; 1,209,901 acres in Arizona). There is a free Museum of Natural History open daily in the National Park Service Building.

Annual temperatures in Boulder City range from 20 to 120 degrees. Winter daytime temperatures vary between 50 and 70 degrees. In the spring and fall the days are pleasantly warm and the nights cool. The weather is warm from 1 June to 15 September, but not nearly so hot as it is nearer the Colorado River. Boulder City is an oasis for birds. During migrations many birds are found in the shrubs and trees of the town.

Las Vegas Wash enters Lake Mead about 10 miles north of Boulder City. Unimproved campgrounds for tents and trailers are available here. In the desert may be found the Gambel's Quail, Road-runner, Say's Phoebe, Verdin, Common Raven, Cactus Wren, Crissal Thrasher, and Loggerhead Shrike. Hemenway Wash, 6.5 miles from Boulder City, is one of the principal recreational developments on the shore of Lake Mead, with boats, campgrounds, and bathhouses. There are few birds on the Lake, but the White Pelican, Brown Pelican, Double-crested Cormorant, Black Brant, Bald Eagle, Bonaparte's Gull, Least Tern, and Caspian Tern have been recorded.

Both Las Vegas Wash and Hemenway Wash may be reached by driving east from Boulder City on US Route 93, then north on State Route 41. Route 41 goes northwest along the shore of Lake Mead, then turns southwest and joins Route 93 northwest of Boulder City.

The Lake Mead Recreational Area extends as far south as the old mining town of Searchlight (elevation 3,560 feet), reached by driving west from Boulder City on Route 93 and south on US Route 95. Within 5 miles of Searchlight to the north and the east there are extensive Joshua-tree forests, along with hop sage and blackbrush. The Joshua tree, a yucca, which grows in close stands and reaches heights of 15 feet, is especially favored by the Scott's Oriole for nest sites. Other birds to be seen in these areas are the Sparrow Hawk, Ladder-backed Woodpecker, and Loggerhead Shrike.

The southern tip of Nevada on the Colorado River, opposite the site of Old Fort Mohave, Arizona, is reached by continuing south on Route 95 to State Route 77, turning east on Route 77, then right (south) on State Route 76, an unimproved road that follows the River south to Needles, California. The COLORADO RIVER VALLEY here is worthy of a visit in winter and early May. Bird finding is also profitable later in the summer for anyone able to endure the humid heat. Environmental conditions have been changed considerably in late years by grazing and by human modifications of the stream. This presents an opportunity to compare recent observations with those made in earlier years when the River was free to control the flood plain.

The River itself attracts fish-eating birds. The willows and cottonwoods on the bottomlands were formerly flooded every summer. Characteristic nesting birds here are Black-chinned Hummingbirds, Bell's Vireos, Yellow Warblers, Brown-headed Cowbirds, and Summer Tanagers. Until recent years the tracts of marshy ground along the edge of the Valley had nesting Yellow-throats, Red-wings, and Song Sparrows (the palest race of all the Song Sparrows). In the winter there were Marsh Hawks, Florida Gallinules, Coots, and Long-billed Marsh Wrens.

Farther away from the River, toward the margin of the bottomland that was formerly flooded, are stands of arrow-weed and low shrubs. On the second bottomland, a narrow belt of land above high-water level, saltbush is prominent. On higher land and in the washes there is a still greater variety of desert woody plants. Some of them reach the size of trees, and together they provide shelter and food supplies for large bird populations. An exploration of this area in early May will yield the following list of nesting birds: Gambel's Quail, White-winged Dove, Road-runner, Screech Owl, Great Horned Owl, Poor-will, Lesser Nighthawk, Black-chinned Hummingbird, Costa's Hummingbird, Gila Woodpecker, Ladder-backed Woodpecker, Vermilion Flycatcher, Verdin, Phainopepla, Bell's Vireo, Lucy's Warbler, Brown-headed Cowbird, Summer Tanager, Blue Grosbeak, Abert's Towhee, and Desert Sparrow.

In addition, at this season there is likely to be a swarm of transients that are on their way to nesting places in the mountains farther north in the state. Concentrations of birds along the River in winter deserve close examination, for they often include many unexpected species.

CARSON CITY. Much of the early ornithological exploration in Nevada was made from headquarters near this city, the smallest capital city in the United States.

The best areas for bird finding are in the vicinity of Minden (15 miles south on US Route 395) and Genoa (12

miles south on Route 395, then 3 miles west on State Route
57), the oldest town in Nevada. In this area, watered by
the Carson River, the Mormon pioneers established farms
and planted orchards, gardens, and many shade trees. About
the habitations in early summer may be found nesting
Mourning Doves, House Wrens, Robins, Cedar Waxwings,
Warbling Vireos, Yellow Warblers, Bullock's Orioles, Western Tanagers, Lazuli Buntings, House Finches, Common
Goldfinches, and Chipping Sparrows. On and about the
ponds near Minden many birds nest or stop in migration;
among these may be found Great Blue Herons, American
Egrets, Black-crowned Night Herons, Canada Geese,
Fulvous Tree-ducks, Mallards, Pintails, Cinnamon Teal,
Killdeer, Willets, Avocets, Wilson's Phalaropes, Northern
Phalaropes, Forster's Terns, and Black Terns. Where the
water is deep and the bulrushes especially rank, Long-billed
Marsh Wrens, Yellow-headed Blackbirds, and Red-wings
nest.

ELKO. The first town of more than 1,000 people that the
bird finder will encounter when crossing Nevada from the
east on US Route 40 is Elko in the northwestern part of
the state. From here visits may be made to numerous places
along the Humboldt River.

The RUBY LAKE NATIONAL WILDLIFE REFUGE
(35,618 acres) may be reached by taking the Lamoille
Highway (State Route 46) south for 5 miles, turning right
on a gravel road (still Route 46), and following signs
for 55 miles to Refuge headquarters. The Refuge is a natural
sump area, fed by springs on the west side and by runoff
from the snow on the surrounding mountains. The water
areas consist of spring holes, channels, and open places
ranging from a quarter acre to several hundred acres,
mainly at the south end of the marsh. The strikingly rugged
Ruby Mountains rise to 11,000 feet to the west of the Refuge. Elevation at headquarters is 6,012 feet. Predominant
types of vegetation are bulrush, sago pondweed, chara,
water milfoil, and water speedwell. These cover approximately 12,000 acres. The rest of the area has native grasses
and sedges, sagebrush, and rabbitbrush. This is one of the
few refuges where Sandhill Cranes nest. Also in summer

there are nesting Canada Geese and a great variety of ducks, among which are Mallards, Gadwalls, Pintails, and Green-winged Teal. There is also a transplanted, captive colony of Trumpeter Swans. Other nesting birds include the White-faced Ibis, Long-billed Curlew, and Willet. These are observed most satisfactorily in May and June. Transient waterbirds should be sought from September to November.

In a recent summer at the Ruby Lake Refuge the following birds were present: Eared Grebe, White Pelican, Canada Goose, Turkey Vulture, Red-tailed Hawk, Ferruginous Hawk, Marsh Hawk, Sparrow Hawk, Killdeer, Wilson's Snipe, Long-billed Curlew, Willet, Lesser Yellowlegs, Avocet, Black-necked Stilt, Forster's Tern, Mourning Dove, Short-eared Owl, Belted Kingfisher, Red-shafted Flicker, Lewis' Woodpecker, Western Wood Pewee, Horned Lark, Violet-green Swallow, Bank Swallow, Barn Swallow, Cliff Swallow, Scrub Jay, Pinyon Jay, Long-billed Marsh Wren, Rock Wren, Sage Thrasher, Loggerhead Shrike, Black-throated Gray Warbler, Western Meadowlark, Yellow-headed Blackbird, Red-wing, Brewer's Blackbird, Lazuli Bunting, Savannah Sparrow, and Sage Sparrow.

ELY. This is a mining community of more than 3,000 population, close to the eastern border of Nevada. Many people stop here to see the huge works where copper is taken from a deep open pit. The town is built in a narrow canyon, where it is protected from the storms of the open valley. There are several hotels and other services, including horses for pack trips into the near-by National Forest areas. The Millard Museum, 614 High Street, has a large collection of minerals and relics.

LEHMAN CAVES NATIONAL MONUMENT (640 acres), at the east base of the SNAKE MOUNTAINS, is about 65 miles from Ely and just 5 miles west of the very small settlement of Baker. It may be reached by following US Route 6 southeast of Ely and turning right on State Route 74. At the Caves are cabins and campsites. Roads and trails lead to numerous places in the Mountains where birds

of special interest are found. The vegetation and the animals here show more affinities with those of the Rocky
Mountain area than with those toward the Pacific Coast.
The high elevations account for conditions considerably
more moist than those in central and southern Nevada.

The Monument contains one section of land, at about
7,000 feet altitude, in a belt of pinyon pine and juniper
woodland. Baker and Lehman Creeks run toward the east
from Wheeler Peak, 13,058 feet, the highest point in the
Snake Mountains and the second highest peak in the state.
In the Mountains there are forests of pine, spruce, fir, and
mountain mahogany. Aside from the trails into the Mountains there is a road (off Route 74, north of Monument headquarters) up to Stella Lake, at 10,750 feet, on the north side
of Wheeler Peak. There is a constructed trail from the Lake
to the top of the Peak.

Among the birds to be found in these Mountains at some
time between May and September are the following:
Goshawk, Blue Grouse, Broad-tailed Hummingbird, Common Sapsucker, Three-toed Woodpecker, Western Flycatcher, Steller's Jay, Scrub Jay, Clark's Nutcracker, Mountain Chickadee, Plain Titmouse, Bush-tit, White-breasted
Nuthatch, Red-breasted Nuthatch, Pygmy Nuthatch,
Brown Creeper, Dipper, House Wren, Robin, Hermit
Thrush, Mountain Bluebird, Townsend's Solitaire, Golden-
crowned Kinglet, Warbling Vireo, Orange-crowned Warbler, Audubon's Warbler, Black-throated Gray Warbler,
Townsend's Warbler, Macgillivray's Warbler, Black-capped
Warbler, Cassin's Finch, Pine Siskin, Red Crossbill, Green-
tailed Towhee, Spotted Towhee, Vesper Sparrow, Gray-
headed Junco, Chipping Sparrow, and Fox Sparrow.

FALLON. The vicinity of Fallon (population about 2,000)
in the LAHONTAN VALLEY of western Nevada was
originally mainly desert, although there was water in Carson
Sink and Carson Lake. About 40 years ago the Truckee-
Carson Irrigation District was developed, and the consequent expansion of agriculture resulted in a great increase
in variety and number of birds in the Lahontan Valley.
Alfalfa is the chief crop, but there are truck farms and some

dairies. In addition to the crops, plantings of many kinds of trees and other cultivated plants have contributed to expansion of the avifauna.

Headquarters for the STILLWATER NATIONAL WILDLIFE MANAGEMENT AREA (204,633 acres) is in Fallon. Here the bird finder may receive permission and directions for visiting the most interesting parts of the Area, which lies north of town. The Area is mainly greasewood desert, sand dunes, and alkali flats, but there are some marsh areas, with cattails, bulrushes, bayonet rushes, and other aquatic plants bordered by salt grass. The 10,000 acres of marsh and open water include numerous lakes and ponds. The five Indian Lakes range from 40 to 100 acres, and Stillwater Point Reservoir is approximately 2,500 acres. Nesting of the waterbirds is mainly from late April through July. Common nesting ducks include Redheads (which have numbered as many as 1,000 pairs), Mallards, Gadwalls, Pintails, and Cinnamon Teal. Canada Geese and Coots also nest here, and an island in Stillwater Point Reservoir is a nesting site for Caspian Terns. Migrating waterbirds are present in March and April and from late August to December.

Birds in great variety and abundance may be watched from many points along the roads in the moist parts of the Lahontan Valley. An especially favorable locality is Stillwater—12 miles east from Fallon, on State Route 42, and then straight north on a dirt road to the edge of Carson Sink. The Soda Lakes, reached by driving west from Fallon on US Route 50 for 8 miles, then north on a dirt road 8 miles, are in the depressions of two old craters. They have no surface inlets or outlets. The larger lake covers about 400 acres and the smaller about 16 acres.

Resident birds easily found in the Lahontan Valley include the Eared Grebe, Western Grebe, Pied-billed Grebe, Great Blue Heron, American Egret, Black-crowned Night Heron, American Bittern, Green-winged Teal, Shoveler, Ruddy Duck, Red-tailed Hawk, Golden Eagle, Virginia Rail, Sora, Burrowing Owl, Horned Lark, American Magpie, Common Raven, Common Crow, Long-billed Marsh Wren, Red-wing, and Brewer's Blackbird. Summer residents that occur commonly are the White Pelican, Double-crested Cormorant, Snowy Egret, White-faced Ibis, Swainson's Hawk, Long-billed Curlew, Willet, Avocet, Blacknecked Stilt, Wilson's Phalarope, Forster's Tern, Black Tern, Yellow-billed Cuckoo, Bank Swallow, Cliff Swallow, and Yellow-headed Blackbird. Winter visitants worth searching for are the Snow Goose, Rough-legged Hawk, Ferruginous Hawk, and Short-eared Owl.

LAS VEGAS. At an altitude of 2,000 feet and surrounded by the desert of southern Nevada, Las Vegas (population about 26,000) has, since the construction of Hoover Dam, developed into a major center for vacations and recreation. There is a great variety in accommodations and supplies for tourists.

MUDDY VALLEY, a farming area with abundant birdlife, may be reached by following US Route 91 for about 50 miles northeast from Las Vegas. At a point 2.6 miles beyond Glendale, turn right on State Route 12 and drive to Lake Mead by way of Logandale and Overton. There are dense growths of tamarisk, mesquite, willow, and greasewood adjacent to the areas of water. The agricultural developments are interspersed with desert washes and river bottomlands. This variety of habitats attracts nearly all the species of waterfowl, shorebirds, and marshbirds that pass through the region, as well as other birds. Any time of year is suitable for bird finding in this section, but because of the heat in the summer the best times are probably spring, fall, and winter. The greatest numbers of birds occur in the latter part of April and the first week of May.

Unimproved campgrounds for tents and trailers are available on Lake Mead at Overton. The State Museum of Archeology shows the history of the Indians that have occupied this arid region.

In the VIRGIN RIVER VALLEY, 80 miles northeast of Las Vegas on US Route 91, between Bunkerville and Mesquite, desert conditions adjacent to a sluggish meandering river make a favorable riparian habitat, which is always attractive to a great variety of birds. Breeding species here include the Gambel's Quail, Barn Owl, Screech Owl, Great Horned Owl, Yellow-billed Cuckoo, Red-shafted Flicker, Western Kingbird, Black Phoebe, Vermilion Flycatcher, Bell's Vireo, Lucy's Warbler, Yellow Warbler, Yellow-throat, Yellow-breasted Chat, Bullock's Oriole, Brown-headed Cowbird, Blue Grosbeak, Abert's Towhee, and Song Sparrow.

PAHRANAGAT VALLEY, a long desert plain divided by a narrow line of green vegetation, is a good bird-finding area. Agriculture, centered at Alamo, has developed rapidly in the last 25 years, and warm springs provide open water the year round. US Route 93, 125 miles north of Las Vegas, passes through this Valley.

At Crystal Springs, 12 miles north of Alamo, there are ponds, green meadows, and trees that attract and hold a great variety of birds, both summer residents and transients. Shallow Pahranagat Lake, about 12 miles south of Alamo, is surrounded by a great desert region.

On the desert around Pahranagat Valley, below 4,500 feet, the most characteristic plant is creosote bush. Other common plants are two kinds of mesquite, catclaw, pea-bush, white bur sage, and bottle stopper. Landbirds that nest commonly in this area are the Swainson's Hawk, Ash-throated Flycatcher, Mockingbird, Bendire's Thrasher, Sage Thrasher, Loggerhead Shrike, Scott's Oriole, and Desert Sparrow. The Vermilion Flycatcher and Blue Grosbeak range as far north as the southern part of this Valley.

Above the creosote-bush desert most of the land in this vicinity is covered with sagebrush, hop sage, and rabbit-brush on the lower places, and juniper, pinyon pine, and mountain mahogany on the higher ground. Among the trees, typical nesting birds are the Cooper's Hawk, Long-eared Owl, Poor-will, Gray Flycatcher, Pinyon Jay, Bush-tit, Black-throated Gray Warbler, and Sage Sparrow.

The CHARLESTON MOUNTAINS west of Las Vegas lie within a division of the Nevada National Forest known as the Charleston Mountain Area. This precipitous range, about 50 miles long and 30 miles wide, extends in a northeast-southwest direction. There are no meadows or lakes and only a few small springs and short streams, but the higher slopes are well covered with trees. The highest point, Charleston Peak, is 11,910 feet, approximately 9,000 feet above the surrounding desert.

Summer headquarters of the Charleston Mountain Area

is at Kyle Canyon Ranger Station. To reach Kyle Canyon which is 35 miles northwest of Las Vegas, go north on US Route 95 for 13 miles, then west on State Route 39. Lee Canyon, north of Kyle Canyon, may be reached from the latter, or by driving north from Las Vegas on Route 95 for 28 miles and turning left on State Route 52. Conditions are much alike in the two areas.

The Charleston Mountains and the Sheep Mountains to the northeast are boreal islands isolated from other boreal areas by at least 100 miles of desert. Below the 6,000-foot line the prominent plants are creosote bush, mesquite, and Mohave yucca, where may be found the Gambel's Quail, Screech Owl, Lesser Nighthawk, Ladder-backed Wood-pecker, Western Kingbird, Traill's Flycatcher (nesting at Indian Springs, 42 miles north of Las Vegas on Route 95), Common Raven, Cactus Wren, Leconte's Thrasher, Crissal Thrasher (rare), Bullock's Oriole (Indian Springs), Brown-headed Cowbird, and Desert Sparrow. On the higher slopes, where sagebrush, juniper, pinyon pine, and mountain mahogany are prominent plants, the resident birds are the Scrub Jay, Plain Titmouse, Bush-tit, Sage Thrasher, Spotted Towhee, Sage Sparrow, and Brewer's Sparrow. Summer residents are the Common Nighthawk, Gray Flycatcher, Horned Lark, Blue-gray Gnatcatcher, Virginia's Warbler, Scott's Oriole, Black-headed Grosbeak, Lazuli Bunting, and Black-chinned Sparrow. From 8,000 to about 9,000 feet, where there are ponderosa pines and white firs, and still higher, where bristlecone and limber pines are domi-nant, may be found about 35 nesting species, including the Goshawk, Saw-whet Owl, Poor-will, White-throated Swift, Costa's Hummingbird, Broad-tailed Hummingbird, Wil-liamson's Sapsucker, Wright's Flycatcher, Pygmy Nuthatch, Brown Creeper, Dipper (one record), Townsend's Soli-taire, Ruby-crowned Kinglet, Cassin's Finch, Red Cross-bill, and juncos.

RENO. The largest city in Nevada, along the Truckee River only 14 miles from the western border of the state, has less than 35,000 inhabitants. Although there are abundant ac-commodations for tourists, the city is sometimes crowded in the vacation season. It is surrounded by easily accessible spots where a variety of birds occurs in good numbers, and field studies are profitable at all seasons. Places for bird finding range from boreal areas in the Sierra Nevada to barren, rocky desert and large lakes and rivers. The UNIVERSITY OF NEVADA, in the northern part of the city, is at University Avenue and Ninth Street. The Biology Museum has specimens of birds collected in Nevada.

Surrounding the city and extending to the east and south are the TRUCKEE MEADOWS, which still have trees and wet grasslands where hay is a prominent crop. On a drive through the area in summer, a long list of birds may be seen, including many species of waterfowl, marshbirds, shorebirds, hawks, owls, flycatchers, swallows, warblers, and sparrows.

PYRAMID LAKE, 30 miles long and 5 to 12 miles wide, is 33 miles northeast of Reno. High mountains rise abruptly on the east and west sides. Drive north from Reno on State Route 33, which leads to the southwest shore of the Lake. From here turn left and follow the shore to Sutcliffe, or turn right and follow the shore to Nixon, the headquarters of the Pyramid Lake Indian Agency. Since Pyramid Lake is a popular fishing spot, boats may be hired at various points.

The ANAHO ISLAND NATIONAL WILDLIFE REFUGE (248 acres) comprises a high rock island in the south-central part of Pyramid Lake, 9 miles north of the mouth of the Truckee River and one mile from the eastern shore. It may be seen from the edge of the Lake. This is the nesting site for most or all of the White Pelicans seen in summer anywhere in Nevada, for these birds wander far in their feeding expeditions. Other birds that have nested at Pyramid Lake in recent years and are likely to be present in summer are the Double-crested Cormorant, Great Blue Heron, American Merganser, and California Gull (on a pinnacle at the north end). The Western Grebe, Canada Goose, Mallard, Gadwall, and Killdeer are possible finds at the Lake. Landbirds common in the vicinity are the Turkey Vulture, Common Raven, Rock Wren, Desert Sparrow, and Brewer's Sparrow.

To see birds of the coniferous forest on the east side of the CARSON RANGE in the Sierra Nevada, Galena Creek

Public Camp Ground is an easily reached station. Take US Route 395 south from Reno for 9 miles and turn west on State Route 27. This road starts through sagebrush, and there is a good view of Mt. Rose on the right. At the Camp Ground there is riparian woodland along the stream, with pine forests in every direction, and some areas of snowbush and manzanita. Summer birds here are the Calliope Hummingbird, Hairy Woodpecker, (Red-breasted) Common Sapsucker, Steller's Jay, Mountain Chickadee, White-breasted Nuthatch, Brown Creeper, House Wren, Townsend's Solitaire, Warbling Vireo, Nashville Warbler, Yellow Warbler, and Chipping Sparrow.

Along the road above the Camp Ground, at the 7,500-foot mark, there are three Ski Clubs on the side of a ridge above Galena Creek. The meadow area here is bordered by an especially good stand of aspens and many willow clumps. It is a place to look for Western Wood Pewees, Warbling Vireos, Black-capped Warblers, White-crowned Sparrows, Lincoln's Sparrows, and Fox Sparrows. At about 8,000 feet, beside a small stream north of Slide Mountain, are red firs, lodgepole pines, and western white pines, along with a growth of shrubs. Here occur Hammond's Flycatchers, Audubon's Warblers, Western Tanagers, and Cassin's Finches.

By the second week of August there have been extensive post-nesting movements of birds in the mountains, and the fall migration is beginning. Some of the species present along Galena Creek then include the Red-tailed Hawk, Poor-will, Common Nighthawk, Robin, Solitary Vireo, Orange-crowned Warbler, Black-throated Gray Warbler, Townsend's Warbler, Hermit Warbler, Lazuli Bunting, Evening Grosbeak, Pine Siskin, Green-tailed Towhee, and Oregon Junco.

Route 27 continues upward to Tahoe Meadows at 8,500 feet on the Lake Tahoe side of the pass; from here a trail leads 5 miles to Mt. Rose, the only peak northeast of Lake Tahoe that extends above the timber line. Along the Mt. Rose trail, above timber line, in mid-July, there are Sparrow Hawks, Prairie Falcons, Clark's Nutcrackers, Rock Wrens, and Mountain Bluebirds.

The road continues south down to Incline (6,250 feet),

a U.S. Forest Service campground at the north end of
LAKE TAHOE. On the slopes north of the lakeshore there
is a remarkably good stand of solid coniferous forest, chiefly
white fir, Jeffrey pine, and sugar pine. In addition to a few
waterbirds attracted to the Lake, species commonly seen
during the summer in the vicinity of Incline include: Moun-
tain Quail, Williamson's Sapsucker, Hairy Woodpecker,
White-headed Woodpecker, Black-backed Woodpecker,
Western Wood Pewee, Steller's Jay, Mountain Chicka-
dee, Bush-tit, White-breasted Nuthatch, Red-breasted
Nuthatch, Robin, Hermit Thrush, Olive-backed Thrush,
Ruby-crowned Kinglet, Warbling Vireo, Nashville Warbler,
Audubon's Warbler, Macgillivray's Warbler, Western
Tanager, Cassin's Finch, Green-tailed Towhee, Oregon
Junco, Chipping Sparrow, and Fox Sparrow.

South of Reno are WASHOE and LITTLE WASHOE
LAKES, connected by marshy land. To reach these bodies
of water, drive 18 miles south of Reno on US Route 395
and turn left on a dirt road (State Route 3B) that runs
along the eastern sides of the Lakes. The water comes from
streams on the eastern slopes of the Carson Range, and
the amount varies greatly from year to year. Mallards, Gadwalls, Cinnamon Teal, Redheads, Ruddy Ducks, and Coots
are common nesters. When the water is low, shorebirds
congregate in great numbers; they include Avocets, Black-
necked Stilts, and Wilson's and Northern Phalaropes. Regularly present in summer are White Pelicans, White-faced
Ibises, and Canada Geese. Back from the Lakes is a stand
of sagebrush with birds characteristic of this habitat.

Contributing authorities: W. D. Billings, Baine H. Cater, Howard
L. Cogswell, Clarence Cottam, Fred G. Evenden, Jr., Thomas C.
Horn, David B. Marshall, Warren M. Pulich.

New Mexico

BY J. STOKLEY LIGON

ROAD-RUNNER

Writing on the historic expedition in search of the 'Seven
Cities of Cibola' over four hundred years ago, a member
of the Coronado Expedition of 1540 referred to 'quail,'
'cranes,' and 'wild geese' on the Rio Grande, in the vicinity
of where Albuquerque is now located. Blackbirds were
listed as 'starlings' and Wild Turkeys as 'cocks with great
hanging chins,' the latter attracting more attention because
of their fine edible qualities. It was almost 300 years after
these first records of birds in New Mexico that the early
naturalists, most of whom were attached to U.S. Army expeditions, laid the ground work for the later publications
on the birds of the state.

369

New Mexico, the fourth largest state, is a land of contrasts and color, a land with great variations in altitude, rainfall, and temperature, which create, in turn, a wide range of habitats for birds. The record of species now stands at approximately 300, of which about 225 nest within the state.

The topography of New Mexico is dominated by two north-to-south drainage systems, the Rio Grande and the Pecos, and by numerous mountain ranges which roughly parallel the Rio Grande on both sides. The Rio Grande almost bisects the state, being a little west of center, while the Pecos rises just east of Santa Fe in the Sangre de Cristo Mountains, crosses into Texas south of Carlsbad, and later joins the Rio Grande.

For most of its length the Rio Grande is bordered by alluvial bottomlands, many of which are now irrigated and used extensively for farming, but here and there occurs a native vegetation consisting of cottonwood, willow, and such low growth as saltbush, acacia, mesquite, and screw bean. Mesquite, acacia, creosote bush, and various yuccas and cacti grow on the drier, lower slopes; juniper and pinyon pine on the higher slopes and ridges. The great Bosque del Apache National Wildlife Refuge (see under Socorro) is the outstanding spot for bird finding in the Rio Grande Valley.

Like the Rio Grande Valley, the upper Pecos River Valley has extensive bottomlands that are used for agriculture, but it is cooler and less arid, although the kinds of plants are much the same. In the lower two thirds of the more than 400 miles of the Pecos Valley a most interesting tree succession has occurred. During the past 25 years tamarisk has encroached upon the flood and reservoir-delta lands and adjacent slopes, forming, in places, all but impenetrable jungles. While the tamarisk does not provide food for birds, mature tamarisk now provides nesting environment, particularly in the McMillan and Avalon delta areas (see under Artesia), which contrasts sharply with the former scant, dwarf, native shrubs dominated by mesquite. Mourning Doves, Yellow-billed Cuckoos, Mockingbirds, Bullock's Orioles, and Blue Grosbeaks nest here in increasing numbers. The adjacent irrigated agricultural land now provides an abundance of food for many species. In addition, irrigation projects in the Pecos Valley have created favorable summer habitats for such birds as the American Egret, Snowy Egret, Green Heron, Black-crowned Night Heron, Virginia Rail, and some ducks—particularly on the Lake McMillan delta. What has occurred in the Pecos Valley is duplicated to some extent on the flood- and wastelands bordering the Rio Grande.

The following list includes many of the birds known to breed regularly in the Rio Grande Valley and, in most cases, in the Pecos Valley.

Pied-billed Grebe
Double-crested Cormorant
Great Blue Heron
American Egret
Snowy Egret
Green Heron
Black-crowned Night Heron
American Bittern
Least Bittern
Mallard
New Mexican Duck
Gadwall
Cinnamon Teal
Ruddy Duck
Gambel's Quail
Ring-necked Pheasant
Virginia Rail
Sora
Florida Gallinule
Coot
Killdeer
Avocet
Black-necked Stilt
Mourning Dove
Yellow-billed Cuckoo
Road-runner
Barn Owl
Screech Owl
Great Horned Owl
Black-chinned Hummingbird
Red-shafted Flicker
Hairy Woodpecker
Ladder-backed Woodpecker

Western Kingbird
Ash-throated Flycatcher
Say's Phoebe
Western Wood Pewee
Horned Lark
Barn Swallow
Verdin (southern parts)
Cactus Wren (southern parts)
Rock Wren
Mockingbird
Crissal Thrasher (southern parts)
Robin
Plumbeous Gnatcatcher (southern parts)
Loggerhead Shrike
Lucy's Warbler (southern parts)
Yellow Warbler
Yellow-throat
Yellow-breasted Chat
Western Meadowlark
Red-wing
Scott's Oriole
Bullock's Oriole
Boat-tailed Grackle
Brown-headed Cowbird
Summer Tanager
Blue Grosbeak
House Finch
Lesser Goldfinch
Spotted Towhee
Desert Sparrow

Besides the Rio Grande and Pecos River, New Mexico is also drained by two other river systems. Waters from the extreme northeastern corner of the state flow into the Cimarron River, while those from the plains-sandhill country lying southward between the Sangre de Cristo Mountains and the Texas line reach the Canadian River. Both rivers have a west-to-east course and are tributaries of the Arkansas River of the Mississippi River system. In their valleys (e.g. the Cimarron River Valley; see under Clayton) may be found birds of eastern affinities not occurring regularly elsewhere in the state. West of the Continental Divide, which passes along the crests of the mountains paralleling the west side of the Rio Grande, are terminal feeders of the San Juan, Puerco, Zuni, Carrizo, San Francisco, and Gila (*hee'-la*) Rivers of the Colorado River system. The Gila River Valley in the southwest is the most favored from the bird finder's point of view because it brings into the state a number of bird species typical of the low, hot country of Arizona. The Valley's floor and lower slopes, with a low native growth of mesquite, creosote bush, acacia, mimosa, saltbush, yucca, and cactus, together with trees (e.g. cottonwood and willow) along watercourses, have nesting habitats for such birds as the Mexican Black Hawk, Elf Owl, Gila Woodpecker, Lucy's Warbler, Hooded Oriole, and Abert's Towhee. On the upper slopes and in shaded canyons, common trees are the live oak, walnut, and hackberry. Here the Arizona Jay and Bridled Titmouse are characteristic birds.

New Mexico east of the Sangre de Cristo Range and the Pecos River Valley is part of the Great Plains, consisting largely of level to rolling terrain, interspersed with sandhills and interrupted by breaks along streams. With an average elevation of about 4,000 feet and an average rainfall of 12 to 16 inches, the country is largely treeless, except where ranchers have created small 'oases' about homes and stock-watering wells. The dominant plant life consists of short grasses, such as grama and buffalo, and stretches of mesquite, catclaw, and buckthorn. On the sandhills the shin oak and sagebrush comprise the perennial cover, much favored by Lesser Prairie Chickens (see under Portales). The acorns of the oak constitute an important

part of the fall and winter diet of these birds. Throughout
the plains are many sinks and deep basins which, during
rainy periods, provide resting and feeding places for Avocets and Black-necked Stilts, but the birds breed around
them only infrequently because suitable nesting cover has
been destroyed by cattle grazing. In the list below are a
few of the species breeding regularly in the plains area east
of the Pecos:

Turkey Vulture	Eastern Kingbird (northern
Swainson's Hawk	part)
Harris' Hawk (southern part)	Western Kingbird
Lesser Prairie Chicken	Scissor-tailed Flycatcher
Scaled Quail	Say's Phoebe
Mountain Plover	Horned Lark
Killdeer	White-necked Raven
Long-billed Curlew (northern	Western Meadowlark
part)	Lark Sparrow
Road-runner	Cassin's Sparrow
Burrowing Owl	Desert Sparrow
Common Nighthawk	
Lesser Nighthawk (southern	
part)	

The extensive mountainous areas in the state, ranging
from 5,000 to over 13,000 feet in elevation, are a source of
multiple interest to the bird finder. Nearly all of them are
in National Forests, which aggregate 8,649,000 acres, or
more than one third of the state.

The loftiest and most extensive mountains in New Mexico
are those of the Sangre de Cristo Range, a southern extension of the Rocky Mountain chain of the same name in
Colorado. The Range lies east of the Rio Grande in the
northern part of the state. Against the awe-inspiring background of these mountains lie the ancient cities of Santa
Fe and Taos, good starting points for trips to observe the
birdlife of the Range in the midst of unsurpassed scenery
from wooded foothills to above the timber line. The Range
is dominated by a north-to-south line of very high ridges
and peaks. Several of the peaks exceed 13,000 feet elevation; one, Wheeler Peak (13,151 feet), is the highest point
in the state. Throughout the length of the Range are high
valleys, long, steep, and frequently rocky slopes, numerous

lakes and ponds, and rushing streams. The forests are distinctly belted. Juniper and pinyon pine, several kinds of yuccas and cacti, sagebrush, and various other shrubs are the characteristic growth on the lower slopes and foothills up to about 7,000 feet, or slightly higher on the warmer slopes. Cottonwoods, ashes, willows, and other deciduous trees, as well as shrubs, abound on canyon bottoms. Ponderosa pine in open stands, mixed with Douglas fir, and cottonwoods along the streams prevail from 7,000 to 8,500 feet on the cooler northeast slopes, 7,500 to 9,700 on the southwest slopes. Here and there are slopes that support groves of Gambel's oak. A spruce-fir association consisting mainly of Engelmann spruce and white fir, with quaking aspens near streams and on slopes that have been burned, extends from 8,500 feet to 11,000 feet (northeast slopes), or 9,700 to 12,000 feet (southwest slopes). For a thousand feet above this association extends a subalpine belt comprising dwarfed Engelmann spruce, limber pine, alpine fir, and bristlecone pine. The upper reaches of this belt are fringed by 'wind timber,' marking the timber line. A typical alpine region, with meadows of brilliant wildflowers and thickets of willows, caps the highest peaks.

Listed below are some of the bird species that may be found breeding regularly at different elevations in the Sangre de Cristo Range. Species marked with an asterisk may also be found at still higher elevations.

BELOW 7,000 FEET ELEVATION:

Sparrow Hawk
*Spotted Sandpiper
Poor-will
*Broad-tailed Hummingbird
*Red-shafted Flicker
Lewis' Woodpecker
Say's Phoebe
*Western Wood Pewee
Scrub Jay
Pinyon Jay
Plain Titmouse

Bush-tit
*Rock Wren
Blue-gray Gnatcatcher
Black-headed Grosbeak
Lazuli Bunting
*Spotted Towhee
Brown Towhee
Sage Sparrow
*Chipping Sparrow
Brewer's Sparrow

FROM 7,000 TO 9,700 FEET:

Sharp-shinned Hawk
Cooper's Hawk

Blue Grouse
Wild Turkey

Great Horned Owl
Band-tailed Pigeon
White-throated Swift
(Red-naped) Common Sap-
  sucker
*Hairy Woodpecker
Wright's Flycatcher
Western Flycatcher
*Violet-green Swallow
*Purple Martin
Steller's Jay
American Magpie
*Common Raven
Black-capped Chickadee
*Mountain Chickadee
White-breasted Nuthatch
Pygmy Nuthatch

Dipper
House Wren
*Robin
*Mountain Bluebird
Solitary Vireo
Warbling Vireo
*Orange-crowned Warbler
Virginia's Warbler
Audubon's Warbler
Grace's Warbler
*Macgillivray's Warbler
Western Tanager
*Pine Siskin
Vesper Sparrow
(Red-backed) Gray-headed
  Junco
Song Sparrow

FROM 8,500 TO 12,000 FEET:

Goshawk
Golden Eagle
Spotted Owl
Williamson's Sapsucker
Three-toed Woodpecker
Olive-sided Flycatcher
Red-breasted Nuthatch
Brown Creeper
Hermit Thrush

Townsend's Solitaire
Golden-crowned Kinglet
Ruby-crowned Kinglet
Evening Grosbeak
Cassin's Finch
Pine Grosbeak
Red Crossbill
Lincoln's Sparrow

ABOVE 12,000 FEET:

White-tailed Ptarmigan
American Pipit
Brown-capped Rosy Finch

White-crowned Sparrow (usually at timber line)

Just west of the Rio Grande, in the northern part of the state, rise the San Juan Mountains, another southern extension of the Rocky Mountain chain, ranging from 10,000 to 11,000 feet in elevation, with a few peaks reaching 11,-500 feet. Above the scrub forests of the lower slopes are open stands of ponderosa pine, succeeded on the highest slopes by Engelmann spruce and white fir. True timber-line and alpine regions are absent. These mountains, with their gentle slopes, are not spectacular, but good roads over their higher parts, numerous campgrounds, cool forests, and picturesque canyons make them attractive spots for bird finding. Species of birds to be found are practically the same as those at similar elevations in the Sangre de Cristo Mountains. Species characteristic of alpine and subalpine regions are, of course, lacking.

South of the Sangre de Cristo Mountains, between the Rio Grande and Pecos Valleys, lies a strip of rough country 300 miles long containing mountains, plateaus, and bolsons (undrained basins). The Manzano and Sandia Mountains (see under Albuquerque), adjacent to the Rio Grande in the northern part, attain altitudes of about 10,000 to 11,000 feet. Coniferous trees cover their higher slopes (spruce-fir down to 8,000 feet; ponderosa pine down to 6,500 feet), while a desert-like vegetation prevails on their lower slopes, as on the arid surroundings from which they rise. The Sierra Oscuro, San Andres Mountains, and Organ Mountains, adjacent to the Rio Grande in the southern part, form an almost unbroken chain of peaks (reaching about 9,000 feet elevation) to the Texas line north of El Paso. Desert or semidesert conditions exist on these mountains from foothills to summits. (For an interesting bird-finding spot in the San Andres Mountains, see under Las Cruces.) To the east of this chain—across the Tularosa Basin, a 125-mile-long desert plain as low as 4,000 feet, with vast alkali flats and stretches of sand dunes—rise the Sierra Blanca, Sacramento, and Guadalupe Ranges to heights between 9,000 and 12,003 feet (Sierra Blanca Peak). Their slopes are rugged, except those on the east, which slant down gradually to the floor of the Pecos Valley. The lower slopes and ridges are either barren or covered with juniper, pinyon pine, Gambel's Oak, and scrub. The upper slopes are well timbered—from 6,000 to 9,500 feet, with ponderosa pine and some Douglas fir, white pine, maple, and oak; from 9,500 feet to the summits, by Engelmann spruce, white fir, and aspen. On Sierra Blanca Peak the trees become stunted and cease to grow some distance below the summit, but the summit is not a true alpine region, being merely bald and grassy. The Guadalupe Mountains extend for some distance into Texas. Three places for bird finding that represent the possibilities are pointed out under Artesia and Carlsbad in this chapter and under El Paso in the Texas chapter.

In western New Mexico, west of the Rio Grande and the San Juan Mountains, are many mountain ranges of varying extent and height. In the northwestern part of the state are several low ranges, including the Zuni and Chuska or Lukachukai Mountains (see under Gallup), which are well forested at their higher elevations and attract a surprising variety of birds. Of special interest to the bird finder, because of their high altitude and extensive forest cover, are the Mogollons (see under Silver City) in the southwest near the Arizona line. The greater part of the range comprises a rough, dissected plateau, 7,000 to 8,000 feet in elevation, with canyons and high ridges. Several peaks, volcanic in origin, reach almost to 11,000 feet. The top of the plateau and adjacent slopes are beautifully forested with open stands of ponderosa pine, mixed sparingly with Douglas fir and Mexican white pine; cottonwood, willow, and alder fringe the streams, and in places there are stands of oak. Most of the higher peaks and ridges, from 8,500 and 9,500 feet to the summits (there is no timber line), support a dense stand of Engelmann spruce and white fir, with quaking aspen in the ravines near streams. The lower and drier slopes of the Mogollons have a characteristic chaparral containing mountain mahogany, scrub oak, manzanita, and other low, thick growth. Some of the breeding birds to be expected in the Mogollons at varying levels, depending on habitat requirements, are listed below. Species marked with an asterisk are confined largely to the higher slopes.

*Golden Eagle	*Hairy Woodpecker
*Blue Grouse	*Three-toed Woodpecker
Mearns' Quail	Western Flycatcher
Wild Turkey	Western Wood Pewee
*Band-tailed Pigeon	*Violet-green Swallow
Screech Owl	*Purple Martin
*Flammulated Owl	Steller's Jay
*Pygmy Owl	Scrub Jay (chaparral)
*Spotted Owl	Arizona Jay
Whip-poor-will	*Mountain Chickadee
Broad-tailed Hummingbird	Bridled Titmouse
*Red-shafted Flicker	Bush-tit
Acorn Woodpecker	*White-breasted Nuthatch
Lewis' Woodpecker	Pygmy Nuthatch

°Brown Creeper
°Dipper
°House Wren
 Bewick's Wren
 Canyon Wren
 Rock Wren
°Robin
°Hermit Thrush
°Western Bluebird
 Blue-gray Gnatcatcher
°Ruby-crowned Kinglet
 Gray Vireo (chaparral)
°Solitary Vireo
°Virginia's Warbler
°Audubon's Warbler

 Black-throated Gray Warbler
°Grace's Warbler
 Red-faced Warbler
 Painted Redstart
°Western Tanager
°Hepatic Tanager
°Black-headed Grosbeak
°Red Crossbill
 Spotted Towhee (chaparral)
 Brown Towhee
 Rufous-crowned Sparrow
°(Red-backed) Gray-headed
 Junco
°Chipping Sparrow

All of northwestern New Mexico, west of the San Juan Mountains, is typical Navajo country, continuous with the area of the same name in northeastern Arizona (see the introduction to the Arizona chapter). Southwestern New Mexico, between the mountain ranges, has wide areas of creosote-bush desert and stretches of grassland—all with scattered buttes and isolated mountains. The few stream beds, usually with water only after heavy rains, are sometimes thinly lined with cottonwoods, willows, and thickets of mesquite and other shrubs. Along stream beds in canyons and in other moist places, vegetation grows in greater profusion with the addition of such trees as live oaks, hackberries, walnuts, and sycamores. On the dry lower slopes of the mountains, manzanita, mountain mahogany, scrub oak, and sumac sometimes abound, together forming a chaparral. At slightly higher elevations, often on ridges, is a 'pygmy' forest of juniper and pinyon pine. In extreme southwestern New Mexico, desert and grassland merge in many places with the vegetation of streamsides and canyons and with the chaparral and pygmy forests of the lower slopes of the Animas and Peloncillo Mountains that extend south through the New Mexico Panhandle to the Sierra Madre of Mexico. Bird finding in this extreme southwestern section of the state (see under Lordsburg) is invariably worth while because many Mexican and Arizona species near the northern or eastern limits of their ranges may be found here. Some of the breeding birds that may be expected are given below. Species marked with one asterisk should be looked for mainly on the lower wooded slopes of mountains, those with two asterisks along wooded stream-beds.

Red-tailed Hawk
Swainson's Hawk
*Zone-tailed Hawk
**Mexican Black Hawk
Sparrow Hawk
Scaled Quail
Gambel's Quail
*Mearns' Quail
*Wild Turkey
*Band-tailed Pigeon
Mourning Dove
**White-winged Dove
Road-runner
Screech Owl
Great Horned Owl
Elf Owl
Poor-will
Lesser Nighthawk
**Black-chinned Humming-
    bird
*Blue-throated Humming-
    bird
*Broad-billed Hummingbird
Gila Woodpecker
Ladder-backed Wood-
    pecker
*Arizona Woodpecker
Western Kingbird
**Cassin's Kingbird
Ash-throated Flycatcher
*Olivaceous Flycatcher
**Black Phoebe
*Western Wood Pewee
**Vermilion Flycatcher

Horned Lark
*Scrub Jay
*Arizona Jay (in oaks)
White-necked Raven
*Bridled Titmouse (in oaks)
Verdin
*Bush-tit
Cactus Wren
Mockingbird
Bendire's Thrasher
Curve-billed Thrasher
Crissal Thrasher
Loggerhead Shrike
*Blue-gray Gnatcatcher
Phainopepla
*Hutton's Vireo
**Yellow Warbler
*Black-throated Gray War-
    bler
*Painted Redstart
(Rio Grande) Eastern
    Meadowlark
**Hooded Oriole
Scott's Oriole
**Bullock's Oriole
**Cardinal
**Pyrrhuloxia
**Blue Grosbeak
*Spotted Towhee
Brown Towhee
Lark Sparrow
*Rufous-crowned Sparrow
Desert Sparrow
*Black-chinned Sparrow

The higher slopes of the Animas and Peloncillo Mountains (maximum elevations in New Mexico about 8,500 and 6,500 feet, respectively) and the cool ravines near their summits support some aspen, Douglas fir, ponderosa pine, Chihuahua pine, and several kinds of oaks—an environment attractive to quite a few bird species found also in the higher montane forests of the Sierra Madre in Mexico, the Mogollon Mountains to the north (see above), and the mountains in southeastern Arizona (see the introduction to the Arizona chapter). Among the breeding birds to be expected are such species as the Band-tailed Pigeon, Flammulated Owl, Whip-poor-will, Broad-tailed Hummingbird, Acorn Woodpecker, Western Flycatcher, Coues' Flycatcher, Steller's Jay, Mexican and Mountain Chickadees, (Mexican) Brown Creeper, Western Bluebird, Olive Warbler, Grace's Warbler, Red-faced Warbler, Western and Hepatic Tanagers, Gray-headed Junco, and Mexican Junco.

Draining from north to south, the Rio Grande and Pecos Rivers constitute the most heavily utilized migratory bird flyways of the entire southwest. This is especially true for Sandhill Cranes, many ducks, and shorebirds. Even though extensive irrigation projects have resulted in the draining of the valley sloughs, marshes, and, at times, the rivers themselves, reservoir impoundments and delta-marsh creations have to some extent compensated for the loss. The Pecos Valley is noted for great flights of Sandhill Cranes, ducks (particularly Mallards, Baldpates, and Pintails), and Long-billed Curlews. Elsewhere in the state, because of the mountainous terrain, migration is for the most part vertical, birds of the higher altitudes descending into the valleys and foothills for the winter.

Many of the northern birds often remain most of the winter in the southern Rio Grande and Pecos River Valleys. At Bitter Lake National Wildlife Refuge (see under Roswell) as many as 12,000 Sandhill Cranes and 90,000 ducks have been found in midwinter. In the Rio Grande Valley southward from Albuquerque (see under Socorro, Truth or Consequences, and Las Cruces), where the mild climate and luxuriant vegetative cover is conducive to wintering, a large resident population is augmented in winter by birds from the north—Lewis' Woodpeckers, Common Crows, Western Bluebirds, Mountain Bluebirds, American Pipits, Audubon's Warbler, Yellow-headed Blackbirds, Brewer's Blackbirds, Lark Buntings, various juncos, White-crowned Sparrows, Lincoln's Sparrows, and Song Sparrows, together with many waterbirds and waterfowl. These immense numbers of birds, easily observed from the roads that border irrigated farms and parallel irrigation and drainage canals, never fail to impress the visiting bird finder.

ALBUQUERQUE. There is a great variety of birds within easy reach of Albuquerque, the largest city in New Mexico, situated on the Rio Grande near the central part of the state. In RIO GRANDE PARK (80 acres; entrance at the end of South 14th Street), which borders the Rio Grande, are two duck ponds that are easy places to see the rare New Mexican Duck and the various hybrids between it and the Mallard. Both the New Mexican Duck and the Mallard can usually be counted on in late fall, winter (unless exceptionally severe), and early spring.

At the base of the SANDIA MOUNTAINS lies the JUAN TABO RECREATIONAL AREA in the Sandia State Game Refuge. The Area, which is about 15 miles from Albuquerque, is reached by driving several miles out of town on North Second Street to a gravel side road marked 'Nazareth Sanatorium.' Turn right onto this road and continue, past the Sanatorium, to the Recreational Area, 9 miles from the turn.

The Area (elevation about 6,000 feet), in pinyon pine, juniper, and oak country, is an excellent place for birds characteristic of lower mountain reaches. Scrub Jays are very abundant. Flocks of Pinyon Jays sometimes come through. Canyon Wrens and Rock Wrens are common. Birds of higher elevations come down to the Area in the winter, when this is an excellent place to see Clark's Nutcrackers, Mountain Chickadees, Robins, Mountain Bluebirds, Townsend's Solitaires, and Gray-headed Juncos.

A steep trail leads along the foot of the Sandia Mountains and up to Sandia Crest Observation Point at the summit (elevation 10,678 feet), from which there is a fine view of the surrounding country. The less adventuresome may drive to the Point, 34 miles from Albuquerque, by going east from the city on US Route 66, through Tijeras Canyon, turning left on State Route 10, and then left again on the Sandia Rim Road (State Route 44). This drive, open only from May to November, passes through forests of ponderosa pine and beautiful groves of aspen. There are picnic areas and campgrounds along the way. Stops in the areas of ponderosa pine may reveal Wild Turkeys, Steller's Jays, and Pygmy Nuthatches. Red-breasted Nuthatches and Gray-headed Juncos breed in the conifers near the summit. Because of winter sports in the Sandia Mountains, more roads are being kept open each year—thus increasing the opportunities for winter bird finding.

The abundance of cottonwoods, willows, and undercover along the many canals and drainage ditches in the RIO GRANDE VALLEY, both above and below Albuquerque, provide summer habitat for a great variety of birds, the most common of which include the Mourning Dove, Yellow-billed Cuckoo, Red-shafted Flicker, Western King-bird, Western Wood Pewee, Mockingbird, Robin, Yellow Warbler, Yellow-breasted Chat, Bullock's Oriole, Summer Tanager, Blue Grosbeak, Lesser Goldfinch, Spotted Tow-hee, and Chipping Sparrow.

ARTESIA. The lower part of the PECOS RIVER VAL-LEY, between Artesia and the Texas border, is becoming increasingly interesting to the bird finder. Two reservoirs, Lake McMillan (5,120 acres) and Lake Avalon (1,600 acres), and artesian wells, with consequent agricultural activities, have been responsible for this change. For many years the Valley above Lake McMillan accumulated silt, forming barrier dykes, which resulted in marshes and small lakes with a profusion of willows and cattails, sedges, and other water plants. During the past 25 years, the delta-spread of approximately 13,000 acres, exclusive of water and marsh, has become a jungle of tamarisk. Great Blue Herons, American Egrets, Snowy Egrets, Green Herons, Black-crowned Night Herons, rails, and some ducks now appear in this area in the summer. Mockingbirds, Bullock's Orioles, Blue Grosbeaks, and great numbers of Mourning Doves find the larger tamarisks good nesting places.

This is not an easy country to get around in. While the open water and marshes are fairly accessible, roads are few, and the tamarisk is almost impenetrable. Several farm-to-market roads, branching east from US Route 285 south of Artesia, provide access to the lakes and marshes. About 19 miles south of Artesia, a road to the left goes 2 miles to the tiny town of Lakewood, on the western shore of Lake Mc-Millan. From Lakewood, the Lake proper can easily be reached, and a long stone and earthen dam with an auto road provides excellent opportunities for observing White Pelicans (during migration), American Egrets, Snowy Egrets, and many ducks.

About the farms in the Pecos River Valley, Cliff Swallows concentrate in such vast numbers in July that the weight of the birds, perching on power lines, literally sways the lines between the poles. Great flocks of Red-wings appear in the fall in the rushes around the marshes and ponds.

A very pleasant spring or summer trip from Artesia (elevation 3,380 feet), one that offers a decided contrast to the Valley, is made by taking State Route 83 across the SACRAMENTO MOUNTAINS and turning south on US Route 54 to tree-adorned Alamogordo, a total distance of 119 miles.

The road passes from semidesert with short grass, cactus, and soapweed into the Lincoln National Forest, where pinyon pine and juniper first appear, and upward into impressive forests of pine, fir, spruce, and aspen. Among the highlights of this scenic drive are the several colonies of Cliff Swallows in the limestone cliffs over the road between Elk and Mayhill. Other breeding birds of interest that may be seen or heard in the higher areas are Mearns' Quail, Wild Turkey, Pygmy Owl, Steller's Jay, Common Raven, (Red-backed) Gray-headed Junco, and, possibly, a Zone-tailed Hawk or Spotted Owl. Cloudcroft (elevation 8,640 feet), a lumber and recreation center on the summit, has accommodations for tourists.

The road winds down the west side of the Mountains, by cozy canyon homes, flower gardens, and apple orchards, and through a tunnel blasted in the canyon wall. The bird finder should stop and visit some of the gardens near Mountain Park (7 miles beyond Cloudcroft), where the red-hot poker plant grows in profusion; in August its brilliant flowers attract hundreds of migrating hummingbirds—the Black-chinned, Broad-tailed, Rufous, and Calliope. The visitor will be impressed by the humming music of their wings and the general atmosphere of belligerency as the more aggressive individuals attempt to defend, by vicious aerial combat, the small segments of garden they have chosen as their own. Other birds to be looked for on the downward trip are Gambel's Quail, Scrub Jays, Canyon Wrens, Rock Wrens, Spotted Towhees, and Brown Towhees.

CARLSBAD. The bird finder in southeastern New Mexico must not miss CARLSBAD CAVERNS NATIONAL PARK, containing the largest, if not the most awesome, limestone caverns in the world. The one natural entrance leads far underground to a mile-long series of giant 'rooms' marvelously festooned with calcite formations. Out of this entrance each evening, beginning at sunset, from about the first of May until the middle of October, stream enormous numbers of bats. At least five kinds are represented, but the great majority are of one species, the Mexican free-tailed. In midsummer the nightly exit comprises hundreds of thousands of individuals (three million, according to one estimate) and is a thoroughly amazing spectacle. During the winter the bats hibernate in remote parts of the Caverns, far from the entrance.

The above-ground area of the Park embraces 45,526 acres of desert country, but it is not without its attractions. In May and June the blooming of the cacti, Spanish bayonet, desert willow, and mountain laurel turn the mesas, limestone hills, and canyons into a gorgeous flower garden. Birdlife, while not particularly varied, merits attention. Canyon and Rock Wrens frequent Walnut Canyon and the ledges forming the entrance to the Caverns. Scaled Quail, Verdins, Scott's Orioles, Pyrrhuloxias, House Finches, Brown Towhees, and Rufous-crowned Sparrows find suitable nesting habitats not far from the entrance.

To reach the Caverns, drive southwest from Carlsbad on US Route 62 for 20 miles, and turn right at White City on State Route 7, which goes up through Walnut Canyon and thence south on a high ridge to the Caverns entrance. Overnight accommodations are available at Carlsbad and White City.

CHAMA. The ancient town of Chama (elevation 7,860 feet), only a few miles south of the Colorado line, is a former lumber center that is fast becoming a recreational and summer resort. One of the few places in extreme northern New Mexico with good tourist accommodations, it is a natural headquarters for the bird finder. The canyons and mountains, with forests of pine, spruce, fir, oak, aspen, cottonwood, and boxelder, the Rio Chama with its clear, rushing tributaries, and the mountain lakes and meadows, coupled with a superb summer climate, provide a fine variety of birds in a truly beautiful setting.

Birds nesting along the Rio Chama, on which the town is located, and in the meadows southward on US Route 84, are the Spotted Sandpiper, Catbird, Yellow Warbler, Yellow-breasted Chat, Yellow-headed Blackbird, Red-wing, Brewer's Blackbird, and Lazuli Bunting. North of Chama, as one goes higher into the SAN JUAN MOUNTAINS on State Route 19 toward famous Cumbres Pass (elevation 10,007 feet), one should look for such birds as the (Red-naped) Common Sapsucker, Williamson's Sapsucker, Hairy Woodpecker, Downy Woodpecker, Violet-green Swallow, Dipper, House Wren, Olive-backed Thrush, Mountain Bluebird, Townsend's Solitaire, Warbling Vireo, Audubon's Warbler, Western Tanager, Pine Siskin, Gray-headed Junco, Lincoln's Sparrow, and Song Sparrow. About the alpine rims may be seen Canada Jays, Common Ravens, and Clark's Nutcrackers. In mid-July the many brilliant flowers that adorn canyon slopes and meadows become animated with great numbers of Broad-tailed, Rufous, and Calliope Hummingbirds. These may be readily viewed from the highway near Cumbres Pass wherever flowers abound.

Twelve miles south of Chama on US Route 84 is the Mexican village of Park View and, easily accessible, the PARK VIEW STATE FISH HATCHERY. Here the several ponds and ample meadows with luxuriant vegetation are bordered by willows and cottonwoods, and have such nesting birds as Mallards, Green-winged Teal, Blue-winged Teal, Barn Swallows, Catbirds, Yellow-throats, Yellow-headed Blackbirds, Red-wings, Brewer's Blackbirds, Savannah Sparrows, and Song Sparrows. This is one of the few places in the state where the Bobolink has been found nesting.

The outstanding place for nesting waterbirds, when there

has been sufficient rain and snow, is LAKE BURFORD, which lies high in the SAN PEDRO MOUNTAINS, just east of the Continental Divide, on the Jicarilla Indian Reservation. This body of water (elevation 7,700 feet), with its several arms and bays, has about 14 miles of shoreline, and in places supports a rich growth of bulrushes and other vegetation that provides a marsh habitat suitable for many water-loving birds. Here nest Redheads and Canvas-backs as well as Mallards, Gadwalls, Green-winged Teal, Blue-winged Teal, Cinnamon Teal, and Ruddy Ducks. Eared Grebes, Pied-billed Grebes, and Coots are common. Also, one may expect to see Black-crowned Night Herons, Virginia Rails, Soras, Spotted Sandpipers, Long-billed Marsh Wrens, Yellow-headed Blackbirds, and Brewer's Blackbirds. The open ridges to the north and west of the Lake, covered with purple sagebrush, are places where Sage Thrashers, Vesper Sparrows, Sage Sparrows, and Brewer's Sparrows may be found. To the east and south are rugged mountains and canyons, heavily forested with ponderosa pine and Douglas fir—the habitat of Wild Turkeys, Lewis' Woodpeckers, Violet-green Swallows, Purple Martins, American Magpies, and Common Ravens. The Prairie Falcon, Duck Hawk, and White-throated Swift occupy the massive canyon walls just southeast and south of the Lake.

Lake Burford is reached by going south from Chama on Route 84 to Park View, thence west on State Route 95. Since the Lake is under the joint administration of the U.S. Indian Service and the Fish and Wildlife Service, anyone wishing to camp or do any extensive bird work should obtain permission from the Indian Service of the U.S. Department of Interior, Albuquerque, New Mexico. Even the bird finder who is just driving through should check on the road conditions before attempting the trip.

Although early June is the best time for a visit, the months of September and October, when the fall migration is at its height, are very pleasant in these mountains.

CLAYTON. From 20 to 40 miles north and west of this plains town in northeastern New Mexico are vast stretches of open country, principally grassland, interrupted by breaks along streams and by mesas and mountains. Most of

the grassland not too greatly disturbed by grazing or agricultural activities is worth exploring in late May and June
for nesting Long-billed Curlews. On the plains of the mesa
country around Mt. Dora and Grenville, northwest of Clayton on US Route 64, a few breeding Mountain Plovers may
be expected at the same time of year.

The deciduous trees and thickets in the CIMARRON
RIVER VALLEY, between Folsom and the Oklahoma line,
comprise a habitat of great ornithological interest. Owing
probably to the west-east course of the River, several east-
ern bird species—for example, the Catbird and Brown
Thrasher—have extended their breeding ranges westward
into New Mexico, following the Valley. Other species nest-
ing regularly in the same habitat include the Sparrow
Hawk, Mourning Dove, Red-shafted Flicker, Red-headed
Woodpecker, Eastern Kingbird, Western Kingbird, Cassin's
Kingbird, Mockingbird, Warbling Vireo, Bullock's Oriole,
Blue Grosbeak, House Finch, and Lesser Goldfinch.

To reach the Cimarron River Valley, drive north from
Clayton on State Route 18 to State Route 325, turn left,
and follow the road west along the River. A right turn on
Route 325 leads to Kenton, Oklahoma, in the Black Mesa
country, a fascinating spot for bird finding (see under Boise
City in the Oklahoma chapter).

GALLUP. Near the Arizona line in the northwestern part
of the state, Gallup (elevation 6,505 feet) is the principal
town in New Mexico's Navajo country where weird, colorful geological formations and relics of an early Indian culture create a land of romance, and where many Indian inhabitants still cling to primitive ways. To the southeast rise
the ZUNI MOUNTAINS, to the north, the CHUSKA
MOUNTAINS (sometimes called the LUKACHUKAI
MOUNTAINS); both reach elevations between 8,000 and
9,000 feet.

The Zuni Mountains, embraced by the Cibola National
Forest, consist mainly of flat-topped ridges with steep sides.
Though relatively dry, their upper slopes and tops support
open stands of ponderosa pine mixed with Douglas fir and,
here and there, groves of Gambel's oak. Grasses and shrubs
provide a low undergrowth. In the few cool places, such as

shaded ravines, are aspen and blue spruce. Typically southern bird species mingle in the Zunis at nesting time with
the more northern species that breed at higher altitudes.
The Mearns' Quail and Painted Redstart, for example, approach their northern range limits in these Mountains,
where there are such breeding birds as the Lewis' Woodpecker, Hermit Thrush, Western Tanager, and Green-tailed
Towhee. Other breeding birds to be found include the
Hairy Woodpecker, Western Wood Pewee, White-breasted
Nuthatch, Pygmy Nuthatch, Western Bluebird, Mountain
Bluebird, Warbling Vireo, Grace's Warbler, Western Tanager, Black-headed Grosbeak, and Spotted Towhee.

The best way to see a cross section of the Zuni Mountains
is to drive east from Gallup on US Route 66 to Thoreau
(about 30 miles distant). Just beyond Thoreau, turn south
on an unnumbered road to Bluewater Lake. Another interesting trip is to drive east from Gallup on Route 66 to Grants
(about 59 miles distant) and turn right on State Route 53
(impassable in winter) to El Morro National Monument,
site of the famous Inscription Rock, a great mass of sandstone rising about 200 feet above the valley floor. This road,
southward from Grants, skirts the edge of a great lava flow
with caves of perpetual ice, and passes through ponderosa-
pine forests. Such birds as the Lewis' Woodpecker, Common Raven, Clark's Nutcracker, and juncos may be observed.

Though lying across the New Mexico–Arizona line, most
of the Chuska Mountains, which comprise primarily a
broad plateau with steep rimrock edges, are in New
Mexico. Somewhat segregated in a vast land of sagebrush-
covered mesas, ridges, and valleys, the Chuskas dominate
the landscape for miles around. Climatic conditions and the
types and distribution of vegetation on the higher slopes
and top of the plateau are much like those on the Zunis.
Breeding birds of the Chuska Mountains include many
species attracted to higher altitudes, namely, Goshawk,
Blue Grouse, Pygmy Owl, Lewis' Woodpecker, Williamson's Sapsucker, Three-toed Woodpecker, Western Flycatcher, Violet-green Swallow, Purple Martin, Clark's
Nutcracker, Dipper, Hermit Thrush, Mountain Bluebird,

Ruby-crowned Kinglet, Audubon's Warbler, Pine Siskin, and (Red-backed) Gray-headed Junco.

The Chuskas are almost entirely within the Navajo Indian Reservation, the headquarters of which are at Window Rock, Arizona, reached from Gallup by going north on US Route 666 for 8 miles, turning left (west) on State Route 68, and then right on the first road after crossing the state line. North from Gallup, Route 666 goes along the eastern foothills of the range, and several side roads (ungraded) lead off to the west, penetrating the range for varying distances. One, leaving the highway 48 miles from Gallup, crosses the range through forested regions over Washington Pass to Crystal. Atop the mountains on either side of Washington Pass are many lakes, on the larger of which Eared Grebes nest. Numerous ducks use these lakes during migration.

Route 666 continues on to SHIPROCK, a weirdly precipitous butte, which looms in striking contrast to the sagelands about it. Birdlife in this immediate area is limited to such species as the Horned Lark, Sage Thrasher, and Sage Sparrow. The Scaled Quail's northwestern limit occurs at about this point.

LAS CRUCES. US Route 85 south from Las Cruces (*las crew'-sees*) goes down the Rio Grande Valley to the Texas border 25 miles distant. Irrigation has added a lush greenness to this area. Passerines nest in the bordering cottonwoods and willow thickets. Ducks congregate on the river during migration and in the winter. The bird finder, driving down the Valley, would do well to inspect the river at every convenient spot.

In striking contrast to the Valley is the SAN ANDRES NATIONAL WILDLIFE REFUGE (57,215 acres), which lies a short distance northeast of Las Cruces, in the SAN ANDRES MOUNTAINS. To reach the Refuge, drive east from Las Cruces on US Route 70 for 6 miles; turn left on a rough but passable Forest Service road and drive northeast 17 miles to the headquarters, at Rope Springs. Additional directions from headquarters will lead the bird finder to interesting places for birds.

The Refuge consists of semidesert, bighorn-sheep-range country, extremely rough and broken by cliffs of limestone. The scant annual precipitation limits the area to semidesert and desert plants such as mountain mahogany, buckbrush, desert willow, creosote bush, mesquite, yucca, century plant, and an abundance of cacti, with some pinyon pine and juniper on the northern slopes of the Mountains.

Despite the fact that a shortage of permanent water eliminates some birds, there have been 113 species recorded on the Refuge, and bird finding should be interesting here, especially during the winter and migration seasons. The Mourning Dove, a very common summer bird, probably numbers 5,000 in fall migration. Such breeding species as the White-throated Swift, Cactus Wren, Rock Wren, Brown Towhee, Rufous-crowned Sparrow, Desert Sparrow, and Black-chinned Sparrow may be seen by those who are willing to scramble over the rugged terrain. Many cliffs and ledges provide nesting sites for the Golden Eagles, which may be seen soaring over the Mountains or the adjacent Jornada Valley. Swainson's Hawks and White-necked Ravens are common nesting birds.

LORDSBURG. A desert city with good tourist accommodations, Lordsburg (elevation 4,249 feet) is the best and about the only headquarters for trips into the southwestern corner of the state.

State Route 180 south from Lordsburg goes for about 70 miles in the ANIMAS VALLEY, between the ANIMAS and PELONCILLO MOUNTAINS, and leads to Cloverdale, an abandoned settlement close to the Mexican border. Some of the birds to be looked for in the desert country along the way include the Red-tailed Hawk, Gambel's Quail, Road-runner, Horned Lark, Ash-throated Flycatcher, Verdin, Cactus Wren, Mockingbird, Curve-billed Thrasher, Loggerhead Shrike, Scott's Oriole, Brown Towhee, and Desert Sparrow.

From Cloverdale (elevation 5,400 feet), at the southeast end of the Peloncillo Mountains, drive west about 2 miles and enter Coronado National Forest, where there is a picnic ground graced by some of the most beautiful live oaks and stately alligator junipers in the southwest. Farther west, in a canyon, accessible by car, is country partly forested with pinyon pine, ponderosa pine, oak, and juniper, together with an abundance of manzanita, mountain mahogany, mescal, and sotol. Deep in the canyon are cotton-woods and sycamores. On the northern slopes of the higher elevations the Chihuahua pine dominates. In this area, above 6,000 feet, an annual precipitation of about 22 inches accounts for the more luxuriant vegetation. Some of the breeding birds to be seen here are the Mearns' Quail, Band-

MEARNS' QUAIL

tailed Pigeon, Olivaceous Flycatcher, Steller's Jay, Scrub Jay, Arizona Jay, Bridled Titmouse, Bush-tit, Hutton's Vireo, Black-throated Gray Warbler, Painted Redstart, Scott's Oriole, and Spotted Towhee.

The Lordsburg-Cloverdale trip should be made in a loop. Drive east from Cloverdale on State Route 79, through San Luis Pass (elevation 5,500 feet) in the Animas Mountains, toward Antelope Wells on the International boundary, thence north on State Route 81 to its junction with US Route 80, and west to Lordsburg. About 18 miles north of Antelope Wells the road passes west of BIG HATCHET

PEAK (elevation 8,366 feet), a conspicuous, all but treeless, desert landmark. This mountain and the desert surroundings, studded with yucca, mesquite, and creosote
bush, are the habitat of the Golden Eagle and are within
the breeding range of Swainson's Hawks, White-necked
Ravens, and Scott's Orioles. On the slopes, Road-runners,
Horned Larks, Cactus Wrens, and Desert Sparrows are
common.

The SAN SIMON MARSHES, in the San Simon Valley,
provide the only suitable nesting place for waterbirds and
waterfowl in this section of the southwest. To reach the
Marshes, drive 35 miles southwest from Lordsburg on US
Route 80 and turn right on an obscure but well-traveled
country road for about 2 miles. (Note: Should the bird
finder miss this road and come to a sign marked 'Cienaga
Ranch,' he should turn around, drive back, and, after crossing a small bridge, take the first road on the left. The bridge
is not more than 2 miles from the sign.)

The Marshes are about 2 miles long, with a dominating
vegetation of cattails and a variety of grasses on the extensive meadows. There are some willows and cottonwoods in
the center and a row of giant cottonwoods along an abandoned ditch on the east side. The valley slopes on the east
are covered with creosote bush and mesquite, while the
sand washes are bordered by skunkbrush, Apache plume,
and desert willow.

This is an area established by the U.S. Soil Conservation
Service solely to protect New Mexican Ducks, which nest
here. Blue-winged Teal, Cinnamon Teal, Red-wings, and
meadowlarks nest in considerable numbers; during migration, Mallards, Baldpates, Pintails, Green-winged Teal,
Shovelers, Coots, and Wilson's Snipe rest and feed. Western
Kingbirds, Western Wood Pewees, Yellow-throats, and
Bullock's Orioles breed in the cottonwoods and brush. Adjacent slopes and sand washes have suitable nesting habitats
for the Gambel's Quail, Lesser Nighthawk, Verdin, Bendire's Thrasher, and Curve-billed Thrasher.

To the north and northwest of Lordsburg lies the GILA
RIVER VALLEY, of special interest because of the rare
New Mexico bird species that may be seen here. Two places
in the Valley are quite easily accessible—Redrock and

Virden (an irrigated section). Redrock may be reached by a good country road (unnumbered) that goes directly north from Lordsburg for 18 miles; to get to Virden go northwest from Lordsburg on US Route 70 for 25 miles, then right on an unnumbered country road for 6 miles. The tree growth in both places consists of cottonwood, sycamore, ash, and mesquite, with a fill-in cover of arrowweed. In the Redrock region nest such birds as the Mexican Black Hawk, White-winged Dove, Screech Owl, Elf Owl, Gila Woodpecker, Black Phoebe, Vermilion Flycatcher, Phainopepla, Bell's Vireo, Lucy's Warbler, Hooded Oriole, Cardinal, and Abert's Towhee. These same species and, in addition, the Inca Dove occur near Virden.

PORTALES. In the east-central part of the state, about 15 miles west of the Texas border, lies an area of plains interspersed with sandhills and tablelands—a dry, treeless country, where the chief land-use is grazing. There is some mesquite, catclaw, buckthorn, and shin oak, but the principal vegetation is bluestem grass, which, together with sand sagebrush, constitute the preferred habitat of the Lesser Prairie Chicken.

State Route 18, south and north from Portales, practically bisects the best Lesser Prairie Chicken country in the state. On early-morning visits to the vicinity of Milnesand (37 miles south of Portales), between mid-March and early June, one is almost certain to see these birds. Their astonishing nuptial displays may be observed from the car along any of the farm and ranch roads that branch from Route 18.

Milnesand is in the heart of the Scaled Quail range. Western Meadowlarks are exceedingly common. Wherever there is short grass, Mountain Plovers may be found nesting; they are probably more common here than elsewhere in the southwest.

In the region around both Portales and Milnesand there is a spectacular mingling of species when, in late winter or very early spring, the population of winter residents— Sage Thrashers, Brewer's Blackbirds, Vesper Sparrows, juncos, White-crowned Sparrows, and McCown's and Chestnut-collared Longspurs—is augmented by the early arrival of birds from the south—Swainson's Hawks, Mountain Plovers, Killdeer, Barn Swallows, Cliff Swallows, Chipping Sparrows, and Brewer's Sparrows.

RATON. A tourist center as well as an important livestock and mining town, Raton is the principal gateway to New Mexico from Colorado. Historic Raton Pass (elevation 7,834 feet) is just a few miles north, on US Route 85.

From Raton, with its mesas and forested mountains, many interesting trips may be made during the summer months. Since the elevations vary greatly (from 6,000 feet in the open country to the south to 10,000 feet on near-by mountains), a great variety of birds may be seen.

Drive southwest on US Route 64 for 48 miles to Cimarron, the entrance to beautiful CIMARRON CANYON. In the forests of pine, fir, and aspen, or along the rushing trout stream, lined with cottonwoods, willows, and alders, may be found such breeding birds as the Spotted Sandpiper, Blue Grouse, Steller's Jay, American Magpie, Dipper, Hermit Thrush, Western Bluebird, Mountain Bluebird, Townsend's Solitaire, Audubon's Warbler, Pine Grosbeak, and Evening Grosbeak. There are camping facilities in the Canyon.

Twelve miles east of Raton, on State Route 72, is JOHNSON MESA, a high tableland rimmed by precipitous breaks and canyons. The Mesa proper, approximately 10 miles wide from east to west, consists of open valleys, ridges, and prairie lands, but adjacent rims and canyons are well forested with ponderosa pine, Douglas fir, aspen, and oak. Horned Larks, Western Meadowlarks, and Vesper Sparrows nest regularly on the Mesa, and it is probably the only place in the state where Sharp-tailed Grouse may be seen. Red-tailed Hawks, Sparrow Hawks, Lewis' Woodpeckers, and American Magpies nest in the adjacent timber. Often a Golden Eagle or two may be seen soaring above some of the rugged canyons that cut deeply into the north shoulder of the Mesa.

CAPULIN MOUNTAIN NATIONAL MONUMENT (680 acres), which embraces one of the most recent and clearly defined volcanic cones in the southwest, is 40 miles from Raton. To reach the Monument, drive southeast on US Route 87 to Capulin Station, turn north on State Route

325, and follow the spiral drive around Capulin Mountain to the crater, a great pit on the summit. Watch for summer-resident Horned Larks, Lark Sparrows, Lark Buntings, and, possibly, Mountain Plovers on the way.

The 8,732-foot SIERRA GRANDE looms to the southeast of the Monument. Its massive symmetrical outline, treeless except for the north slope, rises impressively from an elevated plain, richly covered with grasses. The higher elevations of the north slope have only scattered stands of ponderosa pine and sufficient other tree growth around springs to provide habitat for Wild Turkeys, jays, and other mountain birds. Route 87 passes the north side of the Sierra to the village of Des Moines, where it is possible for the hardy bird finder to arrange for trips, either on foot or on horseback, to the top of the Sierra.

ROSWELL. At any time of year the visitor to Roswell, in southeastern New Mexico, should not miss a trip to BITTER LAKE NATIONAL WILDLIFE REFUGE (23,-923 acres), one of the most important waterfowl refuges in the southwest. To reach headquarters, drive north from Roswell on US Route 285, for 4 miles, turn right on US Route 70 and continue for 5 miles, to the Refuge sign; there take a gravel road for 3 miles. All interesting parts of the Refuge may be reached by car.

The Refuge, which is in two sections, includes 10.5 miles of the Pecos River Valley and 5 miles of the Salt Creek Valley. The Valleys are bordered by low rolling hills and mesas where mesquite, sagebrush, creosote bush, grama grass, yucca, and cactus constitute the chief vegetation. In the Valleys tamarisk, cottonwood, and salt grass are the main cover. Quillreed makes up the marsh vegetation.

In addition to the River and the Creek, the Refuge has 38 so-called 'bottomless' lakes, the largest of which is an acre in extent, and 8 impoundments, which range in size from 22 to 40 acres.

The total water area, constituting 1,200 acres (extensive for the southwest), plus a mild climate and an abundance of food in the near-by irrigated fields, make this Refuge a resting and wintering place for multitudes of waterbirds and waterfowl. A recent January census listed

12,000 Sandhill Cranes, 125 Canada Geese, and 92,000 ducks of all species, with Pintails, Mallards, and Baldpates predominating. While the primary value of the Refuge is for migrating and wintering birds, future developments may attract more nesting birds. At present Avocets and Black-necked Stilts are common summer residents and the area is New Mexico's principal breeding ground of the Snowy Plover.

The DEXTER FEDERAL FISH HATCHERY (640 acres), 18 miles south of Roswell on US Route 285, lies on a paved road just east of the little town of Dexter, and contains a series of lakes and ponds much used by migrating birds, especially ducks and Sandhill Cranes. The land south of the Hatchery is maintained by the state as a refuge for upland game birds. Common birds nesting in the area include the Scaled Quail, Ring-necked Pheasant, Killdeer, Black-necked Stilt, Yellow-throat, Western Meadowlark, and Red-wing. In winter, thousands of Sandhill Cranes congregate each night on the Hatchery grounds.

A very pleasant 75-mile trip from Roswell is to go west on US Route 70 into the SIERRA BLANCA to State Route 37, turn north on Route 37, and drive 1.5 miles beyond the little resort town of Ruidoso to a Lincoln National Forest sign on the left reading 'Cedar Creek Picnic Grounds.' Enter the gate, follow a well-graveled secondary road through meadow and forest past the picnic areas on Cedar Creek, and continue through heavier timber to the end of the road, marked by a ski shelter and a clear running spring. From here, a ski run extending about a quarter of a mile up a small steep valley has been cleared of virgin pine and spruce, affording a lovely vista and an excellent vantage point from which to observe the abundant birdlife on the heavily timbered mountains on either side.

Every yard of the 3-mile drive from the gate is worthy of attention, from the meadows by the gate where Purple Martins and Western Bluebirds abound to the very top of the ski run where Western Tanagers nest. A typical June list might include, in addition to the birds mentioned above, the Sparrow Hawk, Mearns' Quail, Wild Turkey, Mourning Dove, Pygmy Owl, Red-shafted Flicker, Acorn Woodpecker, Hairy Woodpecker, Cassin's Kingbird, Western

Flycatcher, Steller's Jay, Common Raven, Mountain Chick-
adee, House Wren, Hermit Thrush, Audubon's Warbler,
Gray-headed Junco, Chipping Sparrow, and possibly a
Zone-tailed Hawk.

SANTA FE. This old capital city (elevation 6,954 feet),
rich in historic interest, lies at the foot of the Sangre de
Cristo Range. So precipitous are the slopes adjacent to the
city that few roads penetrate the mountains. The best way
for the bird finder to reach the higher altitudes is on foot or
horseback.

The most exciting drive from Santa Fe—one that climbs
into the mountains—is up PECOS CANYON. To reach this
Canyon, take US Route 85 east from Santa Fe for 20 miles
(2 miles beyond Glorieta), and turn left on a paved road
to Pecos, 4 miles distant. From Pecos take State Route 63
north for 20 miles to Cowles, which is in the heart of the
mountains.

As the Canyon narrows, there are dense growths of
scrub oak and juniper where one should look for breeding
Red-shafted Flickers, Lewis' Woodpeckers, Cassin's Kingbirds, Violet-green Swallows, Steller's Jays, Scrub Jays,
American Magpies, Pinyon Jays, Red-breasted Nuthatches,
Mountain Bluebirds, Western Tanagers, House Finches,
and Brown Towhees. Spotted Sandpipers and Dippers may
be observed along the margins of the Pecos River, which
rushes down through the Canyon.

Cowles, where the spruce and aspen begin to appear, is
a resort village, and many of the breeding birds listed for
the Sangre de Cristo Range may be seen about the cabins
and campgrounds—Band-tailed Pigeons, (Red-naped)
Common Sapsuckers, Olive-sided Flycatchers, Hermit
Thrushes, Townsend's Solitaires, Golden-crowned Kinglets,
Ruby-crowned Kinglets, Evening Grosbeaks, and Red
Crossbills.

At Cowles one may make arrangements for trips, on foot
or horseback, into dense forests of pine, fir, spruce, and
aspen, to mountain lakes, and to peaks (Truchas, Pecos,
Baldy, and Lake) where, beginning at the timber line, the
White-tailed Ptarmigan, American Pipit, Brown-capped
Rosy Finch, and White-crowned Sparrow occur.

SILVER CITY. This business center (elevation 5,931 feet) of southwestern New Mexico is a fine headquarters for bird-finding trips into the PINOS ALTOS and MOGOLLON MOUNTAINS (pronounced *moke'-o-yon*), which rise to the north. Late May and June is the best time for observing birds of the lower slopes, valleys, and canyons; June and early July, for nesting birds of the higher slopes.

The Sapello Loop Drive will take the bird finder across the Pinos Altos Mountains, a low range forested with pinyon pine and alligator juniper at middle levels and ponderosa pine and Gambel's oak at higher levels. Drive north from Silver City on State Route 25 to Pinos Altos and Cherry Creek Canyon, where there is a public campground maintained by the U.S. Forest Service; continue thence over the Pinos Altos Range into Sapello Creek Valley to the junction with State Route 61. Turn right on Route 61 to San Lorenzo, then right on State Route 180 to Silver City. The total distance is about 75 miles. Arizona Jays, Bridled Titmice, and Blue-gray Gnatcatchers are numerous in the live oaks around Pinos Altos at the southern edge of the Pinos Altos Mountains. In the vicinity of Cherry Creek Canyon and in the Mountains, such breeding birds should be watched for as the Broad-tailed Hummingbird, Acorn Woodpecker, Steller's Jay, Mountain Chickadee, Hermit Thrush, Solitary Vireo, Red-faced Warbler, Painted Redstart, Western Tanager, Hepatic Tanager, Pine Siskin, and (Red-backed) Gray-headed Junco.

A fine combination of scenic beauty and birdlife of both low and high altitudes may be enjoyed by driving northwest from Silver City on US Route 260 to Glenwood in the SAN FRANCISCO RIVER VALLEY. The several canyons here with their thickets of mesquite, acacia, and other shrubs, together with fine stands of oak, cottonwood, and Arizona sycamore, attract the Gambel's Quail, Gila Woodpecker, Ladder-backed Woodpecker, Black Phoebe, Vermilion Flycatcher, Crissal Thrasher, Abert's Towhee, and other nesting species. Five miles north of Glenwood turn east on State Route 78 and drive over the Mogollons to Willow Creek Canyon high up on the east side. This road, open only in summer, has steep grades and sharp turns, but is safe for careful drivers. From Glenwood the trip is almost entirely within the Gila National Forest, where campgrounds are maintained. There are tourist accommodations in Willow Creek Canyon. (For some of the breeding birds that may be expected in the Mogollons, consult the list in the introduction to this chapter.)

SOCORRO. By far the best area in the Rio Grande Valley for nesting, wintering, and migrating waterfowl is the 57,191-acre BOSQUE DEL APACHE NATIONAL WILDLIFE REFUGE (pronounced *boss'-ke del ah'-pa'-chay*). US Route 85, south from Socorro, bisects this Refuge just beyond the village of San Antonio. A large sign denotes headquarters, which is only 140 yards from the highway. The importance of this Refuge becomes evident when one considers that out of 300 birds listed for the state, 230 have occurred here.

The Refuge includes 13,000 acres of bottomland along the Rio Grande, where impoundment areas are flooded in the fall to form marshes and ponds of about 5,200 acres when filled. Cattails and bulrushes are found in the marshes, and there is an abundant bottomland growth of cottonwood, screw bean, willow, and tamarisk. The remainder of the Refuge slopes up to rough mountains and mesas—mostly desert country. Creosote bush, four-winged saltbush, desert holly, sumac, skunkbrush, and sagebrush are limited to the arroyos on the west side of the river. Black sage dominates the vegetation on the east side.

As water development and impoundment become more extensive, the breeding bird populations increase. Mallards, New Mexican Ducks, Gadwalls, Blue-winged Teal, Cinnamon Teal, Shovelers, and Coots nest regularly. Upland breeding birds include the Scaled Quail, Gambel's Quail, Killdeer, Road-runner, Red-shafted Flicker, Ladder-backed Woodpecker, and Western Meadowlark. Double-crested Cormorants, American Egrets, Snowy Egrets, Black-crowned Night Herons, and Least Bitterns are breeding in increasing numbers. The best time for observing the nesting birds is the first three weeks in May.

Fall migration, September through October, is the most exciting time on the Refuge. Flocks of Canada Geese and concentrations of ducks, representing 14 species, occur.

Sandhill Cranes are often present in large flocks during October and November. Also to be seen are Greater and Lesser Yellow-legs, Least Sandpipers, Dowitchers, Wilson's Phalaropes, Tree Swallows, Yellow-headed Blackbirds, Savannah Sparrows, Sage Sparrows, and Song Sparrows.

Many of the birds remain to spend the winter—a few Whistling Swans and Snow Geese, as well as Green-winged Teal, Blue-winged Teal, Shovelers, Canvas-backs, Buffle-heads, Hooded Mergansers, American Mergansers, Coots, and Marsh Hawks.

It is possible, after obtaining permission and directions from headquarters, to drive along the tops of the dykes through the bottomlands and watch birds directly from the car. The upland roads are not recommended for ordinary passenger cars.

TAOS. Selected for 'colonization' by some of the leading artists of the day, Taos (pronounced *tous*) is also a spot favored by bird finders during the summer and fall. Because it is on a high plateau between the Sangre de Cristo Mountains on the east and the San Juan Mountains on the west, there are many scenic and ornithologically rewarding trips to be taken into high country, in some cases far above timber line. Two trips into the SANGRE DE CRISTO MOUNTAINS are highly recommended.

1. Drive east from Taos (elevation 7,050 feet) on US Route 64, crossing Morreno Valley, to EAGLE NEST LAKE (elevation 8,500 feet), and then down to CIMARRON CANYON (see also under Raton) to Cimarron. The road traverses farm- and rangelands, passes over oak- and juniper-clad hills, and gradually climbs into montane forests of pine, fir, spruce, and aspen. In the vicinity of Eagle Nest Lake, on the right just beyond the town of Eagle Nest, some of the nesting birds are Townsend's Solitaires, Cassin's Finches, Pine Grosbeaks, Pine Siskins, and Red Crossbills. If stops are made while driving down into Cimarron Canyon, one should be able to find, among the breeding birds, the following: Hairy Woodpecker, Steller's Jay, Black-capped Chickadee, Dipper, Virginia's Warbler, Audubon's Warbler, Western Tanager, and Green-tailed Towhee. From Eagle Nest one may travel northwest on

State Route 38, through the magnificent Red River Canyon, to State Route 3 and return to Taos.

2. Drive 12 miles north from Taos on Route 3 to Arroyo Hondo, then take an unnumbered road (right) for about 15 miles to Twining (elevation 9,500 feet), a mining town in upper Hondo Canyon, where there is a public campground. From Twining, go by trail on foot or horseback into the high country. Half a mile above Twining the trail forks. Here sign directions indicate Gold Hill (elevation 12,660 feet) 3 miles to the left, and Wheeler Peak (elevation 13,-151 feet) 6 miles to the right. Both trails, maintained by the U.S. Forest Service, are well-marked. Breeding birds, which may be seen along either trail, are the following: below timber line, the Goshawk, Blue Grouse, Three-toed Woodpecker, Olive-sided Flycatcher, Violet-green Swallow, Canada Jay, Brown Creeper, Hermit Thrush, Townsend's Solitaire, Golden-crowned and Ruby-crowned Kinglets, Evening Grosbeak, Pine Grosbeak, Cassin's Finch, Pine Siskin, Red Crossbill, and Lincoln's Sparrow (in willow meadows or willow thickets along streams); at timber line, the White-crowned Sparrow; above timber line, the American Pipit and probably the White-tailed Ptarmigan and Gray-crowned Rosy Finch. Views of Golden Eagles and Common Ravens along the way are a possibility and, if lucky, one may catch a glimpse of a Spotted Owl.

TRUTH OR CONSEQUENCES. Formerly called Hot Springs, this thriving resort town in the lower Rio Grande Valley is near the mammoth Elephant Butte Dam that forms the ELEPHANT BUTTE RESERVOIR, on which many waterfowl rest during the winter and the migration seasons. The Dam is a short distance northeast of Truth or Consequences, on State Route 52. Cliff Swallows nest under overhanging cliffs adjacent to the Dam and Reservoir, and a pair of Golden Eagles usually have an aerie on Elephant Butte, a conspicuous landmark in the Reservoir just above the Dam.

The HOT SPRINGS FEDERAL FISH HATCHERY, with a series of ponds, the edges of which are well-vegetated with willows and cottonwoods, lies in a game refuge just below the Dam. With permission from headquarters, the bird finder may drive on one or two roads paralleling the ponds and observe a good variety of water-birds, waterfowl, and shorebirds from the car. The very best seasons are fall and spring, but many birds winter here.

An interesting trip may be made from Truth or Consequences into the eastern side of the BLACK RANGE by way of Winston and Chloride. These two villages, relics of past mining activities, now lie in cattle country, but a brief trip up Chloride Canyon brings the bird finder into rugged mountainous land, forested with pinyon pine, alligator juniper, ponderosa pine, white fir, and Douglas fir. Here may be heard or seen such breeding birds as the Mearns' Quail, Wild Turkey, Band-tailed Pigeon, Screech Owl, Great Horned Owl, Spotted Owl, White-throated Swift, Canyon Wren, Rock Wren, Solitary Vireo, Hepatic Tanager, and Western Tanager. To make this trip, drive north from Truth or Consequences on US Route 85 to State Route 52, and turn left to Winston. At Winston, turn left to Chloride, from which point it is possible, except during flood periods, to drive 12 miles up Chloride Canyon to Monument Pass on the Continental Divide.

TUCUMCARI. Just north and east of Tucumcari, US Route 54 passes through an extensive sandhill section, which is one of the best habitats for Scaled Quail in the state. Winter concentrations of this bird may be seen near the State Agricultural Experiment Station (3 miles northeast of Tucumcari on US Route 54) and around many ranch houses and farms. Lesser Prairie Chickens also thrive here, and, where prairie-dog colonies have survived, there are a few Burrowing Owls. Swainson's Hawks and White-necked Ravens nest commonly in the vicinity.

Contributing authorities: George E. Barclay, Raymond J. Fleetwood, John E. Galley, Mrs. John E. (Margret) Galley, John C. Gatlin, Raymond H. Hunter, Jens K. Jensen, Cecil A. Kennedy, Alton A. Lindsey, Gale Monson, J. A. Seery, J. D. Thompson, Jr., H. C. Williams.

North Dakota

AVOCETS

There are numerous places in North Dakota where the prairie dips slightly, forming a shallow basin. Water gathers here from the melting snow and spring rains, stands unreplenished, and becomes highly alkaline. Under clear summer skies, it gradually evaporates. When the water reaches its maximum depth in the spring, Avocets assemble along the shores of these basins. At first there is great activity: courtship antics, during which birds lift their wings, lower their heads, and trip along liltingly in the shallow water, pursuing and circling one another; mild contests, as each pair—the mating bond once established—claims a section of shoreland for private use as nesting territory. Before long the hubbub is over, for the colony is organized and nesting is under way. If the bird finder approaches such an aggregation soon after the eggs have been laid, he is greeted by the unexpected. Instead of fleeing in panic, as is the custom of most colonial birds, the Avocets hold their ground and present forthwith a series of deflection displays ('injury-feigning' performances) that are as remarkably fantastic as they are multifarious. Wing-waving and wing-trailing; careening and falling; bounding ahead on stiffened legs; taking off in erratic, zigzagging flights, and then abruptly 'crash-landing'; flopping on the ground and floundering in the water as if hopelessly maimed—all to the accompaniment of shrill staccato calls and heart-rending moans. To see this avian show, the bird finder need only visit in June one of the alkaline lakes in the Lostwood National Wildlife Refuge (see under Kenmare) or similar localities elsewhere in the state.

Big skies and rolling plains. Treeless horizons with the outlines of grain elevators marking the locations of towns. Brief springs and warm summers with cool nights. Unceasing winds and ever-moving tumbleweeds. Jack rabbits bounding across wide stretches of grassland, 'flickertails' (Richardson's ground squirrels) scurrying about or sitting 'at attention' near the edges of grainfields, and an occasional coyote disappearing over a swell. Birds in abundance. Such are the first impressions of the visiting bird finder in North Dakota, the northernmost state that lies entirely within the interior plains.

The land surface of the state is composed of three plains, which, like three great steps, rise one above the other from Minnesota westward to Montana. The lowermost, with a minimum elevation of 790 feet, is the level Red River Valley bordering the Red River of the North on the eastern boundary. Its breadth in North Dakota varies from about 40 miles near the Canadian line to 10 miles toward the South Dakota line; comparatively speaking, it is a small part of the state. Birdlife is characteristically eastern with respect to the timber and brush species. For example, the Whip-poor-will, Yellow-shafted Flicker, Crested Flycatcher, Baltimore Oriole, Scarlet Tanager, and Indigo Bunting are of regular occurrence. But the birdlife of the open country is marked by the presence of many western species, such as the Western Kingbird, American Magpie,

Sprague's Pipit, Western Meadowlark, Brewer's Blackbird, Baird's Sparrow, and Chestnut-collared Longspur.

The next plain, the Drift Prairie, rises gradually from the western edge of the Red River Valley and extends westward, as gently undulating to hilly country, to meet the third and highest plain, the Missouri Plateau, whose eastern edge (recognized by a succession of hills and hummocks) passes diagonally in a northwest-southeast direction. General elevations of the Drift Prairie range from 1,500 feet to 1,800 feet. This large section of North Dakota is interesting ornithologically because it shows a marked transition between the eastern and western avifaunas. Moreover, it has several physiographic features that are attractive to particular kinds of birds. Northward, straddling the International boundary, are the Turtle Mountains (maximum elevation 2,321 feet), with timbered tracts where a few species of northern affinities nest, among them the Philadelphia Vireo. To the northwest lies the Souris River Valley, where there formerly existed some of the finest marshes on the continent. Drained many years ago for agricultural projects that proved unsuccessful, certain of them have since been restored by the U.S. Fish and Wildlife Service. Through the present management and the protection afforded them as National Wildlife Refuges (see under Kenmare, Minot, and Towner), they are probably more attractive to wildlife now than before they were destroyed. Today they are unquestionably among the topnotch places in the United States for seeing nesting grebes and ducks in exceptionally large numbers, while bird finding in their immediate vicinities—the grassy lowlands, wooded coulees (trenchlike ravines), and adjacent prairie uplands—is as rewarding as anywhere in the state. Much of the Drift Prairie from north to south is dotted with shallow lakes, ponds, and sloughs; owing to the naturally poor drainage of the area, very few contain running water except during the wet seasons. Some become decidedly alkaline and consequently invite Avocet colonies. Nearly all of these water bodies, if they do not go dry by midsummer, have small populations of breeding waterfowl.

The Missouri Plateau, occupying the remaining half of the state, is a part of the Great Plains, with general elevations from 1,800 to 2,700 feet. Going through the area is the broad valley of the Missouri River, which is joined from the west by the valleys of the Little Missouri, Knife, Heart, and Cannonball Rivers. On the west side of the Missouri, the topography of the Missouri Plateau is characterized by rolling surface and by abrupt buttes which increase in size and number toward the southwestern corner, where Black Butte rises to an elevation of 3,468 feet, the highest point in the state. The Plateau is further characterized by many wide valleys in which erosion has cut amazing formations, exposing layers of many-colored soils. The famous Badlands along the Little Missouri (see under Belfield) are the best example. Here is the most spectacular scenery; here also is a spot for bird finding as good as any in extreme western North Dakota. Despite the semi-arid conditions, the avifauna shows a surprising variety of species. The Ferruginous Hawk, Red-shafted Flicker, Say's Phoebe, Rock Wren, Mountain Bluebird, Bullock's Oriole, Black-headed Grosbeak, Lazuli Bunting, and Spotted Towhee are only a few of the characteristic breeding species to be observed regularly.

Timbered areas in North Dakota are limited to the borders of watercourses, to sheltered coulees, and to a few slopes such as those on the Turtle Mountains. Aspen, cottonwood, elm, oak, ash, birch, basswood, and boxelder are some of the dominant trees, while west of the Missouri River, especially in the Little Missouri territory, juniper is common. Various shrubs (e.g. the buffaloberry, wolfberry, silverberry, wild rose) grow extensively on the edges of timbered places or by themselves in draws (shallow ravines). Most of the state was originally prairie grassland, the fertile, better-watered soils of the Red River Valley and Drift Prairie producing tall grasses of lush green, the less fertile, drier soils of the Missouri Plateau producing short grasses of a grayish-green hue. Now the Red River Valley and Drift Prairie show an almost continuous succession of grainfields with intermittent pastures and haylands and, at regular intervals, a cluster of farm buildings partly surrounded by groves of trees that have been introduced as wind breaks. Because of low rainfall, the Missouri Plateau can be more profitably used for grazing than for crop production; hence the original grassland conditions have been less modified. As far as the eye can see there are vast stretches of short-grass prairie. Here prairie birds nest over wide areas, whereas the same species east of the Plateau are restricted mainly to pastures, neglected fields, and other uncultivated places. The following species breed more or less regularly throughout the state in the timbered areas and in the open country (prairie grasslands, pastures, fallow fields, meadow-like lowlands, brushy places, and dooryards):

TIMBERED AREAS

Black-billed Cuckoo
Screech Owl
Hairy Woodpecker
Downy Woodpecker
Least Flycatcher
Blue Jay

Black-capped Chickadee
White-breasted Nuthatch
Red-eyed Vireo
Warbling Vireo
American Redstart

OPEN COUNTRY

Greater Prairie Chicken (un-
    common)
Sharp-tailed Grouse
Killdeer
Upland Plover
Marbled Godwit
Mourning Dove
Burrowing Owl
Short-eared Owl
Red-headed Woodpecker
Eastern Kingbird
Western Kingbird
Horned Lark
Tree Swallow
Barn Swallow
American Magpie
House Wren
Catbird

Brown Thrasher
Eastern Bluebird
Sprague's Pipit
Loggerhead Shrike
Yellow Warbler
Yellow-throat
Bobolink
Western Meadowlark
Common Grackle
Common Goldfinch
Savannah Sparrow
Grasshopper Sparrow
Baird's Sparrow
Vesper Sparrow
Chipping Sparrow
Clay-colored Sparrow
Song Sparrow
Chestnut-collared Longspur

US Routes 2 and 10, crossing the state in an east-west direction, pass over all three plains, thus presenting a satisfying panorama of the North Dakota landscape. Both highways are remarkably straight, the roadbeds are well constructed for easy travel, and there are few wayside obstructions to mar the tremendous sweep of countryside. It is, therefore, an easy matter to see many species of birds from the moving car. In late spring and summer one is almost certain to notice, either in flight or perched on poles and wires, Swainson's Hawks, Ferruginous Hawks, Marsh Hawks, Short-eared Owls, Common Nighthawks, Western Kingbirds, American Magpies, Loggerhead Shrikes, Western Meadowlarks, and Brewer's Blackbirds, while there is always a good chance of noting one or two Burrowing Owls, Upland Plovers, and Marbled Godwits. Before the oncoming car, Horned Larks, Vesper Sparrows, and, not infrequently, Chestnut-collared Longspurs fly up from the roadsides where they have been searching for food. There are years when Lark Buntings and Dickcissels are common, sometimes abundant, along the highways, and other years when they seem to be absent. When driving over either Route 2 or Route 10, the bird finder should stop his car at widely separated points to investigate adjacent wooded coulees and timbered borders of streams and thus determine for himself the range limits of several closely allied eastern and western species. How far west can he find the Baltimore Oriole, Rose-breasted Grosbeak, and Indigo Bunting; and how far east their western counterparts, the Bullock's Oriole, Black-headed Grosbeak, and Lazuli Bunting, respectively? In certain spots, he may find both Orioles, or both Grosbeaks, or both Buntings, in which case he is also quite likely to observe interesting hybrids.

Waterfowl and shorebirds tend to attract the greatest attention during the migration seasons because they appear in such large numbers. Canada, Snow, and Blue Geese are especially abundant in the Devils Lake region (see under Devils Lake), ducks and shorebirds on the lakes, ponds, and sloughs throughout the state. The commonest shorebirds are the Willet, Greater and Lesser Yellow-legs, Pectoral Sandpiper, White-rumped Sandpiper, Baird's Sandpiper, Least Sandpiper, Dowitcher, Semipalmated Sandpiper, Wilson's Phalarope, and Northern Phalarope. Thousands of Sandhill Cranes move through the state to and from their Arctic breeding grounds, a few stopping off in such places as the Des Lacs National Wildlife Refuge (see under Kenmare). Although North Dakota has one

known breeding colony of White Pelicans—at Chase Lake
(see under Jamestown)—large numbers of Pelicans are
observed elsewhere in the state, either passing through
the state to more northern breeding grounds and returning
in the fall, or remaining through the summer on the larger
lakes. Of the many passerine species that have the status
of transients in North Dakota, the following are considered
common to abundant in suitable environments throughout the state: Olive-backed Thrush, American Pipit (particularly abundant in fall), Tennessee Warbler, Orange-
crowned Warbler, Myrtle Warbler, Black-poll Warbler,
Slate-colored Junco, American Tree Sparrow, Harris'
Sparrow, White-crowned Sparrow, White-throated Sparrow, Lincoln's Sparrow, and Lapland Longspur. In
North Dakota, the main migration flights may be expected within the following dates: for waterfowl, 1
April—5 May, 15 September—1 November; for shorebirds, 1 May—1 June, 1 August—15 September; for landbirds, 25 April—1 June, 15 August—1 October.

Only the irrepressible bird finder cares to pursue his avo-
cation in North Dakota between December and April, for
the rewards are meager when weighed against the low,
frequently subzero, temperatures and numbing winds he
must face. No matter how diligently he may strive to obtain a long list of species, the greatest number he can hope
to observe seldom exceeds 15, and rarely 20. All of the
watercourses are frozen over 'for keeps,' thereby restricting
his efforts entirely to landbirds. Aside from a few permanent
residents, the species most likely to be seen are the Rough-
legged Hawk, Golden Eagle, Snowy Owl, Bohemian Waxwing, Northern Shrike, Common Redpoll, and Snow Bunting. Possibly the American Tree Sparrow will be met, but
the vast majority of individuals of this hardy species prefer
the few additional degrees of warmth in the states immediately to the south.

BELFIELD. To the footsore French trappers of bygone
years, the country along the Little Missouri in the extreme
west-central part of North Dakota was 'les mauvaises terres
à traverser' (bad lands to travel through). However dis-
paraging the designation, it has persisted, but in reality,

the Badlands of North Dakota are weirdly beautiful, not dreary or barren as might be supposed from the appellation.

The beauty of the country is due in no small measure to the extraordinary formations that mark its surface—the bizarrely shaped buttes and tablelands, their steep slopes, stark and bare, showing multiple layers of variously tinted sandstone and clay capped by brick-red scoria. The beauty is considerably enhanced by diversified vegetation. Junipers and shrubs such as sumac, wolfberry, buffaloberry, chokecherry, currant, wild rose, and dogwood grow in the cuts and draws; cottonwoods, elms, aspens, ashes, and birches along the streams and on the moist river bottoms. Grasses, sagebrush, and occasionally yucca and cactus occur on the floors of the wider valleys and on the broad tablelands. Nearly all localities having a suitable soil produce pasqueflowers, larkspurs, arnicas, and other wildflowers. In the spring and early summer the blooming of the shrubs, cacti, and wildflowers creates a floral display that rivals in gaiety the blues, yellows, pinks, and reds of the earth formations.

On first entering the Badlands in the late spring and summer, the bird finder will observe a few Ferruginous Hawks, Sparrow Hawks, American Magpies, Mountain Bluebirds, Loggerhead Shrikes, and perhaps one or two Golden Eagles. But most birds are less wide-ranging and conspicuous and must be looked for in suitable situations; Horned Larks occupy the level portions with sparse vegetation, Western Meadowlarks the grassy stretches, Sage Grouse the extensive sagebrush flats, Lark Sparrows the slopes with scattered brush, and Say's Phoebes and Rock Wrens the vicinity of sharply cut banks and cliffs. By far the greatest number of birds inhabit the widely spaced areas grown to bushes and trees; the more extensive and dense the cover the more abundant the birds. Some of the species to be expected regularly are the Catbird, Brown Thrasher, Veery, Yellow Warbler, Yellow-breasted Chat, Bullock's Oriole, Black-headed Grosbeak, Lazuli Bunting, and Spotted Towhee, but occasionally the bird finder will meet other species, some of eastern affinities (e.g. the Least Flycatcher, Black and White Warbler, Oven-bird, Baltimore Oriole, Rose-breasted Grosbeak, Indigo Bunting) and some of western (Lewis' Woodpecker, Western Wood Pewee, Sage Thrasher). Flickers, invariably common, are always of special interest because many individuals are intermediate between the Yellow-shafted and Red-shafted forms.

Theodore Roosevelt, the outdoor-loving, conservation-minded twenty-sixth President of the United States, became so enamored of the Badlands that he chose to establish his ranch, the Elkhorn, in the immediate vicinity. Later, near the end of his life, he wrote, 'I have always said I never would have been President if it had not been for my experiences in North Dakota.' It is wholly fitting that Roosevelt's enduring contributions toward the conservation of the nation's resources should be commemorated by the THEODORE ROOSEVELT NATIONAL MEMORIAL PARK, which embraces country that so greatly appealed to him. As now established, the Park consists of 59,420 acres of federally owned land in three separate units: one, the south unit, near Medora (13 miles west of Belfield on US Route 10); a second, the north unit, southwest of Watford City (about 55 miles north of Belfield on US Route 85); and a third, the Elkhorn Ranch site, about midway between the two, on the Little Missouri. Park headquarters (address: Medora) is situated in Peaceful Valley in the south unit. US Route 10, passing west from Belfield, comes dramatically upon the Badlands before entering this unit. Both the north and the south units have spectacular scenery, but the north unit is better for bird finding. It has many wooded spots and, because it is served only by rough roads that are impassable in wet weather, it is little disturbed by tourists. After passing through the north-unit gate, the road winds along the base of the buttes rimming the little Missouri to the Squaw Creek picnic grounds, in a well-forested area particularly worth investigating for birds. From here the road goes up Cedar Canyon, becoming steeper and with more sharp turns, and leads on and up to Sperati Point, from which may be obtained the most magnificent view the entire Park has to offer. Several canyons with a dense growth of junipers and valleys with sagebrush—all visible from the Point—are excellent for birds, but the bird finder will have to work his own way down to them, since there are no trails.

US Route 85, which passes through Belfield, traverses many miles of rolling prairie both north and south of town. Where the highway crosses streams, the bird finder should look for colonies of Cliff Swallows in the concrete culverts. Just north of Belfield one such culvert, with its roof only four feet above the surface of the stream, usually has about a hundred nests wedged in the angles between the roof and sides. Incubation is normally under way by the first of June. An investigation of the prairie where the grasses are of sufficient density should turn up Sprague's Pipits, Baird's Sparrows, and Chestnut-collared Longspurs. Lark Buntings are common—frequently abundant—along the shoulders of the highway and in adjacent grainfields. Other species that may be observed along Route 85 are the Upland Plover, Burrowing Owl, Eastern and Western Kingbirds, Eastern Bluebird, Bobolink, and McCown's Longspur.

DEVILS LAKE. An excellent place in North Dakota for seeing the spring goose flights is the LAC AUX MORTES NATIONAL WILDLIFE REFUGE (5,882 acres), administered by the Sullys Hill National Game Preserve in Fort Totten, North Dakota. Here in late April and early May, Snow and Blue Geese congregate in immense numbers, sometimes exceeding 200,000. To reach the Refuge from Devils Lake, proceed 13 miles northwest on US Route 2 to Penn, then north on a side road for 12 miles. The birds also congregate, though usually in smaller numbers, in the vicinity of SWEETWATER LAKE, which is passed on the right by State Route 20, going north from Devils Lake to Webster.

DUNSEITH. The TURTLE MOUNTAINS in north-central North Dakota are an island of hills and lake-filled hollows surrounded by boundless stretches of prairie. Extending for 40 miles east and west and 30 miles north and south, the area is cut across by the International boundary; thus about one third lies in Canada. Although farms are numerous in the Turtle Mountains, much of the region is woods-covered, the principal trees being quaking aspen mixed with balsam poplar, hazelnut, and white birch. In certain places oak is abundant, while elm, ash, and box-elder are sometimes common. The trees are largely second growth, having replaced the original forests that were swept by fire at one time or another. These woods-covered lands, together with marginal, shrub-covered lands and many lakes, make the Turtle Mountains one of the important wildlife areas in the state.

Ornithologically, the Turtle Mountains have the distinction of being one of the few spots in the United States where the Philadelphia Vireo is known to breed. The Ruffed Grouse is a regular permanent resident, and in a few localities the Northern Water-thrush, Slate-colored Junco, and White-throated Sparrow are summer residents. Other birds that probably breed here are the Broad-winged Hawk, Crested Flycatcher, Least Flycatcher, Eastern Wood Pewee, Veery, Red-eyed and Warbling Vireos, Chestnut-sided Warbler, Oven-bird, Mourning Warbler, American Redstart, Baltimore Oriole, Rose-breasted Grosbeak, Common Goldfinch, and Eastern Towhee. Broods of the White-winged Scoter may be observed on some of the more undisturbed lakes.

North from Dunseith, State Route 3 passes over wooded hills and by little lakes that are typical of the Turtle Mountains. Many productive bird-finding spots lie near the highway. The WILLOW LAKE NATIONAL WILDLIFE REFUGE (2,848 acres), west of Dunseith, embraces interesting wilderness country that includes Willow Lake with its small rookery of Double-crested Cormorants. Directions for reaching the Refuge, and permission to enter it, may be obtained at the headquarters of the Lower Souris National Wildlife Refuge (see under Towner). The Willow Lake Refuge is administered by the Lower Souris Refuge. The best hotels and restaurants in the Turtle Mountains region are in Bottineau, 22 miles west of Dunseith on State Route 5.

JAMESTOWN. One of the best spots in eastern North Dakota for breeding and transient waterfowl is the AR-ROWWOOD NATIONAL WILDLIFE REFUGE (15,-

934 acres). Refuge headquarters (address: Kensal) may be reached from Jamestown by driving northward on US Route 52 to Edmunds, a distance of 27 miles, then turning right on an improved road and going east for 6 miles to the entrance road. Extending along the James River for 15 miles, the Refuge has several lakes—notably Arrowwood (1,600 acres), Mud (470 acres), and Jim (860 acres)— and DePuy Marsh (360 acres), all formed by damming the River's overflow. The vegetation in DePuy Marsh and in marshy areas around the lakes consists principally of cord grasses, bulrushes, smartweeds, and (especially in Arrowwood Lake) an abundance of sago pondweed. A small amount of timber borders Arrowwood and Jim Lakes. Some of the terrain has numerous coulees and ravines with heavy growths of grasses where co-operative grazing is used as a means to regulate cover for nesting birds. About 900 acres of the Refuge are farmed for grain on a share-crop basis, thus furnishing attractive feeding areas for water-fowl and upland game birds. Ducks nesting regularly are the Mallard, Gadwall, Baldpate, Pintail, Green-winged and Blue-winged Teal, Shoveler, Redhead, Canvas-back, Lesser Scaup Duck, and Ruddy Duck. Many broods of these species may be observed during July. Both spring and fall migrations of waterfowl bring large transient populations, but the fall population is much heavier and is well worth seeing when it reaches its peak in October. The birds begin to arrive in September, and many remain until the freeze-up. Included in the population are flocks of Canada Geese, which rest on the lakes and feed in the surrounding grainfields. As many as 10,000 individuals have been estimated on the Refuge at one time.

During the summer large numbers of White Pelicans commonly appear on the lakes of the Arrowwood Refuge, perhaps coming from a nesting colony on an island in Chase Lake, about 30 miles southwest. Chase Lake is embraced by the CHASE LAKE NATIONAL WILDLIFE REFUGE (375 acres), an area taken care of by the personnel of the Arrowwood Refuge. The island occupied by the pelican colony has a 4-acre surface, which rises only slightly above the water level. Grasses and weeds are the only vegetation. According to a recent census, the colony contained between 700 and 800 nests, while the number of young reaching maturity approximated 1,000. Also on the island were about 100 nests of California Gulls, 400 nests of Ring-billed Gulls, and less than a dozen duck nests. A gravel point on the shore of Chase Lake nearest the island may be reached as follows: Drive west from Jamestown on US Route 10, through Medina, to the intersection with State Route 30, a distance of 29 miles; go north on Route 30 for 9 miles, then turn left and proceed westward for 6 miles. The last 3 miles are over prairie trails, impossible to travel in wet weather and difficult to follow under even the best conditions. On the shore of Chase Lake from late May through July are several Avocet colonies, one of which is usually situated at the point near the end of the road. Since the adult birds are conspicuous, there should be no difficulty in finding the colony.

Visits to the pelican colony must not be undertaken without first obtaining permission from the manager of the Arrowwood Refuge. Generally, visits are discouraged, since human intrusion invariably creates factors that increase the already high mortality rate among the young birds. Each year the personnel of the Arrowwood Refuge makes two trips to the colony, the dates varying according to the earliness or lateness of the spring. The first, between 10 and 20 June, is for census purposes and for banding young gulls; the second, between 4 and 20 July, is for banding young pelicans. Bird finders wishing to accompany the personnel on either trip are welcome, provided they make arrangements with the Refuge manager by correspondence well in advance of the time the trip is to be made.

KENMARE. The DES LACS NATIONAL WILDLIFE REFUGE (pronounced *deh lacks'*) is the summer home of a thousand or more Western Grebes. In June, after they have arrived from their winter quarters, the Refuge is a must for any bird finder.

This fine preserve of 18,841 acres is 35 miles in length, extending from the Canadian border to 7 miles south of Kenmare. Within the area are the Upper, Middle, and Lower Lakes of the Rivière des Lacs, with their peripheral marshes, wooded coulees and draws, and bordering upland.

Roughly, the Lakes and their marshes comprise 8,000 acres; agricultural lands (for wheat and other small grains), 2,000 acres; prairie grassland, 7,000 acres; and tree- and brush-covered lands, 2,000 acres. Since there is no sustained flow of water through the Lakes, their size depends on the vagaries of the weather, a situation that has a profound effect on the abundance of birdlife using the Lakes for feeding and nesting purposes.

The majority of the Western Grebes usually occupy the large marsh at the south end of Upper Lake, where bulrushes, quillreeds, and other emergent plants provide them with ample nesting cover, while numerous channels and wide stretches of open water allow enough space for their courtship displays. Although the Western Grebes are the chief attraction in summer, this marsh has at the same time of year an impressive aggregation of other species: great numbers of Eared and Pied-billed Grebes and usually a few pairs of Holboell's Grebes; an abundance of American Bitterns, Soras, Coots, Black Terns, Yellow-headed Blackbirds, and Red-wings; a heavy population of ducks—Mallards, Gadwalls, Baldpates, Pintails, Green-winged and Blue-winged Teal, Shovelers, Redheads, Canvas-backs, Lesser Scaup Ducks, and Ruddy Ducks—the males of which are conspicuous as they loiter on the open water. The wet, grassy edges of the marsh invariably attract Brewer's Blackbirds and a few nesting pairs of Willets and Wilson's Phalaropes. White Pelicans and Double-crested Cormorants do not nest on the Refuge, but are nevertheless present throughout the breeding season. Tree, Bank, and Barn Swallows can always be seen flying low over the marshes in search of insect food.

Outside the marshes there are also many breeding birds. Species commonly inhabiting undisturbed portions of the prairie grassland are the Sharp-tailed Grouse, Common Nighthawk (on bare knolls), Horned Lark, Sprague's Pipit, Western Meadowlark, Savannah Sparrow (in low grasslands), Baird's Sparrow, Vesper Sparrow, and Chestnut-collared Longspur. Less common are the Upland Plover, Marbled Godwit, Burrowing Owl, Bobolink (in low grasslands), and Grasshopper Sparrow. In coulees where there are cottonwoods, aspens, and other trees, some of the species known to occur are the Screech Owl, Great Horned Owl, Least Flycatcher, Black-capped Chickadee, Veery (uncommon), Red-eyed Vireo, and Baltimore Oriole. Greater in number are the species associated with shrubs—wolfberry, silverberry, hawthorn, and others—on the edges of wooded coulees, in draws, or in isolated thickets; these include the Mourning Dove, Eastern and Western Kingbirds (often perching on wires and fences), Traill's Flycatcher (near wet places), House Wren, Catbird, Brown Thrasher, Cedar Waxwing, Loggerhead Shrike, Yellow Warbler, Yellow-throat (near wet places), Lazuli Bunting (uncommon), Common Goldfinch, Spotted Towhee, Clay-colored Sparrow, and Song Sparrow. A few Say's Phoebes frequent the vicinity of buildings, bridges, and freshly eroded vertical banks. Common as well as conspicuous over much of the Refuge are the Swainson's Hawk (nests usually in stunted trees, occasionally on the ground), the Marsh Hawk and Short-eared Owl (nests on the ground, generally in grassy lowlands or marshes), and the American Magpie (nests in trees or in high thickets).

Spring migration begins in March and continues until June. One of the prominent features is the appearance of thousands of Sandhill Cranes during mid-April. Ducks reach their peak of abundance soon after the ice breaks up in mid-April; shorebirds from late April through May. The common to abundant transient warblers, namely, the Black and White, Tennessee, Orange-crowned, Myrtle, and Blackpoll Warblers and the American Redstart, pass through the Refuge between 25 April and 20 May. Fall migration gets under way in August with the arrival of birds from northern breeding grounds and the departure of several local summer residents. From then until the freeze-up, usually in the first two weeks of November, migration proceeds steadily. Shorebirds are most abundant from late July through August; ducks during the first two weeks of October.

Headquarters of the Refuge may be reached from Kenmare (situated on the northeast shore of Middle Lake) by driving westward on a road across the north end of Middle Lake, then bearing left onto the entrance road. All of the worth-while bird-finding spots on the Refuge are accessible by car, but directions should be obtained at headquarters before attempting to reach them.

On the hilly prairie terrain west of Des Lacs Refuge lies the LOSTWOOD NATIONAL WILDLIFE REFUGE (26,107 acres). This area is dotted with numerous potholes and several alkaline lakes, some of which have excellent marshes. Their water supply depends almost wholly on rainfall and the spring runoff. Like the Des Lacs Refuge, Lostwood has wooded coulees, draws, and thickets, but they are fewer in number and less extensive.

Refuge headquarters is on the west side of State Route 8, overlooking Thompson Lake, at a point 25 miles north of Stanley and 18 miles south of Bowbells. It can be reached from Kenmare, 17.5 miles distant, by driving west over an improved road (not numbered). For route directions, inquire at the headquarters of the Des Lacs Refuge.

The Lostwood Refuge has good breeding grounds for the same species of waterfowl and other birds that are found on the Des Lacs Refuge, except for Holboell's and Western Grebes, which do not nest on Lostwood.

Very near the headquarters is a spot where Sharp-tailed Grouse perform their courtship 'dances' each spring from the time the snow disappears until well into June. Peak activity is usually reached during the last week of April. The dances, which begin in the dusk before sunrise and continue for two or three hours, may be observed at a distance of about 100 yards; if closer views are desired, the observer must conceal himself in a car or blind before the birds arrive.

Associated with the shallow, white-bordered alkaline lakes are two species of special interest: the Piping Plover and the Avocet. Both nest near the water's edge. One of the largest Avocet colonies on the Refuge is along the shore of Dead Dog Slough. The nests, close to 100 in number, are placed on pebbly ground among sparse grasses. By mid-June, the four or five eggs in each nest begin to hatch. Directions for reaching the Slough by car can be secured at headquarters.

MINOT. Like the Lower Souris and Des Lacs National Wildlife Refuges, the UPPER SOURIS NATIONAL

WILDLIFE REFUGE (32,045 acres) northwest of this city embraces extensive marshes, wide stretches of grass-land, and woodlands. Refuge headquarters may be reached from Minot by driving westward on US Route 52 to Foxholm (a distance of 19 miles), then bearing right on an improved road (no number) and going northward for 7 miles to the entrance road.

The Refuge occupies a 40-mile section of the Souris River Valley between points near McKinney on the north and Burlington on the south. A series of dams across the River within the property have created open marshes producing a rich vegetation. There are wooded areas—many of them —in near-by coulees and on bottomlands along the main river channel. The adjacent grassland represents former farmland reverting to the original short-grass prairie. In species of birds and their relative abundance, the Refuge is nearly identical with the Lower Souris and Des Lacs Refuges (see under Towner and Kenmare, respectively).

TOWNER. Of the 75 or so refuges administered by the U.S. Fish and Wildlife Service in North Dakota, the largest is the LOWER SOURIS NATIONAL WILDLIFE REF-UGE of 58,571 acres situated in the north-central part of the state. From the Canadian border, it extends southward along the Souris River to a point not far north of Towner on US Route 2. Refuge headquarters may be reached by proceeding northward from Towner on State Route 14, through the town of Upham (23 miles distant), to the entrance road on the right, approximately 3 miles beyond Upham.

The northern part of the Refuge consists of open water and marshes—formed by damming the Souris River at widely separated points—and adjacent wet meadows and prairie grassland. The southern part contains the wooded bottoms of the Souris River, with numerous meander cut-offs and sloughs, and the surrounding sandhills.

The populations of nesting and transient birds associated with the marshes and their immediate vicinity are tremendous. Two outstanding features of the breeding bird-life are the huge colonies of Franklin's Gulls in the marshes and the rookery of Double-crested Cormorants (nearly

100 pairs) and Great Blue Herons (less than a dozen pairs) occupying a group of dead elms standing in water about a mile from the nearest mainland. Other birds nesting regularly are five species of grebes (Holboell's, Horned, Eared, Western, Pied-billed), eleven species of ducks (Mallard, Gadwall, Baldpate, Pintail, Green-winged and Blue-winged

SHOVELERS

Teal, Shoveler, Redhead, Canvas-back, Lesser Scaup Duck, Ruddy Duck), and the following: American Bittern, Canada Goose (about 40 pairs), Marsh Hawk, Virginia Rail, Sora, Coot, Forster's Tern, Black Tern, Long-billed Marsh Wren, Yellow-headed Blackbird, and Red-wing. A number of Ring-billed Gulls and Common Terns find suitable localities for nests on islands in the marshes. Around the marshes, in wet, grassy situations, are a variety of birds of interest to the bird finder who will take time to search for them. These include the Willet, Wilson's Phalarope, Short-billed Marsh Wren, Bobolink, Brewer's Blackbird, Savannah Sparrow, Leconte's Sparrow, and Sharp-tailed Sparrow.

The upland country immediately beyond the marshes is gently rolling short-grass prairie with patches of brush and tall grasses here and there. Breeding regularly in this type of environment are the Sharp-tailed Grouse, Upland

Plover, Marbled Godwit, Short-eared Owl, Common Night-hawk (nests on bare knolls and in the woods), Horned Lark, Sprague's Pipit, Yellow-throat (in brush near wet places), Western Meadowlark, Grasshopper Sparrow, Baird's Sparrow, Vesper Sparrow, Lark Sparrow (occasionally), Clay-colored Sparrow (in brush), and Chestnut-collared Longspur. The bottoms of the Souris River, with their cover of elms, ashes, and willow thickets, and the near-by sandhills, with their aspen groves and thorny bushes, provide nesting habitats for numerous species, such as the Red-tailed Hawk, Swainson's Hawk, Long-eared Owl, Traill's Flycatcher, Least Flycatcher, Eastern Wood Pewee, American Magpie, House Wren, Catbird, Brown Thrasher, Veery, Cedar Waxwing, Red-eyed and Warbling Vireos, Yellow Warbler, Oven-bird, American Redstart, Baltimore Oriole, Rose-breasted Grosbeak, Common Goldfinch, and Song Sparrow. Both Eastern and Western Kingbirds and the Loggerhead Shrike may be expected on wires and other suitably exposed perches; Eastern and Say's Phoebes near buildings, bridges, and eroded riverbanks; and four species of swallows—the Tree, Bank, Rough-winged, and Barn—continually winging their way low over the marshes in search of insect food.

Waterfowl migrations in the spring and fall bring enormous transient populations of geese and ducks to the Refuge. Snow and Blue Geese are abundant in the spring (usually during mid-April), less so in the fall. Ducks, though appearing in impressive numbers in spring, with peak abundance soon after mid-April, come in far greater numbers in fall. Mallards reach peak abundance in mid October but most other ducks appear in largest numbers during the last week of August. Occasionally there are many Whistling Swans in the spring (mid-April).

Contributing authorities: Claude Alexander, Forrest A. Carpenter, Burns T. Carter, Edward F. Dana, F. Sheldon Dart, Robert T. Gammell, Mrs. Robert T. (Ann M.) Gammell, F. C. Gillett, Don Gray, Merrill Hammond, Allyn F. Hanks, C. J. Henry, William J. Lowe, Nelius B. Nelson, Stanley Saugstad, O. A. Stevens, Dwain W. Warner.

Oklahoma

SCISSOR-TAILED FLYCATCHER

From early spring to late fall no living thing lends greater color or interest to the open country in Oklahoma than the handsome, graceful Scissor-tailed Flycatcher. Trim and sedate, it rests on telephone wires, fence posts, or low trees, then takes flight, revealing the salmon pink of its underwings and flanks and spreading, as it changes course or elevation, the black and white, streamer-like feathers of its deeply forked tail. Unafraid of passers-by, courageous when protecting its nest, skilled in a variety of aerial maneuvers

—by such behavior the bird thus accentuates its unforget-
table appearance.

Much of Oklahoma is open, flat to rolling prairie country, devoted to farming of one sort or another. The wide
differences in the texture and composition of its soils and
in its annual rainfall (about 10 to 15 inches in the northwest, as compared with 50 to 60 in the southeast) make
possible the production of nearly every type of crop raised
in the United States. Yet there are areas within the state
that are rough and generally unsuited to agriculture.

Of the rough areas, four are extensively mountainous and
possess distinctive physiographic features. First, the Ozarks,
in the northeast, a westward extension of the dissected
plateau of the same name in Missouri and Arkansas. These
are broad flat-topped hills, or ridges, separated by the deep,
often narrow, valleys of clear, cold, spring-fed streams. A
few hills attain elevations as great as 1,150 feet. Characteristically the area is timbered, principally with blackjack
and post oaks, black hickories, and winged elms, but about
30 per cent has been cleared for agricultural purposes.

Second, the western chain of the Ouachita Mountains
(pronounced *wash'-i-ta*), in the southeast, the most rugged
relief in the state. Rich Mountain, the highest point, is
over 2,800 feet above sea level. The slopes are littered with
huge rocks, and along the numerous spring-fed streams
rise the sheer cliffs of canyons. Only about 15 per cent of
the Ouachita area is used for farming; the rest is woodland,
the finest in the state, consisting chiefly of short-leaf pines
mixed with white, post, and blackjack oaks, black hickories,
and black locusts. In the extreme southeast (the southern
half of McCurtain County) the Ouachita Mountains border upon 120 square miles of Coastal Plain, which is largely
forested with loblolly and short-leaf pines.

Third, the Arbuckle Mountains (see under Davis), occupying a 35- by 65-mile area in south-central Oklahoma.
Though they reach unspectacular heights (900 feet to
1,300 feet above sea level and no higher than 400 feet
above the surrounding country), the area is scenically attractive, owing to the many deep canyons through which
flow rapid streams with frequent and beautiful plunging

waterfalls. Save in the ravines, gullies, and canyons, trees are scarce.

And fourth, the Wichita Mountains (see under Lawton) 70 miles farther west, in southwestern Oklahoma, a group of low ridges and hills somewhat widely dispersed in a 25- by 65-mile area. A few peaks exceed 2,400 feet above sea level and rise about 1,000 feet above the plains; all, regardless of elevation, are rugged, with granite outcroppings and talus boulders, with steep upper slopes almost devoid of soil, and with a scanty tree growth.

Although the Oklahoma mountains, because of their relatively small extent and moderate elevations, hold no species of birds peculiar to them and show no altitudinal succession in birdlife, they provide opportunities for finding birds not occurring regularly in other parts of the state. In both the Ozarks and the Ouachita Mountains, the Acadian Flycatcher, Black and White Warbler, Parula Warbler, Louisiana Water-thrush, American Redstart, Scarlet Tanager, and Chipping Sparrow are among the breeding birds; in the Ouachita Mountains, the Pine Warbler may be expected in forests where pine is prevalent. The Arbuckle Mountains are notable for Black-capped Vireos and for Rufous-crowned Sparrows. Even more notable are the Wichita Mountains, where bird finding is surprisingly productive in any season and—because of the isolated situation —highly fascinating. Not only can Rufous-crowned Sparrows be found nesting, but also Canyon Wrens, Rock Wrens, and a host of other species, both eastern and western.

In addition to the mountain areas, another rough area warranting mention is the sandstone-hills region, or Cross Timbers, its boundaries not sharply defined, which occupies a large part of east-central Oklahoma and reaches across the Texas line (where it is continuous with the East and West Cross Timbers of that state) and for a short distance across the Kansas line. Fingers of the region extend eastward between the Ozarks and the Ouachita Mountains to the Arkansas line and westward into western Oklahoma as far as Cleo Springs, Camargo, the Wichita Mountains, and other points. The roughness of the region is accounted for by the sandstone hills and escarpments, whose tops and sides are scattered with loose sandstone boulders. Having only relatively dry, sandy soils, these areas support primarily a scrubby growth of post oaks, blackjack oaks, and black hickories, with a floor of short grasses. Between the hills, especially in the valleys of the larger streams, are level to rolling plains with rich clay soils producing tall grasses. Almost 75 per cent of the original woodland cover of the sandstone hills still remains, but the valley grasslands have lost most of their original character through agricultural uses.

Eastern and central Oklahoma, excepting the mountain areas and the sandstone-hills region, is essentially tall-grass prairie in which bluestem, Indian grass, switch grass, and other tall grasses predominate, with a gradual increase westward of such short grasses as buffalo and grama. Bottomlands along the larger streams are often forested with American elms, slippery elms, hackberries, various oaks, sycamores, cottonwoods, and black willows, with extensive cutover areas grown to dense tangles of weeds and shrubs. Most of the tall-grass prairie is now a thriving agricultural land.

Western Oklahoma, excluding the Panhandle and the Wichita Mountains, is on the mixed-grass plains, level to slightly rolling, with deeply eroded channels, sometimes called ravines or canyons. Merging gradually with the tall-grass prairie in the central part of the state and meeting the short-grass plains of the Great Plains in the Oklahoma and Texas Panhandles, these plains represent an area of transition. Cottonwoods and tamarisks are prevalent along the stream margins. On the floors of the deep ravines are isolated strips of forest containing trees typical of the stream bottomlands farther east, in central and eastern Oklahoma, while on the slopes and terraces of the ravines are oaks and, occasionally, junipers. Here and there, notably near the larger streams, are broad, sandy areas, sometimes with dune formations, showing wide variations in cover, from none whatsoever on live dunes to bunch grass, sand sagebrush, and thickets of plum and sumac. Toward the Oklahoma and Texas Panhandles, the sand areas support the so-called 'shinnery' grasslands, where shin oaks are intermixed with grasses, principally of the tall type. Usually the oaks are low (from 2 to 8 feet in height) and grow in mottes (clumps) on small hills of sand. In the extreme southwest (i.e. in southern Harmon and Jackson Counties) and in a few spots farther north and east are the mesquite plains, which are part of an extensive area of that name in Texas. (For a description of the mesquite plains, see the introduction to the Texas chapter.) Nearly three fourths of the western Oklahoma plains are under cultivation; the remainder, together with eroded spots and sandy areas, are used mainly for grazing when used at all.

Very different from the rest of the state is the Oklahoma Panhandle (see under Boise City), which is a strip of high Great Plains that extend northward through the continent from central Texas into Canada. The breaks along the streams and the Black Mesa in the northwestern corner are the only natural interruptions in an otherwise level, tree-less plain.

An unusual spot, ornithologically as well as geologically, is the Great Salt Plains in the extreme north-central part of the state (see under Cherokee). Here, at an elevation slightly lower than the surrounding prairie, is a vast flat, covering some 60 square miles. Part is now covered by a reservoir, but the remainder retains its original appearance—a plain of glistening white (light-colored sand with a wafer-like crust of salt). The Snowy Plover, which breeds only rarely in the interior of the United States and was first discovered nesting on the Salt Plains in 1886, is still a summer resident. Two other birds nest in this strange environment—the Least Tern and the Common Nighthawk.

Most of the breeding birds in the eastern third of Oklahoma are eastern in their affinities, a fact to be expected in view of the great extent of eastern forest and forest-edge environments. Central Oklahoma, with its stretches of scrub oaks, its wooded river bottoms, and its many tree and shrub plantations about settlements, shows a westward continuation of the same avifauna, though it lacks many species found in the forests of the Ozarks and Ouachita Mountains. The western third of Oklahoma and the Panhandle, while possessing over 50 eastern species, have nearly 20 species that are characteristically western.

Listed below are some of the species breeding regularly

in eastern and western Oklahoma (except as indicated), but not in both sections. Those marked with an asterisk extend commonly into central Oklahoma.

EASTERN OKLAHOMA

*Black Vulture (mountainous areas)
Red-shouldered Hawk
Broad-winged Hawk (northeast only)
Greater Prairie Chicken (northeast only)
*Barred Owl
Pileated Woodpecker
Acadian Flycatcher
*Eastern Wood Pewee
*White-breasted Nuthatch
*Wood Thrush
*White-eyed Vireo

Yellow-throated Vireo
Black and White Warbler
*Prothonotary Warbler
Parula Warbler
Cerulean Warbler
Yellow-throated Warbler
Pine Warbler
Prairie Warbler
Louisiana Water-thrush (also in Arbuckle Mountains)
*Kentucky Warbler
American Redstart
Scarlet Tanager
Chipping Sparrow

WESTERN OKLAHOMA (exclusive of Black Mesa country)

*Swainson's Hawk
Lesser Prairie Chicken (northwest only)
Long-billed Curlew
Burrowing Owl
Red-shafted Flicker
Ladder-backed Woodpecker

*Western Kingbird (rare eastward)
White-necked Raven
Western Meadowlark
Bullock's Oriole
Rufous-crowned Sparrow
Cassin's Sparrow

A number of species are statewide in their distribution, nesting in open country (prairie grasslands, pastures, fallow fields, meadow-like lowlands, brushy places, and dooryards) or in woodlands. Those species that breed regularly throughout Oklahoma, excluding the Panhandle, are as follows:

OPEN COUNTRY

Turkey Vulture
Marsh Hawk
Bob-white
Killdeer
Mourning Dove

Road-runner
Barn Owl
Yellow-shafted Flicker
Red-headed Woodpecker
Eastern Kingbird

Scissor-tailed Flycatcher
Eastern Phoebe (rare west-
   ward)
Horned Lark
Barn Swallow
Purple Martin (rare west-
   ward)
Bewick's Wren
Mockingbird
Catbird (rare southward)
Brown Thrasher (rare south-
   ward)
Eastern Bluebird
Loggerhead Shrike
Bell's Vireo
Yellow Warbler
Yellow-throat

Yellow-breasted Chat
Eastern Meadowlark (rare
   westward)
Red-wing
Orchard Oriole
Common Grackle
Cardinal (rare westward)
Blue Grosbeak
Indigo Bunting
Painted Bunting
Dickcissel
Common Goldfinch (rare
   westward)
Grasshopper Sparrow
Lark Sparrow
Field Sparrow

WOODLANDS

Red-tailed Hawk
Cooper's Hawk (chiefly north-
   ern Oklahoma)
Yellow-billed Cuckoo
Screech Owl
Great Horned Owl
Chuck-will's-widow
Red-bellied Woodpecker
Hairy Woodpecker
Downy Woodpecker
Crested Flycatcher

Blue Jay
Carolina Chickadee
Tufted Titmouse
Carolina Wren (rare west-
   ward)
Blue-gray Gnatcatcher
Red-eyed Vireo
Warbling Vireo
Baltimore Oriole (chiefly
   northern Oklahoma)
Summer Tanager

Spring migration in Oklahoma begins about the last week of February when the first birds appear from the south in scattered numbers. The height of landbird migration is reached during the last week of April and the first week of May, at which time the majority of north-bound flycatch-ers, warblers, and fringillids pass through the state and most of the summer-resident species arrive. The fall migra-tion of landbirds starts in late August, when most of the summer-resident species begin leaving. Although Okla-homa is in the path of the central flyway, the birds tend to pass through the state in a widely dispersed fashion, fol-lowing no particular route. Transient waterbirds, water-fowl, and shorebirds may be observed in appreciable numbers at the larger reservoirs. Here, not infrequently, the April and October flights of Franklin's Gulls are so enormous as to be a show in themselves. The many small water impoundments on farms, called 'farm ponds,' provide resting (and sometimes feeding) places for ducks and shorebirds, though the number of individuals attracted to any one pond is never very great. In Oklahoma, the main migration flights may be expected within the following dates: waterfowl, 25 February—1 April, 20 October—15 December; shorebirds, 15 April—15 May, 10 August—15 October; landbirds, 25 March—5 May, 10 September—5 November.

Fairly large populations of geese and ducks pass the winter on, or in the immediate vicinity of, the large reservoirs. Numerous species of northern landbirds, particularly fringillids, winter in the state. For example, in central Oklahoma, one may expect to find between November and April (in order of abundance) Harris' Sparrows, Slate-colored Juncos, American Tree Sparrows, White-crowned and White-throated Sparrows, Common Goldfinches, and Song Sparrows. There are also large concentrations of Robins, bluebirds, meadowlarks, and blackbirds. Cardinals, Carolina Wrens, Harris' Sparrows, and meadowlarks serve to enliven the winters by their frequent singing. In the southeastern part of the state certain species of warblers spend the winter. Christmas bird counts taken in Oklahoma areas that include large bodies of water usually indicate the presence of between 60 and 80 species.

The Oklahoma Ornithological Society, recently organized and steadily growing in membership, meets annually in different parts of the state, usually in April or May. A field trip is invariably held in conjunction with the meeting. The Society may be contacted through the Department of Zoological Sciences at the University of Oklahoma in Norman; the Department of Zoology at Oklahoma Agricultural and Mechanical College in Stillwater; or the Oklahoma Game and Fish Department in Oklahoma City.

ARNETT. The area around Arnett in extreme western Oklahoma, near the Texas Panhandle, is typical shinnery grassland, with gently rolling hills and loose sandy soils covered with grasses and scrub oaks. According to census figures obtained by the Oklahoma Game and Fish Department, the area supports a population of about 600 Lesser Prairie Chickens, the heaviest concentration of which are to be found on, or in the vicinity of, the DAVISON RANCH. Here the birds may be observed on their booming grounds early any morning between March and early June, but preferably on an early April morning, when courtship activities reach their peak.

To observe the Chickens on their booming grounds, leave Arnett an hour or so before dawn, driving south on US Route 283 for 10 miles, and taking any side road to the left. After proceeding for about a mile, locate the grounds (several are near the roads) by listening for the birds. Having determined the direction, drive the car as close as the road will permit and wait for daylight. Invariably the birds can be studied closely with field glasses from the car. One word of caution: the roads leading from Route 283 are very sandy, so have a shovel handy in case the car is stalled.

After sunup, some of the birds likely to be seen in the vicinity of the booming grounds are Mississippi Kites, Swainson's Hawks, Burrowing Owls, White-necked Ravens, Loggerhead Shrikes, and Western Meadowlarks. Watch for the Long-billed Curlew, which may be passing through in migration.

BOISE CITY. The drive westward across the Oklahoma Panhandle on US Route 64 to Boise City is a 150-mile trip over high, short-grass plains where houses are few and towns small and far apart; where winds blow constantly, piling up tumbleweeds against fences and roadside embankments and sometimes lifting up clouds of fine sand; where level horizons shimmer in the heat of the day, frequently creating peculiar mirages. It is a journey of great sameness and yet never without interest to the bird finder. The most abundant bird in any season is the Horned Lark, but in the late spring and summer Long-billed Curlews stalk across the grassy plains; Sparrow Hawks, Western Kingbirds, and Western Meadowlarks perch on wires and posts; colonies of Cliff Swallows nest in the cement culverts under the highway; Swainson's Hawks and Ferruginous Hawks soar over the plains or loiter on telephone poles; and an occasional Burrowing Owl drowses at the entrance of a prairie-dog burrow.

Westward beyond Boise City (elevation 4,164 feet) the level plains suddenly give way to a broken terrain of high mesas, dissected plateaus, gulches, and, occasionally, deep canyons. Unquestionably the choice spot for birds here is the BLACK MESA country, in the extreme northwestern corner of the Panhandle. Here, amid a mountainous setting, the breeding ranges of many eastern and western birds overlap to a remarkable degree. June, when the birds are in full song, is the best time for a visit.

To reach the Black Mesa country, proceed west from Boise City on an unnumbered road to Wheeless, then north and west to the little town of Kenton, just south of the Black Mesa and east of the New Mexico line. The distance from Boise City is 36 miles.

Kenton (elevation 4,349 feet) lies in the broad valley of the Cimarron River, which cuts through the northwestern Panhandle from New Mexico. The valley floor is distinctly plains-like, sparsely covered with grasses and clumps of cacti. Near Kenton the Cimarron is joined by two tributaries —the Carrizzos (pronounced *car'-ris-sos*) and the Tesquesquite (pronounced *tex'-a-keet*). Though usually dry, save for holes of quicksand, the Cimarron and its tributaries hold sufficient moisture to support along their banks thickets of weeds and brush and long narrow groves of such trees as cottonwoods, hackberries, and willows. This part of the Black Mesa country—the valley floor and the lower slopes of the near-by mesas—has a wide variety of breeding birds: in the thickets, or groves, the Great Horned Owl, Broad-tailed Hummingbird, Red-headed Woodpecker, Ladder-backed Woodpecker, American Magpie, Catbird, Brown Thrasher, Warbling Vireo, Brewer's Blackbird, Blue Grosbeak, Lesser Goldfinch, and Clay-colored Sparrow; on the plains and lower slopes, the Scaled Quail, Road-runner, Curve-billed Thrasher, Sage Thrasher, Western Meadowlark, Lark Sparrow, Cassin's Sparrow, and Desert Sparrow; around buildings, the Barn Swallow, Bewick's Wren, Eastern Bluebird, Mountain Bluebird, and House Finch; in gulches with boulders or rocky cliffs, the Canyon Wren,

Rock Wren, and Rufous-crowned Sparrow. Interest in the wide variety of birds here is considerably heightened by the presence of such closely allied eastern and western species as the Yellow-shafted and Red-shafted Flickers and the Baltimore and Bullock's Orioles. Finding hybrids between these species is always a possibility.

The Black Mesa rises 500 feet above the valley of the Cimarron, attaining an elevation of 4,978 feet, the highest point in the state. The Mesa may be reached by driving north from Kenton on an improved gravel road for 2 miles, turning west and proceeding as far as possible in the car, then going the rest of the way on foot. When ascending the Mesa the bird finder will climb on rocky slopes covered in part with low (4 to 5 feet high) scrubby vegetation consisting largely of hackberry mixed with live oak and juniper and also, on the north-facing slopes, with pinyon pine. Once on the Mesa's table-like top, he will enter upon a short-grass plain not unlike most of the Panhandle's surface. During the trip it will be surprising if one or two Golden Eagles do not soar into his view. On the high slopes he will find Pinyon Jays nesting and possibly the following breeding species: Poor-will, Lewis' Woodpecker, Cassin's Kingbird, Scrub Jay, Plain Titmouse, Bush-tit, Gray Vireo, and Brown Towhee. It is also possible that he will discover the Virginia's Warbler and Western Tanager occurring as summer residents.

CHEROKEE. The GREAT SALT PLAINS NATIONAL WILDLIFE REFUGE (31,129 acres), situated east of Cherokee in northwest-central Oklahoma, is surrounded by level, rich farmlands producing an abundance of wheat, corn, alfalfa, and other crops. Lying within the Refuge are the remarkable salt flats (now partially inundated by the Great Salt Plains Reservoir) and the lands immediately adjacent to them. The Reservoir covers from 10,700 acres at 'conservation-pool level' to 29,000 acres at 'flood-control level.' Twenty-two outlying small ponds cover an additional 203 acres. The major streams entering the Reservoir are the Salt Fork (two branches) of the Arkansas River and Sand Creek from the north, and Clay Creek from the west. A few marshy areas in the inlets and coves of the Reservoir,

and in the outlying ponds, support a thin growth of bulrushes, cattails, and smartweeds, but extensive marshes are
non-existent. West of the Reservoir is the best remnant of
salt-encrusted flats. Near the Refuge headquarters on the
northeast side of the Reservoir are grass-covered sand dunes
and stands of trees and shrubs, principally elm, hackberry,
cottonwood, dogwood, and wild plum. In general, the
Reservoir and the remaining salt flats are bordered by salt
grasses and, on the adjacent higher ground that is under
Refuge ownership, by long-grass prairie. Some of the
prairie is cultivated, producing wheat and other small
grains for transient waterfowl; the rest is used by local
farmers for grazing and cutting hay.

On the Refuge, the summer-resident bird that attracts
the greatest interest is the Snowy Plover, which nests on
the salt flats. Two other species nesting in the same habitat are the Least Tern and Common Nighthawk. Elsewhere on the Refuge or in the immediate vicinity, the fol-
lowing species are among those known to nest: Mississippi
Kite, Sparrow Hawk, Avocet, Red-bellied Woodpecker,
Red-headed Woodpecker, Eastern Kingbird, Western King-
bird, Scissor-tailed Flycatcher, Bewick's Wren, Carolina
Wren, Mockingbird, Brown Thrasher, Eastern Bluebird,
Bell's Vireo, Yellow-breasted Chat, Eastern Meadowlark,
Orchard Oriole, Baltimore Oriole, Cardinal, Blue Grosbeak,
Indigo Bunting, Painted Bunting, Dickcissel, and Lark
Sparrow.

Birds visiting the Refuge in considerable numbers during late summer are the White Pelican, and the American
Egret, Black-crowned Night Heron, and other herons. The
spring and fall flights of waterfowl take place between mid-
February and the first of April and between mid-October
and mid-December. Snow and Blue Geese are usually abundant. The predominant ducks in both the spring and fall
flights are Mallards, Gadwalls, Pintails, Baldpates, Green-
winged and Blue-winged Teal, and Shovelers, but the following ducks are also present: Wood Ducks, Ring-necked
Ducks, Canvas-backs, Lesser Scaup Ducks, American
Golden-eyes, Buffle-heads, and Ruddy Ducks. Perhaps the
most impressive spectacle to be witnessed on the Refuge
are the spring (April) and fall (October) flights of

Franklin's Gulls. During the winter, as many as 10,000
Canada Geese, together with a few White-fronted Geese,
remain on the area, loitering on the Reservoir and salt flats
and feeding in the near-by grainfields.

From Cherokee, it is possible to drive around the Refuge
as follows: Go north on US Route 64 to State Route 11,
turn right on Route 11, and continue 10 miles to a point one
mile beyond a series of cement bridges over branches of
the Salt Fork (Arkansas River) and Sand Creek; turn right
and follow the signs to headquarters, 2 miles distant. From
headquarters go one mile east and one mile south to Vining,
thence 2 miles east, 4 miles south, one mile west, and 3
miles south to Route 64. Turn right (west) on Route 64
and return to Cherokee. During the trip, the Reservoir,
the salt flats, and all other worth-while habitats become
readily accessible from the road. Bird finders desiring directions for locating certain species of birds should make inquiries at headquarters.

DAVIS. US Route 77 winds south from Davis through the
ARBUCKLE MOUNTAINS, an area of low, grass-covered
hills and intermittent gullies and canyons studded with red
cedar, blackjack oak, dogwood, redbud, and other trees
and shrubs. The principal ornithological feature of the
Arbuckles is the Black-capped Vireo, which is more common here than anywhere else in the state.

BLACK-CAPPED VIREO

The bird finder who wishes to search for Black-capped Vireos should, in late May or June, make his headquarters in the Arbuckles at Cedarvale (on Route 77, 6 miles south of Davis), where there are cabin accommodations. Chuck-will's-widows are remarkably common here and become vociferous after nightfall. From Route 77, one mile south of Cedarvale, a well-marked dirt road to the right leads through a gorge to Turner Falls, where Honey Creek drops 72 feet into a deep pool, and beyond to a lookout that commands a superb view of the country. Summer-resident Louisiana Water-thrushes are sometimes common along Honey Creek and other streams in the Arbuckles.

Numerous foot trails pass over the Arbuckles from Cedarvale. A walk along any one of these will bring the bird finder to the Vireo habitats—scrubby woodlands or isolated clumps of brush. Not infrequently these same habitats are also occupied by Bell's Vireos and Yellow-breasted Chats. When watching Black-capped Vireos, the bird finder should notice their rather unusual habit of hanging momentarily from the underside of a twig before dropping to the branch below. Another species to be looked for during the walk is the Rufous-crowned Sparrow.

LAWTON. In southwestern Oklahoma, the WICHITA MOUNTAINS WILDLIFE REFUGE (59,099 acres) encompasses the higher Wichitas and a wide interior valley. Included in the Refuge is Mt. Scott, the highest point (2,467 feet). About two thirds of the area consists of hills studded with hardwoods, primarily post and blackjack oaks; the remaining third comprises prairie and 659 acres of water (17 lakes and about 50 ponds) in rocky basins, mainly behind man-made dams. The bluestem and associated grasses that thrive on the prairie form one of the finest examples of long-grass prairie sod remaining on the continent. Extensive marshes are lacking, but the larger lakes have their marshy fringes producing cattails and pondweeds. Standing on the banks of many of the lowland streams are American elms, white ashes, spotted oaks, hackberries, black walnuts, and other woody growth requiring a moist environment.

The area that is now the Wichita Mountains Refuge was proclaimed a Federal game preserve in 1905 by President

Theodore Roosevelt, the primary purpose being to perpetu-
ate suitable habitat for the bison, then in great danger of
extinction. Its present name was acquired in 1935, when
it was placed under the administration of the U.S. Fish and
Wildlife Service. Today the Refuge has a herd of more than
700 bison. It is also a preserve for elk, white-tailed deer,
pronghorn antelope, long-horned cattle, and prairie-dog
towns, and is one of the most productive bird-finding areas
in southwest Oklahoma. Approximately half of the Refuge
is open to the public; there are good roads (including the
winding, scenic highway to the summit of Mt. Scott), well-
marked foot trails, and excellent camping and picnicking
facilities.

Some of the best spots for birds are in the southwestern
part of the Refuge: for example, the area around headquarters and the vicinity of Sunset Camp. Here both Canyon and Rock Wrens are heard singing from April to July.
Other breeding birds that may be observed here at this
same time of year include the Great Blue Heron, Turkey
Vulture, Red-tailed Hawk, Bob-white, Wild Turkey, Killdeer, Mourning Dove, Yellow-billed Cuckoo, Screech Owl,
Chuck-will's-widow, Downy Woodpecker, Western Kingbird, Scissor-tailed Flycatcher (common), Crested Flycatcher, Eastern Phoebe, Eastern Wood Pewee, Barn
Swallow, White-necked Raven, Carolina Chickadee, Tufted
Titmouse, Bewick's Wren, Carolina Wren, Mockingbird,
Eastern Bluebird, Red-eyed Vireo, Western Meadowlark,
Red-wing, Summer Tanager, Cardinal, Painted Bunting
(common), Dickcissel, Lark Sparrow, Rufous-crowned
Sparrow, and Chipping Sparrow. A few Road-runners are
permanent residents in the vicinity and are occasionally seen
by the lucky bird finder.

About the middle of September and again about the
tenth of February, migrating ducks begin to appear at the
Refuge, stopping on the larger lakes. These include nearly
all the species commonly using the central flyway and, in
addition, a few American Golden-eyes, Buffle-heads, and
Hooded Mergansers. Occasionally in both spring and fall
there are large flocks of Robins and, more rarely, small flocks
of Long-billed Curlews and Upland Plovers. For a few days
in early November spectacular flights of Mississippi Kites

are often observed. During open winters the Refuge has a fairly large concentration of Chestnut-collared Longspurs.

The Refuge may be reached from Lawton by driving north through Fort Sill on US Route 281 to State Route 49. Turn left on Route 49 and follow it past Medicine Park to a point 8 miles beyond the eastern boundary of the Refuge, then turn right on a road leading northwest directly to headquarters. Sunset Camp can be reached by a road leading southwest from headquarters. For the bird finders unprepared for camping, there are overnight accommodations available at Medicine Park, Craterville Park, and Lawton.

MADILL. The UNIVERSITY OF OKLAHOMA BIO-LOGICAL STATION, a summer field station on the north shore of the Red River arm of Lake Texoma, offers course work and opportunities for graduate research in ornithology. It is easily reached by driving south from Madill on State Route 99 to Willis, then east for 2 miles on a gravel road. The Station operates for eight weeks, beginning early in June. The mailing address is Willis, Oklahoma.

The region surrounding the Station consists largely of tall-grass prairie with intervening woodlands containing blackjack and post oaks. Bottomlands along the streams that empty into Lake Texoma, farmlands, farm ponds, and marginal wet lands lend variety. Opportunities for ornithological research are particularly inviting in at least two respects: (1) the birdlife of the region has not been thoroughly investigated, and (2) the effects that Lake Texoma—a new reservoir filled to power-pool level as recently as 1945—has had on breeding and transient birds have not been determined. The great number and variety of migrating herons and shorebirds on the mud flats of the fluctuating shoreline are impressive.

NORMAN. For many years the UNIVERSITY OF OK-LAHOMA has encouraged ornithological investigations throughout the state. At least one formal course in ornithology is offered each year. Advanced courses, Investigations in Ornithology and Birds of the World, are intended primarily for graduate students. In the bird range, where all of these courses are given, are about 10,000 bird skins, 800 mounts, and a good working library. The collection of Mexican birds is notable.

Ornithology students working at the University have many good places to visit. Beyond the outskirts of the city are extensive prairie areas which, though cultivated for the most part, contain many farm ponds and pastures. To the south and west are woodlands bordering the South Canadian River. Perhaps the most frequently visited place is OLIVER'S WOODS, a 60-acre tract comprising woodland, swamp, and meadows. This can be reached by driving south out of Norman on Chautauqua Street for 2 miles. Landbirds that may always be expected in this area in the summer are the Yellow-billed Cuckoo, Red-bellied Woodpecker, Red-headed Woodpecker, Scissor-tailed Flycatcher, Eastern Wood Pewee, Carolina Chickadee, Bell's Vireo, Orchard Oriole, Summer Tanager, Blue Grosbeak, Indigo Bunting, and Painted Bunting.

OKLAHOMA CITY. This capital city, the name of which has become almost synonymous with oil, lies on the undulating plain where the remnants of the blackjack and post-oak woodlands meet the tall-grass prairies. Two large reservoirs attract sizable aggregations of waterbirds and waterfowl during the fall, winter, and spring.

LAKE OVERHOLSER (1,700 acres), reached by driving 8 miles west of the city on US Route 66, has large numbers of transient Pied-billed Grebes, Double-crested Cormorants, Great Blue Herons, Canada Geese, Snow Geese, Blue Geese, Mallards, Pintails, Shovelers, Redheads, Canvas-backs, Lesser Scaup Ducks, Ruddy Ducks, American Mergansers, Coots, Ring-billed Gulls, Franklin's Gulls, Least Terns, and Black Terns. In addition, when the water level is low in August and September, it has numerous shorebirds.

LAKE HEFNER (3,500 acres), 6 miles northwest of the city, is reached by driving west on Route 66 to May Avenue, turning right on May Avenue and left on Northwest Highway, from which the Lake can be seen stretching to the north. Any of the gravel roads on the right of the Highway will lead to a roadway that completely encircles the Lake. Flocks of White Pelicans come here occasionally in migration about the last of April and the first of October. The shallow, muddy shoreline attracts a good many shore-birds, among them the Killdeer, Greater and Lesser Yellow-legs, Pectoral Sandpiper, White-rumped Sandpiper, Least Sandpiper, Semipalmated Sandpiper, and, occasionally, the Wilson's Phalarope. The waterbirds and waterfowl commonly seen on Lake Overholser also occur here.

A good place for small landbirds throughout the year is LINCOLN PARK (640 acres), a city recreational area, with low hills partly covered with trees and shrubs. A small lake, a zoo, and the several footpaths increase its attractiveness to the visitor. Some of the common birds that may be looked for in and around the Park are the Yellow-billed Cuckoo, Red-bellied Woodpecker, Western Kingbird, Scissor-tailed Flycatcher, Eastern Wood Pewee, Blue-gray Gnatcatcher, Bell's Vireo, Baltimore Oriole, Summer Tanager, and Lark Sparrow. To reach the area, drive north and east from the city on US Route 62 and turn north on State Route 14, which borders the western side of the Park.

PONCA CITY. The country around this oil center in north-central Oklahoma is gently undulating plain with grain and alfalfa fields and patches of scrub-oak woods. When the roads pass near alfalfa fields that adjoin wooded areas, watch in the summer for both Yellow-billed and Black-billed Cuckoos. The birds may be seen perched on telephone and fence wires, from which they swoop down into the fields in quest of the caterpillars that forage on the alfalfa.

The best area for birds in Ponca City is LAKE PONCA PARK. Lake Ponca, a two-armed reservoir, which is the source of water supply for Ponca City, attracts numerous waterbirds and waterfowl in both spring and fall. The somewhat forested northern part of the Park, and the wooded banks of the Arkansas River east of the Park, should yield, in late spring and summer, a list of birds including the Yellow-shafted Flicker, Red-bellied Woodpecker, Tufted Titmouse, Bewick's Wren, Carolina Wren, Mockingbird, Brown Thrasher, Eastern Bluebird, Baltimore Oriole, and Orchard Oriole.

To reach Lake Ponca Park, drive north from the center of the city on US Route 77 to the Pioneer Woman Statue, turn right on Lake Ponca Road (L.A. Cann Drive) for 2 miles, go left for $\frac{1}{8}$ mile, then turn right and drive one mile, on a winding road.

STILLWATER. OKLAHOMA AGRICULTURAL AND MECHANICAL COLLEGE is in Stillwater, which lies in north-central Oklahoma at a meeting point of tall-grass prairie and scrub-oak woods. Course work relating to birds, centered in the Life Sciences Building, consist of General Ornithology, stressing the classification, identification, distribution, life histories, and conservation of common birds; Wildlife Conservation; and Animal Ecology. Ornithological materials for study purposes include 300 skins and 200 mounts. The College library contains the standard works on birds and sets of the leading ornithological periodicals.

The best place for birds near Stillwater, and the one most frequently visited by bird students, is the LAKE CARL BLACKWELL AREA, a 21,000-acre tract administered by the College. This includes fine stretches of tall-grass prairie and 3,300-acre Lake Carl Blackwell, a water impoundment. Much of the prairie, at the present time subject to a varying degree of experimental grazing, is dissected by timbered ravines and interspersed with patches of oak woods, resulting in a vegetative pattern that is ideal for a wide variety of birds. Nesting species include the Red-tailed Hawk, Marsh Hawk, Mourning Dove, Chuck-will's-widow, Eastern and Western Kingbirds, Crested Flycatcher, Scissor-tailed Flycatcher, Bewick's and Carolina Wrens, Mockingbird, Brown Thrasher, Bell's Vireo, Cardinal, Blue Grosbeak, Painted Bunting, Lark Sparrow, and Field Sparrow. Common during migration, or in winter, are the Snow Goose, Franklin's Gull, Red-shafted Flicker, Spotted Towhee, Common Goldfinch, Slate-colored Junco, American Tree and Harris' Sparrows, and Lapland Longspur. To reach the Area from Stillwater, drive west on State Route 51 for 9 miles, then approximately 2.5 miles north, to the shore of Lake Carl Blackwell. Roads and trails lead around the Lake to many parts of the Area, most of which are open to the public.

TISHOMINGO. Part of the Washita Arm of Lake Texoma, the huge reservoir formed by the Denison Dam across the Red River, is occupied by the TISHOMINGO NATIONAL WILDLIFE REFUGE (13,449 acres). Roughly two thirds of the Refuge consists of the open water of the Lake and its marshy shore. Because the water level fluctuates greatly, typical marsh conditions cannot be permanently established; nevertheless, extensive shoreline plantings of emergent aquatics, such as smartweed and wild millet, provide food that is attractive to ducks. The remaining third of the Refuge is upland—the river-valley terrain lying above the water level. Here there are high hills, heavily forested in places, and numerous small valleys, where creeks flow into Lake Texoma. In the north-central part are flat, open areas, formerly farmlands, now planted with peanuts and various grains for waterfowl.

The principal ornithological attractions in the Tishomingo Refuge are the hordes of waterbirds, geese, and ducks that gather in the late summer and fall. During August and September Great Blue Herons, American Egrets, and Snowy Egrets are especially numerous. By September large numbers of Double-crested Cormorants, Coots, and Franklin's Gulls begin to appear, reaching their peaks of abundance in early October. Frequently the concentrations of Franklin's Gulls are spectacular; on one October day recently, as many as 30,000 individuals were estimated. From September to December the following species of waterfowl appear on the Refuge: Canada Goose, White-fronted Goose, Snow Goose, Blue Goose, Mallard, Black Duck, Gadwall, Baldpate, Pintail, Green-winged Teal, Blue-winged Teal, Shoveler, Wood Duck, Redhead, Ring-necked Duck, Canvas-back, Lesser Scaup Duck, American Golden-eye, Buffle-head, Ruddy Duck, Hooded Merganser, and American Merganser.

At the peak of abundance in November, the duck population usually amounts to at least 65,000 individuals, of which 40,000 are Mallards; the goose population varies from 5,000 to 10,000 individuals, most of which are Canada and Snow Geese. A great many of the waterfowl remain on the Refuge through the winter.

The Tishomingo Refuge is 3 miles southeast from the

eastern edge of the town of Tishomingo. To reach the
Refuge, leave State Route 22 at the edge of town on a
gravel road that leads directly to Refuge headquarters.
Most parts of the Refuge are accessible by road or trail, but
permission and directions for using them should first be
obtained at headquarters. Tables, benches, fireplaces, and
other picnicking facilities are available in an area adjacent
to headquarters.

TULSA. The great oil refineries, modern skyscrapers, fine
suburban homes, and tree-shaded parks of this big municipality occupy the rolling terrain on the east side of the
Arkansas River in northeastern Oklahoma. In the opinion
of the members of the Tulsa Audubon Society, 2,400-acre
MOHAWK PARK, northeast of the city, surpasses all other
areas in or close to Tulsa for bird finding. Although it is
a popular playground, with Recreation Lake (for boating),
a zoo, and numerous picnic grounds, it has relatively undisturbed forested and shrub-covered tracts where landbirds abound in all seasons, and an 80-acre lake attractive
to waterbirds and waterfowl. Such areas are readily accessible by foot trails.

Mohawk Park may be reached from the center of Tulsa
by driving north and east on US Route 169 for about 8
miles, then turning right into the Park on a hard-surfaced
road that leads to the zoo, 1.5 miles distant.

The Tulsa Audubon Society, which may be contacted
through the Central Public Library or the Chamber of
Commerce, sponsors a series of public lectures and conducts numerous field trips in all seasons of the year to
local bird-finding areas.

WILBURTON. On the western edge of the Ouachita Mountains, in a rugged, semi-wilderness area rich in Indian history and legends of outlaws, lies ROBBERS CAVE STATE
PARK, part of an 8,400-acre forest game preserve. A clear
mountain stream, Fourche Maline Creek, cuts through the
Park on an eastward course, forming a picturesque gorge
flanked by high sandstone-limestone cliffs. The surrounding hills and bluffs, ranging in height from 300 to 1,500
feet, are characteristically wooded, steep, and rough with

loose slabs of stone. Common trees are the short-leaf pine, red cedar, black walnut, hickories (scaly bark, white, and pignut), oaks (blackjack, post, and white), elms (American, winged, and slippery), river birch, sugar maple, hackberry, black locust, and sycamore. Shrubs of many kinds (buttonbush, sumac, hawthorn, wild rose, blackberry, and spicebush) grow luxuriantly.

The Park entrance is 4.2 miles north of Wilburton on State Route 2, which runs through the Park. Two miles north of the entrance, on the left of Route 2, is Lake Carlton (52 acres), formed by damming the Fourche Maline Creek. Near the Lake are recreational facilities that include overnight cabins and campgrounds. Four miles farther north, across Fourche Maline Creek, in the center of the Park, is a Boy Scout Camp; just north of it, under an overhanging sandstone cliff, is a deep recess from which the Park gets its name.

Wild Turkeys have been recently introduced in the Park. Lake Carlton attracts a few transient waterbirds and waterfowl in the spring and fall, but the best bird finding is in April and early May, when the landbird migration takes place, and later, in June, when the nesting season is well under way. Some of the birds that should be found breeding in the Park are the Red-tailed Hawk, Red-shouldered Hawk, Barred Owl, Chuck-will's-widow, Crested Flycatcher, Acadian Flycatcher, Eastern Wood Pewee, Blue Jay, Carolina Wren, Mockingbird, Brown Thrasher, Wood Thrush, Eastern Bluebird, White-eyed Vireo, Parula Warbler, Yellow-throated Warbler, Pine Warbler, Kentucky Warbler, Yellow-breasted Chat, American Redstart, Orchard Oriole, Summer Tanager, Blue Grosbeak, Indigo Bunting, Common Goldfinch, Chipping Sparrow, and Field Sparrow.

Contributing authorities: Ernest E. Allen, Frederick M. Baumgartner, Mrs. Marguerite H. Baumgartner, G. B. Bristow, Earl W. Craven, Joe C. Creager, David J. Edwards, John E. Galley, Mrs. John E. (Margret) Galley, Ernest J. Greenwalt, Julian A. Howard, Wallace Hughes, Glenn E. Jones, Orrin W. Letson, Juanita Mahaffey, Carl D. Riggs, C. A. Shockley, George Miksch Sutton, John B. Van den Akker.

Oregon

BY ROBERT M. STORM

TRUMPETER SWAN

It can be said that ornithology was introduced into Oregon when the explorers Meriwether Lewis and William Clark recorded in their journals their impressions of the Oregon country. They reached the headwaters of the Columbia River in October 1805, and worked their way down, amid endless hardships, to arrive at its mouth in November. Here, on the south bank near the present city of Astoria, they built a crude log fort where they passed the winter. On

2 January 1806, they took time from the arduous task of hunting food to write the following in their journal:

The birds which most strike our attention are the large as well as the small or whistling swan, the sandhill crane, the large and small geese, cormorants, brown and white brant, duckauinmallard, the canvass and several other species of ducks. There is also a small crow, the blue crested corvus, and the smaller corvus with a white breast, the little brown wren, a large brown sparrow, the bald eagle, and the beautiful buzzard of the Columbia.

The 'beautiful buzzard of the Columbia' (the California Condor) is gone from the Columbia and from all of Oregon, and the 'large swan' (Trumpeter Swan) may now be seen only in the Malheur National Wildlife Refuge (see under Burns). But the winter bird finder in the Astoria region will still find notable concentrations of wintering waterfowl, as well as the permanent residents of adjacent coniferous forests.

Winter concentrations of waterfowl occur throughout the more than 400 miles of Oregon coastline and in the main valleys of western Oregon; nesting waterfowl collect in impressive numbers on the large alkaline lakes in the southeastern part of the state.

The 96,000 square miles of the state of Oregon are cut into sections by various mountain ranges, the highest of these being the Cascades. Several peaks exceed 10,000 feet; Mt. Hood in the extreme north reaches 11,245 feet, the highest point in the state. About 100 miles inland, the Cascades parallel the coast from the Columbia River, at the northern boundary, to the California line, thus dividing the state into a western section, comprising about one third of the state's area, and an eastern section, which covers the remaining two thirds. West of the Cascades, the climate of Oregon is tempered by prevailing westerly winds from the Pacific Ocean. Winter temperatures are unusually mild for so northern a latitude, and winter rainfall is heavy. The result is luxuriant forest vegetation in most areas, accompanied by birds typical of such a habitat. Much of eastern Oregon lies in the rain shadow of the Cascades, so that rainfall is greatly reduced (to 20 inches or less). The climate here is more subject to influences from the interior of the continent, and low temperatures are the rule during the winter. Much of this part of the state supports only sagebrush or similar sparse vegetation, and the birdlife mirrors this difference in climate and plant cover.

The picture is interrupted in the northeast, however, by the Blue Mountains, which extend southwestward almost to the Cascades from the Rocky Mountains, with which they are contiguous. The highest and most scenic of the Blue Mountains form a group, the Wallowa Mountains, which attain elevations between 9,000 and 10,000 feet.

The mountains of western Oregon form a U. The eastern arm of the U includes the Cascades; the western arm is formed by the lower Coast Range. The average elevation of the Coast Range is 2,000 feet, with the highest point Marys Peak (4,097 feet). These coastal mountains stand very close to the sea, leaving only narrow beaches, or none at all, and a few good harbors such as Coos, Yaquina, Tillamook, and Astoria Bays. The base of the U is disproportionately thick, and is made up of hills running roughly east to west and of higher ridges. The most impressive of these cross-ranges are the Siskiyou Mountains, at the California line; their maximum elevation—reached by Siskiyou Peak —is 7,662 feet. The cross-ranges are interrupted by rivercourses, some of which have formed agriculturally important valleys, such as the Rogue River and Umpqua River Valleys. Between the arms of the U is the well-known Willamette Valley, a relatively flat agricultural area, extending 130 miles south from the Columbia River, and averaging 30 miles in width. The state's largest cities—Portland, Salem, and Eugene—lie along the Willamette River, which rises in the Cascades north of Crater Lake and flows north to join the Columbia.

Of great convenience to the bird finder is US Route 101, which follows the coastline from Washington to California. Throughout the length of the Oregon coastline, huge rocky headlands, such as Capes Arago, Lookout, and Meares, jut into the sea and furnish, together with offshore islands, nesting sites for a multitude of seabirds, including the Fork-tailed and Leach's Petrels, Double-crested Cormorant, Brandt's Cormorant, Pelagic Cormorant, Black Oyster-catcher, Western Gull, Common Murre, Pigeon Guillemot, Cassin's Auklet, and Tufted Puffin. Other birds, such as the Common Loon, Brown Pelican, White-winged Scoter, Surf Scoter, and Marbled Murrelet, find feeding grounds or refuge in these waters. One species, the Snowy Plover, is a permanent resident of the sand beaches. Bald Eagles may frequently be seen feeding along the beaches or resting on some weather-beaten snag just back of the beach. They usually nest in high conifers (e.g. Douglas fir) a mile or so back in the hills from the beach. The vigilant observer can usually spot an Osprey, particularly in the vicinity of the bays. This is also a favorable area for the Common Raven, which finds adequate food in the carrion of various sorts that washes onto the beaches.

Immediately adjacent to some of the open beaches is a narrow strip, usually not more than a mile or two in width, much of which is given over to very dense areas of shrubby growth, salal, shot huckleberry, wax-myrtle, salmonberry, kinnikinnick, hairy manzanita, and rhododendron. The Wren-tit is practically confined to this strip in all but south-western Oregon, and a considerable list of species that prefer brushy habitats can also be encountered. In addition, there are scattered trees and extensive pure stands of lodgepole pine and Sitka spruce, in which Red Crossbills are often common.

The strip merges into the great fir-hemlock forests that cover so much of western Oregon. Typically, before the advent of lumbering, these forests were dominated by splendid forest giants, Douglas fir and western hemlock, with a liberal sprinkling of grand fir and western red cedar, but such mature stands are rapidly being depleted. A recently denuded area is first invaded by such plants as bracken fern, grasses, and various annuals. In a few years, shrubs and deciduous trees take over, and the area is gradually invaded by conifers. Traveling through the coast forest, the bird finder passes through all stages of this suc-cession and the great variety of bird habitats provided. The following bird species may be expected to breed in the coniferous forests of the Coast Range and higher cross-ranges and on the west slopes of the Cascades up to about 5,500 feet.

Goshawk
Blue Grouse
Band-tailed Pigeon
Great Horned Owl
Pygmy Owl
Pileated Woodpecker
Hairy Woodpecker
Hammond's Flycatcher (except Coast Range)
Olive-sided Flycatcher
Steller's Jay
Chestnut-backed Chickadee
Red-breasted Nuthatch

Brown Creeper
Winter Wren
Varied Thrush
Olive-backed Thrush
Golden-crowned Kinglet
Audubon's Warbler
Hermit Warbler
Western Tanager
Evening Grosbeak
Purple Finch
Pine Siskin
Red Crossbill
Oregon Junco

The Willamette Valley and the other large valleys west of the Cascades contain diverse habitats for birds. In addition to extensive farmlands (fields, pastures, orchards, vineyards) are deciduous trees and shrubs growing abundantly along watercourses and roadsides, in city parks and dooryards, and on the adjacent foothills. Among the birds to be expected regularly during the breeding season in the open country (farmlands and shrubby places) and in the more undisturbed wooded areas are the following:

OPEN COUNTRY

Turkey Vulture
Killdeer
California Quail
Mourning Dove
Rufous Hummingbird
Horned Lark
Barn Swallow
Bush-tit
House Wren
Bewick's Wren
Western Bluebird
Orange-crowned Warbler
Nashville Warbler
Yellow Warbler

Macgillivray's Warbler
Yellow-throat
Yellow-breasted Chat
Black-capped Warbler
Western Meadowlark
Lazuli Bunting
Common Goldfinch
Lesser Goldfinch
Spotted Towhee
Savannah Sparrow
Vesper Sparrow
Chipping Sparrow
White-crowned Sparrow
Song Sparrow

WOODED AREAS

Ruffed Grouse
Screech Owl
Red-shafted Flicker

Common Sapsucker
Hairy Woodpecker
Downy Woodpecker

Western Flycatcher	Solitary Vireo
Western Wood Pewee	Warbling Vireo
Black-capped Chickadee	Bullock's Oriole
Olive-backed Thrush	Black-headed Grosbeak

As one travels eastward out of the Willamette Valley and upward into the high Cascades the heavy timber of Douglas fir and western hemlock gives way, at an altitude of 5,500 feet, to a forest of lodgepole pine, western white pine, Engelmann spruce, and silver fir. This is replaced, beginning at 6,000 feet or less, by subalpine forest in which the dominant trees are the alpine fir, mountain hemlock, and (especially at the timber line) the whitebark pine. In these coniferous forests of the high Cascades occur regularly such breeding birds as the Black-backed Woodpecker, Canada Jay, Clark's Nutcracker, Mountain Chickadee, Hermit Thrush, Townsend's Solitaire, Ruby-crowned Kinglet, and Red Crossbill. Where willows and aspens grow about streams and lakes at these high elevations, the White-crowned and Lincoln's Sparrows may be found. Above the timber line, the elevation of which ranges from 6,000 to 7,000 feet according to slope and exposure, is an alpine region of scant vegetation—the summer home of the American Pipit and Gray-crowned Rosy Finch. Throughout the high Cascades of Oregon are a multitude of mountain lakes, varying greatly in size, which attract Barrow's Golden-eyes for nesting purposes, while along the swift streams coming down from the mountains nest Dippers and a few Harlequin Ducks.

On the eastern slope of the Cascades, below the forest of lodgepole pine, western white pine, Engelmann spruce, and silver fir, the vegetation changes rather abruptly to park-like stands of ponderosa pine forming a wide belt in which the following birds are characteristic: Williamson's Sapsucker, Hairy Woodpecker, White-headed Woodpecker, White-breasted Nuthatch, Pygmy Nuthatch, Evening Grosbeak, Cassin's Finch, and Red Crossbill. At its lower edge the pine belt merges with the juniper woodland, of which the western juniper is the principal constituent. Breeding birds typical of this environment are the Ash-throated Flycatcher, Pinyon Jay, and Black-throated Gray Warbler. Below the juniper woodland begins the sagebrush country.

East of the Cascades, ponderosa pine clothes the slopes of

mountains and foothills at similar elevations. The juniper woodland is not generally so noticeable and is sometimes absent. On slopes where it is lacking, pine and sagebrush meet and intermingle, forming a habitat in which the Green-tailed Towhee is a common nesting bird. The high Blue and Wallowa Mountains in the northeast show a vertical succession of vegetation from sagebrush to alpine region that is essentially the same as that on the eastern slope of the Cascades. Numerous breeding birds here are racially distinct from the birds of the Cascades and coastal mountains, and there are a few of different species (for example, the Franklin's Grouse occurs only in the Wallowas); nevertheless most of the species are identical with those of the Cascades and coastal ranges.

The sagebrush country comprises much of eastern Oregon below the pine belt, or (east of the Cascades) below the juniper woodland. Here the most conspicuous and widespread plant is the sagebrush, but where there are alkaline soils such shrubs as greasewood and rabbitbrush thrive. In the sagebrush country, the following nesting birds may be regularly expected:

Red-tailed Hawk	Western Kingbird
Swainson's Hawk	Say's Phoebe
Ferruginous Hawk	Gray Flycatcher
Golden Eagle	Horned Lark
Prairie Falcon	American Magpie
Sharp-tailed Grouse (northern part)	Common Raven
	Sage Thrasher
Sage Grouse	Mountain Bluebird
Mountain Quail	Loggerhead Shrike
Mourning Dove	Lark Sparrow
Burrowing Owl	Sage Sparrow
Poor-will	Brewer's Sparrow

The sagebrush habitat is interrupted by streams and rivers, with a typical riparian association of deciduous brush and trees. Birds inhabiting these situations are quite similar to those in like situations in western Oregon, although there are fewer species. Two conspicuous breeding birds of deciduous growths near streams or around ranch buildings in eastern Oregon are the Eastern Kingbird and House

Finch. In northeastern Oregon, riparian situations of this type bring eastern forms such as the Catbird, Red-eyed Vireo, and American Redstart into the state.

Finally, there occur in southeastern Oregon vast marshy areas, those in the Malheur Lake and Upper Klamath National Wildlife Refuges (see under Burns and Klamath Falls) being the most famous examples. The total area of all the marshes has been greatly diminished by drainage for agriculture, but there remain adequate marshlands to furnish nesting and feeding grounds to great numbers of waterfowl, shorebirds, and marshbirds. The following birds may be expected as regular summer inhabitants of these immense marshes:

Eared Grebe	Marsh Hawk
Western Grebe	Sandhill Crane (limited areas)
Pied-billed Grebe	Sora
White Pelican	Willet
Double-crested Cormorant	Avocet
Great Blue Heron	Black-necked Stilt
American Egret	Wilson's Phalarope
Black-crowned Night Heron	California Gull
American Bittern	Ring-billed Gull
Least Bittern	Forster's Tern
White-faced Ibis	Caspian Tern
Canada Goose	Black Tern
Mallard	Long-billed Marsh Wren
Gadwall	Yellow-throat
Pintail	Yellow-headed Blackbird
Cinnamon Teal	Red-wing
Shoveler	Tricolored Blackbird (Klamath
Redhead	marshes)
Ruddy Duck	

Landbird migrations in Oregon are seldom spectacular and can be very disappointing to one accustomed to the more regular routes and timetable arrivals of the east and midwest, but the flights of waterbirds, waterfowl, and shorebirds are always impressive, in both numbers of species and numbers of individuals. Two main routes are utilized. The majority of waterfowl pass through eastern Oregon, stopping to rest and feed in the large lake and marsh areas of Malheur,

Abert, Summer, Goose, Warner, and Klamath. Practically all of the waterfowl species of the North American continent can be encountered along this route during the migration season, including the Whistling Swan, Canada Goose, White-fronted Goose, Snow Goose, Ross' Goose, and Cinnamon Teal. Several shorebirds also use this inland route, but the greatest number of shorebirds are to be encountered on the coastal route, particularly the Wandering Tattler (on exposed rocks), and (on sandy beaches or mud flats) the Semipalmated Plover, Black-bellied Plover, Ruddy Turnstone, Hudsonian Curlew, Baird's Sandpiper, Least Sandpiper, Red-backed Sandpiper, Dowitcher, Western Sandpiper, and the Northern Phalarope. An Oregon migration timetable would run somewhat as follows: *Eastern Oregon.* For waterfowl, 15 March—20 April; 10 October—25 November; for shorebirds, 1 May—1 June, 1 August—1 October. *Coastal Oregon.* For waterfowl, 1 March—15 April, 1 October—1 December; for shorebirds, 10 April—10 May, 20 July—1 November.

As mentioned earlier, western Oregon winters are mild, and winter visitants include a number of waterbird and waterfowl species; several shorebirds, such as the Surf-bird, Black Turnstone, and Rock Sandpiper, which frequent the coastal rocks, and the Black-bellied Plover, Red-backed Sandpiper, and Sanderling, which prefer sandy beaches or mud flats; the Golden-crowned Sparrow and several subspecies of the Hermit Thrush, Fox Sparrow and Song Sparrow. In addition, almost all of the summer birds that feed on seeds, pupae, earthworms, et cetera remain in Oregon during the winter, moving to the valleys from their mountain breeding grounds when this becomes necessary. The birds that depart from western Oregon during the winter are for the most part those that feed on living insects. The Duck Hawk is a regular (although rather uncommon) winter visitor to the Oregon coast, where it finds an easy food supply among the many waterfowl, waterbirds, and shorebirds wintering there. For similar reasons, the Pigeon Hawk visits the coast in winter. The following is a list of waterbirds and waterfowl that one can reasonably expect to see during the winter in bays and harbors and other protected waters inshore:

Common Loon	Lesser Scaup Duck
Arctic Loon	American Golden-eye
Red-throated Loon	Barrow's Golden-eye
Holboell's Grebe	Buffle-head
Horned Grebe	Harlequin Duck
Eared Grebe	White-winged Scoter
Western Grebe	Surf Scoter
Double-crested Cormorant	American Scoter
Brandt's Cormorant	Ruddy Duck
Pelagic Cormorant	Hooded Merganser
Canada Goose	Red-breasted Merganser
Black Brant	Coot
Mallard	Glaucous-winged Gull
Gadwall	Western Gull
Baldpate	Herring Gull
Pintail	California Gull
Green-winged Teal	Ring-billed Gull
Ring-necked Duck	Short-billed Gull
Canvas-back	Common Murre
Greater Scaup Duck	Marbled Murrelet

Winter visitants in the lowlands of eastern Oregon are quite similar to those encountered in the northern Great Plains: Rough-legged Hawk, Snowy Owl, American Pipit, Bohemian Waxwing, Northern Shrike, Gray-crowned Rosy Finch, and Snow Bunting.

BANDON. On the southwestern coast is one of the most beautiful beaches in Oregon. Just offshore lie huge rocks with nesting colonies of gulls and alcids that can be observed from the mainland. The beach extends south from Bandon, which is on US Route 101. A good place to observe the offshore colonies is COQUILLE POINT. US Route 101, entering Bandon from the east, makes a broad curve to the south within the city limits. Three blocks south of the southern end of the curve, a road going west leads to a dead end, one mile distant. From here, trails go out to the Point, where there is a Coast Guard lookout.

Breeding birds to be looked for on and around the rocks are the Leach's Petrel, Double-crested and Pelagic Cormorants, Black Oyster-catcher, Western Gull, Common Murre, Pigeon Guillemot, and Tufted Puffin. In addition, the following non-breeding birds can usually be observed during the summer on or over the rocks and water: the Sooty Shear-water, White-winged and Surf Scoters, Glaucous-winged Gull, and Marbled Murrelet.

BEND. This lumbering and recreational center, once the home of Klondike Kate, is in central Oregon on the east slope of the Cascades. Scenic mountains rise on the west, the snow-capped Three Sisters (elevation over 10,000 feet) towering over the lesser peaks; to the north and east stretches a vast area of lava rocks, junipers, and sagebrush.

For profitable bird finding, proceed north on US Route 20 from Bend (elevation 3,629 feet) to Sisters, then travel west (straight ahead) on US Route 126 at the west edge of Sisters. Route 126 (open from 1 June into October) goes over the Cascades via McKENZIE PASS. Between Bend and Sisters, much of the route is through juniper country. Here breed such birds as the Pygmy Owl, Ash-throated Flycatcher, American Magpie, Pinyon Jay, Rock Wren, Black-throated Gray Warbler, and Green-tailed Towhee. Westward from Sisters, the vegetation for many miles is largely ponderosa-pine forest. The Williamson's Sapsucker, Hairy Woodpecker, White-headed Woodpecker, Red-breasted Nuthatch, Pygmy Nuthatch, Western Tanager, Evening Grosbeak, Cassin's Finch, Red Crossbill, and Ore-gon Junco should be looked for in this environment.

As one approaches McKenzie Pass, the ponderosa pine gives way rapidly to the smaller firs, hemlocks, and lodge-pole pines of the higher areas. Look for Varied Thrushes here. At the Pass are extensive and comparatively recent lava flows, which are almost devoid of vegetation.

Six miles west of McKenzie Pass, a gravel road leads off to the right (west at this point) to small SCOTT LAKE, a very attractive example of the many lakes in these moun-tains. This road is usually blocked with snow until about 1 July. There is a picnic area and campground at the edge of the Lake, between the water and the extensive subalpine forest. Here, amid the conifers, the Canada and Steller's Jays may be seen stealing food from the picnic tables, and Clark's Nutcrackers may be heard calling overhead. Other birds to be watched for are the Barrow's Golden-eye, Com-mon Raven, Mountain Chickadee, Hermit Thrush, Townsend's Solitaire, Golden-crowned Kinglet, Red Crossbill, Oregon Junco, and Lincoln's Sparrow.

From Scott Lake, there is a good view of the Three Sisters, which lie to the southeast. The adventuresome bird finder will enjoy taking a day to hike south on the Oregon Skyline Trail, which starts at Frog Camp (reached by turning left from Route 126, one mile south of the Scott Lake turnoff) and winds through lava beds and the stunted, subalpine forest.

Route 126 west from the Pass drops down into the Willamette Valley, leading through some of the most magnificent Douglas-fir timber to be seen in Oregon.

BURNS. Famous MALHEUR LAKE NATIONAL WILD-LIFE REFUGE can be reached by driving 2 miles east from Burns on State Route 78, then turning right at the Poison Creek Grange Building on State Route 205 (gravel road). After approximately 28 miles on this road, 3 miles past the town of Narrows (one house), turn left (north) on a marked road to headquarters (3 miles). The headquarters buildings are constructed of stone with Spanish-tile roofs. Consult here with the Refuge personnel about closed areas and the best tours to take at the particular time of the year. All major ponds and marsh areas of the Refuge are accessible by car most of the time.

Malheur Refuge (165,276 acres) is in the arid Harney Basin, bounded by the Blue Mountains on the north and the Steens Mountains on the south, and has no outlet to the sea. The floor of the Basin, though interrupted by occasional rock-capped buttes, is generally flat and is margined with rimrock cliffs. In the shallow waters of Malheur Lake (65,000 acres) are cattail-bulrush marshes. Harney Lake (30,000 acres), a sump of the Basin, is extremely saline and without vegetation except for a few spring-fed bulrush patches. The remainder of the floor of the Basin, aside from smaller bodies of water and marshes, supports a plant growth typical of semidesert areas, containing sagebrush, greasewood, rabbitbrush, and giant ryegrass. At higher elevations western juniper occurs.

Spring migration is at its peak in March and April, fall migration in September and October. To see nesting birds, a visit should be made during May, June, and July. Probably the outstanding species to be observed are the Trumpeter Swan and Sandhill Crane. The Malheur Refuge obtained Trumpeter Swans some years ago from Red Rock Lakes National Wildlife Refuge in Montana. These birds have been confined to a huge spring near headquarters. Inquire at headquarters about the possibilities of seeing these rare birds and the Sandhill Cranes. Other nesting species of particular interest are the Western Grebe, White Pelican, Snowy Egret, White-faced Ibis, Cinnamon Teal, Ruddy Duck, Golden Eagle (over marshes and around rimrock areas), Prairie Falcon (rimrock areas), Sage Grouse (sage-brush areas away from marshes), Long-billed Curlew (grassy areas near marshes), Willet (long-grass areas near marshes), the Avocet and Black-necked Stilt (nesting in scant grasses on alkaline flats), Wilson's Phalarope (near areas of open water), Forster's and Caspian Terns (flying over marshes), Say's Phoebe (around rock formations or old ranch buildings), Canyon Wren, Rock Wren (rocky areas), Sage Thrasher (sagebrush areas), and Yellow-headed Blackbird (cattails and bulrushes).

Some of the best bird finding in the Refuge is along State Route 205, from the turnoff to Refuge headquarters south to Frenchglen (38 miles). The road parallels the Donner und Blitzen River with its pools and adjacent marshes built up by management work. Here may be seen the Sandhill Crane and almost all of the waterfowl, waterbirds, and shorebirds that nest in the Refuge. From the main road, frequent side roads (unimproved and usually impassable when muddy) lead deeper into the marshes and afford more intimate views of the nesting birds. During April and early May, the spectacular courtship display of the Sage Grouse can usually be observed in sagebrush areas near the road, 1.5 to 2 miles south of Frenchglen. Caution: south of Frenchglen the roads are poor and unmarked, and there are vast areas with few, if any, human inhabitants.

US Route 20 eastward from Burns traverses the very flat Harney Valley for some 20 miles. Adjacent to the road (south side) for considerable stretches are extensive marshy areas where the bird finder may see a number of the typical birds of the area without leaving the highway. Many water-

fowl nest here, as well as Willets, Avocets, Wilson's Phalaropes, California Gulls, Forster's and Caspian Terns,
Yellow-headed Blackbirds, and Red-wings.

CORVALLIS. At OREGON STATE COLLEGE ornithology and natural-history courses are taught each year in the
Natural History Building, across from and somewhat east
of the greenhouses. Personnel in this Building will be pleased
to admit the visitor to the Braly Collection, which includes
some 500 mounted specimens of Oregon birds. Study skins
of most Oregon species can be produced for close examination. It will be worth while for the eastern bird finder to
spend some time wandering about the campus in search
of species that may be new to him. During April, when the
elms shed their annual crop of seeds, hundreds of Evening
Grosbeaks invade the campus to feed. The observer can approach within a few feet of large flocks of these striking
birds. Migrating warblers are often common in trees and
shrubbery on the campus, and an hour or two of careful bird
watching will result in a satisfying list.

Classes in ornithology and in natural history often take
field trips to McDONALD FOREST, the closest area with
a typical stand of Douglas fir. Leaving the Benton Hotel in
downtown Corvallis, drive east one block and then turn
north on US Route 99W. At 4.8 miles from the Hotel, a
gravel road goes to the left from a junction known as Lewis-
burg. Follow this road for 1.3 miles to a point where the
road forks. Take the right-hand road, which winds upward
1.6 miles and emerges in a clearing. Here, leading to right
and left, are roads with locked gates barring entrance by
auto. Park in the clearing and walk up the left-hand road,
through a considerable stretch of brushy second growth, to
some stands of relatively old fir. It is advisable to remain on the road, for poison oak grows thickly in some
areas.

From about 10 April to 15 June is the most productive
time for visiting this area. Almost all of the migrating and
resident warblers to be encountered in western Oregon may
be found during the early part of May. In the tangles of
thimbleberry, hazel, and young fir, look for such species as
the Orange-crowned, Nashville, Yellow, Macgillivray's, and

Black-capped. In the conifers, particularly in small clumps of large trees or at the edge of larger stands, search for other species such as the Audubon's, Black-throated Gray, Townsend's, and Hermit. When thimbleberry, salmonberry, red-flowering currant, and other shrubs are in bloom, Rufous Hummingbirds become fairly numerous around them. During the latter part of April, the males perform their spectacular courtship flights. Stop and listen at intervals for the slow, ventriloquial hooting of the Blue Grouse, given as the bird perches motionless near the summit of some high fir. Other birds to be observed, particularly in the coniferous areas, are the Band-tailed Pigeon, Pileated Woodpecker, (Red-breasted) Common Sapsucker, Olive-sided Flycatcher, Canada Jay, Steller's Jay, Winter Wren (on the forest floor near vine tangles or exposed, entwined roots), Varied Thrush, Hutton's Vireo, Solitary Vireo, Warbling Vireo, Western Tanager, Purple Finch, Pine Siskin, Red Crossbill, and Oregon Junco.

EUGENE. This city, the site of the UNIVERSITY OF OREGON, is in the southern end of the Willamette Valley. In Deady Hall, on the campus of the University, is the Prill Collection of some 5,000 bird and mammal skins and bird eggs. This may be seen by arrangement with a member of the Zoology Department.

The best place near Eugene in which to find land- and waterbirds at any season is the FERN RIDGE RESERVOIR. Drive west on 11th Street (at the northern edge of the University campus), which continues westward from Eugene as the road to Veneta, a small town at the southwest corner of the Reservoir, 14 miles from Eugene. The southern edge of the Reservoir will be reached 8 miles from Eugene. This southern portion may or may not contain water, depending on the time of year, but it is usually quite well filled during the summer. It is possible to drive entirely around the Reservoir (approximately 20 miles), stopping where bird finding seems best. One good vantage point can be reached by turning right (east) 0.3 mile north of Veneta, then following this road as far as possible (about 4 miles) onto a point, which extends well into the Reservoir from the south. Another good observation point is on the west side,

3.7 miles north of Elmira, where an unimproved road leads to the right (east) out onto a small point.

Extensive cattail marshes and mud flats of varying size surround much of the Reservoir. On the higher ground, a considerable part of the area is given over to diversified farming; hence farm buildings, open fields, orchards, small woodlots, and fencerows are the prevalent bird habitats. The area to the west of the Reservoir is probably least disturbed; here there are fairly extensive areas of brushy growth, second-growth Douglas fir, and oak scrub and woodland.

Breeding birds to be seen in or near cattail areas of the Reservoir are the Pied-billed Grebe, American Bittern, Marsh Hawk, Virginia Rail, Coot, Long-billed Marsh Wren, Yellow-throat, Yellow-headed Blackbird, and Red-wing. Birds likely to be seen on open mud flats during the summer are the Great Blue Heron, American Egret, Killdeer, and Spotted Sandpiper, while White Pelicans and Double-crested Cormorants may often be seen in the open water or on dead snags in the water. Breeding ducks in the Reservoir area are the Mallard and Wood Duck.

In places where moderately large oak trees are present (e.g. just west of the dam at the north end of the Reservoir), look for the Acorn Woodpecker, which here reaches the northern edge of its breeding range. Other birds to be found in oak habitats are the Scrub Jay, White-breasted Nuthatch, Solitary Vireo, Audubon's Warbler, and Chipping Sparrow. In trees and brushy growth near the water, the following breeding birds may be expected: Traill's Flycatcher, Bewick's Wren, Olive-backed Thrush, Warbling Vireo, Yellow Warbler, Macgillivray's Warbler, Yellow-breasted Chat, Black-headed Grosbeak, Lazuli Bunting, Spotted Towhee, and Song Sparrow.

Fern Ridge Reservoir has important concentrations of wintering waterfowl and shorebirds, including almost all species to be found inland in western Oregon. Fall and spring shorebird transients gather in considerable numbers here.

HOOD RIVER. From the town of Hood River, on US Route 30 adjacent to the Columbia River (elevation 154 feet),

drive south on State Route 35 to the junction with US
Route 26, 45 miles from Hood River. After leaving Hood
River, Route 35 proceeds for several miles through the rich
HOOD RIVER VALLEY, largely given over to fruit or-
chards. Birds of this cultivated section tend to be much
the same as those of the northern part of the Willamette
Valley. One can expect such breeding birds as the California
Quail, Mountain Quail, Vaux's Swift, Rufous Hummingbird,
(Red-breasted) Common Sapsucker, Violet-green Swallow,
House Wren, Robin, Cedar Waxwing, Warbling Vireo, Yel-
low Warbler, Bullock's Oriole, Brewer's Blackbird, Lazuli
Bunting, House Finch, (Willow) Common Goldfinch, and
Chipping Sparrow.

About 6.5 miles from Hood River, the highway winds
upward through about 5 miles of oak-covered foothills, then
descends again into the upper Hood River Valley, where
the elevation is from 1,400 to 1,900 feet. In the sections of
oak woodland, the bird finder should look for the Lewis'
Woodpecker, Downy Woodpecker, White-breasted Nuthatch, Solitary Vireo, Nashville Warbler, Black-throated
Gray Warbler, and Black-headed Grosbeak, all of which
breed.

As the mileage from Hood River approaches 17 or 18
miles, the highway climbs more rapidly, soon leaving cultivated fields and orchards and entering the Douglas-fir forest,
characteristic of the lower slopes of MT. HOOD. The con-
tinuity of this forest is interrupted by ranch clearings and
natural meadows, rushing mountain streams, and loggings
or burns in various stages of reforestation. The birdlife is
therefore varied and should include the following nesting
species: Blue Grouse, Ruffed Grouse, Band-tailed Pigeon,
Pileated Woodpecker, Hammond's Flycatcher, Olive-sided
Flycatcher, Steller's Jay, Brown Creeper, Dipper, Winter
Wren, Varied Thrush, Townsend's Solitaire, Golden-
crowned Kinglet, Hermit Warbler, Macgillivray's Warbler,
Western Tanager, Evening Grosbeak, Cassin's Finch, Pine
Siskin, Red Crossbill, and Oregon Junco.

Somewhat before the junction of Route 35 with US
Route 26, at an elevation on Mt. Hood of about 4,000 feet,
smaller species of conifers become more and more prevalent
until the forest consists almost entirely of such trees as

lodgepole pine, western white pine, Engelmann spruce, grand fir, and mountain maple. In the higher parts of this subalpine forest, mountain hemlock, alpine fir, Sierra juniper, alpine mountain ash, and other trees make their appearance. Breeding birds to be expected here are the Williamson's Sapsucker, Black-backed and Three-toed Woodpeckers, Canada Jay, Clark's Nutcracker, Mountain Chickadee, Hermit Thrush, and Ruby-crowned Kinglet.

One mile west from the junction of Routes 35 and 26, turn right (north) and drive up to Timberline Lodge (elevation 6,000 feet), which, as its name implies, is near the upper level of tree growth. Numerous trails leave the Lodge, including those leading up through the alpine region to the summit of Mt. Hood (elevation 11,245 feet). Vegetation in the alpine region consists of numerous bright-flowering annuals and perennials plus much-dwarfed false heathers. Only one breeding bird is found in this area—the Gray-crowned Rosy Finch.

The best time of the year to investigate the birdlife of Mt. Hood is June and early July, when most species are in full song.

KLAMATH FALLS. Although not nearly so large as the Malheur Lake National Wildlife Refuge (see under Burns), the UPPER KLAMATH NATIONAL WILDLIFE REFUGE (8,140 acres) is more easily reached and includes a good proportion of the bird species that can be seen at Malheur. From Klamath Falls, take State Route 236, which leads around the southwest side of Upper Klamath Lake, for 25.7 miles to a junction with a gravel road; take the right-hand road for 2.9 miles to the town of Rocky Point. Two miles past this, the Refuge cabin and a near-by lookout tower can be seen on the right. No personnel is stationed regularly at the Refuge. The Refuge can be visited at any time from the first part of April to the end of October, but migration flights of waterfowl and shorebirds will, of course, be in evidence only at the beginning and end of this period. The flocks of waterfowl are not nearly so spectacular here as at Malheur, although the bird finder should see most of the migrating species that appear at the larger Refuge.

The Upper Klamath Refuge borders the northwestern

shore of Upper Klamath Lake, where there is a marsh vegetation of cattails and bulrushes. Westward the land rises rapidly to mixed ponderosa pine and fir characteristic of the upper eastern flank of the Cascades. This gives the bird finder opportunity to observe, within a few miles, a number of distinct habitats and their typical birdlife. Several species of waterfowl and waterbirds breed in the marshy areas. On Thomason Creek, near the east side of the Refuge, several hundred Double-crested Cormorants nest each year in a large rookery, which includes lesser numbers of Great Blue Herons, Black-crowned Night Herons, and American Egrets. On the west side of the Refuge, nesting birds include the Pygmy Owl, (Red-naped) Common Sapsucker, Hairy and White-headed Woodpeckers, Olive-sided Flycatcher, Canada and Steller's Jays, Mountain Chickadee, Ruby-crowned Kinglet, and Song Sparrow.

Crater Lake National Park (see under Medford) may be reached from Klamath Falls by traveling north on US Route 97, turning left (west) either on State Route 62, 6 miles north of Modoc Point, or at a well-marked (cloverleaf) junction, 10 miles north of Modoc Point.

LA GRANDE. This city lies in the GRANDE RONDE VALLEY (elevation 2,700 feet) of northeastern Oregon at the foot of the BLUE MOUNTAINS. To the east rise the WALLOWA MOUNTAINS.

The Blue Mountains consist of rolling terrain with open, park-like stands of ponderosa pine and Douglas fir on the slopes up to 5,000 feet or more, where Engelmann spruce and alpine fir appear and extend up to the highest points (over 8,000 feet). Some of the characteristic breeding birds of this area are the Blue Grouse, Ruffed Grouse, Pileated Woodpecker, Williamson's Sapsucker, White-headed Woodpecker, Western Wood Pewee, Olive-sided Flycatcher, Canada Jay, Steller's Jay, Common Raven, Clark's Nutcracker, Mountain Chickadee, Pygmy Nuthatch, Brown Creeper, Hermit Thrush, Golden-crowned and Ruby-crowned Kinglets, Townsend's Warbler, Western Tanager, Cassin's Finch, Red Crossbill, Oregon Junco, and Fox Sparrow. Though the upper part of the Grande Ronde Valley is agricultural country (for grain and fruit raising), there are stretches of greasewood, rabbitbrush, and sagebrush, with intermittent bare areas, where one may find such summer-resident birds as the Sage Thrasher, Bobolink, Lazuli Bunting, Common Goldfinch, Spotted Towhee, Lark Sparrow, and Brewer's Sparrow.

US Route 30 going northwest from La Grande to Pendleton winds upward into the Blue Mountains, where one may easily observe many of the birds of moderately high elevations. Route 30 going southeastward from La Grande to Baker crosses typical sections of the upper Grande Ronde Valley. At North Powder, 30 miles southeast from La Grande, a gravel road turning right (west) proceeds along the North Powder River, then soon rises sharply into another section of the Blue Mountains, where there are a number of attractive mountain lakes bordered by fine stands of conifers. This is the Anthony Lakes Recreation Area (elevation about 7,000 feet) and the road leading in is usually open from 1 July to early October. Forest camps are available here. Bird finding should be rewarding anywhere along this mountain route.

The Wallowa Mountains, east of La Grande, are decidedly more rugged than the Blue Mountains, having precipitous slopes and sharp crests. Several peaks between 9,000 and 10,000 feet are snow-capped and have glaciers, which produce numerous mountain lakes. On the lower slopes the conditions of vegetation and birdlife are similar to those in the Blue Mountains, but on the slopes above 6,000 feet the conditions are different. Here the forests contain extensive stands of lodgepole pine, mountain hemlock, alpine fir, and (at timber line) whitebark pine. Toward the highest peaks, above timber line, are treeless slopes with low herbaceous plants of alpine character. Among the breeding birds to be expected in the higher forests are the Blue Grouse, Black-backed Woodpecker, Three-toed Woodpecker, Canada Jay, Clark's Nutcracker, Red-breasted Nuthatch, Hermit Thrush, Townsend's Solitaire, Ruby-crowned Kinglet, Pine Grosbeak, and Lincoln's and White-crowned Sparrows. Above timber line, the two nesting species of regular occurrence are the American Pipit and the Gray-crowned Rosy Finch. Wherever there are swift mountain streams the Harlequin Duck and the Dipper are relatively common.

One of the few ways to enter the range is to drive north-ward and eastward from La Grande on State Route 82 for 66 miles to Enterprise. (See the Enterprise librarian for information on meetings of the Wallowa County Audubon Society, which meets regularly at homes of various members over the County. Regular field trips are also held.) From Enterprise, continue on State Route 82 to famous Wallowa Lake (10 miles), which lies at the foot of the Wallowa Wilderness Area. This place is kept in its original unspoiled beauty with only trails leading to its many lakes. Horses may be rented at the south end of the Lake, or short trips may be made on foot. The lakes and streams are good places to watch for Harlequin Ducks, and the careful observer may see White-winged Crossbills. The road to Wallowa Lake is kept open throughout the year. During the winter the bird finder may see wintering waterfowl on the Lake.

Traveling toward Wallowa Lake from Enterprise, one may turn left (east) at Joseph (6 miles) on a dirt-and-gravel road that runs down the Sheep Creek Canyon to the town of Imnaha (31 miles), which is hemmed in by towering basaltic cliffs. Take the Hat Point Road (open only during the summer months) up the mountain to Hat Point Lookout (25 miles), which overlooks Hell's Canyon of the Snake River. Here is some of the most spectacular scenery in the state of Oregon. Breeding birds to be watched for on this trip are the Golden Eagle, Burrowing Owl, Canyon Wren, Rock Wren, and Red-eyed Vireo.

LAKEVIEW. Just east of Lakeview in south-central Oregon are the WARNER VALLEY, with its chain of lakes, and the HART MOUNTAIN NATIONAL ANTELOPE REFUGE (240,664 acres).

The Warner Valley (elevation 4,500 feet) covers about 180 square miles, and is 5 to 8 miles wide. A chain of lakes, some of them dry beds, lie on the eastern side. The Valley, which lacks any water outlet, depends upon the surrounding mountains for moisture, and the amount of water in the lakes varies from season to season. Many of the waterways become

Oregon

465

dry in the fall. The floor of the Valley is flat and has various habitats—meadows, lakes bordered with marshy edges supporting bulrushes and flags, and drier sections covered with sagebrush and greasewood. Trees are limited to cottonwoods, willows, and junipers. Chokecherry, wild plum, and wild rose form thickets around the ranch houses and along the streams, which drain down from the mountains.

On the west side of the Valley is the Warner Rim, topped by broad tablelands and the peaks of the WARNER MOUNTAINS, some rising to 8,400 feet. Above an elevation of 5,500 feet, there is an extensive forest of ponderosa pine and white fir to about 7,500 feet, where lodgepole pine and whitebark pine occur to the summits. In the area near Drake Peak Lookout (elevation 8,215 feet) nest such species as the Sage Grouse, Poor-will, Calliope Hummingbird, Steller's and Scrub Jays, Sage Thrasher, Hermit Thrush, Audubon's Warbler, Green-tailed Towhee, Brewer's Sparrow, and Fox Sparrow. Golden Eagles, Prairie Falcons, American Magpies, and Common Ravens are numerous.

On the east the HART MOUNTAINS rise abruptly from the Valley to their highest point, Hart Mountain (8,020 feet). The breeding-bird populations of the Hart Mountain area are of the utmost interest. Here are desert, coniferous-forest, and deciduous-forest birds, all in close proximity. At the site of old Fort Warner (6,600 feet) is a large grove of ponderosa pine that attracts numerous Calliope Hummingbirds, Clark's Nutcrackers, Mountain Chickadees, Cassin's Finches, and Red Crossbills. Within a few hundred feet is a typical sagebrush flat with Sage Grouse, Poor-wills, Horned Larks, Canada Jays, Sage Thrashers, Vesper Sparrows, and Brewer's Sparrows. Also near by are extensive aspen groves with (Red-naped) Common Sapsuckers, Hairy Woodpeckers, Audubon's Warblers, Green-tailed Towhees, and many Swainson's Hawks. Along the many streams lined with willows, alders, and other deciduous growth are vireos, warblers, Black-headed Grosbeaks, Song Sparrows, and other riparian birds.

The Hart Mountain Antelope Refuge includes along its western boundary part of the Warner Valley chain of lakes, and stretches east to embrace Hart Mountain.

Great numbers of waterfowl and waterbirds stop in the

Warner Valley during the spring and fall, and a considerable number remain through mild winters. Many species nest in the area, the most spectacular numbers occurring in the Valley itself. Birds to be seen here commonly in the summer are the Horned Grebe, Western Grebe, White Pelican, Great Blue Heron, American Egret, American Bittern, Canada Goose, Gadwall, Cinnamon Teal, Redhead, Ruddy Duck, Turkey Vulture, Marsh Hawk, Prairie Falcon, Sparrow Hawk, Sage Grouse, California Quail, Sandhill Crane, Coot, Killdeer, Wilson's Snipe, Avocet, Wilson's Phalarope, Ring-billed Gull, Forster's Tern, Mourning Dove, Lewis' Woodpecker, Western Kingbird, Tree Swallow, Bank Swallow, Cliff Swallow, Scrub Jay, American Magpie, Yellow-throat, Yellow-breasted Chat, Yellow-headed Blackbird, Red-wing, Brewer's Blackbird, Bullock's Oriole, and Lark Sparrow. Higher up in the foothills, especially in the ponderosa-pine areas, are Goshawks, Cooper's Hawks, Red-tailed Hawks, Swainson's Hawks, Great Horned Owls, Red-shafted Flickers, Hairy Woodpeckers, Wright's Flycatchers, Audubon's Warblers, Macgillivray's Warblers, and Chipping Sparrows. In the groves of alder and aspen one may find the (Red-naped) Common Sapsucker, Mountain Bluebird, Nashville Warbler, and White-crowned Sparrow.

Pronghorn antelopes are common in most of this area. In late summer and early fall they graze in open bands over the country, and frequently visit the watercourses. The visitor cannot miss them.

To reach the Warner Valley, drive north from Lakeview on US Route 395 for 5 miles, then turn right on the Warner Highway, which crosses the Warner Mountains at 6,500 feet. The road to the Drake Peak Lookout turns north from the Warner Highway, about 10 miles from Route 395. This road is poor, steep, and usable only in the summer. The Warner Highway is paved for at least the first 15 miles, and paving to Adel is in progress. Turn north at Adel and drive 18 miles past the chain of lakes to Plush, then follow the main graveled road from there to Refuge headquarters (address: 252 Post Office Building, Lakeview). These roads are open except during winter storms. The distance from Lakeview to the Refuge headquarters is about 80 miles. The best time of year to visit the area is between 15 May and

1 November. Directions for reaching Hart Mountain may be obtained at headquarters.

Road maps may indicate roads between Hart Mountain Refuge and Frenchglen at the south end of Malheur Refuge, but these roads are usually unimproved, poorly marked, and rough in dry weather, and should *not* be attempted in wet weather.

ABERT LAKE, which is 24 miles north of Lakeview, on Route 395, has a great many nesting Canada Geese, Avocets, and Wilson's Phalaropes.

MEDFORD. Even if one should fail to see birds in CRATER LAKE NATIONAL PARK (250.52 square miles), he would be amply rewarded by lovely scenery. An ornithological famine is extremely unlikely in this splendid place, however, for its avifauna is quite representative of the southern high Cascades.

Crater Lake, with a shoreline of about 20 miles, now partly fills the caldera of the destroyed Mount Mazama. With no inlet or outlet, this fresh-water lake is exceedingly deep (1,996 feet), and around it are spectacular cliffs, 500 to 2,000 feet high. All roads down the side of Mount Mazama drop at least 2,000 feet before leaving the Park.

Besides Crater Lake and its encircling cliffs, the Park has extensive coniferous forests, mountain meadows, and (at high elevations) open pumice flats. The summit of Mount Scott (8,938 feet), the highest peak in the Park, has some of the characteristics of an alpine tundra.

Take State Route 62 from Medford to the west entrance of the Park. The route is kept open throughout the year (automobiles must have chains in winter), but it is impossible (without skis or snowshoes) to get far from the main highway, in the upper parts of the Park, from October through April. The highway from Klamath Falls is also kept open throughout the winter. Other entrance routes, open during the summer months, are indicated on any good road map.

At 'the Rim' above the south shore of the Lake is Crater Lake Lodge. The most conspicuous bird in its vicinity is the Clark's Nutcracker. This species has became accustomed to tourists and feeds boldly on peanuts and other tidbits that come its way. Not as conspicuous, but fully as forward, is the Canada Jay or 'Camp Robber,' which delights the visitor with its fearlessness. Other birds seen commonly around the Lodge are the Rufous Hummingbird, Red-breasted Nuthatch, Robin, Mountain Bluebird, Audubon's Warbler, Cassin's Finch, Pine Siskin, Red Crossbill (in years when cones are abundant), Oregon Junco, and Chipping Sparrow.

Both the Golden Eagle and Bald Eagle are found within the Park and may sometimes be seen soaring above the Lake. Duck Hawks may be observed frequently at Llao Rock overlooking Crater Lake from the northwest. Rim Drive Road (35 miles), a paved highway, completely encircles the Crater and passes through many miles of typical subalpine forests of whitebark pine and mountain hemlock. Within the Crater around the Lake, such birds as the Sparrow Hawk (after the first of August), Western Flycatcher, Olive-sided Flycatcher, Common Raven, Western Tanager, and Gray-crowned Rosy Finch may be discovered occasionally.

On the east side of the Rim, a 2.5-mile trail leads from the Rim Drive to the summit of Mount Scott. During this short climb in the summer the bird finder may come upon a Three-toed Woodpecker, Townsend's Solitaire, Rock Wren, or Gray-crowned Rosy Finch. Even without these birds the view will be magnificent, for it is possible to see the remaining slopes of ancient Mount Mazama. If the ascent is made on a sunny day in late August or early September, the bird finder will be treated to a splendid display of soaring hawks.

Dippers may be seen along all of the streams, even in the highest parts of the Park, until the streams are snowed under in late December or early January.

There is a very interesting open pumice flat, with colorful flowers and intermittent clumps of mountain hemlock and whitebark pine, on Dutton Ridge between the Rim Highway and the Rim. Early in the season, breeding Gray-crowned Rosy Finches and Mountain Bluebirds may be observed. In August and September mixed flocks of chickadees, nuthatches, warblers, and fringillids occur in profusion. This is also a favorite feeding area for Sparrow Hawks,

Lewis' Woodpeckers, and Clark's Nutcrackers in late summer.

In the whitebark-pine forests at high elevations on the Rim and on Mt. Scott the breeding birds include the Mountain Bluebird and occasionally the Red-breasted Nuthatch and Mountain Chickadee; foraging species (late summer), the Blue Grouse, Red-shafted Flicker, Black-backed Woodpecker, Hammond's Flycatcher, Clark's Nutcracker, Common Raven, Golden-crowned Kinglet, Ruby-crowned Kinglet, Audubon's Warbler, Hermit Warbler, Cassin's Finch, Pine Siskin, Oregon Junco, and Chipping Sparrow.

Mount Mazama is completely encircled by a belt of lodgepole-pine forest (5,000 to 6,500 feet elevation). There are relatively few breeding birds in the stands of small, densely growing trees here; in the more mature stands, however, such as along the east entrance highway and in the western part of the Park, the Blue Grouse, Pileated Woodpecker, Hammond's Flycatcher, Canada Jay, Steller's Jay, Brown Creeper, Townsend's Solitaire, Western Tanager, and Oregon Junco (where there is low cover) are among the considerable number of breeding species.

Isolated stands of ponderosa pine occur in the southern and northeastern parts of the Park. A particularly fine stand is along the Fort Klamath highway near the south entrance. Common breeding birds here include the Pileated Woodpecker, Williamson's Sapsucker, Hairy Woodpecker, Hammond's Flycatcher, Steller's Jay, Western Tanager, and (with adequate low growth) the Green-tailed Towhee, Oregon Junco, and Fox Sparrow. During summers when cones are abundant there may be Pygmy Nuthatches, Evening Grosbeaks, and Red Crossbills.

Ponderosa-pine and white-fir forests are primarily in the southern part of the Park and have, as breeding birds, Wright's Flycatchers (where there is suitable understory), Hermit Thrushes, Solitary Vireos, and Nashville Warblers, in addition to the birds that occur in the pure stands of ponderosa pine.

Wherever there are spring-fed mountain meadows with dense willows and a lush growth of wildflowers and sedges, the characteristic breeding bird is the Lincoln's Sparrow;

other nesting species include the Olive-backed Thrush, Macgillivray's Warbler, Black-capped Warbler, and occasionally the Lazuli Bunting.

PORTLAND. Portland bird finders frequently visit SAUVIE ISLAND, at the confluence of the Columbia and Willamette Rivers, north of the city. The Island abounds in sloughs and lush bottomland growth, and is an important crossroads for migrating and wintering waterfowl. Visit the Island between the close of the hunting season and the end of February to see the winter concentrations (mainly ducks) at their best. Avoid visiting the Island during the spring runoff of the Columbia, which usually occurs in late May. During the spring and summer months, the dense deciduous growths along the waterways are excellent habitats for many birds, such as the Traill's Flycatcher, Bewick's Wren, Olive-backed Thrush, Solitary Vireo, Black-headed Grosbeak, Lazuli Bunting, and Spotted Towhee.

To reach Sauvie Island, drive north from the city center of Portland on US Route 30. Approximately 3.5 miles beyond the St. Johns Bridge (across the Willamette River to the right) and one mile beyond the Portland city limits, turn right and cross the well-marked Sauvie Island Bridge. After crossing the Bridge, keep to the right and follow signs indicating the Sauvie Island Game Management Area (about 12,000 acres). Suitable bird-finding habitats will soon appear, mainly on the right side of the road.

The PITTOCK BIRD SANCTUARY, property of the Oregon Audubon Society, is a 25-acre tract of hilly woodland, west of the city, containing fine stands of virgin Douglas firs, a grove of old Oregon maples, and hemlocks, grand firs, cedars, yews, oaks, cascaras, alders, and cherries. Food-producing shrubs have been planted. A small creek meanders through the brushy-edged meadows of the southern section. Marked trails are maintained, and there is a resident caretaker. Some of the birds commonly nesting are Black-capped Chickadees, Chestnut-backed Chickadees, House Wrens, Bewick's Wrens, Robins, Olive-backed Thrushes, Audubon's Warblers, Black-headed Grosbeaks, Purple Finches, Spotted Towhees, White-crowned Sparrows, and Song Sparrows.

To reach the Sanctuary, which is adjacent to Macleay Park, drive north and west on US Route 30 to Lovejoy Street, turn west onto Lovejoy Street (which becomes Cornell Road), and continue almost 2 miles on Cornell Road to the entrance on the right.

The lakes in EASTMORELAND PARK, in the southeast section of the city at US Route 99E (McLoughlin Boulevard) and Bybee Avenue, afford an unusual opportunity for close-up views of waterfowl. The area is protected, and the birds are fed by the city.

The WASHINGTON PARK ZOO has approximately 180 birds of about 50 species, most of which are exotic. State Route 2, west from the center of the city, passes the south side of Washington Park.

The Oregon Audubon Society meets at the Multnomah Public Library, S.W. 10th Avenue between Yamhill and Taylor Streets, the first Friday evening of each month except the summer months, and conducts bird walks each week from 15 March to 4 July. The time and place of the walks are announced in the local papers. The *Audubon Warbler,* published monthly except in July, August, and September, is the official journal of the Society. Members of the organization may be contacted through the Oregon Museum of Science and Industry, E. 9th and Hassalo Streets.

TILLAMOOK. For those who wish to observe seabirds in immense numbers within a small area, a June or July visit to THREE ARCH ROCKS NATIONAL WILDLIFE REFUGE is suggested. Here, on about 17 acres of rocky, offshore islands, is an enormous nesting population of Common Murres, together with smaller numbers of Fork-tailed and Leach's Petrels, Double-crested, Brandt's, and Pelagic Cormorants, Western Gulls, and Tufted Puffins.

The Rocks are too far from shore for satisfactory observations through binoculars or telescope; hence they must be visited by boat. In order to land on them, however, permission must first be obtained from the U.S. Fish and Wildlife Service, Regional Office, Swan Island, Portland 18, Oregon. Inquiry about chartering boats for the trip may be made at Netarts, 7.6 miles from Tillamook on State Route 6.

CAPE LOOKOUT, south of Netarts, is a rugged, narrow strip of rocky headland, extending 1.5 miles straight out to sea. The very tip of the Cape, where sheer cliffs drop into the water, is about 400 feet above the high-tide mark. On the south side of the Cape is an impressive seabird colony containing the three Oregon species of cormorants, Common Murres, Pigeon Guillemots, Tufted Puffins, and Western Gulls.

To reach Cape Lookout from Tillamook, turn west from US Route 101 onto State Route 6 and go 1.8 miles to a fork in the road (just west of the bridge across the Tillamook River). Take the left-hand road for approximately 3 miles to another fork in the road. Bear left here (the right-hand road leads to Netarts) and drive about 4.5 miles to near the south end of Netarts Bay. Leave the car and walk to the shore, then go south along the beach to the mouth of Jackson Creek. Cross this stream and continue southward, between the sea and the edge of the timber, until a trail (poorly marked) is seen leading east through a small clearing somewhat above the level of the beach. Follow the trail eastward for several hundred feet, then southward and upward toward the top of the Cape. From here, proceed to the tip. The entire trip involves about 10 miles of walking and can be made easily in one day. If one wishes ample time to investigate the colony, he should plan to camp overnight on the Cape (no man-made facilities available).

Contributing authorities: William F. Atkinson, Burton Bailey, Robert Bratz, F. Sheldon Dart, Donald S. Farner, Kenneth L. Gordon, Gordon Gullion, Stanley G. Jewett, S. Walter Lesher, P. D. Lewis, Brian McNab, William B. Morse, A. G. Prill, George C. Ruhle, Baird Walker, Kenneth Walker.

South Dakota

FRANKLIN'S GULL

When the eastern bird finder plans a trip west, he should arrange to drive across South Dakota on US Route 14 or 16. No other crossing of the great interior plains of the United States demonstrates in so striking a manner the transition between east and west. First, the highways traverse level, productive farmlands with freshly painted buildings sheltered by groves of trees, with neatly fenced pastures for dairy herds, with spacious fields for grain, corn, and other crops—all in all, a panorama much the same as that of Illinois, Iowa, and Minnesota. But almost imper-

ceptibly the scene changes: the terrain becomes more rolling and the farms less flourishing, the buildings shabbier
and more exposed, the pastures more extensive, and the
croplands more scattered. Then, almost halfway across the
state, the highways suddenly mount grassy, stone-strewn
hills, plunge into the wide, deep valley of the Missouri
River, and climb out in sweeping curves to the high range
country that marks the beginning of 'the wide open spaces.'
Over the steeply undulating grasslands the roads continue
their course, dipping into draws (shallow ravines) and looping over ridges. A herd of cattle appears now and then.
Occasionally visible in the distance is a fence or ranch
house, but generally there is little evidence of human life.
For a short distance the highways pass close to the northern rim of the Big Badlands, giving tantalizing glimpses of
strange, light-colored spires and pinnacles. Finally, the Black
Hills, an outer range of the Rocky Mountains, come into
view; once the highways have entered the mountains, the
range country ceases almost as abruptly as it began.

The changes in birdlife along Routes 14 and 16 are no
less striking than the countryside transitions. From the Big
Sioux River bottoms in eastern South Dakota, where Whip-
poor-wills, Least Flycatchers, Eastern Wood Pewees, Baltimore Orioles, Scarlet Tanagers, Rose-breasted Grosbeaks,
and Eastern Towhees are summer residents, the bird finder
reaches by a journey of 360 miles the Poor-wills, Wright's
Flycatchers, Western Wood Pewees, Bullock's Orioles,
Western Tanagers, Black-headed Grosbeaks, and Spotted
Towhees in the Black Hills. Between these two points, some
of the changes in birdlife are evident from the moving car,
and offer exciting opportunities for observation. In June,
for example, male Lark Buntings in their handsome black
and white livery are usually first seen along Route 14 just
west of the Big Sioux River and steadily increase in numbers until, in the range country west of the Missouri, they
are common. Time after time they flush from the road-
shoulders or adjacent grasslands to repeat their aerial
songs—ascending quickly to heights of 20 to 30 feet, burst-
ing into a medley of tinkling notes, and spiraling down with
stiff, butterfly-like wing movements. One year the estimated
number of males seen on one trip between the Big Sioux

River and the edge of the Big Badlands was 4,125, or roughly 15 per mile.

Physiographically, as well as ornithologically, South Dakota is divided into two nearly equal parts: an eastern and a western. The line of division roughly follows the Missouri River as it cuts down the middle of the state from North Dakota; consequently, South Dakotans frequently refer to the eastern and western parts of their state as the East River and West River, respectively.

Eastern South Dakota is for the most part a continuation southward of the Drift Prairie of North Dakota, with elevations decreasing from about 1,500 feet in the north to 1,200 feet in the south. The surface is flat to gently rolling except near the Minnesota boundary, where the low hills and ridges of the Coteau des Prairies arise. An abundance of lakes and sloughs characterizes the topography of the northeastern corner of the state; many of these are shallow, with a rich growth of marsh vegetation (see under Aberdeen and Waubay), and provide some of the finest breeding grounds for waterbirds and waterfowl in the state. Meandering southward through eastern South Dakota, and parallel to the Missouri, which they eventually join, are two prominent rivers, the James and the Big Sioux, the latter forming part of the state's eastern boundary. Most of eastern South Dakota was originally tall-grass prairie. Willows, cottonwoods, elms, hackberries, boxelders, maples, oaks, basswoods, and ashes occurred—and to some extent still occur—in strips along rivers and streams and in groves around some of the lakes. In the bottomlands of the Big Sioux and Missouri Rivers in the southeastern corner of the state there are a few forests of considerable extent in which the trees attain impressive height and density. Birdlife inhabiting the forest growth in eastern South Dakota is principally eastern in composition, whereas the birdlife of the open country contains many species of western affinities.

Western South Dakota is situated on the Missouri Plateau, a part of the high Great Plains, whose deeply rolling surface suggests a greatly rumpled carpet. The extreme eastern portion of the Plateau is dissected by the Missouri River; thus a strip 15 to 25 miles wide bounds the Missouri River on its eastern side. The western portion is broken by several big rivers, including the Cheyenne and the White, which empty into the Missouri. Elevations of the Missouri Plateau range from 1,400 feet along the Missouri to 3,500 feet near the western boundary. Owing to low rainfall, the soils are relatively dry, produce only a short-grass vegetation, and are normally unsuited to crop production; much of western South Dakota serves, therefore, as grazing land for cattle. Various shrubs, such as wolfberry, silverberry, buffaloberry, sumac, and wild rose, grow in moist draws and hollows, or along streams and riverbeds, where there are also a few willows, cottonwoods, bur oaks, boxelders, and other trees. In these environments may be expected an interesting variety of birds, including the Yellow-breasted Chat, Bullock's Oriole, Lazuli Bunting, and Spotted Towhee.

The Missouri Plateau is interrupted by three distinct regions of irregular surface. The first, in the northwest, is the so-called antelope country (see under Belle Fourche), where picturesque, flat-topped buttes rise to heights of 400 to 600 feet above the plains. A part of this country is noted for its 'gumbo' surface. The second region, in the south, comprises the remarkable Big Badlands (see under Wall), where the plains have been weirdly dissected by erosion. The third region, in the southwest, is the Black Hills, which occupy a section of the Plateau roughly 125 miles long (in a north-south direction) and 60 miles wide. They are not hills but mountains—the highest in North America east of Denver—with a magnificence surpassing their elevation. Unless seen in silhouette they are not 'Black' but deep green, sometimes with tints of purple and blue from their forest covering. Completely surrounded by the Missouri Plateau and more than 100 miles east of the Rocky Mountains, of which they are physiographically a part, the Black Hills have an island-like separateness that gives them a distinct regional character. Ornithologically they are so distinct from South Dakota as a whole that they warrant separate consideration. The reader is, therefore, referred to a special account of the Black Hills under Rapid City.

Although the great majority of birds in South Dakota are not state-wide in their distribution (e.g. many woodland-shrub species found east of the Missouri do not occur regularly west of the River, and *vice versa*), the following species breed more or less regularly throughout the state (or in regions indicated) in timbered areas, or in the open country (prairie grassland, pastures, fallow fields, meadow-like lowlands, brushy places, and dooryards):

TIMBERED AREAS

Black-billed Cuckoo
Screech Owl
Hairy Woodpecker
Downy Woodpecker
Blue Jay
Black-capped Chickadee

White-breasted Nuthatch
Red-eyed Vireo
Warbling Vireo
Oven-bird
American Redstart

OPEN COUNTRY

Swainson's Hawk
Greater Prairie Chicken (uncommon)
Sharp-tailed Grouse
Ring-necked Pheasant
Killdeer
Upland Plover
Mourning Dove
Red-headed Woodpecker
Eastern Kingbird
Western Kingbird
Eastern Phoebe
Say's Phoebe (West River)
Horned Lark
Tree Swallow
Barn Swallow
American Magpie
House Wren
Catbird
Brown Thrasher
Eastern Bluebird
Mountain Bluebird (West River)
Loggerhead Shrike

Yellow Warbler
Yellow-throat
Bobolink
Western Meadowlark
Orchard Oriole (southern South Dakota)
Common Grackle
Cardinal (southeastern South Dakota)
Blue Grosbeak (southern South Dakota)
Indigo Bunting
Dickcissel
Common Goldfinch
Lark Bunting
Savannah Sparrow
Grasshopper Sparrow
Vesper Sparrow
Chipping Sparrow
Clay-colored Sparrow
Field Sparrow
Song Sparrow
Chestnut-collared Longspur

Migration in South Dakota, which lies across the central flyway, is dominated by the spring and fall movements of waterbirds and waterfowl. In eastern South Dakota, geese steal the show as they gather in immense numbers along the valleys of the Big Sioux and James Rivers. Farther west,

Sandhill Cranes are frequently observed along the Missouri Valley from the North Dakota line south as far as Pierre and Chamberlain, where their overland route southward into Nebraska apparently begins. Throughout eastern South Dakota, ducks and shorebirds are abundant on suitable lakes, ponds, and sloughs. Long-billed Curlews and Avocets are conspicuous transients in western South Dakota, where they loiter and feed in the shallow margins of rivers. In a very few places, such as the Lacreek National Wildlife Refuge (see under Martin), both of these splendid shorebirds remain as summer residents. A few hundred White Pelicans nest in the state (see under Aberdeen and Martin), but a far greater number pass through in spring and fall, when they may often be observed on many of the larger lakes. Among the passerine birds the Harris' Sparrow is a common to abundant transient throughout South Dakota, as are the American Pipit, Tennessee Warbler, Orange-crowned Warbler, Myrtle Warbler, Black-poll Warbler, White-crowned Sparrow, White-throated Sparrow, and Lincoln's Sparrow. In South Dakota, the main migration flights may be expected within the following dates: waterfowl, 25 March—20 April, 5 October—15 November; shorebirds, 1 May—1 June, 1 August—25 September; landbirds, 20 April—25 May, 20 August—10 October.

South Dakota's severe winters are not conducive to good bird finding. Except in unusually mild winters, most streams and other bodies of water freeze over, thereby excluding all birds dependent upon them. In making their Christmas counts in the vicinity of Sioux Falls, members of the Sioux Falls Bird Club usually manage to find between 30 and 40 species. Their counts, as well as those made by others elsewhere in the state, almost always include the winter-resident Rough-legged Hawk, Slate-colored Junco, and American Tree Sparrow, in addition to permanent residents. Since very few observations on winter birdlife in the Black Hills have been made, it is impossible to indicate with any certainty the species that reside there between fall and spring.

The South Dakota Ornithologists' Union may be contacted through the South Dakota Department of Game, Fish, and Parks in Pierre. The principal activities of this young organization are an annual meeting, usually held

in May in a different part of the state, and the publication
of *South Dakota Bird Notes,* a quarterly journal.

ABERDEEN. One of the most highly recommended places
for bird finding in the lake country of northeastern South
Dakota is the SAND LAKE NATIONAL WILDLIFE
REFUGE (21,451 acres), which extends along the James
River southward for about 20 miles from a point within a
few miles of the North Dakota line. Two low dams across
the James River within the property have created a total
water surface of about 10,500 acres. Bulrushes, quillreeds,
smartweeds, and other emergent plants, including small
patches of cattails, grow profusely where the water is shallow, producing a dense marsh vegetation. The adjacent,
relatively flat uplands are chiefly grass-covered, except
where they have been cultivated to produce feed for transient waterfowl populations, or planted with trees for shelter
purposes. There is a sparse native stand of trees near the
original borders of the River.

The hordes of transient waterfowl that appear on the
Refuge in the spring present a remarkable spectacle. About
20 March, or soon thereafter, come the first of the geese, and
during the remainder of the month their numbers increase
steadily. Between 1 and 10 April, and occasionally later,
they reach a peak abundance, numbering 250,000 or more
individuals. The greatest number are Blue Geese, followed
(in order of decreasing numbers) by Snow Geese, Canada
Geese (including all races), and White-fronted Geese. While
the goose population is building up, thousands upon thousands of ducks appear daily until they reach maximum concentration—exceeding 150,000, with Mallards and Pintails
predominating. Usually a few Whistling Swans stop briefly.

The waterfowl and waterbirds attracted to the Refuge for
nesting purposes are notable for both variety and abundance. Several pairs of Canada Geese are summer residents,
and the following ducks nest commonly: Mallards, Gadwalls, Baldpates, Pintails, Blue-winged Teal, Shovelers, and
Ruddy Ducks. As many as 500 pairs of White Pelicans and
700 pairs of Double-crested Cormorants have established
a colony on a treeless island (hatching takes place in early
July). There are also several colonies of Franklin's Gulls,

totaling thousands of adults, in different sections of the marshes. Other birds nesting in the marshes, or in their immediate vicinity, are the Horned Grebe, Eared Grebe, Western Grebe, Pied-billed Grebe, Black-crowned Night Heron, American Bittern, Least Bittern, Sora, Coot, Wilson's Phalarope, Forster's Tern, Common Tern, Black Tern, Long-billed Marsh Wren, Yellow-headed Blackbird, and Red-wing.

To reach the Sand Lake Refuge from Aberdeen, drive north on US Route 281 to Barnard (19 miles distant), turn east on State Route 10, and go straight ahead for 9 miles to a junction with a road on the right, which leads to head-quarters. There is a Refuge directional sign at the junction. Route 10 from Barnard goes north from the junction near headquarters and east across the mid-section of the Refuge (including the flooded James River) to Houghton.

If the bird finder is especially interested in the spring migration of geese, he should, in addition to viewing the aggregations in the Sand Lake Refuge, visit PUTNEY SLOUGH, southeast of the Refuge. To reach it from Aberdeen, drive 20 miles east on US Route 12 to the junction with State Route 37, and turn left (north); 16 miles north of the junction the highway crosses the eastern part of the Slough—a vast marshy area. At the height of the goose migration, immense numbers can usually be seen from the highway, or from section-line roads that lead away from the highway on both the north and south sides of the Slough.

ARLINGTON. In May, June, and July, bird finders travel-ing through eastern South Dakota on US Route 14 will notice, west of Arlington, many Franklin's Gulls searching for insects on the farmlands. If the farmers are plowing, Gulls will be eagerly following them overhead and dropping frequently into the newly made furrows for earthworms and grubs. The majority of the Gulls undoubtedly nest at LAKE PRESTON north of the highway. One colony usually oc-cupies the marshy western extremity of the Lake, and may be viewed by turning north from Route 14 half a mile west of the town of Lake Preston, and driving 2 miles; the west end of the Lake will be seen on the right. The colony can be located from the shore by watching the birds as they go to and from their nests in the deep vegetation.

Two and a half miles southwest of Arlington, US Route 14 dips down to cross MUD LAKE on a grade. This small body of water is quite shallow, with marshy shores and a sparse growth of bulrushes. The road grade is an excellent vantage point for observing Mud Lake's summer-resident birds, which include Horned Grebes, Pied-billed Grebes, Mallards, Pintails, Blue-winged Teal, Ruddy Ducks, Coots, Black Terns, Yellow-headed Blackbirds, and Red-wings.

BELLE FOURCHE. North of the Black Hills in northwestern South Dakota, US Route 85 passes northward from Belle Fourche (pronounced *bel' foorsh'*) to the North Dakota line, over a sparsely settled and almost desolate plain from which rise numerous buttes. Often it is referred to as antelope country because herds of the pronghorn antelope are of common occurrence. For the first 40 miles the highway traverses the 'gumbo belt,' where the clay soil, when wet, produces the 'clingingest mud in the world.' Sod is non-existent; what there is of grassy cover is extremely thin. Birdlife is consequently scarce. In draws and near creeks, however, grasses tend to attain greater density, frequently forming thick clumps. The bird finder should inspect these situations, since they often prove to be the habitats of Brewer's Sparrows. The birds are best located by stopping the car near likely spots and listening for the song. After the first 40 miles, the highway passes over well-grassed prairie, used principally for grazing. Birds to be seen commonly along the way include Lark Buntings and Chestnut-collared Longspurs. Small lakes and sloughs in sight from the road have surprising concentrations of birds such as Gadwalls, Pintails, Ruddy Ducks, Coots, and Wilson's Phalaropes. Adjacent to this 100-mile stretch of highway between Belle Fourche and the North Dakota line are several spots used by Sage Grouse for their April courtship performances, but it is impractical to attempt route directions here. The bird finder desiring to witness these astonishing displays may obtain the necessary information from the state game warden in Belle Fourche.

BROOKINGS. SOUTH DAKOTA STATE COLLEGE, located in this attractive town in southeastern South Dakota, offers a course in ornithology during the spring quarter and has an ornithological collection of 225 mounts, 200 study skins, and 300 egg sets. The course is given, and the collection housed, in the Horticultural Building. There are approximately 600 volumes on birds in the College library.

One of the favorite bird-finding areas near Brookings is OAKWOOD LAKES STATE PARK (3,800 acres, of which 3,000 are water). There are two shallow prairie lakes, Lake Oakwood and Lake Tetonkaha, surrounded by marshes containing bulrushes, bur reeds, and quillreeds. Predominating in the woody growth around the Lakes are cottonwoods, elms, and hackberries, mixed with a few hawthorns, plums, and chokecherries.

Although various geese, ducks, and shorebirds are attracted to the Lakes in migration, the best time for a visit to the area is from June to September, when common breeding birds include the Pied-billed Grebe, Western Grebe, Coot, Belted Kingfisher, Yellow-shafted Flicker, Red-headed Woodpecker, Baltimore Oriole, Yellow-headed Blackbird, and Red-wing. On the southwest shore of Lake Oakwood is a large rookery of Double-crested Cormorants and Black-crowned Night Herons. Some of the birds nest in emergent dead trees a quarter of a mile from shore.

To reach the Park, drive west from Brookings on US Route 14 for 7 miles to Volga, turn north on an unnumbered road for 7 miles, then turn west and follow a gravel road around the south shores of both Lakes and one mile beyond. Here signs direct one to the picnic area, where there are tables and fireplaces.

MARTIN. In the extreme southwest-central part of the state, on the northern margin of the Nebraska sandhills, and in the valley of the South Fork of the White River, is the LACREEK NATIONAL WILDLIFE REFUGE (9,442 acres), a productive spot for bird finding. Half of the acreage comprises a series of pools and bordering marshes formed by impounding the waters of Lacreek Creek, a tributary of the South Fork; the other half consists of rolling prairie grassland with scattered willow thickets and small groves of cottonwoods and elms. In late June and early July, large numbers of ducks, representing 8 to 10 species, may be found in the marshes with their broods. A colony of White Pelicans (about 25 pairs) and Double-crested Cormorants (200 pairs) occupies a 2-acre, treeless island in one of the pools. Hatching is usually completed early in July. Among the various birds nesting in the marshes are the Western Grebe, Pied-billed Grebe, Black-crowned Night Heron, American Bittern, Forster's Tern, Black Tern, Long-billed Marsh Wren, and Yellow-headed Blackbird. The grassy edges of the pools are attractive to a few nesting pairs of Willets, Avocets, and Wilson's Phalaropes. Sharp-tailed Grouse are common on the surrounding stretches of prairie, where it is usually possible to see a few breeding pairs of Long-billed Curlews and Upland Plovers. Lark Buntings are sometimes abundant summer residents in the vicinity; small colonies of Cliff Swallows are frequently established under the eaves of Refuge buildings or under the superstructures of the water-control gates.

Many thousands of Mallards, Gadwalls, Pintails, Blue-winged Teal, Shovelers, and smaller numbers of other ducks appear on the pools during their migrations in spring (March—early April) and fall (October—November). Not infrequently 10,000 or more Mallards and a few American Golden-eyes and American Mergansers winter in the Refuge, staying on the open water below the spillways, or in spring-fed channels. Both the Golden and the Bald Eagles are observed regularly during the winter, and an occasional Prairie Falcon is seen in flight over the area.

The Lacreek Refuge may be reached from Martin by driving south on State Route 73 for about 6 miles to a Refuge directional sign, then turning east and proceeding for 7 miles to headquarters. Nearly all parts of the Refuge are readily accessible by roads and trails.

MURDO. US Route 16 traverses the vast stretch of rolling plains between Chamberlain on the Missouri and the Black Hills. Between Murdo and Kadoka the highway is not far north of the WHITE RIVER VALLEY, where there are interesting spots for bird finding. One of the best is reached by proceeding west on Route 16 from Murdo for 21 miles, to the little hamlet of Stamford, and turning left (south) on a dirt road, which, after about 7 miles, drops down into the Valley. On the moderately high bluffs, where there are low shrubs in scattered patches, Blue Grosbeaks are surprisingly numerous. Lark and Field Sparrows occupy the same environment. Close to the White River, amid thin stands of cottonwoods, willows, boxelders, and shrubby thickets, one may locate without much difficulty such birds as Catbirds, Yellow-breasted Chats, Orchard and Bullock's Orioles, Spotted Towhees, and Clay-colored Sparrows.

RAPID CITY. Too many transcontinental motorists think of the BLACK HILLS as mere foothills of the Rocky Mountains. If the traveler comes across the South Dakota plains, the Black Hills only foreshadow the greater sights to come; if he comes from the Tetons, the Big Horns, or Yellowstone National Park, the Hills are an anticlimax. In either event, he hurries on—perhaps after glancing at the great faces on Mt. Rushmore—never realizing that he has missed an area with superb scenery, remarkable geological attractions, abundance of wildlife, and a history as colorful and romantic as that of any other region of the west. Though motorists will doubtless continue to give the Black Hills only passing notice, may the touring bird finder know better! In this mountain range—from edge of plains to crests of ridges—there awaits an exciting avifauna.

The Black Hills, rising about 4,000 feet above the Missouri Plateau, present a varied landscape. On the eastern and southern limits of the range are hogback ridges, interrupted at intervals by water gaps where streams escape to the surrounding plains. Between the ridges, many of which have precipitous escarpments of red sandstone, and the main mass of the range lies the Red Valley, averaging about 2 miles in width. The main mass is domelike, its eastern side dipping rather suddenly toward the Red Valley, its western side declining gently to the plains. Owing to prolonged erosion, the eastern half of the range has features that are unforgettably picturesque. Deep canyons and rugged inter-canyon ridges are everywhere, while the southeastern section is dominated by granite knobs, spires, pinnacles, and bold mountain forms, culminating in Harney Peak, the high-est, with an elevation of 7,242 feet.

Because of their elevation, the Black Hills have a heavier rainfall than the surrounding plains, a fact that is reflected by their dense forest cover. A greater variety of birds is, therefore, to be expected. The predominating tree through-out the Black Hills is the ponderosa pine, often growing in pure stands; two other pines, the limber and lodgepole, are present in limited numbers. Mixed with the pine, espe-cially in ravines, are a few deciduous trees, principally the quaking aspen and white birch. Breeding birds commonly associated with these forests and consequently widespread in the Black Hills are the Western Flycatcher, Western Wood Pewee, White-breasted Nuthatch (uncommon), Olive-backed Thrush, Townsend's Solitaire, Solitary Vireo, Audubon's Warbler, Oven-bird, Macgillivray's Warbler (usually in ravines), Western Tanager, Pine Siskin, Red Crossbill, White-winged Junco, and Chipping Sparrow. (Red-naped) Common Sapsuckers are numerous wherever there are aspens. Along the streams at higher elevations and on cool north slopes are a few pure stands of white spruce. Although birds attracted to the spruces include many species that are also attracted to the pines, and *vice versa,* generally the Canada Jay, Red-breasted Nuthatch, Brown Creeper, and Golden-crowned Kinglet more commonly occur in the spruces. On some of the drier ridges of the foothills (e.g. the hogback ridges on the east and south) grow mountain junipers that provide suitable habitats for Pinyon Jays.

Quite a different variety of breeding birds is found in the deciduous woods on the floors of the wider valleys and can-yons and along the streams emerging upon the plains. Among the willows, cottonwoods, aspens, American elms, bur oaks, and boxelders, with their shrubby undergrowth and bordering thickets, occur the Wright's Flycatcher, Cat-bird, Brown Thrasher, Veery, Red-eyed and Warbling Vireos, Yellow Warbler, Yellow-breasted Chat, American Redstart, Bullock's Oriole, Black-headed Grosbeak, Indigo and Lazuli Buntings, Common Goldfinch, Spotted Towhee, Clay-colored Sparrow, and Song Sparrow (uncommon).

Breeding in suitable situations in many parts of the Black

'Hills are the following species: in the steep-walled canyons, or near precipitous slopes, the White-throated Swift and Rock Wren; along swift-flowing streams, the Dipper; in grassy stretches of the Red Valley and elsewhere, the Sharp-tailed Grouse, Horned Lark, Western Meadowlark, Grasshopper Sparrow, and Vesper Sparrow. Other birds likely to be seen near dwellings or near roads through open country are the Turkey Vulture, Red-tailed Hawk, Swainson's Hawk, Ferruginous Hawk, Golden Eagle (a few), Sparrow Hawk, Red-headed Woodpecker, Eastern and Western Kingbirds, Eastern and Say's Phoebes, Violet-green Swallow, American Magpie, House Wren, Eastern and Mountain Bluebirds, Loggerhead Shrike, Brewer's Blackbird, and Lark Bunting.

Rapid City, lying in the gap between the hogback ridges where Rapid Creek enters the plains, is a convenient place from which trips may be taken to the places that have the most interesting birds and, fortunately, also the greatest scenic appeal.

Overlooking Rapid City from the west is HANGMAN'S HILL, a ridge that has a few rather stunted pines, junipers, and oaks along the crest but is for the most part treeless, the slopes being covered with grasses and scattered shrubby thickets. Skyline Drive, reached by driving west from Quincy Street and turning right, passes up Hangman's Hill to Dinosaur Park. Flickers (mostly hybrids between the Yellow-shafted and Red-shafted) and noisy Pinyon Jays should be looked for in the scrubby trees along the Drive. In Dinosaur Park (where there are five life-sized figures of prehistoric reptiles fashioned in cement), Lark Sparrows are common nesting birds. On the slopes of the ridge, especially on the west side, below Skyline Drive, one may hear or see Western Meadowlarks, Spotted Towhees, Grasshopper Sparrows, and Field Sparrows.

A few miles west of Rapid City are two beautiful spots: DARK CANYON and SOUTH CANYON. Both have a winding course and rushing transparent streams; both are walled by cliffs with irregular strata and numerous crags; both have deciduous trees and shrubs along the streambeds, pines and scattered junipers on the rims. Dark Canyon is the more spectacular, for the cliffs are higher and, in places, the opposing walls draw so close together as to prevent the sun's rays from reaching the floor except for a brief period each day. A pair of Prairie Falcons and a pair of Duck Hawks are known to nest in inaccessible niches not far from each other on one of the highest cliffs. Far up on nearly all of the cliffs, Canyon Wrens are common, their presence revealed by their distinctive song—a series of melodious, cascading notes. Sheer walls are less frequent in South Canyon, many of the slopes being more gradual and at the same time more thickly covered with pines, but Canyon Wrens are nevertheless in evidence. The outstanding orni-thological feature of South Canyon, however, is the Poor-wills, which may be heard chanting regularly during June and July evenings. Birds likely to be seen or heard in both Dark and South Canyons include the Sharp-shinned Hawk, Cooper's Hawk, Pigeon Hawk (one pair recently nested in South Canyon), Great Horned Owl, Long-eared Owl, White-throated Swift, Lewis' Woodpecker, Blue Jay, Pinyon Jay, Rock Wren, Dipper, and Lark Sparrow.

Dark Canyon is reached by taking the Rim Rock Trail (no route number), which branches south from US Route 14 just west of Baken Park in Rapid City. After passing Canyon Lake, the State Fish Hatchery, and the entrance of the drive to Nameless Cave, the road forks at a point 4.9 miles from the city. The left road enters the mouth of Dark Canyon and should be followed if one wishes to look for birds along Rapid Creek in the depths of the gorge. The right-hand road, which is a continuation of Rim Rock Trail (unpaved and very slippery in wet weather), climbs to the north rim of Dark Canyon and follows the Canyon west-ward. Splendid views of the gorge and distant peaks are obtainable all along the way. Stop the car and walk out on one of the spurs that jut into the chasm: there may be Pinyon Jays in the conifers; falcons, swifts, and wrens on the cliffs below.

South Canyon is reached by turning west from US Route 14 at a point 2.4 miles from Rapid City, where a sign indi-cates the direction of the Canyon and the villages of Nemo and Roubaix beyond. After 1.7 miles, the road enters the

Canyon and ascends through it for 4 miles or so. Bird finding is good almost anywhere from the roadside to the highest slopes.

A trip during June and July southwest of Rapid City into the most rugged part of the Black Hills is rewarding ornithologically because it provides the opportunity to study the avifauna of typical pine forests in the Black Hills. Proceed 22 miles south on US Route 16 to the Mt. Rushmore Memorial Highway, which turns west one mile south of Keystone and climbs circuitously for 3 miles to a parking lot in the MOUNT RUSHMORE NATIONAL MEMORIAL (1,278 acres). A few steps from the car, a height of ground affords a dramatic view of the faces of four United States Presidents—Washington, Jefferson, Lincoln, and Theodore Roosevelt—carved in heroic proportions on the towering granite shoulder of Mt. Rushmore (6,040 feet in elevation). White-throated Swifts nest in lofty crevices near these immense sculptures and can be seen frequently as they dash back and forth. Western Wood Pewees, Solitary Vireos, Audubon's Warblers, Western Tanagers, and White-winged Juncos are some of the birds that can be heard in the general vicinity.

From Mt. Rushmore, follow the Memorial Highway westward over a twisting, narrow road through lovely pine forests, passing Horse Thief Lake and wide vistas of HARNEY PEAK, in the distance to the left. Frequent stops should be made along the way to search or listen for Western Flycatchers, Olive-backed Thrushes, Townsend's Solitaires, Oven-birds, Macgillivray's Warblers, Pine Siskins, and Red Crossbills. On reaching US Route 85A, which is about 12 miles from the parking space in the Mt. Rushmore Memorial, bear left, drive 4 miles southward, and bear left again on the Needles Highway. This soon passes Sylvan Lake. If one wishes to climb Harney Peak, the trail, which is very easy to follow, begins at the campground on the northeastern edge of the Lake. Birds along the trail are about the same as those in the Mt. Rushmore Memorial, around Sylvan Lake, and at points between, although Red-breasted Nuthatches and Golden-crowned Kinglets are more numerous here. As the summit is approached, the trail leads out of the tree growth onto bare rock surfaces. (There are no timber-line or alpine conditions comparable to those on higher peaks in the Rocky Mountains.) Birds are relatively scarce, but one is quite likely to see Turkey Vultures, Red-tailed Hawks, White-throated Swifts, and Violet-green Swallows in flight above or below the trail. Mountain Blue-birds and White-winged Juncos are the most common birds about the summit. Situated on the highest point is a glass-enclosed fire-lookout (occupied by a fire warden during most of the summer) from which one may obtain a breath-taking view of the southern Black Hills and outlying plains, and observe the mountain goats that have thrived on Harney Peak since their introduction a number of years ago.

The drive on the Needles Highway beyond Sylvan Lake provides an exciting scenic climax to the trip. One and a half miles beyond Sylvan Lake the road enters a tunnel in a tremendous granite promontory and emerges upon the NEEDLES—gigantean knobs, pinnacles, spires, and other strangely shaped rock masses reaching skyward. A few Audubon's Warblers and Western Tanagers inhabit the scattered, somewhat stunted pines at their bases; White-throated Swifts and occasionally a Duck Hawk or two cut across the deep abysses between them; but in general this uncanny place is not attractive to birds.

Unquestionably the best place for bird finding, if not for sight seeing, in the Black Hills is SPEARFISH CAN-YON, far to the northwest of Rapid City. Extending for 21 miles in a north-south direction between Cheyenne Cross-ing and the town of Spearfish, the Canyon is comparatively open in its upper part near Cheyenne Crossing, but farther on it begins to deepen, the light-colored sandstone and lime-stone walls becoming increasingly steep and close together. Clear, cool Spearfish Creek, descends rapidly through the chasm, and is joined about 4 miles above Spearfish by the waters of Bridal Veil Falls, which spill over the face of the east wall from a considerable height. As in Dark and South Canyons, White-throated Swifts, Dippers, Canyon Wrens, and Rock Wrens are present, but the superiority of Spearfish Canyon as a place for bird finding is due in large measure to its extensive forest growth—the spruces, sometimes in pure stands, sometimes mixed with pines, that occur along Spearfish Creek in the upper part of the Canyon, the decidu-

ous trees and shrub thickets that occur along the Creek
toward the southern part. Thus Spearfish Canyon attracts a
wide variety of breeding birds, as the following selected
list indicates: Saw-whet Owl, Common Sapsucker, Three-
toed Woodpecker, Wright's Flycatcher, Western Flycatcher,

DIPPER

Canada Jay, Black-capped Chickadee, White-breasted Nuthatch, Red-breasted Nuthatch, Brown Creeper, Olive-
backed Thrush, Veery, Townsend's Solitaire, Golden-
crowned Kinglet, Warbling Vireo, Macgillivray's Warbler,
American Redstart, Western Tanager, Black-headed Grosbeak, Lazuli Bunting, Evening Grosbeak, Purple Finch,
Red Crossbill, Spotted Towhee, and White-winged Junco.

Spearfish Canyon may be reached from Rapid City by
driving westward over Rim Rock Trail to US Route 85A,
turning right and following 85A to Lead, then turning left
(west) on US Route 85 to Cheyenne Crossing. The distance
from Rapid City is about 58 miles. From Cheyenne Crossing, Route 85 continues west and south along the west
branch of Spearfish Creek through a delightful valley for-

ested with spruce and pine. Along the first 5 miles of this highway, and in Hellsgate and Deadhorse Gulches, whose entrances are passed on the right, bird finding is very productive. The Spearfish Canyon Road (State Route 89) begins on the right at Cheyenne Crossing and follows Spearfish Creek into the Canyon. Bird finding along the Road, which goes down the Canyon to Spearfish, is as good in one place as in another. Nearly every bridge crossed has a pair of Dippers nesting beneath it. While going through the deepest part of the gorge, stop the car now and then to listen for Canyon Wrens singing far up on the lofty cliffs. At a spot called Savoy (the location of the Latchstring Inn), 5.5 miles down from Cheyenne Crossing, walls of limestone attain heights of 1,000 feet or more. Veeries, Warbling Vireos, Lazuli Buntings, and Black-headed Grosbeaks occupy the deciduous trees and shrubs near the stream. Before continuing down the Canyon past Bridal Veil Falls to Spearfish, take a side trip by turning left at Savoy on a narrow road that follows the winding course of Little Spearfish Creek. After one mile, a short path leads from a parking lot on the left to Roughlock Falls. It is almost a certainty that a pair of Dippers will have a nest behind this 20-foot drop of water and will be searching for food in the series of cascades below. About 4 miles beyond the Falls the road forks. Take the right fork and, a little later, the next left; this climbs rapidly to the crest of Cement Ridge, where there is a fire-lookout (just over the state line, in Wyoming). Townsend's Solitaires are fairly numerous in the pine woods. The higher slopes, though treeless, are richly matted with wildflowers—balsam roots, larkspurs, lupines, chickweeds, bluebells, shooting stars, and pasqueflowers—which bloom profusely in June and July. From atop the Ridge the superlative view of the northern Black Hills is itself well worth the trip.

SIOUX FALLS. In the farming country west of Sioux Falls, the largest city in the state, lie marshy lakes and potholes, considered by members of the Sioux Falls Bird Club to be the most exciting areas for bird finding in the vicinity. They are readily accessible by car; in fact, many of the birds can easily be seen from the car windows.

Drive west from Sioux Falls on US Route 16 for 11 miles to a crossroad; turn left (south) to WALL LAKE, which will soon appear on the right. Follow the section-line roads around the Lake. At the Girl Scout Camp on the east shore, Baltimore and Orchard Orioles are summer residents in the grove of trees and bordering shrubs, Bobolinks in the near-by pastures and haylands. Just southeast of the Lake, a section-line road crosses a marsh (no name) with cattails, quillreeds, and pickerelweeds, where, during the summer months, such birds may be observed as Pied-billed Grebes, Great Blue Herons, Black-crowned Night Herons, American Bitterns, Blue-winged Teal, Coots, Yellow-headed Blackbirds, and Red-wings.

Another marsh may be reached by turning right (north) from Route 16 at the aforementioned crossroad and taking the next road to the right, which crosses the marsh half a mile distant. Virginia Rails, Soras, Black Terns, and Short-billed Marsh Wrens are among the birds that nest commonly here.

Continue west on Route 16 for 4 miles beyond the crossroad that leads to Wall Lake, then turn north on a road to GRASS LAKE, on the left, 3 miles distant. At a point half a mile after turning north, the road passes (on the right) a shallow marsh with muddy shores and flats attractive to shorebirds in May, August, and September. Between this point and Grass Lake are big fields (on the right), where thousands of Snow and Blue Geese stop to feed during the northward migration in late March. Grass Lake itself, an extensive marsh with open water, is attractive to many transient waterbirds and waterfowl. Whistling Swans in late March and White Pelicans in fall are the Lake's outstanding ornithological features.

The Sioux Falls Bird Club, whose members may be contacted through the Pettigrew Museum at North Duluth and 8th Streets, sponsors a series of lectures each year and conducts field trips in the spring and fall.

VERMILLION. The UNIVERSITY OF SOUTH DAKOTA MUSEUM, on the first floors of the west and north wings of the University's Administration Building, has the following ornithological materials, most of them from South Dakota: 571 mounts, 736 skins, and 430 egg sets.

WALL. Between the Cheyenne and White Rivers east and south of the Black Hills is a vast area where the semi-arid plains have been remarkably eroded, forming the Big Badlands of South Dakota. Fine soft clays, capped by a thin sod, have been deeply dissected, producing a succession of V-shaped ravines with most of their walls oddly terraced by plates of sandstone. Between closely adjacent ravines there are sharp crests; between widely separated ravines there remain, as mesas or tablelands, the grassy uncut surfaces, 500 to 600 feet above the riverbeds. One of the most picturesque sections of the Big Badlands is now embraced by the BADLANDS NATIONAL MONUMENT (154,119 acres), which lies north of the White River and 60 miles east of the Black Hills. Here the plains have been cut by numerous tributaries of the White River. When they are looked down upon from the edge of the plains, or are viewed from the broad flat through which the White River wanders, the effect is startling. Between the innumerable ravines looms a veritable wilderness of sculptured formations that suggest spires, turrets, minarets, pyramids, domes, and giant tables. Nearly all have strata of different pale colors—buff, pink, gray, light green—which vary in intensity according to lighting conditions. On late, sunlit afternoons or early mornings when the sky is deep blue, they are at their brilliant best.

US Route 16A, proceeding south from Wall, enters the Badlands Monument (about 7 miles from the town) and soon passes down over the Great Wall into the strange wonderland of the Badlands. For 23 miles the highway winds southward and eastward through the heart of the Monument, giving the traveler every opportunity to view the array of formations. Before the highway ascends Cedar Pass and leaves the Monument, it crosses a section of the grassy flat of the White River and comes to the Cedar Pass Tavern and Cabins.

Birdlife in the Badlands Monument is expectedly limited both in variety of species and in numbers of individuals, yet it is not without interest, especially to eastern bird finders in quest of their first glimpses of Rock Wrens, Say's Phoebes, and Mountain Bluebirds. Rock Wrens nest in fissures of the clay banks; Say's Phoebes and Mountain Bluebirds choose similar nesting sites, though at the Cedar Pass Tavern and Cabins they may be found nesting under the eaves of buildings. Other birds to be seen commonly in the Badlands are Horned Larks and Western Meadow-larks, which occupy the flat of the White River, the tops of the tablelands, and the neighboring grassy plains; Lark Sparrows, which nest on the more gradual slopes where clumps of grasses and brush manage to gain foothold; and Cliff Swallows, which presumably find suitable nesting situations for their colonies on steeply cut banks with over-hanging sandstone plates or sod.

WAUBAY. The name of this town in northeast South Da-kota comes from a word in the language of the Sioux Indians meaning 'where wild fowl build their nests.' The name is indeed appropriate, for Waubay is situated in rolling prairie dotted with many potholes and lakes; much of the upland has the original prairie sod undisturbed by settlement, while the bodies of water, being in most cases shallow, have ex-tensive beds of cattails, bulrushes, quillreeds, and sedges, which provide suitable cover for breeding waterbirds and waterfowl.

Waubay, 11 miles east of Webster, is on the south side of US Route 12. North of the town lies the WAUBAY NA-TIONAL WILDLIFE REFUGE (4,651 acres), reached by turning north from Route 12, $1\frac{1}{4}$ miles east of Waubay, and following a road (no route number) northward for $6\frac{1}{2}$ miles past the Enemy Swim Indian School. A short distance beyond the schoolhouse, take the first turn left, which leads west to Refuge headquarters. The lookout tower near headquarters can be seen at the turn. The Waubay Refuge has several lakes and marshes serving as nurseries for Canada Geese and for many ducks, representing 12 species altogether. Certain of the marshes have the distinc-tion of being among the southernmost breeding grounds of the Holboell's Grebe and American Golden-eye in the United States. Large numbers of Western Grebes nest here.

One section of the Refuge is covered by a stand of native hardwoods and brush, another section by tall-grass sod that has never been plowed. Although bird finders are welcome to enter the Refuge, provided they first obtain permission at headquarters, the best places for birds are not readily accessible by roads; therefore, they are advised to visit two other spots in the general vicinity that are very productive and more easily reached.

BITTER LAKE, south of the town of Waubay, may be approached from Route 12 by turning into Waubay at the directional sign and driving southward through the business section to the south edge of town, turning west for one mile, then turning south on a gravel road (in fair condition), which leads to the north shore of the Lake. From here the road leads south and southwest along the west shore, where a fine marsh merges with an undisturbed prairie. The nesting season extends from May through mid-July. Broods of ducks (e.g. Mallards, Pintails, Blue-winged Teal, Shovelers, Ruddy Ducks) are most numerous from 10 June to 1 July. Among the various marsh, shore, and upland birds to be looked for during the trip are the Pied-billed Grebe, American Bittern, Coot, Piping Plover, Upland Plover, Marbled Godwit, Avocet, Franklin's Gull, Forster's Tern, Black Tern, Common Nighthawk, Horned Lark, Long-billed Marsh Wren, Western Meadowlark, Yellow-headed Blackbird, Red-wing, Brewer's Blackbird, and Chestnut-collared Longspur.

RUSH LAKE is crossed at the south end by Route 12, 2.5 miles west of Waubay. From the road grade one may obtain excellent views of the open water and the marsh vegetation that gives the Lake its name. Black-crowned Night Herons nest on a wooded island 1.5 miles north of Route 12. In the late spring and summer the Lake is occupied by a large population of waterbirds and ducks, the species being the same as those at Bitter Lake. If the water level is low in August and September, shorebirds are numerous on the muddy shores and flats. From spring to fall, a few White Pelicans can always be seen somewhere on the Lake.

Another good location is HEDKE'S PASS, a public shooting area owned by the State Game, Fish, and Parks Commission, between North Waubay and South Waubay Lakes.

This is reached as follows: At a school 5 miles west of Waubay on Route 12, turn north on a gravel road and drive for
about 3.5 miles to a point where a rather poor township
road turns off west; turn onto this road. After 1.5 miles the
road enters Hedke's Pass. To the left, in South Waubay
Lake, is CORMORANT ISLAND, which has a nesting
colony of Double-crested Cormorants (eggs by 1 June),
also a few breeding Forster's Terns and, occasionally, White
Pelicans. Geese, ducks, and shorebirds are usually abundant
along the shores of both Lakes and in a marsh that lies about
a quarter of a mile west of the Pass.

Contributing authorities: Homer L. Bradley, Herman F. Chap-
man, Edward F. Dana, William C. Dilger, Ernest P. Edwards,
J. S. Findley, J. O. Johnson, James W. Kimball, Kenneth Krumm,
Robert B. Lea, Miss Zell C. Lee, W. H. Over, Gerald B. Spawn,
Frederic T. Staunton, Jerome H. Stoudt, Geroge Miksch Sutton.

Texas

SENNETT'S WHITE-TAILED HAWK

Texas, true to its reputation as a land of superlatives, has the longest list of birds of any state—altogether 540 species. Since the total number of bird species known to occur in the United States is about 720, one may say that it is possible to find in Texas three fourths of the nation's birds.

The list of Texas birds, though impressive, is to be expected, for reasons peculiar to the state itself. In the first place, Texas covers an immense and diversified area of some 267,000 square miles. Whether from the northern boundary of the Texas Panhandle south to the mouth of the Rio

Grande, or from the Sabine River in the extreme east to
the westernmost corner of the state near El Paso, the distance across Texas is nearly 800 miles. The state thus brings
within its borders segments of the Coastal Plain, the Great
Plains that sweep north into Canada, the southwestern arid
lands that characterize New Mexico and Arizona, and several environments that are distinctly semitropical or Mexican. From the Gulf Coast to the mountains that tower above
the deserts in the far western part of the state, elevations
range from sea level to over 8,000 feet. Annual rainfall varies
from 50 or more inches in extreme eastern Texas to less than
10 inches around El Paso. Winter days at Amarillo on the
high prairies of the Panhandle are frequently bitter, with
sharp winds and freezing temperatures, while those at Corpus Christi and Brownsville are typically warm and sunny.
In the second place, Texas has vastly different and extensive
habitats: fresh water and salt water; coastal islands, beaches,
marshes, and prairies; lowland, upland, and montane forests; brushlands, grasslands, and deserts. In the third place,
Texas lies in the path of a tremendous number of migrating
species and within the winter range of many others.

The Texas coast, extending for 380 miles between Louisiana and Mexico, has a shoreline of barrier sand beaches.
Many of them are long, slender islands and peninsulas that
parallel the mainland and shelter narrow, intervening
lagoons, usually called bays. Except for interruptions caused
by such bays and by river mouths, these beaches are continuous. All the bays are normally shallow, with low islands;
not infrequently both the bays and their islands are fringed
by grassy marshes. Of the various narrow bays, the longest
is Laguna Madre, which extends south from Corpus Christi
Bay for 130 miles to a point near the delta of the Rio Grande.
Padre Island, reputed to be the longest island for its width
in the world, separates Laguna Madre from the Gulf.
Though averaging 6 miles in width, the Laguna is remarkably shallow—in a few places more than 10 feet deep, but
most of it less than 2 feet. For thousands of waterfowl and
other birds the Laguna is a winter haven, and certain of
its islands—for example, Green Island (see under Brownsville-Harlingen)—hold enormous nesting colonies of waterbirds.

Along the Texas coast, on the beaches and islands, and in the salt or brackish marshes, the birds listed below breed more or less regularly. Species marked with an asterisk nest locally in colonies.

°Olivaceous Cormorant	Snowy Plover
°Brown Pelican	Wilson's Plover
°Great Blue Heron	Willet
°American Egret	Black-necked Stilt
°Snowy Egret	°Laughing Gull
°Reddish Egret	Gull-billed Tern
°Louisiana Heron	Forster's Tern
Green Heron	°Least Tern
°Black-crowned Night Heron	°Royal Tern
°White-faced Ibis	°Cabot's Tern
°White Ibis	°Caspian Tern
°Roseate Spoonbill	°Black Skimmer
Fulvous Tree-duck	Long-billed Marsh Wren
Mottled Duck	Yellow-throat
Clapper Rail	Red-wing
Purple Gallinule	Boat-tailed Grackle
Florida Gallinule	Seaside Sparrow

The interior of Texas may be considered to have four major natural regions: the Coastal Plain, the High Plains Country, the Edwards Plateau, and the Trans-Pecos. All show sharp contrasts in topography and climate and, in turn, great differences in habitats for birds. It must not be inferred, however, that these contrasts exist only *between* these regions and that *within* each region the conditions are relatively uniform. So extensive is each region and so diverse its topography and climate that within each area, though to a somewhat lesser degree, there are marked differences in environmental conditions. In the following paragraphs each of the major regions is described to the extent of depicting its general limits (which are often arbitrary) and some of its more important environments, especially those of interest to the bird finder. In view of the paucity of information on the birds of each region as a whole, a listing of breeding species is not attempted.

A. The Coastal Plain comprises all of eastern and southern Texas, limited on the west by the Balcones Escarpment of the Edwards Plateau, a prominent topographic feature that runs from the Rio Grande near Del Rio eastward to San Antonio and northward through Austin, becoming lower and disappearing west of Waco. Farther north there is no sharp western boundary, but a line drawn northward through Mineral Wells and Nocona to the Red River roughly marks the western limits of the true Coastal Plain. Though a low-lying country throughout, the Coastal Plain may nevertheless be divided into four general areas:

1. Inland for 30 to 50 miles from the beaches and marshes of the Gulf Coast is the flat Coast Prairie, on which lie the cities of Beaumont, Port Arthur, Galveston, Houston, and Corpus Christi. The Coast Prairie is a broad strip of clayey soils and high water table, with small stretches of sandy soils interspersed. It is generally tree-less; salt and marsh grasses thrive near the coast and coarse beard grasses, bull grasses, panic grasses, and others predominate farther inland. The only parts of the Coast Prairie with any extensive tree growth are the valleys of the larger rivers that support luxuriant stands of oak, pecan, elm, and cottonwood, and the Blackjack Peninsula and a few other places between Bay City and Corpus Christi that have huge mottes (clumps) of oak. (For sections of the Coast Prairie with interesting spots for bird finding, see under Port Arthur, Galveston, Houston, Bay City, Port Lavaca, and Rockport.)

2. Extreme eastern Texas (north of the Coast Prairie and west approximately to a line beginning just north of Houston and passing northward to the Red River through Huntsville, Palestine, Mineola, and Clarksville) has sandy soils. Much of the area supports upland forests of pines and hardwoods, with oaks predominating, but river-bottom and swamp hardwoods occupy considerable territory. In the extreme southeast is the Big Thicket (see under Beaumont), which contains an unusually varied forest flora, including large beeches, magnolias, oaks, and pines.

3. The remainder of eastern Texas is mainly the Black-land Prairie area, a belt of calcareous clayey soils running from San Antonio northeast and north to the Red River. This is the most densely populated portion of the state

and includes the cities of San Antonio, Austin, Waco, Dallas, and Fort Worth. North of Waco, the Prairie is split by the East Cross Timbers, a narrow strip of sandy soils covered by post and blackjack oaks. On the west at about the same latitudes, the Prairie is bordered by another strip of sandy soils, the West Cross Timbers, with similar vegetation. The West Cross Timbers extend without a topographical or vegetational break for a short distance westward outside the true Coastal Plain. (For bird finding in this third general area of the Coastal Plain, see under Dallas and Fort Worth.)

4. Southern Texas—the triangular part of the state south and southeast of the Edwards Plateau—is a rolling plain, rising imperceptibly westward to an elevation of almost 1,000 feet near Del Rio. Being covered in most areas with thorny shrubs, often in open stands and mixed with various grasses, yuccas, and cacti such as prickly pear and tasajillo, it receives the name Chaparral Country. The prominent shrub is mesquite; other important kinds are acacia, mimosa, huisache, buckthorn, lignum vitae, granjeno, cenizo, and whitebrush. Bottomlands of the larger stream valleys have many trees, among which are live oaks, pecans, elms, hackberries, and ashes. In the lower Rio Grande Valley, an extensive citrus-fruit and vegetable-raising industry has been developed, but there are still a few undisturbed areas where shrubs—the Texas ebony, retama or Jerusalem thorn, wild olive, anaqua, and many other semitropical or tropical species—grow luxuriantly, forming dense, almost impenetrable tangles. On the flood plain of the lower Rio Grande, trees of immense size still stand in a few places. (For bird-finding possibilities in typical Chaparral Country, see under Crystal City; in the lower Rio Grande Valley, see under Brownsville-Harlingen.)

B. The High Plains Country occupies all of the Panhandle and extends, as the Edwards Plateau, south to the Rio Grande between Del Rio and the mouth of the Pecos River; east and southeast to the Coastal Plain; and west to the Pecos River (which marks the eastern margin of the Trans-Pecos). Within the High Plains Country, excluding the Edwards Plateau, there are at least three natural divisions: the short-grass plains, the mixed-grass plains, and the mesquite plains.

1. The short-grass plains, called in Texas the Staked Plains or Llano Estacado, are a southward continuation of the Great Plains from western Kansas and the Oklahoma Panhandle. In Texas they stretch from the northernmost limits of the Texas Panhandle south to the Edwards Plateau, with which they merge indiscernibly south of Big Spring and Ballinger. On the west, they reach to the New Mexico line and the Pecos River Valley; on the east, they are bounded by 'the Cap Rock,' an abrupt, rock-capped escarpment dropping to the mixed-grass and mesquite plains. In the Panhandle, the Staked Plains are exceedingly flat, interrupted only by a few deep valleys and by scattered, shallow depressions containing temporary (playa) lakes. A short-grass association, with buffalo and grama grasses as the principal constituents, is the natural cover. (For further information on the Staked Plains, together with an indication of the opportunities that await the bird finder in the area, see under Amarillo.)

2. In Texas the mixed-grass plains are limited to the eastern side of the Texas Panhandle between the Cap Rock of the Staked Plains and the Oklahoma boundary, but across the boundary in Oklahoma they include much of the western part of that state. (See introduction to the Oklahoma chapter for a description of the mixed-grass plains.)

3. The mesquite plains lie in north-central Texas south of the Red River. (A small section also extends into the southwestern corner of Oklahoma, north of the Red River.) Like the mixed-grass plains, they are limited on the west by the Cap Rock of the Staked Plains. On the east they merge gradually with the West Cross Timbers of the Coastal Plain; on the south they meet the Edwards Plateau. In general, the country is level to rolling except where gullied or, at higher elevations approaching the Cap Rock, cut by deep canyons. The native vegetation is represented by an abundance of thorny shrubs, mainly

mesquite, growing in open stands that alternate with stretches of grama and other short-grass species. In certain places, especially in gullies, the shrubs grow in dense thickets. The bottomlands along the larger streams support stands of such trees as elms, oaks, hackberries, and cottonwoods; the canyons support a similar growth and, in addition, junipers. (For bird finding on the mesquite plains, see under Abilene and Seymour, two cities situated in this type of country.)

C. The Edwards Plateau in south-central Texas reaches from the Staked Plains and mesquite plains to the Rio Grande between Del Rio and the mouth of the Pecos River. Its western limits are the Pecos River Valley, while its eastern and southern limits are the out-facing Balcones Escarpment, which drops abruptly to the Coastal Plain. The height of the Escarpment increases gradually toward the west, from Austin, where it is 300 feet high, to Del Rio, where it reaches 1,000 feet. Altitudes of the Edwards Plateau show a steady decline southward and eastward from 2,500 feet at the border of the Staked Plains to 1,000 feet just west of Austin and 1,500 feet just north of Del Rio. West of the 100th meridian the Edwards Plateau resembles the Staked Plains, being a little-interrupted, level plain covered with short-grass sod, but farther east it has a rugged surface owing to the numerous out-flowing, many-branched rivers (the San Saba, Pedernales, Blanco, Guadalupe, Nueces, and others) that have cut deeply into the underlying limestone, producing such formations as terraced hills, canyons, and gullies. Vegetation, in addition to the grasses that cover the few remnants of the plain, ranges from heavy forests of live oaks, elms, walnuts, hackberries, and pecans on the canyon floors (many are very wide) to scrub forests of Mexican junipers, Texas oaks, shin oaks, post oaks, blackjack oaks, stunted live oaks, and other trees on the higher, rocky slopes of the hills and canyons. Birdlife on the Edwards Plateau shows an intriguing mixture of the species characteristic of the several adjoining natural regions; only one species, the Golden-cheeked Warbler, is peculiar to the Plateau, and it is apparently found nowhere else in the

United States. (For places on the Plateau in which to find the Golden-cheeked Warbler, as well as a fine variety of other breeding birds, consult the account under Kerrville.)

D. The most rugged and scenic of the four major natural regions in Texas is the Trans-Pecos, which lies west of the Pecos River between the upper Rio Grande and the New Mexico line. In general, it is a region of arid to semi-arid conditions, of varying elevations and discontinuously distributed habitats, of desert, grassland, and montane birds. Aside from the Toyah Basin (a plain about 50 miles wide lying along the Pecos River from New Mexico south to Terrell County) and the Stockton Plateau (geologically a part of the Edwards Plateau, and lying south and southeast of the Toyah Basin in most of Terrell and eastern Brewster Counties), the Trans-Pecos consists of bolsons (undrained basins) and intervening mountain ranges or 'roughlands.' The bolsons have a flat terrain and desert aspect: some stretches yield a thin cover of grasses (chiefly tobosa, galleta, and grama); others, open stands of such shrubs as creosote bush, catclaw, and blackbrush. On low mountain slopes and, not infrequently, on high slopes with southern exposure, similar grass associations occur, together with mesquite and various acacias, but on all high mountain slopes with northern exposure the vegetation features an extensive growth of trees.

The three highest mountain ranges of the Trans-Pecos—the Guadalupe Mountains in the extreme north (see under El Paso), the Davis Mountains in the central part (see under Fort Davis), and the Chisos Mountains in Big Bend National Park in the extreme south (see under Marathon)—show a typical succession of plant associations from desert to mountain top. Although the avifauna of all three mountain ranges is much the same, there are nonetheless a few species that occur in only one or sometimes two of the ranges. This is explained in part by the vast expanse of open country that separates the ranges and thus tends to restrict the dispersal of mountain birds from one range to another. Also, the bird finder will discover that the three ranges show a rough grandeur, but that each one possesses a distinctiveness of topography, color, and general character. Hence the exploration of each range is in itself a matchless adventure.

Lying in the path of the central flyway (sometimes called the 'flyway of the plains'), Texas is in spring and fall the scene of the migratory movements of those avian hordes that breed in the enormous area between the Mississippi River and the Rocky Mountains and the equally great area directly north in Canada. Texas is also a vantage point for viewing the passage of huge numbers of birds that are summer residents east and west of these areas: in eastern Canada and eastern United States; in western Canada and eastern Alaska; in western Montana and Idaho, Wyoming, western Colorado and Utah, and New Mexico. The Wood Thrush, Worm-eating Warbler, Golden-winged Warbler, Blue-winged Warbler, Parula Warbler, Cerulean Warbler, Blackburnian Warbler, Hooded Warbler, Canada Warbler, and Louisiana Water-thrush, which breed mainly in the wooded parts of eastern North America, appear as common transients along the Texas coast and inland for 50 miles; and many waterbirds and waterfowl that nest in the Bear River Marshes of Utah fly in a northwest-southeast direction across the Texas Panhandle and central Texas to and from the Laguna Madre and other coastal areas southward where they winter.

Birds moving through central and west Texas seem to follow no particular mountain ranges, ridges, valleys, or watercourses. Waterbirds, waterfowl, and shorebirds tend to 'hop skip' from one suitable body of water to another lying in the general direction of their flight. Flocks of open-country birds, such as Lark Buntings, pass north and south over the plains, stopping to loiter and feed as the occasion demands. Flycatchers, warblers, and other tree and shrub birds gather temporarily in most forested areas along rivers, or in thickets sequestered in canyons and draws.

Along the Texas coast pass tremendous numbers of migrating waterbirds, shorebirds, and landbirds. The populations of certain species of small landbirds that are observed along the lower Texas coast from Port Lavaca south are sometimes so great as to be almost unbelievable. From

Rockport, for example, come reports in the spring (late March through early May) of 500 Yellow-throats estimated at one time in a 100-foot row of tamarisk, of 57 Bay-breasted Warblers observed in one tree, and of 50,000 Barn Swallows counted within two hours. Along the upper Texas coast such concentrations of small landbirds occur in the spring only during a cold front, or 'norther.' In good weather, apparently, the birds continue north (inland) where the upper coast swings eastward, but when a cold front comes in from the northwest (the usual direction), the birds are forced southeastward off their course and congregate on the upper coast until the weather improves.

Probably a few small landbirds reach the extreme upper Texas coast in the spring in the way that great numbers reach the Louisiana coast—from across the Gulf of Mexico. (For a description of how weather, both good and bad, affects their arrival, see the introduction to the Louisiana chapter.)

A great many shorebirds may be observed in Texas, especially along the coast, in any season except early summer, but they are most abundant in the spring and fall, when their numbers are increased by transient individuals that spend the winter farther south.

The majority of birds that migrate through Texas may be observed within the following dates: shorebirds, 10 March—10 May, 20 August—25 October; landbirds, 15 March—5 May, 15 September—10 November.

Winter bird finding is unusually rewarding in Texas, particularly along the coast, in the sheltered depths of western canyons, and in the lowlands of the Rio Grande Valley. This is because many northern species join a large variety of permanent residents. Among Christmas bird counts taken in different parts of the state, those in the lower Rio Grande Valley yield the highest figures. The record of 172 species (at Harlingen in 1950) is the highest record for Christmas counts throughout the country. Other recent counts at Harlingen range between 128 and 163. At Houston, near the upper Texas coast, Christmas counts usually reach 100 and sometimes higher. Farther inland and north of the lower Rio Grande Valley the counts are always much lower. For example, at Fort Worth and El Paso, during a recent 5-year period, the counts ranged, respectively, from 51 to 83 and 46 to 79.

The wintering populations of certain northern species in Texas are often as impressive as the variety. Geese (mostly Canada, Snow, and Blue) on the coast and Coast Prairie are estimated each winter to be in excess of 300,000. The first flights arrive on the coast during the last two weeks of September; the heaviest flights come during the first two weeks of October; departures begin in late February and continue until mid-May. In the Muleshoe National Wildlife Refuge (see under Muleshoe) between 8,000 and 15,000 Sandhill Cranes usually stay through the winter; another winter concentration of several thousand birds occurs on the Cinco Ranch near Houston (see under Houston).

ABILENE. About midway on US Route 80, which crosses the width of Texas just north of its central area, lies Abilene (elevation 1,719 feet) with its fine tourist accommodations. For the bird finder making his initial trip west it makes an interesting stopping point because it is situated in one of the first stretches of typical mesquite plains.

Any road leading out of Abilene passes groves of mesquite, sometimes hung with mistletoe, and intervening grassy stretches where cacti and yuccas are prevalent. Here are habitats for such regular nesting birds as Road-runners, Scissor-tailed Flycatchers, Horned Larks, White-necked Ravens, Verdins, Loggerhead Shrikes, Orchard Orioles, Bullock's Orioles, Lark Sparrows, and Cassin's Sparrows. Two lakes in the vicinity are worth investigating. One, LAKE FORT PHANTOM HILL, is a reservoir a few miles north of town, reached by taking State Route 351 and turning left onto a marked county road. The other, LAKE ABILENE, in LAKE ABILENE STATE PARK (508 acres), is a reservoir 17 miles south of town, reached by taking US Route 83 and turning right onto a marked road. Both reservoirs have muddy shorelines when the water is receding. Waterbirds, waterfowl, and shorebirds frequent the Lakes during migration, sometimes in impressive numbers. If, during late April, May, August, or September, there are muddy edges, shorebirds may be readily observed. Wilson's Phalaropes are sometimes very common, as are Greater

and Lesser Yellow-legs, Pectoral Sandpipers, White-rumped
Sandpipers, Baird's Sandpipers, Dowitchers, and others.
Avocets and Black-necked Stilts also appear and may nest
in the vicinity. Though both Lakes are surrounded by mesquite country, Lake Abilene has in addition a bordering
growth of oaks, hickories, and other trees; thus the area is
attractive to a greater variety of landbirds. Some of the
species to be looked for here are the Mississippi Kite, Black-
chinned Hummingbird, Ladder-backed Woodpecker, and
Black-crested Titmouse.

AMARILLO. This one large city in the Texas Panhandle
may serve as headquarters for the bird finder desiring to
investigate the Staked Plains, the Palo Duro Canyon, and
the numerous lakes that are widely scattered.

The Texas Panhandle embraces an almost square area,
roughly 165 miles from east to west and 150 miles from
north to south. Essentially it is a segment of the short-grass
Great Plains (3,400 to 3,800 feet elevation), flat to slightly
rolling, and treeless except in dooryards, shelterbelts, and
breaks along streams. The land is used principally for the
grazing of livestock and for crop production. The eastern
edge of the Plains is marked by the Cap Rock trending
north and south, some 30 to 50 miles west of the Oklahoma
line. The cultivated areas and grazing lands of the Staked
Plains show a paucity of breeding birds; the Horned Lark,
Western Meadowlark, Grasshopper Sparrow, Lark Sparrow,
and Cassin's Sparrow are among the few species that are
at all common. Where there are shrubs and trees, however,
additional breeding birds, such as the Mourning Dove,
Western Kingbird, Scissor-tailed Flycatcher, Bewick's
Wren, Mockingbird, Bullock's Oriole, and, occasionally, the
Loggerhead Shrike, may be expected; in fact, there is
scarcely a dooryard with trees that does not have at least
one pair of Western Kingbirds or Mockingbirds. Burrowing
Owls may be found wherever there are prairie-dog towns.
Except during the summer months, hawks may be frequently observed along the highways, either in flight or
perched on telephone poles and fence posts. The Rough-
legged Hawk, Ferruginous Hawk, Marsh Hawk, and Sparrow Hawk are the predominating species, except in the

spring and fall (usually April and October), when there are immense flights of Swainson's Hawks. In May, and again in the late summer and fall, migrating flocks of Lark Buntings that contain hundreds of individuals are frequent on the Staked Plains.

Two large streams cut through the Staked Plains of the Panhandle from west to east. One, the South Canadian River, flows through a narrow, bluff-rimmed valley 20 miles north of Amarillo; the other, a somewhat smaller stream called Prairie Dog Town Creek, courses through an awesome gash in the Plains, known as Palo Duro Canyon, 20 miles south of Amarillo. Neither stream ordinarily carries much water, but both are subject to flash floods during the infrequent periods of heavy rainfall. While birdlife is invariably interesting almost anywhere along these streams, unquestionably the greatest variety of species is to be found in that part of Palo Duro Canyon which is in PALO DURO STATE PARK.

Palo Duro State Park (15,103 acres) includes Palo Duro Canyon's upper section, which is a mile wide and 600 feet deep, the walls precipitous and highly colored—mostly red combined with yellow, gray, lavender, and streaks of white. To reach the Park, drive south from Amarillo on US Route 87 for 19 miles, to the town of Canyon; turn left (east) onto State Route 217 and proceed about 12 miles, to the Park entrance. Once in the Park one may take a broad, well-graded road that passes from the rim of the Canyon to the floor, thence down the chasm for a distance of 10 miles through thickets of mesquite and juniper, crossing and re-crossing Prairie Dog Town Creek at frequent intervals. The stream itself is bordered by chinaberry, hackberry, willow, and cottonwood, while here and there are large, grassy flats.

Bird finding in the Canyon is excellent in any season, including the winter months, when the high walls, trees, and brush afford shelter for hosts of birds from near and far. Among the common winter residents are the Robin, Mountain Bluebird (often in huge flocks), Oregon Junco, and White-crowned Sparrow. Along with these species occur the year-round residents, including the Prairie Falcon, Sparrow Hawk, Scaled Quail, Road-runner, Red-shafted

Flicker, Golden-fronted Woodpecker, Ladder-backed Woodpecker, Black-crested Titmouse, Canyon Wren, Rock Wren, Cardinal, House Finch, and Lesser Goldfinch. Beginning in May, when the nesting season gets under way, the following birds may be looked for: Mississippi Kite, Sharp-shinned Hawk, Yellow-billed Cuckoo, Great Horned Owl, Belted Kingfisher, Ash-throated Flycatcher, Cliff Swallow (large colonies), Blue-gray Gnatcatcher, Yellow Warbler, Blue Grosbeak, and Rufous-crowned Sparrow. April, September, and October bring numerous transient species, including the Common Goldfinch and Chipping Sparrow, the Orange-crowned, Nashville, Myrtle, Audubon's, and Black-capped Warblers, and the Yellow-throat.

Scattered across the broad, seemingly interminable expanse of the Panhandle's Staked Plains are thousands of playa lakes, often called 'wet weather' lakes because of their temporary nature. In addition to these natural bodies of water there are several hundred water impoundments that have proved invaluable to waterbirds, waterfowl, and shorebirds when the playas are dry. A good example of one of the larger impoundments is AMARILLO LAKE, formed by damming Palo Duro Creek just before it joins Prairie Dog Town Creek and enters the Canyon. To reach the Lake from the Post Office in Amarillo, drive southwest on Route 87 for 12.2 miles, turn right (west) about 100 yards north of a small playa lake, and proceed west 6 miles on a well-defined road; then turn left (south) and go one mile to the entrance of Amarillo Lake Park (small admission fee). Amarillo Lake lies in the Park, which is a state game preserve open to the public during the fall and winter. Occupying a wide valley of low relief, the Lake is surrounded by treeless plains, though a few willows and cottonwoods border Palo Duro Creek. The shallow west end of the Lake, edged with mud flats, is the best site for birds. Some of the species appearing regularly here in the fall and spring are the Pied-billed Grebe, Great Blue Heron, Canada Goose, Mallard, Gadwall, Baldpate, Pintail, Green-winged Teal, Blue-winged Teal, Shoveler, Redhead, Canvas-back, Lesser Scaup Duck, Ruddy Duck, Coot, Killdeer, Solitary Sandpiper, Lesser Yellow-legs, Dowitcher, Western Sandpiper,

Avocet (known to nest near some of the larger lakes and possibly near this one), Wilson's Phalarope, Ring-billed Gull, and Franklin's Gull.

ANAHUAC. In the eastern part of Galveston Bay, emerging only slightly above the normal high-tide mark, are the VINGT'UN ISLANDS, mere blobs of mud and shells except for two, which have a total surface area of about 2 acres and are the site, from May to July, of a thriving water-bird rookery.

The two islands are close together and are for the most part densely covered with tall shrubs, in which the birds crowd their nests, and with man-high grasses. During their period of occupancy the islands are deep-greenish humps, flecked with quiet white forms, when viewed from across the yellow-green waters of the Bay; but when approached closely they burst suddenly, discharging birds by the hundreds. White birds, pink birds, and birds of darker colors rise excitedly to form a turbulent, multi-colored cloud. It is a marvelous spectacle, but no more marvelous than the fact that so many birds can nest in so small an area.

The white birds, which greatly outnumber the others, are American Egrets, Snowy Egrets, and White Ibises; the pink birds are the handsome Roseate Spoonbills; and the darker-colored birds are Great Blue Herons, Louisiana Herons, Black-crowned Night Herons, and White-faced Ibises. Decidedly overshadowed by these large birds are numerous pairs of Boat-tailed Grackles, two or three pairs of Gull-billed Terns and Least Terns, and (occasionally) several pairs of Black Skimmers.

The Vingt'un Islands rookery is carefully protected by the National Audubon Society, which employs a warden during the nesting months. Landing on the islands is prohibited, and no one is allowed to approach the islands closely enough to disturb the rookery. Bird finders desiring to see the rookery may accompany the warden on his tour of duty. Permission to do so may be obtained by writing to the Society's headquarters, 1130 Fifth Avenue, New York 28, New York. The warden is stationed at Smith's Point, reached from Anahuac by driving south on Farm Road 562 (hard surfaced) for 22 miles.

AUSTIN. The UNIVERSITY OF TEXAS, on a hill north of the State Capitol, offers graduate work, but no undergraduate courses, in ornithology. The Texas Natural History Collection, maintained by the Department of Zoology in Room 401 of the Biological Laboratories Building, contains 1,100 bird skins, mostly from southern and western Texas and northern Mexico.

There is a great variety of environments for birdlife near Austin, principally because the Balcones Escarpment separating the Edwards Plateau from the Coastal Plain passes through the area. The LOWER COLORADO RIVER AUTHORITY PARK on Lake Travis, about 20 air miles northwest of the city, best represents the various bird associations. The Park is reached from Austin by following US Route 290 west to Oak Hill, turning northwest onto State Route 93, and then turning northeast onto a marked, graded road just before reaching the bridge over the Pedernales River. The Park, part of which has stretches of woods and brush, occupies a peninsula of land bounded by the Pedernales River and Lake Travis. The Golden-cheeked Warbler probably nests here. Other breeding birds include the Roadrunner, Screech Owl, Golden-fronted Woodpecker, Black-crested Titmouse, Bewick's Wren, Canyon Wren, and Rufous-crowned Sparrow.

BAY CITY. Not far from this big town on the southeast Coastal Plain there is a thriving rookery, active in May and June, containing Olivaceous Cormorants, Anhingas, Great Blue Herons, American Egrets, Snowy Egrets, Louisiana Herons, Little Blue Herons, Black-crowned Night Herons, Yellow-crowned Night Herons, White-faced Ibises, White Ibises, and Roseate Spoonbills. The rookery occupies a small, relatively obscure area on the HAWKINS RANCH and may be reached as follows: Drive east out of Bay City on State Route 35, which branches, before leaving the city, into a thin Y. Take the right branch (Farm Route 457), narrow but paved, and follow it for about 3 miles; turn right onto the first hard-surfaced road intersecting from the right and proceed on this road until it intersects another road at right angles. At this intersection there are a few houses and a white painted schoolhouse. Turn right here, drive a few hundred yards, and bear left with the road; go a few hundred yards farther until a low thicket appears 500 yards to the right on the open prairie, which is fenced along the road. Park by the roadside, climb through the fence, and walk to the thicket, which extends into a hollow.

Once at the edge of the thicket, the bird finder will be looking directly down on an aggregation of birds, estimated at 1,500 pairs, nesting in the tops of bushes and small trees —a truly impressive sight. The bird finder's position is elevated and is only a few yards from the birds; he may easily watch nesting activities through field glasses or telescope without concealing himself. While here he should look for Audubon's Caracaras, a few pairs of which always nest in the vicinity.

BEAUMONT. Northwest of industrial Beaumont, with its factories and refineries and its oak- and magnolia-shaded residential districts, sprawls the BIG THICKET, a wilderness area estimated to cover some two million acres. Why, considering its extent, its fascinating complexity of terrain and plant distribution, and its reputed richness in birdlife, it remains an unknown quantity ornithologically cannot be answered.

The Big Thicket consists of both upland and swamp forests cut up by innumerable fresh-water or brackish streams, bayous, and ponds that are bordered with, and not infrequently choked by, waterlilies, hyacinths, cattails, and other herbaceous vegetation. Hardwoods—beeches, magnolias, tupelos, sweet gums, and various species of oaks and ashes—with an undergrowth of shrubs, so dense in places as to be almost impenetrable, are predominant on poorly drained ground, but on ridges or on 'islands' of higher, dry ground are stands of loblolly, short-leaf, and long-leaf pines and post, red, and blackjack oaks. Though lumber and oil operations and fires have taken their toll of timber growth, there are still places where the forest is relatively undisturbed. To state positively just what species of birds may be expected and where they may be found is impossible, but it seems quite likely that one should find such breeding species as the following: along waterways, the Anhinga, Mottled Duck, Wood Duck, Louisiana Heron, Little Blue

Heron, Purple Gallinule, and Prothonotary Warbler; in the hardwoods, the Red-shouldered Hawk, Barred Owl, Pileated Woodpecker, Acadian Flycatcher, Blue-gray Gnatcatcher, Yellow-throated Vireo, Swainson's Warbler, Parula Warbler, Kentucky Warbler, Hooded Warbler, and Summer Tanager; in the pines, the Red-cockaded Woodpecker, Brown-headed Nuthatch, Pine Warbler, and Pinewoods Sparrow. What may be found here during the spring and fall migrations, or during the winter, also remains to be determined.

The main roads leading north and west from Beaumont pass through sections of the Big Thicket, but the following route will give the bird finder the best roadside view of it. From Beaumont, drive north on US Route 69 to Kountze, turn left (west) on State Route 326, and, after 5 miles, turn right on State Route 770 to the town of Saratoga. From here, go north on State Route 787 to Votaw, then east on an unnumbered road to the settlement of Thicket. Between Saratoga and Thicket, typical parts of this wilderness area lie close to the highway and may be readily observed. No attempt, however, should be made to explore far beyond the highway without a guide or map, compass, and general knowledge of the environment.

BROWNSVILLE-HARLINGEN. To see a sample of what birdlife is like in Mexico, without leaving the United States, the bird finder may go to the Brownsville-Harlingen region in the lower Rio Grande Valley. Numerous Mexican birds breed here that are found nowhere else in the United States.

Originally the drier, sandy soils of the region produced an abundance of mesquite thickets, yuccas, cacti, and grasses, while the richer soils along the resacas (old beds of the Rio Grande now cut off and usually filled with water) supported forests of jungle-like density. Remnants of these bird habitats still exist, but they are fast disappearing, destroyed by the rapid growth of cities and by increased agricultural activities. Fortunately for the visiting bird finder in the years ahead, there are two areas in which these habitats will remain relatively undisturbed and which will continue to hold an excellent representation of birds once characteristic of the region. These are two National Wildlife

Refuges, the main headquarters of which are in San Benito.

The SANTA ANA NATIONAL WILDLIFE REFUGE (1,981 acres) lies southwest of Harlingen in a lowland flanking a big bend of the Rio Grande. On the tract there are three lakes—Santa Ana Lake (200 acres), West Lake (150 acres), and North Lake (150 acres)—choked with retama, mimosa, and other plants that die off each time the Rio Grande overflows. Marshes containing duckweeds and naiads are on the periphery of all three of these bodies of water. In addition to the lakes, there is a dense, lowland forest of red elms festooned with Spanish moss, mixed with Texas ebonies, tepeguajes, ashes, and hackberries, and having an understory vine and herbaceous growth. On the drier upland is a typical mesquite association.

Chachalacas are regularly present in the Refuge forests and may be heard at their noisy best in April and May. The trim little Green Kingfisher should always be looked for along the Rio Grande. Other permanent-resident birds are the Least Grebe, Ground Dove, White-fronted Dove, Ferruginous Pygmy Owl, Merrill's Parauque, Golden-fronted Woodpecker, Ladder-backed Woodpecker, Derby Flycatcher, Beardless Flycatcher, Green Jay, Black-crested Titmouse, Sennett's Thrasher, Curve-billed Thrasher, Audubon's Oriole, Red-eyed Cowbird, and Texas Sparrow.

Hooded Orioles arrive in late March or early April and begin making their nests in the Spanish moss. Also putting in their appearance as summer residents at about this same time, or a little later, are the following: Red-billed Pigeon, White-winged Dove, Yellow-billed Cuckoo, Groove-billed Ani, Buff-bellied Hummingbird, Couch's Kingbird, Mexican Crested Flycatcher, Sennett's Warbler, Summer Tanager, and Painted Bunting. For most birds, whether permanent or summer residents, the breeding season is prolonged, continuing through May, June, and July.

Ducks are numerous on the Refuge during the winter months, but by the last of April most of them have departed, with the exception of the Black-bellied Tree-duck, which breeds on the Refuge and is sometimes present throughout the year. Transient passerine birds—flycatchers, warblers, vireos, and others—are abundant during March, April, September, and October.

To reach the Santa Ana Refuge, drive west from Harlingen on US Route 83 to Alamo. On the western edge of this
town, turn left (south) onto South Alamo Road (Alamo
Boulevard); drive 7 miles to the Military Highway (US
Route 281), and turn left; go 0.4 mile to a dirt road (leads
across a field and is impassable in wet weather) intersecting
on the right; turn onto this road, and follow it half a mile,
along a power line and over a levee, down to the Refuge
headquarters, which is just inside the Refuge boundary.
Some of the best bird-finding opportunities are in the vicinity of headquarters, but exploration of the lower part of
the Refuge tract is also worth while. Continue 0.6 of a mile
on the road that goes past headquarters to a fork. The right-
hand road leads immediately to a dry, brushy area in which
Road-runners have nested for a number of years. About
0.7 of a mile beyond the fork, on the right-hand road, park
the car and take a foot trail on the left that goes to West
Lake, a short distance away. The left-hand road from the
fork soon drops down into a shallow swale where the
Acadian Flycatcher has been found nesting (perhaps the
southernmost point of this species' breeding range). About
0.5 of a mile beyond the fork (on the left-hand road), a road
to the left goes for 0.4 of a mile and ends on the bank of
the Rio Grande. Near this termination is a place where a
pair of Rose-throated Becards has been known to nest.

When returning to Harlingen from the Refuge, the bird
finder may go another way, thus increasing the chances of
seeing still other birds. At the top of the levee that was
crossed on entering the Refuge, turn sharp right and drive
along it for about 2.1 miles. At first the levee overlooks Santa
Ana Lake on the right, but later it overlooks two smaller
lakes (on the same side) which are excellent for Black-
bellied Tree-ducks. After 2.1 miles, take a road on the left
that leads down off the levee and reaches the Military Highway, 0.7 of a mile distant. Turn right onto the Highway,
which, 5 miles ahead, cuts through a stretch of chaparral
that holds an association of such typical birds as the Verdin,
Bewick's Wren, Cactus Wren, Curve-billed Thrasher,
Pyrrhuloxia, Varied Bunting, and Desert Sparrow. The Military Highway eventually reaches Brownsville. East of Blue-

town a left turn off the Highway onto a paved road (marked 'to Rangerville') will lead back to Harlingen.

The LAGUNA ATASCOSA NATIONAL WILDLIFE REFUGE has two sections totaling 38,759 acres. Both, lying east of Harlingen and north of Brownsville, embrace grassy, coastal prairies, salt flats covered with tamarisk and salt grass, low ridges supporting thick, thorny shrubs, and stretches of plain on which mesquite, clepe, granjeno, and Texas ebony comprise the principal woody growth, with various kinds of short grasses, cacti, and yuccas abundant in the more open spots. Water areas consist of Laguna Atascosa (3,000 surface acres), Laguna de los Patos (250–300 acres), Cayo Atascosa (some 300 feet to half a mile wide and 6 miles long), western reaches of the Laguna Madre, and several potholes and resacas. Except for the shallow Laguna de los Patos, with its mats of bulrushes and cattails, and the fringes of the many potholes and resacas, there are no extensive marshes.

During the nesting season some of the species of birds to be found on the Refuge in suitable habitats are the Least Grebe, Mottled Duck, White-tailed Kite, Sennett's White-tailed Hawk, Harris' Hawk, Audubon's Caracara, Clapper Rail, Snowy Plover, Wilson's Plover, Florida Gallinule, Willet, Black-necked Stilt, Ground Dove, Road-runner, Groove-billed Ani, Lesser Nighthawk, Golden-fronted Woodpecker, Ladder-backed Woodpecker, Scissor-tailed Flycatcher, Vermilion Flycatcher, Horned Lark, Verdin, Bewick's Wren, Curve-billed Thrasher, Eastern Meadowlark, Blue Grosbeak, Texas Sparrow, Botteri's Sparrow, Cassin's Sparrow, and both the Hooded and Bullock's Orioles. A few ducks arrive on the Refuge by the last of August, but most of them appear between 21 October and 14 November. Many remain through the winter. Such waterbirds as the American, Snowy, and Reddish Egrets, White-faced Ibis, White Ibis, and Roseate Spoonbill may be viewed on the Refuge the year round. An indication of the great numbers of birds that winter on the Refuge is revealed by the Christmas bird count of 1950, when 95,074 individuals, representing 152 species, were recorded.

Nearly all parts of the Laguna Atascosa Refuge that are

productive ornithologically may be reached by dirt roads, except in wet weather, when the roads are impassable. The best road through the Refuge is reached by driving north from Brownsville or south from Harlingen on US Route 77 to San Benito, then east on State Route 345 to Rio Hondo. From Rio Hondo, take the East Road, which, at this point, is also Farm Route 106. When Route 106 turns north, about 3 miles out of town, continue straight ahead. About 9 miles from Rio Hondo, the East Road enters the first section of the Refuge. (The familiar flying-goose sign will denote the boundary.) The country near the entrance is typical chaparral. Look for Botteri's Sparrows in the grassy patches, for Verdins, Curve-billed Thrashers, Blue Grosbeaks, and Texas Sparrows in the shrubby thickets. About half a mile farther on, the road comes to the Cayo Atascosa, which is here a tiny stream flowing toward the Laguna Atascosa about a mile north of the road. A walk along the Cayo to the Laguna passes through excellent shorebird territory. Anywhere near the Cayo or farther east, toward the Laguna Madre, the bird finder is likely to see Harris' Hawks, White-tailed Kites, and Sennett's White-tailed Hawks.

About 3.2 miles east of the Cayo Atascosa, the road comes to a fence and then divides, one road going north, the other south. The north road goes through country similar to that already traversed; the south road leaves the first section of the Refuge. Take the south road for 0.7 of a mile, then turn left (east) into the second section of the Refuge. This road soon passes through an area containing pure stands of salt grass where Botteri's Sparrows abound from May to September. After going 0.4 of a mile turn right (south) and drive 1.7 miles; turn right again (west) and go 1.3 miles; then turn left (south) out of the Refuge and pass through the Bay View Citrus Grove. Beyond this last turn, after a distance of 1.4 miles, the road reaches Farm Route 510. If the bird finder wishes to return directly to Harlingen or Brownsville, he may turn right onto Route 510 to San Benito and take Route 77, but if he desires to look further for birds, the following trip is recommended.

Turn left onto Farm Route 510 and proceed toward Port Isabel. In dry weather, an interesting way is to turn off Route 510 after 4.2 miles and follow a dirt road along the shore of the Laguna Madre to Port Isabel. This trip permits many close views, in any season, of pelicans, cormorants, gulls, terns, Black Skimmers, and shorebirds. If the weather is wet, or if a more direct route is desired, stay on Route 510 to State Route 100, which goes east to Port Isabel. East of the intersection of Routes 510 and 100, Cassin's Sparrows are rather common summer residents in outlying grassland.

From Port Isabel, one may return directly to Harlingen or Brownsville by taking Route 100 west, but a more productive trip for bird finders is as follows: From the Humble Filling Station in the business district of Port Isabel, drive west on Route 100 for 10.1 miles. About 100 yards south of the highway at this point, Avocets may be found nesting along the shore of a lake. Continue west on Route 100 for 2.3 miles and go straight ahead on a dirt road instead of following the highway to the right.

The brushy areas, most of them to the left of this road, will probably hold such breeding birds as Lesser Nighthawks, Cactus Wrens, Curve-billed Thrashers, Botteri's Sparrows, Cassin's Sparrows, and Desert Sparrows. Continue on this road for 7.6 miles, passing Loma Alta Lake on the left. At the junction with Farm Route 511, turn left onto Route 511 and go to the junction with State Route 48; turn onto Route 48 (also becomes Route 511) and proceed a short distance until Route 511 turns off to the right. Follow Route 511 east and then south until it joins State Route 4 (Boca Chica Highway). Turn left onto Route 4 and go 4.5 miles. At this point, several hundred yards to the left (north), lies a long, low, narrow ridge called the Loma de la Montuosa Chica—so named to distinguish it from the larger Loma de la Montuosa just east of it. On the crest of the ridge is a line of mesquite trees. Toward the west end of the crest, near some small shacks, several pairs of Vermilion Flycatchers have nested regularly for many years between April and July. If a walk to this ridge is attempted, beware of rattlesnakes, which are numerous in the vicinity. State Route 4 continues east past the Loma de la Montuosa to Boca Chica Beach, which, like the shore of the Laguna Madre, will yield waterbirds and shorebirds.

In the Laguna Madre about 30 miles north of Port Isabel is one of the National Audubon Society's oldest sanctuaries,

GREEN ISLAND, which has an enormous rookery contain- ing Great Blue Herons, American Egrets, Snowy Egrets, Reddish Egrets, Louisiana Herons, Black-crowned Night Herons, and a few White Ibises. Much of the Island's 30 acres of surface is covered with thick brush, cacti, and yuccas which these birds utilize as supports for their nests. Where there are sand flats without vegetation Least Terns and Black Skimmers nest. Landing on Green Island, or otherwise disturbing the birds, is prohibited, but bird finders interested in seeing the aggregation may accompany the Audubon warden on one of his regular patrols during the nesting season in May, June, and July. Permission to make the trip with him must be obtained from the National Audu- bon Society, 1130 Fifth Avenue, New York 28, New York, and arrangements for the trip made in advance with the warden, whose name and address will be supplied by the Society.

COLLEGE STATION. The AGRICULTURAL AND MECHANICAL COLLEGE OF TEXAS is one of the centers of ornithological research in the state. Courses in ornithology are given each year by the Department of Wild- life Management in the Agricultural Engineering Building, where there are collections of more than 5,000 bird skins, largely from Texas and central Mexico.

CRYSTAL CITY. Millions of Americans bound for Mexico leave the United States by way of Laredo and thence pass along the Pan-American Highway. In order to reach Laredo they cross a part of the Chaparral Country, whether on US Route 81 south from San Antonio, or on US Route 83 south from Uvalde and Crystal City. The few streams in the Coun- try flow mainly in wet seasons, but some water is conserved in small lakes, both natural and artificial. One of the largest watercourses traversing the area from west to east, the Nueces River, is rather narrow and deep, and is lined with live oak, pecan, black walnut, ash, elm, and button willow. Route 83 parallels the River for many miles between Uvalde and Crystal City, and Route 81 crosses it just south of Cotulla. Although some of the Chaparral Country is irri- gated for crop production, much more of it is used for grazing livestock. All in all, it is a thinly settled area of considerable sameness and, to the average tourist, is a part of the trip to be hurried through; but to the bird finder it is not without interest, for it holds an abundance and variety of birds.

When one is traveling on either highway, a number of species may be seen readily from the car. In any season, Mourning Doves and White-necked Ravens are very common and conspicuous, and there is always a chance of identifying a Black Vulture, Red-tailed Hawk, Swainson's Hawk, or Harris' Hawk. Now and then a common species, the Road-runner, dashes across the road ahead. From September to April, Sparrow Hawks and Loggerhead Shrikes are invariably observed sitting on wires, posts, and telephone poles, and Marsh Hawks are regularly seen flying low over the brushy terrain. Familiar sights between March and November are Scissor-tailed Flycatchers resting on exposed perches and making aerial forays for grasshoppers, butterflies, bees, and other insects.

On almost any of the numerous side roads leading off the highways, small birds show up to advantage. Regardless of the season, one can always find such species as the Scaled Quail, Ground Dove, Verdin, Cactus Wren, Mockingbird, Curve-billed Thrasher, Pyrrhuloxia, Lark Sparrow, and Desert Sparrow. The Blue Grosbeak occurs fairly often as a transient in March, April, September, and October.

Both the Common and Lesser Nighthawks are regularly present from May to October; the Poor-will sometimes occurs in the breeding season but is seldom seen. If the road comes to a brush-filled draw where there is a pond or reservoir for cattle, the Vermilion Flycatcher and Bell's Vireo should be looked for.

Near, or within the limits of, the towns through which the highways pass are permanent-resident Inca Doves, Barn Owls, Screech Owls, Bewick's Wrens, and House Finches. Beginning in late April or early May, the summer residents of the tree and shrub plantations in these same localities, or of the citrus orchards, include the White-winged Dove (very noisy and increasing in numbers), Yellow-billed Cuckoo, Black-chinned Hummingbird, Orchard Oriole, Hooded Oriole, Bullock's Oriole, and Painted Bunting. Dur-

ing the winter Cedar Waxwings are often abundant and
there are usually a few Sharp-shinned and Cooper's Hawks,
House Wrens, Robins, Ruby-crowned Kinglets, Myrtle
Warblers, Lesser Goldfinches, and White-crowned Sparrows.

The NUECES RIVER VALLEY, with its woods and
brushy woodland borders, is a likely locality for certain of
the species named above and, in addition, for the Barred
Owl, Belted and Green Kingfishers, Golden-fronted and
Ladder-backed Woodpeckers, Crested Flycatcher, Black-
crested Titmouse, Carolina Wren, White-eyed Vireo, and
Cardinal, which may be found throughout the year. Waterbirds, waterfowl, and shorebirds frequent the River itself
from August to April, but never in very great numbers. The
best spot for these birds is slough-like ESPANTOSA LAKE,
lying in the Nueces River Valley south of Crystal City. Some
of the birds to be expected here are the Anhinga, Little Blue
Heron, Yellow-crowned Night Heron, and Florida Gallinule. Route 83 between Crystal City and Carrizo Springs
parallels this narrow body of water on the west for about
8 miles.

DALLAS. For a big, compact industrial and commercial
center situated on the open prairie, Dallas has an unexpected number of places for bird finding in different seasons. Indicated below are the more productive spots. When
driving to them, the bird finder will find useful a detailed
map published by the Chamber of Commerce.

BACHMAN'S LAKE, within the northern city limits,
is shallow at one end and reed-bordered; when the water
is low, it has extensive mud flats. Though a small body of
water, Bachman's Lake is good for ducks any time between
mid-October and mid-April; sometimes there are as many
as 12 species, including the Mallard, Gadwall, Baldpate,
Pintail, Green-winged Teal, Blue-winged Teal, Redhead,
Ring-necked Duck, Canvas-back, Lesser Scaup Duck, and
Ruddy Duck. If there are mud flats present in April, May,
August, and September, one may expect such shorebirds as
the Wilson's Snipe, Solitary Sandpiper, Lesser Yellow-legs,
Dowitcher, and numerous 'peeps.' The woods and thickets
along Bachman's Creek, which flows into the east end of the

Lake, attract many kinds of small, winter resident land-birds; among them are Brown Creepers, Golden-crowned and Ruby-crowned Kinglets, Myrtle Warblers, Common Goldfinches, Field Sparrows, White-throated Sparrows, Lincoln's Sparrows, and Song Sparrows. To reach Bach-man's Lake from the center of the city, take Harry Hines Boulevard (US Route 77) northwest for about 5 miles, then turn right on Shorecrest Drive. This follows the south-ern edge of the Lake. To reach the woods along Bachman's Creek, continue on Shorecrest Drive across Lemmon Ave-nue.

Another place for ducks is the DALLAS FISH HATCH-ERY on the northeast side of the city at the south end of White Rock Lake. This can be reached from Bachman's Lake by turning northwest (left) on Lemmon Avenue off Shorecrest Drive, driving east (right) on North West High-way (first traffic light) for several miles to Lawther Drive, then turning right on Lawther Drive and following its wind-ing course along the shore of White Rock Lake in White Rock Park. Shortly after passing the junction with White Rock Road (on the right) look for a sign marked 'Dead End Street' and an underpass. On the right, just beyond the underpass, is the Hatchery. Park the car at the entrance, and walk in to look over the pools. Though ducks are present on the pools only from mid-October to mid-April, this spot, and particularly White Rock Creek (just outside the Hatch-ery), with its bordering growth of emergent aquatic plants, shrubs, and trees, will yield interesting birds in winter and summer. Some of the waterbirds that may be expected in summer are the Green Heron, Black-crowned Night Heron, Yellow-crowned Night Heron, King Rail, Purple Gallinule, and Florida Gallinule.

On the southwest side of the city, nestled in mesquite and scrub-oak-covered hills, lies MOUNTAIN CREEK LAKE. Here from May until the last of September there are fair numbers of American Egrets, Snowy Egrets, Little Blue Herons, and Great Blue Herons. Avocets may be present in May, September, and October; Black Terns are numerous during the last three weeks of May and again the last of August and September. The last half of September and the first week of October bring thousands of swallows of several species, the Barn Swallow often predominating. From mid-October to mid-November huge flocks of Franklin's Gulls make the Lake their headquarters while they forage for food in the surrounding countryside. Landbird finding is invariably good near the Lake. The Ladder-backed Woodpecker is a regular year-round inhabitant of the mesquite and oaks. Both Eastern and Western Meadowlarks may be heard singing during May in open grassy places. Scissor-tailed Flycatchers nests are always easy to find—sometimes they are in dead trees standing in the Lake. To reach Mountain Creek Lake from the center of the city, drive west on US Route 80 to Hampton Road, turn left (south) to Illinois Avenue, then turn right (west) and follow Illinois Avenue to the Lake, where it becomes Mountain Lake Road and passes along the eastern shore for several miles.

CAMP KIWANIS, operated by the Girl Scouts, is in the same general direction from the center of the city as Mountain Creek Lake. The hilly terrain in the vicinity is covered chiefly with oak-hickory woods and low shrubs. This is one of the few spots where one may be sure of finding the Black-capped Vireo from mid-April to the first of September. Other birds to be found here in the late spring and summer include the Blue-gray Gnatcatcher, White-eyed Vireo, Red-eyed Vireo, and Summer Tanager. Directions for reaching the Camp and permission to enter the premises may be obtained at the local Girl Scout Headquarters, 4222 Herschel Avenue.

The DALLAS MUSEUM OF NATURAL HISTORY, in Fair Park, has a collection of 3,500 bird skins and 1,000 bird mounts, including a synoptic series of the species of the Dallas area. Among the exhibits of special interest are habitat groups of Texas birds. To reach Fair Park, go east on Main Street and turn right onto First Avenue, which goes directly to the Park.

EL PASO. Although Texas' westernmost city (elevation 3,762 feet) is ringed by arid mountains and extensive deserts, the neighboring Rio Grande, together with numerous irrigation projects, makes its environs attractive to waterfowl and waterbirds, as well as to landbirds.

Winter bird finding is good in ASCARATE PARK, 5 miles

east of the city, on US Route 80. Here, on an artificial lake, grebes (Horned, Eared, Western, and Pied-billed), 12 to 15 species of ducks, Coots, and herons may be seen. In addition to such permanent-resident landbirds as the Scaled Quail, Gambel's Quail, Mourning Dove, Red-shafted Flicker, and Ladder-backed Woodpecker, there are various winter residents—for example, the Mountain Bluebird, Brewer's Blackbird, Spotted Towhee, Baird's Sparrow, Oregon Junco, Brewer's Sparrow, and White-crowned Sparrow —which may be observed in considerable numbers in grassy places, groves of trees, or shrubby thickets. The bird finder will invariably turn up the following species in June and July: the Yellow-billed Cuckoo, Black-chinned Humming-bird, Western Kingbird, Traill's Flycatcher, Mockingbird, Bell's Vireo, Yellow Warbler, Yellow-throat, Yellow-breasted Chat, Bullock's Oriole, Summer Tanager, Blue Grosbeak, and Painted Bunting.

An association of birds typical of the near-by deserts and canyons is found in McKELLIGON CANYON, 7 miles north of the city. This is reached by driving north on Piedras Street and following it as it swings left into the Canyon. Among the birds that commonly occur here at any season are the Scaled Quail, Road-runner, Verdin, Cactus Wren, Canyon Wren, Rock Wren, Brown Towhee, and Desert Sparrow.

For the greatest variety of birds in any season, local bird finders recommend the drive along the levee of the Rio Grande either east or west of the city. From the levee one may watch the river on one side for waterbirds and on the other for birds of the arid country or irrigated farmlands. To reach the levee east of the city, drive east on US Route 80 to the city limits, turn right on Hammet Boulevard, which goes to the top of the levee, then turn left and proceed slowly, stopping when likely spots for birds come into close view. To reach the levee west of the city, drive west on US Route 80A to Country Club Road, turn onto it, and follow it across a bridge to the levee; then turn right at the top of the levee and proceed to Mesilla Dam. On the impounded water here, waterbirds and waterfowl congregate during the migration periods and in the winter.

The El Paso Audubon Society meets the first Tuesday

of each month at 7:30 p.m. in the Museum of Texas Western College, through which institution it may be contacted. Besides publishing a quarterly, *The Road-Runner,* this organization sponsors a series of public lectures, conducts trips to outstanding bird habitats, and promotes a conservation program in the public schools.

From the desert plains about 100 miles east of El Paso rise the abrupt slopes of the GUADALUPE MOUNTAINS, attaining on Guadalupe Peak an elevation of 8,751 feet, the highest point in Texas. Of the Guadalupes' many breathtaking escarpments, the most imposing is the sheer, 1,500-foot face of El Capitan (elevation 8,078 feet), a familiar landmark for many generations of travelers and now probably one of the most photographed mountain features in southwestern United States.

US Route 62 leads east from El Paso to the Guadalupes, crossing low, treeless mountains or foothills and deserts of creosote bush, mesquite, greasewood, agave, cactus, and yucca. Within 10 miles or so of the Mountains the road crosses the SALT FLATS (elevation 3,300 feet)—a desolate stretch of glaring white that contains, after wet weather, shallow blue-green lakes of considerable extent. If there is sufficient water in the late spring, late summer, or early fall, Snowy Plovers, Baird's Sandpipers, Western Sandpipers, Sanderlings, and other shorebirds frequently occur here. Birds that undoubtedly breed in the vicinity include the Scaled Quail, Lesser Nighthawk, White-necked Raven, Mockingbird, Curve-billed Thrasher, and Lark Sparrow. Not far east of the Salt Flats, Route 62 reaches the foothills of the Guadalupes and begins its tortuous ascent through Guadalupe Canyon to Guadalupe Pass, whose elevation is 5,297 feet.

The Guadalupes in Texas (the northern part of the range is across the border in New Mexico) cover a triangular area of some 55 square miles and have many ridges and summits in excess of 8,000 feet altitude. The foothills, the south-facing slopes up to the summits of ridges, and the north-facing slopes up to 6,000 feet support a vegetation in which pinyon pine, juniper, madroña, cane cactus, and catclaw are some of the conspicuous plants. The Desert Sparrow, which seems to be present wherever there is cane cactus, is one of the characteristic birds. The higher peaks, northern slopes above 6,000 feet, and the shaded heads of canyons (often below 6,000 feet) show a different plant association, consisting of ponderosa pine (in some spots attaining a height of about 80 feet), limber pine, Douglas fir, mountain white oak, and buckthorn. An especially fine association of this type is in 'the Bowl' at an elevation of about 8,000 feet.

The Guadalupes, for the most part privately owned, are thinly settled and without parks and other recreational facilities; consequently they have very few roads suitable for an ordinary car. Pine Spring Camp (elevation 5,634 feet) on Route 62, 11 miles north of Guadalupe Pass, offers limited accommodations and, because of its location, makes an ideal base for a visiting bird finder. Here permission and directions may be obtained for a walk up the north wall of Pine Spring Canyon to the summit of a ridge that overlooks the Bowl. This trip permits the bird finder to see the transition in birdlife from the south-facing slopes around the Camp to the coniferous forests on the upper reaches of Pine Spring Canyon and in the Bowl. For breeding birds, the period between late April and the first of June is best.

Nesting birds to be expected around Guadalupe Pass, Pine Spring Camp, and Pine Spring Canyon include the White-throated Swift, Red-shafted Flicker, Ladder-backed Woodpecker, Cassin's Kingbird, Ash-throated Flycatcher, Say's Phoebe (usually near houses), Scrub Jay, Cactus Wren, Crissal Thrasher, Gray Vireo, Scott's Oriole, Brown Towhee, and Rufous-crowned Sparrow. In the upper reaches of Pine Spring Canyon and in the Bowl, the following species breed regularly: Acorn Woodpecker, Hairy Woodpecker, Western Flycatcher, Steller's Jay, Mountain Chickadee, White-breasted Nuthatch, Pygmy Nuthatch, Hermit Thrush, Warbling Vireo, Audubon's Warbler, Grace's Warbler, Western Tanager, and (Red-backed) Gray-headed Junco. Birds that are likely to be observed at almost any elevation during the trip are the Golden Eagle, Poor-will, Broad-tailed Hummingbird, Violet-green Swallow, Bush-tit, House Finch, and Chipping Sparrow.

FORT DAVIS. North and west of Fort Davis (elevation 4,926 feet), which lies in the semi-arid valley of Limpia

Creek, rise the DAVIS MOUNTAINS; the highest peak, Mt. Livermore (Baldy Peak), reaches 8,382 feet, the second highest point in the state. Though little explored ornithologically, the Davis Mountains are known to hold an immense number of opportunities for the bird finder.

Compared with the Chisos Mountains in Big Bend National Park (see under Marathon), the Davis Mountains have a refreshing greenness about them and a less rugged, somewhat kindlier beauty—an over-all impression that has some basis in fact. Despite their rocky surfaces, they have a denser cover of vegetation. This is especially true at elevations above 5,000 feet, where there are many trees, principally scrub oaks and junipers, with a considerable number of pinyon pines, on the north-facing slopes. (Near the summit of Mt. Livermore there is a small grove of aspens.) On the slopes below 5,000 feet the vegetation is characteristically scrub, with thickets of mesquite and acacia often widely separated by grassy stretches containing yuccas and cacti.

A time strongly recommended for bird finding in the Davis Mountains is April and May, when singing is at its height and when a great many desert flowers are in bloom. The Mountain View Lodge on the eastern side of Fort Davis offers clean, neat quarters with excellent meals and makes an ideal headquarters for bird finding. Close by are such resident birds as Common Nighthawks, Lesser Nighthawks, Cassin's Kingbirds, and Crissal Thrashers; the Lodge is also convenient to some of the best spots for Davis Mountain birds. Other accommodations, including camping facilities, are available in Davis Mountains State Park (2,130 acres), a recreational area in the upper part of Limpia Canyon, 5 miles northwest of Fort Davis on State Route 118.

If one has not already searched for desert birds in his trip to the Davis Mountains, all he needs do is drive south from Fort Davis for a short distance across the antelope range on Route 118. Road-runners, Horned Larks, Western Meadowlarks, Cassin's Sparrows, and other birds may be expected.

The most accessible spot for mountain birds may be reached by driving northwest on Route 118 beyond Davis Mountains State Park to a point 17 miles from Fort Davis, then taking a road to the right which leads up Mt. Locke (6,828 feet) to the McDonald Astronomical Observatory, which belongs to the University of Texas. On the slopes and around the summit of this peak are numerous breeding birds—for example, the Mourning Dove (lower slopes), Poor-will, Black-chinned Hummingbird, Rufous Hummingbird, Cassin's Kingbird (one of the most conspicuous birds around the summit), Ash-throated Flycatcher, Olive-sided Flycatcher, Scrub Jay, Black-crested Titmouse, Bush-tit, Bewick's Wren, Canyon Wren, Rock Wren (more frequently on the lower slopes), Hepatic Tanager, Black-headed Grosbeak, Brown Towhee, Rufous-crowned Sparrow, Chipping Sparrow, and an occasional Phainopepla.

From the turnoff to Mt. Locke, one may continue northwestward on Route 118 to State Route 166, turn left onto Route 166, and return to Fort Davis, skirting the western side of the Davis Mountains, including Mt. Livermore. Called the Scenic Loop, the trip totals 74 miles from Fort Davis and back. In addition to certain birds already mentioned, others to be looked for in suitable situations during this trip include the Scissor-tailed Flycatcher, Say's Phoebe, Scott's Oriole, and Lesser Goldfinch.

FORT WORTH. Close to this big city, which lies on the prairie between the East and West Cross Timbers of northeast-central Texas, are several places for diversified bird finding.

Only 2 miles from the business district is the BOTANIC GARDEN (40 acres), reached by driving one mile south from the Tarrant County Courthouse on Main Street, turning right on Lancaster Avenue (US Route 80) and proceeding to University Drive, then turning left on University Drive and going about one mile through Trinity Park to a sign designating the Garden. Turn right here and drive to the Garden Center (a building) about a quarter of a mile distant. In addition to woodlands, the Garden has lawns, pools, lagoons, formal gardens, and a small amount of prairie on the western edge. From late March to mid-May, and from late August through October, as many as 25 species of warblers, together with other small passerine birds, may be identified in migration. Among the birds nesting in the

Garden, or very near by, are the following: Yellow-billed
Cuckoo, Barred Owl, Black-chinned Hummingbird, Red-
bellied Woodpecker, Crested Flycatcher, Tufted Titmouse,
Bewick's Wren, Carolina Wren, Eastern Bluebird, Summer
Tanager, and Painted Bunting. Between October and April,
winter residents include the Red-shouldered Hawk, Yellow-
shafted and Red-shafted Flickers, Common Sapsucker, Red-
breasted Nuthatch, Golden-crowned and Ruby-crowned
Kinglets, Orange-crowned Warbler, Mourning Warbler,
Purple Finch, Pine Siskin, Eastern and Spotted Towhees,
and numerous sparrows such as the Savannah, Field, Harris',
Fox, Lincoln's, and Swamp.

The following trip northwest of Fort Worth leads into
typical Cross Timbers. Drive west from the Courthouse on
West Weatherford Street for 7 blocks to Henderson Street;
turn right on Henderson Street, which becomes the Jacksboro Highway (State Route 199). Once out of the city the
Highway traverses what was once typical prairie country;
here one may expect to see such nesting birds as the Scissor-
tailed Flycatcher, Eastern and Western Meadowlarks,
Painted Bunting, Dickcissel, and Lark Sparrow. Nine miles
from Fort Worth the Highway crosses Nine Mile Bridge.
This spans a portion of Lake Worth, an artificial body of
water with a surface area in excess of 5,000 acres. In the
vicinity are oaks and mesquite on the sandy uplands (part
of the so-called West Cross Timbers) and pecans, hackberries, willows, and various shrubs in the moist lowlands. The
best place in which to look for birds characteristic of these
wooded habitats is LAKE WORTH PARK (2,779 acres),
adjacent to the Lake. The entrance, between two columns
of native rock, is on the right of the Highway, half a mile
beyond the Bridge. Most of the species of birds occurring
in the Botanic Garden may be found here; in addition, the
Whip-poor-will and Poor-will may be observed in the migration season, the Chuck-will's-widow in the summer, and the
Black Vulture the year round.

For waterbirds, waterfowl, and shorebirds, the most productive spot in the Fort Worth area is the FISH HATCH-
ERY of the Texas Game and Fish Commission. This is
reached as follows: Drive north on the Jacksboro Highway
to the Eagle Mountain Service Station (7 miles north of

Nine Mile Bridge); turn right on the Eagle Mountain Dam Road and proceed about 2 miles to the first dam; drive across the dam, make a sharp turn to the right, and go for about 3 miles; turn left and continue for about a mile to the second dam. The entrance to the Fish Hatchery is on the right just before the second dam is reached. Permission to visit the Hatchery ponds must be obtained at the custodian's house near the entrance. In the late summer, many herons (including the Little Blue and Yellow-crowned Night Herons) can be watched in the shallow water of the ponds. Probably the best time for bird finding is from mid-September to mid-November, because during this period many of the pools are being drained, leaving broad mud flats attractive to Golden and Black-bellied Plovers, Solitary Sandpipers, Lesser Yellow-legs, Pectoral Sandpipers, Stilt Sandpipers, Western Sandpipers, and other shorebirds. Also, during this period, many transient and winter-resident ducks arrive, including Gadwalls, Cinnamon Teal, Baldpates, Ring-necked Ducks, American Golden-eyes, Buffle-heads, and Ruddy Ducks. In late October, Ring-billed Gulls, Laughing Gulls, Franklin's Gulls, Bonaparte's Gulls, Least Terns, and Black Terns may be observed.

The Fort Worth Audubon Club publishes the *Texas Nature News* (mimeographed; monthly), meets the first Thursday of each month (except during June, July, and August) at 7:30 P.M. in the Playhouse of the Children's Museum, and schedules field trips on the third Sunday of each month at 2:00 P.M. The organization may be contacted through the Children's Museum, 1306 Summit Avenue, Fort Worth 4.

GALVESTON. Because of its situation on Galveston Island, between Galveston Bay and the Gulf of Mexico, this port city is near many salt-water bays and estuaries, fresh-water ponds, beaches, mud flats, and marshy grasslands where waterbirds, waterfowl, and shorebirds congregate in immense numbers. Outlined below are three trips from Galveston that will lead the bird finder to some of the most rewarding of these spots.

For the first trip (to be made only at hours of low tide), take the BOLIVAR FERRY to Port Bolivar on the BOLI-

VAR PENINSULA. (To reach the ferry dock, drive east
on Seawall Boulevard, following the signs.) During the
3-mile ferry crossing, look for pelicans, cormorants, gulls,
terns, and Black Skimmers, a few of which are almost invariably present in any season. From Port Bolivar proceed
northeastward on the Bolivar Peninsula via State Route 87
for about 3 miles until a group of fishing shacks a few hundred yards on the right (Gulf side) of the road comes into
view; turn in at a gate and go past the shacks out onto the
beach, then swing left and drive along the beach. When
the tide is low, the flats that stretch far out to the waters of
the Gulf constitute an area that attracts a remarkable number of shorebirds. Except in midsummer, two thirds of the
American species of shorebirds, as well as many waterbirds,
may be seen here in countless numbers. Eastward from the
turnoff to the fishing shacks, Route 87 continues to Port
Arthur. (For information on bird-finding possibilities farther
along on Route 87, see under Port Arthur.)

For a second trip, go west on Galveston Island by leaving
the city on S Street Road (also known as Stewart Road).
After crossing 61st Street, watch the ponds on the left for
gallinules and shorebirds. About three quarters of a mile
beyond 61st Street, a paved road slants to the left past the
MUNICIPAL GOLF COURSE, which is worth inspecting
in the winter months for such birds as Black-bellied Plovers,
Long-billed Curlews, Marbled Godwits, Horned Larks,
American Pipits, and Sprague's Pipits, and in the spring
months for Mountain Plovers, Golden Plovers, Upland
Plovers, and Buff-breasted Sandpipers. Continue westward
along the main road for 2 miles to a paved road turning off
right. Drive along this road for about 500 yards to another
road, which intersects from the left. Take this road to its
end where, 300 yards distant, lies SWEETWATER LAKE,
a large body of water with grassy borders. This is one of
the best places near Galveston for a variety of ducks between
October and May. If Ruddy Ducks are anywhere in the
region, they will be found here. Return to the main road and
again continue westward, this time for 1¾ miles to the
next road turning right. Northeast of this intersection are
small marshes flanking the southern end of Sweetwater

Lake. Here Least Bitterns, Purple Gallinules, and Florida Gallinules nest regularly, and Soras are common in the spring.

Follow the road on the right to within 100 yards of West Bay, then turn left on the first road and proceed along it to a dead end about 1¼ miles distant. Of all the places on Galveston Island the marshes and flats near this road are the best for waterbirds and shorebirds. No visitor can come here in any season, except in extreme drouth, without seeing nearly all the species of herons that are common on the Texas coast, as well as rails and (except in the late spring and early summer months) various shorebirds ranging from curlews and the larger plovers to 'peeps.'

Having reached the dead end, turn around and retrace the route; but instead of returning to the main road, turn right onto the first (and only) road one comes to. Follow this somewhat winding road until it rejoins the main road. In spring, especially after a norther, watch the thickets for small landbirds, sometimes seen in enormous numbers. The marshes passed along the way usually harbor Fulvous Tree-ducks and, in proper seasons, Blue-winged Teal and Shovelers, Purple and Florida Gallinules, Black-necked Stilts, and many herons, ibises, and shorebirds. Having reached the main road again, follow it westward for a few miles and take the first road to the left. This leads across some marshes where many marshbirds congregate if conditions are favorable, and where White-faced Ibises and Fulvous Tree-ducks can usually be seen if they are on the Island. This road ends on the Gulf beach; turn around and return to the main road. On the left, a few hundred yards along the main road, is a thicket of bushes and trees (Lafitte's Grove, once the headquarters of the pirate Jean Lafitte). Stop and inspect the thicket, and the ponds on either side of the road, for transient landbirds, Least Bitterns, both species of gallinules, Soras, and Long-billed Marsh Wrens. A few hundred yards farther along the main road, take the first road to the right; it skirts a golf course where Long-billed Curlews are often to be seen, and Black-bellied Plovers, Upland Plovers, Buff-breasted Sandpipers, and Marbled Godwits are present in season. Follow the road to its dead end (three quarters of a mile distant), and inspect the flats beyond, which are usually teeming with waterbirds, shorebirds, and marshbirds.

Return to the main road, and once again continue westward until the road ends (about 12 miles from Galveston) by turning abruptly toward the Gulf and leading out onto WEST BEACH. If the tide is low, it is possible to return to Galveston on the Beach—an ideal trip for observing a wide variety of coastal birds. In the winter months, northern species of gulls and a few diving ducks may be seen. Some species of shorebirds, such as Ruddy Turnstones, Willets, and Sanderlings, can be counted on in any month of the year; others, such as Knots, in the spring and fall; and still others, such as Red-backed Sandpipers and Dowitchers, in the winter. Laughing Gulls, Royal Terns, Caspian Terns, and Black Skimmers are of frequent occurrence any time. If the bird finder grows weary of his drive along the Beach, he can always return to the main road by one of the numerous branch roads connecting it to the Beach.

For a third trip, go to the easternmost extremity of Galveston Island by driving down one of the ramps from the seawall to EAST BEACH (like West Beach, situated on the Gulf side of the Island), and then proceeding eastward on the Beach by car. At the end of the Island, about 3 miles distant, are extensive flats near the jetty guarding the entrance to the shipping channel. Here there are fine places for shorebirds, gulls, terns, and Black Skimmers and excellent vantage points for watching some of the larger waterbirds, such as Brown Pelicans and Olivaceous Cormorants. Snowy Plovers may be seen here regularly except in midwinter.

HOUSTON. The Houston area, on the Coast Prairie about 50 miles inland from the Gulf, has numerous fresh-water and brackish marshes combined with such other environments as tidewater estuaries, large woods, and miles of grasslands. Birdlife is therefore rich both in variety of breeding and wintering species and in the number of individuals. Moreover, Houston lies in the path of spring migration, which in April and early May brings enormous numbers of transients during inclement weather.

HERMANN and MEMORIAL PARKS in Houston are

worth visiting. Hermann Park (545 acres), southwest of the center of the city, on South Main Street between Hermann Avenue and Holcombe Drive, has a stream, pond, and fine pine-hardwood forest, much of it in natural condition. Also in the Park are a zoo, a natural-history museum, and various recreational facilities. Memorial Park, west of the center of the city, may be reached by driving west on Washington Avenue. When, after 3¾ miles, Washington Avenue bears to the right, turn left onto Arnot Street, which leads to the Park. This area is considerably larger than Hermann Park and, though it includes a golf course, has a more extensive pine-hardwood forest. Both areas are excellent for small landbirds, resident and transient, while the pond in Hermann Park is attractive to herons and gallinules the year round, and to a few grebes and ducks in the winter.

When in Houston no bird finder should neglect combining ornithology with history and visiting the SAN JACINTO STATE PARK (402 acres), 22 miles east of the city. This is reached by taking State Route 225 east over a stretch of the Coast Prairie to State Route 134, then north (left) on Route 134 to the Park. Within the area are the San Jacinto Battleground, where, in 1836, the Texans under General Sam Houston defeated the Mexican forces led by Santa Anna; the spectacular 570-foot San Jacinto Memorial Monument with a historical museum in its base; the old battleship *Texas,* permanently anchored and open to visitors; and a continual stream of ocean-going ships passing, within a stone's throw of land, through the Houston Ship Channel between Houston and the open sea. A natural woods of oak and elm in the Park and near-by marshes and prairie attract many birds. The more common herons and egrets may be seen here the year round and pelicans, cormorants, gulls, and terns according to season. The reflecting pool before the Monument is a refuge for ducks during the hunting season. Red-shouldered Hawks, which breed in the Park, may be seen at almost any time of the year. In the winter, Vermilion Flycatchers are often found in the semi-open area on the south side of the Park.

After exploring the Park, return to Route 134, go north for about a mile, and take the LYNCHBURG FERRY (free) across the San Jacinto River. While on the Ferry, one should look for the following: in any season, Brown Pelicans, Laughing Gulls, Gull-billed Terns, Forster's Terns, Royal Terns, and Caspian Terns; from May to October, Black Terns; in winter, Herring Gulls, Ring-billed Gulls, and an occasional Bonaparte's Gull. Once on the other side of the River, take the road (the only one available) which, for about 4 miles, cuts across a vast, grassy marsh containing stretches of open water where there are always herons, a few White-faced Ibises, and, from September to April, Coots, ducks, and other marsh-loving birds. At the first intersection with a concrete road, turn right and proceed to Baytown. At Baytown, turn right on State Route 146, which goes to the HOG ISLAND FERRY (free). On approaching the Ferry, cross a long wooden bridge over a bay. At the far end of this bridge, stop and inspect an adjoining marsh for Long-billed Marsh Wrens in winter and Seaside Sparrows and other marsh dwellers at any season. Proceed to the ferry landing about a mile away, meanwhile inspecting a small beach and open water on the right for Brown Pelicans, Olivaceous and Double-crested Cormorants, Black Skimmers, and numerous gulls, terns, and shorebirds. Near the ferry landing the bird finder may park his car and walk a few hundred yards to the left, along the water's edge, to sand flats that invariably attract shorebirds the year round, though not so many during the summer. Here also, from September to July, will be seen a number of White Pelicans. Cross the Ferry, turn to the right on State Route 225, and return to Houston.

A favorite trip for local bird finders is east from Houston on US Route 90 to Sheldon, 15 miles distant; left on a gravel road across a railroad and straight ahead about 2 miles; left again at the first intersection with another gravel road; and then straight ahead for about 3 miles to the immense SHELDON RESERVOIR on the left. Wintering ducks are often very common here, and Anhingas occur in the spring and summer. Having inspected the Reservoir, back-track for one mile and turn left on a good shell road, which leads north and ends after about 3 miles. Along this road are huge stands of pine and oak in which nest Pileated Woodpeckers, Brown-headed Nuthatches, Parula Warblers, Yellow-throated Warblers, Pine Warblers, and Summer

Tanagers. A few Prothonotary Warblers should be looked
for in a swampy place to the left and near the end of the
road.

An outstanding attraction in the Houston area is the
gathering of thousands of Sandhill Cranes in winter (late
November to early March) on the CINCO RANCH west
of the city near Clodine. To reach this spot, proceed west
on Westheimer Street (becomes Westheimer Road) over a
flat open plain, past Alief, and to a point 6 miles beyond the
village of Clodine. Here a rather poor road, with a white
house and some trees in the distance, slants off to the right
(the first such road beyond Clodine). It is quite possible
that the Cranes will be seen or heard from this point; but,
if not, turn into this road and follow it until it turns sharply
to the right. At the ranch house ask where the larger flocks
of Cranes have been seen feeding. (Permission to go on the
Ranch is readily granted by the owners, who are proud of
their birds and like to have people enjoy them.)

The HOUSTON MUSEUM OF NATURAL HISTORY,
in Hermann Park, has little to interest the bird finder except
for one large and really fine habitat exhibit of the Vingt'un
Islands waterbird rookery.

The Houston Outdoor Nature Club may be contacted
through the Houston Museum of Natural History. This organization meets the third Thursday evening of each month
(except June, July, and August), publishes *The Trail Blazer*
(irregularly), sponsors public lectures, conducts monthly
field trips, and owns and manages a nature sanctuary called
The Little Thicket, situated about 60 miles north of Houston.

KERRVILLE. Picturesquely located on the rugged southeastern part of the Edwards Plateau at an elevation of 1,645
feet, Kerrville is a popular summer resort for Texans. On the
southern edge of town the Guadalupe River cuts through a
deep valley flanked by high limestone hills and eventually
leaves the Plateau through a deep chasm in the Balcones
Escarpment to the east. The hills, especially their upper
slopes, support a scrub growth of Mexican juniper mixed
with Texas oak and stunted live oak, while the River itself
and its tributary streams are bordered by many kinds of
trees, including bur oaks and cypresses, and by mesquite

thickets on the higher terraces. Practically all of the country in the vicinity of Kerrville is occupied by sheep and goat ranches. The necessary permission to enter these private domains may be readily obtained.

The bird of greatest ornithological interest in the region is the Golden-cheeked Warbler, which shares with the Poorwill and Scrub Jay the higher elevations of the juniper-clad hills. The Golden-cheeked Warbler may be easily observed in at least two places near Kerrville. One is the BELL RANCH, reached by going south from town over the big bridge and taking the old Bandera Road for 2 miles to a Ranch gate on the right. Permission to go on the Ranch should be obtained at the house. The other is the DAVIS RANCH, reached by taking State Route 16 north from town for about 3 miles. Permission to enter this property must be obtained from its owner, who manages the Louise Dress Shop, Water Street, Kerrville.

Bird finding during a summer in the Kerrville area will yield almost 90 species, including the following: in the open country, dotted with trees or bushes, the Scissor-tailed Flycatcher and Lark Sparrow; in or near town, the Inca Dove, Bewick's Wren, and House Finch; on the rocky slopes or cliffs, the Canyon Wren and Rufous-crowned Sparrow; in the timber along the River, or in extensive tree plantations, the Wild Turkey, Yellow-billed Cuckoo, Black-chinned Hummingbird (usually near woodland edges), Golden-fronted Woodpecker, Ladder-backed Woodpecker, Carolina Chickadee, Black-crested Titmouse, Carolina Wren, Blue-gray Gnatcatcher, Yellow-throated Vireo, Red-eyed Vireo, and Summer Tanager; in brushy places, sometimes near woods or streams and sometimes on slopes, the Vermilion Flycatcher (usually not far from water), White-eyed Vireo, Bell's Vireo (often in mesquite thickets), Yellow-breasted Chat, Orchard Oriole, Cardinal, Painted Bunting, and Lesser Goldfinch.

MARATHON. BIG BEND NATIONAL PARK, so named because of its location in the huge, U-shaped bend of the Rio Grande in southwestern Texas, embraces some 1,106 square miles—an area greater than the state of Rhode Island.

The chief physiographic feature of the Park is the rugged Chisos Mountains, enormous serrated masses of colorful rock occupying about 40 square miles in the approximate center of the Park. When compared to other mountains in western United States, they are not high—the loftiest point, Mt. Emory, reaches only 7,835 feet—but they stand out above the surrounding, semi-arid plains that are broken only by bluffs and mesas, and by riverbeds that are usually dry. Douglas fir, ponderosa pine, Arizona cypress, maple, and various oaks grow on the higher elevations; below 6,000 feet are pinyon pine, junipers (including the rare weeping juniper), madroña, century plant (maguey), and oaks; the drier, lower slopes support scrub oaks, sotol, cholla, Mexican persimmon, and catclaw. On the plains approaching the Chisos Mountains the sparse vegetation is characterized by creosote bush, mesquite, screw bean, ocotillo, and several kinds of yuccas, with some stretches of tobosa grass and a few cottonwoods and willows near streams.

The Park has a fine variety of landbirds, but no spectacular concentrations of breeding and wintering species or heavy waves of transients. Its sharply contrasting habitat types show correspondingly sharp differences in birdlife; then, too, certain of its habitats, especially those in the Chisos Mountains, hold species of birds that are rare, in some instances non-existent, elsewhere in the United States. Fortunately the habitat types are close enough together to be visited in a day. Bird finding is invariably rewarding the year round. Mid-April to mid-May is the choicest period for breeding birds and late transients; mid-August to mid-September for lingering summer residents and early transients; December and January (when the days are always pleasantly warm and bright) for wintering populations.

Park headquarters is in 'the Basin' (elevation approximately 5,300 feet), a cliff-ringed amphitheater about 4 miles in diameter in the heart of the Chisos. Towering Casa Grande overlooks the Basin from the southeast. Tourist facilities in the Basin include a limited number of housekeeping cabins, a store for supplies, meal service, and a campground. Bird finders not prepared to camp should reserve one of the cabins well in advance. (The address is National Parks Concessions, Box 251, Marathon.) Mail is delivered from Marathon once a week. A few housekeeping cabins, crude but adequate, are available at Hot Springs on the Park's southeastern boundary. There is a trading post selling groceries, gasoline, and oil in the northern part of the Park, 5 miles south of Persimmon Gap.

Although there are two approach roads to Park head-quarters, the one recommended is the shorter road (State Route 227), leading from Marathon (on US Route 90), 80 miles distant. Like so much of southwestern Texas, where the human population averages about one person to a square mile, the country traversed by this road is arid and mainly uninhabited. Consequently, on reaching a filling station, always check on gas, oil, and water, for the next source of supply will be a great many miles away.

During the drive south to the Park from Marathon, it is worth while to investigate GARDEN SPRINGS, a spot that can always be depended upon for good bird finding. Park the car beside the highway (13.2 miles from Marathon) where the tops of the cottonwood trees marking Garden Springs may be seen about half a mile to the east (left) at the foot of a low, east-west ridge. Walk to it (there is no trail) across a pasture. This old cottonwood-willow thicket is a favorite wintering habitat for White-crowned Sparrows, while many of the species of birds found in the Hot Springs area (see below) occur here. Lark Buntings are common in the vicinity during the winter months.

South of Garden Springs, on the approach road to the Park, the Santiago Range and its highest point—flat-topped Santiago Mountain (6,521 feet)—loom on the right. Mean-while watch the desert-like, brush-studded flats along the highway for such year-round birds as the Red-tailed Hawk, Swainson's Hawk, Scaled Quail, Mourning Dove, Road-runner, White-necked Raven, and Loggerhead Shrike. Pyrrhuloxias and Desert Sparrows may be found here upon closer investigation. On reaching Persimmon Gap at 2,971 feet, the entrance to the Park (41.5 miles from Marathon), the road passes through the Santiago Range and permits the first view of the Chisos Mountains. Continue on this road to the Basin.

In and around the Basin itself there is much to delight the bird finder in any season. Near the cabins and campground are permanent-resident Scaled Quail, Road-runners, Bewick's Wrens, Cactus Wrens, Lesser Goldfinches, and Brown Towhees. The adjoining cliff walls and taluses are populated by Canyon Wrens, Rock Wrens, and Rufous-crowned Sparrows in every month of the year. A familiar nighttime sound in April, May, June, and July is the repetitive call of the Poor-will. Transient or winter residents in the Basin area include Mountain Bluebirds, Virginia's Warblers, Macgillivray's Warblers, Green-tailed Towhees, Oregon Juncos, Gray-headed Juncos, Chipping Sparrows, and Black-chinned Sparrows.

Oak Creek, a small stream in a wooded ravine north of headquarters, may be reached by trail in 10 minutes. Once at the stream, follow it down for 2 miles to the Window, a narrow defile in the western rimrock. In the trees and thickets along the bottom of the ravine are such breeding birds as Band-tailed Pigeons, Acorn Woodpeckers, Arizona Jays, Black-crested Titmice, Cactus Wrens, Crissal Thrashers, Western Tanagers, Hepatic Tanagers, Lesser Goldfinches, and Spotted Towhees. Sometimes White-winged and Inca Doves may be found. A bird to be looked for especially is the little Elf Owl, which nests in the dead bloom stalks of the century plants growing on the ravine slopes.

Kibbie Springs, on the western border of Casa Grande Mountain, will produce a variety of birds similar to that of Oak Springs. Take the main road back out of the Basin to the divide (where the road levels off before dipping downhill). Park the car and take a trail that may be seen on the right running parallel with the road about 30 feet away. Walk to the right on this trail, keeping on the Basin side of Casa Grande, for a quarter of a mile to Kibbie Springs, which is in a rock-filled draw marked by good-sized oaks.

No bird finder in the Chisos will wish to miss seeing the Colima Warbler, whose only known nesting place in the United States is at Boot Spring (6,500 feet) on the eastern shoulder of Mt. Emory. This Mexican species, unafraid and easily observed feeding in the maples, oaks, and Arizona cypresses, is present here, according to available records, from the first of May to the first of September. It nests on the ground under an overhanging growth of grasses or other ground cover. Boot Spring, 6 miles from headquarters, is reached by a steep trail. Unless one goes on horseback, an overnight campout is recommended, although this is not absolutely necessary. For precise trail directions and arrangements for pack trips, inquire at Park headquarters.

At Laguna, a mountain meadow midway on the trail to Boot Spring, search for nesting Bush-tits and Townsend's Solitaires. From Laguna to Boot Spring, one should begin watching for Colima Warblers. Other birds to be expected during the breeding season in the Boot Spring area include the Golden Eagle, Band-tailed Pigeon, Screech Owl, Whip-poor-will, White-throated Swift, Blue-throated and Broad-tailed Hummingbirds (often around the blooms of the century plants on which they feed), Acorn Woodpecker, White-breasted Nuthatch, Hutton's Vireo, Western Tanager, and Black-headed Grosbeak. With good luck, one should be able to find a Mearns' Quail. Black-throated Gray and Townsend's Warblers are common transients here, and usually a few Western Bluebirds may be seen in the winter.

Hot Springs (1,800 feet), on the Rio Grande (at the mouth of Tornillo Creek) and about 30 miles from Park headquarters, is a good place for finding birds characteristic of the lower arid country. Late fall and early spring, when the temperature is not too uncomfortable, is the best time. Inquire at headquarters for route directions and the conditions of the road (often hazardous during or just after wet weather).

Tornillo Creek, on which a campground is located, is lined with mesquite, buckthorn (condalia), desert willow, guaya-can, and screw bean; creosote bush, agave, pitahaya, prickly pear, and catclaw grow on the surrounding slopes. Along the Rio Grande are bordering stands of buttonbush, river cane, tobacco tree, cottonwood, and willow. Black-chinned and Broad-billed Hummingbirds and Vermilion Flycatchers regularly nest near the campground, and Scaled Quail frequent the dry washes. Audubon's Warblers are very common around the campground in winter. By exploring the thickets along Tornillo Creek from its mouth to a point about a quarter of a mile upstream, the bird finder should be able to observe numerous resident birds, among them the White-winged Dove, Inca Dove, Road-runner, Great Horned Owl (on the cliffs), Ash-throated Flycatcher, Verdin, Rock

Wren, Curve-billed Thrasher, Crissal Thrasher, Plumbeous
Gnatcatcher, Bell's Vireo, Scott's Oriole, Summer Tanager,
Cardinal, Pyrrhuloxia, and Painted Bunting. By walking
along the Rio Grande half a mile downstream, the bird
finder will come to a willow-cottonwood-mesquite tangle.
This is a good locality for seeing permanent-resident Duck
Hawks (around the cliffs across the Rio Grande on the Mexican side), as well as Zone-tailed Hawks, Mexican Black
Hawks, Ladder-backed Woodpeckers, Black Phoebes, Say's
Phoebes, Canyon Wrens, Yellow Warblers, Orchard Orioles,
Blue Grosbeaks, and Desert Sparrows. A similar resident
bird population will be found by walking upstream from the
campground for three quarters of a mile. Take the trail by
the river's edge for a hundred yards to a branch trail running
up over a hill. Follow this branch along the hills paralleling
the river to a thicket-choked arroyo that usually has a small
flow of water. Lesser Nighthawks nest under the mesquite
trees on a shelf of land on the left bank near the mouth of
this stream. The arroyo is a likely spot for (Dwarf) Red-
shafted Flickers and, in winter, for (Red-naped) Common
Sapsuckers.

Santa Elena Canyon, a great opening through which flows
the Rio Grande, is one of the awesome, scenic features of
the Park. A trail leads up through the chasm on the American side, but the trip is more worth while for sight seeing
than for bird finding. The species most likely to be observed
are the White-throated Swift, Black Phoebe, Common
Raven, Canyon Wren, and House Finch. Specific directions
for reaching the trail may be obtained at headquarters.

MULESHOE. If the bird finder ever has occasion to be on
the Staked Plains in northwestern Texas during the winter,
he should not miss visiting the MULESHOE NATIONAL
WILDLIFE REFUGE, which has one of the greatest wintering concentrations of Sandhill Cranes on the continent.
The Refuge lies on either side of State Route 214, 20 miles
south of Muleshoe. The turnoff to headquarters (2 miles
west of the highway) is indicated by the flying-goose signs.
Fire lanes and patrol roads traverse the Refuge, permitting
easy access by car to all parts.

The 5,809 acres of the Refuge consist mainly of rolling

to hilly plains covered by short grasses, cacti, yuccas, and tumbleweeds. Near the north and west boundaries are rocky outcroppings. The only other prominent interruptions are gullies leading into playa lakes that have no outlets and are dry, except after periods of heavy rainfall. Three of the lakes—Lower Paul's (125 acres), Lower Goose (140 acres), and Lower White (160 acres)—are the result of natural depressions in the ground; three others—Upper Paul's (18 acres), Upper Goose (140 acres), and Upper White (62 acres)—are man-made. When the lakes are receding, after being filled by rainfall, they have mud flats and muddy shores.

A few landbirds may be found on the Refuge (e.g. coveys of Scaled Quail are always present and may be observed around headquarters at almost any time), and enormous numbers of ducks winter on the lakes from November to February (as many as half a million ducks, mostly Mallards, Pintails, and Baldpates, have been estimated in that order of abundance in January). But it is the Sandhill Cranes that provide the signal attraction.

The Cranes usually begin appearing in late September and steadily increase in number until December. Though numerous flocks may continue on southward, as many as 8,000 to 15,000 individuals remain through the winter, unless unfavorable weather conditions cause them to move farther south. By late February or early March, the Cranes start journeying northward.

The Cranes usually roost at night in the shallow water near the shore of one or more of the lakes. At sunrise they depart for their feeding grounds—generally a harvested grainfield; here they stay until mid-morning, when they return to their roosting grounds to loiter and preen. By mid-afternoon they again go to their feeding grounds, returning for a second time to their roosting grounds at sunset. The pleasure in watching these magnificent birds—they are shy and have to be observed from a distance, preferably by telescope—is always heightened by their extraordinary dances, performed individually and sometimes by groups. These dances, with their ludicrous bows and vertical leaps into the air, take place on both the roosting and feeding grounds and are of such frequent occurrence that the watcher need not wait long to see them.

PORT ARTHUR. State Route 87 between Port Arthur and Galveston makes readily accessible the northeastern-most Gulf shore and coastal marshes of Texas. No bird finder can take a trip in any season along this fine highway without seeing the hosts of birds that frequent the marsh grasses, mud flats, lagoons, tidewater creeks and estuaries, shipping canals, beaches, and the open water of the Gulf. When promising spots come into view, the bird finder need only stop his car and scan them with field glasses.

Birds regularly nesting in the coastal marshes from late April to mid-July include the Least Bittern, Mottled Duck, King Rail, Clapper Rail, Long-billed Marsh Wren, Red-wing, Boat-tailed Grackle, Seaside Sparrow, and, occasionally, the Purple Gallinule. Visiting the edges of creeks and lagoons throughout the year, though in greater abundance in the late spring and summer months, are Great Blue Herons, American Egrets, Snowy Egrets, Louisiana Herons, Little Blue Herons, Green Herons, and White-faced Ibises. From October through February these same areas—the marshes and waterways—are a winter haven for great numbers of Canada Geese, Snow Geese, and Blue Geese, for smaller numbers of White-fronted Geese, and for great numbers of ducks—Baldpates, Pintails, Green-winged Teal, Canvas-backs, Lesser Scaup Ducks, and others. Peaks of abundance are usually reached in December and January. Except in June and July, shorebirds galore gather on the mud flats and beaches. The Black-bellied Plover, Ruddy Turnstone, Greater and Lesser Yellow-legs, Semipalmated Sandpiper, and Least Sandpiper are some of the species that may be expected. Along the canals and Gulf shore, Brown Pelicans, Olivaceous Cormorants, Laughing Gulls, Royal Terns, and Black Skimmers may be observed the year round, but more individuals are present in late spring and summer. Other birds to be looked for are the following: White Pelicans (common from October through February); Double-crested Cormorants (October to late March); Man-o'-war-birds (April to September); Wood Ibises and White Ibises (most numerous in the spring and summer); Herring and Ring-billed Gulls (October to April); Bonaparte's Gulls (November to May); Least Terns (April to September).

Typical sections of coastal marshes are crossed by Route 87 as it passes southward from Port Arthur to the fishing village of Sabine Pass, a distance of 14 miles. Bridges over several creeks and lagoons permit good views of bordering shallows and mud flats, where herons and shorebirds often feed. At Sabine Pass, the bird finder should leave Route 87 temporarily, continuing southward a short distance on a shell road to Sabine, another fishing village, which overlooks the entrance waters of Sabine Pass (connecting the Gulf with Sabine Lake). This is invariably a good vantage point for seeing pelicans, cormorants, gulls, and terns at any time of the year, and Lesser Scaup Ducks and other diving ducks during the winter months.

From the village of Sabine Pass, Route 87 goes southwestward, within a few yards of the Gulf's edge, to HIGH ISLAND, 33 miles distant. Stops can be made along the way to inspect the beach on the left and the vast expanse of Coast Prairie and intermittent marshes on the right. Once on High Island, turn right onto State Route 124 and drive to the small town of High Island, 2 miles inland; then turn left to the oil fields on a road that circles close to various creeks and bayous commonly visited by herons and other waterbirds.

High Island has, as the name implies, a somewhat higher elevation than the neighboring marshes and, moreover, supports a cover of live oaks, hackberries, and other trees, together with many shrubs and vines. Because of these features, tremendous numbers of small landbirds congregate here in the spring (April and early May) whenever a norther occurs.

Westward from the turnoff on Route 124, Route 87 continues over the Bolivar Peninsula to Port Bolivar, where a ferry may be taken to Galveston. (For bird-finding opportunities on the Bolivar Peninsula and in the vicinity of Galveston, see under Galveston.)

PORT LAVACA. The ARANSAS NATIONAL WILD-LIFE REFUGE, on the south-central coast of Texas, embraces the last-known wintering ground of the Whooping Crane. This species, one of the largest and unquestionably one of the most spectacular of all North American birds, was once a common summer resident in the marshes of the Canadian prairie provinces and northern prairie states and an equally common winter resident in the marshes of the Gulf states and northeastern Mexico; then the species began to decline in numbers, at first gradually, later alarmingly, until today it is represented by some 20 individuals, all of which choose to winter in the Aransas Refuge. Here, during their stay from October to May, they find their preferred food and coveted isolation—environmental requirements that the Refuge management makes every effort to provide. With the coming of spring all the Cranes, except perhaps two or three individuals, depart for the northern part of the continent to breed.

The 47,261 acres of the Aransas Refuge take in the Blackjack Peninsula, a low-lying, gently rolling section of the Coast Prairie, bordered by grassy marshes, or flats, and surrounded by several bays. Mottes of oak brush (tree and shrub forms of live oak and myrtleleaf oak), separated by stretches of grassland, characterize most of the interior, though stands of blackjack oak (for which the Peninsula was named), mixed with prickly ash and dense thickets of sweet bay, grow in scattered localities. Small bodies of fresh water dot the area. Some are 'wet weather ponds,' others are ponds filled by the overflowing wells that supply water for the cattle, which graze in the Refuge.

The grassy salt flats on the east side of the Peninsula are usually the wintering ground of the Whooping Crane. Averaging a mile or so in width, these flats extend from Mustang Lake (a large lagoon) south for 12 miles to Cape Carlos and are interrupted by numerous tidewater creeks and small, shallow lagoons with wide, muddy shores, and by the Intracoastal Canal, which cuts through their outermost fringes. Except for the ship traffic through the Canal, the flats are remote from disturbances.

The Refuge is reached from State Route 35 between Port Lavaca and Corpus Christi. From Port Lavaca, proceed southwestward on Route 35 for 20 miles to Tivoli, continue one mile beyond, then turn left onto an improved

road and drive 4 miles to the village of Austwell. Drive
through Austwell and along Farm Road 774 for approximately three quarters of a mile; then follow a paved road to
the left in a southeasterly direction for 7 miles, to Refuge
headquarters, situated inside the northern Refuge boundary

WHOOPING CRANES

at the base of the Blackjack Peninsula. The road continues
south on the Peninsula from headquarters and eventually
reaches the eastern flats where the Whooping Cranes ordinarily stay.

In order that the Whooping Cranes shall be as free from
disturbances as possible, the Fish and Wildlife Service and
all other agencies interested in the welfare of the birds have
agreed that the wintering ground shall be closed to the
public. Visiting the eastern flats is, therefore, prohibited.

A visit to the Refuge in the winter will not be in vain even
though Whooping Cranes may not be observed. There are
flats and other wet places adjacent to headquarters (and
not closed to the public) that are invariably attractive to
Sandhill Cranes (as many as several hundred individuals),
herons (including the Reddish Egret), flocks of Canada,
Snow, and Blue Geese, and numerous shorebirds, among
them the Long-billed Curlew, Red-backed Sandpiper, Do-

witcher, and Western Sandpiper. There are also places attractive to Horned Larks, American Pipits, and (more rarely) Sprague's Pipits. Nearly all the ponds scattered over the Refuge have small congregations of ducks—Mottled Ducks, Gadwalls, Baldpates, Pintails, Shovelers, and others. Wild Turkeys inhabit the wooded places and a small number—probably one flock—appear regularly in the vicinity of headquarters. Seldom seen, but common if looked for, are the Woodcock, which pass the winter in the oak-brush mottes and sweet-bay thickets. Usually a walk in winter along the main Refuge road, which passes southward on the Peninsula, will be rewarded by the sight of one or more Sennett's White-tailed Hawks (permanent resident), Bald Eagles, Audubon's Caracaras (permanent resident), Vermilion Flycatchers, and perhaps a Pyrrhuloxia (permanent resident). Other permanent or winter residents to be expected during the trip include the Eastern Phoebe, Brown Thrasher, Hermit Thrush, Ruby-crowned Kinglet, Orange-crowned Warbler, Myrtle Warbler, Brewer's Blackbird, Common Goldfinch, Savannah Sparrow, Seaside Sparrow, Vesper Sparrow, Field Sparrow, White-crowned Sparrow, and Lincoln's Sparrow.

Bird finders visiting the Refuge for any length of time usually stop at Bob Hopper's establishment about midway between Austwell and Refuge headquarters on the west side of San Antonio Bay. Here there are good housekeeping cabins—a rarity in the vicinity of Austwell. It is best to make reservations by writing in advance (address: Austwell) because this is a favorite base for fishermen.

One of the largest waterbird rookeries on the Texas coast occupies three of the five islands in the SECOND CHAIN OF ISLANDS, off the east coast of the Blackjack Peninsula, in Ayres Bay between San Antonio and Mesquite Bays. Like the Vingt'un Islands in Galveston Bay (see under Anahuac), they are small and rise but slightly above the normal high-tide mark. All three occupied islands, the largest of which is Carroll Island, have high brushy thickets; in addition, Carroll Island has considerable grassy cover. The Second Chain rookery is notable for having several hundred pairs of Reddish Egrets. The other waterbirds in the multitude are Brown Pelicans, Olivaceous Cormorants, Great

Blue Herons, American Egrets, Snowy Egrets, Louisiana
Herons, Black-crowned Night Herons, Roseate Spoonbills,
and White Ibises. Great numbers of Boat-tailed Grackles
and a few Mottled Ducks also nest on the Islands. During
May, June, and July, when the rookery is active, White
Pelicans and Wood Ibises frequently loiter on the flats that
extend out from the islands at low tide, but the birds do not
nest in the rookery.

On the highest point on Carroll Island is a monument,
erected by the National Audubon Society in 1938, to the
memory of James J. Carroll of Houston, who was responsible
for instituting the Society's warden service for the Second
Chain rookery and for other bird colonies on the coast of
Texas.

Landing on the Second Chain of Islands or otherwise
disturbing the birds is prohibited, but bird finders desiring
to see the rookery may accompany the warden on one of
his regular tours. Permission must be obtained from the
National Audubon Society, 1130 Fifth Avenue, New York
28, New York, and arrangements for the trip made in advance with the warden, whose name and address will be
supplied by the Society.

Along the Intracoastal Canal, which passes on the east
side of the Blackjack Peninsula, are many so-called shell
bars that have resulted from dredging activities. Though
glaring white, with little or no vegetation, certain of the
larger ones with an extensive surface of moderate incline are
the sites, in late May, June, and early July, of thriving bird
colonies containing one or more, sometimes all, of the following species: Laughing Gull, Gull-billed Tern, Least
Tern, Royal Tern, Cabot's Tern, Caspian Tern, and Black
Skimmer. The dominant species in number of nesting pairs
is usually the Black Skimmer. A pair or two of American
Oyster-catchers frequently nest on the same shell bars.

From year to year the colonies tend to shift to different
sites as the older shell bars are washed away and more
suitable ones are built up by renewed dredging. The best
way to reach the shell bars is by boat, which may be chartered at Hopper's establishment. The proprietor will know
which bars are occupied by the birds.

ROCKPORT. For the bird finder there are numerous meccas in the United States, but none that is quite like Rockport. This coastal town on the Liveoak Peninsula between Copano and Aransas Bays is so situated as to be (1) in the path of the unrivaled coastal flyway, (2) within the wintering range of a great many species from most parts of the United States and Canada, and (3) near the breeding colonies of countless waterbirds. There are, of course, other areas on the Texas coast that are in some respects just as exciting (see under Port Arthur, Anahuac, Galveston, Houston, Bay City, and Port Lavaca), but they are not so frequently visited by bird finders. Why Rockport is unique is a story that goes back to 1935, when Mr. and Mrs. Jack Hagar moved to this town and purchased the Rockport Cottages—pleasant tourist quarters on State Route 35, 1.5 miles south of town. Beach, sand flats, and shell bars with tremendous varieties of water-birds and shorebirds were an 'extension' of their front yard, while a grove of live oaks in their backyard attracted huge aggregations of transient passerine birds. Before long Mrs. Hagar was watching birds from dawn to dusk, and soon there came reports to ornithological journals of her seemingly incredible observations. Ornithologists, great and near-great, came to see for themselves—and have been coming ever since. Now a visit to Rockport is traditional for bird finders whenever they are in southeastern Texas.

The Hagars have listed well over 400 species and sub-species in the Rockport area, a fact that indicates the opportunities for bird finding, yet shows how utterly impossible it is to describe them in a short account. A selection is made here to show what is in store.

Drive north from Rockport on Route 35; at the first intersection, turn right and follow the shore to Fulton and NINE-MILE POINT. Waterfowl to be seen in abundance from the road any time from September through January include the Gadwall, Baldpate, Pintail, Blue-winged and Green-winged Teal, Shoveler, and Lesser Scaup Duck. Herons and shorebirds are present in any season. Return to Route 35 and continue north for 7 miles to the point where the highway crosses CAVASSA CREEK. The environs here comprise a favorite feeding and loitering ground for Canada,

White-fronted, Snow, and Blue Geese from November to March. Also frequenting this spot, as well as the grasslands and cutover fields along the highway (before the Creek and farther north toward Tivoli), are wintering Sandhill Cranes, best seen in the morning or late afternoon, when they are most active. Early in the morning during March and April, Greater Prairie Chickens sometimes feed in the short grasses on the shoulders of the highway.

Bordering MARKET STREET LOOP, about 1.5 miles west of Rockport, are many fresh-water sloughs choked with plants and bordered by shrubs and trees. Horned and Eared Grebes may be found here from October to April, and Least Grebes the year round.

From the center of town take Rattlesnake Road north to RATTLESNAKE POINT on Copano Bay. When about 4 miles out of town, if the trip is between April and November, watch for Roseate Spoonbills and Long-billed Curlews on the adjacent wet meadows. When about 5 miles out of town, if the trip is between November and March, search for Sprague's Pipits on the neighboring short-grass prairie.

The NEW CAUSEWAY ROAD, which goes southwest and west of town, passes, about 4 miles out, dry meadows and prairies covered with short grasses and low catclaw growth. Cassin's Sparrows are found here from April through August. One mile beyond, the highway passes wet meadows and mud flats—probably Rockport's best place for shorebirds from February through April. Mountain Plovers, Upland Plovers, White-rumped Sandpipers, Buff-breasted Sandpipers, Hudsonian Godwits, Avocets, and Wilson's Phalaropes are some of the species to be expected.

In Aransas Bay east of Rockport are numerous shell bars, formed during the dredging of the Intracoastal Canal. Like the shell bars along the Canal east of the Blackjack Peninsula (see under Port Lavaca), they are sites for colonies of terns and Black Skimmers. These bars may be reached from Rockport by chartering one of the small boats available at fishing wharves.

For seeing the unbelievable hordes of landbirds that pass through the Rockport area, there are many places. In March, April, October, and November, huge flocks of hawks— Red-shouldered, Broad-winged, Swainson's, Duck, Pigeon,

Sparrow, and others—may be watched along the coast. Every large grove of live oaks, or big thicket of mesquite and huisache, whether in town or on the outskirts, has throngs of flycatchers, thrushes, kinglets, vireos, warblers, orioles, tanagers, and fringillids from 15 April to 5 May and from 5 September to 15 October. The array of bright-colored birds in these multitudes—the Orchard, Baltimore, and Bullock's Orioles, the Rose-breasted and Blue Grosbeaks, and the Indigo, Lazuli, and Painted Buntings—is in itself a thrill to behold. Few, indeed, are the places in the United States where one may be certain of seeing these species together in the same tree or shrub.

SAN ANTONIO. The SAN ANTONIO ZOO at 3919 North St. Marys Street has, in addition to its famed Monkey Island, a fine collection of about 1,800 birds. Especially well represented are many species of American waterbirds and waterfowl; in fact, the Zoo claims to have one of the largest collections of these birds in the United States.

SEYMOUR. This prosperous farming community (elevation 1,290 feet) of north-central Texas is on the rolling mesquite plains, devoted in part to wheat raising, but chiefly to grazing. Some of the grazing area is open grassland, but much of it supports clumps of mesquite that vary in size and density. Streams are bordered by luxuriant growths of hackberry, willow, cottonwood, and other trees.

For finding nesting birds around Seymour, the best time is late May through June, preferably mid-June. Along all of the out-going highways, Mississippi Kites and White-necked Ravens may be readily observed, either in flight or perched on the mesquite, in which they frequently nest. Bullock's Orioles nest very commonly in the mesquite, as do Mourning Doves, Yellow-billed Cuckoos, Scissor-tailed Flycatchers, and Mockingbirds. Other birds to be looked for in mesquite areas are Road-runners, Poor-wills, Common Nighthawks, Golden-fronted Woodpeckers, Black-crested Titmice, and Lark Sparrows.

Although there is good bird finding along all of the highways, perhaps the best is along US Route 283 north from Seymour, through ranching country, to Vernon. Take this highway, turning off from time to time for bird finding on country roads over grasslands studded with mesquite. Once in Vernon, turn left onto US Route 287. Just outside of town, the highway crosses the Pease River; here, in the trees and brush, several pairs of Mississippi Kites almost invariably nest. Continue west on Route 287 to Quanah, turn left onto State Route 283, and then drive 15 miles to where the highway crosses the Pease River. Under the bridge, on the supporting arches, are the nests of a sizable colony of Cliff Swallows. The Pease River, at this point, has a broad, sandy bed well-covered with tamarisk and walled by rocky, juniper-covered bluffs. This is a good spot not only for Kites but also for Swainson's Hawks, Ferruginous Hawks, and Desert Sparrows.

Contributing authorities: George E. Barclay, W. Frank Blair, Charles R. Bryant, L. Irby Davis, W. B. Davis, John E. Galley, Mrs. John E. (Margret) Galley, Luther C. Goldman, Frank Grimes, Mrs. Jack Hagar, John B. Holdsworth, Julian A. Howard, Paul V. Jones, Jr., George H. Lowery, Jr., E. G. Marsh, Jr., Mrs. Lena McBee, Wm. Larrey McCart, Vincent P. McLaughlin, F. W. Miller, Marcus C. Nelson, Harry C. Oberholser, Fred Mallery Packard, Daniel M. Popper, Mrs. Bruce (Bessie) Reid, Lloyd H. Shinners, George H. Sholly, Alexander Sprunt, Jr., James O. Stevenson, Jerry E. Stillwell, J. D. Thompson, Jr., S. R. Warner, Mrs. John R. (Lovie M.) Whitaker, George G. Williams, Wynn A. Wilson, Mrs. T. E. (Edith) Winford.

Utah

BY WILLIAM H. BEHLE

CALIFORNIA GULLS

There are few bird finders who have not heard of the 'miraculous' appearance of the great flocks of 'sea gulls' in 1848, which descended on the meager grainfields of Salt Lake Valley and destroyed the Mormon crickets that were ravaging the crops of the first white settlers there. These California Gulls are to be seen commonly in northern Utah during the spring and summer months, at parks and school grounds of cities, as well as in marshes and sloughs and around farms. Most interesting in the spring are the flocks of gulls in fields, following the plow and eating the insect larvae and worms from the furrows. Second only to the historical interest of the gulls among Utah's ornithological distinctions is the Bear River Migratory Bird Refuge (see under Brigham), where in February and March concentrations of twenty to twenty-five thousand Whistling Swans occur, and in the spring and fall, Wilson's Phalaropes, Northern Phalaropes, and other shorebirds by tens of thousands. Then there are the colonies of White Pelicans that nest with the gulls on Hat (Bird) and Gunnison Islands in Great Salt Lake. White Pelicans are frequently seen foraging or in flight along the waterways from Utah Lake to the Bear River Refuge. These three features are localized in central northern Utah, but ornithological opportunities exist in almost every section of the state, whose deserts, Great Salt Lake, mountains, high plateaus, rivers, canyons, natural bridges, arches, and bizarre red-rock formations have earned Utah the name 'Center of Scenic America.'

Utah has no natural boundaries and consequently shares the physical features of the surrounding states. The result is a land of great contrasts, with alkaline desert wastes in the west, rugged mountains and high plateaus extending down the middle and across the northeast, and bare-rock canyon country in the southeast. Altitudinally the range is from 2,500 feet along the Virgin River in the southwestern corner to the 13,498 feet of Kings Peak, Uinta Mountains, in the northeast. Less than 3 per cent of the land of the state is suitable for agriculture; most of the land that is so utilized is located in valleys at the base of mountains where water is available for irrigation. Three major physiographic provinces are represented, namely the Great Basin, Rocky Mountains, and Colorado Plateau.

The western third of Utah comprises part of the Great Basin, which ranges for the most part between 4,000 and 5,000 feet. Much of it is a dry wasteland, used for grazing, with north-to-south mountain ranges looming up like islands in the midst of alkaline plains. Indeed, many were once actually islands, for in Pleistocene times, about 25,000 to 50,000 years ago, Lake Bonneville covered most of the lowlands, as shown by shorelines of ancient lake levels, gravel bars, and wave-cut cliffs. Great Salt Lake, locked in an interior basin with no outlet, is its remnant. In this Great Basin portion of Utah one sees a northern desert shrub type of vegetation consisting of sagebrush or *Artemisia* and rabbitbrush on fertile soils, shadscale, greasewood, and gray molly on the alkali flats. This is the habitat for such birds as the Sage Grouse, Burrowing Owl, Horned Lark, Sage Thrasher, Loggerhead Shrike, Western Meadowlark, Lark Sparrow, Vesper Sparrow, Desert Sparrow, Sage Sparrow, and Brewer's Sparrow.

Running from north to south in central-northern Utah is the Wasatch Range, extending from the Idaho border to Mount Nebo east of Nephi, and presenting on the west side a fault scarp, the Wasatch Front, which in places is 6,000 feet high. Several streams, such as Bear, Ogden, Weber, Provo, and Spanish Fork, cut through the Range, flowing east to west. Nearly all the major cities of Utah, containing two thirds of the state's population, are located in the area watered by these streams at the base of the Wasatch Front. These streams are also responsible for much of the marshland of northern Utah; as the streams reach the stagnant levels around the Great Salt Lake, they form such habitats as the Bear River Marshes at the delta of the Bear (see under Brigham).

South of the Wasatch Mountains and continuing down the central part of the state is a series of interconnecting ranges—the Gunnison, Pavant, Tushar, Parowan, and, curling off to the southwest, the Pine Valley Mountains. US Route 91 runs along the base of the mountain chain from Salt Lake to St. George in southwestern Utah. It passes through a series of small settlements located wherever water and a little farmland are available. East of this mountain chain lie the high plateaus of central and central-southern Utah. From the southern border of the state, the Vermilion, White, and Pink Cliffs are like great steps ascending to Markagunt Plateau, where Zion Canyon (see under Hurricane) has been carved by the Virgin River, and to Paunsagunt Plateau, where Bryce Canyon (see under Panguitch) is located. South and east of Bryce Canyon National Park lies Kaiparowits Plateau; to the north are the Aquarius, Avara, Panguitch, Sevier, Fish Lake, and Wasatch Plateaus. The Sevier River, with its two forks, rises in the high plateau country, swings north, cuts west through the mountain front between the Pavant and Gunnison Mountains, and finally turns southwest into the Sevier Desert and the playa Sevier Lake. US Route 89 follows along the Sevier River through central Utah, then passes over the divide, drops down to Kanab, and continues on to the Grand Canyon.

Much of southeastern Utah, part of the Colorado Plateau country, is inaccessible, broken, red-rock country, referred to as the canyon lands. The Green and Colorado Rivers, with tributaries such as the San Juan, Fremont, and Escalante, cut deep through the rock formations; occasional mountain masses rise from 10,000 to 12,000 feet—for example, Navajo Mountain, just north of the Arizona border, and the Henry, Abajo, and La Sal Mountains.

The Book and Roan Cliffs in central-eastern Utah, at the base of which US Route 50 runs from Grand Junction, Colorado, toward Price, Utah, mark the abrupt rise from the canyon lands to the East and West Tavaputs Plateaus and the Uintah Basin. US Route 40 runs east and west across the Uintah Basin, which contains some farming land. Forming the border of this Basin and lying adjacent to the Wyoming border are the Uinta Mountains, an elongated dome, which is unusual in that the main axis extends east and west. This range has been heavily glaciated and contains huge cirques with hundreds of lakes. The dome is about 10,000 to 12,000 feet in elevation, but several peaks project over 13,000 feet. Much of this country is primitive, but a few roads run up to the margin of the wilderness region.

One of the distinctive features of the mountains and plateaus is the belting of vegetation. On the lower mountain slopes and alluvial fans, between 3,200 and 7,000 feet, are distinctive forests of pinyon pines and junipers, aptly designated 'pygmy forest' or 'pygmy conifers' because of the relatively low habit of the trees as compared with the taller coniferous trees found at higher elevations. Associated with this forest may be found sage, cliff rose, antelope brush, serviceberry, and, at high elevations, mountain mahogany. Certain species of birds are restricted to this forest: Gray Flycatcher, Pinyon Jay, Plain Titmouse, Bush-tit, Gray Vireo (southwestern Utah), Black-throated Gray Warbler. Others often found in this habitat are the Poor-will, Common Night-hawk, Say's Phoebe, Scrub Jay, Blue-gray Gnatcatcher, Spotted Towhee, Chipping Sparrow, and Black-chinned Sparrow.

Above the pygmy conifers in southern and eastern Utah, approximately between 6,200 and 8,000 feet, is a belt of ponderosa pine. Gambel's oaks are associated in places with this forest, occurring in dense continuous stands. In addition, there are other scrub types, such as antelope brush, squaw-apple, and manzanita. Essentially, however, the ponderosa-pine forest is open, with little underbrush, and is not rich in birdlife. A few forms occur here regularly (though not all of them exclusively): Band-tailed Pigeon, Williamson's Sapsucker, Steller's Jay, Mountain Chickadee, White-breasted Nuthatch, Pygmy Nuthatch, Western Blue-bird, Audubon's Warbler, Gray-headed Junco.

In central-northern Utah, where ponderosa pine does not occur and scrub oaks are extensive, one finds the introduced California Quail and the Mourning Dove, Scrub Jay, American Magpie, Virginia's Warbler, Black-headed Grosbeak, Green-tailed Towhee, and Spotted Towhee.

Above the ponderosa-pine and oak belt in southern and eastern Utah, and above the pygmy-conifer and mountain-mahogany stands in the mountains of western and central-northern Utah is a conifer-aspen forest. The conifers are principally Colorado blue and Englemann spruces, white and alpine firs, Douglas firs, and bristlecone, limber, and lodgepole pines, depending on the geographic location and the elevation. At lower elevations, tongues of conifers and aspens push down into the cooler environments along the streams. The coniferous forest is very rich in variety of birdlife, and the following species are to be expected in Utah wherever this type of cover occurs.

Goshawk	Calliope Hummingbird
Sharp-shinned Hawk	Red-shafted Flicker
Cooper's Hawk	(Red-naped) Common Sapsucker
Red-tailed Hawk	
Blue Grouse	Williamson's Sapsucker
Ruffed Grouse	Hairy Woodpecker
Great Horned Owl	Downy Woodpecker
Broad-tailed Hummingbird	Black-backed Woodpecker

Hammond's Flycatcher
Wright's Flycatcher
Western Flycatcher
Western Wood Pewee
Olive-sided Flycatcher
Violet-green Swallow
Canada Jay
Steller's Jay
Clark's Nutcracker
Mountain Chickadee
Red-breasted Nuthatch
Brown Creeper
House Wren
Robin
Hermit Thrush

Olive-backed Thrush
Townsend's Solitaire
Golden-crowned Kinglet
Ruby-crowned Kinglet
Warbling Vireo
Orange-crowned Warbler
Audubon's Warbler
Black-capped Warbler
Western Tanager
Cassin's Finch
Pine Grosbeak
Pine Siskin
Red Crossbill
Gray-headed Junco
White-crowned Sparrow

Cutting back through the mountain escarpments are canyons with the streams along their bottoms lined with willows and cottonwoods at the lower elevations; maples, river birch, and alder in the higher reaches; thickets of rose and dogwood filling in. In this habitat, lying between 5,000 and 7,000 feet, one finds Song Sparrows and sometimes Soras if there are wet grassy areas associated with the willows, Dippers along the swifter moving streams, and a number of other birds, as follows: Traill's Flycatcher, Black-capped Chickadee, American Magpie, Catbird, Olive-black Thrush, Solitary Vireo, Yellow Warbler, Macgillivray's Warbler, Yellow-breasted Chat, American Redstart, Lazuli Bunting, and Fox Sparrow.

Following the roads up the canyons to the tops of the mountains or plateaus, one can pass through several vegetative belts in the space of a few miles and study representatives of the birdlife in each situation. As far as climate, vegetation, and birdlife are concerned, such a trip is equivalent to one north through the great transcontinental coniferous forests of Canada to the Arctic tundra. For example, in the St. George region and up to the mouth of Zion Canyon, semitropical conditions prevail; the rim of Bryce Canyon, at about 8,000 feet, is in the ponderosa-pine belt; Cedar Breaks (see under Cedar City), at 10,700 feet, and the slopes of Brian Head, extending to 11,315 feet, represents an approach to Arctic-alpine conditions. Thus, in making a circuit of Zion and Bryce Canyon National Parks and the Cedar

Breaks National Monument, one passes through five climatic situations with their attendant birdlife.

Birds that are more commonly seen around farmlands and outskirts of cities (in dooryards, fields, wet meadows, bushy areas, orchards, and roadsides) are the following:

Red-tailed Hawk	Robin
Swainson's Hawk	Mountain Bluebird
Marsh Hawk	Yellow Warbler
Sparrow Hawk	Western Meadowlark
California Quail	Bullock's Oriole
Killdeer	Brewer's Blackbird
California Gull	Black-headed Grosbeak
Mourning Dove	Lazuli Bunting
Broad-tailed Hummingbird	House Finch
Red-shafted Flicker	Pine Siskin
Western Kingbird	Savannah Sparrow
Say's Phoebe	Vesper Sparrow
Horned Lark	Lark Sparrow
Barn Swallow	Chipping Sparrow
American Magpie	Song Sparrow
Common Raven	

In almost all regions there are seasonal changes in the local avifauna as a result of migration. In Utah a great many of the waterbirds, hawks, shorebirds, hummingbirds, flycatchers, swallows, wrens, thrushes, vireos, warblers, finches, and sparrows are only summer residents and leave for the winter. A few other species move in from the north as winter visitants. Some of the more common of these are the Rough-legged Hawk, Ring-billed Gull, Common Crow, Bohemian Waxwing, Cedar Waxwing, Northern Shrike, Evening Grosbeak, Gray-crowned Rosy Finch, Black Rosy Finch, Oregon Junco, American Tree Sparrow, and Snow Bunting.

Utah is on the fringe of the Pacific flyway; in the series of marshes at the base of the Wasatch Front many kinds of transient waterbirds and shorebirds may be seen in spring and fall. Possibly they fly along the Sevier River on their journeys. The Colorado-Green River system serves as a migratory lane in the eastern portion of the state. The best time to see migrating waterfowl and shorebirds is late February to April and August to September. A few landbirds migrate through the state—for example, the Rufous Hummingbird, Townsend's Warbler, and northern races of geographically variable species. An interesting feature is the altitudinal migration of landbirds such as woodpeckers, chickadees, creepers, pipits, and rosy finches, which move down from the mountains into the lowlands for the winter.

BRIGHAM. Outstanding among the country's National Wildlife Refuges is the BEAR RIVER MIGRATORY BIRD REFUGE on the delta at the mouth of the Bear River on Great Salt Lake. Established by special act of Congress in 1928, the Refuge now includes nearly 65,000 acres, or about 100 square miles, and constitutes one of the most completely developed bird refuges in the world. Headquarters is 15 miles west of Brigham. Turn west at the county court house. The surfaced road eventually follows along the Bear River to its mouth. Some birds, such as Snowy Egrets, Avocets, and Coots, will be noticed in spring and summer in small marsh areas along the road. Long-billed Curlews are common in the dry flats. Canada Geese may be seen along the River. At the Duckville Gun Club, Cliff Swallows nest under the eaves and in May gather mud near the bridge across the diversion canal. Others nest on the buildings at Refuge headquarters. White Pelicans and Black-crowned Night Herons are frequently observed fishing or resting in the water near the dam across the River.

At headquarters is an administration building, where visitors must register. Descriptive leaflets and an annotated check-list of birds known to occur on the Refuge are available. Maps of the region, charts showing migration, pictures, mounted specimens, study skins, and sets of eggs are other items of interest. A 100-foot tower, which visitors may climb, gives a marvelous panorama of the marsh area. Among other buildings at headquarters is the much publicized duck hospital, an open building next to a wire-enclosed pond. Sick birds are treated for botulism here and banded before release. From 1929 to 1948, over 35,000 birds were banded, with nearly 3,000 returns.

There are approximately 40 miles of dykes in the Refuge, forming five units. Roads cap the dykes; except during the hunting season, visitors are usually allowed to drive the several miles around Unit 2, which is adjacent to head-quarters. The dykes were constructed by scooping up the dirt on either side, the results being deep channels on either side of the dykes. This makes it possible to see at close range from the car such diving forms as Western Grebes and Ruddy Ducks, in addition to many common species of water-fowl, which spring up or sneak away into the vegetation as the car passes. Overhead are gulls, terns, and sometimes White Pelicans. In shallow water are Coots and shorebirds. In the open water a thrilling sight in May is the Canada Geese convoying their broods away from the dykes, one parent in front and one behind. If lucky, the bird finder may see young Western Grebes riding on the back of a parent.

The best time to visit the Refuge is during the breeding season in late May and June; then on the drive around Unit 2 one can count on seeing about 50 species, of which the following are the most common: Western Grebe, White Peli-can, Double-crested Cormorant, Great Blue Heron, Snowy Egret, Black-crowned Night Heron, White-faced Ibis, Can-ada Goose, Mallard, Gadwall, Pintail, Cinnamon Teal, Shoveler, Ruddy Duck, Marsh Hawk, Coot, Killdeer, Willet,

BLACK-NECKED STILTS

Avocet, Black-necked Stilt, Wilson's Phalarope, California Gull, Franklin's Gull, Forster's Tern, Black Tern, Short-eared Owl, Cliff Swallow, Long-billed Marsh Wren, Yellow-headed Blackbird, and Red-wing.

February is the great month for migratory waterfowl, March for marshbirds, and April for shorebirds. Not only do the summer residents listed above arrive, but thousands of transients pass through, including the Snow Goose, Bald-pate, Canvas-back, Greater Scaup Duck, Lesser Scaup Duck, American Golden-eye, Buffle-head, American Merganser, Red-breasted Merganser, Black-bellied Plover, Solitary Sandpiper, Greater Yellow-legs, Lesser Yellow-legs, Pectoral Sandpiper, Baird's Sandpiper, Least Sandpiper, Red-backed Sandpiper, Dowitcher, Western Sandpiper, Marbled Godwit, Sanderling, Northern Phalarope, Ring-billed Gull, and Bonaparte's Gull. As previously mentioned, probably more Whistling Swans concentrate here in February and March than anywhere else on the continent.

August and September mark the southward migration of northern-breeding shorebirds, as well as the exodus of the locally breeding species. Tremendous concentrations of Western Sandpipers, Wilson's Phalaropes, and Northern Phalaropes occur. Many hawks and corvids are numerous then, such as the Red-tailed Hawk, Rough-legged Hawk, Prairie Falcon, Duck Hawk, American Magpie, and Common Raven. Certain ducks, such as Buffle-heads and American Golden-eyes, appear even later in November.

Unless snowdrifts block the roads, the Refuge may be visited during the winter months and one may then see the following species: Great Blue Heron, Whistling Swan, Canada Goose, Mallard, Green-winged Teal, American Merganser, Bald Eagle, Marsh Hawk, and Common Raven.

CEDAR CITY. To reach CEDAR BREAKS NATIONAL MONUMENT (6,172 acres), 26 miles from Cedar City, take State Route 14 east, and turn left (north) on State Route 55. The road mounts ever higher to the very edge of the Markagunt Plateau in the Pink Cliffs formation, where the huge amphitheater of Cedar Breaks suddenly appears in all its splendor from Point Supreme View. The rim ranges from 10,400 to 10,700 feet in elevation. Brian Head, a near-by peak on the north, rises to an altitude of 11,315 feet (a road leads to its summit). Two other vantage points can be reached—Sunset View and Desert View—but Point Supreme View is generally regarded as the best. Cedar Breaks is not accessible until about 1 June, and snows may close the roads by late September. At the rim is an information office and temporary museum. The Utah Parks Company offers accommodations and serves meals from 1 June to 20 September.

The approach to Cedar Breaks is through ponderosa pine at lower elevations, changing to a heavy forest of Engelmann spruce, alpine fir, and bristlecone pine, with some open, park-like clearings, where one may glimpse Mountain Bluebirds, Vesper Sparrows, and occasional Sparrow Hawks or Common Ravens. Birds seem to be especially common in the forest and on the edges. The following are to be expected: Hairy Woodpecker, Canada Jay, Steller's Jay, Clark's Nutcracker, Mountain Chickadee, Red-breasted Nuthatch, Pygmy Nuthatch, Brown Creeper, Hermit Thrush, Townsend's Solitaire, Golden-crowned Kinglet, Ruby-crowned Kinglet, Audubon's Warbler, Cassin's Finch, Pine Siskin, Red Crossbill, Gray-headed Junco, and White-crowned Sparrow. The White-crowned Sparrows seem most common on wind-swept slopes where there are stunted patches of spruce. Sometimes Blue Grouse are seen along the forested edge of the rim. The White-throated Swift occurs around the cliffs, and the Violet-green Swallow nests in the region. Broad-tailed Hummingbirds are common in patches of flowers along the rim and around Brian Head.

HEBER. ROUND VALLEY, where this town is located, has an abundance of water, so that wet meadows are common, and willow and cottonwood stands abound along the streams. This region yields good bird finding in May and June. Birds are perhaps more easily seen at Midway, 3 miles west on State Route 113. Here are the HOT POTS and two resorts—Luke's Hot Pots, on the north edge of town, and The Homestead (formerly Schneitter's), at the base of the foothills on the west; both feature swimming and meals. Cliff Swallows nest under the dome-shaped limestone roof of these hot springs. About a mile northwest of the big Hot Pot at the Homestead is Snake Creek Canyon, with oaks and stream-side thickets.

About half a mile south of Midway is the MIDWAY STATE FISH HATCHERY, where sizable springs give rise to a stream that winds down through the fields to enter the Provo River at Deer Creek Reservoir near Charleston. Along the stream, in the wet fields, or in the shrubbery or cottonwoods, the following birds should be seen in the late spring and summer: Great Blue Heron, Black-crowned Night Heron, Ruffed Grouse, Cinnamon Teal, Virginia Rail, Sora, Killdeer, Spotted Sandpiper, California Gull, Broad-tailed Hummingbird, Red-shafted Flicker, Traill's Fly-catcher, Western Wood Pewee, Violet-green Swallow, Rough-winged Swallow, Cliff Swallow, American Magpie, Black-capped Chickadee, House Wren, Catbird, Yellow Warbler, Yellow-throat, Yellow-breasted Chat, Bobolink, Western Meadowlark, Yellow-headed Blackbird, Red-wing, Brewer's Blackbird, Black-headed Grosbeak, Common Goldfinch, Savannah Sparrow, and Song Sparrow. Belted Kingfishers are usually present along the Provo River just below Deer Creek Dam.

Thirty miles east of Heber, through Daniels Canyon on US Route 40, is the STRAWBERRY VALLEY NATIONAL WILDLIFE REFUGE. This embraces 14,080 acres of sagebrush country and includes Strawberry Reservoir south of the highway. There is no headquarters. Primitive roads lead down either side of the Reservoir. There is little marsh-land, and Sage Grouse are the chief attraction of the Ref-uge; their nesting season extends from the middle of April to the middle of July.

HURRICANE. From Hurricane take State Route 17 north to State Route 15, then go right on Route 15 to the south entrance of ZION NATIONAL PARK (94,881 acres). A more colorful setting than Zion Canyon can scarcely be conceived, with the red, pink, and white rock formations making up the canyon walls and the projecting dome-like masses exposed by the Virgin River as it scoured out this tremendous gorge. The Canyon extends for about 20 miles from its mouth northward into the Markagunt Plateau. Near its mouth the valley is over a mile wide. Upstream it narrows to a mere slit about 50 feet wide, and here the Canyon is 2,000 feet deep. The walls are nearly perpendicular, with talus slopes at the base of the wider portions. The Virgin River, lined with cottonwoods, winds along the Canyon floor. A few tributary canyons have small streams. Seepage water from springs collects in pools or drips down over the rock surface, making hanging gardens consisting of such plants as mosses and ferns, false Solomon's seal, and columbines. A few swampy areas occur on the Canyon floor, but it is mostly covered with a forest of deciduous trees and shrubs. In a few cooler places at higher pockets, there are isolated patches of coniferous forest—ponderosa pine, Douglas fir, and white fir. On the protected northerly talus slopes grow stands of Gambel's oak, serviceberry, maple, and ash, forming a deciduous thicket, whereas on the exposed southerly slopes are stands of pygmy conifers. At the Canyon mouth grows typical desert scrub vegetation. Hence a variety of environmental situations and habitats exists in a short distance, which favors good bird finding.

Zion Canyon is open to visitors, and accommodations are available at the South Entrance Camp the year round. The lodge, however, is open only between 30 May and 30 September. A paved highway follows along the length of the Canyon, extending for about 7 miles beyond Park headquarters to the beginning of the narrows. Occasional short side branches lead to points of interest. At Park headquarters, 2 miles beyond the south entrance and at the junction of the Mt. Carmel tunnel road and the main road, is a modest museum in which attention is given to the wildlife of the Park, including the birds. Several publications on the history, geology, biotic relationships, plants, and animals of the Park and surrounding region are offered for sale by the Zion-Bryce Natural History Association. A small reference collection of birds is available for study with permission of the naturalist in charge. Evening illustrated lectures at the lodge and campground frequently touch on birds.

Several footpaths and trails lead to all the points of interest on the valley floor, while four ascend to the rims or to mountain tops. They are all good bird walks, but those on the valley floor through vegetated areas afford the greatest number of birds. Short walks through the campgrounds, to the Wylie Retreat, or up and down the Virgin River from the lodge, are recommended.

Some of the more likely prospects for early-summer birds along these trails and roadways are the following. In the desert areas are Gambel's Quail, Road-runners, Costa's Hummingbirds, Mockingbirds, Blue Grosbeaks, and Desert Sparrows. Spotted Sandpipers and Dippers are present along the streams. Canyon Wrens are common on the cliffs. Red-wings frequent the few cattail areas, one of which is near the lodge. In the deciduous vegetation of the valley floor occur commonly such species as the Black-chinned and Broad-tailed Hummingbirds, Western Wood Pewee, Solitary Vireo, Warbling Vireo, Yellow Warbler, Bullock's Oriole, Black-headed Grosbeak, Lesser Goldfinch, and Chipping Sparrow. The deciduous thickets of the talus slopes attract the Spotted Towhee, Blue-gray Gnatcatcher, Bewick's Wren, Ash-throated Flycatcher, and Yellow-breasted Chat, whereas the pygmy conifers are attractive to the Scrub Jay, Pinyon Jay, Bush-tit, Black-throated Gray Warbler, Black-headed Grosbeak, and Chipping Sparrow. Turkey Vultures may be seen soaring overhead, while White-throated Swifts dive past the rocky exposed areas as one climbs the rim trails. Violet-green Swallows are to be seen here, too.

The most popular walk is one from the end of the highway at the Temple of Sinawava to the narrows, a distance of one mile. This is an easy, all-weather trail. Nature walks, taking about two hours for the round trip, are conducted usually twice daily along this trail by ranger naturalists during the summer months. The shortest walk is to Weeping Rock, only a quarter of a mile from the parking area, over a surfaced trail. From the Weeping Rock parking area a fairly strenuous, one-mile trail over steep grades and switchbacks leads to Hidden Canyon. For this, cross the footbridge, climb to the East Rim Trail sign, and follow along to the turnoff into Hidden Canyon, which has many birds. The East Rim Trail itself is 3.5 miles long and climbs to Observation Point at 6,508 feet. The spring at the old sawmill is a good location for bird finding. Near the Grotto Camp Ground and the Utah Parks Company Lodge (4,275 feet) another trail starts westward across the Virgin River by footbridge to the Emerald Pools, formed by two falls. The lower pool is one mile distant and the round trip takes about two hours. The upper pool is 1.5 miles from the bridge and the trip takes about three hours. There are few steep grades. From the Grotto Camp Ground a strenuous 8-hour trip leads 6¼ miles to the West Rim. It is necessary to cross the River on the footbridge and then proceed northward. The West Rim Trail from Scout Lookout to the ranger station, particularly the first stand of aspens beyond Scout Lookout, is good for warblers in May and early June. Along the way the Trail branches, the right-hand trail leading to Angels Landing, 5,785 feet, a 2.5 mile climb, fairly strenuous and steep. The trail is hard surfaced for half the distance. The most strenuous trail, even for experienced hikers, is from the lodge across the River over the footbridge to the lofty summit of Lady Mountain, 6,940 feet. The last trail is to the Great Arch of Zion, an easy 1.5-mile walk from the parking area at the upper end of the mile-long Mt. Carmel tunnel.

A peculiarity of Zion Canyon is the altitudinal migration: certain species that nest very early move to the plateaus above. This unfortunately results in a scarcity of birds in late summer, when the tourist season is at its height; during July, August, and September, birds are at a minimum. The best time for bird finding is from 10 May to 10 June. October marks the influx of southbound migrants, such as Red-breasted Nuthatches, Townsend's Solitaires, juncos, and White-crowned Sparrows. The best months to see these birds (in the order named) are May, April, June, and October.

KAMAS. MIRROR LAKE and the high-mountain country on the west side of the UINTA RANGE may be reached by driving east on State Route 150, 33 miles from Kamas. Mirror Lake is but one of 75 lakes within a radius of six miles. It lies at the base of Bald Mountain, whose summit is 11,947 feet. The pass over which the road leads is 11,000 feet. The area is heavily forested with lodgepole pines. There are U.S. Forest Service camps at Mirror and Tryol Lakes; cabins, meals, supplies, and boats are available at both places. Trails lead to the summit of Bald Mountain.

Summer residents in the Mirror Lake region are: Osprey, Blue Grouse, Hairy Woodpecker, Black-backed Woodpecker, Hammond's Flycatcher, Olive-sided Flycatcher, Canada Jay, Clark's Nutcracker, American Pipit, Cassin's Finch, Pine Grosbeak, Black Rosy Finch, Pine Siskin, Red Crossbill, Gray-headed Junco, White-crowned Sparrow, and Lincoln's Sparrow.

KANAB. Located near the Arizona line in central-southern Utah and nestling in an indenture of the Vermilion Cliffs where Kanab Creek emerges from the plateau country is Kanab, the gateway to Zion and Bryce National Parks from the Grand Canyon country to the south. It is a convenient place to stop overnight, and many bird species can be found in the vicinity.

As US Route 89 enters town from the direction of the Arizona line, it passes along a straight stretch bordered on the west (left) by a row of huge cottonwood trees, beyond which are fields and Kanab Creek. On the east are fields and finally sagebrush rangelands. In the cottonwoods, as summer residents, are Red-shafted Flickers, Western Wood Pewees, Western Kingbirds, Yellow Warblers, and Bullock's Orioles. In the fields and orchards, such species as the Ring-necked Pheasant, Mourning Dove, Eastern Kingbird, Vermilion Flycatcher, Horned Lark, Mockingbird, Phainopepla, Loggerhead Shrike, Blue Grosbeak, and Lark Sparrow may be found.

About 3 miles south of town and a quarter of a mile east of the highway is the LOWER RESERVOIR, to which one must walk. The water cannot be seen from the road, although a cottonwood or two and some willows indicate its presence. Just on the southern outskirts of town, hidden away scarcely 100 yards from the east side of the road, is the UPPER RESERVOIR. A variety of migrating shorebirds and waterbirds stop temporarily at these Reservoirs, in April and May and September and October. During the summer the following birds nest in the vicinity: Marsh Hawks, Soras, Coots, Killdeer, Spotted Sandpipers, Yellow Warblers, Yellow-throats, Yellow-headed Blackbirds, and Red-wings.

An interesting and fruitful bird walk is south of town

along KANAB CREEK. The stream has washed out a huge gorge, which is 75 feet deep in places and 50 to 100 yards across. Seepage water, together with water remaining after diversion, fosters considerable vegetation in the stream bottom.

Birds found along Kanab Creek include the Turkey Vulture, Sparrow Hawk, Gambel's Quail, Spotted Sandpiper, Mourning Dove, Road-runner, Say's Phoebe, Violet-green Swallow, Rough-winged Swallow, Cliff Swallow, Common Raven, Mockingbird, Yellow Warbler, Yellow-throat, Western Meadowlark, Red-wing, Brewer's Blackbird, House Finch, Lesser Goldfinch, and Brewer's Sparrow.

About 5 miles northwest of Kanab along US Route 89 in THREE LAKES CANYON are the THREE LAKES, which are adjacent to the highway on the west (left). These are the only bodies of water along the road, and the vicinity is a good spot for bird finding, with diverse environmental situations such as the pools of water partly situated under the cliffs, a marsh, willow thickets, cottonwoods, wet meadows, cliffs, oak brush, and pygmy forest. Birds commonly seen here are the Wilson's Snipe, White-throated Swift, Traill's Flycatcher, Violet-green Swallow, Cliff Swallow, Scrub Jay, Yellow Warbler, Brown-headed Cowbird, Lazuli Bunting, Spotted Towhee, and Song Sparrow.

LOGAN. CACHE VALLEY contains a small remnant of the grassland that once characterized much of the state, and in this habitat Sharp-tailed Grouse still survive. On a Lake Bonneville level overlooking Cache Valley is the UTAH STATE AGRICULTURAL COLLEGE. The museum, in the Administration Building on the west side of the Quadrangle, has a collection of about 1,000 study skins and a few mounted birds. An elementary course in ornithology is given in the spring quarter. A Co-operative Wildlife Unit conducts graduate work on game birds in the region.

East of the College is beautiful LOGAN CANYON, through which US Route 89 passes to the Bear Lake region (see under Montpelier in the Idaho chapter). Bird finding is good nearly everywhere in the Canyon, but a very good spot for mountain birds is just west of the summit, where the U.S.A.C. School of Forestry has a summer camp. Here is a lake surrounded by rocky, sparsely timbered country, one of the few places where Purple Martins have been seen in the state.

MOAB. Nestled in a little valley at the base of red cliffs adjacent to the COLORADO RIVER is the town of Moab. It is important as the gateway to many scenic areas of the region, where birds may also be seen. The bird finder can expect interesting results from working along the River and through the river bottoms, except in spring when the latter are flooded. On the western outskirts of town is a bridge across the River. State Route 128, which passes up the east side of the River, is not a good route for the bird finder, but on the west side he can walk upstream a short distance and probably see Canyon Wrens. In working southward along the tamarisk thickets, willows, and cottonwoods he should see Yellow Warblers, blackbirds, and other streamside species.

Southward from Moab extends US Route 160. To the east on the Colorado border lie the LA SAL MOUNTAINS, with Mount Peale reaching 13,089 feet. The belting of vegetation is very apparent on the western slope. U.S. Forest Service campgrounds have been established in these mountains in two areas.

Northwest of Moab lie the approaches to the ARCHES NATIONAL MONUMENT (34,249 acres) and DEAD HORSE POINT, both over dirt roads. For the former, turn right over State Route 93, 10 miles from Moab. The area includes 83 arches and strange rock formations. The bird finder must walk short distances to the principal sights and in so doing should see many open-country birds such as Red-tailed Hawks, Say's Phoebes, and Brewer's Sparrows. The area supports sparse desert-shrub and pygmy-forest vegetation.

For the road to Dead Horse Point turn left from US Route 160, 15 miles north of Moab, and proceed about 30 miles over a rough road. In some respects the view out over the gorge of the Colorado River equals that of the Grand Canyon. On a trip to Dead Horse Point the bird finder may see the following: Sparrow Hawk, Great Horned Owl, Say's Phoebe, Horned Lark, Scrub Jay, Pinyon Jay, Plain Titmouse, Bewick's Wren, Canyon Wren, Sage Thrasher, and Spotted Towhee.

MONTICELLO. At the east base of the ABAJO or BLUE MOUNTAINS on US Route 160 lies Monticello (pronounced *mon-ti-sell'-o*). A ponderosa-pine forest covers much of the mountain slopes. From Monticello, State Route 47 continues on to Blanding, Bluff, Mexican Hat, across the San Juan River to the unique Monument Valley. Near Mexican Hat are the geologically interesting Goosenecks of the San Juan, great bends in the River. Roads beyond Bluff are narrow and rough and cross some sandy washes. The sand in Monument Valley makes it necessary for the bird finder to remain on the road. This is wild and isolated country; the only lodgings available in Monument Valley are at Gouldings, near the Arizona state line.

Fifty miles west of Blanding is the NATURAL BRIDGES NATIONAL MONUMENT (2,649 acres). An improved dirt road, State Route 95, climbs up to Elk Ridge and Bear's Ears Pass, an elevation of about 9,000 feet, which affords an inspiring view over the Monument Valley country. The road is through ponderosa pine much of the way, but the National Monument is in a pinyon-pine and juniper environment. The road goes only to Owachomo (Edwin) Bridge, necessitating a hike or horseback trip to the other natural bridges.

OGDEN. Utah's second city in size has Ogden Canyon at its backdoor and Ogden Bay at its front, with the Ogden and Weber Rivers passing through town. The Canyon (State Route 39) lies east of 21st Street and contains the PINEVIEW RESERVOIR. East of the Reservoir the Canyon opens out into a round valley where Huntsville is located. In addition to Belted Kingfishers and Dippers along the River, the Reservoir attracts some waterfowl. A road to the right (south) near the east end of the Reservoir, about 10 miles from Ogden, leads to SNOW BASIN, at an elevation of 8,000 feet back of Mount Ogden. Here the usual

574 A Guide to Bird Finding

spruce-fir-aspen forest prevails, with the common species likely to be encountered, as listed for that environment in the introduction of the chapter.

BIRCH CREEK HOLLOW is a productive area for birds within the city. From the business district proceed south along Washington Boulevard to 40th Street, turn left (east) one block past the Birch Creek School, then go right (south) a quarter of a mile to the north end of the Country Club Golf Course. One can then work up Birch Creek to the foothills for a long bird walk or veer to the east at the end of the road and engage in bird finding in the few acres surrounding three small ponds. Along the stream and the ponds among the cottonwoods, willows, birches, and dogwoods may be found the Ring-necked Pheasant, Killdeer, Great Horned Owl, Long-eared Owl, Saw-whet Owl, Downy Woodpecker, Scrub Jay, American Magpie, Blackcapped Chickadee, Yellow-throat, Yellow-breasted Chat, Western Meadowlark, Red-wing, Black-headed Grosbeak, Spotted Towhee, and Song Sparrow. Most of these are permanent-resident species, and their numbers are augmented in fall, winter, and spring by an influx of birds such as the Goshawk, Brown Creeper, Ruby-crowned Kinglet, Townsend's Solitaire, Oregon Junco, and White-crowned Sparrow.

The WEBER RIVER BOTTOMS, on the south and west sides of Ogden, afford good bird finding. Drive south on Wall Avenue to 33rd Street, turn right (west) half a mile to the railroad tracks, and continue another half a mile or so to the River. Work southward on either side of the River to the Riverdale Road or north on the west side of the River to the viaduct on 24th Street. Here there are the same species as mentioned for Birch Creek Hollow, and in addition such species as the Pied-billed Grebe, Virginia Rail, Cooper's Hawk, Red-tailed Hawk, Sparrow Hawk, California Quail, Screech Owl, Belted Kingfisher, Redshafted Flicker, Dipper, Yellow Warbler, American Redstart, Brewer's Blackbird, Lazuli Bunting, and Common Goldfinch.

PANGUITCH. The 36,010 acres of BRYCE CANYON NATIONAL PARK (from Panguitch south on US Route

89 to State Route 12, and east on Route 12) comprise a huge amphitheater at the edge of the pink cliffs of Paunsagunt Plateau, with a view from the rim of highly colored, delicately and fantastically eroded rock formations. In approaching Bryce National Park, the Route passes through a ponderosa-pine forest, where characteristic birds may be seen, such as Williamson's Sapsuckers, Steller's Jays, White-breasted Nuthatches, Pygmy Nuthatches, Western Bluebirds, Audubon's Warblers, Western Tanagers, Red Crossbills, and Gray-headed Juncos. A short walk from the parking lot near the lodge to the rim at Sunset Point (8,000 feet) also leads through this forest.

From the rim looking out over Bryce Canyon and the Paria Valley beyond, Violet-green Swallows can be seen slowly soaring along and an occasional White-throated Swift passing by in rapid flight.

A surfaced road follows the rim to the southeast for about 18 miles from the checking station, with turnouts or stops for Sunset, Inspiration, and Bryce Points, Paria View, the Natural Bridge, Rainbow Point, and Yavimpa View. Rainbow Point rises to 9,105 feet, and among its spruces and firs Clark's Nutcrackers are frequent. A dirt-road drive of about one mile extends eastward from near the checking station to Fairyland.

Numerous trails of varying lengths radiate from Sunset Point, some leading along the rim, others into Bryce Canyon; the Navajo-Comanche Loop and return is 1.5 miles; Inspiration Point is one mile; Sunrise Point, half a mile; Bryce Point, via Peek-a-boo Trail, 3¾ miles; the Campbell Canyon-Fairyland Loop and return is 6 miles. None of these is particularly good for birds. More birds may be seen by wandering around the lodges and cabins or around the museum, campfire, campground, and cafeteria areas. During the summer season short nature walks, usually starting from Sunrise Point, are conducted into Bryce Canyon daily. Evening illustrated lectures frequently feature the birds of the region.

Bryce Canyon is open from about 15 April to 15 November, the dates varying according to weather conditions. The cafeteria and adjacent cabins are in operation from about 1 May to 30 October. The lodge is operated from about 30

May to 25 September. Birds are best seen from mid-May through early June.

PROVO. The most spectacular mountain of the Wasatch Range is Mount Timpanogos, just south of which is the town of Provo. This is the home of BRIGHAM YOUNG UNIVERSITY, which has a collection of about 2,000 study skins, 500 mounted birds, and 125 sets of eggs in the Brimhall Building on the Upper Campus at 8th North and 2nd East Streets. An elementary course in ornithology is given in the spring, and graduate work is conducted the year round.

West of Provo is UTAH LAKE, a body of fresh water whose outlet, Jordan River, flows into Great Salt Lake. The Provo River enters Utah Lake west of the city. Near its mouth there is good bird finding in the riverside thickets, tamarisk stands, and marshes along the lake shore. Drive west along Center Street from 5th West Street across the viaduct and on for about 3 miles. About 3 miles offshore is ROCK ISLAND, which at low-water stages has served as the nesting site of California Gulls, Forster's and Caspian Terns, and a few other species, but of recent years the Island has been submerged, and the colony of California Gulls has moved to the dyke of the Geneva Steel Plant. The area along the Jordan River near its origin is good for birds; it is reached by driving west from Lehi 4 miles along State Route 73 until the highway crosses the River.

US Route 189 passes eastward through PROVO CANYON with its precipitous walls. Many birds are to be found along the river in the shrubbery. From Wildwood, 13 miles up from Provo, the Alpine Drive (State Route 80) circles back of Mt. Timpanogos into AMERICAN FORK CANYON, an exceptionally beautiful drive in the fall of the year. Glacier-carved 'Timpie' looms up 12,008 feet, and at its eastern foot, on State Route 80, is the Brigham Young University's Alpine Summer School, where courses in ornithology are frequently offered. This is a splendid area for bird finding, and trails lead to the summit of the mountain, passing through the various vegetative belts with their characteristic birds.

RICHFIELD. Drive north on US Route 89 for 8 miles to Sigurd, then turn right (southeast) on State Route 24 for about 71 miles to the CAPITOL REEF NATIONAL MONUMENT (36,393 acres), known locally as Wayne Wonderland, an area that someday may be as popular as Zion and Bryce. This country, in the Fremont River Basin, is essentially undeveloped for tourists, but there is a wealth of colored rock formations, gorges, vertical walls, reefs, arches, temples, buttes, petrified trees, and archeological ruins of great interest. The road into the Monument climbs the Fish Lake Plateau, the summit of the road reaching 8,410 feet. It then drops down to the Fremont River through a series of small towns—Loa, Lyman, Bicknell, Torrey, and Fruita, the last in a delightful setting, at the base of red cliffs in a protected little valley. One tourist court offers accommodations here. As the name suggests, there are orchards, along with fields of alfalfa. These and the natural habitat offer a rich area for bird finders. Canyon and Rock Wrens are common. Other birds of common occurrence here are the Prairie Falcon, Broad-tailed Hummingbird, Say's Phoebe, Violet-green Swallow, Scrub Jay, House Wren, Yellow Warbler, House Finch, and Spotted Towhee.

State Route 24, a dirt road, continues beyond the Monument to Hanksville through some drab country, crosses the Fremont River, and after 60 rough, sandy miles reaches Greenriver on US Routes 50 and 6.

SALT LAKE CITY. Among the advantages of Salt Lake City are the many areas for bird finding at relatively short distances from the center of the city. In Temple Square is the famous Seagull Monument. Within half a mile of this and other historical points of interest is the mouth of CITY CREEK CANYON, just east of the Capitol. Turn right at State and North Temple Streets and proceed north along Canyon Road half a mile to Memory Grove. From here a bird walk can be made over trails upstream past cottonwoods, grassy hillsides, and scrub oaks. The Utah Audubon Society's field trips to this area in fall and spring usually result in lists of 30 to 35 kinds of birds. Bohemian Waxwings are frequently found here in winter.

Several other canyons exist on the outskirts of the city; those whose roads are open to the public are (from north to south): EMIGRATION, PARLEY'S (US Route 40), MILL CREEK, BIG COTTONWOOD, and LITTLE COTTONWOOD. At the mouth of Emigration Canyon along the Wasatch Drive at the east end of Sunnyside Avenue is HOGLE ZOO, with numerous native birds in the surroundings. Across the street is the 'This is the Place' Monument. There is an unsurpassed view from here over the tree-filled city and valley, with the extensive marshland and Great Salt Lake beyond. At the southern end of the Lake are the smelters and mills. Even the location of the Utah Copper Mine in the Oquirrh Mountains can be seen.

Close by Emigration Canyon is the UNIVERSITY OF UTAH, the entrance of which is at the head of Second South and University Streets. In the Biology Building is a research collection of birds from the state numbering about 10,000 study skins, together with a few mounted specimens, and 2,000 sets of eggs. A course in Utah birds is given each spring quarter and occasionally in the summer. Graduate work is also given in ornithology. The Utah Audubon Society meets here monthly, September through May. In the Geology Building Museum is a huge relief map of central and northern Utah that will help one to visualize the physiography of the state.

US Route 40 enters Salt Lake Valley through Parley's Canyon. At the mouth of the Canyon there is a good place for bird finding upstream from the Country Club. About 25 miles east of Salt Lake City through Parley's Canyon on US Route 40, at Snyderville, is PARLEY'S PARK, an important collecting station of Robert Ridgway in 1869. The area abounds in birds and is known to local bird finders as the 'Ridgway Trail'; over 90 species of birds have been seen in the Park and 120 in the Park and surrounding country. The common species are the same as those listed for Midway (see under Heber).

The OLD MILL area at the mouth of Big Cottonwood Canyon, on State Route 152 about 8 miles southeast of Salt Lake City beyond Holladay, abounds in cottonwoods along the streams and in oaks, sumac, and squawbush in drier situations; it affords good bird finding. BRIGHTON, in a mountain-surrounded amphitheater at the head of Big Cottonwood Canyon, 8,730 feet, about 28 miles from the city, at the end of State Route 152, is a different type of bird-finding area, with dense spruce-fir-aspen forests, meadows, and lakes such as Silver Lake. There are many summer cabins here, and lodges offer accommodations for visitors both summer and winter, since this is an important skiing area. One can expect about 65 species of breeding birds (see introduction to chapter). In winter, Mountain Chickadees, Steller's Jays, and Clark's Nutcrackers reward the bird finder.

ALTA, at the end of State Route 210, lies over the divide from Brighton, at the head of Little Cottonwood Canyon at an elevation of 8,583 feet. This spot 17 miles east of Sandy, or about 30 miles southeast of Salt Lake City, is an old mining camp, now a summer picnic area and superb skiing resort. Lodges afford accommodations, but there are no cabins. Birds appear in large numbers on the valley floor and in the surrounding forest areas, which are less dense than those at Brighton. The Old Mill and Brighton or Alta could be combined in an all-day bird trip.

Liberty Park contains the TRACY AVIARY, which is at 6th East and 13th South Streets. There are about 2,000 birds representing 475 kinds. Most are exotic species, but all the local ducks, many marshbirds, and a few landbirds are present.

GREAT SALT LAKE, about 15 miles west of Salt Lake City, is in barren surroundings. While driving along US Route 40 to the resort areas at Saltair, Sunset, and Black Rock Beaches, one may get glimpses, during spring and summer, of such birds as the Red-tailed Hawk, Swainson's Hawk, Ferruginous Hawk, Golden Eagle, Marsh Hawk, Prairie Falcon, Horned Lark, Common Raven, and Brewer's Blackbird. At times during migration, April to May and August to September, tremendous flocks of Eared Grebes, ducks, phalaropes, and sandpipers alight on the Lake. The rookeries on the islands are not accessible.

ST. GEORGE. The area along the Virgin River in south-western Utah, particularly the St. George region, is known as Utah's Dixie, because the climate is semitropical and in pioneer days cotton was grown and cloth produced here, in keeping with the plan to make the region self-sustaining. DIXIE JUNIOR COLLEGE is on East Tabernacle Street, one and a half blocks south of US Route 91. A collection of approximately 500 bird skins and a few sets of eggs are housed in the Science Building on East Tabernacle Street.

About 3 miles south of St. George, along East Tabernacle Street, lies the junction of SANTA CLARA CREEK and the VIRGIN RIVER. Along the banks of the Virgin River are thickets of tamarisk and willows. Small cattail marshes exist near the confluence of the two streams. Westward from here along the Santa Clara river bottoms is a dense tangle of brushy types, providing cover for many species, such as the Gambel's Quail, Barn Owl, Screech Owl, Great Horned Owl, Red-shafted Flicker, Western Kingbird, Black Phoebe, Traill's Flycatcher, Vermilion Flycatcher, Rough-winged Swallow, Bell's Vireo, Lucy's Warbler, Yellow Warbler, Yellow-throat, Yellow-breasted Chat, Yellow-headed Blackbird, Red-wing, Bullock's Oriole, Black-headed Grosbeak, Blue Grosbeak, Lesser Goldfinch, Abert's Towhee, and Song Sparrow.

During migration, shorebirds and waterbirds may be seen along the Virgin River. In the winter months there is a concentration of Ruby-crowned Kinglets, Oregon Juncos, White-crowned Sparrows, and Song Sparrows in the river bottoms, with Loggerhead Shrikes, American Pipits, and various species of broad-winged hawks in the more open fields. Mockingbirds and Vermilion Flycatchers are probably more common in the St. George area than elsewhere in the state. Any of the lanes or roads to ranches in the surrounding country afford good bird finding, especially those leading to the fields south of the hamlet of Washington, which lies 5 miles east of St. George along US Route 91.

An interesting side trip for one wishing to make a long stay in southern Utah is to go north from St. George along State Route 18, through Diamond Valley, with its black craters and red-rock formations, to Central, then right (east) to Pine Valley, and east 3 miles to the U.S. Forest Service Camp. In this delightful setting are fields, meadows, willow-lined streams, cottonwood groves, and ponderosa-pine forest, with the many types of birds associated with these environmental conditions. Hikes may be made over good trails into the Pine Valley Mountains through spruce-fir forests to high mountain meadows around 9,500 feet.

VERNAL. This is the principal city of the Uintah Basin in northeastern Utah. The FIELD HOUSE OF NATURAL HISTORY, on the north side of US Route 40, just east of the business district, features exhibits on the geology and resources of the region, and also contains a few ornithological items.

Ten miles northwest of Vernal at the junction of Dry Fork and Ashley Creek, north of Maeser, is MERKLEY PARK, a picnic and recreation area in an extensive grove of cottonwoods. Downstream are wet meadows, willow patches, and pasturelands. In the general vicinity may be seen Soras, Broad-tailed Hummingbirds, Belted Kingfishers, Black-capped Chickadees, House Wrens, Catbirds, Mountain Bluebirds, Solitary Vireos, Warbling Vireos, Virginia's Warblers, Macgillivray's Warblers, American Redstarts, Spotted Towhees, and Song Sparrows.

State Route 44 leads into the eastern section of the UINTA MOUNTAINS en route to Manila and Wyoming. The dirt road climbs abruptly through pygmy forest to an extensive stand of ponderosa pine and finally to a dense lodgepole-pine forest. There are a few cabins at GREEN LAKE. A road near here leads from the highway to a lookout point over RED CANYON, where Green River, 1,500 feet below, cuts through the Uinta Mountains. Birds to be seen in the Green Lake area are the Williamson's Sapsucker, White-breasted Nuthatch, Townsend's Solitaire, Western Tanager, Cassin's Finch, and Pine Siskin.

US Route 40 crosses the Green River at Jensen, 13 miles east of Vernal. Many waterfowl and shorebirds migrate along the River in spring and fall. The road leading south on the west side of the River extends 2 miles to STEWART LAKE, a state game refuge. A short distance beyond, best reached by walking, are the ASHLEY SLOUGHS, where Ashley Creek enters the River. In the river bottoms and the surrounding area one should see Sharp-shinned Hawks, Coots, Red-shafted Flickers, Western Kingbirds, House

Wrens, Bewick's Wrens, Long-billed Marsh Wrens, Sage
Thrashers, Yellow Warblers, Yellow-breasted Chats, West-
ern Meadowlarks, Yellow-headed Blackbirds, Red-wings,
Bullock's Orioles, Savannah Sparrows, Lark Sparrows, and
Brewer's Sparrows.

From Jensen, State Route 149 leads north 7 miles to the
DINOSAUR NATIONAL MONUMENT (209,744 acres).
A small temporary museum features dinosaur bones and
geological specimens. Though this is barren country with
greasewood and scattered junipers, one may see such birds
as Mourning Doves, Say's Phoebes, Pinyon Jays, Bewick's
Wrens, Sage Thrashers, Loggerhead Shrikes, Black-throated
Gray Warblers, House Finches, Green-tailed Towhees,
Lark Sparrows, and Brewer's Sparrows.

Contributing authorities: Arthur F. Bruhn, Russell K. Grater,
Clifton Greenhalgh, C. Lynn Hayward, Charles W. Lockerbie,
Alden H. Miller, Richard D. Porter, Clifford C. Presnall, Robert
Selander, Randall L. Turpin, Arthur C. Twomey, Calvin Wilson,
Vanez T. Wilson, Angus M. Woodbury.

Washington

COMMON MURRES

Probably no other state shows greater contrasts of environment than Washington. Elevations range from sea level to peaks well above 10,000 feet. Average precipitation ranges from extremes of 142 inches a year—the heaviest in the United States—in one part of the state, to 6 inches in another. There are some places so densely forested as to appear tropical and others so arid in character as to be desertlike. Birdlife (for example, Common Murres, White-tailed Ptarmigan, Bush-tits, Hermit Thrushes, and Sage Sparrows), responding to these extremes or the intergrading conditions that lie between them, is equally diversified.

Running through the interior of Washington from the northern to the southern boundary are the Cascade Moun-

tains. About 100 miles wide toward the northern and southern boundaries and, like an hourglass, narrowed between to
a width of 60 miles, they divide the state into western and
eastern sections, the latter being slightly the larger. Western Washington, favored by prevailing moist sea winds, has
a high humidity and moderate temperatures at all seasons.
Cloudy weather is of common occurrence. But eastern
Washington, lying in the rain shadow of the Cascades, is
comparatively dry and subject to extremes of heat and cold.
Strong winds and clear skies are often the rule.

In general, the peaks and ridges of the Cascades, though
exceedingly abrupt and rugged, form a relatively uniform
skyline with an average level of 8,000 feet in the north,
gradually descending to 5,000 feet in the south. This typical evenness is broken, however, by five lofty volcanic cones,
one of which—Mt. Rainier—reaches 14,408 feet, the highest point in the state. On the eastern side of the Cascades
are several long spur ranges extending in a southeastwardly
direction parallel to deep, steep-sided valleys.

In western Washington, the Cascades slope down to
a long, broad valley called the Puget Trough, which is continuous southward with the Willamette Valley in Oregon.
The northern part of the Trough is occupied by Puget
Sound; the southern part, while above sea level, rarely exceeds 500 feet elevation, except in a few hilly areas. West
of Puget Sound is the Olympic Peninsula, with the Olympic
Mountains rising from its central portion. Many of the
Olympic ridges reach heights between 4,500 and 5,000 feet,
and a few peaks extend well above 7,000. In their sharp-
ness and steepness, the Olympics strongly resemble the
Cascades. South of the Olympic Peninsula and west of the
Puget Trough are the rough Willapa Hills, a northward extension of the Coast Range in Oregon, and generally low
(under 3,000 feet).

The higher peaks and ridges of both the Cascade and
Olympic Mountains have alpine regions characterized by
glaciers, permanent snowfields, and a vegetation of hardy
shrubs and herbaceous plants. A few such regions in the
Cascades are known to support nesting pairs of White-
tailed Ptarmigan, Horned Larks, American Pipits, and Gray-
crowned Rosy Finches; in like places on the Olympic Moun-

tains, Horned Larks are known to breed and it is not unlikely that further investigation will reveal Ptarmigan, Pipits, and Rosy Finches breeding there, too. Below the alpine regions exists a vertical succession of tree associations, or belts. (For a description of typical succession on the moist western slopes of the Cascades and the slopes of the Olympic Mountains, see under Tacoma and Port Angeles; for a description of succession on the drier, eastern slopes of the Cascades, see under Okanogan.) A peculiar feature of vegetation on the lowlands of western Washington, which enjoys a cool, humid climate, even in the summer, is the presence of coniferous forests, extending almost to the edge of the sea. Before settlement and lumbering operations, Douglas fir, western hemlock, and western red cedar covered vast areas. Deciduous trees and shrubs grew mainly in ravines and valleys near streams, rarely on higher ground. Areas of native grasses (i.e. prairies) were of minor extent. Along the coast where the rainfall is heaviest (e.g. on the west side of the Olympic Mountains), both coniferous and deciduous growth attained remarkable density and luxuriance. While excellent samples of these original conditions may still be seen today in Olympic National Park (see under Port Angeles) and offer an unusual opportunity for bird finding, most of the lowland forests of western Washington have since been replaced by second-growth woods, or by agricultural lands.

In the coniferous forests of the Cascade and Olympic Mountains and the lowlands of western Washington, the bird species listed below breed regularly unless otherwise indicated. Species marked by an asterisk occur mainly at higher elevations.

Goshawk
Sharp-shinned Hawk
Cooper's Hawk
Blue Grouse
Franklins Grouse (east slopes of Cascades)
Band-tailed Pigeon
Pygmy Owl
*Saw-whet Owl
Pileated Woodpecker
Williamson's Sapsucker (east slopes of Cascades)
White-headed Woodpecker (east slopes of Cascades)
Olive-sided Flycatcher
Canada Jay
Steller's Jay
Common Raven
*Clark's Nutcracker
*Mountain Chickadee

Chestnut-backed Chickadee (west side of Cascades)
Red-breasted Nuthatch
Pygmy Nuthatch (east slopes of Cascades)
Brown Creeper
Winter Wren
Varied Thrush
°Hermit Thrush
Olive-backed Thrush
°Townsend's Solitaire
Golden-crowned Kinglet
Ruby-crowned Kinglet (east slopes of Cascades)
Solitary Vireo
Audubon's Warbler
°Townsend's Warbler
Black-capped Warbler
Western Tanager
Evening Grosbeak
Purple Finch (west side of Cascades)
Cassin's Finch (east slopes of Cascades)
Pine Siskin
Red Crossbill
Oregon Junco
White-crowned Sparrow
°Fox Sparrow
°Lincoln's Sparrow

The Washington coast has a varied and highly scenic topography. Fronting on the Pacific in the southwest are many long, straight beaches, backed by sand dunes; reaching inland behind them in several places are large bays, bordered frequently by mud flats and occasionally by salt marshes. In the northwest are high, rocky bluffs and headlands, and, seldom far offshore, numerous giant rocks or ledges boldly projecting above tide level. Cape Flattery, the westernmost tip of the Olympic Peninsula—and of the United States—is notable for its rugged and generally bleak appearance. Undoubtedly the outstanding feature of the Washington coast is its great indentation, Puget Sound, in reality a deep, drowned valley severely gouged by glacial action. The northern portions, known as the Straits of Georgia and San Juan de Fuca, are broad channels separating the state from Vancouver Island. The remaining portion, extending southward into the state for a hundred miles, is exceedingly irregular, its many bays and 'canals' forming a shoreline of 1,750 miles. While most of these inlets are flanked by precipitous banks, often of impressive height, a few, having become partly filled by silt, show mud bars and marshes along their edges. Occasionally an inlet has been cut off by sediments and forms a body of water such as Lake Washington, east of Seattle. The Sound also embraces hundreds of islands, including the San Juans (see under Anacortes). Some are large and support farms and resorts, but the majority are small pieces of wooded land, or bare rock. All have a picturesque northland charm.

The bluffs, headlands, small islands, and rocks of the Washington coast are as attractive ornithologically as they are scenically, for they provide the isolation that many sea-birds prefer when nesting. Between mid-May and mid-July, the following species may be found breeding regularly in such areas:

Fork-tailed Petrel (not common)
Leach's Petrel
Double-crested Cormorant
Brandt's Cormorant (not common)
Pelagic Cormorant
Glaucous-winged Gull (northern coast only)
Western Gull (not common)
Common Murre
Pigeon Guillemot
Cassin's Auklet
Rhinoceros Auklet (not common)
Tufted Puffin

The northern third of eastern Washington—east of the Cascades and the Okanogan River Valley; north of the Columbia River Valley (where its course is east to west) and the Spokane River—comprises the Okanogan Highlands. A western extension of the northern Rocky Mountains in Montana and Idaho, with many elevations reaching above 6,000 feet, the Highlands consist mainly of several small ranges and other uplands trending north and south, paralleled by intervening valleys. They have no alpine regions. As on the east slopes of the adjacent Cascades (see under Okanogan), the climate here is somewhat arid, a fact that has a marked effect on the vegetation. Such conifers as Douglas fir, western larch, and lodgepole pine are replaced, except at higher elevations, by park-like stands of ponderosa pine, and occasionally by grasslands or sagelands. Breeding birds of the coniferous woods include the Williamson's Sapsucker, Steller's Jay, Pygmy Nuthatch, Audubon's Warbler, Western Tanager, Fox Sparrow, and many other species found also on the east slopes of the Cascades.

The extreme southeastern corner of Washington is occupied by the Blue Mountains, the northern fringe of the range with the same name in Oregon (see introduction to the Oregon chapter). In Washington they attain elevations between 5,000 and 6,500 feet. On the north and west slopes and the tops of many ridges are heavy stands of Douglas fir, grand fir, Engelmann spruce, lodgepole pine, and western larch; on the highest ridges, alpine fir is the most common tree. Usually the south and east slopes are either barren or covered with open ponderosa-pine forests. Throughout the Blue Mountains are many deep canyons well wooded with conifers down to their bottoms, where there are cottonwoods and willows. The birdlife of the Blue Mountains (see under Walla Walla) is very much like that of the Cascades.

The remainder of eastern Washington is a semi-arid plateau, most of which is below 2,000 feet in elevation and is underlain by laval rock. North of the Snake River, which crosses the southeastern part of the state to join the Columbia River, the plateau is known as the Palouse Country. Here the surface, rolling in broad, wave-like swells, contains fine-textured soils used extensively for wheat production. From the Palouse Country north and west to the Columbia, the plateau is desert-like and, at least at one point, receives an average precipitation of 9 inches or less a year. Conditions of surface and vegetation show considerable variation. Certain parts have extensive dunes, owing to shifting sands; others have a peculiar type of erosion topography called channeled scablands (see under Spokane); and still others have a gently rolling surface suggesting the Great Plains east of the Rocky Mountains. In the northwest, embraced by the 'big bend' of the Columbia, are two striking geological phenomena—Moses Coulee and the Grand Coulee. Great gashes running across the plateau from northeast to southwest, they are former beds of the Columbia. In the southwest, between the Columbia and the southern Cascades, the plateau has southeastward-trending ridges, 1,000 to 3,000 feet in height, drained for the most part by the Yakima River. Throughout the plateau, with the exception of the Palouse Country and other areas that have been modified for agricultural purposes, vegetation is more or less of the desert type. Sagebrush and bunch grass constitute the predominant growth, with admixtures of greasewood, foxtail, cheat grass, and cacti. Pines may be found on ridges, and cottonwoods and willows along streams, but otherwise trees are scarce. Among the bird species that may be considered typical of the sagebrush and bunch-grass areas are the following:

Swainson's Hawk	Sage Thrasher
Ferruginous Hawk	Savannah Sparrow
Sage Grouse (uncommon)	Lark Sparrow
Burrowing Owl	Sage Sparrow
Poor-will	Brewer's Sparrow
Horned Lark	

In widely scattered localities of eastern Washington are lakes, ponds, sloughs, potholes, and marshes, in some cases created or improved by artificial means, which attract surprisingly large nesting populations of waterbirds, waterfowl, and marsh-loving birds. Moses Lake (see under Moses Lake), Twelve-Mile Slough (see under Pullman), and the ponds and potholes in the Turnbull National Wildlife Refuge (see under Spokane) are among the better known. The fact that these watery environments and their associated birdlife exist in an otherwise arid region contributes in no small degree to their interest.

As in western Washington, many natural areas east of the Cascades have been converted into agricultural lands. There are now many farmlands (fields, meadows, and pastures) where there were once sagelands or grasslands. Deciduous trees, formerly prevalent only along watercourses, now stand in dooryards and parks and comprise orchards. At the present time, throughout both western and eastern Washington (unless otherwise indicated), birds that may be found breeding regularly in the open country (farmlands, brushy areas, orchards, parks, and dooryards) and deciduous woods are listed below. Species marked by an asterisk breed also in the mountains.

OPEN COUNTRY

Turkey Vulture
Marsh Hawk (eastern Washington)
California Quail
Killdeer
*Mourning Dove
Short-eared Owl
Eastern Kingbird (mainly eastern Washington)
Western Kingbird (eastern Washington)
Say's Phoebe (eastern Washington)
Barn Swallow

*American Magpie (eastern Washington)
Bush-tit (western Washington)
*House Wren
Bewick's Wren
Catbird (eastern Washington)
Western Bluebird (mainly western Washington)
*Mountain Bluebird (eastern Washington)
Loggerhead Shrike
Orange-crowned Warbler
Yellow Warbler
*Macgillivray's Warbler

Yellow-throat
Yellow-breasted Chat (mainly eastern Washington)
Bobolink (eastern Washington)
Western Meadowlark
Lazuli Bunting (eastern Washington)
Common Goldfinch
Spotted Towhee
Savannah Sparrow
Vesper Sparrow
*Chipping Sparrow
Song Sparrow

DECIDUOUS WOODS

Ruffed Grouse
Screech Owl
Red-shafted Flicker
Common Sapsucker
*Hairy Woodpecker
Downy Woodpecker
*Hammond's Flycatcher
Western Flycatcher
Western Wood Pewee
Black-capped Chickadee

*White-breasted Nuthatch
Red-eyed Vireo (eastern Washington)
Warbling Vireo
*Nashville Warbler
American Redstart (eastern Washington)
Bullock's Oriole
Black-headed Grosbeak

Bird transients through Washington, unlike transients through the states in the same latitude on the Atlantic Coast, include very few landbird species nesting exclusively in regions to the north. The Golden-crowned Sparrow is one of the few, but even this species is a common transient only in western Washington. Migration is notable mainly for the movements of waterfowl, waterbirds, and shorebirds. Geese and ducks stop off on lakes and other water areas in eastern Washington, though not in the abundance to be observed west of the Cascades, in Puget Sound, Grays Harbor, and similarly sheltered coastal indentations. Whistling Swans sometimes congregate in the mouth of the Columbia River. At ocean-front spots such as Point Chehalis (see under Aberdeen), Sooty and Pink-footed Shearwaters are often seen passing by in immense numbers. Transient

Parasitic Jaegers and Short-billed Gulls are common to abundant in Puget Sound and elsewhere on the coast. Shore-birds, including Semipalmated and Black-bellied Plovers, Surf-birds, Black Turnstones, Hudsonian Curlews, Wandering Tattlers, Pectoral, Least, and Red-backed Sandpipers, Dowitchers, Western Sandpipers, and Sanderlings, frequent many of the beaches for feeding and loitering while on their way north or south. In Washington, the main migratory flights may be expected within the following dates: waterfowl, 20 March—25 April, 15 September—15 November; shorebirds, 1 May—1 June, 1 August—15 September; landbirds, 15 April—1 June, 15 August—1 October.

Eastern Washington is within the winter ranges of a few landbird species, such as the Rough-legged Hawk, Bohemian Waxwing, Common Redpoll, American Tree Sparrow, and Snow Bunting. Its water areas (e.g. in Turnbull National Wildlife Refuge), if they fail to freeze over, hold moderately large populations of geese and ducks. Western Washington, which has relatively mild winters, can be rewarding to winter bird finders, especially along the coast and on Puget Sound. Here are opportunities to see loons (Common, Arctic, and Red-throated), grebes (Holboell's, Horned, Eared, and Western), over 20 species of ducks, gulls (Glaucous-winged, Western, Herring, Short-billed, and Bonaparte's), a few shorebirds and alcids, and a variety of landbirds, such as Band-tailed Pigeons, Chestnut-backed Chickadees, Bewick's Wrens, Varied Thrushes, Cedar Waxwings, Hutton's Vireos, Purple Finches, and Song Sparrows. As an example of just how successful winter bird finding can be in western Washington, a party of 29 people, taking a Christmas bird count recently in the Seattle area, recorded 21,718 individual birds, representing 93 species.

The Pacific Northwest Bird and Mammal Society is not a state organization, but half of its members are Washingtonians. This organization, which publishes *The Murrelet* (triannually), holds an annual meeting in April at the University of Washington in Seattle and regional meetings in other months of the year at institutions elsewhere in the state and in Oregon, Idaho, Montana, and British Columbia. The Society may always be contacted through the

Washington State Museum, University of Washington, Seattle 5.

ABERDEEN. One of the most productive places for shore-birds on the Washington coast is POINT CHEHALIS (known to local bird finders as the 'Westport Area'), near the northern end of a long, narrow, sandy peninsula that guards Grays Harbor on the south and west. From Aberdeen, drive south on US Route 101 and, after crossing a bridge over the Chehalis River, turn right on State Route 13A to Cohasset, 20 miles distant, where the road comes to a T. Turn right here (leaving Route 13A) and drive north to Westport and beyond this tiny fishing village on a gravel road up the peninsula.

Although bird finding on Point Chehalis is good any time of the year, it is best in May, August, and September. There is an outer beach, which is attractive to Sanderlings. From this outer beach, a great stone jetty, called Damon's Point, projects over a mile into the ocean. Surf-birds, Ruddy Turnstones, Black Turnstones, and Wandering Tattlers are seen along its shore, which is dangerous during storms since giant waves break over it. In October, Sooty Shearwaters migrate by the hundreds past the end of the jetty.

The inner beach, adjacent to backwater lagoons, is lined with mud flats where Hudsonian Curlews, Semipalmated Plovers, Least and Red-backed Sandpipers, Dowitchers, Western Sandpipers, and Sanderlings may be found. The lagoons are particularly worth investigating during storms since many birds seek shelter here.

ANACORTES. Persons who enjoy looking for birds on islands will find to their liking the rocky SAN JUAN ISLANDS, between the northwestern Washington mainland and Vancouver Island. Varied in size and (in some cases) quite undisturbed by human activities, they attract an avifauna in excess of 150 species and subspecies. A few of the islands are accessible by car and ferry, but most may be visited only by chartered boat.

About 170 of the several hundred San Juan Islands are large enough to be habitable; the others, which may be

called simply rocks, either are tide-washed or have high
and precipitous walls, with little level surface. Orcas Island (56 square miles) and San Juan Island (55 square
miles) are the largest. Since the San Juan Islands represent
a partly submerged, severely glaciated mountain range, all
show a rough topography. Their shorelines, consistently irregular, are cut by many long, narrow, steep-sided inlets,
while their interiors have numerous low mountains or hills
and intermittent valleys with basins containing lakes,
marshes, and bogs. Mt. Constitution on Orcas Island attains the highest elevation (2,409 feet) and there are several other mountains on Orcas Island and on other islands
that reach above 1,000 feet. All the larger islands support
coniferous forests, though these are much less extensive
than they were formerly, owing to the development of
agriculture. Douglas fir is the principal tree, with an ad-
mixture of western red cedar, western hemlock, and grand
fir. In certain areas, Pacific madrone, Oregon white oak, and
big-leaf maple are a conspicuous deciduous growth. Since
most of the rainfall occurs in winter, parts of the San Juan
Islands are surprisingly arid in the summer—arid enough
to support one species of cactus, *Opuntia fragilis.*

A suggested trip to the San Juan Islands via Anacortes is
described below. Ample time should be allowed for transportation by ferry to the larger islands and short excursions
by chartered boat to several of the small islands or rocks.

Drive north from Seattle on US Route 99 to State Route
11. Turn left and at Mukilteo take the car on the ferry to
WHIDBEY ISLAND. Parasitic Jaegers are likely to be seen
from the ferry if the trip is in the spring or fall. Once on
Whidbey Island, drive north on State Route 1D for about
48 miles to Deception Pass State Park (about 2,000 acres),
which lies on the north end of Whidbey Island and the
south end of FIDALGO ISLAND. The two islands are
connected at this point by a bridge over a channel through
which tides rush and churn. In the Park, the coniferous
woods are well worth exploring for such breeding birds as
Chestnut-backed Chickadees, Red-breasted Nuthatches,
Brown Creepers, Olive-backed Thrushes, Golden-crowned
Kinglets, Orange-crowned Warblers, Audubon's Warblers,

Hermit Warblers, Oregon Juncos, and White-crowned Sparrows. Many trails lead to quiet coves where bird finding is good. The bridge over Deception Pass is a fine vantage point in any season for seeing, especially at low tide, Glaucous-winged Gulls and other waterbirds.

Continue north on Fidalgo Island by Route 1D to State Route 1; turn right here, then left to the sand spits at the head of a peninsula. In May, July, August, and September, this is a good spot for Pectoral Sandpipers and other shorebirds and, in the early spring, late fall, and winter, for thousands of Black Brant.

In near-by Ship Harbor is the WALLA WALLA COLLEGE BIOLOGICAL STATION. To reach it, return to Route 1 and proceed to Anacortes; in Anacortes, turn left on 12th Street and drive 3 miles on a paved road to a sign marking the turnoff to the Station. A six-weeks' course in ornithology is offered here each summer, beginning in mid-June. Opportunities for the study of seabirds are especially good. Field trips to Mt. Baker in the western Cascades and to the Olympic Peninsula are part of the course work. The summer address is Anacortes, Washington; the permanent address is Walla Walla College, College Place, Washington.

From Anacortes the bird finder may ferry his car to several of the larger San Juan Islands, among them Orcas, Lopez, and San Juan. Ferry schedules vary with the season and weather. Once on these islands, where hotels and cabins are available, he may hire a powerboat and a guide for reaching some of the offshore rocks that are inhabited only by seabirds.

BARE ISLAND, off the northwestern shore of Orcas Island, is a rock where Pelagic Cormorants, Glaucous-winged Gulls, Pigeon Guillemots, and Tufted Puffins may be found nesting in June, July, and August. There is evidence that Marbled Murrelets breed somewhere on the Island or in its vicinity. Common Murres are often seen offshore.

Among the several good bird rocks off Lopez Island is COLVILLE ISLAND. Here the breeding species, which are identical with those on Bare Island, were recently found to have over 2,000 nests.

On the main county road, just northwest of Friday Harbor (the ferry landing on San Juan Island), is the University of Washington Oceanographic Laboratories.

There are many vantage points on all the larger San Juan Islands where one may observe offshore in winter a wide variety of such waterfowl and waterbirds as Red-throated Loons, Holboell's Grebes, Horned Grebes, Black Brant, American Golden-eyes, Buffle-heads, Old-squaws, Harlequin Ducks, White-winged Scoters, Surf Scoters, American Scoters, Red-breasted Mergansers, Short-billed Gulls, and Bonaparte's Gulls.

BELLINGHAM. In extreme northwestern Washington, on the Strait of Georgia, is Bellingham, well known as a shipping center and also as a starting point for a climb, via State Route 1, up the western Cascades and the lower spurs of MT. BAKER, a massive, snowy volcanic cone rising 10,750 feet. Since the whole area traversed has many popular resorts for camping, hiking, fishing, and skiing, numerous good roads and well-marked trails lead off the main highway. At the highway's end on Kulshan Ridge (elevation 5,000 feet), which extends between Mt. Shuksan (elevation 9,038 feet) to the southeast and Mt. Baker to the southwest, a trail goes on to higher altitudes. The views obtained during this climb and at Kulshan Ridge are the finest from any highway in the northern Cascades.

This 59-mile drive on State Route 1 east from Bellingham winds past hills and farmlands and, beyond the town of Deming, follows the Nooksack River. Just east of Glacier, stop at the U.S. Forest Service office for maps, trail directions, information on camping places, and regulations for building fires. Beyond Glacier, as the elevation increases, the forests become heavy, containing magnificent stands of western red cedars (some of the tallest in the state), Douglas firs, and western hemlocks. Near Austin Pass, however, the forests begin to thin out. The Heather Meadows Winter Sports Area lies just below Kulshan Ridge, which forms its southern wall, and is a superb example of alpine meadow with its profusion of hardy wildflowers. The chief tree growth consists of scattered groups of mountain hemlocks. Some of the birds to be looked for in the immediate vicinity

of the Sports Area are Blue Grouse, Olive-sided Flycatchers, Townsend's Solitaires, Townsend's Warblers, Macgillivray's Warblers, Fox Sparrows, and Lincoln's Sparrows. On
the rocky alpine fields and slopes above the Sports Area,
which are reached by trail, White-tailed Ptarmigan, Horned
Larks, and Gray-crowned Rosy Finches may be expected.

CLARKSON. US Route 410 east from Clarkson to Lewiston, Idaho, crosses the SNAKE RIVER CANYON. On its
steep walls during June and July are Canyon and Rock
Wrens and enormous breeding colonies of Cliff Swallows.
With the coming of winter many of the Swallow nests are
used as sleeping quarters by Gray-crowned Rosy Finches.
State Route 3, southward from Clarkson, proceeds downhill to the Snake River and, at a point in the Canyon about
3 miles distant, passes on the right the base of a high cliff
that rises sharply above the road and supports one of the
larger Cliff Swallow colonies.

GRAND COULEE. Any bird finder in northeast-central
Washington will want to see Grand Coulee Dam, which
holds back the waters of the Columbia River for a great
many miles. If he has time, he should not fail to take the
interesting trip down the Grand Coulee to Soap Lake, 50
miles south. From the settlement of Grand Coulee, 2 miles
south of the Dam, drive south on State Route 2F to Coulee
City; turn right in Coulee City on US Route 2, and then
left on State Route 7 to Soap Lake.

The Grand Coulee is a huge canyon formed by the
Columbia River when the last great ice sheet blocked its
northern course and forced it into a new channel. Following the retreat of the ice, the Columbia returned to its original bed, leaving the channel—now the Grand Coulee—
dry and desert-like except for a number of lakes. The
UPPER GRAND COULEE, between Grand Coulee (the
settlement) and Coulee City, is 2 to 5 miles wide, with
sheer rock walls 400 to 800 feet high. Since it is being partly
flooded at the present time for reclamation purposes, future
bird-finding possibilities here cannot be indicated with
certainty. In view of what has happened in the vicinity of
other irrigation projects, the area will no doubt see an in-

flux of farmland birds; at the same time, however, those places above the reach of water will retain their desert character—and birds.

The best spot for bird finding in the Upper Grand Coulee, now and probably for many years to come, is the vicinity of Steamboat Rock, about 9 miles south of Grand Coulee (settlement) near Route 2F. Steamboat Rock is a giant butte rising from the floor of the Grand Coulee at its widest part. Opposite Steamboat Rock, in the eastern wall of the canyon, opens a lateral chasm called Northrup Canyon, which is about a mile wide at the mouth. In the Northrup Canyon area are many habitats—sagebrush-covered areas, small groves of ponderosa pine and Douglas fir, deciduous thickets, cliffs, and rocky slopes. May or June, before the hot, dry, summer weather, is a good time for bird finding. Then White-throated Swifts may be observed darting about overhead near the higher canyon walls, Canyon and Rock Wrens singing, and Poor-wills chanting in the evening. Other birds to be found by watching, searching, or listening in suitable areas are Prairie Falcons, Great Horned Owls, Western Kingbirds, Say's Phoebes, Cliff Swallows, Loggerhead Shrikes, Common Goldfinches, Sage Sparrows, and Brewer's Sparrows.

LONGVIEW and *KELSO*. These two cities are near the Columbia River in southwestern Washington. US Route 830 west from Longview traverses relatively level country with willow-bordered sloughs and creeks that are breeding grounds for many pairs of Wood Ducks.

Far to the northeast of these cities rises MT. SAINT HELENS (9,671 feet) amid a vast wilderness area that will delight any bird finder. Drive north from Kelso on US Route 99 to Castle Rock (11 miles), then take State Route 1R (right) for 25 miles to the south side of SPIRIT LAKE (elevation 3,199 feet), a lovely body of water close to the northern slope of Saint Helens' volcanic cone. A campground maintained by the U.S. Forest Service and cabin-camps are available here. Broods of Harlequin Ducks and American Mergansers are likely to be seen on the Lake at any time during the summer months. Although the highway ends at Spirit Lake, a fairly good road extends 1.5 miles from the campground to the timber line on Saint Helens, giving ready access to mountain meadows where Horned Larks and American Pipits nest, as well as to subalpine forests inhabited by such birds as Canada Jays and Clark's Nutcrackers.

MOSES LAKE. This booming city in southeast-central Washington is known to local bird finders as a base for investigating MOSES LAKE. Shaped like a curve-stemmed pipe, about 20 miles in greatest length and averaging half a mile in width, Moses Lake fills part of what was once a bed of the Columbia River. Being generally shallow, it is choked in several places with emergent aquatic plants and has a few small islands covered with grasses, brush, and a few low trees. Although the surrounding land rises rather abruptly from the water's edge, leaving little shore, there is a border of trees and shrubs. Considering the suitable habitats available, it is not surprising that, from May through July, Moses Lake abounds with a rich variety of nesting birds.

There are scattered colonies of Great Blue Herons and Black-crowned Night Herons on the islands, in the marshes, and in the trees around the Lake. A colony of Ring-billed Gulls and a few pairs of Caspian Terns usually occupy at least one of the islands. Many pairs of Avocets establish loose colonies, especially on islands where there are flats crusted with alkali. White Pelicans are always present, but apparently do not breed. Other common nesting birds are Western Grebes, Virginia Rails, Soras, Coots, Wilson's Phalaropes, Black Terns, Long-billed Marsh Wrens, Yellow-headed Blackbirds, Red-wings, and many ducks, including Gadwalls, Cinnamon Teal, Shovelers, and Redheads.

US Route 10, going west from the city of Moses Lake on the east shore, crosses the Lake, and is a good vantage point for observations. Improved country roads follow the lakeshore on all sides. The bird finder, however, will achieve the best results if he rents a powerboat. This will give him opportunity to get into the marshes (wading is not feasible because of the soft bottom) and to visit the islands.

The undulating sagebrush plains around Moses Lake are rapidly becoming agricultural lands, but at the south end

there still remain stretches of sand and numerous dunes
where Burrowing Owls may be found.

OKANOGAN. This town in the Okanogan River Valley
makes a good base for the bird finder wishing to explore,
in the late spring and summer, both the scenic east slopes
of the northern Cascades and the Okanogan Highlands.

A short trip on an unnumbered road northwest from
Okanogan leads up through the SALMON CREEK VAL-
LEY in the eastern Cascades and passes irrigated lands
with innumerable apple orchards, which bloom in early
May. Just before reaching Conconully, 17 miles from
Okanogan, the road crosses a stream connecting Conconully
Lake, a natural body of water on the right, with Conconully
Reservoir on the left. The country in the vicinity of Conconully (elevation 2,358 feet) is relatively rough with
numerous steep-sided ridges and peaks, some attaining altitudes in excess of 7,000 feet. In addition to the orchards
and other plantings introduced by man, the lower areas
show, along the watercourses, cottonwoods, willows, alders,
and shrubby thickets. Sagebrush predominates on the adjacent hillsides (the rangelands) just above the reach of
irrigation, and is succeeded by open stands of ponderosa
pine as the elevation increases. The higher slopes support a
wider variety of conifers, such as lodgepole pine, Douglas
fir, and western larch. Birds regularly observed during the
breeding season on the agricultural and rangelands, in
brushy places near the road, and in wooded stream borders include the Red-tailed Hawk, Swainson's Hawk,
Sparrow Hawk, California Quail, Poor-will, Common
Nighthawk, Calliope Hummingbird, Lewis' Woodpecker,
Eastern Kingbird, Western Kingbird, Say's Phoebe, Western Wood Pewee, Violet-green Swallow, Rough-winged
Swallow, Black-capped Chickadee, House Wren, Catbird,
Veery, Warbling Vireo, Macgillivray's Warbler, Yellow-
breasted Chat, Brewer's Blackbird, Vesper Sparrow, Lark
Sparrow, Brewer's Sparrow, and Song Sparrow. An improved road, going northward out of Conconully and open
only in the summer, reaches altitudes above 5,000 feet
where, in coniferous forests, one may find such breeding
birds as the Blue Grouse, Franklin's Grouse, Williamson's

Sapsucker, Canada Jay, Clark's Nutcracker, Mountain Chickadee, Red-breasted Nuthatch, Pygmy Nuthatch, Winter Wren, Varied Thrush, Mountain Bluebird, Townsend's Solitaire, Ruby-crowned Kinglet, Townsend's Warbler, Cassin's Finch, Red Crossbill, Oregon Junco, and Fox Sparrow. Also in the forests, but more often at lower elevations, one may find the Ruffed Grouse, Pileated Woodpecker, Wright's Flycatcher, Steller's Jay, Solitary Vireo, and Western Tanager.

PORT ANGELES. The westernmost extremity of Washington, the mountainous Olympic Peninsula, is a vast wilderness penetrated by few roads and interrupted only by scattered fishing, lumbering, and farming settlements. Port Angeles, on the Strait of Juan de Fuca, is the largest city on the Peninsula and the headquarters of OLYMPIC NATIONAL PARK, which lies to the south.

Covering about 1,321 square miles, Olympic Park encompasses most of the higher, snowy Olympic Mountains —a disorganized group of sharp ridges, crags, and peaks rather than a range. Elevations in the Park extend from 300 feet to 7,954 feet, at the summit of Mt. Olympus, situated almost in the center of the Park. The area has been severely glaciated and even today several of the high peaks support active glaciers. Though not lofty as compared with the Cascades, the Olympic Mountains are no less majestic, their heights rising abruptly from sea level.

The dense forests of Olympic Park, containing some of the finest remaining virgin stands in the Pacific Northwest, rival its mountains as the principal wilderness feature. Douglas fir, western hemlock, western red cedar, and Sitka spruce are the predominating species in the lower valleys up to 1,500 feet, and appear occasionally at higher altitudes in the valleys of big rivers. On the western side of the Park, these trees, deluged by as much as 142 inches of rainfall annually, attain their maximum size and shade an understory of mosses, lichens, and deciduous shrubs so luxuriant as to suggest a tropical rain forest. On the eastern side of the Park, which is drier, coniferous trees predominate on the slopes, but a thick deciduous growth of trees and shrubs—big-leaf maples, red alders, willows, flowering dogwoods, and others—line the streams and cover various areas on the valley floors. Western hemlock, western red cedar, and silver fir constitute the chief forest growth of the Park from 1,500 to 3,500 feet; from that elevation to the timber line, the forests are interspersed with beautiful mountain meadows which, in the summer, are colored by the countless blooms of wildflowers. At elevations above timber line, the vegetation is limited to low shrubs, grasses, sedges, and a few hardy wildflowers.

Enhancing the pristine splendor of Olympic Park's mountains and forests are the many blue lakes and the glacier-fed streams with their falls and cascades. The largest stretch of water in the Park is Lake Crescent in the northwest. Ringed by conifers and with the Olympic peaks in the background, it is undoubtedly one of the most beautiful lakes in western Washington.

The Olympic Loop Highway (US Route 101) goes along the east, north, and west sides of the Peninsula, passes through Port Angeles, and encircles Olympic Park outside its boundaries, crossing the Park at only one point—the northwest corner along the south shore of Lake Crescent. Spur roads lead off the highway into the Park, via the main river valleys, for short distances; at their ends begin 400 miles of trails leading to some of the most remote parts of the wilderness area. Hotels, lodges, chalets, and cabins are available in the Park and near by. Information on accommodations and rates may be obtained from the Olympic Peninsula Resort and Hotel Association, Colman Ferry Terminal, Seattle. Campgrounds with camping facilities are located along most of the spur roads, while conveniently spaced on the main trails are numerous rustic shelters.

Of places in Olympic Park accessible by car and good for the observing of high-mountain birds, probably the best is Hurricane Ridge. This is reached by driving west and south from Port Angeles on Route 101 for 9 miles to the Elwha River, then turning left and driving up the River 4 miles to the Elwha Ranger Station. Near here a road leads by a very steep grade up Hurricane Ridge and then forks. The road to the right runs along the top of the Ridge (elevation 5,000 to 5,500 feet) for 9 miles to Obstruction Point, passing forests at timber line and meadows; the road to the left goes for 2 miles to Hurricane Hill (5,751 feet). From the road, the views of Mt. Olympus' three peaks on the south and the Strait of Juan de Fuca on the north are superlative. Some of the birds that may be expected in this high country from mid-June through July are the Red-tailed Hawk, Bald Eagle, Sparrow Hawk, Blue Grouse, Black Swift, Vaux's Swift, Rufous Hummingbird, Horned Lark, Violet-green Swallow, Canada Jay, Common Raven, Robin, Mountain Bluebird, Orange-crowned Warbler, and Oregon Junco. Another place for high-mountain birds in Olympic Park, also accessible by car, is Deer Park (elevation 5,400 feet), reached by driving east from Port Angeles on Route 101 for 5 miles, then going south on a well-marked road for 17 miles. Deer Park, a winter sports area, has bird habitats not unlike those on Hurricane Ridge.

Nearly all the spur roads into Olympic Park are in valleys where one may find many of the bird species regularly frequenting coniferous forests of lower slopes and the thickets and open areas of valley floors. Better results will be obtained, however, if one takes a trail into a more remote valley area where there are fewer disturbances. Strongly recommended is the Elwha River Trail, which begins at Whiskey Bend, 4.5 miles from the Elwha Ranger Station and 9 miles from Route 101, on the road that leads up Hurricane Ridge. This Trail follows the Elwha River past the Elkhorn Station (12 miles from the road) into the heart of the Park. Birds that should be readily observed along the River, or in its immediate vicinity, include the Great Blue Heron, Harlequin Duck, Blue Grouse, Spotted Sandpiper, Band-tailed Pigeon, Common Nighthawk, Vaux's Swift, Rufous Hummingbird, Red-shafted Flicker, Western Flycatcher, Olive-sided Flycatcher, Violet-green Swallow, Barn Swallow, Cliff Swallow, Chestnut-backed Chickadee, Dipper, Winter Wren, Robin, Olive-backed Thrush, Varied Thrush, Warbling Vireo, Macgillivray's Warbler, Black-capped Warbler, Western Tanager, Black-headed Grosbeak, Pine Siskin, Common Goldfinch, Chipping Sparrow, and White-crowned Sparrow.

Outside of Olympic Park on the ocean side of the Peninsula is the LAPUSH AREA, centered about the little fishing hamlet of Lapush just south of the mouth of the Quillayute

River. Lapush is 73 miles from Port Angeles, from which it may be reached by driving west and south on Route 101 to within one mile of the town of Forks, then turning right on State Route 9B. In the Lapush Area is a great variety of bird habitats, such as coniferous forests and their brushy borders, fields, a broad beach, mud flats, the open water of the River mouth and the ocean, and the jagged rocks and wooded islands offshore. Bird finding is good at any time of the year. From vantage points along the River mouth and ocean, some of the birds that may be seen, except during the nesting season, are the Arctic Loon, Holboell's Grebe, Baldpate, Green-winged Teal, Greater Scaup Duck, American Golden-eye, Buffle-head, American Merganser, Red-breasted Merganser, Bald Eagle, Glaucous-winged Gull, Herring Gull, California Gull (particularly in the late summer and fall), and Short-billed Gull. Both Double-crested and Brandt's Cormorants may be seen in any season. Among the shorebirds that are sometimes fairly numerous on the beaches and flats in May, July, August, and September are the Semipalmated Plover, Surf-bird, Black Turnstone, Knot (most numerous in May), Pectoral Sand-piper (most numerous in the late summer), Least Sandpiper, Red-backed Sandpiper, Dowitcher, Western Sandpiper, and Sanderling. Alcids—for example, the common Murre, Pigeon Guillemot, and Tufted Puffin—probably nest on some of the offshore islands or rocks, and are occasionally seen close to shore. Breeding landbirds to be looked for in suitable habitats inland include the Ruffed Grouse, Bush-tit, Western Meadowlark, and Savannah Sparrow.

Some of the best of Olympic Park's rain forests may be reached by continuing south on Route 101 from Forks for 14 miles, then taking the Hoh River Road for 18 miles to the Hoh Ranger Station. Here are enormous, moss-draped spruces, firs, and hemlocks, standing so tall and so close together as to shut out the sun. Along the mossy trails that begin at the Ranger Station and wind through this forest spectacle, a remarkable stillness prevails day and night regardless of season.

If the bird finder is anxious to see Black Oyster-catchers, he should visit CAPE FLATTERY on the western tip of the Olympic Peninsula. A wild desolate place, it is the only spot in Washington where these big shorebirds may be found at any time of the year. The Cape is reached from Port Angeles by driving west 39 miles on State Route 9A to a point about 5 miles beyond Pysht. Turn right here to Clallam Bay and Neah Bay (25 miles distant) on an un-numbered road which, between Clallam Bay and Neah Bay, runs for the most part along the Strait of Juan de Fuca. If the tide is low, stops should be made at intervals to scan the beach and outlying waters for birds. At Neah Bay, a quiet Indian settlement, ask how to reach the road that leads toward the Cape, 5 miles away. Once on this road, begin watching carefully for a sign, on the left, marked 'To the Cape' and indicating the start of the foot trail. Take this path, which leads to the tip of the Cape—a high, lonely bluff. Without getting too close to the edge, since it overhangs dangerously, inspect the rocks below for Oyster-catchers. Common Ravens, Double-crested and Brandt's Cormorants, Tufted Puffins and other alcids, and (depending on the season) various loons, ducks, and gulls may also be observed from this fine vantage point.

PULLMAN. This city in the Palouse Country of southeast-ern Washington is the home of THE STATE COLLEGE OF WASHINGTON. In Science Hall the Charles R. Con-ner Museum of the Department of Zoology has an ornitho-logical collection of about 2,500 study skins, 100 skeletons, and 400 mounted specimens on display. Two courses in ornithology are given by the Department of Zoology.

The SNAKE RIVER CANYON near Wawawai, about 21 miles from Pullman, has steep, basaltic cliffs, bunch-grass slopes, and brushy bottomlands where such birds as Prairie Falcons, Say's Phoebes, Cliff Swallows, Canyon Wrens, and Rock Wrens may be found. To reach Wawawai, drive south from Pullman on US Route 195; about one mile north of Colton, turn right on a gravel road. This goes down to the Snake River at Wawawai, then follows the River upstream to Lewiston, Idaho. Since the road is rather rough, the trip from Wawawai to Lewiston requires about one and a half hours of driving.

One of the finest places in eastern Washington for waterbirds, waterfowl, and shorebirds is TWELVE-MILE SLOUGH, about 75 miles from Pullman via US Route 195 to Colfax, US Route 295 to the turnoff (right) to Mockonema, then by unnumbered road (through Diamond, Endicott, and Winona) to Benge. At Benge, inquiry is necessary for directions to the Slough. Nesting birds associated with this marshy body of water include various species of ducks, together with Eared Grebes, Coots, Wilson's Phalaropes, and Ring-billed Gulls. In August and early September, the Slough's extensive mud flats attract large numbers of shorebirds representing many species.

SEATTLE. The largest metropolis on the Pacific Coast north of San Francisco and one of the leading shipping centers of the United States, Seattle lies east of Puget Sound on a wide strip of hilly land between Puget Sound and Lake Washington. Puget Sound is connected to Lake Washington by the Lake Washington Canal running through the city, first to Lake Union, and then Lake Union to Union Bay, an arm of Lake Washington.

Undoubtedly the best landbird finding in the Seattle area is in the north part of the city on the 582-acre UNIVERSITY OF WASHINGTON CAMPUS (on the west shore of Union Bay north of the Washington Canal; main entrance at 15th Avenue Northeast and East 40th Street) and in the 267-acre UNIVERSITY OF WASHINGTON ARBORETUM (on the west shore of Union Bay, opposite the campus on the south side of the Canal; reached from Lake Washington Boulevard). Two spots in these areas are especially productive: (1) In the northeast part of the Campus, 30 acres of coniferous trees, Douglas fir predominating, with deciduous trees and shrubs intermixed. (2) In the Arboretum, a small point of land called 'Foster Island,' extending into Union Bay and covered with a deciduous thicket. Birds that may be found any time of the year in, or in the vicinity of, these spots are the California Quail, Screech Owl, Steller's Jay, Black-capped Chickadee, Chestnut-backed Chickadee (in conifers), Bush-tit, Winter Wren, Bewick's Wren, Golden-crowned Kinglet (in conifers), Purple Finch, Pine Siskin, Spotted Towhee, Oregon Junco, and Song Sparrow. Among the common summer residents (May to September) are the Rufous Hummingbird, Western Flycatcher, Olive-sided Flycatcher, Violet-green Swallow, Barn Swallow, Olive-backed Thrush, Solitary Vireo, Warbling Vireo, Orange-crowned Warbler, Yellow Warbler, Audubon's Warbler, Black-headed Grosbeak, Common Goldfinch, Chipping Sparrow, and White-crowned Sparrow. In the spring (April and May) and fall (September and October) some of the transients that show up regularly are the Hermit Thrush, Cedar Waxwing (also in the winter), Black-throated Gray Warbler, Black-capped Warbler, and Golden-crowned Sparrow.

Along the shore of Union Bay adjoining the Campus and Arboretum, and flanking Foster Island, are extensive marshy flats with cattails, bulrushes, and willows where Pied-billed Grebes, Green Herons, American Bitterns, Mallards, Coots, Traill's Flycatchers, Long-billed Marsh Wrens, Yellow-throats, and Red-wings may be found nesting. Great Blue Herons and Glaucous-winged Gulls may be seen along the shore in any season.

While Union Bay is a good place for observing waterbirds and waterfowl in the fall, winter, and spring (September to April), a far better place, because it permits closeup views, is GREEN LAKE (250 acres), a body of fresh water in the northern residential area of the city. Despite the fact that it is a municipal recreational center, with bathing beaches and playgrounds on its eastern and southern shores, it is attractive to the following: Eared Grebe, Canada Goose, Snow Goose, Baldpate, Pintail, Green-winged Teal, Shoveler, Canvas-back, Lesser Scaup Duck, American Golden-eye, Buffle-head, American Merganser, Red-breasted Merganser, California Gull, Ring-billed Gull, and Bonaparte's Gull. US Route 99 north from downtown Seattle passes the west shore of Green Lake for a short distance. Green Lake Way from Route 99 encircles the rest of the Lake. There are many good vantage points along these roads.

Southwest of Green Lake in Woodland Park (crossed by Route 99 before reaching Green Lake) are the ZOOLOGICAL GARDENS, with fine exhibits of about 500 different kinds of birds. The Gardens are most easily reached by

turning west on East 50th Street from Route 99, then turning north into the Park opposite Fremont Street.

Seattle bird finders seem agreed that the best vantage
point on PUGET SOUND for seeing alcids and sea ducks
(e.g. Old-squaws and the three species of scoters) in
winter is Beach Drive, from Alki Point south to Lincoln
Park. This road passes very close to Puget Sound and
frequent stops may be made to scan the open water. To
reach Beach Drive, take US Route 99 south from downtown
Seattle, then go west on Spokane Street (which becomes
Admiral Way) to Alki Point.

The WASHINGTON STATE MUSEUM, on the campus
of the University of Washington, has an ornithological collection of 6,106 skins, 926 mounts, and 1,294 egg sets representing the Pacific Northwest, particularly Washington.
In the Museum library, which supplements the main library
of the University, are the principal reference works on
birds. The Museum is open on week days from 9:00 A.M.
to 5:00 P.M. and on Sundays from 1:00 to 5:00 P.M. The
bird collection and library are not open on Saturdays and
Sundays.

The Seattle Audubon Society, which may be contacted
through the Washington State Museum, meets the third
Thursday of each month at 7:30 P.M. in the Plymouth Con-
gregational Church, Sixth Avenue and University Street.
Field trips are taken once a week, usually on Sunday, to
points of interest in or near Seattle. Both the meetings and
the trips are discontinued in June, July, and August.

If the bird finder has time, he should take the 5-hour trip
from Seattle to VANCOUVER ISLAND, British Columbia, by car ferry (either the Canadian Pacific Steamship
or Black Ball Ferry). On the way he will have a good opportunity to observe many seabirds in Puget Sound. In
Victoria, where the ship docks, is the PROVINCIAL MU-
SEUM OF NATURAL HISTORY AND ANTHRO-
POLOGY, located in the Parliament Buildings. Its ornithological collection includes over 10,000 skins and 500
mounts, chiefly from British Columbia. In the vicinity of
Victoria are the only nesting populations of Skylarks in
North America. These birds prefer open fields not regularly

cultivated. Being non-migratory, Skylarks may be found at any season, but the best time to observe them is in the spring and summer. The three nesting grounds most conveniently reached from City Hall by bus are the following: (1) Open fields bounded by Landsdowne, Shelbourne, and Richmond Roads; reached by Mount Tolmie bus to Landsdowne Road. (2) Open fields bordering Cedar Hill Cross Road near Uplands Golf Course; reached by Uplands bus or Cadboro Bay bus to Cedar Hill Cross Road. (3) Open country bordering Wilkinson Road north of Burnside Road; reached by Wilkinson Road bus.

SOUTH BEND. The WILLAPA NATIONAL WILDLIFE REFUGE (7,123 acres) is a favorite wintering and resting place for waterfowl on the coast. It is easily reached by driving west and south on US Route 101, which soon passes along the eastern side of Willapa Bay and the Refuge boundary. Refuge headquarters, marked by the flying-goose sign, is on Route 101.

The Refuge, which includes the southern section of Willapa Bay and Long Island, has a terrain that varies from sand dunes, mud flats, and tidal marshes to the heavily timbered ridges of Long Island. On the benchlands bordering the flats and marshes, the cover is thick brush and second-growth spruce and alder. Douglas fir, western hemlock, and other conifers characterize the heavy forest farther back on the uplands.

Mallards, Hooded Mergansers, and Band-tailed Pigeons are among the regular nesting birds in the Refuge area. During migration shorebirds are very abundant; in the winter there are large numbers of Black Brant, Baldpates, Pintails, and other waterfowl.

SPOKANE. The Spokane Bird Club meets the second Tuesday of every month, September through May, at 7:30 P.M. in the museum of the Eastern Washington State Historical Society, West 2316 First Avenue, Spokane 43, and schedules field trips twice monthly, except in midsummer. Both meetings and field trips are open to visitors, who may contact the Club at the address given above.

The TURNBULL NATIONAL WILDLIFE REFUGE,

about 25 miles south of Spokane, has one of the best water-fowl nesting grounds in eastern Washington. Its 15,964 acres comprise a section of the channeled scablands, where the force of ancient streams cut deep gullies down to bare lava in some places (now dry for the most part) and piled sediments high in others, leaving a succession of ponds and potholes. Within the Refuge are several bodies of water whose levels are now controlled by dams and dykes and which have a total surface of about 5,000 acres. An abundance of cattails, bulrushes, and other aquatic plants, including submersed types, provides excellent cover and food for marsh-loving birds.

Waterfowl that breed commonly on the Refuge are Canada Geese, Mallards, Gadwalls, Baldpates, Green-winged, Blue-winged, and Cinnamon Teal, Shovelers, Red-heads, Lesser Scaup Ducks, and Ruddy Ducks. The Geese begin nesting in early April, the ducks in mid-April. Other birds nesting in the marshes or their wet borders are Hol-boell's Grebes, Eared Grebes, Pied-billed Grebes, American Bitterns, Soras, Coots, Wilson's Phalaropes, Black Terns, Long-billed Marsh Wrens, Yellow-headed Blackbirds, and Red-wings. During the fall migration in September and October, congregations of transient Canada Geese, Mallards, Baldpates, Pintails, and Coots are especially large.

Although the birds associated with the marshes are the principal attraction of the Refuge, there is a considerable variety of landbirds to be found in the willows, cottonwoods, and aspens bordering some of the lakes, in the open stands of ponderosa pine that cover much of the upland area, in scattered thickets of serviceberry, snowberry, and wild rose, and in the near-by farmlands.

To reach the Refuge from Spokane, drive southwestward on US Route 395 to Cheney, a distance of 15 miles; in Cheney, turn left on Badger Lake Road and proceed 6 miles to Refuge headquarters. Inquiry here will determine the most promising places for birds, many of which are accessible by car.

TACOMA. SPANAWAY PARK (339 acres), on the right side of State Route 5 about 8 miles south of Tacoma, is a popular recreational area. Along its west side is SPANA-

WAY LAKE, 1.5 miles long and half a mile wide, bordered by woods of Douglas fir and scrub oak and sections of open prairie. Both the Park and the borders of the Lake have productive spots for bird finding in May, June, and July. Such breeding birds as Western Flycatchers, Steller's Jays, Bush-tits, Brown Creepers, Hutton's Vireos, Solitary Vireos, Orange-crowned Warblers, and Pine Siskins may be observed without too much difficulty. With careful searching a pair or two of Hermit Warblers may be found. Horned Larks are common on the adjacent prairie.

Southeast of Tacoma towers Mt. Rainier, the 'king' of all the slumbering volcanoes in the United States. Though 40 miles away, it reaches so high—14,408 feet—that the city seems almost in its shadow. For bird finders no less than for sightseers, MOUNT RAINIER NATIONAL PARK, which embraces this massive dome, is a 'must'; in fact, no other place in the three Pacific states offers a better opportunity for finding so many mountain birds conveniently in a glorious setting.

Mt. Rainier occupies about one fourth of the 377 square miles of the Park. Built up by its own volcanic activity and rugged with many perilous slopes, the mountain when viewed from any direction has an aspect that belies its harshness, for its summit is capped by perennial snow and its flanks—all but the most prominent crags and ridges—are blanketed by 26 glaciers, more than are possessed by any other single peak in the country. Most of the glaciers extend down to elevations of 4,000 feet, well below timber line.

The melting of Mt. Rainier's snow and glaciers in the warmer months gives rise to numerous streams, which, in the heat of the day, increase in volume and turbulence as they descend into the deep ravines and valleys. This water supply, supplemented by the heavy moisture that characterizes the prevailing climate of the vicinity, accounts in no small measure for the richness of vegetation below the ice and snow-covered slopes, and that, in turn, for the great abundance of birds.

The lowland forests of the Park, from the lower valleys at 1,700 feet to about 3,000 feet on Mt. Rainier, are dense and shady, their trees frequently tall and often branchless for

over half their height. Grand fir, Douglas fir, western hemlock, and western red cedar are the predominating growth.
Occasionally along streams is a lower deciduous growth
consisting of red alder, black cottonwood, big-leaf maple,
and willow. At middle elevations, from 3,000 to 4,500 feet,
the forests are still dense, but the predominant trees change
to Alaska yellow cedar, mountain hemlock, silver fir, noble
fir, western white pine, and lodgepole pine. Around 4,500
feet, subalpine conditions appear: the trees begin to show
reduction in size; alpine fir and mountain hemlock become
the principal species, joined by a scattering of whitebark
pine as the elevation increases. Between 5,000 and 6,500
feet, depending on the exposure and conditions of mountain
surface, comes the interspersion of subalpine forests and
subalpine meadows, the latter being by far the most exciting
places on Mt. Rainier. These open spots are the first vantage
points for awe-inspiring scenery. Birds here, while probably
no more numerous than in other places in the Park, are certainly more conspicuous. And the wildflowers, in their great
abundance and variety, are famous the world over. From
early June to early August, they produce great carpets of
gorgeous colors, which change from day to day as different
species come into bloom. Above 6,000 feet, the average
elevation at timber line, is the alpine region, where severe
winds and chilling temperatures are common even in midsummer. Only the hardiest of wildflowers, which are no
match in color for those in the subalpine meadows, can
tolerate this bleak climate.

Mount Rainier National Park has five principal entrances,
two on the west side and three on the east. Since no west-
east roads run through the Park, one cannot, for example,
come in by an eastern entrance and go out by a western.
Both west and east sides of the Park may be conveniently
reached from Tacoma by separate highways, but from Yakima only the east side is readily accessible (see under
Yakima).

The Park has 80 miles of paved roads; and there are
numerous trails, some leading to its most isolated sections.
Campgrounds, inns, lodges, eating places, and grocery
stores are conveniently located on both sides of the Park;

housekeeping cabins are available only at Ohanapecosh Hot Springs on the east side. Rates and reservations at the overnight concessions may be obtained by writing to Rainier National Park Co., Box 1136, Tacoma 1.

As in all National Parks, there are naturalists' services, including guided trips and illustrated talks on natural features of the Park. The Park naturalist's office is at Park headquarters in Longmire. Here the Park Museum houses a small collection of bird skins, mounted birds, and egg sets, all taken in the Park.

The best time of the year for finding nesting birds is from early June to mid-July. All the higher elevations that may be reached by car are usually clear of snow by mid-June, occasionally not until early July. When entering the Park, the bird finder should obtain a map at the checking station and a schedule of naturalists' activities.

A fair number of bird species may be found in the Park in suitable habitats from almost any elevation to the timber line. These include such nesting birds as the Sharp-shinned Hawk, Cooper's Hawk, Red-tailed Hawk, Golden Eagle, Sparrow Hawk, Great Horned Owl, Saw-whet Owl, Vaux's Swift, Rufous Hummingbird, Red-shafted Flicker, Violet-green Swallow, Canada Jay, Chestnut-backed Chickadee, Red-breasted Nuthatch, Brown Creeper, Dipper, Winter Wren, Robin, Varied Thrush, Hermit Thrush, Golden-crowned Kinglet, Pine Siskin, Red Crossbill, and Oregon Junco. Many other species, however, are confined to suitable habitats at one elevation or another. Three places, if investigated thoroughly, should yield most of the birds regularly breeding in the Park:

1. Longmire Meadows (elevation 2,760 feet), on the southwest side of the Park via the Nisqually River entrance (adjacent to headquarters); reached from Tacoma by driving south on State Route 5 for 60 miles. Longmire Meadows is a clearing of about 5 acres, surrounded by a heavy coniferous forest, and containing old beaver ponds partly filled by cattails and bordered by a few alders. Some of the breeding birds that may be located, either in the open area or in the neighboring woods, are the Band-tailed Pigeon, Hairy Woodpecker, Downy Woodpecker, (Red-breasted) Common Sapsucker, Western Flycatcher, Steller's Jay, Black-

capped Chickadee, Yellow Warbler, Red-wing, Western Tanager, Black-headed Grosbeak, and Song Sparrow.

2. Paradise Valley (elevation 5,557 feet) in the south part of the Park; reached by driving over a well-marked road from Longmire. Paradise Valley has several hundred acres of beautiful subalpine meadows—among the most spectacular for flowers—and forests of alpine fir and mountain hemlock. The Blue Grouse, Saw-whet Owl, Calliope Hummingbird, Olive-sided Flycatcher, Clark's Nutcracker, Mountain Chickadee, Mountain Bluebird, Townsend's Solitaire, Orange-crowned Warbler, Townsend's Warbler, and Lincoln's Sparrow should be among the birds observed here. The Paradise River, cutting down through the area, is a favorite haunt of Dippers. White-tailed Ptarmigan, American Pipits, and Gray-crowned Rosy Finches may be found in the vicinity of the Edith Creek Glacial Cirque, or Amphitheater, just above Paradise Inn, and on the higher slopes of the Valley.

3. Yakima Park (elevation 6,000–6,500 feet), on the east side of the Park; reached from Tacoma by driving east on State Route 5 to the White River entrance, a distance of 60 miles, then following a well-marked road in Mount Rainier Park. Yakima Park is on a long, relatively flat-topped ridge that supports wide meadows interspersed with low stands of alpine fir and whitebark pine—conditions that are typical of the timber line. Common Ravens are sometimes seen here, as are most of the species observed at Paradise Valley. At higher elevations on the ridge, reached by the Burroughs Mountain Trail, are some of the best places in Mount Rainier Park for White-tailed Ptarmigan, Horned Larks, Mountain Bluebirds, and American Pipits.

WALLA WALLA. In College Place, located just 2 miles southwest of Walla Walla, is WALLA WALLA COLLEGE, which has an ornithological collection of about 2,500 bird skins (mainly from the Pacific Northwest), 100 mounts, and 350 egg sets. The material is housed in the Biology Building, where a course in ornithology is given each spring. The College operates a Biological Station (see under Anacortes) and a unique Field School of Biology. The latter is a traveling school limited to 20 students interested in field studies of plants and animals. One trip of three months' duration is made each year, sometimes to points as far away as southern Mexico.

Walla Walla lies west of the BLUE MOUNTAINS, which are difficult to reach because of the poor roads. There is, however, one trip into the Mountains from Walla Walla that will be rewarding to the bird finder.

From Walla Walla take an unnumbered county road 3 miles east, and then turn south into Mill Creek Canyon, where there is an area known as Kooskooskie. Here among the open, ponderosa-pine forests and shrubby thickets of the Canyon's floor may be found, in May and June, such breeding species as the Red-tailed Hawk, Sparrow Hawk, Great Horned Owl, Pygmy Owl, Vaux's Swift, Red-shafted Flicker, Pileated Woodpecker, Wright's Flycatcher, Western Flycatcher, Steller's Jay, Brown Creeper, House Wren, Olive-backed Thrush, Veery, Solitary Vireo, Orange-crowned Warbler, Audubon's Warbler, Macgillivray's Warbler, Western Tanager, Cassin's Finch, Pine Siskin, Red Crossbill, Spotted Towhee, Oregon Junco, and Chipping Sparrow. From Mill Creek Canyon numerous logging roads lead into the higher areas. By walking a mile or two up any of these roads one may reach elevations well over 3,000 feet where Douglas fir and white fir are the principal timber. Birds to be expected here are the Blue Grouse, Calliope Hummingbird, Three-toed Woodpecker, Hammond's Flycatcher, Olive-sided Flycatcher, Canada Jay, Clark's Nutcracker, Mountain Chickadee, Red-breasted Nuthatch, Varied Thrush, Hermit Thrush, Mountain Bluebird, Townsend's Solitaire, Townsend's Warbler, and Evening Grosbeak.

WENATCHEE. Because this city in the center of the state is the distributing point of a famous apple-growing area, its name is practically synonymous with apples. Orchards blanket for miles the irrigated valley of the Columbia River, in which Wenatchee lies, as well as the valley of the Wenatchee River, which merges with the Columbia north of the city. In summer, the green of countless fruit trees contrasts sharply with the grayish, comparatively barren hills of the range country that flanks the valleys and with the blue-tinted mountain peaks rising beyond.

STEMILT CREEK CANYON, opening on the Columbia River south of the city, is excellent for breeding birds in the late spring and early summer. It is reached by driving 5 miles down the west side of the Columbia River on an unnumbered road toward Malaga, then turning right at a little sawmill where Stemilt Creek joins the Columbia. When the road begins winding up through the Canyon, stops should be made to look or listen for such birds as Veeries, Yellow-breasted Chats, Warbling Vireos, Black-headed Grosbeaks, Lazuli Buntings, and Song Sparrows, which inhabit the cottonwoods, wild-rose thickets, and other deciduous trees and shrubs bordering the stream. Farther up the Canyon, where pines and firs predominate, similar stops should be made for Olive-backed Thrushes, Audubon's Warblers, and other birds preferring cooler environments.

YAKIMA. From Yakima, on the eastern side of the Cascades, US Route 410 leads to the Chinook Pass entrance to Mount Rainier National Park (see under Tacoma for an account of the Park).

For a very worth-while trip from Yakima, take US Route 97 north through Ellensburg for 68 miles, to Liberty. This route, from a city surrounded by sagebrush-covered hills, winds up the lush Yakima Valley, famous the country over for its wonderful fruits. Beyond Teanaway (56 miles from Yakima) the road passes forests of ponderosa pine and fairly damp, green meadows. At Liberty, an old gold-mining town, obtain information from the U.S. Forest Service office about the road to TABLE MOUNTAIN (elevation 6,243 feet).

If this road is passable, drive up several miles until it runs beside an extensive hellebore meadow on Hurley Creek. The surrounding forests are of the arid type, containing an abundance of ponderosa pine. This is an excellent area in May and June for an interesting variety of breeding birds, including the following: Franklin's Grouse, Ruffed Grouse, Great Horned Owl, Saw-whet Owl, Williamson's Sapsucker, White-headed Woodpecker, Hammond's Flycatcher,

Wright's Flycatcher, Olive-sided Flycatcher, Canada Jay,
Steller's Jay, Clark's Nutcracker, Pygmy Nuthatch, Hermit
Thrush, Veery, Black-throated Gray Warbler, Townsend's
Warbler, and Hermit Warbler. On the sage- and grass-
covered top and slopes of the Mountain, the Brewer's Spar-
row may be found.

Contributing authorities: James R. Beer, Ernest S. Booth, Earl M.
Brooks, G. Clifford Carl, Russell T. Congdon, Donald S. Farner,
Miss Martha R. Flahaut, John B. Hurley, Mrs. Paul J. Keating,
Earl J. Larrison, Preston P. Macy, Fred J. Overly, John C. Preston,
Wilbert A. Rodgers, Theodore H. Scheffer, Ralph C. Winslow.

Wyoming

SAGE GROUSE

Though mounting agricultural and industrial activities have changed many states in recent times, they have made few inroads on the open plains and mountain fastnesses that comprise Wyoming. Over its entire rectangular area there are only 220 cities and towns; of these only 137 are occupied by 100 people or more, and only three—Cheyenne (the capital), Laramie, and Casper—by more than 14,000. The plains, making up two thirds of the state, are in general so arid and so thin of soil and cover that as many as 50 acres are declared necessary for the grazing of a single cow. All in all, elbow room is never at a premium in Wyoming!

Any bird finder intent on observing a wide variety of Wyoming birds must count on many miles of travel, yet if he plans a late-spring or early-summer trip that will include diversified types of plains areas and several of the high mountain ranges that are readily accessible by car, the rewards for his efforts can be gratifying, for there is much birdlife to see by the way. In the sagelands of the Wyoming Basin north of Rock Springs, Sage Grouse conduct their remarkable courtship performances in an environment shared with such birds as the Sage Thrashers, Sage Sparrows, and Brewer's Sparrows; and on the grassy Laramie Plains, where Mountain Plovers nest, the flight displays of McCown's Longspurs are a familiar and ever delightful spectacle. Probably there is no stretch of the Plains that is not regularly frequented by the larger predators— Swainson's Hawks, Ferruginous Hawks, Prairie Falcons, and even one or two Golden Eagles—types of birds all too seldom found in most parts of the country. Despite the extent of the Wyoming plains, hardly a spot anywhere is very far from mountains that have an entirely different association of birds, for Wyoming has many mountain ranges, high and low, and they are widely scattered over the state. The higher uplifts have in common a marked ruggedness, a coniferous forest cover, and many kinds of birds, such as Olive-backed Thrushes, Audubon's Warblers, and Western Tanagers. Yet each also has a distinct topography and tree growth and certain peculiarities with respect to its avifauna. In the Black Hills (including their western extension, the Bear Lodge Mountains) in the northeastern corner of the state, the summer-resident junco is the White-winged, but in the Big Horn Mountains in the north-central part of the state it is the Oregon, and in the Laramie and Medicine Bow Mountains in the southeast-central part of the state, it is the Gray-headed. What the bird finder discovers in one Wyoming mountain range is, therefore, never exactly duplicated in another.

The Wyoming plains east of the Big Horns and the Laramie Mountains are part of the Great Plains, with average elevations between 5,000 and 6,000 feet; they incline gradually, however, from 3,100 feet, in the extreme northeast, to about 7,000 feet at the base of the Laramie Mountains in

the south. (The Missouri Plateau, a northern section of
the Great Plains, includes the Wyoming plains east of the
Big Horns and extends, roughly, as far south as Lusk and
Douglas.) Drainage, provided chiefly by the Powder, Belle
Fourche, and North Platte Rivers and their tributaries, is
northward or eastward into the Missouri River system. The
country is best described as an undulating prairie interrupted by sandhills, buttes, and talus ridges and by rocky
bluffs and rough badlands near watercourses. Rainfall is
moderate. Cottonwood, willow, boxelder, and various deciduous shrubs line most of the larger streams; juniper,
mountain mahogany, and, occasionally, ponderosa pine
occur in scattered stands on bluffs and ridges; but on the
open expanses the principal plants are short grasses, chiefly
grama and buffalo, mixed (in numerous localities) with
sagebrush, rabbitbrush, greasewood, yucca, and other
shrubby growth. Where water has been put on the land
through irrigation projects, crops are now produced; elsewhere the prairie is used mostly for livestock grazing, if it
is used at all.

The Wyoming plains west of the Big Horns and the
Laramie Mountains occupy the floors of the Big Horn
Basin (3,500 to 5,500 feet elevation) and of the Wyoming
Basin (6,000 to 7,500 feet). The Big Horn Basin, a segment of the Great Plains, lies west of the Big Horns and
drains northward into the Yellowstone River; the Wyoming
Basin lies west of the Laramie Mountains and drains in three
different directions: north to the Yellowstone via the Big
Horn River, east to the Platte River, and south to the Colorado via the Green River. Both Basins are almost completely
rimmed by mountain ranges, while the Wyoming Basin
is also encroached upon by mountain ranges and studded
with isolated peaks. As a whole, the plains have a level to
undulating surface with scattered buttes and ridges and
ranges of low hills. Along the larger streams the plains have
been much roughened by erosion, producing colorful badlands and rugged canyons. Owing to scant rainfall the aspect
of this section is decidedly arid. Though wide grassy
stretches may be found, more generally the vegetation is of
the shrubby, bunch-like, desert type, consisting of such
plants as sagebrush, greasewood, and rabbitbrush, with

juniper, pinyon pine, and mountain mahogany on bluffs
and ridges. Willow and cottonwood, bordering the streams,
are among the very few common trees. The country, on the
whole, has little use save for grazing livestock.

The distribution of birds on the Wyoming plains, ridges,
bluffs and mountain foothills varies greatly according to
vegetative cover. Where the plains are grassy (e.g. the
Laramie Plains) will be found species that do not occur on
plains dotted with sagebrush (e.g. the sagelands north of
Rock Springs), and *vice versa*. Slopes and ridges with
scattered juniper and pinyon-pine associations are habitats
for at least a few Poor-wills and Pinyon Jays. On the slopes
of the hot and dry Green River Valley, near the Colorado
line in southwestern Wyoming, the juniper and pinyon-pine
associations also attract Scrub Jays, Plain Titmice, and Bewick's Wrens. Listed below are other species that breed
regularly in Wyoming's open country (prairie grasslands,
sagelands, agricultural lands, wet lowlands, brushy places,
woodland edges, and dooryards) and in wooded tracts (deciduous trees along streams and in plantations). Species
marked with an asterisk also breed in the mountains.

OPEN COUNTRY

Turkey Vulture
Swainson's Hawk
Ferruginous Hawk
Marsh Hawk
Sharp-tailed Grouse (chiefly
    northeast Wyoming)
Sage Grouse
Mountain Plover
Killdeer
Long-billed Curlew (uncom-
    mon)
Upland Plover (eastern
    Wyoming)
Mourning Dove
Burrowing Owl
Short-eared Owl
Red-headed Woodpecker
    (eastern Wyoming)
Eastern Kingbird
Western Kingbird

Say's Phoebe
*Horned Lark
Barn Swallow
*American Magpie
*House Wren
Mockingbird (southern Wyo-
    ming)
Catbird
Brown Thrasher (eastern
    Wyoming)
Sage Thrasher
*Mountain Bluebird
Loggerhead Shrike
Yellow Warbler
Yellow-throat
Yellow-breasted Chat
Bobolink (uncommon)
Western Meadowlark
Common Grackle (eastern
    Wyoming)

Dickcissel (eastern Wyoming)
House Finch (southern Wyoming)
Common Goldfinch
Green-tailed Towhee (western Wyoming)
Spotted Towhee
Lark Bunting
Savannah Sparrow
Grasshopper Sparrow (mainly northeastern Wyoming)

Vesper Sparrow
Sage Sparrow
°Chipping Sparrow
Clay-colored Sparrow (eastern Wyoming)
Brewer's Sparrow
Song Sparrow
McCown's Longspur (eastern Wyoming)
Chestnut-collared Longspur (eastern Wyoming)

WOODED TRACTS

°Cooper's Hawk
Black-billed Cuckoo (eastern Wyoming)
Screech Owl
Red-shafted Flicker
°Hairy Woodpecker
°Downy Woodpecker
Wright's Flycatcher
°Western Wood Pewee

Blue Jay (eastern Wyoming)
Black-capped Chickadee
°White-breasted Nuthatch
Red-eyed Vireo
Warbling Vireo
American Redstart
Bullock's Oriole
Black-headed Grosbeak

All of Wyoming's mountain ranges belong to the Rocky Mountain system, but most of them are peculiarly separated. The Black Hills (and Bear Lodge Mountains) rise by themselves in the northeast, and the immense Big Horns tower alone above the plains in the north-central part of the state. The Absaroka, Teton, Gros Ventre, Wind River, Wyoming, and Salt River Ranges in the northwest and west are, as a group, cut off by the plains of the Wyoming Basin from another parallel group—the Laramie, Medicine Bow, and Sierra Madre Ranges—which extends into Colorado from the southeast-central part of the state. Moreover, the ranges within these groups tend to stand apart from one another. For example, the Wind River Range is so encompassed by the Wyoming Basin as to be almost disconnected from others in the group; and the Laramie, Medicine Bow, and Sierra Madre Ranges are largely isolated from each other by intervening fingers of the Wyoming Basin.

Of the many mountain ranges in Wyoming, those that

reach elevations above 6,000 feet support extensive conifer-ous forests. Plateaus (e.g. the Yellowstone Plateau) and valleys (e.g. Jackson Hole) that attain the same heights have a similar growth. Six mountain ranges—the Big Horns, Absaroka, Teton, Gros Ventre, Wind River, Medicine Bow —and several isolated peaks in Yellowstone Park reach above tree growth and are capped by an alpine region. The altitude at which the tree growth ceases and the alpine regions begin varies in a general way with latitude. Thus in the southern mountains (e.g. Medicine Bow Range) the trees become stunted between 10,000 and 10,500 feet and fail to grow at all above 10,500 to 11,000 feet; in the north-ern mountains (e.g. the Big Horns) these points of change are respectively lower by 1,000 feet. The most extensive alpine region occurs in the Wind River Range, the highest and most massive of all the ranges. Above timber line here are a great many broad ridges and lofty peaks, including Gannett Peak, which reaches 13,785 feet, the highest point in the state.

The vegetation of all the higher mountain ranges shows a more or less uniform succession of tree species from the sagebrush- and juniper-covered lowest slopes to the sum-mits. Merging with the sagebrush and juniper of the lowest slopes there is a belt of ponderosa pine. Above this is lodge-pole pine with quaking aspen along streams and in groves, followed at higher levels by Engelmann spruce, sometimes in pure stands. Mixed with these trees at all altitudes is Douglas fir. In the subalpine belt of stunted tree growth, limber pine, alpine fir, and whitebark pine become promi-nent and, at timber line, make up for the most part the char-acteristically twisted and one-sided 'wind timber.' Much of the alpine region is rock-strewn and barren, yet there are slopes with ample turf for a luxuriant growth of mosses, grasses, and sedges, low matted willow thickets, and count-less wildflowers. On three ranges, the Absaroka, Teton, and Wind River, the alpine regions are of sufficient height and exposure to hold extensive snowfields and even small glaciers in the shaded heads of valleys.

Owing in a large measure to the discontinuity of moun-tain ranges in Wyoming, breeding birdlife is rarely the same from one range to another, particularly if the ranges are far apart. The differences in species of juncos, referred to early in this chapter, are a notable example. Other examples are: the apparent absence of Steller's Jays in the Black Hills (and Bear Lodge Mountains) and the Big Horns; the reported occurrence of the Gray-crowned and Black Rosy Finches only in the northwestern and western mountains, and of the Brown-capped Rosy Finches only in the Medicine Bow Mountains. Listed below are birds that may be found in the forests of most of the major mountain ranges, unless otherwise indicated.

Goshawk
Sharp-shinned Hawk
Blue Grouse
Ruffed Grouse
White-tailed Ptarmigan (above timber line)
(Red-naped) Common Sapsucker (generally below 9,000 feet)
Williamson's Sapsucker (except in Black Hills and Big Horns)
Three-toed Woodpecker
Olive-sided Flycatcher
Violet-green Swallow
Canada Jay
Steller's Jay (except in Black Hills and Big Horns)
Common Raven
Clark's Nutcracker (except Black Hills)
Mountain Chickadee
Red-breasted Nuthatch
Pygmy Nuthatch (below 9,000 feet)
Brown Creeper
Hermit Thrush

Olive-backed Thrush
Townsend's Solitaire
Golden-crowned Kinglet
Ruby-crowned Kinglet
American Pipit (above timber line)
Solitary Vireo (generally below 9,000 feet)
Audubon's Warbler
Oven-bird (mainly Black Hills)
Macgillivray's Warbler (in deciduous thickets below 9,000 feet)
Black-capped Warbler (mainly above 9,000 feet, in deciduous thickets)
Western Tanager (mainly below 9,000 feet)
Cassin's Finch
Pine Grosbeak (subalpine forest)
Pine Siskin
Red Crossbill
White-crowned Sparrow
Lincoln's Sparrow (in deciduous thickets)

Two great recreational centers in the state—Yellowstone and Grand Teton National Parks (see under Yellowstone Park and Jackson)—are hardly less outstanding for bird finding than they are for their superlative scenic attractions. Both areas hold not only an impressive variety of Rocky

Mountain birds and birds characteristic of sagelands but also such breeding birds as Trumpeter Swans, Sandhill Cranes, and (in Yellowstone Park) White Pelicans and California Gulls.

Though Wyoming lies across the central flyway that is used by birds breeding in Montana and northwestern Canada and wintering in places to the south, there is no information available on the routes taken through the state. Undoubtedly a vertical migration occurs in the higher mountain ranges, but no studies of it have been reported. Apparently the principal migratory movements in the state take place within the following dates: waterfowl, 10 March—20 April, 10 October—25 November; shorebirds, 1 May—1 June, 1 August—1 October; landbirds, 15 April—20 May, 25 August—20 October.

Winter bird finding in the wooded river valleys of the plains and Rocky Mountains will yield, with moderate effort, a list of between 30 and 40 species, rarely more. With luck, flocks of rosy finches may be found, together with other interesting fringillids such as Evening Grosbeaks and Red Crossbills. The Golden Eagle and Northern Shrike should be on the list and, if there are suitable lakes and reservoirs that do not freeze over, perhaps an American or Barrow's Golden-eye, or both.

CHEYENNE. An excellent place for bird finding between this capital city and Laramie is the POLE MOUNTAIN FEDERAL GAME REFUGE, a 52,819-acre tract in the Laramie Mountains under the management of the U.S. Forest Service and called the Pole Mountain Unit of the Medicine Bow National Forest. Of the many good spots for birds in the Refuge, one that is both picturesque and readily accessible from US Route 30—the main highway from Cheyenne to Laramie—is Vedauwoo Glen, part of which has been developed as a picnic area. To reach it from Route 30, take the Vedauwoo Glen Road for 2.2 miles. If one is driving west from Cheyenne, the Road turns off right 6.3 miles west of Buford; if one is coming from Laramie, it turns off left 6.2 miles below Summit Inn, where the highway crosses the Laramie Mountains at an elevation of 8,835 feet.

Vedauwoo Glen is a natural amphitheater walled by unusual granite formations and containing aspen glades and forests composed of Douglas fir, ponderosa pine, lodgepole pine, and limber pine. In October, the Glen teems with juncos—White-winged, Oregon, and Gray-headed—and other birds such as Steller's Jays, Clark's Nutcrackers, Mountain Chickadees, Pygmy Nuthatches, and Cassin's Finches. Except for the White-winged and Oregon Juncos, most of these birds are present in June, together with such summer residents as the Olive-backed Thrush, Ruby-crowned Kinglet, Audubon's Warbler, and Western Tanager.

JACKSON. Majestic, ruggedly beautiful mountains and a wealth of wildlife—such are the attractions of GRAND TETON NATIONAL PARK (484 square miles), which embraces, on the west, the most scenic section of the Teton Range and, on the east, part of a wide valley known as Jackson Hole.

The Teton Range, close to the Idaho line and not far south of Yellowstone National Park, extends in a north-south direction for 40 miles. It rises abruptly on the east side, more gently on the west. The highest peak, Grand Teton, reaches 13,766 feet; numerous subordinate peaks attain elevations above 10,000 feet. Altogether they comprise a massive, jagged crest of granite. In many a lofty crevice, snow persists the year round. Numerous glaciers are a characteristic feature of the high eastern slopes.

Jackson Hole, 8 to 10 miles wide, parallels the Teton Range from north to south and is so encompassed by mountains as to give the impression of being a huge basin. The Teton Range walls the valley on the west side; on the north, east, and south the valley is bordered by the Absaroka and Gros Ventre Ranges. This mountainous encirclement of Jackson Hole seems accentuated by the valley floor, which is remarkably flat—a level plain except for several widely separated buttes. Elevations of the valley floor range from 6,000 feet near Jackson at the southern end to 7,000 feet at the north, but the changes in elevation are almost imperceptible to the eye. Jackson Lake, a large body of water in the northern section, is a broadening of the Snake River, which flows southward through the valley, receiving streams from the adjacent highlands along its winding course. Small lakes and beaver ponds dot the valley floor, especially on the west side of the Snake River. Some are quite shallow, with marshy edges.

The Park offers a diversity of habitats. Much of the valley floor consists of gravelly stretches covered with sagebrush, but along the Snake River and around the lakes is a coniferous-deciduous growth of lodgepole pine, blue spruce, Douglas fir, alpine fir, cottonwood, aspen, and willow. Fine stands of conifers (lodgepole pine, limber pine, Engelmann spruce, alpine fir), mixed with aspen, grow on the slopes of the Teton Range, extending up to the timber line at 10,000 to 11,000 feet, where there is also whitebark pine. Above the timber line, on the west slopes of the peaks, and in some basins on the east slopes, are true alpine meadows matted with grasses and wildflowers. In midsummer (20 July—15 August), when the snow has disappeared, such plants as Indian paintbrush, Parry's primrose, larkspur, and saxifrage bloom in profusion. The mountains to the east and south of Jackson Hole have more gradual slopes. Their forests and their alpine meadows are more extensive. The isolated buttes in Jackson Hole are notably rocky, with some cliffs. Scattered brush grows on their slopes and the more shaded, northern sides have stands of lodgepole pine, with scattered Douglas fir and aspen.

Adjoining the Park in the southeastern part of Jackson Hole is the NATIONAL ELK REFUGE (23,648 acres), administered by the U.S. Fish and Wildlife Service. Headquarters is on the eastern outskirts of the town of Jackson, reached by driving east from town on an improved road (no route number) to the directional sign indicating the entrance. The Refuge is a wintering area for elk, which arrive in late October or November, depending on the snowfall, and depart in late April and early May for the mountain country in the northern part of Jackson Hole, where they pass the summer.

The main tourist drive through Grand Teton National Park is US Route 187, which passes up through the valley from Jackson to the junction with US Route 287, near

Moran; 16 miles from Jackson this highway comes to Park headquarters (post office: Moose, Wyoming) and, 5 miles farther along, the Jenny Lake Museum, which houses natural history exhibits pertaining to the surrounding region. In summer, ranger naturalists give nature talks each evening in an open-air amphitheater adjacent to the Museum, and conduct daily nature hikes and auto caravans to special spots of interest in the Park.

To show the unlimited possibilities for bird finding in and around the Park, a number of vantage points and trips are suggested in the paragraphs below. Before following the directions given, the bird finder will be wise to visit the headquarters or Museum and there obtain maps and supplementary information.

Several pairs of Trumpeter Swans are permanent residents on Flat Creek and adjacent small ponds in the Elk Refuge. To assure their protection, the Refuge is closed to the public; bird finders are admitted only after obtaining special permission at Refuge headquarters. Generally a pair or two may be seen on the Refuge from Route 187 where it passes close to the western boundary just north of Jackson. Look for the birds on any of the ponds that come into view, or on Flat Creek, which the highway crosses at Jackson. (The bridge is immediately west of the point where the Creek leaves the Refuge.) Also look for Cinnamon Teal, a few of which breed on the Refuge. Although three or four pairs of Sandhill Cranes are summer residents on the Refuge, they are not frequently seen while nesting is under way.

Route 187 north from Jackson passes entrance drives (on the left) to the following big lakes: Jenny (21 miles from Jackson), String (24 miles from Jackson), Leigh (reached by a hike of about a mile from the end of the road at String), and Jackson Lake (30 miles from Jackson). Birds to be seen at these lakes in the summer are White Pelicans, Canada Geese, and Great Blue Herons, numerous swallows—the Violet-green, Tree, and Barn—and broods of Barrow's Golden-eyes and American Mergansers. Several pairs of Ospreys have their aeries near the shore of Jackson Lake. Where the shores of these lakes are bordered by marsh vegetation and, on higher ground, by brush, the following species may be expected: Yellow Warbler, Yellow-throat, Red-wing, Brewer's Blackbird, White-crowned Sparrow, and Lincoln's Sparrow.

The forests along the Snake River and around the bigger lakes in the Park hold a large number of bird species, including the following, which nest between the first of June and mid-July: Swainson's Hawk, Ruffed Grouse, Red-shafted Flicker, (Red-naped) Common Sapsucker, Williamson's Sapsucker, Western Wood Pewee, Canada Jay, Steller's Jay, Clark's Nutcracker, Black-capped and Mountain Chickadees, White-breasted and Red-breasted Nuthatches, Hermit Thrush, Ruby-crowned Kinglet, Warbling Vireo, Audubon's Warbler, Western Tanager, Cassin's Finch, Pine Grosbeak, Pine Siskin, Oregon Junco, and Chipping Sparrow. One of the best and most accessible forests is reached from the bridge over the Snake River at Moose (on Route 187, 15 miles north of Jackson). Leave the car near the bridge and proceed on foot through the forest, which lies on either side of the River. Another easily explored forest is on the eastern edge of Jackson Lake; 30 miles north of Jackson, Route 187 begins to pass through fine sections of this forest.

The buttes rising from the floor of Jackson Hole are interesting ornithologically, for their thick brush, cliff shelves, and rocky crevices attract such nesting species as the Red-tailed Hawk, Prairie Falcon, Violet-green Swallow, Cliff Swallow, Common Raven, and Green-tailed Towhee (rare). Sage Grouse, Horned Larks, Sage Thrashers, Vesper Sparrows, and Brewer's Sparrows inhabit the wide stretches of sagebrush that surround the buttes. East Gros Ventre Butte (elevation 7,398 feet), north of Jackson, is easily reached by driving north on Route 187 for 3 miles, to the summit of 'Boucher Hill' (the north end of the Butte). Leave the car here and walk west from the highway, exploring the cliffs and brushy slopes. Blacktail Butte (elevation 7,676 feet) may be reached by driving 6 miles farther north on Route 187. The Butte, which looms on the right (east), must be approached on foot.

The population of Sage Grouse within the Park has recently been estimated at about 500 individuals. The most accessible strutting ground of this species is the north end of the Western Airlines airstrip, on the left of Route 187,

8 miles north of Jackson. About 70 males perform here from late March until June (peak activity in late April).

A brushy stream bottom south of Jackson offers fair prospects for finding Lazuli Buntings. This stream is reached by driving south from Jackson on Route 187 for about 8 miles, then turning left on a dirt road that follows Game Creek for about 3 miles. Stop the car anywhere along the Creek, since one spot is about as good as another. Watch also for Dippers, which are known to frequent the stream.

For the person who wishes to combine bird finding with mountain climbing, a trip to Lake Solitude in the high glacial 'back country' on the east side of the Teton Range is recommended. Here conditions are typically alpine. From the west side of Jenny Lake (reached by boat or by the Lakes Trail, which begins at the Museum on the east side of Jenny Lake and passes around the Lake) take the Cascade Canyon Trail (suitable for travel on foot or on saddle horses). The Trail ascends sharply, by a series of switchbacks, through Cascade Canyon, the deepest chasm in the Teton Range. Below the Trail, Cascade Creek rushes downward in a series of cascades. The Trail leads to the base of Hidden Falls, where Cascade Creek makes a roaring plunge from a lofty glacial bench. Eventually the Trail approaches the bases of the massive peaks that divide the Canyon into the north and south forks. The Trail enters the north fork and continues upward, coming finally to Lake Solitude (elevation 9,024 feet), the headwaters of the north fork of Cascade Creek. The distance from the Jenny Lake boat landing is about 7 miles if one crosses Jenny Lake by boat. Birds to be looked for during the ascent to Lake Solitude are Dippers in Cascade Creek and at Hidden Falls, and Blue Grouse and Ruffed Grouse in the coniferous forests that penetrate the Canyon. The Hermit Thrush and White-crowned Sparrow are very common along the Trail. Seeing one or more Golden Eagles in flight over the jagged, precipitous slopes is always a possibility. Above the timber line, on the alpine meadows, American Pipits may be found. Quite likely Black Rosy Finches will be noticed searching for insect food on the alpine turf, or moving to and from their nesting sites in cliffs and in talus walls. A trip to Lake Solitude cannot be undertaken until July, when the Trail is clear of snow and ice. Before making the trip, it is essential that inquiries about climbing conditions and routes be made at the Jenny Lake Museum or at Park headquarters. Persons inexperienced in mountain climbing are advised to obtain guide service, which is available in the Park.

Within the Park, in the northeastern part of Jackson Hole, is the JACKSON HOLE WILDLIFE PARK (1,500 acres), sponsored by the New York Zoological Society, the Jackson Hole Preserve, Inc., and the Wyoming Game and Fish Commission. Four hundred acres are fenced in for the purpose of showing elk, moose, deer, antelope, and bison. To reach the Park, drive north from Jackson on Route 187 to the junction with US Route 287, and turn right (east). Soon after this turn, the highway traverses the fenced area, in which there are places to park and an information center.

About 38 miles east from the Jackson Hole Wildlife Park and outside the confines of Grand Teton National Park, US Route 287 begins to wind through TOG-WO-TEE PASS (elevation 9,658 feet) on the Continental Divide. Although the highway never climbs above timber line, one may leave the car at the top of the Pass and, by climbing on foot for 1,000 feet or more, can easily reach timber line and alpine conditions, where the birdlife is much the same as on the high slopes of the Teton Range.

LARAMIE. This southeastern Wyoming city is the seat of the UNIVERSITY OF WYOMING, which offers an introductory course in ornithology and training in wildlife management and research. The work is centered in Agricultural Hall on the campus at the northeastern edge of Laramie. Ornithological materials include 1,800 skins and 150 mounts, representing chiefly southeastern Wyoming.

A drive west from Laramie on State Route 130 (the Snowy Range Road) crosses 30 miles of the LARAMIE PLAINS, the elevation of which ranges from 7,000 to 7,500 feet. The best time to make the trip is between 15 June and 15 July, when this grassy, undulating country is brilliantly colored with wildflowers and when the Horned Larks and McCown's Longspurs, the most abundant birds, are repeating their flight songs. Mountain Plovers, which begin nesting in May, are fairly common but inconspicuous and therefore must be searched for carefully. Swainson's Hawks, Golden Eagles, Prairie Falcons, and Sparrow Hawks will probably be seen. If stops are made to investigate the alkaline lakes that dot the Plains along the way, Eared Grebes, Great Blue Herons, Black-crowned Night Herons, several species of ducks, Spotted Sandpipers, Avocets, and Yellow-headed Blackbirds may be expected.

Beyond the Laramie Plains the highway comes to the foot of the Snowy Range of the MEDICINE BOW MOUNTAINS at Centennial (elevation 8,000 feet), 32 miles from Laramie, and then proceeds to cross the Range via Snowy Range Pass (highest point, 10,800 feet). Bird finding along this mountain highway and at points to be reached by side trips on foot will yield a fine variety of birds typical of the coniferous forest and alpine meadows of the Rocky Mountains. The best time is from 20 June to 20 July, when the birds are in full song. Meals and lodging may be obtained along the highway at Snowy Range Lodge and Brooklyn Lodge on the east slope and at Medicine Bow Lodge on the west.

Lodgepole-pine forests, interspersed with aspen groves, predominate in the Snowy Range from 8,000 to 9,000 feet elevation; above them are forests of spruce and fir that, from 10,500 feet to the timber line at 11,500 feet, become stunted, forming a typical subalpine forest. Route 130 at its highest point passes through a part of this forest. Extending above the timber line to the summits, the highest of which is Medicine Bow Peak (12,005 feet), are extensive alpine meadows. Some of the characteristic breeding birds to be looked for in the forests are the Goshawk, Blue Grouse, Canada Jay, Clark's Nutcracker, Mountain Chickadee, Hermit Thrush, Olive-backed Thrush, Mountain Bluebird, Townsend's Solitaire, Ruby-crowned Kinglet, Cassin's Finch, Pine Grosbeak, and Gray-headed Junco. White-tailed Ptarmigan occur above the timber line. In order to see them, turn right on a secondary road that branches off to the north from Route 130, 8.7 miles from Centennial at a point just beyond Brooklyn Lodge. This road terminates at Brooklyn Lake. From here take a 2-mile foot trail to the top of Brooklyn Ridge, where the birds are found. During the trip White-crowned Sparrows will undoubtedly be observed at timber line. American Pipits may be seen on Libby Flats, which the highway traverses soon after the turnoff to Brooklyn Lodge.

On the eastern slope of the Snowy Range, Route 130 passes the UNIVERSITY OF WYOMING SCIENCE CAMP, 8 miles from Centennial. This is situated within the 771-acre Snowy Range Natural Area (elevation 9,500 feet), which embraces a fine tract of Engelmann spruce. The Camp (address: Centennial, Wyoming), which is in operation from late June to late August, offers field courses in zoology, botany, and geology, and provides facilities for persons wishing to undertake independent biological investigations.

ROCK SPRINGS. One of the largest known populations of Sage Grouse in Wyoming, or anywhere else, occurs in the upper GREEN RIVER VALLEY of the Wyoming Basin in the southwestern part of the state. Here the habitat is semi-arid sagebrush prairie and foothills (elevations from 6,000 to 8,000 feet), scarred by streambeds, sometimes dry, and by variously colored badlands consisting of valleys and benchlands, and of buttes, mesas, ridges, and bluffs, often with precipitous slopes. The Sage Grouse may be observed commonly in the spring, when they assemble on permanently established strutting or display grounds, and at other seasons.

Each year about 30 strutting grounds are used in the vicinity of Eden and Farson on US Route 187, 36 and 40 miles north from Rock Springs. As a rule, the strutting grounds are bare spots, either on exposed ridges, knolls, and small buttes, or in the flat sagebrush areas. The maximum daily strutting activity takes place on these grounds during an hour period beginning soon after daybreak, from late March until early June. Display activities may be watched at close range from a car. One strutting ground frequented by over 200 males is 2 miles northwest of the state highway maintenance garage in Farson; another, frequented by about 100 males, lies adjacent to the west side of Route 187, about 3 miles north of Farson. From June to October, thousands of Sage Grouse visit alfalfa fields near Eden and Farson to feed. Further details about the locations of these and other strutting and feeding grounds may be obtained from the Eden and Farson postmasters, both of whom have visited many of the areas and are very familiar with them.

The Sage Grouse shares this sagebrush country with a number of other breeding bird species. The most common is probably the Horned Lark, followed by the Brewer's Sparrow and Sage Thrasher. Other characteristic birds to be found include the Killdeer, Mourning Dove (often nests on the ground among sagebrush), Loggerhead Shrike, Lark Bunting, and Sage Sparrow. Mallards and Pintails regularly nest in sagebrush areas, sometimes a mile or two away from the water. Commonly seen in flight over the sagebrush prairie are the Red-tailed Hawk, Swainson's Hawk, Ferruginous Hawk, Marsh Hawk, and Prairie Falcon. Another predator, uncommon but seen regularly, is the Pigeon Hawk, which nests in cottonwoods near watercourses.

SHERIDAN (BY ROBERT M. MENGEL). A traveler headed west in northern Wyoming will encounter the BIG HORN MOUNTAINS as the first great mountain mass in his path. Perhaps he has recently passed through the picturesque Black Hills of South Dakota, where gentle slopes and forests of ponderosa pine have given him his initial experience with the west, and where the bird fauna was an interesting mixture of eastern and western species. Beyond the Black Hills a long haul across open plains—antelope country— on US Routes 14 and 16 toward Sheridan brings him within view of the massive, tumbled peaks of this eastern outpost of the Rocky Mountains.

The Big Horns should be traversed, rather than bypassed, by the bird finder. For the newcomer to the west they offer a cross section of true Rocky Mountain scenery and fauna (with only a few characteristic species, such as Steller's Jay, missing); for anyone, the pleasant scenic and climatic relief from the hot summer plains will more than repay a few extra miles and hours.

On the lower slopes of these mountains the bare, upsweeping plains give way, at 4,000 or 5,000 feet, to steep, rocky inclines grown up with sagebrush and spotted with juniper and scrubby pines. These slopes are the homes of innumerable chipmunks, jack rabbits, and ground squirrels, of

American Magpies and Rock Wrens, of European Partridges (introduced), Common Nighthawks, Sage Thrashers, Green-tailed and Spotted Towhees, Lark Sparrows, and other species. Particularly good bird-finding spots at these levels are afforded by canyons containing streams and clumps of cottonwood and willow. In such situations nesting Say's Phoebes, Bullock's Orioles, Western Tanagers, and Black-headed Grosbeaks may be encountered.

On the higher slopes, irregularly distributed according to soil and moisture conditions, is the forest of lodgepole pine and Engelmann spruce (the two predominant timber species), Douglas fir, ponderosa pine, and alpine fir, which comprises the million-acre Big Horn National Forest. These areas of Rocky Mountain forest are rich in birdlife. Characteristic and readily observed breeding species are the Blue Grouse, Three-toed Woodpecker, Western Wood Pewee, Canada Jay, Clark's Nutcracker, Mountain Chickadee, Red-breasted Nuthatch, Brown Creeper, Hermit Thrush, Townsend's Solitaire, Audubon's Warbler, Pine Siskin, and Oregon Junco. In shrubby areas, White-crowned Sparrows, Lincoln's Sparrows, and Song Sparrows are common, and Dippers occur along the streams. Snowshoe rabbits and porcupines are often seen from the roads.

The broad tops of the mountains, particularly in the northern parts of the range, are wide, gently rolling table-lands of subalpine meadows, which are valuable for grazing purposes; decorated with stark patches of fir and littered with boulders, the meadows are very beautiful. In places the mountains rise to rocky crags well above the timber line. Horned Larks, Mountain Bluebirds, American Pipits, and Vesper Sparrows are typical summer residents of these high meadows, which are riddled with the holes of mountain marmots. To the south the elevations are higher and the country more primitive, culminating in mighty Cloud Peak (elevation 13,165 feet), which can be reached only by pack trip.

The following routes for a summer trip through the Big Horn Mountains are suggested:

1. Drive north and west out of Sheridan on US Route 14, a good road, to Greybull, 99 miles distant. Outside of Dayton the traveler makes a spectacular climb from 3,900 feet

to 8,200 feet, proceeding over the Mountains for some 50 miles (highest point, Granite Pass, 8,950 feet), and emerging through scenic Shell Canyon to the plains. Food, gas, and lodging are available on top, at the pleasant Arrowhead Lodge.

2. Drive south from Sheridan on US Route 87 to Buffalo, then west on US Route 16 over the Big Horns (Powder River Pass, elevation 9,666 feet), emerging at Ten Sleep Canyon onto the plains again; continue 28 miles to Worland, where a right turn on US Route 20 leads to Greybull. Information, lodging, and supplies are available at two fine lodges on this route, the Pines, and South Fork Inn, about 17 miles west of Buffalo. Both of these arrange pack trips to the primitive Cloud Peak area, the most magnificent part of the Big Horn range, where mountain sheep and White-tailed Ptarmigan may be seen by the fortunate. These lodges had best be contacted well in advance for reservations (Buffalo, Wyoming). There is excellent bird finding in any woodland along this or the preceding route.

3. Drive north and west on US Route 14 to a point 5 miles beyond Arrowhead Lodge, and turn right on a gravel road, State Route 14, to Lovell. This route is the best way to see the wilderness country from a narrow but perfectly passable road with relatively little traffic. Elk and mule deer are frequently seen on this drive, especially at dusk. Ferruginous Hawks, Golden Eagles, Prairie Falcons, and Common Ravens occur regularly about the many rugged cliffs and peaks close by the road. Beaver-dammed trout streams are numerous. Near interesting Medicine Wheel Peak (accessible by a 3-mile side trip marked by Forest Service signs, and well worth the trouble) the road rises over Baldy Pass (elevation 9,700 feet) and then descends the mountain (with some of the finest views in the Big Horns), through Five Springs Canyon, to the plains. On Medicine Wheel Peak the bird finder is likely to see many White-throated Swifts executing truly breath-taking flight performances over the knife-edge ridge above the timber line. Black Rosy Finches are also a possibility. This third route is perfectly safe throughout for careful drivers. It is not, however, recommended for inexperienced drivers, or those who are unduly frightened by heights.

SUNDANCE. The BEAR LODGE MOUNTAINS in the northeastern corner of Wyoming represent an extremity of the Black Hills of South Dakota (see under Rapid City in the South Dakota chapter). Like the Black Hills, they are forested principally with pine, except for their highest summits, the Warren Peaks (maximum elevation 6,673 feet), which are treeless and grass-covered. Aspens and birches thrive in ravines, or on slopes that were once burned over; scrub oaks predominate on several high ridges and in numerous draws on the outskirts of the range. Unlike the Black Hills, the Bear Lodge Mountains are without deep canyons and stands of spruce; hence they do not have a great variety of bird species. One of the best sections for bird finding may be reached from US Route 14 at Sundance by turning north on the Reuter's Canyon Road (no route number; dirt surface) to Warren Peaks, 6 miles distant. After traversing agricultural lands for the first 2.5 miles, the road crosses a draw grown to oaks and shrubs where such breeding birds as the Wright's Flycatcher, Blue Jay, Veery, Warbling Vireo, Black-headed Grosbeak, Lazuli Bunting, and Spotted Towhee may be found. Beyond the draw the road begins to climb through Reuter's Canyon, a wide ravine with deciduous trees bordering a streambed and pines on the slopes. From the road in the evening, Poor-wills may sometimes be heard calling. Among the summer birds to be looked for are the Western Flycatcher, Olive-backed Thrush, Oven-bird, Macgillivray's Warbler, Western Tanager, Pine Siskin, and White-winged Junco. As the road approaches the treeless heights of the Warren Peaks, Ruffed Grouse are fairly numerous. Frequently individuals may be heard drumming, even as late in the breeding season as the last of June. The fire lookout tower on the highest point of the Warren Peaks permits a fine view, which includes to the northwest one of the most extraordinary geologic formations on the continent—the Devils Tower.

Variously likened to such massive objects as 'a huge fluted monumental shaft,' or 'a gigantic petrified tree stump,' the Devils Tower is in reality what is left of an ancient lava intrusion. Measuring 865 feet from bulging base to top, and looming 1,280 feet above the near-by Belle Fourche River (locally pronounced *bel' foorsh'*), it is an astonishing topographic feature when observed from a distance; when studied close at hand, it is even more amazing, for its sides are then seen to be composed of enormous columns of remarkable design and symmetry. The Tower and the adjacent land—altogether 1,194 acres—comprise the DEVILS TOWER NATIONAL MONUMENT.

The rolling landscape in the immediate vicinity of the Tower is covered largely with ponderosa pine, mixed in certain places with aspens, oaks, and other deciduous growth including shrubby thickets. Some of the bird species to be found regularly in the summer near the base of the Tower are the Hairy Woodpecker, Western Wood Pewee, Pinyon Jay (a few), Black-capped Chickadee, Brown Thrasher, Warbling Vireo, Audubon's Warbler, Yellow-breasted Chat, Western Tanager, Pine Siskin, White-winged Junco, and Chipping Sparrow. No birds are known to nest among the ferns, grasses, and shrubs that grow in the acre and a half of surface on top of the Tower, but a pair or more of Rock Wrens nest either in the niches on its near-perpendicular sides or among the talus of broken columns below. From time to time Prairie Falcons and Duck Hawks have been reported nesting on the sides of the Tower, where there are numerous situations apparently suitable for falcon aeries; both species should be looked for.

The Devils Tower National Monument may be reached from Sundance by proceeding west on US Route 14 for 21 miles, then turning north on a road that is paved but has no route number, and driving for 7 miles to the entrance road, which passes around the south side of the Tower and up the hill to the museum and office near the west base. Soon after entering the property and crossing the Belle Fourche River, the road traverses an open grassy stretch occupied by a thriving prairie-dog colony. Lark Sparrows are common in its vicinity. A foot trail encircling the Tower and an additional 4.5 miles of nature trails give the bird finder every opportunity to enjoy the natural features of the Monument.

North of the Monument on the Belle Fourche River is a large Cliff Swallow colony. This may be reached by continuing north on the road that leads from Route 14 to the Monument's entrance. Drive through the town of Hulett to a point 2.5 miles beyond, where the road rises high above the east side of the River. Below the road, under overhanging cliffs, 500 or more pairs of Cliff Swallows build their nests in mid-June. The colony may be easily observed from below by back-tracking on the road to lower ground, leaving the car, and approaching the colony on foot along the River's edge.

YELLOWSTONE PARK. Established in 1872, YELLOWSTONE NATIONAL PARK is the oldest of all National Parks. It is also the largest, with a total area of 3,472 square miles. Though most of the Park is in the northwestern corner of Wyoming, its northern and western boundaries embrace small strips of the adjoining states of Montana and Idaho. Coupled with Yellowstone Park's supremacy in age and size is its singular standing as the most celebrated showplace among all American wildernesses. Considering the natural features that lie within its confines —the imposing array of mountains, lakes, rivers, canyons, and waterfalls, the amazing geysers and hot springs, and the tremendous abundance of wildlife—the reputation seems wholly justified.

Yellowstone Park occupies the high, volcanic Yellowstone Plateau (altitudes between 7,000 and 8,500 feet), partly ringed by mountain ranges that reach from 2,000 to 4,000 feet above the general level. These are, on the north, the Madison, Gallatin, Snowy, and Beartooth Ranges; on the east, the rugged Absaroka Mountains; and, on the south, the majestic Tetons. In the Park loom a great many isolated peaks, several of which exceed 10,000 feet, the highest being Eagle Peak, with an elevation of 11,360 feet. Of the several rivers providing drainage, the chief one is the Yellowstone, whose headwaters, rising in the Park, are soon interrupted in their northwest course by the natural dam that forms Yellowstone Lake, 139 square miles in surface area and 7,731 feet above sea level, the largest body of water at such an altitude on the continent. North of Yellowstone Lake, the River churns down through Hayden Valley and then plunges 500 feet in two thundering cataracts, Upper and Lower Yellowstone Falls, into the Grand Canyon of the Yellowstone. For spectacular beauty this enormous chasm has few competitors in the world. Its

1000-foot walls from the blue-green torrents at the base to the deep-green conifers at the rim have a dazzling yellow-whiteness tinted with a multitude of pastel shades.

The 10,000 or so hot springs, geysers, steam vents, mud volcanoes, and 'paint pots,' nearly all located in the west and south-central part of the Park, comprise an unrivaled aggregation of thermal phenomena. Of these, 100 are geysers large enough to have names.

Nearly three fourths of Yellowstone Park is forested, primarily with lodgepole pine, mixed with Douglas fir in cool canyons. Deciduous trees, such as aspen, cottonwood, willow, and alder, line many of the watercourses, while groves of aspen are prevalent on the floors of wide valleys or on the slopes, where they appear as light-green patches among the dark pines. At higher altitudes, on the mountains, Engelmann spruce and alpine fir become increasingly common and, as the timber line is approached, are intermixed with whitebark pine, which, together with the spruce and fir, here exhibits the peculiar, dwarfed, matted, and one-sided condition characteristic of wind-beaten subalpine trees. Natural open areas in Yellowstone range from lush meadows and dry, gray sagelands to bleak alpine meadows above the timber line. Amid these environments, which over the years have been given rigid protection through Federal ownership, wildlife thrives in variety as well as numbers.

Almost as great an attraction to Park visitors as the canyons and geysers are the black bears, including the brown or cinnamon bears that are actually a color phase of the same species. Many of these big quadrupeds are seen by the roadsides, lumbering along unconcernedly. Though they seem friendly enough, they are potentially dangerous if molested or fed. Other big mammals—moose, elk, mule deer, grizzly bear, bighorn sheep, pronghorn antelope, and bison—are to be seen, usually back from the roads, or on trails, away from tourist traffic. The visitor cannot be in the Park very long before he will see red squirrels, ground squirrels, chipmunks, marmots, and, in certain localities, beavers and pikas.

Throughout the Park in the summer the Clark's Nutcracker and Mountain Bluebird are perhaps the most conspicuous of the passerine birds, the former for its grating calls, the latter for its brilliant hue. Many other birds may be seen without much difficulty. Swainson's Hawks are the most common of the predators. No large stand of pines is without Audubon's Warblers and Western Tanagers, no rocky outcrop without Rock Wrens, no swift stream without Dippers, no campground without Canada Jays ('Camp Robbers'), no dry, grassy stretch without Western Meadowlarks and Vesper Sparrows, no wet meadow without Savannah Sparrows, and no canyon of any size without Belted Kingfishers, Spotted Sandpipers, Violet-green Swallows, Common Ravens, and at least a view of one or two Ospreys.

Automobile roads in Yellowstone are usually clear of snow only from the first of June to mid-October, except the road from the north entrance to the northeast entrance, which is kept open the year round. Bird finding in the Park is best during the height of the singing period, from 15 June to 15 July, but there are many birds present at all times of the year except in the winter. When coming into the Park at any one of the five entrances, obtain a detailed map at the checking station. This will show the locations of the several spots for summer bird finding indicated below.

The East Entrance Road (reached from Cody, Wyoming, via US Route 14 and 20) skirts the northeastern shore of Yellowstone Lake and proceeds to the village of Lake, where it joins the Grand Loop Road (the 142-mile main road system is laid out in a figure 8). By turning left on the Loop Road, one may continue along the west side of Yellowstone Lake to Thumb and thereby obtain additional views of this great basin of water.

The shore of Yellowstone Lake is a fine vantage point for seeing a number of waterbirds and waterfowl. Outstanding among them are the White Pelicans, which nest on the Molly Islands in the Lake's South East Arm. At least a few of the 300 to 400 adults belonging to this colony may be seen anywhere around the Lake, since they wander afar in search of food. California Gulls and Caspian Terns also have colonies on islands in the Lake and are likewise easily observed. Visiting the colonies is forbidden by Park authorities, but bird finders may inquire at headquarters (located at

Mammoth Hot Springs) about arrangements for a boat trip near enough to the colonies for the pirds to be readily observed from the boat. Other birds likely to occur anywhere on the Lake, though more often near its remote and undisturbed marshy edges, include the Eared Grebe, Western Grebe, Baldpate, Pintail, Blue-winged Teal, Cinnamon Teal, Barrow's Golden-eye, Ruddy Duck, Hooded Merganser, and American Merganser.

The Loop Road from the village of Lake to the village of Canyon goes down through Hayden Valley close to the Yellowstone River. Bald Eagles, Ospreys, California Gulls, Ring-billed Gulls, and Common Ravens should be observed along the way. The LeHardy Cascades (indicated by a directional sign) is an excellent place for Harlequin Ducks. At 'the Monad,' where the Road crosses Trout Creek, there are in view, from the parking area, overhanging ledges under which thousands of Cliff Swallows nest. At the ranger station in Canyon inquire about trail directions to Grebe Lake, to the northwest, where Trumpeter Swans are known to breed.

Between Norris and Mammoth Hot Springs the Loop Road follows Obsidian Creek for a considerable distance and at the same time passes many grassy meadows, willow flats, and small lakes. Beaver Lake, on the west side of the road, opposite Obsidian Cliff, has such birds nesting in its vicinity as Canada Geese, Mallards, and Green-winged Teal. Swan Lake, on the west side of the Road 5.5 miles north of Beaver Lake, has a pair or two of Trumpeter Swans, which can usually be seen from the highway. Between Beaver Lake and Swan Lake there are extensive willow flats, the favorite haunts of the Traill's Flycatcher and Black-capped Warbler. Occasionally these flats are visited by moose. Other birds to be watched for, especially around the lakes and meadows, are Sandhill Cranes (never common, but there is always a possibility of locating one or two), Yellow-throats, Yellow-headed Blackbirds, Brewer's Blackbirds (very common), White-crowned Sparrows, and Lincoln's Sparrows. On near-by brushy slopes a few Green-tailed Towhees may be found.

A good opportunity to observe birds of the mountain

slopes is provided by hiking to the summit of Mt. Washburn (10,317 feet elevation) on the old Mt. Washburn Road, which is now closed to cars. This leaves the Loop Road at Dunraven Pass, between Canyon and Tower Junction. The north side of the mountain is treeless, except for scattered groves of lodgepole pine, Douglas fir, and quaking aspen on the lower slopes, and Engelmann spruce and whitebark pine on the higher slopes to the timber line at about 9,800 feet, but the southern side is more or less continuously forested with the same succession of trees from base to timber line. Among the birds to be expected during the climb are the following: Blue Grouse, Ruffed Grouse, Williamson's Sapsucker, Wright's Flycatcher, Steller's Jay, Mountain Chickadee, Red-breasted Nuthatch, Hermit Thrush, Townsend's Solitaire (higher slopes), Ruby-crowned Kinglet (higher slopes), Cassin's Finch (higher slopes), Pine Siskin, Oregon Junco, and (at the timber line) White-crowned Sparrow. Above the timber line, American Pipits occur, and there is always a chance of discovering Black Rosy Finches or spotting a soaring Golden Eagle.

Yellowstone Park's various naturalist services, available during the Park's main season, from 20 June to 10 September, are centered at Mammoth Hot Springs, Norris Geyser Basin, Madison Junction, Old Faithful, West Thumb, Fishing Bridge, Canyon, and Camp Roosevelt. Activities at most of these points include field trips by car or on foot, illustrated lectures, and campfire programs. When entering the Park, obtain a full schedule of activities. Museums containing bird exhibits are maintained at Fishing Bridge, Norris Geyser Basin, Old Faithful, and Mammoth. Books and other published information on birds are available at the museum in Mammoth Hot Springs.

In addition to 15 improved campgrounds and 30 smaller sites scattered throughout the Park (available as soon as the roads are clear of snow), there are hotels, lodges, and tourist cabins (open during the main season) at the principal points of scenic interest. For information concerning exact locations, accommodations, and rates, and for reservations (which should be made well in advance), write to the Yellowstone Park Co., Yellowstone Park, Wyoming (from 1 May to 30 September).

Contributing authorities: Floyd M. Blunt, Maurice Brooks, Edward F. Dana, William R. Eastman, Jr., Reed W. Fautin, C. E. Hope, Emerson Kemsies, Karl H. Maslowski, John S. McLaughlin, Robert M. Mengel, A. B. Mickey, Olaus J. Murie, Robert L. Patterson, Clifford C. Presnall, Edmund B. Rogers, John W. Scott, James R. Simon.

Suggested Reference Material

BOOKS FOR FIELD STUDIES AND IDENTIFICATION

A Field Guide to the Birds. By Roger Tory Peterson. 1947. Houghton Mifflin Co., Boston.

A Field Guide to Western Birds. By Roger Tory Peterson. 1941. Houghton Mifflin Co., Boston.

Birds of the West. By Ernest Sheldon Booth. 1950. Stanford University Press, Stanford, California. (A handbook for the identification of birds by means of keys. The species covered are those from the western edge of the Great Plains—Montana, Wyoming, Colorado, and New Mexico—to the Pacific Ocean.)

Birds of the Pacific States. By Ralph Hoffmann. 1927. Houghton Mifflin Co., Boston.

Audubon Bird Guide: Small Land Birds of Eastern and Central North America. By Richard H. Pough. 1946. Doubleday & Co., Garden City, New York.

Audubon Water Bird Guide: Water, Game, and Large Land Birds of Eastern and Central North America from Southern Texas to Central Greenland. By Richard H. Pough. 1951. Doubleday & Co., Garden City, New York.

A Guide to Bird Songs. By Aretas A. Saunders. 1951. Doubleday & Co., Garden City, New York.

Birds' Nests. A Field Guide. By Richard Headstrom. 1949. Ives Washburn, New York.

Birds' Nests of the West. By Richard Headstrom. 1951. Ives Washburn, New York.

How to Know the Birds. An Introduction to Bird Recognition. By Roger Tory Peterson. 1949. Houghton Mifflin Co., Boston.

The Ducks, Geese, and Swans of North America. By Francis H. Kortright. 1942. American Wildlife Institute, Washington, D.C.

The Hawks of North America. By John B. May. 1935. National Audubon Society, New York.

644

A *Guide to Bird Watching.* By Joseph J. Hickey. 1943. Oxford University Press, New York.

A *Laboratory and Field Manual of Ornithology.* By Olin Sewall Pettingill, Jr. 1946. Burgess Publishing Co., Minneapolis.

Bird Hiking. By Leon Augustus Hausman. 1948. Rutgers University Press, New Brunswick, New Jersey. (Useful hints on where to go on bird walks, how to get close to birds, how to identify birds, etc.)

Exploring Our National Parks and Monuments. By Devereaux Butcher. 1949. Houghton Mifflin Co., Boston. (Emphasizes items of major interest in each area. In addition to excellent photographs there is a list of books and articles for further reading.)

The National Parks: What They Mean to You and Me. By Freeman Tilden. 1951. Alfred A. Knopf, New York.

Wildlife Refuges. By Ira N. Gabrielson. 1943. Macmillan Co., New York. (Concerned largely with the development of the National Wildlife Refuges administered by the U.S. Fish and Wildlife Service. Contains considerable information about each of the important refuges.)

Naturalist's Guide to the Americas. Assembled and edited by Victor E. Shelford. 1926. Williams and Wilkins Co., Baltimore. (Each state is described with respect to physiographic features, biota, natural areas, and other topics. Unfortunately the treatment varies in thoroughness. For example, the predominant vegetation in certain states is satisfactorily indicated, but not in others. The work is well worth consulting, however, if the bird finder desires an understanding of a particular state's natural history.)

REGIONAL PUBLICATIONS

MINNESOTA, IOWA, NORTH AND SOUTH DAKOTA, NEBRASKA

The Birds of Minnesota. By Thomas S. Roberts. 1932. Two volumes. University of Minnesota Press, Minneapolis. (This great work is unfortunately out of print, but most ornithological libraries have copies available for consultation.)

Where to Find Birds in Minnesota. Compiled by Kenneth D. Morrison and Josephine Daneman Herz. 1950. Webb Publishing Co., St. Paul. (An indispensable work for the bird finder in this state.)

Birds of the Canadian Border Lakes. By W. J. Breckenridge. 1949. The President's Quetico-Superior Committee, 919

North Michigan Avenue, Chicago 11, Illinois. (A fine booklet, distributed free of charge, pertaining to the Quetico-Superior Canoe Country in northern Minnesota and southern Ontario.)

The Common Loon in Minnesota. By Sigurd T. Olson and William H. Marshall. 1952. Minnesota Museum of Natural History (Minneapolis), Occasional Papers No. 5. (Based on a two-year study in the Quetico-Superior Canoe Country and Itasca State Park.)

The Birds of Iowa. By Rudolph M. Anderson. 1907. Davenport Academy of Sciences, Davenport, Iowa. (For sale by the Pierce Book Company, Winthrop, Iowa. Although out of date, it is the only readily available work on the birds of the entire state.)

A Revised List of the Birds of Iowa. By Philip A. DuMont. 1933. University of Iowa (Iowa City) Studies in Natural History. (A very useful work, but now rare since only a thousand copies were printed.)

Waterfowl in Iowa. By Jack W. Musgrove and Mary R. Musgrove. 1943. Des Moines, Iowa. (Published by the State Conservation Commission, Des Moines, and may be purchased directly from the Commission. An informative little volume, handsomely illustrated in color by Maynard F. Reece.)

A Preliminary Survey of the Bird Life of North Dakota. By Norman A. Wood. 1923. University of Michigan (Ann Arbor) Museum of Zoology, Miscellaneous Publications No. 10.

Birds of South Dakota. By William H. Over and Craig S. Thoms. 1946. University of South Dakota Museum, Vermillion.

Check-List of the Birds of Nebraska. By F. W. Haecker, R. Allyn Moser, and Jane B. Swenk. 1945. Reprinted from *The Nebraska Bird Review*, vol. 13. (May be obtained from the Nebraska State Museum, University of Nebraska, Lincoln.)

MISSOURI, ARKANSAS, LOUISIANA, KANSAS, OKLAHOMA, TEXAS

Check-List of the Birds of Missouri. By Rudolf Bennitt. 1932. University of Missouri (Columbia) Studies. (Out of print.)

Guide to St. Louis Birding Areas. Compiled by James Earl Comfort, Marshall and Ernestine Magner, Hattie Ettinger, and William Neal Kelley. 1950. (A four-page folder obtainable from the St. Louis Audubon Society, 1207 N. 7th Street, St. Louis 6.)

The Prairie Chicken in Missouri. By Charles W. Schwartz.
1944. Published by the Conservation Commission, State of
Missouri, Jefferson City. (An album of photographs of the
Greater Prairie Chicken's life history, including a superb
series on courtship activities.)

The Ecology of the Prairie Chicken in Missouri. By Charles W.
Schwartz. 1945. University of Missouri, Columbia. (The
results of a five-year investigation; of interest to anyone
looking for birds in the northeastern, north-central, and
southwestern regions of the state.)

Birds of Arkansas. By W. J. Baerg. 1951. University of Arkansas College of Agriculture, Fayetteville.

The Bird Life of Louisiana. By Harry C. Oberholser. 1938.
Department of Conservation, City Courts Building, New
Orleans. (Out of print, but available in most ornithological
libraries.)

The Ivory-billed Woodpecker. By James T. Tanner. 1942. Research Report No. 1 of the National Audubon Society, New
York. (Largely a report on a study made in the Singer Preserve, Louisiana.)

Audubon: An Intimate Life of the American Woodsman. By
Stanley Clisby Arthur. 1937. Harmanson, New Orleans.
(Among the several biographies of John James Audubon,
this one is highly recommended to the bird finder visiting
Louisiana. It deals authoritatively and in detail with the
great ornithologist-artist's activities in the state he so loved.)

Check-List of Kansas Birds. By W. S. Long. 1940. Transactions
of the Kansas Academy of Science, vol. 43.

Notes on the Birds of Southwestern Kansas. By Richard and
Jean Graber. 1951. Transactions of the Kansas Academy of
Science, vol. 54.

The Birds of Oklahoma. By Margaret Morse Nice. 1931. University of Oklahoma Press, Norman.

Notes on the Birds of the Western Panhandle of Oklahoma.
By George Miksch Sutton. 1934. Annals of the Carnegie
Museum, Pittsburgh, Pennsylvania.

A Survey of the Game and Furbearing Animals of Oklahoma.
By L. G. Duck and Jack N. Fletcher. 1943. Oklahoma Game
and Fish Commission, Oklahoma City. (Game birds included are the Greater and Lesser Prairie Chickens, Bob-
white, Scaled Quail, Ring-necked Pheasant, Wild Turkey,
Woodcock, and Mourning Dove. The description of the
state's different wildlife habitats will be particularly instructive to a visiting bird finder.)

Birds of the Austin Region. By George Finlay Simmons. 1925.

University of Texas, Austin. (The most comprehensive work on any region in Texas.)

Check List of Birds of Dallas County, Texas. By Jerry E. Stillwell. 1939. Published by the author. (May be purchased by contacting the author, whose address is R.R. 2, Fayetteville, Arkansas.)

Checklist of the Birds of the Central Coast of Texas. By Conger N. Hagar and Fred M. Packard. 1952. (Privately printed; may be obtained from Mr. Packard, 1840 Mintwood Place, N.W., Washington 9, D.C.)

The Flame Birds. By Robert Porter Allen. 1947. Dodd, Mead & Co., New York. (The Roseate Spoonbills of the Texas Gulf Coast and Florida Bay; how the author studied them and what he learned.)

The Whooping Crane. By Robert Porter Allen. 1952. Research Report No. 3 of the National Audubon Society, New York. (Contains an excellent report on the winter life of this species at the Aransas National Wildlife Refuge in Texas.)

Birds of the Guadalupe Mountain Region of Western Texas. By Thomas D. Burleigh and George H. Lowery, Jr. 1940. Louisiana State University (Baton Rouge) Museum of Zoology, Occasional Papers No. 8.

The Birds of Brewster County, Texas. By Josselyn Van Tyne and George Miksch Sutton. 1937. University of Michigan (Ann Arbor) Museum of Zoology, Miscellaneous Publications No. 37. (Useful for anyone visiting Big Bend National Park.)

Texas Bird Adventures in the Chisos Mountains and on the Northern Plains. By Herbert Brandt. 1940. The Bird Research Foundation, 2425 North Park Boulevard, Cleveland 6, Ohio. (Good reading for the bird finder interested in Big Bend National Park.)

The Biotic Provinces of Texas. By W. Frank Blair. 1950. Texas Journal of Science, vol. 2.

MONTANA, WYOMING, IDAHO, WASHINGTON, OREGON

A Distributional List of the Birds of Montana. By Aretas A. Saunders. 1921. Pacific Coast Avifauna No. 14, Cooper Ornithological Club, Berkeley, California. (An up-to-date work on the birds of the state is greatly needed, but this one is still useful.)

Wyoming Hawks. By Ralph B. Williams and Clyde P. Matteson. 1948. Wyoming Game and Fish Commission, Cheyenne. (An unusually attractive, well-illustrated booklet, giving extensive information on each predator.)

Wyoming Bird Life. By Otto McCreary. 1939. Revised edition.

Burgess Publishing Co., Minneapolis. (This mimeographed
publication, now out of print, is the only recent work covering the state.)

The Sage Grouse in Wyoming. By Robert L. Patterson. 1952.
Sage Books, Inc., Denver, Colorado.

A Check List of the Birds of Idaho. By M. Dale Arvey. 1947.
University of Kansas (Lawrence) Publications, Museum of
Natural History.

Distributional Check-List of the Birds of Washington. By
E. A. Kitchen. 1934. Northwest Fauna Series No. 1, Pacific
Northwest Bird and Mammal Society. (Obtainable at the
Washington State Museum, University of Washington,
Seattle 5.)

Birds of the Olympic Peninsula. By E. A. Kitchen. 1949.
Olympic Stationers, Port Angeles, Washington.

Field Guide to Birds of Puget Sound. By Earl J. Larrison.
1952. Seattle Audubon Society. (Obtainable at the Washington State Museum, University of Washington, Seattle 5.)

Union Bay: The Life of a City Marsh. By Harry W. Higham
and Earl J. Larrison. 1951. University of Washington Press,
Seattle. (Deals entertainingly with birds and other wildlife
of the Union Bay Marsh in Seattle, Washington.)

Waterfowl and Their Food Habits in Washington. By Charles
F. Yocom. 1951. University of Washington Press, Seattle.

Mammals of Washington. By Walter W. Dalquist. 1948. University of Kansas (Lawrence) Publications, Museum of
Zoology. (The introductory sections dealing with the state's
physiographic regions, climate, and vegetation will be useful
to any visiting bird finder.)

Birds of Oregon. By Ira N. Gabrielson and Stanley G. Jewett.
1940. Oregon State College, Corvallis.

Birds of the Portland Area, Oregon. By Stanley G. Jewett and
Ira N. Gabrielson. 1929. Pacific Coast Avifauna No. 19,
Cooper Ornithological Club, Berkeley, California.

The Birds of Crater Lake National Park. By Donald S. Farner.
1952. University of Kansas Press, Lawrence. (May be purchased from the Crater Lake Natural History Association,
Ft. Klamath, Oregon.)

COLORADO, NEW MEXICO, UTAH, ARIZONA, NEVADA, CALIFORNIA

The Birds of Denver and Mountain Parks. By Robert J.
Niedrach and Robert B. Rockwell. 1939. Colorado Museum
of Natural History, Denver. (Of great value to any bird
finder visiting the eastern slopes of the Rocky Mountains in
Colorado.)

The Birds of Rocky Mountain National Park. By Fred Mallery

Packard. 1950. Rocky Mountain Nature Association, Estes Park, Colorado. (This is a pocket-sized, annotated check-list of 219 species.)

Birds of New Mexico. By Florence Merriam Bailey. 1928. New Mexico Department of Game and Fish, Santa Fe. (An excellent work, long out of print, but available in most ornithological libraries.)

Annotated Check-List of the Birds of Utah. By Angus M. Woodbury, Clarence Cottam, and John W. Sugden. 1949. University of Utah, Salt Lake City.

Birds of the Pine Valley Mountain Region, Southwestern Utah. By William H. Behle. 1943. University of Utah, Salt Lake City.

Birds of the Uinta Basin, Utah. By Arthur C. Twomey. 1942. Annals of the Carnegie Museum, Pittsburgh, Pennsylvania.

The Birds of Zion, Bryce, and Cedar Breaks, Utah. By Russel K. Grater. 1947. Zion-Bryce Museum, Springdale, Utah.

A Distributional List of the Birds of Arizona. By Harry S. Swarth. 1914. Pacific Coast Avifauna No. 10, Cooper Ornithological Club, Berkeley, California. (A supplement to this list, by Anders H. Anderson, was published in *The Condor,* 1934, vol. 36, no. 2.)

Birds Recorded from the Santa Rita Mountains in Southern Arizona. By Florence Merriam Bailey. 1923. Pacific Coast Avifauna No. 15, Cooper Ornithological Club, Berkeley, California.

Arizona and Its Bird Life: A Naturalist's Adventures with the Nesting Birds on the Deserts, Grasslands, Foothills, and Mountains of Southeastern Arizona. By Herbert Brandt. 1951. The Bird Research Foundation, 2425 North Park Boulevard, Cleveland 6, Ohio.

Birds of Montezuma Castle and Tuzigoot National Monuments. By Henry H. Collins, Jr. 1951. Southwestern Monuments Association, Santa Fe, New Mexico. (A pamphlet covering two areas in Arizona.)

Birds of the Navajo Country. By Angus M. Woodbury and Henry Russell Norris, Jr. 1945. University of Utah, Salt Lake City. (This work covers southeastern Utah and northeastern Arizona. The Navajo country in northwestern New Mexico, while not covered here, is ecologically similar.)

The Birds of Nevada. By Jean M. Linsdale. 1936. Pacific Coast Avifauna No. 23, Cooper Ornithological Club, Berkeley, California. (A supplement to this work has been published by the same author in *The Condor,* 1951, vol. 53, no. 5.)

Birds of the Charleston Mountains, Nevada. By A. J. van

Rossem. Pacific Coast Avifauna No. 24, Cooper Ornithological Club, Berkeley, California.

The Distribution of the Birds of California. By Joseph Grinnell and Alden H. Miller. 1944. Pacific Coast Avifauna No. 27, Cooper Ornithological Club, Berkeley, California.

A Revised List of the Birds of Southwestern California. By George Willet. 1933. Pacific Coast Avifauna No. 21, Cooper Ornithological Club, Berkeley, California. (Covers the Pacific slope from, and including, Santa Barbara County to the Mexican boundary, and from the summits of the mountains to the ocean; also covers all the islands of the Santa Barbara group.)

Directory to the Bird-Life of the San Francisco Bay Region. By Joseph Grinnell and Margaret Wythe. 1927. Pacific Coast Avifauna No. 18, Cooper Ornithological Club, Berkeley, California.

The California Deserts. A Visitor's Guide to the Mohave and Colorado Deserts. By Edmund C. Jaeger. 1938. Stanford University Press, Stanford, California.

MAPS, GUIDES, AND MANUALS FOR TRAVELING, EXPLORING, AND CAMPING

Nearly all road maps issued by oil companies and available gratis at gasoline stations are suitable for use with this book, but the latest Rand McNally Road Maps are recommended because they have been the basis for the route directions given. (A great many of the oil-company maps are Rand McNally products.) Especially convenient is the spirally bound *Rand McNally Road Atlas of the United States, Canada, and Mexico* (Rand, McNally & Company, Chicago), which contains a collection of individual state maps.

For bird finders planning intensive explorations of particular areas, the colored, three-dimensional, topographic maps published and sold by the United States Geological Survey are indispensable. These show natural features by contour lines and shaded relief and in many instances indicate trails, cliff dwellings, buildings, and other man-made features. An index to topographic maps available for any state, as well as a checklist of available topographic maps of National Parks and Monuments, will be sent upon request of the Director, Geological Survey, Washington 25, D.C.

Frequently helpful when looking for birds in different states are the individual state guides of the American Guide Series, compiled by the Workers of the Writers' Program, or the Workers of the Federal Writers' Project of the Works Progress Administration. These were published by various companies during a five-year period immediately preceding the Second World War. The descriptions of each state's natural setting are usually instructive, but not always reliable. Some of the guides give attention to parks, refuges, and scenic spots where bird finding is good.

Two very useful publications for bird finders who may wish to camp or 'rough it' are the following: *Campground Guide* (1953), published by Campgrounds Unlimited, Box 415-E, Blue Rapids, Kansas. This lists the locations and various facilities of the 2,000 campgrounds (most of them free) in the United States and Canada. *Way of the Wilderness* (1952) by Calvin Rutstrum, published and distributed by Burgess Publishing Company, 426 South Sixth Street, Minneapolis 15, Minnesota, is an exceptionally comprehensive camping manual, dealing with such matters as suitable clothing, foods and equipment for cooking, and how to travel by canoe and pack animals. It is available in a waterproof case.

Index